The Book of Daniel

THE BOOK OF DANIEL

An Archaeological Commentary

PATRICK MAZANI

Foreword by Randall Younker

WIPF & STOCK · Eugene, Oregon

THE BOOK OF DANIEL
An Archaeological Commentary

Copyright © 2026 Patrick Mazani. All rights reserved. Except for brief quotations in critical publications or reviews, no part of this book may be reproduced in any manner without prior written permission from the publisher. Write: Permissions, Wipf and Stock Publishers, 199 W. 8th Ave., Suite 3, Eugene, OR 97401.

Wipf & Stock
An Imprint of Wipf and Stock Publishers
199 W. 8th Ave., Suite 3
Eugene, OR 97401

www.wipfandstock.com

PAPERBACK ISBN: 979-8-3852-5623-5
HARDCOVER ISBN: 979-8-3852-5624-2
EBOOK ISBN: 979-8-3852-5625-9

VERSION NUMBER 010226

Scripture marked "NKJV" taken from the New King James Version®. Copyright © 1982 by Thomas Nelson. Used by permission. All rights reserved.

Scripture quotations marked "ESV" are from The ESV® Bible (The Holy Bible, English Standard Version®), © 2001 by Crossway, a publishing ministry of Good News Publishers. Used by permission. All rights reserved.

Scriptures marked "TNIV" taken from the HOLY BIBLE, TODAY'S NEW INTERNATIONAL VERSION®. Copyright © 2001, 2005 by Biblica®. Used by permission of Biblica®. All rights reserved worldwide.

CONTENTS

Archaeological Timetable | viii
World Empires | ix
Months of the Year | x
Tables | xi
Foreword by Randall Younker | xiii
Abbreviations | xiv
Preface | xix

Introduction
ARCHAEOLOGY AND THE BOOK OF DANIEL | xxi
    The Text and Its Geography | xxii
    The Text and Its Setting in Life | xxiv
    The Text and Its Archaeology | xxiv
    The Text and Its Concern | xxvi
    The Text in the Appendices | xxviii

Daniel 1
JUDAH UNDER ATTACK | 1

Daniel 2
DREAMING SUCCESSION | 42

Daniel 3
IMAGE OF GOLD | 67

Daniel 4
CENTER OF THE EARTH | 87

Chapter 5
FALL OF BABYLON | 106
    Belshazzar in Business | 112
    Belshazzar's Offerings | 121

Chapter 6
PLOT AGAINST THE INNOCENT | 138

Chapter 7
POLITICAL SUCCESSION | 156

Chapter 8
VISION IN TIME AND LOCATION | 178

Chapter 9
PROPHETIC PRACTICE | 197

Chapter 10
CONTENDING POWERS | 228

Chapter 11
FIGHTS 'TIL END TIMES | 238
    Literary Pattern of Daniel 11 | 238
    Context of Daniel 11 | 239

Chapter 12
END OF THE TIME OF THE END | 268

Appendix A
THE COMPOSITION OF THE BOOK OF DANIEL | 283
    Datable Events in Daniel | 285
    Dating Problem | 285
    Multilingualism in Daniel | 289
    Greek Translation of Daniel | 290
    Sources for the Study of Daniel | 293
    Daniel Outside the Book of Daniel | 309

Appendix B
DANIEL AND ANCIENT NEAR EASTERN LITERATURE | 312
    The Legend of Aqhat | 312
    The Story of Ahikar/Ahiqar | 313
    Daniel and Related Ugaritic Literature | 314
    The Text of Daniel at Qumran | 315
    Nonbiblical Qumran Texts Associated with Daniel | 321
    The Prayer of Nabonidus | 323
    Apocryphal Additions to the Text of Daniel | 327
    Daniel in the Pseudepigrapha | 329
    Daniel as an Apocalypse | 331
    Pseudo-Danielic Apocryphal Apocalypses | 337

Appendix C
INTERPRETATION VIEWS ON DANIEL | 345
    The Maccabean Hypothesis Approach | 345
    Historical Arguments | 346
    Linguistic Arguments | 346
    Literary Arguments | 348
    Theological Arguments | 349
    Exegetical Arguments | 350
    Antiochus IV Epiphanes Omission | 350
    The Major Schools of Interpretation on the book of Daniel | 356

Bibliography | 361

Index | 397

ARCHAEOLOGICAL TIMETABLE

STONE AGE

Neolithic	8000–4500 BC
Early Chalcolithic	4500–3800 BC
Late Chalcolithic	3800–3200 BC

COPPER/BRONZE AGE

Early Bronze	3200–2200 BC
Middle Bronze	2200–1550 BC
Late Bronze	1550–1200 BC

IRON AGE

Iron I	1200–1000 BC
Iron II	1000–586 BC

WORLD EMPIRES

Neo-Babylonian/Exilic Period	586–539 BC
Medo-Persian Period	539–332 BC
Greek/Hellenistic Period	332–37 BC
Hasmonean Period	141–37 BC
Roman Period	37 BC–AD 324
Byzantine Period	AD 324–640
Islamic Period	AD 640–1918
Crusader Period	AD 1099–291
Ottoman Period	AD 1517–917
British Mandate Period	AD 1917–48
Modern	AD 1948–Present

MONTHS OF THE YEAR

JEWISH	BABYLONIAN	PERSIAN	JULIAN
Nissan	Nissanu	Adukanaisha	March/April
Iyyar	Ayyaru	Thuravahara	April/May
Sivan	Simanu	Thaigacish	May/June
Tammuz	Du'uzu	Garmapada	June/July
Ab	Abu	Turnabazish	July/August
Elul	Ululu	Karbashiyash	August/September
Tishri	Tashritu	Bagayadish	September/October
Marheshvan	Arakhsamna	Vrkazana	October/November
Kislev	Kislimu	Asiyadiya	November/December
Tebeth	Tebetu	Anamaka	December/January
Shebat	Shabatu	Thwayauva	January/February
Adar	Addaru	Viyax(a)na	February/March

TABLES

Table 1: Dating Conventions | 3
Table 2: Synopsis of the Neo-Babylonian Chronology | 5
Table 3: Nebuchadnezzar's Name | 21
Table 4: Chronological Kingdoms: Symbolism and Parallels | 63
Table 5: Daniel 3 List of Musical Instruments | 75
Table 6: The Neo-Babylonian Kings | 105
Table 7: Biblical Eponymous Practice | 134
Table 8: Kings of Persia | 241
Table 9: Roman Procurators in Palestine | 249
Table 10: Dated Events in Daniel | 286
Table 11: Sources for the Study of Daniel | 299
Table 12: Qumran Scrolls on Daniel | 316
Table 13: Nonbiblical Qumran Texts Associated with Daniel | 322
Table 14: The Four Interpretation Strains | 358

FOREWORD

Daniel is one of those books that have excited Bible believers through the ages—mainly because through its prophecies it purports to tell the future from the time of Daniel himself (biblically dated to the late seventh into the sixth centuries BC) to the end of time and the return of the Messiah.

Daniel's visions proved so uncannily accurate that skeptics, who believed that divinely inspired foreknowledge of the future is impossible, went to great lengths to show that Daniel was really a *vaticinium ex eventu* —that the prophecies must have been written after the events they describe, not before. One of the ways that believers in Daniel's prophecies have countered such claims is through archaeology. In the case of Daniel, this means a focus on those archaeological evidences that support the idea that Daniel was a real person who lived in the sixth century BC as Daniel's internal chronology suggests.

There have been several attempts to show that parts of Daniel do indeed represent a sixth-century authorship. However, in this work, Patrick Mazani has attempted one of the most comprehensive examinations of all the archeological evidence pertaining to the book of Daniel—not only those evidences that supports sixth-century composition of the book, but also those finds that help in understanding the message of Daniel in its true historical context. This book will be a valuable aid to anyone interested in understanding the fuller context of this special biblical book.

Randall Younker,
Professor of Archaeology and History of Antiquity;
and Director, Institute of Archaeology

ABBREVIATIONS

QUMRAN DOCUMENTS

CD	Damascus Document
1Q, 2Q, 3Q, 4Q, etc.	Number of Qumran Cave (usually followed by number or abbreviated document)
1QapGen	Genesis Apocryphon
1QDan$^{a, b, etc.}$	Daniel (first, second copy, etc.)
4QDibHam	Words of the Luminaries
4QFlor	Florilegium (or Eschatological Midrashim)
1QH	Hōdāyôt (Thanksgiving Hymns)
1QM	Milḥāmāh (War Scroll)
11QMelech	Melchizedek
1QpHab	Pesher on Habakkuk
4QPrNab	Prayer of Nabonidus
1QPs^a	Psalms (first copy)
4QpsDan^c ar	Pseudo-Daniel (third copy Aramaic)
1QS	Serek Hayyaḥad (Rule of the Community Manual of Discipline)
1QS^a	Appendix A to 1QS (Rule of the Community Manual of Discipline)
11QT	Temple Scroll
11QtgJob	Targum of Job

ABBREVIATIONS

ABD	*Anchor Bible Dictionary*
ADAJ	*Annual of the Department of Antiquities of Jordan*
AfO	*Archiv für Orientforschung*
ANE	Ancient Near East
ANE	*The Ancient Near East: c. 3000–300 BC*
ANEP	*Ancient Near East in Pictures Relating to the Old Testament*
ANET	*Ancient Near Eastern Texts Relating to the Old Testament*
ASOR	American Schools of Oriental Research
AUSS	*Andrews University Seminary Studies*
BA	*Biblical Archaeologist*
BAR	*Biblical Archaeology Review*
BASOR	*Bulletin of the American Schools of Oriental Research*
BDB	*The Brown-Driver-Briggs Hebrew and English Lexicon*
BHS	*Biblia Hebraica Stuttgartensia*
Bib	*Biblica*
BM	British Museum
BN	*Biblische Notizen*
BSA	*Bulletin on Sumerian Agriculture*
CAD	*The Assyrian Dictionary of the Oriental Institute of the University of Chicago*
CAH	Cambridge Ancient History
CANE	*Civilizations of the Ancient Near East*
CBQ	*Catholic Biblical Quarterly*
COS	*The Context of Scripture*
CTA	*Corpus des tablettes en cunéiforms alphabtiéques découvertes à Ras Shamra-Ugarit de 1929 à 1939*
CTM	*Concordia Theological Monthly*
DANE	*Dictionary of the Ancient Near East*
DDD	*Dictionary of Deities and Demons in the Bible*
DJD	Discoveries in the Judaean Desert
DSS	Dead Sea Scrolls
EA	Tell el-Armana tablets

ABBREVIATIONS

EDNT	*Exegetical Dictionary of the New Testament*
ErIsr	*Eretz Israel*
HALAT	*Hebräisches und aramäisches Lexikon zum Alten Testament*
HAM	Horn Archaeological Museum
HTR	*The Harvard Theological Review*
HUCA	Hebrew Union College Annual
IDB	*Interpreter's Dictionary of the Bible*
Int	Interpretation
IVP	InterVarsity Press
JANES	*Journal of the Ancient Near East Society*
JAOS	*Journal of the American Oriental Society*
JATS	*Journal of the Adventist Theological Society*
JETS	*Journal of the Evangelical Theological Society*
JBL	*Journal of Biblical Literature*
JCS	*Journal of Cuneiform Studies*
JJS	*Journal of Jewish Studies*
JNES	*Journal of Near Eastern Studies*
JNSL	*Journal of Northwest Semitic Languages*
JPS	Jewish Publication Society
JQR	*Jewish Quarterly Review*
JSOT	*Journal for the Study of Old Testament*
JSS	*Journal of Semitic Studies*
JTS	*Journal of Theological Studies*
MSS	Manuscripts
MT	Masoretic Text
MUSJ	*Mélanges de Université Saint-Joseph*
NEAEHL	New Encyclopedia of Archaeological Excavations in the Holy Land
NEASB	Near East Archaeological Society Bulletin
NIDNTTE	*New International Dictionary of New Testament Theology and Exegesis*
NIDOTTE	*New International Dictionary of Old Testament Theology and Exegesis*
NIV	New International Version

ABBREVIATIONS

NTS	*New Testament Studies*
OEANE	*The Oxford Encyclopedia of Archaeology in the Near East*
OG-Dan	Old Greek Daniel
OTL	Old Testament Library
PEFQS	Palestine Exploration Fund Quarterly Statement
PSBA	Proceedings of the Society for Biblical Archaeology
PEQ	*Palestinian Exploration Quarterly*
RA	*Revue d'assyriologie et d'archéologie orientale*
RB	*Revue biblique*
RQ	*Revue de Qumran*
SBL	Society of Biblical Literature
SBLMS	Society of Biblical Literature Monograph Series
SBT	Studies in Biblical Theology
SDABC	*Seventh-day Adventist Bible Commentary*
TDNT	*Theological Dictionary of the New Testament*
TDOT	*Theological Dictionary of the Old Testament*
Th-Dan	Theodotion Daniel
TLOT	*Theological Lexicon of the Old Testament*
TWOT	*Theological Workbook of the Old Testament*
TZ	*Theologische Zeitschrift*
VAB	Vorderasiatische Bibliothek
VAT	Vorderasiatische Abteilung, Thontafelsammlung
VT	*Vetus Testamentum*
VTSup	Supplements to Vetus Testamentum
WA	Western Asiatic
WTJ	*Westminister Theological Journal*
YBC	Yale Babylonian Collection
YOS	Yale Oriental Series, Texts
ZA	*Zeitschrift für Assyriologie*
ZAW	*Zeitschrift für die alttestamentliche Wissenschaft*

PREFACE

THE BOOK OF DANIEL is fascinating to read. Young people master easily the stories in the first half of the book while adults continue to be amazed and/or puzzled by messages in the last half of the book. These messages from antiquity continue to be relevant to the times. Despite the fact, some inquisitive minds have suspected the authenticity of the claims of the author. Debates on issues drawn from the study of Daniel are not only sometimes outrageous, but inconclusive. However, there is beauty in the book of Daniel that edifies and inspires the reader on a spiritual journey. This has attracted me to spend some time carefully examining the text of Daniel and some material finds in relation to this book. I decided to approach the study of the book of Daniel from a different angle. This time I am focusing on what archaeology and history of antiquity have to say on the writings of Daniel.

It is always informing to examine history, religion, political developments, social and cultural trends, and anthropological models in light of the material remains from the ancient world Daniel lived in. Many archaeological finds, as this book points out, give credence to the writings of Daniel in an independent way. It feels good many times when we have support for our convictions. On the other hand, it may be disturbing to encounter that which does not subscribe to our own beliefs. The way to handle such situations is to objectively find different and effective ways of analyzing the data presented. It is refreshing to look at Daniel from a different perspective. Archaeology is very helpful with regard to illuminating the text of Daniel. It broadens our view and understanding on what Daniel recorded.

There is always something that tends to bother those who study the book of Daniel. This is the nature with Scripture anywhere else. In light of this, there are some passages in the book of Daniel that have no archaeological discoveries so far to support what the author wrote. The world has been violent, even from antiquity. Some of the material remains that might have shed light to the text of Daniel have been unfortunately destroyed for good, either through wars, natural disasters, vandalism, or accidents. So, we hang on to what we have, hoping that what we have not, will someday, somehow, appear to us. The missing archaeological finds with regard to Daniel do not obliterate or discredit its message in any way. The images in this commentary are representative of the many extant materials that can help us understand Daniel.

I started studying the book of Daniel from a very young age. I am not sure whether I understood it or not. It was through a Bible correspondence school. All I did was to read and find the answers from the text of Daniel and mail my answer sheets. It was easy to get the right answers because the questions directed me to the specific passages in Daniel. However, this study planted in me a great interest and profound respect for the biblical book of Daniel. The desire to make this book understood is still in me today. This commentary is a product of my continued effort to understand the book of Daniel. It is beneficial to study the book of Daniel along with the book of Revelation. These two books are apocalyptic and continue to capture the interest of those who want to trace human history and want to know what the future holds.

In my academic journey, I had mentorship from some of the finest minds in the academic world, who groomed me to do a more serious work in understanding the Bible. Just to name a few of the professors I rubbed shoulders with, Richard Davidson, Jacques Doukhan, Roy Gane, Jiří Moskala, Joel Musvosvi, and Jon Paulien. I am most grateful to Randall W. Younker, the director of the Institute of Archaeology at Andrews University, who initiated and groomed me in the study of archaeology. His ingenious insight and support are one of a kind.

A dear friend and colleague, Efrain Velazquez, shares the same burden with me, that scholars need to write more biblical archaeological commentaries for the people. This commentary is an attempt to fulfill that conviction. I am so grateful for my family for being very supportive to me in my personal and spiritual endeavors.

Introduction

ARCHAEOLOGY AND THE BOOK OF DANIEL

ARCHAEOLOGY IS A SCIENCE which studies past remains and attempts to reconstruct the history behind them. In relation to the Bible, the task of archaeology is not to prove, but to illuminate the biblical text.[1] It validates the biblical events in their proper political, historical, geographical, religious, anthropological, or cultural context. When archaeology is utilized appropriately in relation to the biblical text, the student will develop confidence and trust in the Bible as the consistent word of God.

Most biblical scholars share the opinion that archaeological finds "provide the only contemporary witnesses"[2] for many events found in the Bible. In other words, the things that archaeologists find allow readers to better understand what the Bible says because they are from the same time and culture within which it was written. Archaeology presents a new perspective on the meaning of the biblical passages by illuminating and deepening our understanding of the biblical text in its original context. William G. Dever describes archaeology as a "valuable tool"[3] that "still provides an invaluable service"[4] in the interpretation of the Bible. He further concludes that many puzzling passages have been made easier to understand by the discovery of parallel nonbiblical texts and artifacts that make the meaning of the biblical

---

1. Kaiser Jr., *Old Testament Documents*, 97–108.
2. Laughlin, *Archaeology and the Bible*, 15.
3. Dever, *Recent Archaeological Discoveries*, 26.
4. Dever, *Recent Archaeological Discoveries*, 33.

text clearer.[5] Israel Finkelstein affirms that "archaeology speaks with real-time evidence, and in many cases, it provides the most important testimony, sometimes the only evidence"[6] available for the biblical text.

Unfortunately, archaeology has further been described as a "great untapped resource"[7] that could cast "light on the social, religious, and economic setting in which the political events took place."[8] Scholars who write biblical commentaries often seem to neglect the use of archaeology as a means of understanding the real meaning of the text.[9] The lack of an archaeological commentary for the book of Daniel, for instance, has led scholars to create an inflated list of problems regarding many aspects of the book. These include authorship, dating, anachronisms, linguistics, historical inaccuracies, lack of unity, identification of certain individuals, the predictive nature of the message, semantics, terminology, sources, literary dependence, genre, chronology, intervention of divine beings in human activities, canonization, and content.[10] While archaeology does not solve all the problems cited here, its remarkable contribution is noted in providing some artifacts which indeed increase our understanding of the text of Daniel.

THE TEXT AND ITS GEOGRAPHY

Another area in which archaeology provides important insights concerns the geographical references mentioned in the book of Daniel. Some scholars believe that many of these locations should be understood symbolically.

---

5. Dever, *Recent Archaeological Discoveries*, 33. See also Dever, "Whom Do You Believe," 43–47, and Holden and Geisler, *Popular Handbook*, 181–87.

6. Finkelstein, interview by Hershel Shanks, "'Centrist,'" 42.

7. King, *Amos, Hosea, Micah*, 13.

8. King, *Jeremiah*, xxiv.

9. Gaalyahu Cornfeld attempted using archaeology to explain the book of Daniel but highlights Antiochus IV Epiphanes as relevant to understanding Daniel. See his *Archaeology of the Bible*, 231–36. On the other hand, Gonzalo Baez-Camargo's *Archaeological Commentary on the Bible* tried to cover all books of the Bible in 288 pages. He commented on the book of Daniel in a single paragraph on p. 180. Randall Price and H. Wayne House cite a few extant literary evidences on Daniel in *Zondervan Handbook of Biblical Archaeology*, 176–80.

10. The literature which highlights some of these problems is discussed in Mazani, "Book of Daniel," 1–11.

For example, the Great Sea (Dan 7:2),[11] Ulai River/Canal (8:2, 16),[12] Plain of Dura (3:1),[13] Kittim (11:30),[14] and Uphaz (10:5)[15] have not been taken to be what the author said they were. Are these the names of real physical locations as Daniel claimed them to be? If not, is it possible to discover what the author implied when he mentioned these names in the text? By comparatively examining the names of places and people mentioned in the text of Daniel in light of related archaeological artifacts, this commentary aims to improve our understanding of these references as they are presented by the author.

Some events, perplexing words or passages, and individuals mentioned in the text of Daniel have caused persistent problems with interpretation. The author writes with the assumption that his audience understands the times. He does not provide details or proof of his claims. As an example, in Daniel 1:1–5, he mentions the third year of Jehoiakim king of Judah (v. 1), Nebuchadnezzar laying siege against Jerusalem (v. 1), temple articles (v. 2), temple of Nebuchadnezzar's god in Babylonia (v. 2), treasure house of Nebuchadnezzar's god (v. 2), Ashpenaz (v. 3), court officials (v. 3), language and literature of Babylonians (v. 4), daily food rations (v. 5), wine (v. 5), three-year training (v. 5), and king's service (v. 5). No details are provided in the text concerning any of these items. As a result, interpreters often feel free to reject or emend the text. Many make assumptions based upon their own worldview and religious beliefs about what the author of Daniel intends. Therefore, comparing the text of Daniel with some related ancient evidence can clarify what the author is communicating and bring about a more coherent understanding of the text.

---

11. Interpreters are divided on the identity of the Great Sea. Those who take the Great Sea to be the Mediterranean Sea are represented by Goldingay, *Daniel*, 160, and Lubetski, "Mediterranean Sea" (*ABD*, 4:664). On the other hand, those who claim the Great Sea to be the mythic sea includes Ginsberg, *Studies in Daniel*, 57; Hartman and Di Lella, *Book of Daniel*, 223–24; and Porteous, *Daniel*, 102–3.

12. Bill T. Arnold briefly outlines the issues surrounding the identity of Ulai in scholarly discussions; see his "Ulai" (*ABD*, 6:721).

13. Several places in the ancient Near East are called "Dura"; if this is so, then it makes it more cumbersome to identify the Plain of Dura in Dan 3. See Henry O. Thompson, "Dura" (*ABD*, 2:241).

14. Is Kittim as it appears in Dan 11:30 a gentilic, geographical, or figurative reference? Although these alternative references to Kittim seem plausible, the question is, which reference was in the mind of the author of Daniel?

15. Collins argued that the appearance of the word "Uphaz" in Dan 10:5 is a corruption of the word "Ophir" in Job 28:16; see Collins, *Daniel*, 373.

THE TEXT AND ITS SETTING IN LIFE

There has been a long-lasting debate between those who support the sixth-century BC date—which the book of Daniel claims—and those who assign a much later date of composition, sometime in the second century BC. The author of the book of Daniel claims to be contemporary with certain historical individuals mentioned in the text. The setting depicts Neo-Babylonian and Medo-Persian court life. The text references specific people, events, places, and cultural practices in a sixth-century BC context. The debate includes questions such as: How accurate is the text regarding the people, events, places, and cultural practices of the times? How familiar is the author with the Neo-Babylonian or Medo-Persian cultural setting?

Perhaps a question pertinent to readers today is: Can the postmodern interpreter understand the text of Daniel when there seem to be so many recurrent problems with interpretation?

The interaction of nations as they are portrayed in contemporary ancient Near Eastern literature and the artifacts from sixth-century BC Babylon which are brought to light by the archaeologists must be considered in order to bring to light a clearer understanding of the text. Some astronomical and various other texts on cuneiform tablets have accurately fixed Nebuchadnezzar's regnal years synchronically with his Jewish contemporaries, pointing to 605 BC as his first attack on Jerusalem.[16]

THE TEXT AND ITS ARCHAEOLOGY

The aim of this commentary is to engage in a more illuminating way the discussion between the text of Daniel and archaeological finds. Avraham Biran observes that "by establishing a dialogue between biblical studies and archaeological research, we are able to obtain a better picture of the historical and cultural setting of the Bible."[17] A consistent, informed, and objective analysis of the historical and archaeological data available to us can help solve some interpretive problems in Daniel. This commentary examines the literary text of the book of Daniel, and where possible, comparatively relates this text to relevant archaeological artifacts and/or documentation not found in the Bible. The underlying principle is to let both the literary texts and the archaeological evidence speak for themselves and in dialogue with each other.[18]

---

16. Horn, *Light from the Dust Heaps*, 63.
17. Biran, "What Is Biblical Archaeology?," 2.
18. Dever, *Who Were the Early Israelites*, 26. See also Zimansky, "Archaeology,"

ARCHAEOLOGY AND THE BOOK OF DANIEL

Several ancient documents can be used as research material on the book of Daniel. Some of these texts are records written by travelers and historians who visited the Bible lands. Some are preserved copies of the book of Daniel and other texts recovered by archaeologists. Nevertheless, the recurrent problems in interpretation of the book of Daniel can be minimized when the text is analyzed objectively considering archaeological and material finds from the ancient Near East. Raymond E. Brown writes of a "stock of difficulties"[19] that has emerged against the biblical text as archaeological information perceived to be more accurate is discovered. However, many of these difficulties in the interpretation of Daniel are caused by an inappropriate and/or uninformed use of archaeological evidence. The bibliographic reference used in this commentary includes archaeological technical reports, inscriptions, seals, iconographic texts, as well as interpretive information necessary for a comparative analysis with the text of Daniel. Archaeology fulfills its task by reconstructing history through analyzing recovered material remains. These artifacts include but are not limited to tools, weapons, human remains, animal bones, ceramics, architecture, grains, coins, sites, and texts.

Comments are made on specific people, places, historical events, and objects which impact the text of Daniel. Evidence for or against the book of Daniel is analyzed to present a balanced and accurate viewpoint of the author. All available evidence is given a fair examination whether it be authentic or otherwise.

To an extent, *The Book of Daniel: An Archaeological Commentary* follows the traditional chapter-by-chapter and verse-by-verse commentary style. However, it analyzes independently the verses or passages that form a coherent thought in relation to the corresponding archaeological discoveries. The verses or passages without related archaeological data are left out of the discussion. Other relevant topics related to the book of Daniel are also interspaced in the commentary to give a comprehensive understanding on the book of Daniel.

Minimal analysis of grammar and patterns of speech, along with an exploration of literary devices, is useful for solving some problems with semantics. Some words encountered in this commentary have been analyzed to discover their full archaeological and biblical meaning and context. Relevant exegetical and linguistic tools have been consulted for semantics and etymology. A comparative analysis of each literary unit and related archaeological information is used to show the relation between the text

308–26.
19. Brown, *Recent Discoveries*, 69.

and the archaeological data. The images, illustrations, chronological charts, and tables graphically offer valuable help in understanding the subject. The sampling and analysis of the literary sources for the study of Daniel highlight the interpretive issues with scholarship on the book.

Archaeology does not provide prophetic insight. Its focus is in analyzing the past. Prophecy specializes in outlining future events beforehand. The book of Daniel challenges the student of archaeology because it is mostly prophetic. The tantalizing dreams and visions in a sixth-century BC Babylonian context point to the future. When prophetic events come to pass, they become history. The reconstruction of such historical events can be a challenging phenomenon, especially if the events are obscured by the remote past and lack of contemporary records.

A question may be asked about the availability or authenticity of some sources for reconstructing that history. Some common sources for the historical past which may be available include contemporary texts as well as material remains. However, the examination of some of these sources varies between two extremes: raw fundamentalism (accepting evidence uncritically) and outright skepticism (adamant rejection of evidence). The problem of interpretation is made more challenging because most interpreters come to the research with a set of personal presuppositions. The book of Daniel has been a battleground for a long time now, particularly concerning its date of composition. There are two main groups—those who advocate for an earlier date (sixth century BC) and those who point to a later date (second century BC). Both sides often argue from the same recovered evidence and draw conflicting conclusions depending on their presuppositions and worldview.

It is fascinating to note how archaeology illuminates parts of the text of Daniel and highlights the historical events in a credible way. From the evidence that has been so far discovered in relation to the book of Daniel, it is safe to conclude that time, resources, and research will yield more remains from antiquity, which will help scholars in their search for truth. There remain yet other textual questions which may not be archaeologically settled.

THE TEXT AND ITS CONCERN

Unless otherwise indicated, the verse order in this commentary follows the English translation of the Hebrew Bible. The first half of Daniel (chapters 1–6) is mainly comprised of Babylonian court stories.[20] The idea that these

---

20. Shea, *Daniel*, 17–31. John J. Collins argues that the stories in Dan 1–6 are not

stories are not historical continues to dominate scholarly thinking.[21] Even so, an objective comparison of the book of Daniel with related archaeological data seems to provide some helpful insights in the interpretive process.

The last half of Daniel (chapters 7–12) presents prophetic insights of end-time events. These chapters relate Daniel's personal dreams and visions which seem to complement those of Nebuchadnezzar. There is adequate archaeological information to illuminate some passages in this section of Daniel.

Daniel 1—2:4a and 8–12 were originally written in Hebrew while Daniel 2:4b—7:28 in Aramaic. Moreover, there are some foreign words scattered in the entire text. Here in *The Book of Daniel: An Archaeological Commentary*, the author translated the text from the original Hebrew and Aramaic languages in consultation with the New King James Version (NKJV), English Standard Version (ESV), and Today's New International Version (TNIV).

Most scholars accept a date for the composition of Daniel in the second century BC to comfort the Judeans undergoing persecution by Antiochus IV Epiphanes.[22] However, there is sufficient evidence pointing to the setting and composition in the sixth century BC.[23] The *NIV Archaeological Study Bible* (2005) illustrates on a large scale the interaction between the biblical text and archaeological finds. This study Bible incorporates several artifacts, historical texts, and inscriptions which are relevant to the biblical text. However, when it comes to the book of Daniel, this archaeological Bible cites only a small portion of the relevant archaeological data. It unquestioningly accepts a date of setting and composition contemporaneous with Antiochus IV Epiphanes in its interpretation process.[24] As we shall see later, this uncritical approach can lead to serious interpretive problems. The *ESV Archaeology Study Bible* (2017) also highlights Antiochus Epiphanes IV in its reconstruction of ancient history. The *Archaeology and Cultural Background Study Bible* (2022) presents a few relevant artifacts that highlight the text of Daniel.

---

historical but are meant only to be exemplary; see his *Introduction to the Hebrew Bible*, 555.

21. Collins, "Current Issues," 1:13, 14, and Hartman and Di Lella, *Book of Daniel*, 8.

22. Grabbe, "Dan(iel) for All Seasons," 1:229–44; Collins, *Apocalyptic Imagination*, 88–89; and Goldingay, *Daniel*, 326–29.

23. Baldwin, *Daniel*, 35; Longman III, *Daniel*, 21–24; Ferch, "Authorship," 3–21; and Hasel, "Establishing the Date," 84–164.

24. For example, Antiochus IV Epiphanes is read into Dan 8, 9, 11 and 12; see *NIV Archaeological Study Bible*, 700, 1406, 1408, and 1551.

The book of Daniel repeats a message relating to the chronological succession of four world political empires leading up to the coming of the divine kingdom at the end of time (Dan 2, 7, 8, 11). Crucial to Daniel's chronology is the sequence of the four empires. There is little consensus among scholars on the identification of these four empires.[25] The great divide among scholars is between what is called: (1) Greek view, which outlines the kingdoms as Babylon, Media, Persia, and Greece; and (2) Roman view, which has Babylon, Medo-Persia, Greece, and Rome. It is interesting to see how archaeology contributes to the dialogue on the chronological succession of empires in the book of Daniel. The present lack of evidence on some events, places, or persons does not diminish the concern of the book of Daniel, which is the chronological succession of the earthly kingdoms from Neo-Babylonia to the end of time. Missing evidence does not prove that some event has not taken place.

THE TEXT IN THE APPENDICES

There are three sections at the end of this commentary that further some of the discussion presented in this introduction. "Appendix A: The Composition of the Book of Daniel" addresses the questions of dating, linguistics, translations, and sources with regard the text of Daniel. On the other hand, "Appendix B: Daniel and the Ancient Near Eastern Literature" deals with extant documents discovered by archaeologists that one way or the other are related to the book of Daniel. Apocryphal additions to the book of Daniel and related pseudepigrapha are also addressed in this section. Apocryphal books have no theological value. They tend to contradict the canonized Scripture. However, these later additions present information on what was going on during the intertestamental times. An analysis on the interpretation strains reveals that the interest in the study of Daniel continues to excite all people everywhere. Finally, "Appendix C: Interpretation Views on Daniel" addresses different approaches used in an attempt to understand the book of Daniel. The role of Antiochus Epiphanes IV in the understanding of the book of Daniel is highlighted here.

---

25. The main proponents of the Greek view include Rowley, *Darius the Mede*, 67–173; Porteous, *Daniel*, 45–52; and Collins, *Daniel*, 166–70. Those who hold the Roman view are represented by Boutflower, *In and Around*, 13–23; Baldwin, *Daniel*, 161–62; and Hasel, "Establishing the Date," 155–58.

Daniel 1

JUDAH UNDER ATTACK

Soon after Nebuchadnezzar was crowned king, he embarked on the expansion of his territories to the north and west of Babylon. While he was in conflict with several nations in the west, his main concern was with Egypt and its allies, which included the kingdom of Judah. After each conquest, Nebuchadnezzar neglected the territories he subdued in terms of development and the welfare of the people. He focused more on exploring local resources for building the city of Babylon into a world-class capital. Information about Nebuchadnezzar's administration in the west, as well as his interaction and treatment of some of his captives, is portrayed in the biblical text, as well as in nonbiblical literature and material evidence from this period.

1:1. In the third year. The Babylonian attacks on Jerusalem (Dan 1:1) began in the third year of the reign of Jehoiakim, king of Judah (605 BC). This event is also recorded by Jeremiah the prophet (Jer 25:1), and by Josephus.[1] However, these authors date the attacks in the fourth year of Jehoiakim, which was also the first year of Nebuchadnezzar, king of Babylon. The Babylonian Chronicle[2] and the biblical text (Jer 46:2) are in agreement that Nebuchadnezzar defeated Pharaoh Necho at the Battle of Carchemish in 605 BC, which Jer 46:2 also dates in the fourth year of Jehoiakim.

---

1. Josephus, *Josephus*, 10.6.1.84–86.
2. Concerning the early years of Nebuchadnezzar, see Chronicle BM 21946, obverse, lines 1–5 in Grayson, *Assyrian and Babylonian Chronicles*, 99, and Wiseman, *Chronicles of the Chaldaean Kings*, 67.

How can Jehoiakim's third year (Dan 1:1) also be his fourth year (Jer 25:1; 46:2)? Or, how can Jehoiakim's third and fourth years of reign both be Nebuchadnezzar's first year as king of Babylon? Many commentators believe that this discrepancy cannot be settled.[3] John J. Collins affirms that Daniel's statement about Jehoiakim's third year "cannot be reconciled with any plausible reconstruction of the course of events."[4] Some scholars take 606 BC to be the third year of Jehoiakim when Nebuchadnezzar had not yet become the king of Babylon, while others think that the whole event is not historical at all. Some interpreters have tried to defend the biblical text by modifying the texts so as to fit the chronology better. Such changes have not brought forth satisfying results.

Since Nebuchadnezzar became king in the fourth year of Jehoiakim (Jer 25:1; 46:2), it has been suggested that "in the third year" (Dan 1:1) does not refer to Jehoiakim's reign but to his vassal revolt against Nebuchadnezzar. However, the etymological and semantic range of *lᵉmalḵût* ("of the reign") does not accommodate such a rendering.

From the Babylonian Chronicles it can be ascertained that Nebuchadnezzar became king following the death of his father in 605 BC. The chronological puzzle here can be resolved by realizing that there were several different time-reckoning systems employed by different writers in ancient times; in fact,

> two systems of reckoning were used for the Hebrew kings, accession-year reckoning (postdating), and non-accession-year reckoning (antedating). Since in the latter system the year in which a ruler began is termed his first official year, that year is counted twice, for it is also the last year of the previous ruler. Thus in a country where this system is used, one year must always be deducted from the official total of every reign in order to secure actual years. Totals according to accession-year reckoning, however, equal actual totals.[5]

The period from the time Jehoiakim became king in 609 BC to the end of that very year was considered as the accession year leading to 608/607 BC, his first full year of ruling. In the non-accession-year system, the first year of the king starts the moment he sits on the throne. See Table 1.

---

3. Montgomery, *Critical and Exegetical Commentary*, 113–119; Charles, *Critical and Exegetical Commentary*, 4; Porteous, *Daniel*, 25; Hartman and Di Lella, *Book of Daniel*, 47, 48; and Collins, *Daniel*, 45.

4. Collins, *Daniel*, 131; see also Montgomery, *Critical and Exegetical Commentary*, 113–119.

5. Thiele, *Mysterious Numbers of the Hebrew Kings*, 14.

Table 1
DATING CONVENTIONS

Accession Reckoning Dan 1:1	Accession Year	First Year	Second Year	Third Year
Jehoiakim's First Years	609/608 BC	608/607 BC	607/606 BC	606/605 BC
Non-Accession Reckoning Jer 25:1, 9; 46:2	First Year	Second Year	Third Year	Fourth Year

Table 1 indicates that Dan 1:1 (Babylonian setting) used the accession system whereas Jer 25:1 and Josephus (Palestinian setting) used the non-accession time reckoning. Nebuchadnezzar was enthroned as king in Babylon on the first of Elul, which corresponds with September 7, 605 BC. Soon after this he went back to Palestine until the month of Sebat (February to March 604 BC).

Babylon expanding west. The Neo-Babylonian Empire (626–539 BC) emerged into political and international prominence after a series of conflicts with the Assyrians, who had been the dominant political power in the ancient Near East until then. An important source of information on the wars between Assyria and Babylonia is the Synchronistic History Chronicle which came from the library of Ashurbanipal in Nineveh.[6] Vital social, cultural, religious, and political background to the Neo-Babylonian Empire is gained through an understanding of the Assyrians. Some of this background is essential to understanding the book of Daniel. Even though Daniel does not make any direct reference to their Assyrian historical background or cultural heritage, some of the geopolitical struggles and developments in Judah and its neighbors discussed in Daniel's book can be better understood in light of the preceding historical developments in the ancient Near East.

In 605 BC, Nebuchadnezzar, the Neo-Babylonian Crown Prince, marshaled his forces for a decisive battle at Carchemish. There he defeated the coalition forces of Pharaoh Necho II (610–595 BC) of Egypt and the Assyrians (Jer 46:1–10) followed by the defeat of the fleeing Egyptians again at Hamath.

---

6. Grayson, *Assyrian and Babylonian Chronicles*, 157–70. Other relevant works discussing the political career of the Assyrians just prior to the rise of the Neo-Babylonians include Oppenheim, *Ancient Mesopotamia*, 168–70; Brinkman, "Babylonia in the Shadow of Assyria," in *CAH*, 3/2:1–70; Oates, "Fall of Assyria," in *CAH*, 3/2:162–93; Roux, *Ancient Iraq*, 300–17; and Kuhrt, *Ancient Near East*, 2:483–546.

While chasing the Egyptians, Nebuchadnezzar received a message that his father, Nabopolassar, had died, so he summoned a few of his men and hurried back to Babylon. Upon his arrival, Nebuchadnezzar was immediately crowned king on the first of Elul (September 7), 605 BC. Despite the defeat at Carchemish, the Egyptians continued to influence the Mediterranean kingdoms which were subordinate to Babylon. In light of this, the kingdom of Judah also resisted Babylon. This led Nebuchadnezzar to lay siege to Jerusalem in 605 BC, 598 BC, and 588 BC (Dan 1:1-2; 2 Kgs 24:1, 10-11; 25:1-3). The Babylonian account of the siege of Jerusalem is contained in Chronicle 5, Tablet BM 21946, in the British Museum. This Chronicle narrates the reign of Nebuchadnezzar from 605 BC to 595 BC, the tenth year of his reign.

BABYLONIAN CHRONICLE OF NEBUCHADNEZZAR
This cuneiform tablet records some political activities of Nebuchadnezzar II from 605-595 BC including the conquest of Jerusalem and the surrender of Jehoiakim, king of Judah, in 597 BC. (Credit: Zev Radovan)

Berossus, a Babylonian priest who lived in the third century BC, wrote that Nabopolassar's son, "Nabukodrossoros[,] ruled for forty-three years; and gathering an army, he marched out and took prisoner the Jews, the Phoenicians, and the Syrians."[7] Nebuchadnezzar was successful in battles, and funded extensive building projects, mainly in Babylon, his administrative center. Babylon was a prosperous city until he died in 562 BC. Table 2 presents a synopsis of the Neo-Babylonian Empire.

Table 2
SYNOPSIS OF THE NEO-BABYLONIAN CHRONOLOGY

DATE	EVENT
626 BC	Nabopolassar seized the Babylonian throne following the power vacuum created by the deaths of Assurbanipal king of Assyria (668–627 BC) and Kandalanu, king of Babylonia (747–627 BC).
616 BC	Nabopolassar began attacks on Assyrian-held territories with assistance from Median forces. The clashes between the Assyrians and Babylonians continued until 605 BC.
614 BC	Allied Babylonian and Median (led by Cyaxares) forces besieged Nineveh.
612 BC	The fall of Nineveh, attacked by Babylonians, Medes, and Scythians.
610 BC	Harran attacked by both the Babylonians and Scythians.
609 BC	Pharaoh Necho of Egypt slew King Josiah of Judah at Megiddo (2 Kgs 23:29–35; 2 Chr 35:20–24; 36:1–4). Necho proceeded to Carchemish where he defeated the Babylonians. After three months, Necho deposed Jehoahaz, king of Judah, and replaced him with Jehoiakim.
605 BC	Nebuchadnezzar, the crown prince, mustered the Babylonian army in the decisive victory against the Egyptians at Carchemish. Nabopolassar, who had stayed in Babylon, died. Nebuchadnezzar at once returned to Babylon and was enthroned as king. Nebuchadnezzar then returned to Palestine for his first visit to Jerusalem. Daniel and others were deported to Babylon along with some vessels and treasures from the temple (Dan 1).
604 BC	Babylonians razed Ashkelon and several other cities in Palestine to drive out all Egyptian presence.
603 BC	Nebuchadnezzar made an unopposed march into Palestine. Daniel interprets King Nebuchadnezzar's dream (Dan 2).
602 BC	Nebuchadnezzar marched into Palestine and collected much treasure.

7. Burstein, *Babyloniaca of Berossus*, 26.

601 BC	Babylonians battled Egyptians at the Egyptian frontier and both armies suffered severe losses.
600 BC	Nebuchadnezzar stayed home and let his troops recuperate.
600–593 BC	Nebuchadnezzar began extensive construction of temples in Babylonia.
599 BC	Nebuchadnezzar went to Palestine and scoured the deserts collecting animals, gods, and treasure from Arabs.
598/7 BC	Nebuchadnezzar attacked and conquered Jerusalem, captured King Jehoiachin and appointed Zedekiah in his stead (2 Kgs 24:8-17; 2 Chr 36:9–10). He collected much tribute and went back through Lebanon, taking cedars to Babylon.
596 BC	Nebuchadnezzar went up the Tigris River and camped against the king of Elam who withdrew from him panic-stricken. Nebuchadnezzar made another march into Palestine.
595 BC	Nebuchadnezzar renovated the old palace in Babylon and used Greek architectural designs on the frontage of the throne room. He also quelled a rebellion in Babylonia and made another trip to Palestine to collect tribute.
594 BC	Nebuchadnezzar marched into Palestine. He summoned Zedekiah to Babylon (Jer 51:59).
588 BC	The Babylonian army marched through Lebanon, Wadi Brissa Inscription A was cut, and more cedars were ferried back to Babylon from 588–586 BC.
588/7 BC	Jerusalem besieged by the Babylonians (2 Kgs 25; 2 Chr 36:17–20; Jer 39:1–10; 52:4–21).
587/6 BC	Jerusalem destroyed by Nebuchadnezzar, who appointed Gedaliah as governor of the land of Judah and established Mizpah (Tell en-Naṣbeh) as his administration base. Wadi Brissa Inscription B was cut. The siege of Tyre began.
586–573 BC	Tyre was under siege by Nebuchadnezzar (Ezek 29:17–20).
568/7 BC	Ahmose II (Amasis) (570–526 BC) defeated Nebuchadnezzar, who had invaded Egypt.
562 BC	Nebuchadnezzar died on October 8 and was succeeded by his son Amel-Marduk (biblical Evil-Merodach, 2 Kgs 25:27; Jer 52:31). Jehoiachin released from prison.
560 BC	On August 7, Amel-Marduk was assassinated by his brother-in-law Neriglissar, who succeeded him as king on August 13.

JUDAH UNDER ATTACK

556 BC	Neriglissar died on April 16 and was succeeded by his son Labashi-Marduk on May 3. Labashi-Marduk was murdered by a usurper, Nabonidus, on June 20, and Nabonidus ascended the Babylonian throne.
539 BC	The fall of Babylon on October 12/13. Belshazzar was murdered on the same day and Medo-Persians took over the kingdom.

Hezekiah, King of Judah. Some events antedate the Babylonian siege of Jerusalem mentioned in Dan 1:1. Archaeologists have discovered an inscribed clay artifact (prism) of Sennacherib, king of Assyria (704–681 BC), which tells of an earlier siege on Jerusalem. The prism mentions *Ha-za-qi-(i)a-ú* ^{amel}*Ia-ú-da-ai*, "Hezekiah the Jew," whom Sennacherib made a prisoner in *Ur-sa-li-im-mu*, "Jerusalem," his royal residence, and caged him there like a bird (2 Kgs 18:17—19:37). Hezekiah (716–686 BC) is best known for his fortifications, constructions, and religious reforms in Jerusalem (2 Kgs 18— 19; 20:20; 2 Chr 29—31; 32:30). A clay seal impression in Hebrew bearing Hezekiah's name was found in Jerusalem by the archaeologist Eilat Mazar.

KING HEZEKIAH BULLA
Bulla inscribed in Hebrew: "Belonging to Hezekiah (son of) Ahaz, king of Judah." (Credit: Zev Radovan)

The most sophisticated of his architectural developments is the Siloam Tunnel. This 1,750-foot (539 meters) rock-hewn underground conduit drains water from the Gihon Spring into the city (2 Kgs 20:20; 2 Chr 32:30; cf. Isa 22:11). The Siloam Tunnel is also mentioned in the Apocrypha, in Sir 48:17. The Siloam Inscription relates the dramatic completion of this tunneling. This tunnel helped Jerusalem get its water supply from outside the city during times of siege by enemies. Several pools have been identified through the ages in connection to the Siloam Tunnel. The New Testament makes a reference to one such (John 9:7, 11; cf. Luke 13:4).

SILOAM INSCRIPTION
The inscription describes how two crews of workers completed tunneling water through the bedrock from Gihon Spring to the Pool of Siloam.
(Courtesy of HAM)

THE SILOAM INSCRIPTION

1. [ ] the tunneling, and this was how the tunneling was completed: as [the stonecutters wielded]
2. their picks, each crew toward the other, and while there were still three cubits to g[o], the voices of the men calling
3. each other [could be hear]d, since there was an increase (in sound) on the right [and lef]t. The day the
4. breach was made, the stonecutters hacked toward each other, pick against pick, and the water
5. flowed from the source to the pool [twel]ve hundred cubits, even though the
6. height of the rock above the heads of the stonecutte[rs] was a hundred cubits.

Marduk-apla-iddin, king of Babylon (721–710 BC), is the biblical Merodach-Baladan (2 Kgs 20:12–19; Isa 39:1–8), who contacted Hezekiah, king of Judah, under the guise of public relations. He sent his envoys to Jerusalem with letters and a gift to congratulate the king on a miraculous recovery from his deadly illness. The real agenda for this visit is not explicit.

After the visit of the Babylonians, Isaiah the prophet confronted Hezekiah and informed him that his hospitality to them was going to have devastating repercussions in the future (Isa 39). Micah (750–686 BC), the prophet from Moresheth in Judah, also informed Hezekiah that Jerusalem was going to be reduced to a heap of rubble (Mic 3:12). Later, Jeremiah the prophet quoted what Micah had said before (Jer 26:18). The Babylonians would raid and rob Jerusalem of its treasures and take captive some of the inhabitants. Nevertheless, Hezekiah did not live to see the attack by the Babylonians, which is implied in Dan 1:1.

1:1, 2. Jehoiakim, King of Judah. Daniel 1:2 simply says that the Lord gave Jehoiakim into Nebuchadnezzar's hands. The binding of Jehoiakim with bronze fetters (2 Chr 36:6) might have happened in 605 or 604 BC, but he could have been loosed when he swore his allegiance to Nebuchadnezzar (2 Kgs 24:1). It is possible that Jehoiakim was carried to Babylon along with the vessels of the temple (Dan 1:2; 2 Chr 36:7; 2 Kgs 24:13), but he could have come back to Jerusalem to serve Nebuchadnezzar for the following years in his reign.

According to the Babylonian Chronicle, Nebuchadnezzar invaded the land of Palestine in 605 BC soon after he was made king. The siege he laid against Jerusalem did not last for a long time, possibly because the king may have appeased him with heavy tribute. However, Nebuchadnezzar managed to break into the city and carry away temple treasure and vessels along with a number of people. In his first year of reign (604 BC), Nebuchadnezzar marched back into Palestine unopposed, and all the kings there gave him heavy tribute. At this time, it is most likely that Jehoiakim, king of Judah, became Nebuchadnezzar's vassal. This relationship continued for the next three years (2 Kgs 24:1), that is, probably 604–602 BC.

When the Egyptian army clashed with Nebuchadnezzar's army at the Egyptian frontier in 601 BC and both armies suffered terrible losses, Nebuchadnezzar withdrew to Babylon. He did not come back to Palestine the following year (600 BC) because he was consolidating his forces. Pharaoh also stayed home and did not make any political interference in Palestine (2 Kgs 24:7). Jehoiakim miscalculated the political terrain of the region and might have thought that Nebuchadnezzar was so defeated and humiliated that he would not try to maintain his authority over Palestine. Jehoiakim rebelled and ceased to send tribute to Nebuchadnezzar from 601 BC onwards. In the meanwhile he suffered economic damage from Babylonian, Aramean, Moabite, and Ammonite marauding bands (2 Kgs 24:2).

Nebuchadnezzar resumed his operations in Palestine in 598/7 BC. This time his main focus was on crushing Jehoiakim's rebellion. He laid a siege against Jerusalem, but it is not certain how long it took him to break through. The chronicle[8] asserts that in his seventh year, in the month of Kislev (December 598–January 597 BC), Nebuchadnezzar headed with his army to Palestine and camped against the city of Judah. On the second day of Adar (March 16, 597 BC) he seized the city and captured its king. On the throne in Jerusalem, Nebuchadnezzar placed a king of his own choice (2 Kgs 24:17).

Jehoiachin, King of Judah. Jehoiachin succeeded his father Jehoiakim on the throne in Judah. The chronicle BM 21946 gives a hint regarding the end of Jehoiachin's reign. Lines 11–12 of the reverse side read: "In the seventh year, the month of Kislev, the king of Akkad mustered his troops, marched to the Ḫatti-land, and camped against (i.e. besieged) the city of Judah and on the second day of the month of Adar he seized the city and captured the king."[9] Nebuchadnezzar's seventh year, according to the accession system, is 598/7 BC, and the month of Kislev is equivalent to November/December of 598/7 BC. The second day of the month of Adar, when Jerusalem was taken by the Babylonians, would be Saturday, March 16, 597 BC. If the end of Jehoiachin's reign was on March 16, 598/7 BC, then his three-month rule (2 Kgs 24:8), or three-month-ten-day rule (2 Chr 36:9), must have, in consideration of the Babylonian calendrical conventions, started sometime in early December 598/7 BC. Jehoiachin, his mother Nehushta, his attendants, nobles, and officials chose to surrender peacefully to Nebuchadnezzar on March 16, 598/7 BC, and the siege was lifted. Regardless of this gesture, Jehoiachin was taken captive to Babylon. With him went his mother, his wives, the chiefs, the royal family, nobility, priests, prophets, eunuchs, seven thousand warriors, and one thousand craftsmen and smiths (2 Kgs 24:12, 14–16; Jer 24:1; 27:20; 29:1, 2). The number of captives totaled ten thousand.

---

8. BM 21946, reverse, lines 11–13, in Wiseman, *Chronicles of Chaldaean Kings*, 73.

9. Wiseman, *Chronicles of Chaldaean Kings*, 73. Pritchard, *ANEP*, 127–28, has pictures of Assyrians taking female captives from Hamath, soldiers taking booty, and also a siege engine attacking. In the attack against Jerusalem, the Neo-Babylonians may have had military activities similar to those of the Assyrians.

JEHOIACHIN'S RATION TABLET
A Cuneiform tablet that lists daily rations Jehoiachin, king of Judah, and dependents received from the Babylonian Palace. (Credit: Zev Radovan)

Babylonian king was kind to Jehoiachin and offered him daily rations of food from the palace (cf. Dan 1:5). His dependents also received clothing, housing, and other necessities. Archaeologists discovered a cache of three hundred cuneiform tablets which bear record of a distribution of sesame oil and barley to various captives and skilled workers living in and around Babylon. These documents are dated from Nebuchadnezzar's tenth year (595 BC) to the thirty-fifth year of his reign (570 BC). The tablets confirm that the captives had daily rations of food from the royal court as indicated in Dan 1:5. Interestingly, among these records, Babylon 28122, obverse (on the front side), lines 29–33, reads:

... t[o?] *Ia-'-ú-kin*, king ...
... to the *qîpūtu*-house of ...
... for Shalamiamu, the ...
... for 126 men from Tyre ...
... for Zabiria, the Ly[dian] ...[10]

Another text, Babylon 28178, obverse ii, lines 38–40, reads:

10 (*sila* of oil) to ... [*Ia*]-'- *kin*, king of *Ia*[...]
2½ *sila* (oil) to [... so]ns of the king of Judah (*Ia-a-ḫu-du*)
4 *sila* to 8 men from Judah (*amelIa-a-ḫu-da-a-a*) ...[11]

10. Pritchard, *ANET*, 308.
11. Pritchard, *ANET*, 308.

Also, Babylon 28186, reverse ii, lines 13–18, reads:

> 1½ *sila* (oil) for 3 carpenters from Arvad, ½ *sila* each
> 11½ *sila* for 8 ditto from Byblos, 1 *sila* each
> 3½ *sila* for 7 ditto, Greeks, ½ *sila* each
> ½ *sila* to *Nabû-êṭir* the carpenter
> 10 (*sila*) to *Ia-ku-ú-ki-nu*, the son of the king of *Ia-ku-du* (i.e. Judah)
> 2½ *sila* for the 5 sons of the king of Judah (*Ia-ku-du*) through Qana'a [. . .].[12]

Zedekiah, King of Judah. The Babylonian Chronicle informs us that on March 16, 597 BC, Nebuchadnezzar seized the city of Jerusalem, captured its king, and "appointed there a king of his own choice (lit. heart), received its heavy tribute and sent (them) to Babylon."[13]

King Jehoiachin was captured by Nebuchadnezzar and made a prisoner (2 Kgs 24:15). In 597 BC Nebuchadnezzar appointed the twenty-one-year-old Mattaniah "Gift of Yahweh," an uncle to Jehoiachin (1 Chr 3:15), and made him king in his stead (2 Kgs 24:17; cf. Dan 9:1). In 2 Chr 36:10 Mattaniah is identified as Jehoiachin's brother, but "his brother" can also mean "his kinsman," or "his relative." Nebuchadnezzar changed this new appointee's name to Zedekiah. The reason for the change of name is not explicit. One would expect this appointee to be given a Babylonian name like those in Dan 1:6, 7. Jeremiah 51:59 announced that Zedekiah once made a trip to Babylon in 594 BC, possibly to be interrogated by Nebuchadnezzar. Although Zedekiah ruled for eleven years (597–586 BC), he did evil (2 Kgs 24:18, 19) and was not humble before Jeremiah, who was God's spokesperson (2 Chr 36:12; Jer 37:2). He rebelled against Nebuchadnezzar and secured support from Egypt (Ezek 17:11–18; 2 Kgs 24:20—25:21).

When the Chaldeans besieged Jerusalem in 588 BC, Zedekiah sent Jehucal ben Shelemiah and Zephaniah ben Maaseiah to Jeremiah to plead for an intercessory prayer over the ominous situation (Jer 37:3). In the meantime, the Egyptian military contingency came to Jerusalem and intercepted the siege (Jer 37:5). The Babylonians temporarily withdrew from Jerusalem, but Jeremiah warned the people that Pharaoh would return to his homeland and the Babylonians would come back to destroy the city (Jer 37:6–21). Jeremiah became so unpopular when he delivered this message that he was imprisoned.

Zedekiah released Jeremiah from the prison and offered him minimal hospitality. Despite Jeremiah's persuasion to submit to the Babylonians,

---

12. Pritchard, *ANET*, 308.

13. Wiseman, *Chronicles of the Chaldaean Kings*, 73; and Grayson, *Assyrian and Babylonian Chronicles*, 102.

Zedekiah remained adamant, thinking that the Egyptians would help do away with the Babylonian threat. In 2 Kgs 25:8 it is mentioned that on the seventh day of the fifth month of Nebuchadnezzar's nineteenth year, i.e., August 14, 586 BC, the Chaldeans under Nebuzaradan, the captain of the guard, broke into Jerusalem and destroyed the city (cf. 2 Kgs 25:1–21; 2 Chr 36:17–20; Jer 39:1–10; 52:4–21). When the Chaldeans managed to break the walls, Zedekiah and his army fled at night through the gate which led to his garden and went towards the Arabah.

The Babylonians later pursued the escapees and rounded up some of them in the plain of Jericho, but the army was scattered. Zedekiah was brought before Nebuchadnezzar at Riblah, where he received his sentence. Zedekiah's children were mercilessly slain before him, then the Babylonians gouged out his eyes and took him captive to Babylon. He was carried to Babylon and kept in prison until he died (Jer 39:7; 52:11). Ezekiel 12:12–16 had prophesied the capture of Zedekiah and that he would be brought to Babylon but would not see that land. Also, Ezek 17 is an illustrative parable on Zedekiah's behavior. Again, the biblical text and the Babylonian Chronicles complement each other to help us understand the contemporary world of Daniel.

Gedaliah, the Governor. Nebuchadnezzar appointed Gedaliah son of Ahikam governor of Judah at Mizpah (2 Kgs 25:22, 24). Other governors attested in the ancient Near East include Milik-etiri, governor of Kadesh, and the governor of Arpad. When Zedekiah retracted his vassalage and was captured, Nebuchadnezzar did not appoint another king over Judah but "set," "entrusted," "made overseer," or "appointed"[14] Gedaliah ben Aḥikam over those people in the land of Judah whom he did not carry into captivity in 586 BC (2 Kgs 25:22, 23; Jer 40:5, 7, 11; 41:3). Jerusalem was in ruins because of the destruction by the Babylonians, so Gedaliah took residence as governor of Judah at Mizpah (Tell en-Naṣbeh), a city located about 7.5 miles (12 kilometers) north of Jerusalem. Gedaliah had some Babylonians there who acted as Nebuchadnezzar's overseers (2 Kgs 25:24, 25; Jer 41:3).

While he was at Mizpah, his administrative center, many people came to Gedaliah to acknowledge his leadership. Those who offered their allegiance to him included some military personnel who had escaped to neighboring countries from Nebuchadnezzar's fury. Gedaliah promised them goodwill.

Johanan, son of Kareah, told Gedaliah about an assassination plot commissioned by Baalis, king of the Ammonites. Gedaliah discredited Johanan,

---

14. Brown et al., BDB, 821–22.

who acted as his counselor and confidant. The governor did not want to believe that Ishmael ben Nethaniah and his gang would have any sinister plans against him. Gedaliah refused Johanan permission to counterattack Ishmael. Eventually, Ishmael and his dissidents murdered Gedaliah, some Judeans, and the Babylonians who were at Mizpah in 582 BC.

The death of Gedaliah marked the end of "a surviving Jewish community in Judah."[15] The remaining people made a reverse exodus back to Egypt in fear of Babylonian revenge (2 Kgs 25:26). It seems that Nebuchadnezzar never attempted appointing another administrator over Judah. Daniel indicates that by 539 BC Judah had not recovered from Nebuchadnezzar's devastation (Dan 9:18).

Ezekiel, the Prophet. Ezekiel was one of the captives who probably left Jerusalem in 598 BC along with King Jehoiachin. He was from a priestly family and lived among the Jews who had settled at Tel-abib by the Kebar Canal (Akkadian *Nâru Kabari*) near the ancient city of Nippur (Ezek 1:1-3; 3:15).

Ezekiel was called to the prophetic office possibly in 594 BC (Ezek 1:1-2), and might have continued to serve until about 571 BC.[16] He was a contemporary of both Daniel and Jeremiah. The book of Ezekiel offers some chronological data which are relevant for dating some events contemporary with Daniel. Ezekiel's writings can be dated with astounding precision. For example, Ezek 24:1-2 precisely dated the Babylonian siege of Jerusalem on January 15, 588/7 BC (cf. 2 Kgs 25:1; Jer 39:1-2; 52:4-5). His wife died on August 14, 586 BC, the same day Jerusalem was burnt (Ezek 24:18). According to Ezek 33:21, a report that Jerusalem was taken came to the exiles in Babylon on January 8, 585 BC. The twenty-fifth year of Ezekiel's captivity coincided with the fourteenth year after the fall of Jerusalem and can be dated April 573/2 BC (Ezek 40:1-2).

Ezekiel indicated that Nebuchadnezzar appointed Zedekiah king over Judah and made a treaty with him (Ezek 17:12, 13). Such suzerainty treaties, imposed upon vassal kings by more powerful governments, were a common phenomenon in Assyria and Babylonia.

Through the parable of an eagle plucking a cedar tree from Lebanon (Ezek 17), Ezekiel showed how a Mesopotamian king "transplanted" exotic

---

15. Mulzac, "Gedaliah," in *Eerdmans Dictionary of the Bible*, 488.

16. Ezekiel 1:1-2 poses a chronological enigma. What the "thirtieth" year refers to has been a matter of hypothesizing. It could be a reference to Ezekiel's age, the captivity, or something else. If v. 2 duplicates the same date that is in v. 1 as a literary technique, then the difficulty of the dating may be solved by suggesting that when Ezekiel was thirty years old, in the fifth year of King Jehoiachin's captivity, that is, 593/2 BC, he had his visions of God on the fifth day of the fourth month and received his call to the prophetic ministry a month later. See Boadt, "Ezekiel, Book of" (*ABD*, 2:711, 713).

trees to his own homeland. This imagery is attested in the Wadi Brisa inscription, where Nebuchadnezzar is depicted as felling a tree in Lebanon to carry it off to Babylon.

Ezekiel 21:18–23 speaks of Nebuchadnezzar using three methods of divination to help him decide whether to attack Jerusalem or Rabbah of the sons of Ammon (modern Amman). Nebuchadnezzar would shake the arrows (cf. 2 Kgs 13:14–19), consult his household gods, and "shall look at the liver" (Ezek 21:21). It was commonly believed in Mesopotamia that the sun god "wrote" the future on the entrails of sheep. The innards were examined and given a particular meaning, a process known as "extispicy."

Although Ezekiel was a deportee living in Babylonia, his work focused more on Nebuchadnezzar's imperial administration than on the life of the Jews in captivity. Tradition holds that Ezekiel was buried in a tomb at al-Kifl in the vicinity of Babylon near the modern town of Ḥilla in Iraq.

1:1. Judah under Babylonian attack. Nebuchadnezzar's campaigns in the west from 605 BC were mainly to thwart Egyptian efforts to establish a presence in the large area known today as the Middle East. His initial attack on Jerusalem was in 605 BC during the reign of Jehoiakim, king of Judah (Dan 1:1).

Between 603–601 BC Nebuchadnezzar destroyed some of the Philistine cities including Aphek, Ashdod VI, Ekron, Tel Batash-Timnah II, Gaza, and Tel Seraʻ. In 1942 a fragmentary Aramaic letter on papyrus was discovered in Saqqara, Egypt, which King Adon of Ascalon (Ashkelon) had sent to the Pharaoh in Egypt appealing for military help to fight against the advancing Babylonian army. The letter to the Pharaoh (who remains unidentified) reads:

> To Lord of kings, Pharaoh, your servant Adon, king of [. . . The welfare of lord of kings, Pharaoh, may . . . and all the gods] of heaven and earth and Baalshamayn, the [great] god, [seek at all times; and may they make the throne of lord of kings,] Pharaoh, enduring like the days of heaven. What . . . [the forces] of the king of Babylon have come; they have reached Aphek and (encamped) . . . they have taken . . . For lord of kings, Pharaoh, knows that your servant . . . to send an army to deliver me. Let him not abandon me . . . and your servant has kept in mind his kindness. But his territory . . . a governor in the land, and as a border they have replaced it with the border.[17]

---

17. Kuhrt, "Ancient Mesopotamia" (*CANE*, 2:591). See also Gibson, *Textbook*, 2:110–116; and Porten, "Identity of King Adon," 36–52.

Many other cities in Judah and the surrounding areas show evidence of the Babylonian destruction in the sixth century BC, including Akko, Arad, Ashdod, Ashkelon, Beth-Shemesh, Dor, Ein Gedi, Ekron, Gezer, Hazor, Jerusalem, Kadesh Barnea, Lachish, Megiddo (II), Meṣad Hashavyahu, Ramat Raḥel, Tell Batash, Tell el-Hesi, Tell ʿErani, Tell er-Ruqeish, Tell Jemmeh, Tell Keisan (IV), Tell Malhata, and Tell Seraʿ.[18]

At Lachish (Tel ed-Duweir) John L. Starkey discovered in 1935 twenty-one inscribed ostraca which are now commonly known as the Lachish letters. Letter 4 relates that the writer was watching for the signals from Lachish but there were no such signs seen from Azekah. Lines 6–12 of the Lachish letter 4, which is on military reports, read: "As for Semakyahu, Shemayahu has seized him and taken him up to the city. Your servant cannot send the witness there [today]; rather, it is during the morning tour that [he will come (to you)]. Then it will be known that we are watching the (fire)-signals of Lachish according to the code which my lord gave us, for we cannot see Azeqah."[19]

LACHISH OSTRACON
An ostracon written in biblical Hebrew dating from the sixth century BC that deals with the fate of one of the prophets whose name is unfortunately not clear. (Credit: Zev Radovan)

---

18. Mazar, *Archaeology*, 458–60; Stern, *Archaeology*, 2:307–11; Negev and Gibson, *Archaeological Encyclopedia*; and Betlyon, "Neo-Babylonian Military Operations," 263–83.

19. Hallo and Younger Jr., *COS*, 3:80.

The biblical text mentions this incident in Jer 34:7. Lines 19–21 of the Lachish letter 3 read: "(Herewith) I am also sending to my lord the letter of Tobyahu, servant of the king, which came to Shallum son of Yada from the prophet and which says 'Beware.'"[20] During that time Jeremiah the prophet was a political and religious critic who was dispensing unpopular messages to the nation facing a crisis. The letter from an unidentified prophet could be from Jeremiah (cf. Jer 29:1).

1:1. Jerusalem. The book of Daniel begins with a major conflict between Babylon and Jerusalem in 605 BC (Dan 1:1). Jerusalem was defeated in this military confrontation, while Babylon gained part of Jerusalem's population and temple resources (Dan 1:1–2; 5:2, 3). More Babylonian attacks on Jerusalem in 598 BC and 588 BC led to its final destruction in 586 BC (2 Kgs 25; 2 Chr 36:17–20; Jer 39:1–10; 52:4–21). Jerusalem lost its political, economic, and religious autonomy to the Babylonians. Excavations have revealed massive fire damage caused by the Babylonians in the city of Jerusalem and in "almost every late-monarchic site excavated in Judah: in the Beersheba valley, in the Shephelah, and in the Judahite highlands."[21]

The main attack against the walls of Jerusalem was made on the northern side of the city, which was the most vulnerable part of the city's defense systems. Archaeologists have unearthed a thick layer of ashes, charred wood, and debris containing bronze and iron arrowheads. These discoveries witness to the battle that raged in the front of the walls.

Nebuchadnezzar demolished and burned the temple, palaces, and houses of Jerusalem (2 Kgs 25:9; Jer 39:8). The destruction was so complete that he had to establish Mizpah (Tell en-Naṣbeh) as an alternative administration center for that region. There he left Gedaliah, his appointee, to rule over the province of Judah (2 Kgs 25:22–24). Mizpah continued as the capital of the Judean province from 587–445 BC.

Jerusalem was an important religious center to the author of the book of Daniel. He is seen in 539 BC still praying with his face towards that city (Dan 6:10; cf. 1 Kgs 8:44–45). The author mentioned the name "Jerusalem" as a geographical place several times in prayer (Dan 9:2, 7, 12, 16, 25). He was hoping for favorable political conditions to allow the Jewish community to return from Babylon back to Jerusalem.

1:1. Besieged. See also 11:15. Besieging enemy cities was a common ancient war tactic (Deut 20:19; 1 Kgs 15:27; Ezek 4:1–3). It involved enclosing

---

20. *COS*, 3:79; see n. 14 for highlights on the debate on this text.

21. Finkelstein and Silberman, *Bible Unearthed*, 294. See also Kenyon, *Digging Up Jerusalem*, 166–71.

or confining people in their city and causing distress until they surrender (Deut 28:52–55; Jer 19:8, 9). Nebuchadnezzar's initial siege on Jerusalem was in 605 BC (Dan 1:1). The last one was in 588 BC, the seventeenth year of Nebuchadnezzar's reign. He besieged Jerusalem to quell the rebellion of his vassal king, Zedekiah of Judah (597–586 BC). According to the biblical record (2 Kgs 25:1; Jer 39:1; 52:4; Ezek 24:1–2) this military blockage began on the tenth day of the tenth month in the ninth year of Zedekiah, king of Judah, that is, on December/January 15, 588/7 BC. Nebuchadnezzar's last siege against Jerusalem ended after eighteen months.

At first those trapped in the city were not afraid of the enemy attack. They had enough resources and water to last for a long time. The walls of Jerusalem seemed impregnable, and also, they cherished the hope that they were going to be delivered somehow. The siege lasted for eighteen months. Many perished from hunger, and from the enemy's darts, which were hurled randomly into the city from the towers. The Sumerian Lamentation of Ur had a similar experience to Jerusalem: "Ur—inside it is death, outside it is death, inside we die of famine, outside we are killed by the weapons of the Elamites."[22] The biblical book of Lamentations passionately expresses grief over the destruction of Jerusalem and the exile of people from Judah. About half of the Psalms are lamentations that express sorrow for different circumstances.

THE LAMENT FOR UR
This tablet is a Sumerian lament over the destruction of the city of Ur. The Bible has similar expressions of abject grief over devastation.
(Credit: Zev Radovan)

22. *ANET*, 618, lines 402–4.

The Babylonians built towers and war engines to attack the wall so as to break through into the city. They breached the walls of Jerusalem on the ninth day of the fourth month in the eleventh year of King Zedekiah, that is, July 19, 586 BC (2 Kgs 25:2; Jer 39:2; 52:5, 6). This date corresponds with the nineteenth year of Nebuchadnezzar's reign.

When the wall of Jerusalem was breached, it seems that Nergal-Sharezer of Samgar; Nebo-Sarsekim, a chief officer; Nergal-Sharezer a high official, and all the other Babylonian officials rallied together at the point of breach near the Middle Gate in the northern wall. This gave opportunity for Zedekiah and the city's inhabitants to flee southwards in the night through the gate leading to the Arabah (Jer 39:2–4).

After Jerusalem was defeated, Nebuchadnezzar targeted the city of Tyre. For thirteen years (586/5–572 BC), Tyre resisted the siege, but was finally captured (Ezek 26:7–14). Ezekiel 29:18–20 prophesied that God was going to give the wealth of the land of Egypt to Nebuchadnezzar for defraying his expense in besieging Tyre.

1:1. Archaeological finds in Jerusalem. Some recovered finds attest to the "fierce conflagration"[23] by which Nebuchadnezzar destroyed Jerusalem in 586 BC (2 Kgs 25:8–10; 2 Chr 36:18–19; Jer 52:12–17). In the city of David, excavations showed several seventh-century BC structures including the four-roomed house of Ahiel, which had "small finds and dozens of pottery vessels."[24] Remains of a Burnt Room included charred wooden beams and furniture (probably the wood was imported from Syria), "pottery, stone and bone vessels, and a metal spoon."[25]

Some excavations near the temple plaza showed Roman-times luxurious homes which must have been occupied by rich people. Some imported items, including sigillata and marble, indicate possible trade with foreign merchants. The baths for ritual purification conform to the standards established by the rabbis. Recently, some small figurines of horses have been recovered from a pagan cultic center just outside one of the ancient walls of Jerusalem (see 2 Kgs 23:11).

Also, an assemblage of animal bones from the excavations has been analyzed. The bones show that domestic animals were the source of meat along with wild game and chicken. The lack of pig bones and other non-kosher animals from around Jerusalem not only inform us about the diet

---

23. Shiloh, "Jerusalem (Topography)" (*NEAEHL*, 2:708).

24. The complete pottery assemblages by strata parallel vessels from other sites in Judah such as Lachish III–II, Ein-Gedi IV, Ramat Rahel V, and Arad VII–VI; see *NEAEHL*, 2:708, 709.

25. *NEAEHL*, 2:708.

then, but show that the population was Jewish.[26] Further, the analysis of these bones contributes to our knowledge about the social, economic, and religious life of the people who lived there.

A possible archive or public office, now known as the House of the Bullae, located between the Upper City and the Ophel, had fifty-one bullae that had seal impressions with identifiable Hebrew names. One such name was that of "Gemareyahu ben-Shapan the scribe" (Jer 36:9–12, 25). This scribe had chambers in Jehoiakim's court in 604 BC. Babylonian arrowheads were also found in abundance in a tower that was part of the defense works to the north of the city.[27] Similar arrowheads were also found at Ein Gedi, a Judahite site destroyed by the Babylonians shortly after they had destroyed Jerusalem in 586 BC.[28]

Excavations in Jerusalem show that the Neo-Babylonians did not rebuild the city they had destroyed. In fact, minimal evidence shows their presence in the region.

1:1. Nebuchadnezzar/Nebuchadrezzar, the name. Some scholars have observed that the author of the book of Daniel is not consistent in spelling of the name Nebuchadn/rezzar. The Hebrew text reflects this inconsistency too. In fact, the Hebrew and Aramaic text has seven different spellings for the Akkadian name *Nabû-kudurri-uṣur* (Nebuchadrezzar). See table 3.

BRICK WITH NEBUCHADNEZZAR'S NAME
In Nebuchadnezzar's construction works, bricks were stamped with his name.
(Courtesy of HAM)

---

26. Spiciarich, "Jerusalem Diet," 43.

27. For more archeological finds from the eighth to the sixth centuries BC through the Persian period, see Shiloh, "Jerusalem (Topography)" (*NEAEHL*, 2:704–12); and Geva, "Jerusalem: Tombs" (*NEAEHL*, 2:712–16).

28. Shanks, "Ein Gedi's Archaeological Riches," 65. See also Barkay and Dvira, "Relics in Rubble," 52.

Table 3
NEBUCHADNEZZAR'S NAME

$N^eb\hat{u}kadne'ṣṣar$ appears 14 times (2 Kgs 24:11; 25:22; 2 Chr 36:6, 7, 10, 13; Esth 2:6; Jer 27:6, 8, 20; 28:3; 29:1, 3; Dan 1:1);
$N^eb\hat{u}kadneṣṣar$ appears 31 times (Ezra 1:7; 2:1 in parentheses; 5:12, 14; 6:5; Neh 7:6; Dan 2:28, 46; 3:1, 2 two times, 3 two times, 5, 7, 9, 13, 16, 19, 24, 26, 28, 31; 4:1, 15, 25, 28, 30, 31; 5:2);
$N^eb\hat{u}k\check{a}dn\check{e}ṣṣ\hat{o}r$ appears once (Ezra 2:1);
$N^ebukadne'ṣṣar$ appears 7 times (2 Kgs 24:1, 10; 25:1, 8; Jer 28:11, 14; Dan 4:34);
$N^ebukadneṣṣar$ appears 5 times (Dan 1:18; 2:1 two times; 3:14; 5:11);
$N^eb\hat{u}kadre'ṣṣar$ appears 33 times (Jer 21:2, 7; 22:25; 24:1; 25:1, 9; 29:21; 32:1, 28; 34:1; 35:11; 37:1; 39:1, 5, 11; 43:10; 44:30; 46:2, 13, 26; 49:28 in parentheses, 30; 50:17; 51:34; 52:4, 12, 28, 29, 30; Ezek 26:7; 29:18, 19; 30:10); and
$N^eb\hat{u}kadre'ṣṣor$ appears once (Jer 49:28).

The various spellings can mean "Nabû protect my child,"[29] "Nabû protect the crown prince,"[30] "Nabû protect my boundary stone,"[31] or "O Nabû protect my heir!" It was a common practice in the ancient Near East to have different spellings of the same name. Since the frequency of Nebuchadnezzar in the Hebrew Bible is far more than that of Nebuchadrezzar, this work uses Nebuchadnezzar for convenience.

1:2. Nebuchadnezzar as servant of deity. The author of Daniel claims that it was the God of Israel who delivered King Jehoiakim into the hands of Nebuchadnezzar (Dan 1:2). Contrary to this idea is Nebuchadnezzar's own understanding on his achievements. Nebuchadnezzar accredited to his gods all his conquests. The Etemenanki cylinder lists the provincial cities and their contribution of corvée workers and supplies for the construction of Marduk's temple in Babylon. Part of the Etemenanki cylinder text reads:

> The widespread peoples whom Marduk, my lord, entrusted to me, whose shepherdship the hero Šamaš gave me, the totality of countries, the whole of all inhabited regions, from the Upper Sea to the Lower Sea, remote countries, the peoples of the widespread inhabited regions, kings of distant mountain regions and faraway islands in the Upper and Lower Sea—whose lead ropes Marduk, my lord, placed into my hands in order to pull his

---

29. Sack, *Images of Nebuchadnezzar*, 13.
30. Selms, "Name Nebuchadnezzar," 226.
31. Oppenheim, "Nebuchadnezzar" (*IDB*, 3:529–30).

chariot pole—I conscripted... for the building of Etemenanki I imposed the work-basket on them.[32]

KING NEBUCHADNEZZAR STELE
A stele dated ca. 604–562 BC, showing Nebuchadnezzar II on the right and Babylon's great ziggurat (the Etemenanki) on the left. (Credit: Zev Radovan)

The concept of labeling Nebuchadnezzar as a servant of the Babylonian gods is also attested on several clay tablets found in the ziggurat of Borsippa. One such inscription reads:

> Nebuchadnezzar, king of Babylon, the loyal shepherd, the one permanently selected by Marduk, the exalted ruler, the one beloved by Nabû, the wise expert who is attentive to the ways of the gods, the tireless governor, the caretaker of Esagil and Ezida, the foremost heir of Nabopolassar, king of Babylon, I, when Marduk, my great lord, duly created me and ordered me to take care of him, Nabû, the administrator of the totality of heaven and the netherworld, put in my hands the just scepter.[33]

In the inscription, Nebuchadnezzar gives credit to Marduk, his god. In direct contradiction of this idea, the book of Daniel paints a picture of Daniel's God handing Jehoiakim into Nebuchadnezzar's hands (Dan 1:2). In the following three chapters of the book, we see God working in

32. Vanderhooft, *Neo-Babylonian Empire*, 36–37.
33. *COS*, 2:309.

Nebuchadnezzar's life to show him who is the One True God and true sovereign of the world. The God of Israel calls Nebuchadnezzar His servant (Jer 25:9; 27:6; 43:10). Nebuchadnezzar may be seen as the servant of the God of Israel in the sense that his destructive actions against Judah were in accordance with God's plan for that nation (cf. Hab 1:5–11). In Ezek 29:19–20 God remunerates Nebuchadnezzar and his army for destroying Judah and other nations.

KING NEBUCHADNEZZAR INSCRIPTION
Cuneiform inscription praising King Nebuchadnezzar II (605–562 BC) as king of justice, wise, pious, and strong. (Credit: Zev Radovan)

Unfortunately, there is no record on Nebuchadnezzar specifically giving offerings to the God of Daniel (see Dan 2:46). However, he did give lavish provisions of daily offerings to the Babylonian gods. His inscription now housed in the British Museum (BM 45690) reads:

> In his presence every day without fail among the food were abundant mighty oxen, fat sheep . . . chicken, duck, *marratu*-birds, [pigeons], dormice, strings of fishes, fruits of the orchard in large quantity, [the luxuriance] of the plantations, [apples], figs, pomegranates, grapes, dates, Tilmun-dates, raisins, dried figs, abundant vegetables, [the profusion] of the gardens, fine quality mixed beer, honey, butter, refined oil, first quality milk, sweet *ulušinnu*-beer, "first" beer, grain, wine, the best of the mountains and all lands, the best that he had, the pleasant luxuries of mountains and seas he gave to eat, in abundance he offered it before the great gods.[34]

---

34. Lambert, "Nebuchadnezzar King of Justice," 9, rev. col. V, lines 4–16.

He also laid before his god, Marduk, all the articles he had brought from the house of God in Jerusalem (Dan 1:2). However, according to Daniel, Nebuchadnezzar acknowledged the God of the Hebrew captives as "the God of gods, the Lord of kings, and a revealer of secrets" (Dan 2:47), "the Most High" (4:34), and "the King of heaven" (4:37). The story of Nebuchadnezzar ends with him praising, extolling, and honoring Daniel's God (4:37).

1:2. Nebuchadnezzar's god. Marduk was the chief god of the Babylonian pantheon and the patron god of all ancient Mesopotamia. Marduk's original Sumerian name was *amar.udak.ak*, which meant "calf/son of the sun" or preferably "calf of the storm."[35] His wife was Zarpanitu. Nabu (Nebo) was Marduk's son. Nothing much is known about Marduk's origin, except that he was the son of Enki (Akk Ea) and also a minor Sumerian god. Marduk became prominent from 2000 BC during the Old Babylonian period. His elevation to the supreme god status in Babylonia is portrayed in the Enuma Elish (the Babylonian Creation Epic). In the Old Testament Marduk (Merodach) is known as Bel, "Lord" (Isa 46:1; Jer 50:2; 51:44). Bel appears in names such as "Belteshazzar" (Dan 1:7; 4:8) and "Belshazzar" (Dan 5).

1:2. Daniel's God. See 9:2. YHWH. Daniel means "My judge is El" or "El is my judge." El or Il(u), "god," is a generic designation for the deity in many parts of the ancient Near East. There is a definite distinction between El, the chief god of the Canaanite pantheon, and the God of Daniel, although similar attributes have been ascribed to both. No evidence has been recovered anywhere of an anthropomorphic graven statue of Daniel's God. In fact, the making of an image of God and any graphic design, form, picture, or depiction of God, for whatever motive, is prohibited (see Exod 20:4, 5; Deut 4:15–19; 5:8, 9).

1:2. Shinar. The origin of the name "Shinar" in Dan 1:2 is a puzzle to scholars. It has been suggested that "Shinar" was derived from "Sumer." But this idea has been rejected by most linguists.[36] "Shinar" is the biblical geographical name for Babylonia[37] (Gen 11:2; 14:1, 9; Isa 11:11; Zech 5:11). The name "Shinar" was mostly applied to the southern part of Mesopotamia, that

---

35. Abusch, "Marduk" (*DDD*, 543).
36. Davila, "Shinar" (*ABD*, 5:1220).
37. Zadok, "Origin," 240–44.

is, south of Baghdad in Iraq. "Shinar" in Egyptian records is rendered as "Shankhar"[38] or "Shanhar."[39]

1:2. Treasure house of his god. The book of Daniel begins with a shift from the house of God in Jerusalem to the house of Marduk, the Esagila, in Babylon (Dan 1:2). From 605 BC onwards the Babylonians robbed and defaced the Jerusalem temple. It was finally burned down in 586 BC (2 Kgs 25:9; 2 Chr 36:19). The Babylonian temple, the Esagila, was used to house all the treasure and utensils carried from Judah (Dan 1:2). The Esagila measured 282 feet (85.8 meters) long and 260 feet (79.3 meters) wide. On each brick was stamped Nebuchadnezzar's name as "the fosterer of Esagila."[40]

Some ancient records shed light on the carrying away of temple treasure as indicated in Dan 1:2. The India House Inscription of Nebuchadnezzar reads:

> Silver, gold, costly precious stones, bronze, mismakannu—and cedar wood, all conceivable valuables, great (?) superabundance, the product of the mountains, the wealth of the sea, a heavy burden, a sumptuous gift, I brought to my city of Babil before him, and deposited in Esagila, the palace of his lordship, a gigantic abundance. Ekua, the chamber of Marduk, lord of the gods, I made to gleam like the sun.[41]

The vessels from the Jerusalem temple were still in the Babylonian temple in 539 BC when the Neo-Babylonian Empire collapsed (Dan 5). Cyrus ordered the rebuilding of the Jerusalem temple. He also ordered that the utensils taken by Nebuchadnezzar be carried back (Ezra 1:2–7). Temples acted as administration, worship, and community life centers. To destroy a national temple meant to incapacitate the nation's entire infrastructure and autonomy. The Babylonians never ventured to repair the temple they destroyed in Jerusalem. They were not interested in resuscitating religiopolitical autonomy in Judah.

1:2. House of God. The Jerusalem temple was first built by King Solomon about 953 BC (1 Kgs 6—8). The architectural descriptions of this tripartite temple are similar to some Canaanite temples found in Palestine and in

---

38. This appears on the list of countries subdued by different Egyptian kings, but caution must be used because some of the Egyptian records are mostly propagandistic; see *ANET*, 243, 247.

39. The stele of Amen-hotep II (1447–1421 BC) states that Shinar was one of those distant countries whose prince begged for peace with Egypt (*ANET*, 247).

40. Koldewey, *Excavations at Babylon*, 210.

41. Koldewey, *Excavations at Babylon*, 210–11.

Syria. The temple continued to be in use until it was destroyed by King Nebuchadnezzar in 586 BC. However, no remains of this temple have been recovered. In its place, the Second Temple was established after the Babylonian exile. This postexilic reconstruction of the temple is attributed to Zerubbabel about 516 BC (Zech 4:6–10). Then Herod the Great refurbished that temple beginning about 20 BC. This Herodian structure ran its course until its catastrophic destruction by the Romans in AD 70. For this temple, the only remarkable remains today are a Herodian platform and part of the Western Wall.

1:2. Carried temple vessels away. See Dan 5:2, 3, 23. Earlier, Shishak, king of Egypt (945–924 BC) had robbed the treasuries from the temple and the palace in Jerusalem (1 Kgs 14:25, 26). Then came Nebuchadnezzar who also plundered the temple of Jerusalem in 605 BC and carried part of the vessels to Babylon (Dan 1:2; cf. Jer 20:4–6). In 598/7 BC the Babylonian Chronicle (BM 21946 reverse, lines 12–13) recorded that Nebuchadnezzar carried off to Babylon "vast tribute" from Hattu.[42] The plunder included more treasures from the Jerusalem temple. These Nebuchadnezzar placed in the treasure house of his god Marduk in Babylon (Dan 1:2; 2 Chr 36:7, 10). Some texts from Mari as well as the Cyrus Cylinder indicate that when people were defeated, their sacred objects, including idols and temple vessels, were taken away from them. See Isa 46:1, 2. The conquerors did this to demonstrate dominance over the defeated gods of their enemies.

An elaborate account of the Jerusalem temple's utensils is found in 1 Kgs 7:40–51 and 2 Kgs 25:13–17 (cf. Jer 52:17–23; 1 Esd 2:13–14). The counted vessels described in Ezra 1:7–11 were 5,400. This also gives an idea of some of the vessels that Nebuchadnezzar might have carried to Babylon: 30 golden dishes; 1,000 silver dishes; 29 silver pans; 30 golden bowls; 410 matching silver bowls; and 1,000 other articles. These temple articles may have been taken bit by bit during the several Babylonian attacks against Jerusalem from 605–587/6 BC. Nothing is said in the biblical account about the capture of the ark, a war talisman for Israel. The ark had both religious and military functions. Neither archaeology nor Rabbinical traditions have offered any evidence regarding the fate of the ark. Either King Josiah, under the direction of the prophetess Huldah, hid the ark in a rock cave under the Mosque on the Temple Mount, or it was carried to Babylon.[43] However, Eupolemus mentioned that "the gold, silver, and bronze of the Temple he [Nebuchadnezzar] sent to Babylon as tribute. Except the ark and the tablets

---

42. Grayson, *Assyrian and Babylonian Chronicles*, 100.
43. Williams, *Holy City*, 1:53. See also Price, *Stones Cry Out*, 203–19.

therein; these Jeremiah retained"[44] (2 Macc 2:4–8). The conclusion that seems plausible is that the ark might have been secretly hidden in a cave before the Babylonian attack, and has never been recovered.[45] Jeremiah 3:16 mentions something about the future of the ark.

The Babylonians did not repair the temple in Jerusalem, nor did they return the equipment and the treasure they confiscated. Nevertheless, in 538 BC Cyrus ordered all the temple utensils to be taken back to the Jerusalem temple (Ezra 6:5). The Cyrus Cylinder indicates that Cyrus returned the looted sacred objects and the gods to their respective places of origin.

1:3. Ashpenaz. A few Neo-Babylonian officials and their roles are mentioned in the biblical text. Ashpenaz appears as *rab*, "the chief, lord, master or owner of the eunuchs" (Dan 1:3), or *śar*, "the chief, ruler, official, captain, prince or leader of the eunuchs" (Dan 1:7, 8, 9, 10, 11, 18). The name "Ashpenaz" is attested in the cuneiform texts from Nippur as *Ashpazanda*[46] and as *'spnz* on an Aramaic incantation bowl from Nippur dated 600 BC.[47] The origin and development of the name has been debated. It may have come from the Old Persian *ašpinja*, "inn," which could imply an innkeeper.[48] Daniel and Ashpenaz had a relationship similar to that of Joseph and Potiphar, the Pharaoh's officer in Egypt (Gen 39:1, 4). Ashpenaz seems to have been very accommodative to the wishes of the Hebrew captives.

1:3–11, 18. Eunuchs. Some question whether Daniel and his three friends were eunuchs. There is no indication in the text regarding the marital status of Daniel and his friends. However, the prophet Isaiah, son of Amoz, warned King Hezekiah of Judah (716–686 BC) that his sons would be taken and made eunuchs in the palace of the king of Babylon (Isa 39:7; 2 Kgs 20:18). Perhaps this prophecy was fulfilled when Nebuchadnezzar commanded his chief of the eunuchs to select from the exiles from Judah some young men "from the sons of Israel and from the royal seed and from the nobles" (Dan 1:3) who had no *m'ûm*, "defect" or "blemish," but were of good appearance (Dan 1:4). The implication is that the young men should have no physical deformity.

Figuratively, the word *m'ûm* implies defilement or having a moral stain. The word *m'ûm* is used to imply any physical disfigurement either natural or human-initiated, and any such individual could be disqualified

---

44. Wacholder, *Eupolemus*, 237. Cf. Kang, *Divine War*, 208–12.
45. White, *Story of Prophets and Kings*, 453.
46. "Ashpenaz" (*SDABC*, 4:757).
47. Isbell, *Corpus*, 24, 25; and Coxon, "Ashpenaz" (*ABD*, 1:490–91).
48. Coxon, "Ashpenaz" (*ABD*, 1:491).

from priestly roles (Lev 21:17, 18, 21, 23; 24:19, 20) or if it be an animal, it would be rejected for a sacrificial offering (Lev 20, 21; Num 19:2; Deut 15:21; 17:1). These selected individuals were to be in the palace, but nothing is mentioned about whether Daniel, Hananiah, Mishael, and Azariah were castrated (Dan 1:3–7). There is substantial information that broadens our understanding on eunuchs in the ancient world. A thirteenth-century BC satirical letter from Egypt indicated that for one to qualify for being a scribe, one should be "a youth distinguished of appearance and pleasing of charm, who can explain the difficulties of the annals like him who composed them."[49]

The Neo-Assyrian and the Neo-Babylonian societies had three genders: the male, female, and eunuchs. Eunuchs were treated differently from other men, although their grammatical gender was still masculine. Reliefs and seals show them in men's dress but they are always depicted beardless in contrast to the *ša ziqni*, the bearded officials. A man was castrated for committing adultery, inappropriate behavior towards another man's wife, or for homosexuality.

The word *saris* is an Aramaic loanword from an unused root which means to "castrate," "emasculate," "geld."[50] The Arabic meaning of the verb is "to be impotent."[51] A eunuch, therefore, was intentionally incapacitated as a preventive measure against any procreation with the king's wives or women in the harem. The most common way to castrate was to crush the testicles before puberty to minimize mortality. In biblical times the eunuch was a high-ranking official in the king's court who was sometimes a foreigner (2 Kgs 9:32; 18:17; Jer 38:7; 41:16; 52:25). It should be noted that eunuchs were entrusted with the most important offices at court, and that they were known to be faithful (cf. Dan 6:4). Without a family of his own, a eunuch would give undivided attention to the king's business. As the text shows, it is difficult to determine whether Ashpenaz himself was a eunuch or simply "the chief" of the eunuchs (Dan 1:3, 7, 8, 9, 10, 11, 18).

1:3. Nobles. The masculine plural noun *happărtᵉmîm*, "the nobles," is a loanword from Old Persian *fratama*, which means "first," and it also appears in Esth 1:3 and Esth 6:9. One of the Hebrew adjectives which could have been used in its place is *ădîr*, "great, mighty, powerful; distinguished; splendid, glorious, majestic."[52] *ădîr* is used of God or the Messiah (Jer 30:21), of men, kings, princes, the godly (Ps 16:3), or of inanimate objects like water,

---

49. *ANET*, 475.
50. BDB, 710.
51. BDB, 710.
52. Wilson, *Old Testament Word Studies*, 189.

cedars, etc., but the word is from the root 'dr, which denotes being wide or great.[53] *Happărtᵉmîm* in Dan 1:3 refers primarily to the Jewish royalty and nobility. It has been argued that the use of the Persian word *happărtᵉmîm* is evidence for a late date for the composition of Daniel. However, Daniel served in the Neo-Babylonian and Persian courts and was well informed on contemporary language and protocol. He could have been acquainted with Persian loanwords on a daily basis.

1:3, 6. Israel and Judah. The names Judah and Israel seem to have been understood to refer to the same people. Archaeology evidence shows that many residents from the Northern kingdom of Israel fled to Judah during the Assyrian attacks and deportations. This makes Judah a composite remnant of the twelve tribes. For example, when the name Israel is mentioned in the context of prayer in Dan 9:7, 11, 20, it specifically refers to the community of exiles from Judah who then lived in Babylon. Daniel was from Judah (Dan 1:6), but he referred to everyone from his homeland as "my people Israel" (Dan 9:20). Daniel's people diffracted God's covenant of love (Dan 9:4–6). This led them into a disaster. The Sefire Treaty III warns of covenant unfaithfulness and subsequent consequences (*ANET*, 660–61; cf. Dan 11:23, 30).[54]

The transition from Neo-Babylonian to Medo-Persian dominance saw Judah being organized into the Persian province of *Yehud*.[55] Cyrus II gave permission in 538 BC for the people of Judah to return to their homeland and to rebuild the temple[56] (Ezra 1).

1:3. Some of the children of Judah. See **2:25. Captives.** The deliberate move to select some of the young people from the captives was based on merit.

1:3, 4. Social distinctions. Despite the Babylonian social restrictions, it seems that some of the people from Judah whom Nebuchadnezzar had deported were allowed to function without any barriers. These included Daniel (Dan 2:48; 5:29; 6:1–3; 6:28), Shadrach, Meshach, and Abednego (Dan 2:49; 3:30), who came from either the royal family or "the nobles" (Dan 1:3). *Happărtᵉmîm*, "the nobles," is a loanword from Old Persian *fratama*, which basically meant "first" (Dan 1:3; Esth 1:3; 6:9). These four

---

53. Wilson, *Old Testament Word Studies*, 189.
54. *ANET*, 660–61; cf. Dan 11:23, 30.
55. For the discussion on Judah under Persian imperial administration see related essays in Lipschits and Oeming, *Judah and the Judeans* (2006).
56. See commentary on **10:1. Cyrus, king of Persia.**

men became highly trained, top Neo-Babylonian and Medo-Persian government officials.

The Judaean exiled professionals (2 Kgs 24:14–16; Jer 24:1; 29:2) may have adopted the cultural traits of the land of their exile and assimilated into the Neo-Babylonian working class. It seems that the imperial administrators in the ancient Near East had more regard for the individual's ingenuity than one's social class.

Several archaeological finds give insights into the social setting of some of the exiles. Some hundreds of inscribed clay tablets dating from Artaxerxes I (464–424 BC) to Darius II (423–404 BC), about the time of biblical Ezra and Nehemiah, were discovered at Nippur in 1893.[57] These documents became known as the Murashu tablets and they highlight the economic life of some Jews in Mesopotamia. Jewish names appear on legal documents as royal officials, principals, contracting parties, buyers, sellers, agents, witnesses, and tax collectors with Murashu and sons, bankers, and brokers.[58]

None of the Judean seals have pagan impressions or symbols.[59] Also, the Judean documents were not issued on Saturdays or Jewish holidays, nor do they contain any oaths to foreign gods.[60] Zadok identified several different occupations and professions of the Judaeans in Babylonia.[61] These included businessmen and business partners, holders of land property, rent collectors, debtors, guarantors, those in charge of the king's poultry, royal merchants or commercial agents, summoners for taxes or corvée work, foremen, gardeners, shepherds, fishermen, scribes, army, seal makers, *gardu-workmen*, and slaves. There were several locations for Judean settlers in Babylonia. A 498 BC administrative text has been published from a place called "Judahtown" (Babylonian *āl-Yāḫūdu*).[62]

The Neo-Babylonian society was created by and for men, therefore women were at a disadvantage. A few specific women appear in the book of Daniel but without personal names (Dan 5:2, 3, 10, 23; 6:24; 11:6, 37). Women from the "nobility" are never mentioned or selected for special

---

57. Hilprecht and Clay, *Business Documents*, 9:13–45.

58. Coogan, *West Semitic Personal Names*, 11–41; cf. Zadok, *Earliest Diaspora Israelites and Judeans*, 11–80.

59. Zadok, *Earliest Diaspora Israelites and Judeans*, 57–61.

60. Zadok, "The Earliest Diaspora: The Judeans in Babylonia and Their Neighbors," Lecture, Horn Archaeological Museum, Andrews University, October 5, 2004; and Zadok, *Jews in Babylonia*, 82.

61. Zadok, *Earliest Diaspora Israelites and Judeans*, 54–56. See also Zadok, "Representation of Foreigners," 471–589.

62. Pearce, "How Bad Was the Babylonian Exile?," 52.

training according to the text. Nevertheless, in the Neo-Assyrian as well as the Neo-Babylonian societies, women could acquire or dispose of property, engage in any business transaction, and sue or be sued. There is no record, however, showing that women could stand as witnesses in legal documents. The Babylonian elite married foreign women but did not give their daughters to foreigners in marriage. The book of Daniel, then, seems to reflect accurately the social distinctions prevailing in Neo-Babylonia.

1:3, 4, 6, 7. Young men of Judah. A select few of the exiled young Judeans were sponsored for Babylonian education by King Nebuchadnezzar (Dan 1:3-7). They were chosen on the grounds of their noble birth, physical appearance, mental aptitude, and readiness to learn. The orientation to the Babylonian training began with the change of their Hebrew personal names (Dan 1:6-7) to Babylonian ones. Daniel, "God is my judge" or "My judge is God," became *balaṭ-su ṣur*, "protect his life," or *balaṭ-šar-uṣur*, "protect the life of the prince," that is, "Belteshazzar."[63] Hananiah, "Yahweh has been gracious," was called Shadrach, possibly the Assyrian *šādurāku*, "I am greatly frightened," "command of Aku (Sumerian moon-god)" or the Babylonian *šūdurāku*, "I am put into much fear."[64] Mishael, "Who is like God?" or "Who is what God is?," was called *mēšāku* (Meshach), "I am of little account" or "Who is what Aku is?" Azariah, "Yahweh helps," was named *'abednego* (Abednego), "servant of the shining one"[65] or "servant of Nego/Nebo." The suggestion that Ardi-Nabu, the official of the crown prince listed in the Istanbul Prism, was Abednego lacks substantive evidence.[66]

The use of Babylonian names was widespread among the Judean exiles. It was not limited only to Daniel, Hananiah, Mishael, and Azariah. The Judeans lived in several communities and participated in the economic and social life. A document was recovered that relates the marriage of the daughter of a Judean royal merchant. His daughter's name, "Kasshaya," is the same as one of Nebuchadnezzar's daughters.

1:4, 17. Language and literature. The curricula of Daniel and his colleagues was based on the literature and the language of the Babylonians (Dan 1:4), and might not have been limited to these only. Recovered texts reveal that the Neo-Babylonians had an extensive education system which

---

63. Collins, *Daniel*, 141; and Pfandl, *Daniel*, 16.
64. Hasel, "Book of Daniel," 213; Collins, *Daniel*, 141.
65. Hasel, "Book of Daniel," 213.
66. Stefanovic, *Daniel*, 23, 143-44. For the Istanbul Prism inscription see *ANET*, 308.

they had inherited from the Old Babylonian kingdom and other contemporary states. Important centers of education were Babylon, Warka, and Hipparene.

The curricula included the study of astronomy, business, economics, history, government, law, lexicography, mathematics, medicine, music, natural phenomena, and religion. Babylonian mathematics was very advanced. Babylonian literature covered a very wide spectrum and might have been multilingual. Aramaic, which had adopted the Canaanite-Phoenician script developed about 1100 BC, was the official language in a multinational Babylon. Classical literature was in Sumerian and Akkadian cuneiform. Akkadian, however, was the language of the Chaldeans. It was imperative for foreigners who worked in that society to learn the language of the Chaldeans (Dan 1:4). Akkadian, or the Babylonian language, used the cuneiform script, which was a complex system of ideograms (pictures or symbols representing an idea) and syllograms (syllabic signs that were used for early development of the alphabet). Years of study were required to become proficient in this language of the Chaldeans.

Besides language and literature, they studied astrology, prognostication, and divination. The Babylonian wise men relied on astrological and cosmological predictions based on omens from natural phenomena such as shooting stars, earthquakes, dreams, storms, and the like. The king would depend on their interpretations and predictions in decisive matters. Just as Daniel indicates, ancient Near Eastern literature shows that the training of capable foreigners and placing them in royal courts was a common practice.

1:4, 17, 20. Wisdom. Jewish education had to do with the application of wisdom in daily life. The human heart is taken to be the citadel of morality and decision-making. Wisdom, therefore, resides in the heart (Ps 90:12; Prov 2:10; Eccl 1:17; 8:16). God dispenses wisdom (Dan 2:14, 20, 21, 30; 5:11, 14). There are several words for wisdom in Hebrew,[67] including: *hokmāh*, "wisdom," "skill," "shrewdness," or "prudence"; *bînāh*, "understanding"; *da'at*, "knowledge"; *m^ezimmāh*, "plan," "thought," or "prudence"; and *mûsār*, "correction."

The Hebrew Scriptures taunted the Chaldean city of Babylon that it would not remain the "mistress of the kingdoms" (Isa 47:1, 5), and that its wisdom and knowledge would be misleading (Isa 47:10). In fact, the wisdom and knowledge of the Chaldeans was fraught with divination and magical characteristics. Some technical terms incorporated in the description of the custodians of the Chaldean wisdom and knowledge include

---

67. Von Rad, *Wisdom in Israel*, 53; and Denning-Bolle, *Wisdom in Akkadian Literature*, 32.

"sorcerers," "those with great spells" (Isa 47:9, 12), "the dividers of the heavens," "the star gazers," and "those who foretell the omens which come with the new moon" (Isa 47:13).

Archaeological evidence shows that in the Neo-Assyrian and Neo-Babylonian empires the king was associated with the intelligentsia who always provided decisive advice on critical matters concerning the kingdom and often reported or interpreted omens of all kinds. For Daniel, it is his God who grants wisdom (Dan 2:19-23, 28) and reveals secrets (Dan 2:19, 22, 27, 28; cf. Amos 3:7).

Mesopotamian or Babylonian concepts of wisdom are contrasted with Jewish concepts of wisdom in the book of Daniel. Wisdom in Jewish circles is applied in daily living. The Mesopotamian wisdom tradition emphasizes craftsmanship, cleverness, and technical know-how. All skill, technical prowess, and wisdom are attributed to the gods Ea or Marduk. In the *Enūma eliš* 2.116, Ea describes Marduk as *mār īmudū gimri uznu*, "my son, (thou) who knowest all wisdom."[68] In Mesopotamia the ear was taken to be the seat of intelligence. The Ugaritic *ḥkm*, "to be wise," is usually associated with the high god El and also aging.[69]

Mesopotamian wisdom and knowledge were basically composed of the academic and folk strands. The academic strand involved the rigorous acquisition of knowledge and skills through instructed curriculum in different disciplines and literature. The folk strand included the mastering of linguistics, either from literary sources or from oral traditions. Daniel excelled in wisdom and he was promoted to be the chief administrator over all the wise men in Babylon.

1:4. Chaldeans. The Hebrew name *kaśdîm*, "Chaldeans" (Dan 1:4), is etymologically close to its Aramaic equivalent *kaśdā'în* (Dan 2:4).[70] The Greek term *Chaldaioi*, "Chaldeans," seems to come from the Akkadian *Kaldû*.[71] Nebuchadnezzar's instructions with regard to the Hebrew youths included teaching them "the writing and the tongue of the Chaldeans" (Dan 1:4). According to Daniel, the tongue of the Chaldeans is Aramaic (Dan 2:4). The first mention of the term "Chaldeans" in 878 BC appears in the annals of Ashur-nasir-pal II (883-859 BC) who referred to the southern part of Babylonia as "the land of *Kaldû* (the Chaldeans)."[72] Grant Frame pointed out that

---

68. *ANET*, 64.

69. Müller, "חכם *chākham*" (*TDOT*, 4:366).

70. Rainey, "Chaldea, Chaldeans" (*Encyclopaedia Judaica*, 5:330-31); and Hess, "Chaldea" (*ABD*, 1:886-87).

71. See Millard, "Daniel 1—6 and History," 69-71.

72. Saggs, *Babylonians*, 153; Johns, "Chaldea" (*Encyclopaedia Biblica*, 1:720-21);

from the ninth century BC onwards, evidence of the Chaldeans continued to be seen in cuneiform sources until the time of Darius II (423–405 BC) in the Persian period.[73]

Sennacherib (704–681 BC) claims to have devastated the Chaldean territory and taken eighty-eight walled cities and 820 villages from all the tribes. He further claims to have deported 208,000 captives, along with thousands of animals, which included cattle, sheep, horses, and camels.[74] Other cities in Babylonia which were occupied by the Chaldeans included Ḥursagkalama, Kish, Nippur, Sippar, and Uruk.

The word "Chaldeans" was sometimes used in the book of Daniel as synonymous with "Babylonians" (Dan 3:8; 5:30; Isa 13:19; 23:13; 47:1, 5; 48:14, 20). The context provides clues which make it clear when this was the case. "Chaldean" was also a technical term used for the practitioners of traditional crafts. For example, the astrologers, sorcerers, diviners, and magicians of Dan 2:2, 4, 10; 4:7; and 5:7–11 were called "Chaldeans." These Chaldeans appear in the council of the king along with the wise men. The Babylonian priests as well as magical arts practitioners continued to be described as Chaldeans by ancient writers such as Herodotus (1.181–83), whose writings are dated somewhere around 450 BC. Strabo (16.1), Diodorus Siculus (2.29), and the Palmyrene Inscriptions also used the term "Chaldeans."[75] The writers in the Hebrew Bible interchangeably used "Chaldeans" to imply either the Neo-Babylonian Empire or its citizens (e.g., Gen 11:28, 31; Ezra 5:12; Job 1:17). The author of Daniel seems to have used the term "Chaldeans" contextually and in accordance with the contemporary application of that term.

1:5–16. King assigned them a daily portion of food. The four Hebrew youths were provided with royal food and residence during their three-year training at the king's court in Babylon (Dan 1:3–7). It is with regard to their voluntary abstention from certain foods that one discovers that the Babylonian diet was omnivorous. Flesh foods in Neo-Babylonia in the first millennium BC included poultry, fish, sheep, goats, cattle, pigs, and horses.

Daniel and his friends chose to maintain their dietary heritage (Gen 1:29; 9:4; Lev 3:17; 11:1–46; 17:10–14; Deut 14:1–21). From the foods

---

Brinkman, *Political History of Post-Kassite Babylonia*, 260.

73. Frame, "Chaldeans" (*OEANE*, 1:482–84). See also Oates, *Babylon*, 111–14; and Arnold, *Who Were the Babylonians?*, 87–91.

74. Saggs, *Babylonians*, 157.

75. Hillers and Cussini, *Palmyrene Aramaic Texts*, 26, Ber '34 p 38 IV, line 7; and 126–27, C4357, line 5.

they were offered, they opted for *hazzērō'îm*, "the vegetables"[76] (Dan 1:12, 16; cf. Gen 1:29, 30). *Hazzērō'îm* included "plants raised from seed," "seed-bearing plants," or "sown seeds" (cf. Lev 11:37; Isa 61:11; Gen 1:11–12, 29). Information on the principal foodstuffs and diet of the ancient Mesopotamians is available through large numbers of written documents and archaeological remains recovered from the ancient Near East. This evidence includes royal registry ration texts, art, material remains, and over five hundred documents recovered from various places in ancient Mesopotamia. While there is adequate information on the ingredients available to the ancient cuisine, there is no illumination on the preparation of the meals.

The recovered finds provide necessary information to understanding Daniel's alternative diet. Archaeologists who study ancient forms of plant life (archaeobotanists) show that barley, both naked and hulled *Hordeum distichum* and *Hordeum vulgare* (Sumerian *še*, Akkadian *uṭṭatu/uṭṭetu*), was the most important cereal in the low-lying regions of Mesopotamia. In these areas, irrigation was prevalent from as early as the Old Babylonian period to the Hellenistic period. The word *še* was used as the generic term for grain.[77] Barley was more popular than wheat, not only for its "low irrigation requirements"[78] and "low rate of evapotranspiration"[79] but because it outproduced wheat, and it ripened about three weeks earlier than wheat.

In ancient Mesopotamia the archaeobotanical evidence of wheat (Sumerian *zíz*, Akkadian *kunāšum* or *zízum/zizzum*) dates back to the early Neolithic period. The most common type was the domesticated emmer wheat, *Triticum dicoccum*.[80] Although wheat was less popular than barley, the crop thrived in the dry conditions of southern Mesopotamia. This wheat was known by the generic name (Sumerian *gig*, Akkadian *kibtu*).[81]

Other wheats like einkorn, wild *Triticum boeoticum*, and domesticated *Triticum monococcum* (small spelt) have been attested from as early as the Samarran and Ubaid periods, about 6000–4000 BC, but have not yet been identified in the cuneiform texts.[82]

D. T. Potts pointed out that in southern Mesopotamia there were various legumes which included lentil (*Lens esculenta*), common or field pea

---

76. See BDB, 282–83; Holladay, *Concise Hebrew and Aramaic Lexicon*, 92; and Preuss, "זרע" (*TDOT*, 4:143–48).

77. Potts, *Mesopotamian Civilization*, 59.

78. Potts, *Mesopotamian Civilization*, 60.

79. Potts, *Mesopotamian Civilization*, 60.

80. Potts, *Mesopotamian Civilization*, 60.

81. Potts, *Mesopotamian Civilization*, 62.

82. Maekawa, "Cereal Cultivation," 73–96; and Powell, "Sumerian Cereal Crops," 48–72.

(*Pisum sativum*), chickpea (*Cicer arietinum*), and broad bean (*Vicia faba*), which may have been eaten as "green vegetables, raw or cooked, or used as dried seeds."[83] Two texts were found in northeastern Iraq at Tell Shemshara that had a list of legumes grown there.[84] The field pea was a winter crop. It was used as "a food offering in the Royal Cemetery at Ur (Pu-Abi's grave), in Early Dynastic and Old Akkadian levels at Tell Taya and at Old Babylonian Tell ed-Der."[85]

Besides barley and wheat, the list of the agricultural produce in Neo-Babylonia included dates, flax, grapes, millet, onions, palms, pulses, sesame, and spelt.[86]

In the Neo-Babylonian period there were two types of common vegetables: vegetables eaten freshly from the garden, and pulse crops (edible seeds and legumes). The first book written by Berossus portrays Babylonia as lying between the Tigris and Euphrates rivers where there was a high yield of wheat, barley, ocrus, sesamum, and edible roots called gongæ, which were just as nutritious as barley.[87]

The archaeological finds with regard to food remains seem to indicate that the alternate diet for Daniel and friends included a wide variety of vegetables, fruit, and grains that were adequate for balanced nutrition.

1:5–16. Wine. Daniel's resolve against the king's wine (Dan 1:8) can be better understood in light of some material and literary discoveries. Wine was the main beverage served to the members of the king's court (Dan 1:5, 8, 10, 16). It was not offered as part of the meal for nutritional purposes but for sacral (libations) and social purposes. For the Babylonians, wine was a prestige drink that was served for the king and his officials, but kept away from common people. They always poured a portion of the wine on a pagan altar.

Lower Babylonia was not conducive to wine production. Although there is evidence for some vineyards in southern Babylonia, grape production level was too low for any meaningful wine production. Instead of grapes, they used the fermented juices of dates to make wine. Herodotus recorded: "Oil came from sesame rather than from the olive and . . . fruit, 'wine,' and 'honey' were furnished by the date-palm rather than by figs, grapes and bees."[88]

---

83. Potts, *Mesopotamian Civilization*, 62–63.
84. Eidem, "Note on the Pulse Crops," 141–43.
85. Potts, *Mesopotamian Civilization*, 63.
86. Adams, *Heartland of Cities*, 186.
87. Burstein, *Babyloniaca of Berossus*, 13; and Horne, *Babylonia and Assyria*, 1:19.
88. Herodotus, *Herodotus*, 1.193–94.

In the Chaldean and Persian times, the vine was still being grown, and because it was more expensive to produce the vine, the Babylonians had to resort more to barley and dates. They imported wine and there are some letters from a merchant in Babylon to his agent in Sippar notifying him of the arrival of the "wine boat" and instructing him to purchase wine and bring it to Babylon.[89]

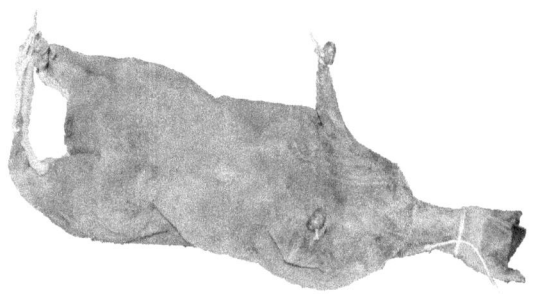

WATER OR WINE SKIN
A water or wine skin was made from a leathered animal, e.g., a sheep or goat, and used to store or transport water or wine in the ancient times.
(Courtesy of HAM)

Nebuchadnezzar's wine came from foreign countries.[90] He dedicated and offered the wine that was bright and pure to the Babylonian gods like the uncountable waters of a river.[91] Another text indicates that Nebuchadnezzar presented abundant wine as a daily offering to the great gods.[92] Wine was an expensive import and was mainly for the gods and the rich. Besides being imported, wine also came to Babylonia as booty or taxes from the countries which the Babylonians subdued. Herodotus (1.193–94) visited Babylonia later in the fifth century BC and wrote that wine came into Babylonia from upriver, being floated downriver via round skin boats in date palm containers.

The refusal of the wine might not have been based solely on Daniel's religious heritage. In fact, only the priests (Lev 10:9), those who administer justice (Prov 20:1; 31:4, 5), and the Nazarite (Num 6:1–4; Judg 13:3–5) were restricted from drinking wine in the Hebrew Bible. There might have been

89. Leemans, *Foreign Trade*, 103–4.

90. See also "Wine Down the Tigris and Euphrates," in McGovern, *Ancient Wine*, 168–73.

91. Powell, "Wine and the Vine," 102. See also "The Care and Feeding of the Gods," in Oppenheim, *Ancient Mesopotamia*, 183–98.

92. Lambert, "Nebuchadnezzar King of Justice," 9, rev. col. v, lines 13–16.

some people who abstained from drinking wine based on some traditional practices (Jer 35). Daniel seems to have decided not to take the wine based more on the Babylonian reasons known to him. As already mentioned above, wine was dedicated to the gods, and a conscientious Jew would not partake of anything offered to idols.

The Babylonian wine was prone to causing some psychodynamic effects which Daniel might not have wanted to experience. Xenophon wrote that wine was imported from the north of Babylonia but date palms and grain were plentiful in the area. He pointed out that there was a lot of sourish date wine and yet another sweetish drink that caused headaches, but no grapes or grape wine originated in Babylonia.[93] Moreover, in the ancient days, wine was fermented by adding to it much sugar-rich fruit and herbs. This made it very syrupy, more or less sweet, and intoxicating.

Wine could be diluted, spiced, or resinated, hence "spiced wine" (Song 8:2), as can be demonstrated by the parallels from Old Babylonia. That which was referred to as "good wine" (Song 7:9) was also spiced or resinated wine.

1:8. Not defile himself. The Hebrew verb here is *gāʾal*, "defile," "pollute," "stain," "desecrate."[94] In the ancient Near East the word "defile" was widely used to imply ceremonial pollution in a physical or metaphorical sense that could be incurred through the breaking of the moral code or ceremonial law. All wrongdoing defiles (Lev 11:44; Ezek 37:23; Zeph 3:1; Neh 13:29; Isa 52:11). Some priests whose genealogy could not be confirmed were considered defiled while they were in exile (Ezra 2:62; Neh 7:64). The Temple Scroll from Qumran states that the city where God chooses to establish His name and His sanctuary must be pure from all impurity[95] (cf. Rev 21:27).

All the wine, oil, and food that enter into that designated city must be clean and pure. Also from Qumran, the Damascus Document adds: "No man shall defile himself by eating any live creature or creeping thing, from the larvae of bees to all creatures which creep in water."[96] Provisionally, the defiled person could go through certain prescribed rituals in order to restore a state of ritual purity and come back to the community of faith. Daniel was aware of possible contaminants with the food and made a personal decision not to break the rules. He was so courageous to stand for his convictions.

---

93. See Xenophon, *Anabasis*, 2.3.14–16, 2.4.28, 3.4.31, 4.2.22, 4.4.9, 4.5.26, quoted in Powell, "Wine and the Vine," 102.
94. Wilson, *Old Testament Word Studies*, 113.
95. Vermes, *Complete Dead Sea Scrolls in English*, 206.
96. Vermes, *Complete Dead Sea Scrolls in English*, 141.

Babylonians used ceremoniously unclean animals for food. Moreover, the clean animals were not slaughtered or prepared according to Jewish laws.

1:11, 16. Steward. *Hammelṣar* means "the steward." Daniel had to tactfully approach *hammelṣar* (Dan 1: 11, 16), probably "the keeper," "overseer," "steward," or "guardian," to make known of his dietary request. *Hammelṣar* is not a personal name, but a Babylonian title to one of the officials. The article *ha*, "the," is placed in front of the noun *melṣar*.[97] The title probably comes to us from the Akkadian *maṣṣaru*, "guardian" or "warden." It was Ashpenaz who appointed this overseer/guardian to take care of Daniel and his friends (Dan 1:11, 16). The steward may have secured permission from Ashpenaz to change the diet of these four Jewish youths.

1:12. Ten days. The time suggested by Daniel was short for developing significant physical improvement, but it worked well for him and his friends. Daniel could have based his decision on the healthy lifestyle he and his friends were already practicing. It is possible that Daniel may have asked for full time for him and his friends to prove themselves in their vegetarian diet. In the ancient Near East, the number ten was considered to imply completeness or fullness. Also, at the end of their three-year education in the king's court, Daniel and his friends were ten times wiser than their colleagues and all the magicians (1:20).

1:17. To these four young men. God enabled Daniel, Hananiah, Mishael, and Azariah to comprehend Babylonian literature and language in exceptional ways. Their competence in understanding astrology and divination by dreams was outstanding. However, on practical tests on interpretation and prediction, and on solving complex riddles and enigmas, omens and dreams, neither the Babylonian gods nor literature were all that helpful. Daniel and his friends received special revelation from their God that distinguished them in the field (Dan 2:11, 47).

1:20. Magicians. The Hebrew *ḥarṭummîm*, "magicians," and Aramaic *ḥarṭummîn*, "magicians," both appear in the text of Daniel. See Dan 2:2–10; 4:6–7, 18; 5:7–15. The word is borrowed from Egyptian language. Egyptian magicians (Gen 41:8, 24; Exod 7:11) were renowned for dream interpretation, divinatory practices, and magical performances. See Exod 7:8–12. Akkadian language has *ḥarṭibi*, "interpreter of dreams."[98] In the ancient Near East *ḥarṭummîm* were considered well advanced in science and

---

97. BDB, 576. The Assyrian *maṣ(ṣ)aru*, the Persian *mulsaru*, or the Akkadian *maṣṣaru*, "guardian" or "warden," could be the equivalent titles to the Neo-Babylonian *melṣar*.

98. *CAD*, 6:116; and *NIDOTTE*, 2:273.

mysterious arts. Each time the king had an emergency, he would consult with the magicians, who were among the wise men. In the book of Daniel, the word "magicians" is used parallel to astrologers, sorcerers, soothsayers, and Chaldeans. Daniel is appointed to be the chief of magicians because of his superior knowledge and wisdom (Dan 2:48; 5:11). Archaeological evidence shows the presence of Egyptians in Neo-Babylonia in the first half of the first millennium BC. Deuteronomy 18:10–11 shows a wide range of vocabulary on magicians. These people claimed to deal with occult knowledge. However, the book of Daniel shows that magicians were limited as far as knowledge of secret divine messages.

1:20. Conjurers/astrologers. The plural Hebrew noun 'aššāpîm, "conjurers of spirits," "enchanters," "necromancers," "magicians," or "astrologers"[99] has an equivalent meaning with its Aramaic counterpart 'ašāpîn. These words appear only in Dan 2:20 and Dan 5:11 and are always in a list with words that clearly indicate the mantic or divination practice (Dan 1:20; 2:10, 27; 4:7; 5:7, 11, 15). Astrologers were Babylonian magicians who were skilled in tracing and predicting the movements the sun, moon, planets, and stars as indicators of the will of gods in human life. This group practiced mantic or divination arts. The conjurers and/or astrologers functioned in the Babylonian court and were always summoned to resolve enigmas faced by the king (Dan 2:1–2; 4:6, 7; 5:6, 7). The ineffectiveness of this group in their role is apparent in the text of Daniel.

1:21. King Cyrus. See 10:1. Cyrus, king of Persia. Daniel went into captivity in 605 BC. After his three years of training, he served the Babylonian government for about sixty-four years. He must have been around eighty years old when the Neo-Babylonian kingdom fell in 539 BC. He then continued to serve King Cyrus in the Medo-Persian era.

1–2:4a. The Hebrew of Daniel. Daniel 1:1–2:4a and 8–12 are the Hebrew parts of the book. Some scrolls recovered at Qumran confirm the Hebrew and Aramaic parts of the text of Daniel just as they appear in the Masoretic Text. 1QDan[a] (Dan 1:10–17; 2:2–6) shows the transition from Hebrew to Aramaic at 2:2b while both 4QDan[a] and 4QDan[b] preserve the shift from Aramaic back to Hebrew at Dan 8:1.[100] Chapters 8–12 are mainly written in Hebrew because they deal with matters that have to do with God's chosen people. The hypothesis that the Hebrew of the Danielic text was a translation from the Aramaic original document has been discarded for lack of

---

99. Baker and Carpenter, *Complete Word Study Dictionary*, 827.
100. Ulrich, "Text of Daniel," in Collins and Flint, *Book of Daniel*, 2:579.

supportive linguistic evidence. Aramaic shares not only the script with Hebrew but also the vocabulary. As sister languages, Aramaic and Hebrew have close affinities that when objectively analyzed may help determine the date of the composition of Daniel.

Daniel uses some contemporary exilic phrases that were also commonly employed by Ezekiel. These include:

- son of man (Dan 8:17; Ezek 2:1)
- time of the end (Dan 8:17; 11:35, 40; 12:4; Ezek 21:25, 29)
- beautiful [thing] (Dan 8:9; 11:41; Ezek 20:6, 15)
- burnished bronze (Dan 10:6; Ezek 1:7)
- clothed in white linen (Dan 12:6, 7; Ezek 9:3, 11; 10:2, 6, 7)[101]

Montgomery, who followed Franz Delitzsch, acknowledged Daniel's literary use of Ezekiel. Nevertheless, he dated Daniel, along with Chronicles, Ezra, Nehemiah, and Esther, as having been written shortly before the beginning of the Greek period.[102] W. F. Martin analyzed the words in Daniel which are used to support a late date for the book. Martin concluded that there was nothing extraordinary in the Hebrew of Daniel which would deny a sixth-century BC date.[103] Thus, there is no evidence to show that any words in Daniel which may be classified as consistent with the second century BC or later were not already in use in the sixth century BC or earlier.

Hebrew is a human language that serves as God's vehicle of revelation to people. It has close affinity to other ancient Near Eastern languages. It even shares some similar vocabulary. Just like any other ancient language, Hebrew is subject to some common linguistic laws and adapts well to sociocultural and religiopolitical influences down through history.[104] This language has continued being used and has developed into spoken contemporary Hebrew that has significant linguistic changes.

---

101. Collins, *Daniel*, 20, n. 200.
102. Montgomery, *Book of Daniel*, 14, 15; and Collins, *Daniel*, 20.
103. Martin, "Hebrew of Daniel," 28–30.
104. Joosten, "How Hebrew Became a Holy Language," 46.

Daniel 2

DREAMING SUCCESSION

THE MAIN THEME IN the book of Daniel turns out to be the succession of the geopolitical kingdoms from the time of Nebuchadnezzar until the time of the end of the world and their subsequent replacement by the divine one. The interpretation of the dreams in light of ancient evidence should be consistent with the history of geopolitical developments beginning from the time of Nebuchadnezzar and Daniel onwards. The dreams in the book of Daniel transcend their time, shedding light throughout human history. They show the end-time destruction of the geopolitical world, and climax in the establishment of a divine kingdom.

2:1. Second year. That is, 603 BC. The Babylonians used the accession year system. See table 1.

2:1. Interpretation of dreams. See also **7:1. Daniel's dreams/visions.** The ancient Near East put significant importance on dreams and their interpretation. The analysis of dreams from the extant ancient literary sources offers an informed understanding of the treatment of dreams recorded in the book of Daniel. In the ancient Near East, dreams were categorized as three types: divine revelations, reflections of the state of the dreamer's mind (symptomatic), or mantic (related to divination) in which forthcoming events are prognosticated. Dreams were generally viewed either as prognostic or symptomatic in nature. The prognostic dreams were perceived as clear messages which did not necessitate interpretation, while the symbolic message dreams were those which required decoding. Dream omens were often interpreted from the dream books. On the other hand, the symptomatic dreams were classified simply as pleasant or bad dreams.

There were trained experts in different techniques and methods of interpretation of dreams. Both the Babylonians and Egyptians had dream books which were compilations of dreams and keys to their interpretation. In ancient Mesopotamia astrology and the interpretation of dreams were seen as methods of divination (cf. Gen 44:5, 15). In Dan 2 and 4, Nebuchadnezzar dreamed, and then demanded from his specialists the interpretations of his dreams (Dan 2:2, 5; 4:3). A small unbaked tablet (YBC 2192)[1] shows the practice of interpreting dreams to the king:

> In the month of Tebet, day 15th, year 7th of Nabonidus, king of Babylon, Shumukin says as follows: the great star, Venus, Kaksidi, the moon, and the sun in my dream I saw, and for favor of Nabonidus, king of Babylon, my lord, and for favor of Belshazzar, the son of the king, my lord, may my ear attend to them. On the 17th day of Tebet, year 7th of Nabonidus, the king of Babylon, Shumukin says as follows: the great star I saw, and the favor of Nabonidus, king of Babylon, my lord, and the favor of Belshazzar, the son of the king, my lord, may my ear attend.

An Old Babylonian omen text (VAT 7525 of the Berlin Museum) states that "if a man cannot remember the dream he saw (it means): his (personal) god is angry with him."[2] It was a common practice in the ancient Near East for kings to call their counselors to interpret the dream. Herodotus wrote about Astyages, king of Persia, who dreamed, and then assembled his magi, who had the gift of interpreting dreams.[3]

Mesopotamian texts on the interpretation of dreams are usually introduced by *kī anni piširšu*, "this is the [pertinent] solution (in the sense of 'answer')"[4] (cf. Dan 2:36; 4:24; 5:26). The root *pēšer* is common in several Semitic languages, including Aramaic, Hebrew, and Arabic. It can mean "to interpret" and can be applied to either a dream or a difficult passage in a text. Usually, interpreters identified the central theme of the dream and figured out the meaning of the dream, and of the symbols it contained. They would not only explain the dream but also dispel all evil consequences

---

1. Clay, *Miscellaneous Inscriptions*, 1:55–56. Other relevant works to the discussion on interpretation of dreams include: Finkel, "Pesher of Dreams and Scriptures," 357–70; Zeitlin, "Dreams and Their Interpretation," 1–18; and Miller, "Dreams and Prophetic Vision," 401–4.

2. Oppenheim, *Interpretation of Dreams*, 232; Husser, *Dreams and Dream Narratives*, 118–22; and Butler, *Mesopotamian Conceptions of Dreams*, 15–41.

3. Herodotus, *Herodotus*, 1.106.

4. Oppenheim, *Interpretation of Dreams*, 220.

through magical arts or discern the message from a deity suggesting the suitable response for the dreamer to take.

Egyptian interpreters were renowned throughout the ancient Near East. On the Dog River Stela, an Assyrian king, Esarhaddon (680–669 BC), relates how he fought and plundered Egypt during the time of Tarqû "Tirhakah" (690–664 BC), and he lists the "divination-experts" to have been among the pharaoh's outstanding officials he encountered there.[5] They were called in and consulted in the Assyrian court before and after the time of Ashurbanipal (668–631/627 BC). Pharaoh was once asked to send to Cyrus (559–530 BC) a diviner who was specialized in observing eagles.[6]

King Ashurbanipal recorded his dreams in his historical documents. In both the Assyrian and the Egyptian court settings there were *ḥarṭummîm*, "the magicians," who would interpret the dreams (Gen 41:8; Exod 7:11, 22; cf. Dan 2:2, 10, 27; 4:6; 5:11, 12). The biblical account accurately reflects the reality of the past when it describes ancient kings who threatened their officials for failing to give interpretation of their dreams.

The importance of the interpretation of dreams and visions in the book of Daniel can be seen in the frequent use of the Aramaic loanword *pēšer*, "solution" or "interpretation."[7] It is repeated about thirty-two times in the first half of the book. *Pēšer* appears in relation to giving the meaning of Nebuchadnezzar's dreams (Dan 2:4, 5, 6, 7, 9, 16, 24, 25, 26, 30, 36, 45; 4:6, 7, 9, 18, 19, 24), and Belshazzar's writing on the wall (Dan 5:7, 8, 12, 15, 16, 17, 26). Although the author seemed to be perplexed over his own ambiguous visions and dreams in the last half of the book, the word *pēšer only* appears in relation to them in Dan 7:16.

It is interesting to note that Nebuchadnezzar and Belshazzar pleaded for someone to give them an interpretation. Daniel as well struggled to understand his own dreams and visions but was aided by divine beings.

2:1–3. Nebuchadnezzar's dreams. The dreams in Daniel are highly symbolic and their interpretation is essential for a complete understanding of the message of the book. Although the dreams of Nebuchadnezzar are extant only in the biblical text (Dan 2; 4), they can be understood more clearly in light of related ancient literary texts. In fact, in the Neo-Babylonian era, the texts on royal dreams are common only from the time of Nabonidus (556–539 BC). Nebuchadnezzar "dreamed dreams" in 603 BC (Dan 2:1). His spirit was troubled and he could not sleep any more after dreaming.

5. *ANET*, 293.

6. Oppenheim, *Interpretation of Dreams*, 224.

7. BDB, 833. It has been argued that in the Qumranic literature *pēsher/pittārōn* could mean "presage" or "prognostic." See Rabinowitz, "*Pēsher/Pittārōn*," 219–32.

There are a number of parallels in the narratives of the dreams of Pharaoh (Gen 41) and Nebuchadnezzar (Dan 2; 4). In Mesopotamia, from the third millennium BC, dreams were considered to be sent by the gods. The messenger for bringing dreams was Zaqiqu. Such dreams caused fear on the one who received them. The dreamer would quickly want to know the fate. The conclusion of a dream was crucial because it expressed that transition from dreaming to wakefulness. In Akkadian, that moment was referred to as *negeltû*, "to wake up with a start."[8] When Nebuchadnezzar's dream ended, he could not sleep and he could not remember what he had dreamed (Dan 2:1).

Literary conventions identify the characteristics of dreams through describing the setting of the dream, the circumstances which led the person to dream, and also the dream content. In addition, the reaction of the dreamer, the result of fulfillment, and the involvement of the divine are included in the analysis. Daniel reminded Nebuchadnezzar that when he went to bed the night of his dream, his mind was preoccupied with what would take place in the future (Dan 2:29).

It is clear in the ancient Near Eastern literature that dreams were sometimes taken as products of the dreamer's psychological and physiological factors. One Akkadian text reads: "Remove [wo]e and anxiety from your heart (literally: from your side), [wo]e and anxiety create (only bad) dreams!"[9] Nebuchadnezzar's mind might have been wondering over some issues with regard to his succession or the like, but his symbolic dream is said to have been of supernatural origin (Dan 2:28). His dreams have both apocalyptic and theological overtones.

Tertullian (ca. AD 160–ca. 225) commented: "It is from God that the dreams proceed which edify us and reveal truth; the latter are also sent to infidels, as for instance to Nebuchadnezzar, who dreamt a dream from God, and many people have come to know God in this way (on the other hand, the faithful are tempted in dreams by the devil)."[10]

Nebuchadnezzar's dreams are symbolic and enigmatic. They sometimes "conceal with strange shapes and veil with ambiguity the true meaning of the information being offered and require an interpretation for its understanding."[11]

Dreams have three components that belong together: the dream content, the interpretation, and the fulfillment in life setting. All three originate

---

8. Oppenheim, *Interpretation of Dreams*, 191.
9. Oppenheim, *Interpretation of Dreams*, 227, 237.
10. See Waszink, *Quinti Septimi Florentis Tertullian*, 480.
11. Oppenheim, *Interpretation of Dreams*, 206.

from the same source. The God of Heaven sent dreams or visions to Nebuchadnezzar (Dan 2; 4), Belshazzar (Dan 5), and Daniel (Dan 7—12). The same God designated Daniel to give the interpretation of Nebuchadnezzar's dreams and the vision of Belshazzar. As for Daniel, he received the understanding of his dreams/visions from a divine agent. God also regulates all circumstances to fulfill the dreams. It was God's responsibility to arrange for those dreams/visions to come true in the future. In the context of Neo-Babylonian culture, Shamash, the sun god of the Babylonians, is perceived as sending a dream to someone who then goes to the priest for interpretation. The priest, in turn, seeks an interpretation from Shamash.[12] A text relates Nebuchadnezzar appearing after his death in Nabonidus's dream:

> With regard to the conjunction of the Great Star and the moon, I became apprehensive (but in a dream) a man (1-*en eṭ-lu*) stood (suddenly) beside me and said to me: "There are no evil portents (involved) in the conjunction!" In the same dream, Nebukadnezzar, my royal predecessor and one attendant (appeared to me) standing on a chariot. The attendant said to Nebukadnezzar: "Do speak to Nabonidus so that he can report to you the dream he has had!" Nebukadnezzar was agreeable (literally: listened to him) and said to me: "Tell me what good (signs) you have seen!" I answered him saying: "In my dream I saw with joy the Great Star, the moon and the planet Jupiter (literally: Marduk) high up in the sky and it (the Great Star) called me by my name [ ]."[13]

This text offers an example of a dream, and an interpretation in another dream. Nabonidus dreamed of his dream being interpreted, in this case, by Nebuchadnezzar, a deceased predecessor. In the Babylonian Talmud, R. Yohanan speaks of "a dream that one has in the morning, and a dream that someone's friend had about him, and a dream that is interpreted through a dream."[14]

Nebuchadnezzar's dream in Dan 2 covered long historical periods of time, so he did not live to see its fulfillment. In this dream, Nebuchadnezzar marveled at the great image, and was stunned when a stone suddenly appeared and smashed the image at its feet, which were partly iron and partly clay. In real life, he managed to outlive only the fulfillment of the dream that is recorded in Dan 4, but not that of Dan 2.

---

12. Oppenheim, *Interpretation of Dreams*, 222.

13. Oppenheim, *Interpretation of Dreams*, 250. Other texts involving the appearance of the deceased include 1 Sam 28:11-20; and Gilgamesh and Enkidu, in Oppenheim, *Interpretation of Dreams*, 247-49.

14. Neusner, *Talmud of Babylonia*, 1:373.

2:2. Magicians. See **1:20. Magicians.** It has been argued that the use of "the magicians" in Dan 1:20; 2:2, 10, 27; 4:7, 9 reveals a clear literary dependence on the Joseph/Pharaoh story of Gen 41:8, 24 and the Moses/Pharaoh cycle of Exod 7:11, 12; 8:7, 18, 19; 9:11. A close analysis of the texts and each context shows that the stories are not borrowing from each other. Evidence shows that there were magicians all over the ancient Near East.

2:2, 10, 27. Sorcerers. See **1:4. Chaldeans.** Also 4:6–7; 5:7–15. The meaning of the word "sorcerer" is obscure but it seems to point to the use of supernatural powers to achieve something. Sorcery implies witchcraft or casting of evil spells. It was common in the ancient Near East and was inseparable from the practice of religion. Sorcerers practiced magic arts and charms with the intention of doing mischief to humans and animals. They attempted to delude or pervert the mind. Sorcery is a practice of witchcraft that was violently condemned by the biblical text (Deut 18:10). The sorcerers spoke in Aramaic because that was the language commonly understood by many people at that time. The failure by the sorcerers to execute the king's requirement was fatal. Daniel intervened and spared the lives of these occult practitioners. Sorcerers appear in the time of the end among those who would be destroyed by God (Rev 21:8; 22:15).

2:4b—7:28. The Aramaic of Daniel. The book of Daniel records that Aramaic was the language the Chaldeans spoke to King Nebuchadnezzar in the court (Dan 2:4b, attested in 1QDan^a).[15] Why the writer switched from Hebrew to Aramaic at this point in the text is not clear. There has been a deliberate attempt to explain the bilingualism in Daniel and Ezra through different approaches. The text in Daniel continues in Aramaic even after the speech of the Chaldeans is ended. At the beginning of chapter 8, the author switches back from Aramaic to Hebrew (attested in 4QDan^a and 4QDan^b).[16] He then continues in Hebrew to the end of the book. The six chapters written in Aramaic address issues of importance to the gentiles in Neo-Babylonia who could easily understand that language.

The book of Ezra has a literary format similar to that of Daniel. Ezra 4:8—6:18; 7:12–26 is written in Aramaic. The rest of the document is in Hebrew. Textual analysts had long identified the two distinct sections of the book of Daniel, namely, the historical court stories (chapters 1–6) and the prophetic/apocalyptic part (chapters 7–12). The Hebrew and Aramaic portions of the book, however, do not follow these two literary conventions.

---

15. DJD, 1:150–51; and Trevor, "Completion," 323–44.

16. Ulrich, "Daniel Manuscripts in Qumran Part 1," 17–37; Ulrich, "Daniel Manuscripts from Qumran Part 2," 3–26; and DJD, 16:239–89.

Some have suggested that the author of Daniel introduced Aramaic to strive for authenticity in reporting the speech of foreigners. This explanation fails to account for the author's continued use of the Aramaic when the foreigners had stopped speaking. However, it has been noted that the author of Daniel was bilingual, and used Aramaic as a rhetorical device to show his literary views. See Appendix A, "Multilingualism in Daniel."

Gerhard F. Hasel[17] traced the old debate with regard to the Aramaic of Daniel. He identified Samuel R. Driver as the one who sparked this ongoing debate in 1897. Driver stated that

> the verdict of the language of Daniel is thus clear. The *Persian* words presuppose a period after the Persian empire had been well established: the Greek words *demand*, the Hebrew *supports*, and the Aramaic *permits*, a date *after the conquest of Palestine by Alexander the Great* (B.C. 332). The Aramaic is also that which was spoken *in or near Palestine*. With our present knowledge, this is as much as the language authorizes us definitely to affirm; though συμφωνία, as the name of an instrument (considering the history of the term in Greek), would seem to point to a date somewhat advanced in the Greek period.[18]

Driver's conclusion led more scholars to the comparative study of the Aramaic of Daniel. Soon, new literary evidence that was being recovered by archaeologists further informed the discussion. It became clear that Driver's conclusion was limited to the evidence he had during his time. Despite a growing catalogue of evidence concerning the date and use of the Aramaic language, scholars reached various conclusions on the nature and date of the Aramaic of Daniel. Driver, affirmed by R. D. Wilson[19] and H. H. Rowley,[20] maintained that the Aramaic of Daniel was consistent with a date of 331 BC or much later. Joseph Fitzmyer suggested that the Aramaic of Daniel should be dated at 200 BC but that this conclusion should not be pressed too rigidly.[21] On the other hand, Montgomery thought that Daniel's Aramaic was from about 400 BC. More evidence is pointing further back to the sixth century BC for the authorship.

---

17. Hasel, "Establishing a Date," in Holbrook, *Symposium on Daniel*, 130–39. See also Stefanovic, *Aramaic of Daniel*, 17–27.

18. Driver, *Introduction*, 508. Emphasis original.

19. Wilson, "Aramaic of Daniel," in Princeton Theological Seminary, *Biblical and Theological Studies*, 303.

20. Rowley, *Aramaic of the Old Testament*, 98.

21. Fitzmyer, *Wandering Aramean*, 61, 77.

The scholarly contention with regard to the dating of the book of Daniel shifted toward a greater concern with the type of Aramaic used in the book. Discussion considered its relation to the dating and authenticity of the entire document.

Despite several recovered Aramaic documents, there is no clear-cut outline of the developmental phases the Aramaic language has gone through. Neither are there definite ways to determine "scribal updating" with regard to the transmission of the Aramaic of Daniel.[22] Little is known about phonological and orthographical differences that may have existed during the writing or transmission of the text of Daniel. Determining whether Daniel's Aramaic dialect is of eastern or western origin may not have a major impact in solving the problems of the dating. The study of the word order in the Aramaic of Daniel has also failed to yield any positive impact on the dating of the document.[23]

The temptation to take the Aramaic portion of the book of Daniel (2:4b—7:28) as an independent book is crippled by the fact that the literary unity of the entire book outweighs any suggestion otherwise. The book of Daniel is not "a composite, but an intentionally constructed book,"[24] which has a consistent literary and a theological momentum throughout the entire text. Stefanovic conducted a study in which he correlated the literary, grammatical, and syntactical constructions of some Old Aramaic texts (900–700 BC) in comparison with the Aramaic of Daniel. This work, though grossly misunderstood by John J. Collins,[25] has made a significant contribution to our understanding of Daniel's use of Aramaic. Stefanovic has shown that the book of Daniel has closer linguistic ties to the Old Aramaic and Official Aramaic (700–300 BC) than to the Middle Aramaic (300–200 BC), the Late Aramaic (200 BC–AD 700), and the Modern Aramaic (AD 700 to the present).[26]

The use of the Aramaic language as a device to advocate for the late date of the book of Daniel has clearly failed to offer substantive evidence. On the other hand, overwhelming evidence shows that the Aramaic of Daniel is more closely related to the Official Aramaic and Old Aramaic than to any other periods of that language's development. Aramaic became the common language of the entire ancient Near East and was used by the

---

22. Stefanovic, *Aramaic of Daniel*, 14, 15.
23. Cook, *Word Order*, 2-16.
24. Arnold, "Use of Aramaic," 9.
25. Collins, *Daniel*, 16, n. 156.
26. Stefanovic, *Aramaic of Daniel*. See also Kitchen, "Aramaic of Daniel," in Wiseman, *Notes on Some Problems*, 31-79.

succeeding Medo-Persian Empire. The wise men who gathered before Nebuchadnezzar were from various ethnic backgrounds and it was fitting for them to communicate in Aramaic, the official language at that time.

2:4b. O king, live forever. These words, a customary salutation of respect and endearment, mark the beginning of the Aramaic language in the book of Daniel. The Aramaic continues to Dan 7:28. Such a phrase is used when addressing kings (Dan 3:9; 5:10; 6:21). See 1 Sam 10:24; 1 Kgs 1:31; and Neh 2:3. The Babylonians have an elaborate formula on their inscriptions which reads: "May Nabu and Marduk give long days and everlasting years to the king my lord."[27]

2:5, 12. Destroying wise men. As long as a dream remained uninterpreted, it was perceived as being dangerous. This is why Nebuchadnezzar threatened to destroy all his counselors should they fail him with regard to his dreams (Dan 2:5, 9, 12, 13). Richard Ellis indicated that "rulers in southern Mesopotamia from Gudea to Nabonidus, laid great stress on the dreams and other omens that sanctioned their projects."[28] Nebuchadnezzar ordered that the men be cut limb from limb for failing to tell and interpret the dream he had forgotten (Dan 2:5; cf. Ezek 16:40; 23:47). On another incident, Nebuchadnezzar threatened all people by being cut to pieces if they spoke amiss about the God of the three Hebrews (Dan 3:29).

Several examples show that those who were suspected of conspiracy were executed. Herodotus writes about Darius I who executed a magus who had successfully seized the throne. Also, Xerxes is reported to have killed all the engineers that had built a bridge that fell down in the storm. Josephus tells of a similar incident during the time of Herod when a man was cut limb from limb and thrown to the dogs to be eaten.[29] The Bible stories are no exception to this. King Saul destroyed all the priests whom he suspected allegiance to David (1 Sam 22:13-19).

2:9. Law. Ancient legal texts seem to show that Daniel was well acquainted with the court law and protocol of the time during which he claims to have written his book. An understanding of a number of words from the ancient Aramaic, Akkadian, and Old Persian facilitates our understanding of Daniel's position in time and government. The Aramaic word *dāt*, "the law" (Dan 2:9, 13, 15; 6:5, 8, 15), *dātu* (Old Persian) and *dīntu* (Akkadian) is attested in the Behistun Inscription, where it seems to refer to

---

27. *SDABC,* 4:767.
28. Ellis, *Foundation Deposits in Ancient Mesopotamia,* 6.
29. Josephus, *Antiquities of the Jews,* 15.8.4.

a comprehensive legal institution.[30] *Dāṯ* is an Old Persian loanword with a wide range of meanings, including a royal *ṭaʿam*, "decree," "command," or "judgment" (Dan 3:10, 29; 4:6; 6:26); *gᵉzeraṯ*, "decree" (Dan 4:17, 24), the state law (Dan 6:8, 12, 15), the Torah or the law of Moses (Dan 7:25; 9:11, 13; cf. 6:5); *qᵉyām*, "regulation," "edict," "statute," "commission," "command," "order," or any public proclamation by authority (Dan 6:7, 15); and *ʾᵉsār*, "an interdict" or "decree" (Dan 6:7, 8, 9, 12, 13, 15).

In accordance with the traditions of the ancient Near East, the Chaldean king was the supreme judicial authority, hence the epithet *šar mīšari*, "king of justice." The king's crucial responsibility was *rāʾim*, "to love," *mukīn*, "establish," and maintain *kitti u mīšari*, "truth and justice," impartially to all his subjects on behalf of the gods.[31] Daniel reminded Belshazzar that Nebuchadnezzar had all his subjects dealt with at his discretion. He would kill or spare as he saw fit (Dan 5:19). The Bible asserts that the king is not above the law but must be submissive to it (Deut 17:18-20).

In AD 1901 the French excavators found in Susa a diorite stele about 9 feet (2.82 meters) high with 282 laws inscribed on it which were promulgated by Hammurabi (1792-1750 BC).[32] The Elamites had taken this monument as war booty from Babylon to Susa, Iran.

---

30. King et al., *Sculptures and Inscription*, 1-91 (Persian text), 93-157 (Susian text), 159-210 (Babylonian text); and Voigtlander, *Bisitun Inscription*, 11-51 (see lines 8, 9, pp. 12, 13, and translation on p. 54, sec. 8, 9).

31. Voigtlander, *Bisitun Inscription*, 11-51 (see lines 8, 9, pp. 12, 13, and translation on p. 54, sec. 8, 9). See also Lambert, "Nebuchadnezzar King of Justice," 1-11.

32. See Oppenheim, "Hammurabi" (*IDB*, 2:517-19); Meier, "Hammurapi" (*ABD*, 3:39-42); Sasson, "King Hammurabi of Babylon" (*CANE*, 2:901-15); and Millard, "Hammurabi" (*DANE*, 138-39).

CODE OF HAMMURABI
This black diorite stele has the longest extant legal code in the ANE. The top part shows the king standing in front of a seated deity while the rest of the stele has the Laws of Hammurabi. (Credit: Zev Radovan)

Hammurabi's concern was to eradicate economic and social unfairness. He claimed on the prologue to his laws that he was *šar mīšarim*, "king of justice," who would "establish justice in the land."[33] Some of the laws of Hammurabi have very close parallels with some of the biblical laws found in Exod 21–23; Lev 17–26; and Deut 12–26.

No code of laws has yet been discovered which was written by the Neo-Babylonian kings. Nebuchadnezzar, however, *riksātu urakkis*, "drew up regulations." He was viewed as the "king of justice"[34] on a nameless Babylonian tablet which mentions a just king and his code of laws.[35] Also,

---

33. *ANET*, 163–80, 269–71; Arnold and Beyer, *Readings from the Ancient Near East*, 111–14, 151–52; and *COS*, 2:256–58, 335–53.

34. Lambert, "Nebuchadnezzar King of Justice," 1–11; Beaulieu, *Reign of Nabonidus*, 7, n. 15; and Vanderhooft, *Neo-Babylonian Empire*, 43–45.

35. Lambert, "Nebuchadnezzar King of Justice," 1–11.

a reference is made to the "law of Nebuchadnezzar, king of [Babylon], the king their lord" on a "Promise of Guarantors to Pay Debt of Silver" transacted in Babylon in the twelfth year of Nebuchadnezzar.[36] Nebuchadnezzar's political career in the west gave him dominance over Judah and the surrounding territories. His political prowess is well noted. Not much is known, however, about his imperial legislative and administrative policies and style. Several of Nebuchadnezzar's officials are listed in the extant texts as well as the biblical text.

During the sixth year of the reign of Nabonidus, king of Babylon, an appeal was made to "the judges of *Nabûna'id*, King of Babylon" for a legal decision.[37] Nabonidus may have inherited and modified the Babylonian legislature. The Seleucid king, Antiochus I, continued the Babylonian kingship traditions and prayed for *šarrūt mīšari*, "a government of justice."[38]

Before the seventh century BC legal documents known as *kudurrus* were usually inscribed on a stele or stone shaped like a tablet. The *kudurrus* could be decorated with reliefs and publicly displayed, especially in the Babylonian temples. These included private contracts, legal transactions, dialogue documents, business documents, economic or administrative texts, and letters. Large numbers of legal documents from the seventh to the fifth century BC have been found at Ea-ilūta-bani (Borsippa), Egibi (Babylon), Murašû (Nippur), and in temple settings at Ebabbar in Sippar,[39] Eanna in Uruk, and also other scattered Babylonian temples.[40]

A preserved copy of what is probably a school tablet dated 536 BC was recently discovered. This Neo-Babylonian law fragment is still a puzzle to scholars who have not reached consensus with regard to its origins.[41] It might serve as evidence for the existence of the legal institution in Neo-Babylonia. Daniel, who claims to have been a high-ranking royal official, seems to have been well acquainted with the contemporary legislation.

2:10, 35, 39. Earth. See **4:1, 10–23, 35. In all the earth.** The Aramaic word used here is *yabeshta'*, "the earth," or "the dry land." Verses 35 and 39 use *'ar'*, which also means "earth." Another Aramaic word for earth is *'raq*

---

36. Moore, *Neo-Babylonian Business and Administrative Documents*, 43.

37. Moore, *Neo-Babylonian Business and Administrative Documents*, 89.

38. Oelsner et al., "Neo-Babylonian Period," in Westbrook, *History of Ancient Near Eastern Laws*, 2:915.

39. Bongenaar, *Neo-Babylonian Ebabbar Temple at Sippar* (1997).

40. Oelsner et al., "Neo-Babylonian Period," in Westbrook, *History of Ancient Near Eastern Laws*, 2:913–14.

41. Oelsner et al., "Neo-Babylonian Period," in Westbrook, *History of Ancient Near Eastern Laws*, 2:915, 916.

(Jer 10:11). The Chaldeans believed that no one from the whole world was able to do what the king wanted.

2:14, 20, 21, 30. With counsel and wisdom. See 1:4, 17, 20. **Wisdom.** Daniel exhibited wisdom in all his interactions with high-ranking officials. This paved his way to being appointed the chief administrator of the elite in Babylon (2:48).

2:14, 15, 24, 25. Arioch. Possibly from Akkadian *Eri-A-ku*, "servant of the Moon god." He was the chief of Nebuchadnezzar's bodyguard. He was sent to execute all wise men for failing to meet the demands of the king. One of the Mesopotamian kings who appeared centuries earlier was called Arioch (Gen 14:1, 9).

2:18, 19, 28, 37, 38. Heaven. See also 4:11–37; 5:21, 23; 6:27; 7:2, 13, 27; 8:8, 10; 9:12; 11:4; 12:7. The Bible broadly describes heaven as the space above the earth and also as the supreme dwelling place of God. Daniel uses "heaven" metaphorically (Dan 2:38; 4:11–37; 5:21; 7:2; 8:8; 11:4) as well as literally (Dan 2:18, 19; 5:23; 6:27; 7:13, 27; 12:7). The ancient Near Eastern worldview depicted heaven being above, the earth in the middle and water all around and below. A tenth-century BC Phoenician inscription from Byblos attests to the "God of Heaven" with regard the god Ba'alšamēm.

The title "God of Heaven" (Jonah 1:9; Dan 2:18, 19, 37) is more popular from the Persian period onwards (Ezra 1:2=2 Chr 36:23; Neh 1:4). It is also attested in the Elephantine papyri. One of the letters from the Elephantine fortress to Bagavahya governor of Judah has a fourfold salutation: "The welfare of our lord may the God of Heaven seek after abundantly at all times, and favor may He grant you before Darius the king and the princes more than now a thousand times, and long life may He give you, and happy and strong may you be at all times."[42]

Daniel demonstrated that his God was the God of Heaven who was indeed God of gods; Lord of lords and King of kings. The term "heaven" was sometimes a Jewish way of referring to God or His residence. Nebuchadnezzar became a witness that there was no god that saves like the God of the Hebrews (Dan 3:29). He finally declared: "Now, I, Nebuchadnezzar, praise and extol and honor the King of Heaven, for all His works are truth, and His ways are just; and those who walk in pride He is able to humble." (Dan 4:37).

---

42. *COS*, 3:125–26.

2:19, 22-28, 47. Secret revealed. *Raz* ("secret") is a Persian loanword. The wise men of Babylon could not make known to King Nebuchadnezzar his forgotten dream despite the death threat (Dan 2:5, 12). They reasoned that what the king wanted was impossible to be accomplished by humans. They concluded that the revealing of the dream and its interpretation was only possible by the gods which did not dwell with humans (Dan 2:11). A seventh-century BC Akkadian letter to a god shows the widespread Mesopotamian belief that gods could reveal signs. It reads:

> Speak to Ida (the river god) my lord: Thus Zimri-Lim your servant. I herewith send a gold cup to my lord. At an earlier date I wrote my report to my lord; my lord reveal[ed] a sign. May my lord make the sign which he revealed come true for me. Moreover, may my lord not neglect to protect my li[fe], may my lord not turn [his f]ace elsewhere, besides me may my lord have need of no one el[se].[43]

Nebuchadnezzar's wise men could not name the gods who were able to meet his needs. When Daniel approached the king, he did not hesitate to declare before the king that the wise men were incapable of performing the assignment that he had requested of them (Dan 2:27). He went further and pointed out that there was "a God in heaven who reveals secrets" (Dan 2:28). Nebuchadnezzar finally affirmed that Daniel's God was "God of gods, the Lord of kings, and a revealer of secrets" (Dan 2:47; cf. Amos 3:7).

2:19. Night vision. See **8:1. Vision.** Visions could occur any time of the day and in any location the recipient happened to be. At night, a dream and a vision could be distinguished in that a vision could be more vivid and dramatic in physical manifestations.

2:20-23. Hymn to God. Some Hebrew writers placed hymns to God or "psalms of thanksgiving in positions immediately *prior* to the resolution of an episode's plot, at points where divine deliverance is expected but not yet accomplished."[44] An example of this practice is seen in Dan 2:20-23. The apocryphal additions to Daniel, the Prayer of Azariah and the Song of the Three Jews 1:1-68, follow the same pattern. Nebuchadnezzar praised the God of Shadrach, Meshach, and Abednego before he reversed the death sentence that he had imposed on them (Dan 3:28-30). He also praised the

---

43. *ANET*, 627.

44. Watts, "'This Song' Conspicuous Poetry," in de Moor and Watson, *Verse in Ancient Near Eastern Prose*, 355. Emphasis original. See also Prinsloo, "Two Poems," 93-108; and Towner, "Poetic Passages of Daniel 1—6," 325.

Most High God at the moment his reasoning power came back to his mind (Dan 4:34–35).

Gideon praised the Lord for victory before defeating his enemies, when he had just overheard at night his enemies talk to each other about him defeating them with the help of the God of Israel (Judg 7:15). In 2 Chr 20:20, 21, Jehoshaphat, king of Judah (870/69–848 BC), praised God for victory even before the battle with Moab and Amon was fought. The act of praising God before the final execution of the action is meant to show the faith of the participant in the promises of one's God that God will fulfill his promises.

In the Mesopotamian-Babylonian ancient literature, the writer of the Hymn to Marduk from Ugarit[45] stated the problem of the fatal illness, how Marduk intervened, and then finally gave praises and thanks for what Marduk had done. In the book of Daniel, however, the expression of praise and gratefulness guarantees beforehand that God has already resolved the problem.

2:21. Changes times and seasons. God alone changes what He constituted. He controls times, seasons, and human destiny by His supreme authority. To attempt to change what God established (Dan 7:25) is an exercise of futility.

2:25. Captives. There were both minor and major deportations from Judah by Nebuchadnezzar from 605 BC onwards. Daniel and his friends were exiled to Babylon in 605 BC (Dan 1:1–3), but no mention is made of the number of individuals taken in this, or the subsequent deportations when Nebuchadnezzar made his annual conquest rounds in Palestine. Moreover, there are conflicting statistics in the biblical account. In 598/7 BC King Jehoiachin, his mother, personal attendants, nobles, and his officials, soldiers, craftsmen, and artisans, a total of ten thousand people, were deported to Babylon (2 Kgs 24:12–14). Further, seven thousand soldiers and one thousand craftsmen and artisans were also carried away into captivity (2 Kgs 24:16).

Jeremiah 52:28–30 seems to summarize a few but not all deportations during Nebuchadnezzar's reign: seventh year (598/7 BC) 3,023 people; eighteenth year (587/6 BC) 832 people; and twenty-third year (583/2 BC) 745 people. The total number reflected here (4,600 people) may be for males only who were involved in the specified vocations. Women, children, and others who were taken into captivity might not have been counted.

---

45. Dietrich, "Babylonian Literary Texts from Western Libraries," in de Moor and Watson, *Verse in Ancient Near Eastern Prose*, 62–67.

Several archaeological finds illustrate the concept of carrying people into captivity as mentioned in Dan 1:2, 3. Nebuchadnezzar claimed that his gods, Marduk and Nabû, had commissioned him to take people into captivity. An inscription by Nebuchadnezzar reads: "When my great lord Marduk selected me, (and) Nabû, the supervisor of the totality of heaven and the underworld, put in my hands the lead-rope of the numerous people,"[46] and led them into captivity.

The Istanbul Stele of Nabonidus, col. 9, lines 31–41, reads: "2850 of the captive warriors of the land of Ḫu-me-e, whom the lord Marduk had granted to me above the kings who had preceded me and had delivered into my hands, I presented to the gods Bêl, Nabû and Nergal, my gods who go at my side, in order to serve as brick carriers."[47] Albert Champdor argued that because of the many people deported there, Babylon became a city of half a million residents and the first world commercial center.[48]

Nebuchadnezzar made intensive campaigns to the west during the early years of his reign, not only to crush every possible rebellion there but also for economic reasons. The Babylonian Chronicle (BM 21946)[49] records Nebuchadnezzar's military activities in Hattu during the early part of his reign. He may have deported people in each campaign he made. After every campaign in Hattu, the Chronicle records that Nebuchadnezzar took back to Babylon much booty. Deportation and looting of temple treasure reflected in the book of Daniel were a common phenomenon in the ancient Near East.

2:27. Gazers. The Aramaic *gāzᵉrîn*, "gazers," "astrologers," "soothsayers," "prognosticators," "seers," "determiners," or "deciders," were perceived as determiners of fate or future events in the ancient Near East. These Chaldean diviners cast "nativities from the place of the stars at one's birth, and by various acts of computing and divining, foretold the fortunes and destinies of individuals"[50] (cf. Num 24:17; Matt 2:1–10). This group is also known as those who consult livers (haruspex) for divination (Ezek 21:21). The astrologers were much needed with regard to the interpretation of dreams and enigmas (Dan 4:4; 5:7, 11). The vocabulary on magicians is voluminous but the distinction between the practices is quite vague (Deut 18:10–11).

---

46. Beaulieu, "New Inscription," 96, col. ii, lines 42–54.

47. Albright, "Cilicia and Babylonia," 23.

48. Champdor, *Babylon*, 96.

49. Grayson, *Assyrian and Babylonian Chronicles*, 99–102; Wiseman, *Chronicles of the Chaldean Kings*, 46–48; Wiseman, *Nebuchadrezzar and Babylon*, 21–41.

50. Wilson, *Old Testament Word Studies*, 405.

However, Daniel outshined these mantic and divination experts and proved himself before kings to be a legitimate apocalyptic seer.

2:31. Great image. See also 3:1. Gigantic image of gold. In Akkadian, dreams are normally "seen." Nebuchadnezzar "was seeing" in his dream "a great image" that had four different metals and clay (Dan 2:32, 33). Dreaming of gigantic images was not a unique phenomenon in the ancient Near East. The Sumerian Gudea dreamed of seeing a man "like the heaven was his surpassing (size), like the earth was his surpassing (size)."[51]

In ancient Egypt the pharaoh Merneptah (1213–1203 BC) saw in a dream the gigantic image of the god Ptah "standing in the presence of the Pharaoh, (and) he was as high as . . . ,"[52] while Ptolemy Soter (305–285 BC) "saw in a dream the colossus of the god Pluto in Sinope but because he had not seen it before he did not understand (the meaning of) its form."[53] The temple of Bel in Babylon had a golden statue of a man that was twelve cubits high. Interpreters have rightly concluded that Nebuchadnezzar's giant statue differs from the others because it did not represent a god. It represented chronological history.

2:31–43. Four-kingdom schema. The gigantic statue of Nebuchadnezzar's dream was segmented into four distinct metals, namely, gold, silver, bronze, and iron. In the feet of the statue, the iron was partly combined with clay (Dan 2:32–33). The metals seem to indicate a decline in value from the head to the toes. Also, the metals, from head to toes, progress in toughness and durability. This has led some to associate Nebuchadnezzar's metals with those of Hesiod, which represent the stages of human moral declivity. Hesiod, who is thought to have written much later than Daniel, is said to have followed the same sequence of metals.[54] His Age of Gold is the utopian age, followed by those of silver, bronze, heroes (demigods), and iron.[55] Hesiod's fourth age is represented by gigantic heroes. The fifth age, represented by iron, would be the current age, which is fraught with social unrest.

Several statues from the ancient Near East show mixed metals. A second-millennium Hittite prayer has a promise to give a life-size image

---

51. For the inscription see Wilson, *Cylinders of Gudea*, 30, lines 13–15; and Edzard, *Gudea and His Dynasty*, 72, Cylinder A, col. v, lines 13–15.

52. Oppenheim, *Interpretation of Dreams*, 251; see also 192.

53. Oppenheim, *Interpretation of Dreams*, 252.

54. Hartman and Di Lella, *Book of Daniel*, 146; and Montgomery, *Book of Daniel*, 187–89. Some suggest that Hesiod wrote his *Works and Days* no later than the seventh century BC or perhaps even earlier; see Lambert, *Background of Jewish Apocalyptic*, 8.

55. See Hesiod's *Works and Days*, 67–74, lines 109–80; and Ovid, *Metamorphoses*, 1:9–27.

of the king with head, hands, and feet of gold, while the rest of the statue is silver. A small calf figurine was recovered at Ashkelon with a bronze body and copper extremities. The whole image was coated with silver.

A striking similarity is also noticed between the four metals of Nebuchadnezzar and those of the Persian Zarathushtra (Zoroaster). Zoroaster dreamed of seeing the trunk of a tree which had four branches of gold, silver, steel, and mixed iron respectively. The four metals of Zoroaster represent his idea of four epochs of history. These epochs would come in the millennium of Zoroaster. At this time King Vistap, King Artakshir, King Khvashry, son of Kavat, and the "divs" who have disheveled hair would be ruling respectively.[56]

A different view of this tradition identifies seven branches representing seven periods. Each branch, or period, is represented by one of the metals: gold, silver, brass, copper, lead, steel, and mixed iron.[57]

The Cyprus Stela of Sargon II (721–705 BC) has been considered as possible evidence in understanding the four-kingdom schema in Daniel. This stela lists gold, silver, ebony, and boxwood as the objects of booty,[58] but these have nothing to do with the representation of successive kingdoms. Esarhaddon (681–669 BC) carried away as booty on his Syro-Palestinian campaign gold, silver, precious stones, elephant hides, ivory, ebony, and boxwood, garments and personal valuables.[59] He boasted of a statue he made of himself that was composed of gold, silver, and copper. This image was supposed to be placed before his gods.

The India House Inscription of Nebuchadnezzar names silver, gold, glitter of precious stones, copper, *mismakanna*-wood, and cedar.[60] These are said to be gifts Nebuchadnezzar collected for Marduk from subdued kingdoms. Scholars consider that the four metals of Nebuchadnezzar represent an outline of successive political kingdoms in the real historical setting (Dan 2:36–42). They disagree, however, on their sequence. The first kingdom is unequivocally identified in the text as that of Nebuchadnezzar (Neo-Babylonia): "You (are) that head of gold" (Dan 2:38). Herodotus wrote about how gold was lavishly used in Babylon. He said that the image of a god, the throne he sat on, the table, and the altar were all made of gold.[61]

---

56. Collins, *Daniel*, 163.
57. Lambert, *Background of Jewish Apocalyptic*, 8.
58. *ANET*, 284.
59. *ANET*, 290.
60. Horne, *Babylonia and Assyria*, 1:442, col. 2, lines 30–40.
61. Herodotus, *Herodotus*, 1.181, 183; 3.1–7.

Daniel 2:38 begins the chronology of the book's successive kingdoms. Neo-Assyria is eliminated from Daniel's chronology because the beginning point is Neo-Babylonia, the head of gold. The remaining three kingdoms are not explicitly named but they follow in succession after the displacement of Neo-Babylonia (Dan 2:39–42). It can also be noted that Daniel's chronology contradicts the Dynastic Prophecy, which has Assyria, Babylon, Elam (Persia), and the Hanaeans (Macedonians = Greeks).[62]

Medo-Persia is represented by the chest and arms of silver (Dan 2:32, 35, 39). Silver is a fitting symbol for Medo-Persia because the Persians were renowned for their tax system which was paid in silver.[63]

The Greeks, "a third kingdom of bronze" (Dan 2:39), are known to have extensively used bronze for commercial and military purposes (Ezek 27:13). Psammetichus I, king of Egypt (664–610 BC), referred to the Greek pirates as the men of bronze who came from the sea and were foraging the land.[64]

On June 22, 168 BC, at the battle of Pydna, the Romans under General Aemilius Paulus became the next world power. They completely defeated the Greeks under Persus, king of Macedonia.[65] Thus the Greeks, according to the history of antiquity, as well as Daniel's chronology, were displaced by the Romans, the fourth kingdom that parallels the legs of iron in Dan 2:33–35, 40.

The motif of the kingdoms in succession is prevalent and recurrent in the dreams and visions of Daniel. Different symbols are used to convey the same message. In Dan 7:2–7, 17, the four kingdoms are represented by hybrid animals. The first is like a lion, the next like a bear, the third like a leopard, and finally a nondescript beast.

The lionlike beast had wings of an eagle (Dan 7:4), which is a fitting symbol for Neo-Babylonia. Babylonian art is full of objects which combine the forms of a lion and an eagle. The walls of the Processional Way from the Temple of Marduk to the Ishtar Gate were decorated with striding lions.

Daniel 8:3–10 has a different set of animals: a ram with two horns representing the kings of Media and Persia (Dan 8:20), and a shaggy goat representing Greece (Dan 8:21). The history of antiquity confirms that after the collapse of Neo-Babylonia, the unified Medo-Persia took control of the region in 539 BC. The Greeks overthrew the Medo-Persian kingdom in 331

---

62. Grayson, *Babylonian Historical-Literary Texts*, 24–37.
63. Herodotus, *Herodotus*, 3:89–94.
64. Herodotus, *Herodotus*, 2:152.
65. Perrin, *Plutarch's Lives*, 6:15–23; Livius, *History of Rome*, 44.41–46; Polybius, *Histories*, 29.14–21; and Holleaux, "Rome and Antiochus," in *CAH*, 7:199–240.

BC and continued as the world's dominant power until they were defeated by Rome, the fourth kingdom (Dan 2:40; 7:23).

The four-kingdom schema appeared in the writing of Aemilius Sura (dated between 189–171 BC). This writing was preserved by Velleius Patercilius (1.6.6). It lists the kingdoms as Assyria, Media, Persia, and Greece, which were all displaced by Rome.[66] Although several ancient sources used metals for designating ages or kingdoms, there is no literary evidence that the book of Daniel had any direct dependence on them.

C. C. Caragounis laid the premise that the four-kingdom schema has to be identified on the basis of three evidences: first, the clues given by the author himself; second, by the actual course of history; and last, by the author's dynamic interpretation of that history.[67] Surprisingly, Caragounis failed to follow this methodology. He asserted an ambiguous "thesis" which is supported neither by the biblical text nor his own methodological analysis. Caragounis's outline of the four kingdoms is: Babylon, Media, Persia, and Greece. He contradicts Daniel, who presents the Medes and Persians as a single kingdom (Dan 5:28; 6:8, 12, 15; 8:20). Likewise, Marshall D. Johnson said that the sequence of historical epochs in the entire book of Daniel was clear in Nebuchadnezzar's dream in chapter 2. Unfortunately, Johnson failed to correlate the chronological outline of the book to history.[68] His world history ended with the Greek kingdom, which he concluded was crushed by the supernatural stone.

Sibylline Oracles, book 4, outlined the world kingdoms beginning with the Assyrians, followed by the Medes, then the Persians, the Greeks, and the Romans, who would destroy the Jerusalem temple.[69] Although this list began with the Assyrian empire, it omitted the Neo-Babylonian Empire which displaced the Assyrians.[70]

Josephus seemed to follow the biblical text but never mentioned the clay that was mixed with iron.[71] Further, he pointed to Babylon as the head

---

66. Collins, *Daniel*, 167. Lucas examined the sources for the four-kingdom schema in "Origin of Daniel's Four Empires," 185–202.

67. Caragounis, "History and Supra-History," in Van de Woude, *Book of Daniel*, 388.

68. Johnson, *Making Sense of the Bible*, 76.

69. Collins, "Sibylline Oracles," in Charlesworth, *Old Testament Pseudepigrapha* 1:385–87.

70. Similar chronology is supported by Swain, "Theory of the Four Monarchs," 1–21. Walton outlined the four kingdoms as Assyrian, Median, Medo-Persian, and Greek, and he also took the ten horns (Dan 7:7) to represent ten kingdoms of Alexander the Great. See his "Daniel's Four Kingdoms," 25–36.

71. Josephus, *Antiquities of the Jews*, 10.10.4.

of gold, yet he was reluctant to identify the other kingdoms represented by the subsequent metals. He referred anyone who was keen to identify these kingdoms to explore the text of Daniel itself.

The Palestinian Targum and the Pseudo-Jonathan Targum of the Pentateuch on Gen 15:12 list the kingdoms as Babylon, Media, Greece, and Edom.[72] The Peshitta of Daniel outlines the four kingdoms as Babylon, Media, Persia, and Greece.[73] The *midrashim* consistently list the four kingdoms as Babylon, Persia, Greece, and Rome.[74] The Medes are ignored in this reconstruction.

Some scholars subscribe to what could be classified as the Grecian Scheme, which lists the kingdoms as Babylonian, Median, Persian, and Greek.[75] Others prefer the Roman Scheme which has Neo-Babylonian, Medo-Persian, Greek, and Roman. The Grecian Scheme highlights only Antiochus IV Epiphanes under the Greeks, whereas the Roman Scheme highlights both Antiochus IV Epiphanes under the Greeks and the papacy under the Romans.

To conclude that the four animals were contemporaneous kingdoms: the lion, Egypt (south); bear, Persians (east); leopard, Romans (west); and the anonymous beast, Syria (north), ignores the historical reality and chronology of the book of Daniel. The main concern or theme presented in the book of Daniel is the chronological succession of the ancient kingdoms. This can be clearly understood in light of the political developments of the historical kingdoms suggested by the text. Interpreters would better understand the chronology of Daniel (see table 4) if they consider Medo-Persia as a single kingdom that defeated Neo-Babylonia in 539 BC (Dan 5:28; 6:8, 12, 15; 8:20).

---

72. Clarke, *Targum Pseudo-Jonathan of the Pentateuch*, 16.

73. Taylor, *Peshiṭta of Daniel*, 200; and Gurney, "Four Kingdoms," 39–45. Charles calls this the older and true interpretation; see his *Critical and Exegetical Commentary*, 167.

74. Goldwurm, *Daniel*, 199. Also, Wilson, *Studies in the Book of Daniel*, 258–64.

75. Those who argue for the Grecian view include Rowley, *Darius the Mede*, 67–173; Porteous, *Daniel*, 45–52; Collins, *Daniel*, 166–70; and Caragounis, "History and Supra-History," 387–97.

Table 4
CHRONOLOGICAL KINGDOMS: SYMBOLISM AND PARALLELS

KINGDOM	ERA	DAN 2	DAN 7	DAN 8	DAN 11, 12
NEO-BABYLONIA	605–539 BC	Head of Gold vv. 31–32 Identified vv. 38, 39	Beast Like a Lion v. 4		
MEDO-PERSIA	539–331 BC	Chest & Arms of Silver v. 32	Beast Like a Bear v. 5	Ram vv. 3–4, 6–7 Ram Identified v. 20	Persian Kings 11:1–2
GREECE	331–168 BC	Belly and Thighs of Bronze vv. 32, 39	Beast Like a Leopard v. 6	Goat vv. 5–8 Goat Identified v. 21	Greek Kings vv. 3–19
FOURTH KINGDOM Divided Fourth Kingdom	168 BC—Stone Kingdom	Legs of Iron vv. 33–35, 40 Feet and Toes of Iron and Clay vv. 33, 34, 41–43	Indescribable Beast vv. 7, 19 10 Horns vv. 7, 8, 20, 24 Little Horn vv. 8, 11, 20, 21, 24–26	Little Horn vv. 9–12	Fourth Kingdom Kings vv. 20–45
DIVINE KINGDOM	Stone Kingdom—Forever	The Mountain v. 35	Son of Man Enthroned vv. 13, 14, 27	Ruler of Rulers v. 25	Michael the Great Prince 12:1–2

2:34. A stone cut out not by human hands. The stone was not part of the statue. It came to destroy the statue and establish itself. The Gilgamesh Epic records a dream in which Enkidu comes as a meteor and rests on Gilgamesh's feet.[76] Unlike the stone in Dan 2, there was no destruction. The stone in Daniel represents divine displacement of human history. The twelfth-century BC Uruk Prophecy relates the coming of four kings. These kings would fail politically. Another king would succeed them and bring

76. *ANET*, 76.

back the statue of Ishtar from Babylon to Uruk. The prophecy concludes by saying that the son of the successful king would establish his kingdom forever. A later interpretation of this dream claims Nebuchadnezzar to be that everlasting king. However, the stone in Dan 2 demarcates human political history and ushers in divine sovereignty.

2:35. Blowing winds of Daniel. See **7:2. Four winds of heaven**, and also 11:4. The book of Daniel presents the wind in both literal and symbolic senses. Considering some related ancient finds can be very informative in the attempt to capture what the author intended to communicate.

In Dan 2:34, 35, the stone struck the feet of the image (the weakest part) but broke down the whole image. The crushed pieces were "like chaff from the summer threshing floors" and "the wind" (singular) took them away never to be found again (Dan 2:35). In the Gilgamesh Epic, the coming of Enkidu is seen in a dream as a falling star that lands at the feet of Gilgamesh but causing no destruction.

The wind in Dan 2:35 is a cleaning agent, removing the debris from the image that was destroyed by the stone. The great stone, however, was not moved by the wind. Similarly, the strong east wind that blew all night in the exodus story drove away the water and left the dry ground (Exod 14:21–22).

2:46. Worshiped. See **3:5-7. Worship.** King Nebuchadnezzar was overwhelmed by Daniel's ability to tell and interpret his dream. His extemporaneous reaction was to fall down before Daniel and worship him.

2:46. Grain offering. The biblical tradition is familiar with the generic concepts of *minḥâ*, "grain offering," "tribute," "offering" (any kind), or "gift," and *nîḥōḥîn*, "incense," ordered by King Nebuchadnezzar. See Lev 2:1, 9; 6:15. Nebuchadnezzar's request for grain offering and incense to be offered to Daniel is a puzzle. Usually in the ancient Near East cereal offerings and incense were made to the gods or the dead.

Grain offering was usually prepared from semolina grains, olive oil, and frankincense. Some of the grain offering was burnt on the altar and the rest was used as food for the priest. Grain offering could easily be distinguished from sacrifice. The latter dealt with slaughtering an animal and offering it to the deity. The sacrifice and offering portrayed in the Hebrew Bible point to the Messiah (Heb 10:1–14).

2:46. Incense. Ancient texts mention that frankincense and myrrh were common. The trees for making *nîḥōḥîn*, "incense," grew in south Arabia, east Africa, Anatolia, the Levant, and Mesopotamia. The process of making the incense included the incising of the bark of the tree to bleed out "the 'tears' of resin" which were collected when dry.

Incense ingredients usually comprised of fragrant raisins, aromatic wood, spices, and other odiferous substances. See Exod 30:34–38. Incense was spread and burned on charcoal on the altar or in other kinds of portable incense burners. Incense was used mainly at funerals, divine worship, and festivals. It was also used in magical rituals to drive away evil spirits. Some ancient people also used incense cosmetically.

INCENSE SHOVEL
This bronze shovel associated with ancient Roman culture had multiple uses, including burning incense and collecting ashes. (Courtesy of HAM)

2:48, 49. Daniel made great. See also Dan 5:16, 29; 6:3. King Nebuchadnezzar was overwhelmed by the ability of Daniel to retrieve and interpret the dream that was lost to his memory. The king, however, kept his promise about rewarding whoever was going to solve the puzzle of the forgotten dream (Dan 2:6). He promoted Daniel to be the ruler of Babylon and also the chief prefect of all the wise men in Babylon (Prov 22:29). He lavished Daniel with many presents. Also, for his outstanding prophetic ministry, Jeremiah was given gifts by the Babylonians (Jer 40:5).

The idea of honoring or awarding individuals for their outstanding performance and contribution was a common practice in the ancient Near East. An Egyptian inscription of Neferhotep (1700 BC) reads: "The reward of one who does is that (things) are done for him." Daniel also requested Nebuchadnezzar to promote Shadrach, Meshach, and Abednego because they were his supportive prayer partners in requesting their God to reveal the forgotten dream and its interpretation.

ISHTAR GATE
The walls were amazingly decorated with different animal figures in glazed bricks. (Picture by Sigfried Horn, Courtesy of HAM)

2:49. At the gate. Ancient cities usually had open spaces near the gates. Such spaces were used for social, commercial, and judicial interaction (Gen 19:1, 2; Deut 12:15, 17, 21; 16:5, 18; 2 Sam 19:8). Archaeologists have often found benches near the gate areas. This is where the elders of the city would sit and discuss important matters including judiciary proceedings. See Job 29:7; Ruth 4:1, 2, 11; Lam 5:14. Daniel was an official at King Nebuchadnezzar's gate. Babylon had eight gates around but the Ishtar Gate was the main gate, which was elaborately decorated.

Daniel 3

IMAGE OF GOLD

Nebuchadnezzar's dream of a statue with different metals had geopolitical connotations that would stretch from his time even to the very end of the world. However, ignoring the interpretation of the dream, he constructed an image of all gold and organized worship of it. The location of the event for the dedication of Nebuchadnezzar's image is still a challenge. Considerable evidence shows that instrumental music at public gatherings was common. Many different images have surfaced from the ancient Near East's vast area, despite the fact no image has been found that has political implications like the one in Nebuchadnezzar's dream.

3:1. Gigantic image of gold. See **2:31. Great image.** There are several gigantic images discovered in the ancient Near East. The Great Sphinx at Giza in Egypt is 66 feet (20 meters) high and 240 feet (73 meters) long. The Colossus of Rhodes had a metal exterior. This image measured about 110 feet (34 meters) high.[1]

---

1. Pliny, *Natural History,* 34.18.

THE GREAT SPHINX AT GIZA, EGYPT
The Great Sphinx is one of the extant wonders of the ancient world. It has a human face and the body of a lion. (Credit: Zev Radovan)

In Assyrian and Babylonian periods they used to make images of their kings and displayed them in their temples to stand before the deities. As it were, the image of the king before the god would be requesting the wellbeing of the king. Also, some images of the kings were erected to commemorate them. In Assyria they erected stelae or statues to exalt their rulers. At the Balawat Gates the reliefs show that offerings were made before the images of the king who is present but the offering is made to his image.

Several golden images have also been discovered. These can be considered in relation to Nebuchadnezzar's gigantic ṣelem, "image," set up in the Plain of Dura (Dan 3). Nebuchadnezzar invited his officials (Dan 3:2–4) to the dedication/consecration (Dan 3:2; cf. Num 7:10; Neh 12:27; 1 Kgs 8:63; 2 Chr 7:9) of the image. The golden image's dimensions were 90 feet (27 meters) high and 9 feet (2.7 meters) wide. It has been suggested that the date for the worship of Nebuchadnezzar's great image might have been in 594/3 BC.[2] It was set up on the Plain of Dura in Babylon. The word ṣelem appears on two seventh-century BC inscribed reliefs from Nerab, which is located about 4.5 miles (7 kilometers) southeast of Aleppo. These reliefs are now housed in the Louvre in Paris.

At the specified musical signal, all people, without exception, were supposed to worship the golden image (Dan 3:5, 6). The image might have been that of Nebuchadnezzar himself. In this case all of his subjects would

---

2. Shea, *Daniel*, 74.

bow and swear loyalty when he was away. The image was never identified as a god although it was to be worshiped (Dan 3:5, 7, 14, 15, 18). Insubordination was violently penalized. In the Wadi-Brisa Inscription, Nebuchadnezzar talks about the statue he had made with an inscription that mentioned his name. The statue was erected for his personal posterity so that the future kings would respect his name and also worship the gods.[3]

Whether or not the great image was actually made completely of gold is difficult to ascertain. Collins is of the opinion that the image was overlaid with gold.[4] Several gold face masks have been recovered from the ancient Near East. Some of these are now housed in the British Museum. Examples include: BM 139535, BM 123894, BM 123895, etc.[5]

Contrary to the biblical story, Champdor reported that the Babylonians were so grateful to have a person such as Nebuchadnezzar for their king that they erected in his honor a solid golden statue weighing four tons. The statue stood on a hill dominating the plains to the south of Babylon. In Champdor's report, the existence of the image, and the devotion of Nebuchadnezzar's subjects, resulted in masses of people coming to bow down before the image.[6]

Several golden statues have been recovered from the ancient Near East. King Esarhaddon of Assyria (680–669 BC) made an image of himself of silver, gold, and copper and placed it before the gods to petition on his behalf.[7] During the reign of Ashurbanipal (668–627 BC), a dream is recorded of a golden statue of the god Sin that had an inscription on its base. That inscription predicted the failure of a Babylonian insurrection. In Susa, a golden statue of a man carrying a baby goat was recovered from a pavement of a ruined tomb near the temple of Inshushinak of the Acropolis. This image is dated about the twelfth century BC.[8] A golden figure of a Persian king in a long robe was discovered at Takht-I Kuwad on the northern bank of the Oxus river.[9] Herodotus reported on the golden image of Zeus sitting at a golden table with a golden footstool and chair. Everything in this ensemble weighed eight hundred talents of gold.[10] He further reported on a

---

3. Wiseman, *Nebuchadrezzar and Babylon*, 110; and *ANET*, 307, (x).

4. Collins, *Daniel*, 181.

5. Curtis, "Gold Face-Masks," in Campbell and Green, *Archaeology of Death*, 226–31.

6. Champdor, *Babylon*, 114.

7. Walton et al., *IVP Bible Background Commentary*, 733.

8. Roaf, *Cultural Atlas of Mesopotamia*, 211.

9. Roaf, *Cultural Atlas of Mesopotamia*, 220.

10. Herodotus, *Herodotus*, 1.183.

statue of solid gold from the time of Cyrus. The statue was said to be twelve cubits high.

It is possible that Nebuchadnezzar may have erected a golden statue with most of the gold coming either from the booty or the tribute of the nations he conquered.

The archaeological discoveries regarding golden images show that the story in Daniel is not a farfetched one. In fact, the requirement for worshiping images in Babylon was still enforced in the third century AD. Philostratus related a story about Apollonius, an ambassador from the Roman governor who visited Babylon. Apollonius was about to enter the city, but "the official in charge of the great gates, learning that he had come as a sightseer, held out to him a golden statue of the king before which one had to do obeisance, or he was forbidden to enter."[11] Apollonius refused to bow down to the image, as was expected. As a result, he was immediately escorted to the king for interrogation. He finally secured an exemption from bowing down to the king's golden statue.

3:1. Plain of Dura. Daniel's description of the great golden image set up by Nebuchadnezzar on the Plain of Dura includes details about which the Babylonian records are silent. There are no Babylonian records of a vast assemblage of people, government officials, and musical instruments as found in Dan 3. The dedication ceremony of the colossal image is never mentioned, and neither is the execution of the offenders who failed to bow down to the image. The silence of the Babylonian records regarding this event does not necessarily discredit its historicity.

The date and location of the place for the great image set by Nebuchadnezzar are still a puzzle to scholars. Some take 593 BC as the date for the event on the Plain of Dura, while others, basing their argument on Jer 51:59, prefer 594 BC. The LXX and the Peshitta identifies 587 BC as the year for the event on the Plain of Dura in Dan 3.

Clues for identifying the Plain of Dura are drawn from semantics of the text as well as the geography of the area. The Akkadian word *dūru*, which means "city wall," "fortification wall," or "inner city wall,"[12] can also be used to refer to any common place in Mesopotamia. Many Babylonian cities had names compounded with *Dur*.[13] Examples include Dur-Katlimmu, Dur-Kurashu, Dur-Kurigalzu, and Dur-Sharruken. Also, Dura-Europos in Syria was an ancient city on the banks of the Euphrates. The writer of Dan 3:1 must have been aware of an open public place in the vicinity of Babylon. To locate

11. Philostratus, *Life of Apollonius of Tyana*, 1.27.
12. *CAD*, s.v. "*Dūru*."
13. Cheyne, "Dura," *Encyclopaedia Biblica*, 1:1142–43.

the site at some great distance from Babylon seems unlikely. The place called Dura on the far side of the Tigris in Persia could have been too distant to be associated with an occasion such as that described in Dan 3.[14]

Edward M. Cook suggested reading Dan 3:1 as "in the plain of the wall in the city of Babylon," that is, "the plain between the outer wall—the wall *par excellence*—and the city proper."[15] This reading seems to follow the LXX Septuaginta (Rahlfs) of Dan 11:24 which translated *mᵉdiynāh* "province" or "district of an empire"[16] as *tēn polin*, "the city."[17]

The assembling of large crowds for royal occasions was a common phenomenon in ancient times. Such places of assembly were usually within or in the vicinity of the royal cities. The Plain of Dura may have been an open area inside the outer wall of Babylon. It could also have been just outside the city. These possibilities are credible even though the name "Dura" survived in the name of a tributary called *Nahr Dūra*, which joins to the Euphrates five miles (eight kilometers) below Hilla. Also, some local hills in that area bear the same name.[18]

Although there has been nothing found from extrabiblical sources corroborating Daniel's account of the golden image, such a practice was not unusual in the ancient Near East. Also, while it is difficult to know the exact location of the Plain of Dura, the evidence seems to suggest that this plain was located within or near the wall of ancient Babylon.

3:2, 3. Satraps. See **6:1–7. Satraps.** The Hebrew or Aramaic word *ahashdarpan*, "satrap," is borrowed from Old Persian. The list of invited officials appears in rank order, the satraps being the first. Satraps were the provincial governors in the Persian Empire (Ezra 8:36; Esth 3:12; 9:3; Dan 6:1–7).

3:2. Dedication. In the Old Testament "dedication" carries both the idea of "training" (Gen 14:14; Prov 22:6) and "putting into use" or "formal opening of a new house, etc." (Num 7:10, 11; Deut 20:5; 1 Kgs 8:63; 2 Chr 7:5; Ps 30 [title]; Ezra 6:16, 17; Neh 12:27). A fifteenth-century BC tablet that was discovered at Taanach in Israel uses "dedication" with the meaning of

---

14. *Ammianus Marcellinus*, 3:25.6.5–9. See also Paton, *Polybius*, 3:5.48.16; and Layard, *Discoveries in the Ruins*, 469.

15. Cook, "In the Plain of the Wall," 116.

16. Holladay, *Concise Hebrew and Aramaic Lexicon*, 183; and BDB, 1087–88.

17. See also Fitzmyer, *Genesis Apocryphon*, 122–23. The phrase εἰς πόλιν Ἰούδα in Luke 1:39 may have originated from the Hebrew "to the province of Judah" and thus should have rightly been translated as εἰς τὴν χώραν τῆς Ἰουδαίας, "to the province of Judah"; see Torrey, "Medina," 83.

18. "Plain of Dura," *SDABC*, 4:780.

"training."[19] In Arabic, the concept of dedication is associated with rubbing the palate of a newborn baby with chewed dates or oil to initiate or accustom the infant to sucking milk. The concept of dedication points to consecration or setting apart for special or sacred purpose. King Nebuchadnezzar invited guests for the dedication of the image of gold he had made. His image might have resembled himself or what he saw in the dream. It was never designated to be a god or divine. Those who administered the dedication event subtly incorporated worship of the image as an occasion to expose and destroy the Hebrew officials for their noncompliant allegiance to idol worship. However, those who were dedicated to God (Dan 3:12) did not bow down to worship the image (Exod 20:4, 5).

3:4. Herald. *Kārôzā'* (from Old Persian *khrausa*, "caller") is one who makes public announcements. Ancient textual evidence shows that the idea of using an announcer for disseminating important announcements existed in ancient Babylon. At the dedication of Nebuchadnezzar's golden image, a "herald" was sent out for public announcements or proclamations. This appears to have been a long-standing Babylonian tradition. In the Atrahasis epic, Atrahasis ordered the elders at the gate to command the heralds to proclaim and make a loud noise in the land.[20]

3:4, 7, 29. Peoples, nations, and languages. See 4:1; 6:25. The text uses an all-inclusive language here. No one is left out. Babylon had become an international city whose population included diverse ethnic groups. Aramaic was the official language. The biblical text expresses the idea of peoples, nations and languages. Genesis 10 is a table of nations. Genesis 11 paints a picture of the multiplication of languages. Israel as a nation craved to have a king like other nations around them (1 Sam 8:5). In Dan 4 Nebuchadnezzar addresses his testimony to all people living on the earth. See Matt 28:18–20. The New Testament records a convocation of many people from different nations and the speaking of their languages (Acts 2).

Nebuchadnezzar's rhetoric indicates that he believed his gods gave him dominance over many different nations. Along with that, he considered that his gods commissioned him to build temples for the gods. On the Etemenanki cylinder Nebuchadnezzar boasts of drawing a large number of captives from "remote countries, the peoples of widespread inhabited

---

19. *TDOT,* 5:21.

20. Arnold and Beyer, *Readings from the Ancient Near East,* 26, 27. See also Wiseman, *Nebuchadrezzar and Babylon,* 111; and Ali, "Blowing the Horn for Official Announcement," 66–68.

regions."[21] He credits all his political, economic, and religious success to his chief god, Marduk.

At the dedication of Nebuchadnezzar's image in Babylon the crowd was from peoples, nations, and languages. These people were later threatened not to speak amiss against the God of the Hebrews (Dan 3:29). The implication of Nebuchadnezzar's message was that all peoples, nations, and languages should acknowledge the God of Daniel. A few other nations mentioned also in the book of Daniel include Judah (Israel); Medes and Persians; Greeks; Edom; Moab; Ammon; Libyans; Egyptians; and Ethiopians. Some of these nations may have had captives in Babylon. When the Medes and Persians took over Babylon, they maintained having people from different parts of their realm (Dan 6:25). On the Cyrus Cylinder, King Cyrus boasted that he was "king of the world," that is, "king of all quarters (of the earth)."[22] Daniel's idea that Babylonians interacted with numerous nations is in keeping with evidence from ancient times.

3:5, 7, 10, 15. Musical instruments. Daniel 3:5 gives a list of musical instruments assembled for worship before the image of Nebuchadnezzar:

- *qarnā*, "the horn"
- *mašrôqitā*, "the pipe"
- *qitārôs*, "zither"
- *śabbᵉkā*, "the lyre"
- *pᵉsanᵉtterin*, "the harp"
- *sûmpōnᵉyâ*, "bag-pipe"

The list appears again in Dan 3:7, 10, 15. In all its occurrences, this list is appended by the words: "and all kinds of music." Table 5 shows minor discrepancies in the listing: the omission of *sûmpōnᵉyâ* in v. 7, and the different spellings as indicated by the words in brackets [ ]. This omission of an instrument and all spelling differences in these texts can be attributed to scribal carelessness.

Recovered texts and pictographs show that the ancient Near East had a long tradition of music. When these finds are considered, it is easier to understand the references to instruments and "all kinds of music" in Dan 3:7, 10, 15. The musical instruments can be categorized into "the

---

21. Vanderhooft, *Neo-Babylonian Empire*, 36.
22. *ANET*, 316; and *COS*, 2:315.

percussive (drums, cymbals, gongs, metal, and wooden clackers), the winds (of wood and reed), and the strings (harps, lyres, lutes)."²³

CYMBAL-LIKE MUSICAL INSTRUMENT
This musical instrument was used in Egypt from ca. twelfth–tenth century BC. (Credit: Zev Radovan)

Music from recovered texts can be divided into clear categories. There were "hymns, laments, jubilation and love songs, which could be accompanied by instrumental music or performed *a cappella*, solo, or in unison."²⁴ In fact, from 1800 BC onwards, music was part of the Mesopotamian school curriculum. The musical sounds of antiquity are lost, but archaeologists have managed to recover the names of the musical instruments and their artistic representations. The Hittite Festival of the Warrior-god shows the king and the queen in a procession. Also shown are noblemen, palace servants, and the guardsmen following the royals. Farther back in the procession are musicians playing instruments such as the *arkammi*, *ḫuḫupal*, *galgalturi*, and tambourines.²⁵

3:5, 7, 10, 15. Horn. The Aramaic *qarnā*, Hebrew *qeren*, or Akkadian *qarnu* is rightly translated "the horn." In Dan 3 this word appears in a musical context where it specifically refers to the name of a musical instrument that

---

23. Kilmer, "Strings of Musical Instruments," in Güterbock and Jacobsen, *Studies in Honor of Brenno Landsberger*, 262.

24. Kilmer, "Strings of Musical Instruments," in Güterbock and Jacobsen, *Studies in Honor of Brenno Landsberger*, 261.

25. *ANET*, 358.

IMAGE OF GOLD

was made from the horn of an animal. Late Assyrian reliefs show long horns/trumpets/cornets that could have been made from either wood or metal.[26]

Table 5
DANIEL 3 LIST OF MUSICAL INSTRUMENTS

Dan 3:5	Dan 3:7	Dan 3:10	Dan 3:15
The Herald	The Author	The Chaldeans	Nebuchadnezzar
qarnā (horn)	qarnā (horn)	qarnā (horn)	qarnā (horn)
mašrôqitā (pipe/flute)	mašrôqitā (pipe/flute)	[mašrôqitā] (pipe/flute)	mašrôqitā (pipe/flute)
qitārôs [qăt^{e}rôs] (zither/harp)	qitārôs [qăt^{e}rôs] (zither/harp)	qitārôs [qăt^{e}rôs] (zither/harp)	qitārôs [qăt^{e}rôs] (zither/harp)
[sabb^{e}kā] (lyre)	śabb^{e}kā (lyre)	śabb^{e}kā (lyre)	śabb^{e}kā (lyre)
p^{e}san^{e}tterin (harp)	[p^{e}san^{e}ṭerin] (harp)	p^{e}san^{e}tterin (harp)	p^{e}san^{e}tterin (harp)
Sûmpōn^{e}yâ (bag-pipe)	X	[sîpōn^{e}yâ] [sûpōn^{e}yâ] (bag-pipe)	[sûmpôn^{e}yâ] (bag-pipe)

The Akkadian *qarnu* has no musical references known yet, but it was blown in the streets by the heralds to draw people's attention for public announcements.[27]

The horn was a common musical instrument in the ancient Near East and is attested dating back to a second-millennium BC drawing at Mari.[28] Oxhorns were used as musical instruments in Egypt during the reign of Amenhotep IV (1352-1336 BC).[29] A Sumerian temple hymn refers to a bull's horn as a musical instrument that made the sound *"gumga."*[30] Another Sumerian hymn has the chief musician play an ibex horn, while other

26. Wellesz, *Ancient and Oriental Music*, 242; and Engel, *Music of the Most Ancient Nations*, 217.

27. Ali, "Blowing the Horn for Official Announcement," 67, lines 2 and 3, read: "According to the word of the Assembly, the bailiff blew the horn in the streets." Kilmer, "Music and Dances" (*CANE*, 4:2603).

28. Mitchell and Joyce, "Musical Instruments in Nebuchadnezzar's Orchestra," in Wiseman et al., *Notes on Some Problems*, 20, 21.

29. Marcuse, *Survey of Musical Instruments*, 747-49.

30. Kilmer, "Music and Dances" (*CANE*, 4:2603).

musicians play lyres, drums, and clackers accompanying singers.[31] An animal horn used as a musical tool is also attested on the ninth/eighth-century BC stone relief at Carchemish.[32]

3:5, 7, 10, 15. Pipe/flute. The word *mašrôqitā*, "the pipe" or "flute," is translated in the LXX as *syrigx*, while the Vulgate has *fistula*. Both of these imply "a row of pipes of different lengths bound together, which produce a piccolo-type sound capable of birdlike twittering and running scales."[33] The term has been associated with the Hebrew verb *šrq*, "to hiss" or "whistle," which implies that this kind of instrument produces a whistling sound like a pipe or flute.[34]

3:5, 7, 10, 15. Zither/harp. The term *qitārôs*, "zither," "harp," or "lyre," is rendered *Kitharas* in the LXX and is thought to have been a loanword from the Greek. The word meant a kind of lyre or lute.[35] *Kitharas* appears in Homer (eighth century BC), Herodotus (fifth century BC), and many other Greek works.[36] Lyres were common in Mesopotamia, but the Greek *kithara* must have been of a prestigious kind, and this might have prompted the Babylonians to import them. Ashurbanipal's (668–ca. 631 BC) relief from Nineveh has two musicians, one playing an eight-stringed, and another, a five-stringed lyre.[37]

When Alexander conquered the Persian Empire, it was not the first time Greeks and Macedonians had appeared in the region. They had visited the area for centuries as travelers, mercenaries, and merchants. Yamauchi cited evidence of Greek presence in the ancient Near East before the time of Alexander the Great, and he argued that the Greek loanwords in Daniel are inadequate for dating that book.[38]

3:5, 7, 10, 15. Lyre. The term *śabbᵉkā*, "the lyre," appears in the text with varied spellings, which may be an indication of its foreign origin.[39] In

---

31. Kilmer, "Music and Dances" (*CANE*, 4:2603).
32. Braun, "Musical Instruments" (*OEANE*, 4:75).
33. Jones, "Musical Instruments" (*ABD*, 4:938); see also Jones, "Musical Instruments in the Bible," 101–16.
34. BDB, 1056.
35. Holladay, *Concise Hebrew and Aramaic Lexicon*, 419.
36. Blackie, *Homer and the Iliad*, 310, bk. 13, v. 731; Merry, *Homer: Odyssey*, 1.153; and Dyer, "Musical Instruments in Daniel 3," 430–31.
37. Mitchell and Joyce, "Musical Instruments in Nebuchadnezzar's Orchestra," 24.
38. Yamauchi, "Daniel and Contacts," 37–47.
39. Mitchell and Joyce, "Musical Instruments in Nebuchadnezzar's Orchestra," 24–25.

Daniel 3:7, 10, and 15 the word is spelled with **ś** (śin) while in verse 5 it is spelled with **s** (*samek*). This is a type of lyre which is triangular, with four strings and a bright tone. The LXX translates this instrument as *sambykē* which has been easily associated with the Roman *sambuca*, a horizontal and angular harp.[40] Since the Greeks looked down upon the *sambykē*, it has been suggested that the Greeks might have borrowed the instrument from the ancient Near East[41] or, according to Strabo, from Phoenicia.[42] The Assyrian harp may have had more strings than the *sambykē*, which was known to have only four strings.[43]

3:5, 7, 10, 15. Harp. Another stringed instrument is *pᵉsanᵉtterin* "the harp," which is transliterated in Persian as *santur*, Arabic *santīr*,[44] the LXX and the Vulgate *psaltērion*.[45] This was a kind of triangular-shaped harp that was like "a trapezoid-shaped dulcimer either plucked or played with plectra."[46]

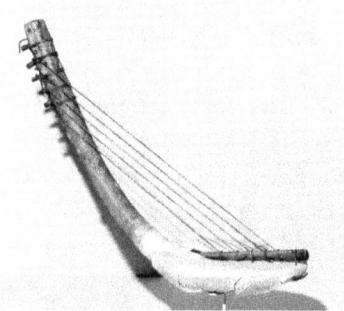

MUSICAL INSTRUMENT
This harp like musical instrument was found in Egypt ca. tenth century BC.
(Credit: Zev Radovan)

3:5, 10, 15. Bag-pipe. The debate on the Aramaic *sûmpōnᵉyâ*, "bag-pipe" or "double pipe," is still unsettled. The discussion centers mainly on the origin and etymology of the word. On the other hand, it is not clear whether *sûmpōnᵉyâ* was an instrument, an assemblage of musical instruments,

40. Dyer, "Musical Instruments in Daniel 3," 431.
41. Dyer, "Musical Instruments in Daniel 3," 432.
42. Strabo, *Geography of Strabo*, 10.3.17.
43. Wellesz, *Ancient and Oriental Music*, 245; Engel, *Music of the Most Ancient Nations*, 31; Mitchell and Joyce, "Musical Instruments in Nebuchadnezzar's Orchestra," 25; and Dyer, "Musical Instruments in Daniel 3," 432.
44. Dyer, "Musical Instruments in Daniel 3," 433.
45. Mitchell and Joyce, "Musical Instruments in Nebuchadnezzar's Orchestra," 25.
46. Dyer, "Musical Instruments in Daniel 3," 433; and Mitchell, "Music in the Old Testament Reconsidered," 137.

sound of an instrument, or an orchestra that may have included voices and instruments.[47] Its association with the Greek *sûmpōnias* has caused intractable problems. Ivor H. Jones is of the opinion that the two words are unrelated[48] and must therefore be treated differently. The Greek does not denote a musical instrument but music in general (Luke 15:25).[49]

Several differing suggestions on the meaning of *sûmpōn*e*yâ* have been considered. Some think that the word means a "bag-pipe," "double pipe," or "pan's pipe,"[50] which may be associated with the present-day Italian *sampogna*.[51] A second-millennium BC Hittite relief at Eyuk, twenty miles north of Boghazköy in central Anatolia, shows a dog-skin bag-pipe.[52] Polybius listed the symphony as an independent instrument along with the hornpipe (*keration*). He writes that Antiochus IV Epiphanes would appear in public without announcement to join the naked dancers where these instruments were being played, but those involved in dancing would disappear from the scene.[53]

All musical instruments in Dan 3 are non-Israelite. Some may have corrupted spelling forms,[54] but they all date before the Seleucid era. Three names of the musical instruments, *qitārôs*, *p*e*san*e*tterin*, and *sûmpōn*e*yâ*, have been identified as Greek loanwords. This has subsequently led to the argument that since the Greeks conquered the ancient Near East in 332 BC, they could only then have brought their musical culture into the area.

The author of Daniel is said to have been aware of the Greek instruments only after the Greeks had conquered Babylon. The trend of this idea ultimately leads to the conclusion that Daniel was written in the second century BC. This conclusion is used to augment support for the idea that the book of Daniel was written to encourage the Jews during the time of Antiochus IV Epiphanes. Adequate discussion on this has already been given by K. A. Kitchen, who pointed to the evidence of the presence of some Greeks in the ancient Near East from the seventh century BC onwards.[55]

---

47. Spicq, *Theological Lexicon of the New Testament*, 3:324-28; and Braun, *Music in Ancient Israel/Palestine*, 34.

48. Jones, "Musical Instruments" (*ABD*, 4:938).

49. Kamphausen, *Book of Daniel*, 21.

50. BDB, 1104; Holladay, *Concise Hebrew and Aramaic Lexicon*, 414; and Driver, *The Book of Daniel*, 39.

51. Keil and Delitzsch, *Ezekiel and Daniel*, 570.

52. Garstang, *Hittite Empire*, 137, Plate xxx.

53. Polybius, *Histories*, 26.10 and 31.4.

54. Braun, *Music in Ancient Israel/Palestine*, 35.

55. Kitchen, "Aramaic of Daniel," 44-50; and Grabbe, "Of Mice and Dead Men," in Grabbe, *"Like a Bird in a Cage,"* 120-25.

Music has been a long tradition in the ancient Near East, and impressive evidence seems to support Daniel's idea of an assemblage of musical instruments at a royal occasion.

3:5–7. Worship. The verb "worship" (Aramaic *sᵉghid*; Hebrew *sāgad*) is not only confined to falling or laying prostrate before a divine being or submission to a superior person. Worship also entails the concept of profound adoration, intense love, and extreme admiration. Significantly, the gesture of worship expresses the individual's inward attitude (Isa 29:13). Nebuchadnezzar, obviously overwhelmed by Daniel's ability to retrieve his forgotten dream and give a logical interpretation of it, fell on his face and worshiped Daniel (Dan 2:46). He ordered some offering and incense to be presented to Daniel. With Nebuchadnezzar, worship happened as a spontaneous response. Worship is that extemporaneous response of awe in the presence of God, who is our ultimate and supreme authority, deserving of all glory, honor, and majesty forever.[56]

Obeisance or paying homage also expresses the idea of physically bowing or prostrating oneself before the deity or a very important individual. The earliest extant ancient picture of an Israelite demonstrating worship is that of Jehu (842–815 BC), king of Israel (2 Kgs 9, 10). The second register of the Black Obelisk basalt stone monument of Shalmaneser III (858–824 BC), king of Assyria, shows Jehu prostrating before him as he was bringing in tribute in 841 BC. The gesture of worship was practiced by many ancient nations for different reasons and occasions. In Egypt the gesture was known as "kissing the ground."

JEHU, KING OF ISRAEL
On the Black Obelisk of Shalmanesser III, Jehu, the king of Israel, prostrates before Shalmanesser III as he brings him tribute. (Courtesy of HAM)

---

56. Mazani, *On the Plains of Moab*, 43–46.

In the ancient Near East, when an inferior prostrates in the presence of a superior it could also imply panic or fear. Falling to the ground on one's face before one's conqueror meant absolute submission. Whether the defeater wants the submitting one to live or die, it was up to his or her own wish (cf. Dan 5:19). In war situations, when an individual bows down and surrenders at the feet of a conqueror, he or she did not expect to rise up again but to die. If the conqueror makes the surrendering person rise up from the ground, then this spared person had all reasons to celebrate and express profound gratitude. The spared one would also show willingness to comply with the terms of the conqueror. Covenantal relationships were then established. Worship of the image set up on the Plain of Dura was mandatory to all who were present (Dan 3:5-7, 10-12, 14-15, 18, 28). The three Hebrew officials deliberately rejected worshiping the image of the king and were thrown into the burning fire. They miraculously survived. Praising, extolling, honoring (Dan 4:37; 5:4, 23); petitioning, giving, praying, as well as fasting (Dan 6:7, 10-13; 9:3-4), are vital components of worship.

3:6-26. Fiery furnace. The furnace of burning fire (Dan 3:6, 11, 15, 17, 19, 20, 21, 22, 23, 26) may have been a trap set up specifically for the purpose of eliminating the Hebrew officials. On the other hand, it is possible that the furnace had been used for the construction of the statue.[57] It may have been one of those massive furnaces used for burning glazed bricks.

Chaldean men approached Nebuchadnezzar and reported on Shadrach, Meshach, and Abednego's noncompliance to the royal religious obligation. These men who informed the king may have been part of the whole scheme involving the setting up of a furnace at an event designed for dedication (Dan 3:8, 12; cf. 1 Macc 2:59).

In the Hebrew Bible, human beings were burned by fire for either religious practice (Gen 22:2; Lev 18:21; Deut 12:31; 18:10; Judg 11:31, 34, 39; 2 Kgs 16:3; 17:17; 21:6; 23:10; 2 Chr 28:1-3; 33:6) or for punishment. In a rage, Judah ordered his daughter-in-law Tamar to be burned for prostitution (Gen 38:24). This was in accordance with the Levitical codification (Lev 20:14; 21:9). Also, fire destroyed the cities of the plain as punishment for their violence and immorality, and the dense smoke rose up like that from a great furnace (Gen 19:28).

The Philistines were familiar with the custom of burning offenders (Judg 15:6). Jeremiah predicted that the false prophets Ahab, the son of Kolaiah, and Zedekiah, son of Maaseiah, would be roasted in the fire to death by Nebuchadnezzar (Jer 29:20-23).

---

57. Stefanovic, *Daniel*, 125.

It is interesting to note that it was the God of the Hebrews who destroyed with a conflagration fire the population of Sodom and Gomorrah, along with the adjacent cities (Gen 19:28, 29). Later, this Hebrew God also burned Nadab and Abihu with fire (Lev 10:1–2). Yet this same God protected Shadrack, Meshach, and Abednego from Nebuchadnezzar's fire, which was heated up "seven times as much" (Dan 3:19).

Many interpreters seek to understand what Daniel's fiery furnace looked like. They also express the desire to be informed on the primitive practice of burning people in ancient times. The architectural structure of the furnace built on the Plain of Dura for Nebuchadnezzar's celebration over his golden statue may have been like a large oven in the shape of a "kiln." Several potters' kilns with different plans and sizes were discovered at the Phoenician industrial city of Sarepta along the Mediterranean coast.[58] The largest kiln in Israel associated with the Philistines was discovered at Tell Jemmeh (Iron Age I) and is ovoid in shape.[59] King Solomon had large industrial smelters at Tell el-Kheleifeh (Ezion-geber).

There were two types of kilns used by ancients to burn ceramics and bricks. These may be traced back to the Early Bronze Age. The vertical, or updraft, kiln stood several meters above the ground and had either a dome or a flat top. Beneath this structure was a fire box that had an opening for building the fire. The temperature in the kiln was regulated by the intensity of the fire, given the amount of the fuel and the air current allowed in.[60] In Mesopotamia oil from open wells was used to fire the brick kilns.

The horizontal, or downdraft, kiln was dug and built into the ground or was constructed on the ground, rising slightly above it. The fire box was located at its front while the exit flue would be at the back.[61] A kiln was discovered at Nippur dating about 2000 BC. It was an elongated rectangular tunnel with one end open and the other closed. Charcoal was used to heat such kilns to extremely high temperatures.

There is little extant evidence on capital punishment by fire in Neo-Babylonia, despite the fact that the Code of Hammurabi, king of Babylon, ordered that any person who appropriates to oneself the goods from a burning house should be thrown into the fire.[62] Such a death is prescribed also

---

58. Pritchard, *Recovering Sarepta*, 111–30.
59. Van Beek, "Jemmeh, Tell" (*NEAEHL*, 2:667–74).
60. Wood, "Kiln" (*ABD*, 4:38–39).
61. Wood, "Kiln" (*ABD*, 4:38–39), and Franken, *Excavations at Deir 'Alla*, 94–97.
62. *ANET*, 167, law 25; and *COS*, 2:338. The stela with the Code of Hammurabi is housed in the Louvre Museum.

for a nun who opens a tavern or who goes into a tavern to drink,[63] or both a man and his mother if they lie together after his father's death.[64]

Rim-Sin, king of Larsa, a contemporary of Hammurabi, issued a letter with a brief message: *aššum ṣuharam ana tinûrim iddu attunu* ˡᵉˢ̌ *wardam ana utûnim idia*; "Since they have thrown a young slave into the oven, do you throw a slave into the furnace?"[65] The word used here for "furnace," *atûnum*, has linguistic affiliations with the Aramaic *'attûn* used in Dan 3 and is from a common root found in Arabic, Aramaic, Babylonian, Ethiopian, and Syriac.[66] In Mesopotamia, dating from the third millennium to the sixth century BC, there existed a practice for establishing the guilt of an accused person. This practice, known as the river ordeal, was for use in cases where evidence of what had happened was lacking except for the testimony of the accuser. Both the plaintiff and the defendant were taken and plunged under water at a mysterious place near the bitumen source at Hit. Whoever was able to emerge was vindicated.[67]

A text attributed to the time of Nebuchadnezzar relates that an accused man plunged into the river and disappeared, but his body emerged hours later looking like it was burned by fire.[68] The body might have been burned due to the hot bitumen springs at Hit, the traditional place for the river ordeal.[69] Kuhrt stresses the point that in the Mesopotamian river ordeal, the guilty sank or drowned while the innocent swam and survived.[70] In the book of Daniel, the three accused young men survived the fire, possibly because of their innocence (Dan 3:24-27). The three stood by their conviction: "Our God whom we serve is able to deliver us from the burning fiery furnace" (Dan 3:17). See Isa 43:2 and Ps 91.

An inscription points out that the Assyrian king Assurnasirpal II (883-859 BC) burned some prisoners.[71] Also, Nebuchadnezzar's son-in-law, Nergal-shar-uîur, claimed to have burned some adversaries and disobedient

---

63. *ANET*, 170, law 110; and *COS*, 2:342.

64. *ANET*, 172, law 157; and *COS*, 2:345.

65. Alexander, *Early Babylonian Letters and Economic Texts*, 3, Plate V, no. 10; and Alexander, "New Light on the Fiery Furnace," *JBL* 69 (1950) 375-376.

66. Alexander, "New Light on the Fiery Furnace," 376.

67. Heimpel used the word "ordalist" for the defendant, the person who is ordered to get into the river ordeal; see his "The River Ordeal in Hit," *Revue d'Assyriologie* 90 (1996) 7.

68. Lambert, "Nebuchadnezzar King of Justice," 9, rev. col. iv, lines 17-20.

69. Oelsner et al., "Neo-Babylonian Period," in Westbrook, *History of Ancient Near Eastern Laws*, 2:925.

70. *ANE* 1:117, n. 11.

71. Rawlinson, *Cuneiform Inscriptions of Western Asia*, 1.19.

individuals.[72] The Persians executed some offenders by destroying them through fire.[73] Cyrus the Persian took Sardis and captured the ruler Croesus. He then set the ruler up, along with seven Lydian boys, to be burned on a great pyre. Taking compassion on them, Cyrus pardoned all and ordered the fire to be put out.[74] Second Maccabees 13:3–8 tells of a certain Menelaus who was burned to death by Antiochus IV at Beroea for troublemaking.

That the three Hebrew men were not burned, and that they had no smell of the fire, puzzled Nebuchadnezzar. He immediately lifted the punishment and ordered all people not to speak amiss of the God of Shadrach, Meshach, and Abednego (Dan 3:27, 28).

The Prayer of Azariah and the Song of the Three Young Men are apocryphal additions to the story of the biblical Shadrach, Meshach, and Abednego. However, it is easier to understand the story of the fiery furnace in Daniel in light of the related archaeological data.

3:8. Accused. Certain Chaldeans accused the three Jews for not worshiping the golden image. The text here depicts the Chaldeans displaying not only a racial slur but also a malicious intent against their Jewish colleagues. The Aramaic idiom *waʼakalu qartsehon di yehudaye*, "and they ate the pieces of the Jews," precisely implies a kind of verbal cannibalism usually done by accusers on those whom they want to destroy. See also Dan 6:4, 24. From antiquity jealousy and murder among court officials was very common (cf. Esth 5:9–14). Sometimes it was survival of the fittest!

3:8. Jews. After the death of King Solomon, the kingdom split into two (1 Kgs 12). The ten tribes occupying the northern part of the country became known as Israel. The two tribes in the south became known as Judah, named after the main tribe there. The terms "Judah" and "Israel" have both been used to imply national and religious commitment. Usually, "Israel" is used by the people in referring to each other as God's covenant people, while on the other hand, gentiles or non-Jewish people contemptuously use the term "Jew," "Jewish," or "Judean" to refer to the people of Israel. Sennacherib (704–681 BC) boasts on his prism:

> As to Hezekiah, the Jew, he did not submit to my yoke, I laid siege to 46 of his strong cities, and walled forts and to the countless small villages and their vicinity, and conquered (them) by means of well-stamped (earth-)ramps, and battering-rams brought (thus) near (to the walls) (combined with) the attack

---

72. "Fiery Furnace," *SDABC*, 4:782.
73. Collins, *Daniel*, 185.
74. Herodotus, *Herodotus*, 1.86.

by foot soldiers, (using) mines, breeches as well as sapper work. I drove out (of them) 200,150 people, young and old, male and female, horses, mules, donkeys, camels, big and small cattle beyond counting, and considered (them) as booty. Himself I made a prisoner in Jerusalem, his royal residence, like a bird in a cage.[75]

A first-person account of Nabonidus's (556–539 BC) affliction and healing indicates that "a diviner, who was himself a Jew fro[m among the exilic community of Judea], provided an interpretation, and wrote (instructions) to render honor and greatness to the name of G[od]."[76] A letter by Hanani[ah] on a strip of papyrus dated 419 BC is addressed to Yedoiah and the Jewish garrison and it discusses the authorizing of a festival of unleavened bread for the Jewish people.[77] Esther 3 is a story of a conspiracy against the Jews. It is clear that Daniel, who was himself Judean, knew the distinction between the terms "Israel" and "Judah" (Dan 9:7), but chose to address his country people as "my people Israel" (Dan 9:20).

3:9. O king, live forever. See **2:4b. O king, live forever.**

3:12, 14, 18. Gods of Babylonians. The Babylonians had a multiplicity of temples. They cherished a polytheistic religious culture. Each temple had a god or several gods. These gods were inanimate idols that were regarded as representation of the divine. The priests took care of the gods. The priests awakened the gods in the morning and put them to bed at night.[78] The gods were fed and were dressed royally. There was an annual parade of the gods during the New Year's Festival. Gods were collected from their different cities and assembled in Babylon. Marduk, the chief god, led the procession of the gods through the city. An Assyrian relief shows a procession of gods mounted on animals[79] (see Isa 46:1–2). On the night Babylon fell to the Medo-Persians, they had an assembly of different gods made of gold, silver, bronze, iron, wood, and stone (Dan 5:4). The Hebrew captives rejected worshiping the Babylonian idols and were persecuted for that (Dan 3:12, 14, 18).

Why Daniel was absent from the worship scene is not explained. There is no account again implicating him to take a loyalty oath to the image of Nebuchadnezzar in Babylon. The Assyrian king Ashurbanipal once

---

75. *ANET*, 288; and *COS*, 2:303.
76. *COS*, 1:286.
77. *ANET*, 491.
78. Cornfield, *Archaeology of the Bible*, 162.
79. Cornfield, *Archaeology of the Bible*, 163.

gathered his chief officials in Babylon to take a loyalty oath.[80] He wrote a letter to one official who was absent to make arrangements to take the oath in the presence of a palace official and images of the gods. It is noted that the official did what was required of him.

3:15. Then what god will be able. Such boasting is characteristic of ancient Mesopotamian kings. The Old Testament registered some of the taunts from proud Assyrian rulers (2 Kgs 18:33–35; Isa 10:8–11; 36:18–20). The saying that "pride goes before falling" (Prov 16:18) has been true from ancient times.

3:15, 17, 28. Deliver. See also **12:1. Deliver.** The Aramaic verb *shezib* was borrowed from Neo-Assyrian about eighth century BC.[81] It means "to deliver" or "rescue" and is always used with a direct object, hence, "to deliver from" or "rescue from." The implication is that of protecting or saving someone from danger, sickness, poverty, enemies, or death. Nebuchadnezzar did not know of any god that could deliver anyone from him; see Dan 5:18, 19. On the other hand, King Darius believed that Daniel's God would deliver Daniel from lions (Dan 6:16, 20, 27). Many Babylonian personal names have the theophoric element and *shezib*, for example, Shuzub-Adad, "delivered by Adad," and Shuzub-Marduk, "delivered by Marduk." The biblical name Mushezib-Il (Meshezabel), "the one who delivers is God" (Neh 3:4; 10:21; 11:24), is typically Akkadian.[82] The biblical text shows Daniel's God delivering His people from current danger (Dan 3:28, 29; 6:27) and finally at the end of time (Dan 12:1). The idea here is that God protects His people from danger; whether they are in the fire (Dan 3:17, 28, 29) or in the lions' den (Dan 6:22, 27), they suffer no harm (Isa 54:17). See Ps 91. Jesus came to save His people from their sins (Matt 1:21).

3:19. Seven times. See **4:16, 23, 25, 32. Seven times.** The phrase "seven times as much" might have been a call to increase the heat intensity by adding more fuel, or it might mean that the fate of the three men was irrevocable. However, a similar phrase, "seven times as much," rendering the same meaning, has been used in the fifth-century BC Aramaic letter from Elephantine.[83] In the ancient times seven was a number for completeness or fullness. Many open wells of oil all over ancient Mesopotamia could have

---

80. Walton et al., *IVP Bible Background Commentary*, 735.
81. *TDOT*, 16:757.
82. *TDOT*, 16:759.
83. Muraoka and Porten, *Grammar of Egyptian Aramaic*, 92, 241; and "One Seven Times More," *SDABC*, 4:784.

easily supplied the fuel needed to increase the heating of the fiery furnace. In the Hebrew Bible the furnace could also be seen as a metaphorical instrument for the people's purification (Deut 4:20; 1 Kgs 8:51; Isa 31:9; 48:10; Jer 11:4; Ezek 22:18-22).

3:21, 27. Mantles, tunics, turbans, and clothes. Everything worn by Shadrach, Meshach, and Abednego did not catch on fire. The Aramaic word *sarbālēyhôn*, "the turbans," is possibly of Akkadian origin, *karballatu*, "cap," "headgear."[84] The term appears on the Naqsh-i-Rustam inscription of Darius I (522-486 BC) designating a helmet, but the late Babylonian texts render it as "hat."[85] The three men were well dressed for the occasion but they would not comply with the expectation to worship an image set by the king (Exod 20:3-6). The list of what they were putting on serves to show that the materials were flammable. The king and everybody present testified that nothing on these three men was burnt by the fire.

3:25. Like son of the gods. King Nebuchadnezzar saw four men in the fiery furnace and identified one of them as looking "like the son of the gods" (Dan 3:25). Nebuchadnezzar's expression reflects his polytheistic worldview. However, he noted the distinctiveness of the fourth individual in the furnace. The expression "son of the gods" is the Semitic way of saying that one is a divine being. In fact, the Ugaritic "expression *bn qdš* refers primarily to members of the heavenly assembly and can be translated as 'son of holiness,' 'son of gods,' or simply 'gods,' 'holy ones.'"[86] Nebuchadnezzar further refers to the same individual as God's angel or messenger (Dan 3:28) in the sense that this divine individual came to rescue or save Shadrach, Meshach, and Abednego, servants of the Most High God.

3:29. Cut to pieces. See **2:5, 12. Destroying wise men.** Such rushed and empty threats from ancient rulers may have never materialized. However, the ancient practice of destroying people for not complying in worshiping a deity is still maintained today in several countries.

---

84. *CAD*, K, 8:215.
85. "Hats," *SDABC*, 4:784.
86. Kornfeld, "*qdš*," (*TDOT*, 12:525).

Daniel 4

CENTER OF THE EARTH

Here, extant material on Nebuchadnezzar's personal testimony is intriguing. The challenge, however, is that Babylonian Chronicles are silent on Nebuchadnezzar's final events and death. It is possible that some records were deliberately destroyed in the course of time. Fortunately, the biblical record presents substantive information. The focus is on Nebuchadnezzar himself and the city of Babylon.

4:1. Nebuchadnezzar the king. "Nebuchadnezzar, the King" (Dan 4:1); "I, Nebuchadnezzar" (Dan 4:4); "I, King Nebuchadnezzar," or "I, Nebuchadnezzar, the King" (Dan 4:18) are common biblical attestations which also appear on the inscription on the Commemoration of the Restoration of Emah in Babylon: "I, Nebuchadnezzar, king of Babylon, king of the country of Sumer and Akkad, the wise, the pious, who lives according to the trust(worthy oracles) of his lord, the great lord Marduk, and of Nabu, the foremost heir who loves kingship, (and) who constantly seeks after their godhead."[1] Here, Nebuchadnezzar uses the appositional independent personal pronoun "I." The use of the personal pronoun is very common in ancient Near Eastern literature. Nebuchadnezzar was a worshiped hero and some parents named their sons "Nabu-kur-usur-ilu," which is "Nebuchadnezzar is God," or "Nabukudur-usur-Shamshi," "Nebuchadnezzar is my sun," and also "Nabuch-abni," "Nebuchadnezzar is my creator."[2] The author of Daniel uses Nebuchadnezzar's royal title in a way similar to its use in the ancient literature.

1. Beaulieu, "New Inscription of Nebuchadnezzar II," 95.
2. Champdor, *Babylon*, 114.

NEBUCHADNEZZAR COMMEMORATIVE CYLINDER
The cylinder begins: "I am Nebuchadnezzar, king of Babylon, the great, the might..." It continues to relate his great achievements.
(Courtesy of Toledo Museum of Art)

4:1. Peoples, nations, and languages. See 3:4, 7, 29. Peoples, nations, and languages. Nebuchadnezzar was open to having his testimony shared with all people, everywhere. He concluded by declaring his decision to worship the God of Heaven, whom he got acquainted with through his personal experience. See Matt 28:18-20 and Rev 14:6, 7.

4:1, 10-23, 35. In all the earth. See 2:10, 35, 39; 6:25, 27; 7:4, 17, 23; 8:5; 12:2. In Semitic languages the noun "earth" has many meanings. It can apply to an individual's home region, empire or country, neighboring territories, and eventually every territory of human habitation. "Earth" can also be land, ground, or soil.

The kings of the ancient Near East could view themselves as rulers of the whole earth, implying their whole domain. Nebuchadnezzar boasted on the Etemenanki cylinder text that his gods Marduk and Shamash gave him rulership over "the totality of countries, the whole of all inhabited regions."[3] This text implies the concept of the control of all the earth but evidence shows that Nebuchadnezzar meant the territory under his control only. Nebuchadnezzar's royal rhetoric also states: "From the kings of the

---

3. Vanderhooft, *Neo-Babylonian Empire and Babylon*, 36.

four corners, from all peoples, let me receive their heavy tribute within it (the palace)."[4]

The word "earth" in Daniel is used both literally and figuratively in accordance to the traditions of the ancient Near East people. The context of each passage where "earth" is mentioned is a good indicator of what the author implies.

4:1. Your peace be increased. See 6:25; 10:19. Semitic languages use formal expressions in their greetings that vary from place to place. The Hebrew word *shālôm* and its Aramaic equivalent *sh^{e}lām* express the idea of "completeness," "soundness," "welfare," "peace," "safety," "healthy," "prosperity," "quiet," "contentment," "tranquility."[5] The root *slm* is also used for greetings in its varied forms by several other languages. The ancient Near East has several other different forms of greetings.

The greetings could be said personally or written in correspondence. There were always some gestures that accompanied the saying of the greetings and these served to express honor and humility. An archive of correspondence documents written in Akkadian, now known as Amarna letters, have the greeting: "At the feet of the king, my lord, and my Sun-god, seven times and seven times I fall."[6] The king of Tyre's court correspondence to the king of Ugarit greets him thus: "May it be well with you."[7] Also, the king of Hatti greets the king of Ugarit by the expression: "With the Sun everything is very well."[8] A governor wrote a letter to the queen and greeted her: "[A]t the feet of my lady I fall. With my lady may it be well."[9]

The Lachish letters were written during the time when the Babylonians were invading the land of Judah. The usual greeting on these letters read: "May Yahweh give you good news at this very time."[10] King Artaxerxes replied to a letter that had come from those who opposed the rebuilding of Jerusalem. He saluted them: "Peace, and now" (Ezra 4:17). Another letter by the same king to Ezra has, "Perfect, and now" (Ezra 7:12). Even in the New Testament times letters have greetings such as: "Grace to you and peace from God our Father and the Lord Jesus Christ" (Rom 1:7).

The practice of well-wishing and greetings in addressing others is an ancient tradition in the Semitic world. Kings maintained order and peace.

4. Vanderhooft, *Neo-Babylonian Empire and Babylon*, 46.
5. BDB, 1022, 1023.
6. *ANET*, 483–490.
7. *COS*, 3:93.
8. *COS*, 3:95.
9. *COS*, 3:107.
10. *COS*, 3:78–81.

Several names have the element of peace. The most common word used in both biblical text and nonbiblical texts for the greetings is *shalom*, "peace." During the Neo-Babylonian period there is plenty of evidence on statements containing peace in prayers and building inscriptions. Daniel 4:1 records Nebuchadnezzar sending to all people on earth a greeting wishing their peace to increase.

4:3, 34. Generation to generation. Aramaic *dār* means "generation." The Akkadian equivalent is *dūr dāri*, "forever," "eternity," "ever," "continuously," or "duration." Hebrew *dor* basically means "circle" or "circle of people," that is, "an assembly," "congregation," or "a generation." *Dor* later developed to *dôr* meaning "lap in a race," "cycle of time," or "lifetime." "From generation to generation" is an expression common in the recovered ancient Near Eastern literature meaning "a long time," "for all generations," "for ever and ever," "everlasting," or "eternity."[11] After the seven years of animal-like life, Nebuchadnezzar's reason came back to him and he acknowledged that the kingdom of the Most High God in Heaven is Powerful and Eternal.

4:4. I, Nebuchadnezzar. Besides Nebuchadnezzar I (1126–1105 BC) and Nebuchadnezzar II (605–562 BC), there were several other individuals who claimed the name "Nebuchadnezzar." One was a Babylonian chanter mentioned in a letter to King Marduk-šapik-zeri. This was possibly during the reign of Esarhaddon (680–669 BC) or Ashurbanipal (668–ca. 627 BC). Another one was an officer at the Nabû Temple of Kalhu. This was also during the reign of Esarhaddon or Ashurbanipal. Also, an Urukean during the reign of Ashurbanipal claimed the name of "Nebuchadnezzar." A Babylonian, probably the father of Bel-ibni, claimed to be Nebuchadnezzar during the reign of Ashurbanipal. A gate guard to the commander in chief, acting as a witness (possibly after the reign of Ashurbanipal), said that he was Nebuchadnezzar.

The Septuagint is the Greek version of the Hebrew Bible which was translated in Alexandria in the third and second century BC. This manuscript, often referred to as the LXX, gives useful information with regard to the name of Nebuchadnezzar.

For the Akkadian name "Nabi-uv-ku-du-ur-ri-u-tsu-ur," usually spelled "Nabû-kudurri-uṣur," the LXX has "Nabouchodonosor," which became "Nabuchodonosor" in the Vulgate. "Nabuchodonosor" is said to be nearer to the true Assyrian pronunciation than the Masoretic "Nebuchadnezzar." There should, however, be an "r" instead of the second "n." Indeed, the "r" is preserved in Jer 49:28. The use of the second "n" in Nebuchadnezzar's

---

11. See *TDOT*, 3:169–81.

name is attested on an Aramaic tablet which is dated the thirty-fourth year of Nebuchadnezzar's reign (571 BC). The shift from "r" to "n" is also attested in several Aramaic transcriptions of Babylonian names.

Nebûkadre'ṣṣar/Nebûkadre'ṣṣor, as found in the books of Jeremiah and Ezekiel, is considered to be a close transliteration of King Nebuchadnezzar's name. The Aramaic Sefire clay tablet dated 571–570 BC has "[Ne]buchadrezzar king of [Baby]lon," a title similarly used in Dan 1:2. A. van Selms suggests that the name "Nebuchadnezzar" was a nickname which meant "Nabû protect the mule," because he was of mixed extraction. This idea can safely be rejected on the basis that such a practice is not found in Babylonian royal names. Further, it is a fact that Nebuchadnezzar was named after a highly honored king of the Isin Dynasty.

Moshe Garsiel discussed the concept of "midrashic name derivation," a phenomenon in the biblical literature where "an interpretation infuses a name with meaning in relation to past events, or looks forward to some future incidents." It is understood that the name giver invented a name to give a message or meaning. We see that many names in the biblical text are followed by an explanation why they were given to the individuals concerned. The midrashic name derivation was different in that it focused more on hidden meanings or wordplays that associate the individual with one's actions or circumstances.

In Ezra 2:1, the last three letters of *Nebûkădnĕṣṣôr* are exploited by making them a verb *ṣôr*. The meaning of this verb would be to "lay a siege." This is illustrated in many texts including Jer 21:2–4, 9; 32:1–2; 39:1; 2 Kgs 24:10–11; etc. Further, the last three letters of the name *Nebûkadne'ṣṣar*, that is, *'ṣr*, are used to form the noun *ôṣṣār*, meaning "treasure." With regard to this, Nebuchadnezzar is known to have plundered all the treasures (*'wṣrwt*) of the house of the Lord and the treasures (*'wṣrwt*) of the king's house (2 Kgs 24:13)[12]. Ester Rabbah I wrote: "Said R. Tanhuma, 'Nebuchadnezzar—may his bones rot—collected all the money in the world, and he was stingy about spending his money.'"[13]

4:4, 29–30. Nebuchadnezzar's palace. The kings of Babylonia used to build their own palaces in cities of their own choice. Nebuchadnezzar's father, Nabopolassar (626–605 BC), built his palace in Babylon. When he died, Nebuchadnezzar used and renovated that palace, but he abandoned the project when he decided to build his own palace adjacent to it. The new palace was not only elaborate and impressive, but had no rival in the ancient Near East. It served as Nebuchadnezzar's royal residence and administrative

---

12. Garsiel, *Biblical Names*, 19.
13. Neusner, *Esther Rabbah I*, 64.

center. Robert Koldewey did extensive excavations in the city of Babylon.[14] He describes Nebuchadnezzar's architectural designs and fortifications of his palace.

The excavations revealed some small, unstamped burnt bricks, 32x32 centimeters that were used in the construction of the foundation of the palace. Asphalt was plastered over the walls. In the northwest corner of the palace there was massive brickwork which excavators traced down and found a pottery coffin of an unusual size. This coffin was bricked up by Nebuchadnezzar's bricks. It was a burial of his time. They discovered that the burial had been robbed before. In the rubbish around the immense sarcophagus were found some gold beads and many small circular and rectangular gold plates that had holes in them. These plates used to be sown into some materials to form impressive decorations. The rectangular plates had some moldings of either a bearded man presenting some offering to Marduk or a gateway of a fortress that has towers and battlements. From the look of it, the burial discovered underneath Nebuchadnezzar's palace must have been of some significant figure. The small portion of the garment found there was spangled with gold ornaments. It is possible that this could be the burial of Nabopolassar, Nebuchadnezzar's father.

Nebuchadnezzar's palace buildings had several courts, towers, and fortification walls. The great hall was part of the western court. The palace complex buildings were roofed over with corbelled flat bricks that were laid on parallel cedar beams. The palace court had ostentatious decorations of unimaginable beauty and ambition. No wonder Nebuchadnezzar paced about on the roof of his palace marveling at his creative achievements (Dan 4:29–30). Prior to this, King David of Israel also paced on the roof of his palace and marveled over a beautiful woman (2 Sam 11:2).

Nebuchadnezzar's inscription reads: "In Babil, my favourite city, that I love, was the palace, the house of the marvel of mankind, the centre of the land, the shining residence, the dwelling of Majesty, upon the Babil place in Babil."[15] He continued to declare:

> Facing the water I laid its foundations firmly, and raised it mountain high with bitumen and burnt brick. Mighty cedars I caused to be laid down at length for its roofing. Door leaves of cedar overlaid with copper, thresholds and sockets of bronze I placed in its doorways. Silver and gold and precious stones, all that can be imagined of costliness, splendour, wealth, riches, all

---

14. Koldewey, *Excavations at Babylon*, 113–27.
15. Koldewey, *Excavations at Babylon*, 113.

that was highly esteemed I heaped up with it, I stored up immense abundance of royal treasure within it.[16]

By the fall of Babylon in 539 BC, Nebuchadnezzar's palace was still of brilliant beauty.

4:6, 7. Magicians. See **1:20. Magicians.**

4:8. The name of my god. See **1:2. Nebuchadnezzar's god.** Nebuchadnezzar makes a distinction between his god, Marduk, and the Holy God of Daniel. Marduk is known by the Semitic term "Bel" (Lord) in the Old Testament (Isa 46:1; Jer 50:2; 51:44). Belteshazzar (Daniel) and Belshazzar (King) were named after Bel.

4:8, 9, 18. Holy gods. See **5:11, 14.** Daniel was able to interpret the dream because of "the spirit of the holy gods" which was in him (Dan 4:8, 9, 18; 5:11, 14). See also Gen 41:37–39; Num 27:18; Job 32:8. In Dan 6:3 Daniel was also characterized as having "superb spirit." The Aramaic expression *ᵉlāhîn qaddîšin*, "holy gods," is equivalent to *hʾlnm hqdšm*, which is on the sarcophagus of Enshmunazar of Sidon.[17] As already noted, *ᵉlāhîn qaddîšin* is translated as "holy gods" to depict the polytheistic worldview of Nebuchadnezzar, the queen mother (Dan 5:11), and Belshazzar (Dan 5:14). Surprisingly, *ᵉlōhîm qᵉdōšim*, "Holy God," is also used in Josh 24:19 to denote God of Israel in the magisterial plural sense.

4:10. Tree. The events of Dan 4 have been dismissed by several scholars as unhistorical, fictional, and mythical. In this chapter, Nebuchadnezzar related his terrible dream of a gigantic tree that was located in the center of the earth (Dan 4:10). Its height reached to the heaven (Dan 4:11; cf. Gen 11:4). The gigantic tree's central location parallels that of the city of Babylon, which the cosmographic *mappa mundi*, "Map of the World," located at the center of the universe.[18]

Ancient Mesopotamian religion had the myth of the garden of paradise, which was supposedly situated at Eridu between the mouths of the Tigris and the Euphrates Rivers. The clay tablets relate of the garden where a sacred palm tree grew. The Akkadian version of a Sumerian text reads: "In Eridu there is a black *kiškanu*-tree, growing in a pure place, its appearance is lapis-lazuli, erected on the *Apsû*."[19] The trunk of the tree was decorated with

---

16. Koldewey, *Excavations at Babylon*, 113.
17. Gibson, *Textbook*, 3.107.
18. See commentary on **4:30. City of Babylon.**
19. The *kiškanu* tree (Akkadian) is equivalent to the *giš-kin* (Sumerian) and

metal bands and fillets[20] (cf. Dan 4:15, 23, 26). The king was obviously the custodian and caretaker of the garden where this tree of life was growing. This mythical idea virtually equates the king to the tree of life, as can be seen from the personal name ᴰŠulgi-ú-nam-til (Šulgi-ú-namtil-la), "the divine Šulgi is the Plant of Life."[21] Other texts that compare the king to a tree are "Šulgi, the king, the graceful lord, is a date palm planted by the water ditch,"[22] and "Like a cedar rooted by abundant water, of pleasant thou art (Šulgi)."[23] Both the Babylonian mythology and Nebuchadnezzar's dream seem to have some allusions to the biblical creation story (Gen 2:9).

The motif of the king being associated with a tree is further illustrated by Assyrian and Babylonian glyptic art, reliefs, and seals where kings appear by a sacred tree or simply holding a tree or its branch.[24] In Ezek 31 the Pharaoh of Egypt is likened to a great tree that has to be felled. The Wadi Brisa rock relief probably shows Nebuchadnezzar cutting down a tree.

Daniel interpreted the king's dream. He pointed out that Nebuchadnezzar was represented by the great tree, and that the fate of the tree prefigured his own fate. There are similarities in the imagery of Dan 2:37-38, where Nebuchadnezzar was represented by the head of gold, and Dan 4:20-22, where he was represented by the tree. The king was to leave his throne and change into a beast of the forest. Then, after seven years, he would regain his sanity and come back to his throne. Nebuchadnezzar was "to learn the basic truth that the complex of human power is always fragile."[25]

4:11. Reached to the sky. This phrase was often used of a Mesopotamian temple-tower, the ziggurat, which was taken as a stairway for the gods from heaven to earth.

4:13, 17, 23. Watcher. See also 8:13. This is an angel or messenger of God, depicted as an executor of God's assignment. Apocalyptic and prophetic writings exhibit a lot of angels interacting with humans. Daniel interacted with angels, the heavenly beings. Several writings discovered at Qumran

---

identical to the tree of life; see Widengren, *King and the Tree of Life*, 5-6.

20. Smith, "Notes on the Assyrian Tree," *Bulletin of the School of Oriental Studies* 4 (1926) 69-76.

21. Widengren, *King and the Tree of Life*, 42.

22. Widengren, *King and the Tree of Life*, 42.

23. Widengren, *King and the Tree of Life*, 42.

24. James, *Tree of Life*, 42, 97-99. For Assyrian, Babylonian, and Achaemenian seals depicting a combination of motifs including the tree, see Smith, "Relation of Marduk, Ashur, and Osiris," 43-44; and Wiseman, *Cylinder Seals of Western Asia*, 66-104.

25. Coxon, "Great Tree of Daniel 4," in Martin and Davies, *Word in Season*, 109.

express the blessedness of communicating with angels as a privilege reserved for the members of the community there (1QS 11:7, 8; 1QSa 3:3–11; 1QH 3:21, 22; 6:12, 13; 11:10–14).

4:15, 23, 26. Stump and its roots. The imagery of the stump and roots that were to remain of the whole tree that was cut down depicts the hope that the tree would develop new shoots (Job 14:7–9; Isa 6:13; 11:1). This biblical motif points to recovery. The stump here is symbolically protected by some metal bands to assure its preservation in anticipation of future restoration. Since the tree represented Nebuchadnezzar (Dan 4:22), his survival is assured despite the ordeal he would encounter. In ancient times some kings somehow survived heavy blows in their reign while others were not that fortunate.

4:15, 23, 25. Dew of heaven. The expression "dew of heaven" appears on a Ugaritic myth tablet CTA 3 with the meaning "falling rain,"[26] similar to that in Dan 4:15, 23, 25. Nebuchadnezzar was made wet each time it rained throughout his stay in the open field where he lived with animals (Dan 4:25, 32). Ancient people believed that the deity sent rains from heaven.

4:16. Heart of a beast. The heart was considered to be the seat of intelligence for humans. Nebuchadnezzar was informed that he was going to be transformed to have the mind of an animal. Boanthropy is a psychological or delusional disorder that makes an individual believe that he or she is an ox or a cow and behaves like that animal. The seven times for Nebuchadnezzar's lycanthropy (living like a wolf), or boanthropy (acting like an ox), animalization or monomania, have been understood to be a literal period of seven years.[27] Josephus, too, took the time to state the period as seven literal years.[28] Nebuchadnezzar was given the mind of an animal, lived with wild donkeys, and ate grass like an ox for seven years (Dan 5:21). Babylonian literature never mentions Nebuchadnezzar's animal-like behavior.

4:16, 23, 25, 32. Seven times. See **3:19. Seven times.** The number seven was always accorded a predominant and sacred position in the ancient Near East. The Babylonians, who ascribed cosmic significance to the number seven and equated it to the concept of *kiššatu*, "fullness" or "totality," had inherited its use from the Sumerian *imin*, "seven," which was used

---

26. *COS*, 1:251.
27. Holladay, *Concise Hebrew and Aramaic Lexicon*, 415–16; and BDB, 1105.
28. Josephus, *Antiquities of the Jews*, 10.10.6; and Josephus, *Against Apion*, 1.20.

symbolically to mean "all."[29] Nebuchadnezzar commanded the furnace to be heated up seven times more than usual for destroying the Hebrew men who failed to comply with his orders (Dan 3:19). He would be herbivorous for seven times, that is, seven literal years (Dan 4:16, 23, 25, 32). It took King Solomon seven years to build the temple in Jerusalem (1 Kgs 6:38). Likewise, Nebuchadnezzar lived like an animal for seven years.

4:27. Break off your sins. Daniel pleaded earnestly with the king to consider the advice he presented. Perhaps the sentence determined upon the king could be ameliorated. Daniel's proposal focused on two requirements. Nebuchadnezzar's potential escape from the impending doom was predicated upon his willingness to separate himself from sins and iniquities (Dan 4:27). The Aramaic peal imperative verb *prq* (Dan 4:27) was widely used in the ancient Near East. The Aramaic root *prq* means "to separate," "scatter," "drive off," "tear away," or "break off" while the New Hebrew denotes "to remove" a burden or a load. Similarly, Akkadian *paraqu* means "to separate" or "detach"; Ugarit *prq*, "break"; Syriac *peraq*, "loose" or "rescue"; Samaritan *frq*, "save" or "rescue"; Arabic *faraqa*, "separate" or "divide"; and Ethiopic *faraqa*, "free," "rescue." When used with regard to something detrimental or undesirable, *prq* means to detach oneself from that thing aggressively. It was thus that Daniel urged Nebuchadnezzar to separate himself from his sins. By using the verb *prq*, Daniel most probably demanded that Nebuchadnezzar initiate a "violent self-liberation" or "snatching out or tearing away associated with rescue" from his own sins and iniquities. It may well have been a difficult and painful process but it was at least possible and, in the end would have been very rewarding. That, for Nebuchadnezzar, would have been a saving act or a rescuing process.[30]

4:27. Iniquities. From ancient times iniquities have been understood to mean "evil," "wickedness," "mischief," "trouble," and "idolatry."[31] Iniquities are actions that oppose that which is good and true. Iniquities are offenses against God and humanity. They may manifest as rebellion, abject recklessness, or manipulative, antisocial behavior. God deals with this wicked conduct if the person does not respond positively to the offer for repentance (Job 4:8; Prov 22:8; Gal 6:7-9). Nebuchadnezzar needed to change his behavior (Dan 5:18-20). Daniel offered him the opportunity to conform to righteousness. See Titus 2:11-15.

---

29. Rengstorf, "ἑπτά" (*TDNT*, 2:627-28); McComiskey, "Seventy 'Weeks,'" 37-38; see also *CAD*, 8:457, texts RA 16 166 ii 24=CT 18 29 ii 19.
30. Mazani, "Nebuchadnezzar's Deficits," 68-69.
31. *TWOT*, 1:23.

4:27. Righteousness. See **9:7, 14, 16, 18, 24. Righteous/ness.** Righteousness is right doing. It is the antidote for sin. For Nebuchadnezzar, moral uprightness was required to bring favorable change to his fate. From antiquity prevails the belief that the deity checks on human behavior and rewards each individual accordingly. Wrongs could be righted by rituals and correct behavior.

4:30. City of Babylon. The book of Daniel seems to recognize the outstanding development of the city of Babylon. Nebuchadnezzar boasted, "Is this not Babylon the great that I have built for the royal palace by the might of my power and for the honor of my majesty?" (Dan 4:30). Here the author of Daniel seems to have preserved important information on Nebuchadnezzar as the extensive builder of Babylon. The Grotefend Cylinder confirms Nebuchadnezzar's boast on Babylon with language or sentiments strikingly similar to Dan 4:30. On the cylinder Nebuchadnezzar states: "Then built I the palace the seat of my royalty, the bond of the race of men, the dwelling of joy and rejoicing."[32] In the India House Inscription, Nebuchadnezzar declares that "in Babylon, my dear city, which I love was the palace, the house of wonder of the people, the bond of the land, the brilliant place, the abode of majesty in Babylon."[33] The idea that Nebuchadnezzar built Babylon to its grandeur seems to have been lost to the Hellenistic writers including Herodotus, Ctesias, Strabo, and Pliny, who did not ever refer to Nebuchadnezzar as the builder of Babylon.[34] This may indicate that the book of Daniel contains an older tradition which preserves unique information which was unknown to later writers.

Under Nebuchadnezzar, Babylon underwent massive reconstruction and expansion. It grew to cover 850 hectares (over three square miles). The city was enclosed by double walls and moats. Its history stretches more than two thousand years. Ancient records indicate that Babylon was founded some time before 2500 BC, and it was not destroyed until 331 BC. The Babylonian *mappa mundi*, "Map of the World," takes Babylon to be at the center of the world. The history of Babylon reveals that

---

32. Schrader, *Keilinschriftliche bibliothek*, 3/2:39.

33. Horne, *Babylonia and Assyria*, 1:451–52, col. vii, lines 34–40. See also Wiseman, *Nebuchadrezzar and Babylon*, 51–80.

34. Pfeiffer, *Biblical World*, 126; and Hasel, "Book of Daniel," 38. For example, Herodotus, *Herodotus*, 1.178–87, extensively describes the architectural remains of Babylon, but never refers to Nebuchadnezzar as the builder. He ascribes the major monuments of Babylon to Queen Nitocris. Diodorus (*Diodorus of Sicily*, 2.7.2–11; 2.10.1) credits Queen Semiramis for the building program at Babylon.

most of this time it maintained a high standard of civilization, surviving one conquest after another, absorbing its conquerors because it was intellectually superior to them, and exporting its culture throughout the ancient world. Its language was the language of international diplomacy; its religion, astronomy, astrology, and jurisprudence dominated the civilized nations until the rise of Greece.[35]

BABYLONIAN MAP OF THE WORLD
This clay tablet shows the Map of the World (*mappa mundi*) with Babylon at its center, surrounded by water. The map is from the time of King Sargon, the first king of Akkad. (Credit: Zev Radovan)

Babylon is said to be the longest-lived capital in history.[36] Its ancient ruins can still be seen by the Euphrates River, about fifty-six miles (ninety kilometers) southwest of modern Baghdad in Iraq. In the sixth century BC Babylon became the greatest city in the ancient Near East. Babylon was described by Robert Koldewey as "perhaps the most celebrated city in the world."[37] It was a large city for its time, and gained a larger-than-life reputation for being an immense and beautiful city of legend. Nebuchadnezzar's building program was so extensive and ostentatious that it far surpassed what the Assyrians had previously done. Babylon became a public spectacle of the ancient world. The beauty of the city's ramparts, palaces, multiple temples, and the hanging gardens invoked the pride of achievement.

---

35. Wellard, *Babylon*, 12.
36. Westenholz, "Babylon," in *Royal Cities of the Biblical World*, 197.
37. Koldewey, quoted in Wellard, *Babylon*, 11.

Archaeologists have recognized that some of Herodotus's descriptions of Babylon do not match well with the results of excavation.[38] A great many inscriptions have been recovered from Nebuchadnezzar's building works. These provide valuable evidence for his military campaigns and also furnish insights into his building activities.

EAST INDIA HOUSE INSCRIPTION
This foundation tablet, dating ca. 604–562 BC, was found in ancient Babylon. It describes Nebuchadnezzar's outstanding construction achievements.
(Credit: Zev Radovan)

Babylon had a quadrilateral layout. Several remarkable features in the topography of Babylon[39] included:

- 43 cult centers of the great gods in Babylon;
- 55 daises of Marduk;
- 2 circumvallations (ramparts or other defensive entrenchments);
- 3 rivers;
- 8 city gates;
- 24 streets of Babylon;

---

38. Herodotus, *Herodotus*, 1:178–87. Koldewey has cited several instances where excavation finds in Babylon do not match what Herodotus described. See his *Excavations at Babylon*, 2–5, 31, 64, 82, 98, 102, 193–97, 201, 210, 212, 222, 242, 280. For a different opinion on Herodotus's descriptions, see Kuhrt, "Ancient Mesopotamia" (*CANE*, 1:58); and Wiseman, *Nebuchadrezzar and Babylon*, 73.

39. The tablets BM 38442 and BM 34789 contain the text Tintir = Babylon (Topography of Babylon); see Westenholz, "Babylon," 204–6.

- 300 daises of the Igigi and 600 daises of the Anunnaki;
- 180 shrines of Ištar;
- 180 stations of Lugalgirra and Meslamtaea;
- 12 stations of the Divine Heptad;
- 6 stations of Kubu;
- 4 stations of the Rainbow;
- 2 stations of the Evil God;
- 2 stations of the Watcher of the City.

This list makes it clear that Babylon was called "the place of creation of the gods"[40] for good reason. Each of the eight city gates was named after a deity:

- North: Ishtar, the goddess of fertility and battle, and Sin, the moon god;
- East: Marduk, the patron deity of the city of Babylon and Ninurta, the god of hunting and warfare;
- South: Urash, the patron deity of the city of Dilbat, Enlil, the god of wind and sky, and Shamash, the sun god;
- and West: Hadad, the storm god.

MUSHUSHU DRAGON
Mushushu is a mythical hybrid dragon found decoratively glazed on the brick walls of Babylon. (Picture by Connie Gane, Courtesy of HAM)

The ziggurat dominated the center of the city of Babylon. It had several temples associated with it, while the administrative buildings and the

40. Westenholz, "Babylon," 204.

royal palaces were located near the walls. Neither the book of Daniel nor the discovered cuneiform tablets refer to one of the seven wonders of the ancient world, the hanging gardens of Babylon. Benjamin of Tudela from Spain traveled to China between AD 1160 and 1173. He was the earliest known European to describe Babylon as follows:

> This is the ancient Babel, and now lies in ruins; but the streets still extend thirty miles. The ruins of the palace of Nebuchadnezzar are still to be seen; but people are afraid to venture among them on account of the serpents and scorpions with which they are infested. Twenty thousand Jews live within about twenty miles from this place, and perform their worship in the synagogue of Daniel, who rests in peace. This synagogue is of remote antiquity, having been built by Daniel himself; it is constructed of solid stones and bricks. Here, the traveler may also behold the palace of Nebuchadnezzar, with the burning fiery furnace into which were thrown Hananiah, Mishael, and Azariah; it is a valley well known to everyone.[41]

However, in 594 BC the prophet Jeremiah wrote in a book about the destruction of the city of Babylon "that none shall remain in it, neither man or beast, but it shall be desolate forever" (Jer 51:59–64). The author of Daniel, unlike contemporary cartographers, seems to see the city of Babylon in its sixth-century BC imperial setting in a more realistic light which is supported by the archeological records.

4:32–33. From men to beasts. The story of Nebuchadnezzar becoming like an animal has sometimes been confused with that of the so-called Prayer of Nabonidus.[42] Daniel told Nebuchadnezzar that he would live like an animal in the field, grazing like a bull for seven times (Dan 4:25; 5:21; cf. Job 30:29–31). Some scholars have argued that it was Nabonidus who was mad and not Nebuchadnezzar.

The Midrash Rabbah indicated that when Adam heard the divine sentence after he had sinned (Gen 3:18), he broke into a sweat and exclaimed, "What! Shall I be tied to the feeding-trough like a beast!"[43] On the other hand, Pseudo-Jonathan wrote that Adam responded by begging for mercy: "O Lord, let me not be considered like the animals (or, as cattle) to eat the grass of the open field. Let me rather stand up and work and let me eat

---

41. See Benjamin Tudela, quoted in Lundquist, "Babylon in European Thought" (*CANE*, 1:68); also quoted in Komroff, *Contemporaries of Marco Polo* (1989).
42. See Appendix B, "The Prayer of Nabonidus."
43. Freedman and Simon, *Midrash Rabbah*, 168.

food from the work of my hands; and thus let there be a distinction before you between human beings and animals."⁴⁴ The *Chronicles of Jerahmeel*, a collection of apocryphal and pseudo-epigraphical books, indicates that Nebuchadnezzar became different from other men "in his appearance, in his mind, and in his language. He appeared to men like an ox as far as his navel (or stomach), and from his navel to his feet like a lion."⁴⁵

Over a hundred winged, human-headed bulls and lions have been recovered from the Assyrian palaces at Kalhu (modern Nimrud), Dūr Šarukēn (modern Khorsabad), Nineveh (opposite present-day Mosul), and Susa (modern Shush).⁴⁶ These symbolic emblems have provided scholars with opportunity for much study, and have been considered the origin of the iconographic motif in the ancient Near East.⁴⁷ Shalmaneser III (858–824 BC) stated that "Ninurta and Palil, who love my priesthood, have given me all the beasts of the field"⁴⁸ (cf. Dan 2:38; 4:15, 23, 25).

The Tablet BM 34113 has Nebuchadnezzar's name partly restored, but the whole text is too fragmented.⁴⁹ The extant text, although badly damaged, seems to relate an unusual behavior by a king. It is not clear whether the strange behavior in this text refers to Nebuchadnezzar or his son Evil-Merodach. However, there is a suggestion that this text may have reference to Nebuchadnezzar's madness.⁵⁰ Grayson thinks that the text makes a reference to Evil-Merodach's mismanagement of public affairs.⁵¹ On the whole, Nebuchadnezzar's dream of the gigantic tree and its implications with regard to him and his kingdom point to the King of Heaven as the one who controls human destiny (Dan 4:3).

4:36. Royal officials. Some of Nebuchadnezzar's officials are attested on a prism that was found in Babylon and is now housed in the Istanbul Museum (no. 7834).⁵² Some of the names on this prism have been associated

---

44. Macho, *Neophyti*, 1 1:17.
45. Gaster, *Chronicles of Jerahmeel*, 205.
46. Roaf, *Cultural Atlas*, 162–63; Black and Green, *Gods, Demons and Symbols*, 48–51; *ANEP*, 212–13; and Saggs, *Greatness That Was Babylon*, 313, and plate 53.
47. Danrey, "Winged Human-Headed Bulls of Nineveh," 133–39.
48. "Beasts of the Field" (*SDABC*, 4:772).
49. Grayson, *Babylonian Historical-Literary Texts*, 89; and Wiseman, *Nebuchadrezzar and Babylon*, 102.
50. Horn, "New Light on Nebuchadnezzar's Madness," 39–40; Maxwell, *God Cares*, 1:73–74; and Stefanovic, *Wisdom to the Wise*, 169.
51. Grayson, *Babylonian Historical-Literary Texts*, 87; see also Wiseman, *Nebuchadrezzar and Babylon*, 102; and Josephus, *Against Apion*, 1.20.146–47.
52. *ANET*, 307–8.

with biblical characters. These include Nabuzeriddinam (Nebuzaradan, Jer 39:9–13; 40:1), Hanunu (Hananiah, Dan 1:6, 7, 19; 2:17), and Nergalsharusur (Nergal-Sharezer, Jer 39:3, 13). There is also a building text, which is usually called "Nebuchadnezzar's Court Calendar."[53] This gives a partial list of Nebuchadnezzar's officials and their responsibilities in Neo-Babylonia.

Recently, Michael Jursa deciphered a cuneiform tablet which proved to be a receipt of payment in the form of gold. This payment was made to the temple by Nabu-sharrussu-ukin (biblical Nebo-Sarsekim, Jer 39:3). Nebo-Sarsekim was Nebuchadnezzar's chief eunuch, and was present at the siege of Jerusalem in 587/6 BC.[54] The cuneiform tablet is dated 595 BC. It has been observed that Ashpenaz might have been Nebo-Sarsekim's predecessor in the office of chief eunuch.[55]

Nebuchadnezzar had "men of might/valor who (were) in his army" (Dan 3:20). Flavius Josephus mentions the names of some of Nebuchadnezzar's army officials, especially those who were involved in besieging Jerusalem. Among these were Nergal Sharezer, Sangar Nebo, Rabsaris, Sarsechim, and Rabmag.[56]

The name Nebuzaradan (Akkadian: Nabû-zer-iddinam) means "Nabu has given me offspring/seed." The man with this name was the general for the army and was the one responsible for all the war operations. According to Josephus, he was responsible for appointing Gedaliah governor to oversee the province of Judah. Nebuzaradan appears as the "chief of the guardsmen or bodyguards" for Nebuchadnezzar (see 2 Kgs 25:8, 10, 11, 12, 15, 18, 20; Jer 39:9, 10, 11, 13; 40:1, 2, 5; 41:10; 43:6; 52:12, 14, 15, 16, 19, 24, 26, 30). The "guardsmen or bodyguards" were originally the "royal slaughterers." This was a commanding position also similar to that of Potiphar of the Egyptians (Gen 37:36). Nebuzaradan was responsible for all military operations in Jerusalem and Judah. He also appeared as the chief cook or baker on a prism that was found in Babylon, now housed in the Istanbul Museum, No. 7834.[57]

Recovered ancient texts reveal that in the Neo-Assyrian Empire about sixteen wise men formed the inner circle of the king. These included "a chief interpreter of celestial and terrestrial omens (who was the closest to the king), a chief liver diviner, or haruspex, a chief exorcist, a personal exorcist whom the king consulted about the health of the royal children, and several

---

53. *ANET*, 307–8.
54. Resig, "Cuneiform Tablet Confirms Biblical Name," 18.
55. Govier, "Babylonian Official Mentioned in the Bible," 15.
56. Josephus, *Antiquities of the Jews*, 8.2.135.
57. *ANET*, 307, 308.

more exorcists, two doctors, a chief chanter and at least two astrologers."[58] It is possible that these officials could be replaced by their sons, who were in turn highly trained for administrative tasks.

The author of Daniel mentioned some of the offices in Nebuchadnezzar's administration which were functional in Neo-Babylonia. He seems to have been acquainted with the court system of the day and indicates personal interaction with some of the high-ranking government officials. His knowledge of the Neo-Babylonian court administration is backed up by several related archaeological discoveries, and these offer a better understanding of the biblical text.

4:36. Restored. Nebuchadnezzar was brought back to the throne after being absent for seven years. Besides raising objections on the spelling and historical significance of the name "Nebuchadnezzar," some interpreters have also disputed the last events of his life, as recorded in Dan 4. According to the author of the book of Daniel, Nebuchadnezzar became proud of his achievements, subsequently became mad, and then regained his sound mind after seven years. Nebuchadnezzar's later life is not commented upon in any literature outside the Hebrew Bible. Nevertheless, the last events of Nebuchadnezzar's life as described in Dan 4 cannot be merely dismissed for lack of extrabiblical documentation.

Another problem is that the book of Daniel is silent on Nebuchadnezzar's death and succession. It seems, however, that Jer 27:7 outlines Nebuchadnezzar's dynasty. This information seems to tally with the ancient sources. According to Jer 27:7, Nebuchadnezzar would be followed on the Babylonian throne by his son and then his grandson. Amel-Marduk (biblical Evil-Merodach, Jer 52:31) indeed replaced his father Nebuchadnezzar on the throne. Amel-Marduk was not succeeded by his son but by a kinsman. The Hebrew word for "son" can also mean "grandson" or even a distant relative.

A fragment of Megasthenes (358-280 BC) was preserved by Abydenus in his history of the Assyrians and it reads:

> That Nabucodrosorus (Nebuchadnezzar), having become more powerful than Hercules, invaded Libya and Iberia, [sic] (Spain), and when he had rendered them tributary, he extended his conquests over the inhabitants of the shores upon the right of the sea . . . he expired, and was succeeded by his son Evilmarchus (Evil Merodach), who was slain by his kinsman, Neriglisares (Neriglissor), and Neriglisares left a son, Labassoarascus (Labarosoarchod), and when he also had suffered death by

---

58. Kuhrt, *ANE*, 2:524; see also Parpola, *Letters from Assyrian Scholars*, 2:xiv-xvi.

violence, they made Nabannidochus king, being of no relation to the royal race.[59]

The dating formulae on the economic texts from the Neo-Babylonian period have also enabled the reconstruction of the following chronology of the kings as shown in table 6. It seems, then, that several problems raised against the person of Nebuchadnezzar in Daniel are plausibly highlighted by some archaeological discoveries.

Table 6
THE NEO-BABYLONIAN KINGS

KING	REIGN
Nabopolassar	May 17/ Nov 22 (?), 626–August 15, 605 BC
Nebuchadnezzar	September 7, 605–October 8, 562 BC
Amēl-Marduk	October 8(?), 562–August 7, 560 BC
Neriglassar	August 13, 560–April 16, 556 BC
Labashi-Marduk	May 3, 556–June 20, 556 BC
Nabunaid	May 25, 556–October 13, 539 BC
Belshazzar	Co-regent with his father, Nabunaid

4:37. Able to put down. The Aramaic language uses the verb *shapel*, "be low," "bring low," or "humble," in a figurative sense to mean "humiliate" (Dan 4:37). God humiliates the proud (Job 40:11, 12; Prov 29:23; Jas 4:6). It is reported that Nebuchadnezzar went too far in disciplining Judah (Isa 47:6; Zech 1:15) and that he humiliated people at will (Dan 5:19). On the other hand, Belshazzar failed to humble himself even though he was exposed to the history of God's dealings with the proud Nebuchadnezzar (Dan 5:22) and how he was disciplined for that. Qumran (4Q542 11.6) advises the young to hold on to religious heritage if they are not to face humiliation in the future.

---

59. Cory, *Ancient Fragments*, 71–72; also quoted in Sack, *Images of Nebuchadnezzar*, 32.

Chapter 5

FALL OF BABYLON

THE BOOK OF DANIEL presents a political and chronological succession of terrestrial kingdoms. The message of the book is that the succession of these kingdoms leads up to an eschatological and celestial kingdom. An outline of the rise and fall of the historical kingdoms from the Neo-Babylonian Empire onwards is provided with such tantalizing accuracy that it has perplexed many scholars through the years. The fall of Belshazzar, and subsequently the city of Babylon, is in keeping with the theme of the book. Several recovered material finds can improve our understanding on the identity of certain persons and events discussed in the text. These also help to clear up some enigmatic passages. They shed light on some socioreligious, historical, and political developments of the ancient Near East which are discussed in the text of Daniel.

5:1. Belshazzar, identity. Many scholars believed that Belshazzar was a fictitious figure until archaeologists discovered the Yale Babylonian Collection (YBC 3765) tablet.[1] This find was dated about 559 BC, which corresponds with Neriglissar's accession year. The tablet identified a certain *Bêl-šar-uṣur*, that is, Belshazzar. This Belshazzar happened to have been a chief officer of King Neriglissar. The tablet does not tell us whether or not Belshazzar, the chief officer of Neriglassar, was the son of Nabonidus and the biblical Belshazzar, but the facts are strongly in favor of such a conclusion. This tablet records a transaction relative to Belshazzar's money which

---

1. Dougherty, *Nabonidus and Belshazzar*, 67–70. "Additional Note on Chapter 5," *SDABC*, 4:806–8, traces the scholarly divergent opinions on the person of Belshazzar in light of the discoveries of archaeological literary texts which had that name.

was administered by a man identified as Nergal-dânu. The main part of this inscription reads:

> (As to) one mina (and) seventeen shekels of silver, which are in one shekel pieces, belonging to Belshazzar, the chief officer of the king, (charged) against Rîmût, the son of Enlil-kidinnu, the silver which is from Nergal-dânu, the son of Mukîn-zêr, for the road, whatsoever he shall gain upon it, half of the profit he shall share with Nergal-dânu.[2]

There has been speculation as to the identity of the actual mother of Belshazzar. The only sibling attested for Belshazzar is his sister, Bêl-šalṭi-Nannar, who was dedicated to the gods by Nabonidus, her father. The text also relates how Nabonidus built her a dormitory near the E-gi-par temple at Ur. Nabonidus dedicated his daughter to the gods Nannar, Sin, Shamash, Adad, and Nikkal. He ended his prayer by saying: "May Bêl-šalṭi-Nannar, the beloved daughter of my heart, be strong before them, and may her command prevail. May her deeds be good, a faithful votary; may she not commit sin."[3] Not much else is known about Belshazzar's family life.

NABONIDUS, KING OF BABYLON
Stele of King Nabonidus of Babylon, praying to the moon, sun, and stars. Nabonidus (ca. 556–539 BC) was Belshazzar's father. (Credit: Zev Radovan)

A letter written by Belshazzar reads: "Letter of Belshazzar unto Nabu-shar-utsur. May the gods decree thy prosperity! On the day thou seest my

---

2. Dougherty, *Nabonidus and Belshazzar*, 67–68.
3. Clay, *Miscellaneous Inscriptions*, 1:74–75.

message do not observe a holiday but the *TU-E* staff, the advisory elders, without their *manzallati*, bring with you and come quickly."[4]

Overwhelming evidence show that Belshazzar was a historical figure who participated in Babylonian social, economic, political, and religious life. He featured as king at the fall of Babylon in 539 BC.

5:1. Belshazzar the king. Serious objections have been raised against some Greek and Jewish sources as well as the Aramaic text of Dan 5. Some scholars have believed that these texts erroneously identified Belshazzar as king of Babylon.

The texts that identify Belshazzar as king read:

- "Belshazzar the king" (Dan 5:1);
- "King Belshazzar" (Dan 5:9);
- "Belshazzar king of the Chaldeans" (Dan 5:30);
- "Belshazzar king of Babylon (Dan 7:1);
- "in the third year of the reign of Belshazzar the King" (Dan 8:1).

Baruch 1:11, which seems to follow the biblical text, also refers to Belshazzar (Balthasar) as the son of Nebuchadnezzar. It reads: "And pray for the life of King Nebuchadnezzar of Babylon, and for the life of his son Belshazzar, so that their days on earth may be like the days of heaven." It has been noted that "individual Chaldeans cited their genealogy in most cases simply by calling themselves 'son' of their tribe's eponymous ancestor (thus: Ea-zera-iqisha 'son' of Amukanu)."[5]

In the ancient Near East, it was politically necessary for any ruler to express familial links with his predecessors even when there was no direct linkage. For instance, there is a second-millennium BC inscription of Hutelutuš-Inšušinak (ca. 1120–1110 BC), king of Elam. His father was never a king, but he addressed his predecessors, Kutir-Nahhunte (1155–1150 BC) and Šilhak-Inšušnak (1150–1120 BC) as his fathers.[6] In this way, a usurping king like Nabonidus or his vice-regent Belshazzar, while obviously not "in direct royal line[,] had an opportunity to establish his legitimate right to the throne by claiming political succession using familial terminology."[7] Such could have been the case with Belshazzar, who might have claimed

---

4. Dougherty, *Nabonidus and Belshazzar*, 133.

5. Brinkman, *Prelude to Empire*, 15.

6. Grillot, "A propos d'un cas de 'Lévirat' élamite," 61–70; and Brosius, *Women in Ancient Persia*, 22.

7. Brosius, *Women in Ancient Persia*, 22.

Nebuchadnezzar as his father, even though his real father was Nabonidus. Belshazzar might have been related to Nebuchadnezzar. It has been suggested that Nabonidus was Nebuchadnezzar's son-in-law. If this was the case, then Belshazzar's mother was Nebuchadnezzar's daughter.[8]

The Harran Inscriptions of Nabonidus, Nabonidus H2 A, col. 1, lines 7–10, read: "I (am) Nabonidus, who have not the honour(?) of (being a) somebody, and kingship is not within me, (but) the gods and goddesses prayed for me, and Sin to the kingship called me."[9]

There is need, however, for evidence to support Paul-Alain Beaulieu's assumption that Belshazzar was the ringleader of the friends who plotted and killed King Lābaši-Marduk (556 BC). Also in doubt is the idea that Belshazzar was chosen to replace the king, but that he declined and let Nabonidus take the throne because he could not be king while his father was still alive.[10] Several Neo-Babylonian archaeological records identify Belshazzar as *mâr šarri*, "the royal prince," or "the son of the king," but never as *šarru*, "king." It is possible that Belshazzar was appointed king of Babylon by his father Nabonidus.

In the ancient Near East, some kings used to appoint "sub-kings" for part of their realm. For example, Sennacherib, king of Assyria (704–681 BC), appointed Bel-ibni, a Babylonian nobleman who was raised in Nineveh, to be the king of Babylon in 702 BC. Likewise, Ashur-nadin-shumu appointed his son to the same post in 699 BC.[11] Esarhaddon (680–669 BC) appointed his younger son Shamash-shum-ukni to be the king of Babylon under the auspices of his older brother Ashurbanipal (668–ca. 627 BC), who was king over Assyria.[12] Neriglissar called his father Bel-shum-ishkun "king of Babylon." However, there is no evidence for this except that Bel-shum-ishkun could have been a sub-king in Babylon.

In Dan 5, Belshazzar is portrayed as the last king of Babylon. He was slain as Neo-Babylonia fell into the hands of the Medo-Persians in October 539 BC. Serious objections have been raised against the author of Daniel for identifying Belshazzar as king. These objections are based on the Nabonidus Chronicle which reads: "The ninth year: Nabonidus, the king, (was) [in] Tema (while) the prince, the officers, (and) the army (were) in Akkad. The king did not come to Babylon in the month Nisan. Nabu did not come

---

8. White, *Story of Prophets and Kings*, 522, 529; and Millard, "Daniel 1—6 and History," 71–72.

9. Gadd, "Harran Inscriptions of Nabonidus," 57.

10. Beaulieu, *Reign of Nabonidus*, 153–55, 166.

11. Boutflower, *In and Around*, 118.

12. Boutflower, *In and Around*, 118.

to Babylon. Bel did not come out. The Akitu festival did not take place."[13] In light of this, it has been argued that Belshazzar could not officiate on the Akitu festival in Babylon because he was not the king.

Several ancient discoveries do, however, attest that Belshazzar was Nabonidus's son and the actual ruler of Babylon in his father's place. These finds seem to shed light on Daniel's reasons for designating Belshazzar as king.

One of the foundation cornerstones recovered from the temple was inscribed with Nabonidus's prayer for his son: "Furthermore, as for Belshazzar, the first son proceeding from my loins, place in his heart fear of thy great divinity and let him not turn to sinning; let him be satisfied with fullness of life."[14] Nabonidus seemed to have been a very religious person, but his radical ideas on religion might have made him unpopular in Babylon. This may have resulted in his stay away for ten years at Tema in northeast Saudi Arabia. Nevertheless, he offered many intercessory prayers on behalf of the people as well as his son Belshazzar. A dream report attests Belshazzar as a crown prince:

> In the month of Tebitu, the 15th day, of the 7th year of (the rule of) Nabonidus, king of Babylon, Shumukin reported as follows: "In a dream I saw the Great Star, Venus (i.e. Diblat), Sirius, the moon and the sun and I shall (now) study this (constellation) with regards to a favorable interpretation for my lord Nabonidus, king of Babylon, as well as to a favorable interpretation for my lord Belshazzar, the crown prince!" The 17th of the month Tebitu of the 7th year of (the reign of) Nabonidus, king of Babylon, Shumukin reported as follows: "I have observed the Great Star and I shall study (this) with regard to a favorable interpretation for my lord Nabonidus, king of Babylon, as well as to my lord Belshazzar, the crown prince!"[15]

Beaulieu lists thirty-seven archival texts that attest Belshazzar attending to royal duties during his father's sojourn in Tema.[16] Several contract tablets relate to the person of the Babylonian *Bilu-šarra-uṣur* (Belshazzar)

---

13. Grayson, *Assyrian and Babylonian Chronicles*, 107, BM 35382, col. 2, lines 10–11.

14. Dougherty, *Nabonidus and Belshazzar*, 93, 94. See also Horne, *Babylonia and Assyria*, 1:438.

15. *ANET*, 309–10, n. 5. See also Clay, *Miscellaneous Inscriptions*, 1:55, no. 39.

16. Beaulieu, *Reign of Nabonidus*, 244.

as the son of the king. At least one reference to Belshazzar in 544 BC, the twelfth year of Nabonidus, reads, "O Bel, defend the king."[17]

The *Verse Account of Nabonidus* was probably composed by the priests of Marduk in the Esagila to justify the Persian occupation of Babylon. Nevertheless, the *Verse Account of Nabonidus* highlights the fact that while Nabonidus was in Tema he entrusted the kingship of Babylon to his crown prince, Belshazzar.

Nabonidus became the king of Babylon in 556 BC, which was his accession year. The *Verse Account of Nabonidus* shows that Nabonidus ruled Babylon in absentia for most of the time, but he had entrusted the kingship to his son Belshazzar. It asserts:

> After he had obtained what he desired, a work of utter deceit, had built (this) abomination, a work of unholiness—when the third year was about to begin—he entrusted the "Camp" to his eldest (son), the first born, the troops everywhere in the country he ordered under his (command). He let (everything) go, entrusted the kingship to him and, himself, he started out for a long journey, the (military) forces of Akkad marching with him; he turned towards Tema (deep) in the west.[18]

The Nabonidus Chronicle informs us that Nabonidus was already in Tema, Arabia, in his seventh year as king while Belshazzar, his son, remained in charge at Babylon. It reads: "The seventh year: the king (was) in Tema (while) the prince, his officers, (and) his army (were) in Akkad. [The king] did not come to Babylon."[19] Nabonidus was away from Babylon for ten years. His stay in Tema and adjacent cities is attested in the Harran Inscriptions of Nabonidus: "Ten years I went about amongst them, (and) to my city Babylon I went not in."[20]

The year of Nabonidus's departure for Tema is also the first year in which Belshazzar reigned as king (Dan 7:1). Establishing this fact has not been an easy task. The Sippar Cylinder indicates that Nabonidus was ordered by the gods Marduk and Sin to build the temple in Harran in the third year, which is the same year Cyrus defeated the Medes.[21] This year can be equated to Nabonidus's sixth regnal year, 550/549 BC. Analyzing the evidence from the Nabonidus Chronicle, the *Verse Account of Nabonidus*, and the Sippar Cylinder, it can be concluded that Nabonidus moved to Tema

---

17. Horne, *Babylonia and Assyria*, 1:457–59.
18. *ANET*, 313, ii.
19. Grayson, *Assyrian and Babylonian Chronicles*, 106, lines 5–6.
20. Gadd, "Harran Inscriptions of Nabonidus," 59.
21. Oppenheim, *Interpretation of Dreams*, 250.

and commissioned Belshazzar with kingship in his sixth regnal year, which is 550/549 BC. Therefore, the first year of Belshazzar's kingship (Dan 7:1) was 549 BC, while his third year (Dan 8:1) was 547 BC. Daniel had dreams and visions in the "first year of Belshazzar king of Babylon" (Dan 7:1) as well as "in the third year of the reign of King Belshazzar" (Dan 8:1). Belshazzar is introduced as "the king" in Dan 5:1. The same chapter identifies him at his death as "Belshazzar the king of the Chaldeans" (Dan 5:30).

Several suggestions have been made regarding the reasons for Nabonidus to stay in Tema for ten years. These range from economic to military purposes. It is clear that his son, the crown prince, administered the kingdom during his absence. Nabonidus must have returned to Babylon in 540 BC, shortly before its fall. The offer made by Belshazzar to Daniel to be the third ruler in the kingdom (Dan 5:16) implied that Nabonidus was the first and Belshazzar the second.

BELSHAZZAR IN BUSINESS

Some Recovered Contract Tablets Mentioning Belshazzar

1. Sale of a Tract of Land to Belshazzar's Servant

(As to) the reeds which Marduk-êriba, the son of Rîmût, son of Miṣrâ, corresponding to his share, which (he has jointly) with Bau-êṭrat, his sister, which adjoin (the house of) Nabû-aḫê-iddin, the son of Shulâ, son of Egibi, and (also) adjoin the house of the son of the king, at the proportion of reeds for two-thirds of a mina and six shekels of silver to Bêl-riṣûa at the full price he sold (them), of his own free will [the document of one-third of a mina] and seven shekels of silver [together with] the former document of one-third of a mina and five shekels of silver, Marduk-êriba as the price of the house from Bêl-riṣûa, the servant of Belshazzar, the son of the king, received. The best of the reeds shall be brought. The record of the receipt they shall seal and whatever money is in excess [or lacking], according to the stipulated price, they shall compensate one another. Dated Babylon, 26th day of Adar, the first year of Nabonidus King of Babylon (possibly 555 BC).

2. Loan of Money from Belshazzar's Secretary

(As to) the house of Nabû-aḫê-iddin, the son of Sulâ, son of Egibi, which adjoins the house of Bêi-iddin, the son of Rîmût, the son of the *dikû* official, for three years to Nabû-mukîn-aḫi, the scribe of Belshazzar, the son of the king, for one and one-half minas of silver he gave (it) with the provision that there should be no rent for the house and no interest on the money. The woodwork of the house he shall renew and (any) crack (of the wall) of the house he shall close up. After three years the money, amounting to one and one-half minas Nabû-aḫê-iddin to Nabû-mukîn-aḫi shall give and Nabû-mukîn-aḫi shall leave the house at the disposal of Nabû-aḫê-iddin. Dated Babylon, 21st day of Nisan, the 5th year of Nabonidus, King of Babylon (possibly 550 BC).

3. Transaction of Business by Belshazzar's Officials

(As to) two-thirds of a mina (and) five shekels of silver, the tithe of Bêl, Nabû, Nergal, and Bêlit of Erech, the claim of Nabû-ṣâbit-qâti, the steward of Belshazzar, the son of the king, which is (charged) against Nabû-mukîn-aḫi . . . the scribe (and) servant of Belshazzar, son of the king, which for the price of Nabû-karâbi-šimê, his servant, was given, the money, amounting to two-thirds of a mina (and) five shekels, Nabû-ṣâbit-qâti, the steward of Belshazzar, the son of the king, from Nabû-aḫê-iddin, the son of Shulâ, son of Egibi, (as a charge) against Nabû-mukîn-aḫi has received. In the presence of Dikîtum, the wife of Nabû-mukin-aḫi. Dated Babylon, 9th day of Shebat, the seventh year of Nabonidus, the King of Babylon (possibly 549 BC).

4. Belshazzar Grants a Loan of Money

Twenty minas of silver, the price of wool, the property of Belshazzar, the son of the king, which (are) from Nabû-ṣâbit-qâti, the steward of Belshazzar, the son of the king, and the scribes of the son of the king, (are charged) against Iddin-Marduk, the son of Iqîsha, son of Nûr-Sin. In the month Adar of the eleventh(?) year the money, amounting to twenty minas, he shall pay. The house . . . his slave, and whatsoever is his of city and plain, as much as there is, (is) the pledge of Belshazzar, the son of the king, until Belshazzar shall be paid his money. On whatsoever money . . . is lacking(?) he shall pay the interest.

Dated Babylon, the 29th day of the month . . . , the 11th year of Nabonidus, King of Babylon" (possibly 545 BC).

> ### 5. Monetary Transaction by Belshazzar's Steward
>
> (As to) one mina and sixteen shekels of silver, principal and interest, the claim of Nabû-ṣâbit-qâti, the steward of Belshazzar, the son of the king, which (are charged) against Bêl-iddina, the son of Bêl-shum-ish-kun, son of Sin-tabni, and (for which) the seed field which (is) between the city gates has been taken as a pledge, the money, amounting to one mina and sixteen shekels, Nabû-ṣâbit-qâti from Itti-Marduk-balâṭu, the son of Nabû-aḫê-iddin, son of Egibi, has received (as a charge) against Bêl-iddina.
> Dated at Babylon the 27th day of the second Adar (intercalary month Ve-Adar), the 12th year of Nabonidus, King of Babylon (possibly 544 BC).
>
> ### 6. Record of Food Delivered to Belshazzar
>
> Provisions which (were given) to... and Shamash-iqîsha, who the food of(?)... to the son of the king delivered(?), the twenty-sixth day (of the month?), the fourteenth year of Nabonidus, the king of Babylon. Serve *gur* of dates (were given) from the storehouse of the king as food which (is the allowance for) the month Nisan until the month Tishri of the fourteenth year. [Tablet is so broken that it is difficult to decipher the rest of the message.] Dated Babylon (possibly 542 BC).
> Dougherty, *Nabonidus and Belshazzar*, 81–86. See also Pinches, *Old Testament*, 430–51.

5:1. Great feast. Daniel 5 records a great feast King Belshazzar made for a thousand of his officials (cf. Esth 1:1–5). Although the purpose of Belshazzar's feast is not disclosed, archaeology reveals that such royal functions were common in the ancient Near East. Mesopotamian court life was known for its "refined and sophisticated pleasures."[22] Several archaeological finds depict kings having banquets with their subjects. An inscription of Ur-nanshe, king of Lagash (ca. 2500 BC), related that he made a feast to celebrate the construction of the temple of Ningirsu.[23]

The British Museum contains a wooden object ornamented with lapis lazuli. This artifact depicts people bringing in war booty. Donkeys can be seen carrying sacks of grain. There are sheep, oxen, and a man carrying

---

22. Kuhrt, *ANE*, 1:35.
23. See Cooper, *Pre-Sargonic Prescriptions*, 22–33; and Kuhrt, *ANE*, 1:34.

fish. The final register on this object shows a banquet scene with the king being conspicuous. He holds a cup in his hand while facing his attendants. A musician with a bull-headed lyre entertains the people in the banquet.

An Assyrian bas-relief (now in the British Museum, BM 124920) portrays a banquet scene where King Ashurbanipal II (668–627 BC) was with his queen Ashur-shurrat. The queen was sitting on a high-backed chair and holding a vessel to her lips. At the opening of his new palace festival, Ashurnasirpal II claimed to have fed 69,574 people for ten days.[24] Ctesias and Dinon reported that the Persian king "used to dine in company with 15,000 men, and 400 talents were expended on the dinner."[25]

These banquets show that Belshazzar's feast was not a far-fetched idea crafted by the author of Daniel. In fact, both Xenophon and Herodotus concur with Dan 5 that Babylon was captured at night when the Babylonians were celebrating a festival[26] (Dan 5:30–31; cf. Jer 50–51). Daniel's account of Belshazzar's feast states that the revelers were drinking wine during the feast, and that they proceeded to worship all the different kinds of gods that were assembled in Babylon at that time (Dan 5:4).

Akitu festival. The biblical text is not explicit on the purpose of Belshazzar's feast in Dan 5. There is an inclination to suggest that this banquet, attended by a thousand nobles, was an Akitu festival. However, evidence to support this suggestion has been wanting. Nabonidus Chronicle, however, shows that the New Year festival was already celebrated in the spring of 539 BC, the seventeenth year of Nabonidus.[27] Both the Sumerian Á-KI-TI and the Akkadian *akītū(m)* (pl. *akiā ti*) may refer either to the festival of *akītū* or to the temple where the celebration was being held.

---

24. Dalley, "Banquets and Feasts" (*DANE*, 47); and "Great Feast" (*SDABC*, 4:801).

25. Ctesias and Dinon, quoted in Collins, *Daniel*, 244.

26. Xenophon, *Cryopaedia*, 7.5.15, 26–33; and Herodotus, *Herodotus*, 1.191. See Stronach, *Pasargadae*, 291.

27. Grayson, *Assyrian and Babylonian Chronicles*, 109, *Nabonidus Chronicle*, col. iii, line 8; and Stronach, *Pasargadae*, 290.

NABONIDUS CHRONICLE
The text on this clay tablet in cuneiform writing reports of Nabonidus's reign in the Neo-Babylonian Empire and his stay away in Tema, Arabia, which caused the disruption of the Akitu Festival in Babylon. The text relates also the surrender of the army to Cyrus. (Courtesy of HAM)

Each year, the first twelve days of the first month (Nisan) were devoted to the celebration of the *akītū* festival. In Babylon the festival was celebrated for the cult of Marduk, while in other Mesopotamian cities it was celebrated for different patron deities.

Ancient texts show that *akītū* had its ancient origins in the Sumerian religion (ca. 2500–1800 BC). The earliest references to *akītū* appear in the Ur III (ca. 2100–2000 BC) economic texts. Here the festival for the god Nanna seems to have been undertaken twice a year, when planting and harvesting barley. Jacob Klein[28] points out that the annual dual performance of the *akītū* has its parallel in the Hebrew Bible (Exod 12:2; 23:16). The first month and the seventh month (Nisan and Tishri) were important events in the agricultural year.

During the first millennium BC, the *akītū* in Babylon gradually merged with the Akkadian *zagmukku/zammukku* (borrowed from the Sumerian term for New Year, "ZAG-MU-K," literally, "the end limit of the year").[29] It came to be celebrated once a year in Nisan.

The climax of the festival was the great procession. The king played the key role of "seizing the hand of Bēl," that is, Marduk, and accompanying the statue to the *akītū* temple. The ceremony included performing several rites for the agricultural year. There was a reading before the god of some

---

28. Klein, "Akitu" (*ABD*, 1:138).
29. Klein, "Akitu" (*ABD*, 1:138).

portions of the Enuma Elish, the reciting of prayers and incantations to Marduk. Offerings were presented to the statue, and hymns were sung. Another significant part of the festival was a dramatization of Marduk dying. He was depicted as visiting the underworld, and then resurrecting, just as Dumuzi/Tammuz was thought to have done. See Ezek 8:14.

On the fifth day of the festival, the king came before the statue of Marduk. The *šešgallu*, "high priest," removed the royal insignia from the king and struck him on his cheeks and pulled his ears so that he should shed tears. Then, in humility, the king would bow down to the ground and profess that he had not neglected the worship of the god nor done any damage to the city or the people. If the king cried, the high priest would bless the king and assure him that Marduk would make him prosperous and would destroy his enemies. The king offended the god if he would not cry. In that case, the high priest would assure him of the wrath of the god.

As shown above, extant evidence seems to indicate that the gods which had been assembled for an *akitu* festival at the beginning of 539 BC could have been the very ones Belshazzar and his guests worshiped in Dan 5. However, the banquet of Belshazzar could have been one of those occasions when the king just wanted to recognize the officials at his royal service, or to celebrate his anniversary and achievements. Worshiping gods at such events was also common (Dan 5:4).

5:1–4. Wine. See **1:5–16. Wine.** Wine was used for the social function that led to the fall of Babylon in 539 BC (Dan 5:1, 2, 4, 23). Such occasions where the king offered wine to his guests are attested in the ancient Near East literature. In fact, Ashurnasirpal II served about ten thousand wineskins to 69,574 guests in his palace.[30] Nabonidus, Belshazzar's father, said that wine, the excellent "beer" of the mountain (regions) of which his country had none,[31] became abundant during his reign. At the *akitu* festival, possibly held in the year of the fall of Babylon, the Nabonidus Chronicle reported that there was an abundance of wine and many gods in Babylon.[32] Belshazzar drank wine with his officials at a state banquet (Dan 5). For some unknown reason he decided to drink the wine from the gold and silver goblets that Nebuchadnezzar had looted from the Jerusalem temple. Their revelry and drunkenness invoked the praise and worship of several of the assembled gods. On the other hand, it provoked God's divine judgment, which led to the downfall of the Neo-Babylonian Empire that very night (Dan 5:30).

30. Bienkowski, "Wine" (*DANE*, 319).
31. Powell, "Wine and the Vine," 101.
32. Dougherty, *Nabonidus and Belshazzar*, 169.

GOLD RYTON
A drinking horn used in the Achaemenid Period, Iran (sixth–fifth century BC).
(Courtesy of HAM)

5:2, 3, 23. Gold and silver vessels. See **1:2. Carried temple vessels away.** Ancient texts from Mari, the Cyrus Cylinder, as well as the biblical text (1 Sam 5:1-2; Ezra 1:6-11; Isa 46:1, 2; Dan 1:1-2; 5:1-4) reveal that when a nation was defeated, gods or temple vessels would be taken hostage by the conqueror. These scared vessels would then be deposited into the victor's temple. The temple vessels taken from Jerusalem appeared, being used at Belshazzar's banquet in Babylon in October 539 BC.

5:2, 3, 23. King's wives and concubines. In Dan 5:2, 3, 23, reference is made to the fact that Belshazzar's wives and concubines attended the final banquet of Babylon. By delineating two categories, the text in Daniel suggests that there was a distinction between the royal women, "his wives and his concubines" (Dan 5:2).

There are several extant texts that help us understand the role and purpose of these women in the royal court.[33] The concubine was at the bottom of the social strata within the harem. There was another class of women in

---

33. For example, the collection of laws from Mesopotamia and Asia Minor discusses women in their different marital statuses; see *ANET*, 159-98; *COS*, 2:106-19, 332-69, 408-14. See also Roth, *Babylonian Marriage Agreements*, 3-134; and Marsman, *Women in Ugarit and Israel*, 49-192, 701-10.

Babylon who were considered even lower in status than the concubines. This class was (Akkadian) "*ṣerretu* 'the rival,' *tappatu* 'girlfriend' and the *qinīti* 'girl who is the object of a wife's jealousy.'"³⁴

Concubinage is the "practice of a man cohabiting with a woman who is regarded only as his sexual partner, or as a secondary wife in his household, of lower station than his primary wife."³⁵ There was no limit on the number of wives and concubines a man could take, even though monogamy was the standard practice in the first millennium BC in Mesopotamia. Concubines had no authority in the household. They could easily be dismissed away by their husbands. Their children could be excluded from the family heritage. Usually, concubinage was the result of the bareness of the first wife who was looking for children from her maidservants. The concubine's social protocol did not carry moral stigma.

The number of Belshazzar's wives and concubines in the banquet hall is lost to antiquity. When Daniel said "your wives and your concubines" (Dan 5:23), he was implying that Belshazzar was the "lord and owner" of all of them. In the ancient Near East, the husband was regarded as *baal*, "the owner" or "master" of his wife or concubine. In ancient Egypt the husband was also regarded as the legal owner of his wife. The Hebrew Bible shows some kings in the practice of hoarding wives and concubines (2 Sam 5:13; 1 Kgs 11:1–3), but advises against it (Deut 17:17; Prov 31:3).

In the ancient Near East the king's wives and concubines were of less importance than the primary wife, the queen. According to recovered literary sources, marriage could be monogamous. Several marriage contracts and laws highlight issues with regard to marital relationships. The British Museum holds tablet (BM 61176 [82-9-18, 1152] and its duplicate BM 67388 [82-9-18, 7384]) from Sippar. This is dated "Month XII, day 4, year 20 of Nebuchadnezzar, king of Babylon" (584 BC). It relates that Qul-dibbīja-ile'i-Nusku son of Sîn-aḫḫē-iddini married Bazītu daughter of Iddin-Nergal on condition that she will die by the dagger if she was found with another man other than her husband. On the other hand, if Qul-dibbīja-ile'i-Nusku found another wife, he was bound to give Bazītu six minas of silver for a divorce settlement.³⁶

Similar to Qul-dibbīja-ile'i-Nusku and Bazītu's marital conditions are those of Nabû-aḫ-iddini, son of Aplā, and Banât-Esagil, daughter of Dalīli-ššu, who both swore by the gods Nabû and Marduk, and also by Nebuchadnezzar, the king, not to contravene their marital commitment.

---

34. Marsman, *Women in Ugarit and Israel*, 123.
35. *Baker Encyclopedia of the Bible*, s.v. "Concubinage."
36. Roth, *Babylonian Marriage Agreements*, 1–134. See pp. 44–49.

Nabû-aḫ-iddini and Banât-Esagil's agreement is from Opis and is on tablet Strassmaier Liverpool 8 (29-11-77, 4) now in the Liverpool Museum, and is dated "month II, day 13, year 41 of Nebuchadnezzar, king of Babylon" (564 BC).

Ancient marriages were also bigynous. Such a term was used in place of "bigamous" because in the ancient Near East, a man could marry two women but no woman could be married to two men. An example of the bigynous/bigamous marriage agreement in Babylon is tablet VAT 5049 in the Staatliche Museen, Berlin. It is that of Nabû-zēr-kitti-lišir whose first wife, Esagil-banāta, had no son. So, in need of one, he took for marriage the maiden Kullā, daughter of Bēl-iqīša, on "month II, day 14, year 2 of Nabopolassar, king of Babylon" (624 BC).[37]

The other category of marriages was polygynous. From the laws of Hammurabi, a man was to have one wife, but it was also possible for a man to have multiple wives and concubines. A man could have children with the (Akkadian) *amtu*, "handmaid," and could add many of these to his harem.

There was a marked difference in Akkadian between *aššatu*, "wife," and *esirtu*, "concubine." The latter was not legally married to the husband, and her children did not have legal claims to their father's property. The wife had full jurisdiction over the dowry and could pass it on to her children.

Several factors motivated the ancient Near Eastern men to enter into plural marriages. The reasons for Belshazzar's plural marriages are not explicit but may include some of the following: (1) longing for more children; (2) desire for a harem; (3) to fill in the place of a sterile primary wife; (4) to have sons if the primary wife had daughters only; (5) the women might have been captives from war; (6) if there was no dowry or bride-price to be paid; (7) the women might have been taken to settle debts; (8) traditional marriages; (9) the women might have been slaves/servants who took care of the house; (10) the girls might have been purchased from poor families; (11) a license for sexual freedom; (12) for prestige or power; and (13) the need to establish political and diplomatic relations. Daniel 5 and related evidence from the ancient Near East indicate that Belshazzar might have been acculturated to the contemporary practice of hoarding wives.

Belshazzar offering. That Belshazzar may have been a religious practitioner can be shown by the tithe and offering receipts of the silver, gold, and sacrificial animals he presented to the temples. Despite all the religiosity displayed in his records, Belshazzar made a critical blunder. He consistently ignored the warnings sent by the Most High God to the Babylonian Empire

---

37. "Bigynous" was the term Marsman used in *Women in Ugarit and Israel*, 122. Roth, *Babylonian Marriage Agreements*, 41–42.

beginning in the days of Nebuchadnezzar (Dan 5:18–21). On the fateful night of his banquet, Daniel reminded Belshazzar that even though he "knew all this" (Dan 5:22), he did not humble himself.

BELSHAZZAR'S OFFERINGS

> Receipts for Belshazzar's Contribution to the Temples
>
> ### 1. Belshazzar Presents Silver to the Temple in Erech
>
> A receipt of the tithe Belshazzar, son of Nabonidus, offered at the temple in Erech reads: "One mina of silver, the tithe of Belshazzar, the son of the king, Shulâ, the son of Êa-shum-iddin in Êanna received. The twenty-ninth day of Elul, the fifth year of Nabonidus, the king of Babylon" (551 BC).
>
> ### 2. Belshazzar Presents Animals to the Temple in Sippar
>
> At the temple in Sippar, Belshazzar presented some animals: "One perfect ox (and) five sheep of the son of the king Nabû-iddin to Êbabbarra gave. The ox (was) young and (was) in the storehouse. The twelfth day of the month Shebaṭ, the seventh year of Nabonidus, the king of Babylon" (549 BC).
>
> ### 3. Oxen and Sheep Presented as an Offering by Belshazzar
>
> Another record of Belshazzar's offering from the temple of Shamash in Sippar reads: "Two perfect oxen four years old, thirty-three sheep, the offering of the son of the king, on the eleventh day of the month Iyyar in the great gate of Êbabbarra were apportioned. The sheep to the stable shall go. From Bêl-shar-bulliṭ, (the man in charge) of [the food] of the king, they were brought to the palace. The oxen in Êbabbarra shall be at the disposal of Shamash-êriba. Dated: The twenty-second day of the month Iyyar, the ninth year of Nabonidus, the king of Babylon" (547 BC).

> ### 4. Belshazzar Presents a Tongue of Gold to Shamash
>
> A valuable monetary contribution from Belshazzar has been recorded: "One tongue of gold, one mina (being) its weight, on the eleventh day of Iyyar, the son of the king gave to Shamash" (547 BC).
>
> ### 5. Payment for the Transportation of Belshazzar's Offerings to Sippar
>
> "One shekel (and) a quarter of silver for the hire of the ship of the three oxen and twenty-four sheep, the offering of the son of the king, which in the month Nisan to Shamash and the gods of Sippar went, in the presence of Bēl-shar-bulliṭ, (the man in charge) of the food of the king, to Shamash-iddin and Dannu-Adad, were given. One [*gur*] (and) twenty-four [*qa*] of dates for their food were given. The ninth day of the month Nisan, the tenth year of Nabonidus, king of Babylon" (546 BC).
>
> ### 6. Record Referring to the Tithe of Belshazzar
>
> "(Concerning) seventy rams and ewes, which Nabû-nâṣir, the son of Lâqîpi, to the messengers of Zêrîa, the administrator of Êana, did not show and did not brand, twenty sheep, the balance of the tithe of the son of the king for the twelfth year of Nabonidus, the king of Babylon, which are at the disposal of Enurtîa, the shepherd of the son of the king, the documents are established, (and) a total of ninety rams and ewes, the property of the Bêltu of Erech and Nanâ, (are charged) against Nabû-nâṣir, the son of Lâqîpi. In the month Nisan of the fourteenth year of Nabonidus, the king of Babylon, the sheep, numbering 90, with . . . (to) the fold he shall bring and at the gate of the canal Nashkapiru he shall brand (them)" (542 BC).
> Dougherty, *Nabonidus and Belshazzar*, 87–92.

5:4. Gods at the final party. On the night of October 12/13, 539 BC, when the Neo-Babylonian Empire fell to Medo-Persia, Belshazzar is reported to have had a banquet that was attended by many officials. He commanded his servants to bring the Jerusalem temple's gold and silver vessels to the banquet hall so that he and his party could use them for drinking wine (Dan 1:2; 5:2, 3). While they were drinking, they praised the gods of gold,

FALL OF BABYLON

silver, bronze, iron, wood, and stone which did not see, hear, or know (Dan 5:4, 23) about the impending fate of the Babylonians. See Ps 115:4–8.

Not much is known about Belshazzar's gods. However, there are several archaeological finds that can possibly inform us on which gods were involved, as implied by the author of Daniel. For example, a jar with beautifully carved figurines in stone, gold, and lapis lazuli beads[38] was discovered at Mari. This find serves to affirm the idea of multiplicity of gods as shown in the book of Daniel. The Iraq Museum contains a clay relief (#9574), a duplicate of which was found at Eshnunna, now housed in the Louvre Museum (#AO12442). The relief shows the goddess Ninḫursag, who was later assimilated into Ishtar. This clay goddess has five other beings depicted with her on the relief. Keš in southern Babylonia was Ninḫursag's cultic center. There she was known as the mother of wild things, of the increase of animals and of human beings. The latter she is said to have created out of clay mixed with the flesh and blood of a slain god. Nabonidus reports that for seven years he was praying to the "gods of silver and gold, [bronze, iron,] wood, stone (and) clay, because [I was of the opini]on that th[ey] were gods [ ]."[39]

KING MARDUK STELE
King Marduk in the center is chartering land to an official in Uruk, Southern Mesopotamia, ca. 850 BC. On the left are the emblems of the four principal Babylonian deities. (Credit: Zev Radovan)

The Nabonidus Chronicle reports the presentation of offerings to the gods of Babylon and Borsippa (column ii, lines 7–8, 12, 20–21, 24–25) and the coming of several gods to Babylon for the Akitu Festival (column iii,

---

38. Kuhrt, *ANE*, 1:41. Some of these finds at Mari might have come from Southern Mesopotamia. Among these discoveries was an inscription by Mesanepada, king of Ur, on one of the lapis lazuli beads. Kuhrt, *ANE*, 1:41.

39. Lines 7 and 8 of The Prayer of Nabonidus (4QPrNab); see Appendix B, "4Q242 (QPrNab) Text."

lines 5–11).⁴⁰ The date for this was most likely 539 BC. It is probable that these were the same gods being praised on the fateful night when Cyrus entered Babylon. The same Nabonidus Chronicle describes the capture of Babylon (column iii, lines 15–20). It says also that "from the month of Kislev to the month of Adar, the gods of Akkad which Nabonidus had brought down to Babylon returned to their places" (column iii, line 21).⁴¹ This literary evidence seems to verify what the author of Daniel implied when he mentioned the worship of various gods that were made from different materials.

Assyria and Babylonia interchanged and assimilated their cultic, cultural, polytheistic, linguistic, and socioeconomic heritage. Gods from either territory were revered (2 Kgs 17:25-33). The gods in the ancient Near East were thought to be territorial and could be involved in cultural, religious, military, fertility, and natural phenomena. Gods were also hierarchical, and each could be linked to a city. The chief god in Mesopotamia was Enlil, the patron of Nippur. Other chief Babylonian gods were Marduk at Babylon, Nabû at Borsippa, Ištar at Uruk, Sin at Ur, Šamash at Sippar, and Nergal at Cuthah. Different titles were ascribed to these gods. Each god was understood to have different epithets whereby the god would display its power.

From the third millennium BC, Babylon was viewed as a holy city that was protected by Marduk. This patron god of Babylon (cf. Dan 1:2) was seized by Assyrian soldiers in 689 BC. The seizure of deities by foreigners was interpreted to mean that the people were abandoned by their god for specific reasons. The divine images were sometimes returned to their homeland after some time.

---

40. Grayson, *Assyrian and Babylonian Chronicles*, 104–11.
41. Grayson, *Assyrian and Babylonian Chronicles*, 110.

BABYLONIAN BOUNDARY STONE
A seated person, perhaps a priest, is worshiping the four main Babylonian deities: Ishtar, the goddess of love and fertility, symbolized by the star; the moon god Sin; the sun god Shamash; and the goddess Ishara, symbolized by the scorpion. (Credit: Zev Radovan)

The defeat and deportation of a nation was taken as another form of divine retribution. The god could let the people be exiled or murdered. This motif is conspicuous in the book of Daniel, for it is the Lord God who delivered the people of Judah into the hands of Nebuchadnezzar (Dan 1:2). Each city had a patron god, but all the gods were "together ordered in pantheons based upon function, genealogy, or an imagined heavenly household."[42] Nabu was "the god of writing, the scribal god."[43] He was centered at Ezida temple in Borsippa near Babylon. Nabu was considered to be the son of Marduk, and became very popular in Babylonia and Assyria in the first millennium BC. An inscription of Nabu states: "Whoever you are, after me, trust in the god Nabu."[44]

Parallel to Nabu's sanctuary in the Ezida temple complex is a smaller sanctuary ascribed to Tašmetum, Nabu's wife. Sin (Semitic name) was the moon god whose Sumerian name was Nannar. Some divine epithets for Sin (*mār rubê*, "Son of the Prince," *Namra-ṣēt*, "Bright-Light," and *Inbu*, "Fruit")[45] can be identified from Nabonidus's inscription. This inscription

---

42. Van de Mieroop, *History of the Ancient Near East*, 49.
43. Oates and Oates, *Nimrud*, 111.
44. Oates and Oates, *Nimrud*, 114, 122.
45. Reiner, *Your Thwarts in Pieces*, 7.

also relates the appointment of the god's daughter as the high priestess at the request of Sin. The inscription has four columns and 86 lines.

The introductory part of it reads:

> When Nannar requested a high priestess
> the Son of the Prince showed his sign to the inhabited world;
> the Bright-Light manifested his reliable decision.
> To Nabonidus, king of Babylon, provider for Esagil and Ezida,
> the reverent shepherd, who shows concern for sanctuaries of the great gods
> Nannar, the lord of the crown, who bears the signal for all peoples,
> revealed his sign concerning his request for a high priestess.[46]

On the whole, the ancient texts and the author of Daniel show that the assembling and plurality of gods in Babylon was a common practice.

In light of this discussion, the Nabonidus Chronicle reports on the several gods that remained in Babylon because they had been brought for the *akitu* festival in the seventeenth year of Nabonidus. This was the same year in which Babylon fell to the Medes and Persians. The date was October 12/13, 539 BC. It is possible that the gods which the Babylonians had assembled in Babylon for the *akitu* festival could be the very ones that were being praised in Dan 5.

5:5. Lampstand and the plaster on the wall. Excavations at Babylon have shown what could easily be identified as the throne room. It was a hall measuring about 170 feet (52 meters) by 55 feet (17 meters). This throne room had a central main entrance and two side doors. It was windowless. Across from the main entrance was a recessed niche in the wall where the throne could have been easily pitched on a raised platform. The throne would be well seen by all in the room. The walls of the throne room were neatly painted in white gypsum. There were elaborate and impressive colorful decorations on the walls. The reconstructed facade of Nebuchadnezzar's throne room is now in the Vorderasiatisches Museum in Berlin. It is ornamented with multicolored glazed bricks.

The setting in the throne room resembled that of a temple. The image of the god would be set where the throne was. The lampstand and the incense altar would be close by. During this time Babylonians used oil lamps which could be mounted on a stand. The lampstand may have been placed on the platform to project ample light in the room. It is reasonable

---

46. Reiner, *Your Thwarts in Pieces*, 2.

to assume that the divine hand incised the writing on the plaster on the wall conspicuous to the king and the audience.

5:5–8, 15–17. Writing on the wall. See 5:25–28. A mysterious hand inscribed something on the wall of the banqueting hall. This terrifying incident caused Belshazzar to summon the conjurers, Chaldeans, and fortune tellers (Dan 5:7). According to Koldewey's excavations, the throne room where Belshazzar had his banquet was about 170 feet (52 meters) long and 55 feet (17 meters) wide. In Dan 5:5, the mysterious hand wrote on the plaster of the wall opposite the lamp-stand (cf. Num 8:2, 3). Daniel 5:5 presents a literary motif where the revelation of the divine will is put in writing (cf. Exod 31:18).

A dream report in the annals of Assurbanipal (668–627 BC) records that a young man saw in a dream an inscription which was written on the pedestal of the image of the moon god, Sin, but no deity appeared on the scene.[47] The inscription describes in detail the fall of Babylon during the time of Assurbanipal. Archaeological discoveries have produced several texts which show Mesopotamian gods revealing their will to humanity through various media. The supernatural writing on the wall seems to have been for the purpose of warning Belshazzar with regard to his fate (Dan 5:22–24).

Although the king and his attendees could not read "the writing" (Dan 5:7), one cannot conclude that every person in the banqueting hall was illiterate. The literacy level of an individual or a nation is not measured by the type or complexity of one script alone. In fact, archaeology has shown that there are still several archaic writings that remain, to this date, undeciphered. These writings include proto-Elamite from Iran,[48] the Harappan or Indus Valley script from Pakistan and India, the proto-Sinaitic script found in the Sinai (only partially), the pseudo-hieroglyphs from Byblos (modern Jubayl), and Minoan Linear A from Crete.[49]

Still other existing scripts can be "read" because the alphabet is familiar, but no one is yet able to understand the language. These include Etruscan, Elamite, Hurrian, Urartian, Iberian inscriptions from Spain,

---

47. Oppenheim, *Interpretation of Dreams*, 201–2.

48. Walker, *Cuneiform*, 41; and Damerow and Englund, *Proto-Elamite Texts from Tepe Yahya* (1989).

49. Nemet-Nejat, *Daily Life in Ancient Mesopotamia*, 51; and Rendsburg, "'Someone Will Succeed in Deciphering Minoan,'" 42, who concludes that the Minoan inscriptions "continue to allure."

various Greek scripts from Anatolia, and Meroitic in Nubia, which used the Egyptian script.⁵⁰

According to archaeological finds, writing was not limited to clay tablets. Texts could be incised on stone, wood, glass, ivory, metal, papyrus, bricks, and walls. An example of writing on plaster walls was discovered at Deir 'Alla in the Jordan Valley. This text mentioned Balaam, son of Beor (Num 22–24). The value of this text ranges widely including archaeological, biblical, historical, linguistic, paleographical, and philological parameters. Archaeology also exhibits many epigraphic inscriptions on the walls of the late Assyrian palaces and monuments. Such inscriptions would only be accessible to the public through a well-trained scribe who could read and give the interpretation.

Writing was invented in Mesopotamia about the end of the fourth millennium BC. At that time geographical and environmental factors were favorable for humans to settle and engage themselves in economic activities. Around 3200 BC the Sumerians invented the cuneiform script from which the Akkadian cuneiform was developed. Writing was the solution to the recording and keeping of information for either administrative or economic purposes. It was a way of preserving and passing on information to future generations. Nebuchadnezzar's concluding remarks on the Wadi Brisa Inscription to Marduk seem to encourage those after him to remember him and his establishments: "I wrote an inscription mentioning my name, . . . I erected for posterity. May future [kings] re[spect the *monuments*], . . . may my name be remembered in future (days) in a good sense, may my offspring rule forever over the black-headed."⁵¹

Marc-Alain Ouaknin argues that writing "only started when an organized system of signs or symbols was created that could be used to clearly record and fix all that the writer was thinking, feeling, and capable of expressing."⁵²

The difficulty in reading the writing on the wall in Dan 5 can be better understood in light of some literary material from the ancient Near East. At Uruk IV level, Jemdet Nasr and Tell Uqair in Mesopotamia, we find the earliest examples of a kind of writing where numerals and pictographs were impressed by a reed or wooden stylus on clay tablets. As the art of writing developed, so did the art of deciphering the written text.

Special knowledge was required in order to understand written secret messages (Dan 5:8, 17). People could access such literacy only through the

---

50. Daniels, "Decipherment of Ancient Near Eastern Scripts" (*CANE*, 1:81–93).
51. *ANET*, 307.
52. Ouaknin, *Mysteries of the Alphabet*, 18.

specially trained professional scribes. Education for this kind of writing was usually obtained in *edubba*, "the tablet house," either in the temple or king's palace. The script was composed of pictograms (signs), which were systematically given phonetic values, and ideograms (symbols for words), which could mean several different things.

5:7, 11, 15. Astrologers. See **1:20. Magicians**; and **2:2, 10, 27. Sorcerers.** Astrologers were part of the elite whom the king relied on in times of emergencies.

5:7, 11. Soothsayers. See **2:27. Gazers.**

5:7, 16, 29. Purple. Belshazzar offered Daniel a purple gown and a golden necklace in exchange for information about the supernatural writing on the palace wall. Expensive dye was used in making purple clothing. The Neo-Assyrian *rab*, "chief," was clothed in a purple garment. Being clothed in "purple" was a royal custom for the Babylonians as well as the Medes and the Persians (cf. Esth 8:15). Such a practice was also common with the Greeks. In the biblical tradition kings (Judg 8:26) and rich people (Prov 31:22; Luke 16:19; Rev 18:16) put on purple attire. Lydia seemed to have been a well-to-do businesswoman who sold purple clothes (Acts 16:14). See also **2:48, 49. Daniel made great.**

5:7, 16, 29. Gold chain. This was a symbol of authority. There were several symbols for the transferring or sharing of royal power, including a signet ring (Gen 41:42; Esth 3:10), a robe (Gen 41:42; Esth 6:11), and a gold chain (Gen 41:42; Dan 5:7, 16, 29). Medes and Persian kings also honored individuals of outstanding contribution (Esth 6:7–11). Belshazzar's proposal was to integrate Daniel into the Babylonian royal hegemony.

5:7, 16, 29. Third ruler. Nabonidus (556–539 BC) was the king of Babylon. He went for an extended expedition to Tema in northeast Saudi Arabia for ten years. While he was away, he left his son Belshazzar in charge of the entire kingdom. Belshazzar, being second-in-command, could only offer to Daniel the third-highest-ranking position.

5:10. Queen mother. It is difficult to identify the queen/queen mother in Dan 5:10. She was not on the list of those who attended Belshazzar's banquet (Dan 5:2, 3, 23). Furthermore, the Aramaic word *malk^{e}tā'* could refer to either "the queen" or "the queen mother." In Neo-Assyria and Neo-Babylonia, it was uncommon for the king to dine with the queen.

Extant literary and biblical texts do attest occasions where some kings and queens dined together on festivals. For example, Ashurbanipal and his Queen Ashur-shurrat are portrayed as celebrating in a banquet after the defeat of the Elamites.[53] King Ahasureus, by special invitation, ate with Queen Esther (Esth 5:4-8; 7:1-2). It was also obvious that wives usually did not dine with their husbands except at banquets or special occasions.[54]

The Hebrew Bible uses several different words to identify the queen. For example, *malkᵉtā*, "queen" (Septuagint *basilissa*), is used to describe only "foreign queen regnants and consorts,"[55] namely: Queen of Sheba (1 Kgs 10:1-13; 2 Chr 9:1-12); Vashti (Esth 1:9-22); Hadassah or Esther (Esth 2:4, 17, 22; 9:12, 29-32); and the queen/queen mother (Dan 5:10). About sixty hypothetical "queens" are referred to in Song 6:8. The prophet Jeremiah condemns the Judeans living in Judah and those in Egypt under the Pharaoh Hophra of the twenty-sixth dynasty (589-570 BC) for the veneration of "the queen of heaven" (Jer 7:18; 44:17, 18, 19, 25).

From the ninth century BC and onwards, the term *gᵉbirāh*, "lady," "queen," or "queen mother," is used sparingly as an official title.[56] In the Hebrew Bible "Tahpenes the Queen" (*gᵉbirāh*) is the wife of Pharaoh, the king of Egypt (1 Kgs 11:19). For the Israelites, the term was possibly used only for Jezebel[57] (2 Kgs 10:13). The Judeans used *gᵉbirāh* for the king's mother, Maacah (1 Kgs 15:13 = 2 Chr 15:16), and also for Nehushta, Jehoiachin's mother (2 Kgs 24:8, 17-18; Jer 13:18; 29:2).[58] The Hebrew and Chaldean word *gᵉbirtāh*, "her lady," "queen," "mistress," or "woman," appears in its varied forms in the Mesha Inscription (line 16)[59] as well as in Isa 47:5, 7;

---

53. See commentary on **5:1. Great feast.**

54. Wilson, *Nimrud Wine Lists*, 6. The idea that wives do not dine with husbands is prevalent in many parts of the world. In certain parts of Africa, especially in rural settings where the traditional ties are strong, men do not sit down and eat together with their wives; for example, in some rural villages in Zimbabwe, village men usually eat in the evening at *padare/enkundleni*, "the courtyard." Women bring food to the courtyard but are not welcome to sit there and eat unless on special invitation. Any other male, even a small boy, may be welcome there.

55. Schearing, "Queen" (*ABD*, 5:583).

56. Brenner, *Israelite Woman*, 18. It must be noted that the meaning of *gᵉbirāh* as "queen" or "queen mother" in the Hebrew Bible has no parallel in the ancient Near Eastern literature.

57. Avigad, "Seal of Jezebel," 274-76. See also Korpel, "Fit for a Queen," 32-37.

58. *DBD*, 150. See also Schearing, "Queen" (*ABD*, 5:583); and Ackerman, "Queen Mother," in Bach, *Women in the Hebrew Bible*, 179-94.

59. Jackson and Dearman, "Text of the Meshaʻ Inscription," in Dearman, *Studies*, 94.

Gen 16:4, 8, 9; 2 Kgs 5:3; Ps 123:2; Prov 30:23; and Sir 41:18.[60] Also, *šegal*, "queen" or "consort," is used for King Artaxerxes's wife in Neh 2:6. In Ps 45:9 *šegal* is sung in a wedding song.

In the ancient Near Eastern literature, including the Hebrew Bible, the king's wife was an important royal figure. Her family, political, social, economic, administrative, and religious roles were limited only to domestic affairs. It was common but not always consistent that the son of the king's principal wife, the queen's son, would be heir to the throne.

The distinction between the queen (king's principal wife) and the queen mother (king's mother) in the texts is often not clear since both were queens. However, with regard to social status, the queen mother did not share her position with any other woman in the kingdom. The queen, on the other hand, had to share her husband the king with his other wives and concubines. The king's mother was of more importance than the king's wife, and would generally be second-in-command to her son, the king. The king's right to rule was often viewed in the context of his heritage of political power and legitimacy based upon his royal biological descent.

In the ancient Near East, kings sometimes married foreign women through international treaties. In such a political marriage, the woman could possibly attain the position of queen, or she could just be one of the king's wives. Texts recovered by archaeologists show that at Mari, the king was *šarru* and his wife *šarratu*, "queen." In Neo-Assyria the queen was addressed as *aššati šarri*, "wife of the king," as well as *ša ekalli*, "she-of-the-palace," or *issi ekalli*, "the woman of the palace."[61] It is possible that *šegal*, "queen," discussed above is a transcription from *ša ekalli*. At Ugarit the queen was called *mlkt*, which is the feminine of *mlk*, "king." Alternatively, the term *mtt*, "lady," was used for Hariya, the wife of King Kirtu, and also for Danatiya, the wife of King Dani'ilu.[62]

The idea that the queen mother came to advise Belshazzar is not a far-fetched idea (Dan 5:10–12). Archaeological sources reveal that it was a common practice for queen mothers to be involved in critical court issues. In Assyria, some queen mothers include Samuramat, the wife of King Shamshi-Adad V (823–810 BC). Samuramat ruled for five years when her

---

60. Wilson, *Old Testament Word Studies*, 336, suggests that *gᵉbirāh* means "female ruler" or "reigning queen." The Hebrew Bible has three meanings for the word *gᵉbirāh*: (1) mother or wife of the ruling king (1 Kgs 11:19; 15:13; 2 Kgs 10:13; Jer 13:18; 29:2; 2 Chr 15:16); (2) mistress in relation to a female slave (Gen 16:4, 8, 9; 2 Kgs 5:3; Isa 24:2; Ps 123:2; Prov 30:23); (3) ruler, regent (referring to Babel in a metaphorical sense in Isa 47:5, 7). Marsman, *Women in Ugarit and Israel*, 360.

61. Marsman, *Women in Ugarit*, 326. Cf. *CAD*, 4, E, 61–62; 17, Š pt. 2, 72–76.

62. Marsman, *Women in Ugarit*, 334, 335. See also Moor, *Rise of Yahwism*, 93–97.

son Adad-nirari III was still a minor.⁶³ King Sennacherib (704–681 BC) was possibly influenced by his wife Naqi'a/Zakutu to choose her younger son Esarhaddon as the crown prince instead of the older son Arda-Mulishshi.⁶⁴ Naqi'a/Zakutu was known as *ummi šarri*, "mother of the king," in the Assyrian court from 681 BC when Esarhaddon became king.⁶⁵ A bronze relief in the Louvre Museum, AO 20185, shows Esarhaddon with his mother, Naqi'a/Zakutu. The Harran Inscriptions of Nabonidus⁶⁶ highlight Adad-guppi as Nabonidus's mother. After Nebuchadnezzar II died in 562/561 BC, three successive family members reigned, each of them for a very short time.

It appears that Adad-Guppi may have been influential in the appointment of Nabonidus as king. Her personal testimony in the Harran Inscriptions of Nabonidus sheds light on who she was, but does not help in identifying her husband or her familial antecedents. Adad-Guppi was the mother of Nabonidus (col. i, line 1). She was a devotee of the gods Sin, Ningal, Nusku, and Sadarnunna (col. i, lines 3, 4). Further, Adad-Guppi must have lived to be over a hundred years old (col. i, lines 29–33). She was born in the twentieth year of the reign of Ashurbanipal (668–627 BC) and must have lived:

> 'til the forty-second year of this king;
> 'til the third year of Aššur-etel-ilāni;
> 'til the twenty-first year of Nabopolassar;
> 'til the forty-third year of Nebuchadnezzar;
> 'til the second year of Amēl-Marduk;
> 'til the fourth year of Neriglassar.⁶⁷

All things considered, Adad-Guppi must have been about ninety-five years old when her son Nabonidus became king in Babylon. She died in the ninth year of the reign of Nabonidus. She is therefore eliminated as a possible candidate for the queen mother of Dan 5.

Several other women could be suggested as possible candidates for the woman who came to Belshazzar's banqueting hall. It could have been

---

63. Weinfeld, "Semiramis," in Cogan and Eph'al, *Ah, Assyria* . . . , 99–103; Grayson, "Assyria" (CAH, 3/1:271–76); Grayson, *Assyrian Rulers*, 2:200–38; and Millard, "Adad-nirari" (*DANE*, 3).

64. See Kuhrt, *ANE*, 2:521–22; 526–28.

65. Marsman, *Women in Ugarit and Ancient Israel*, 34.

66. Gadd, "Harran Inscriptions of Nabonidus," 46–69; *ANET*, 562, 563; Zawadzki, *Fall of Assyria*, 25; and *COS*, 1:477, 478, 482.

67. Zawadzki, *Fall of Assyria*, 25; and Gadd, "Harran Inscriptions of Nabonidus," 69.

Belshazzar's grandmother, according to Josephus.[68] It is most unlikely that it was Belshazzar's wife. Since *malkᵉtā* implies the queen mother, the woman could have been either Nabonidus's wife (Belshazzar's mother) or Nebuchadnezzar's wife. Herodotus indicated that Nitocris was the last great queen of the Neo-Babylonian Empire,[69] but evidence is still lacking for her identity with the queen of Dan 5.

Whoever she may have been, the wisdom and resourcefulness of this "queen mother" was timely and clearly demonstrated. She knew of a man in the kingdom who had the extraordinary qualities required to solve the king's problem (Dan 5:11–12).

5:10. O king, live forever. See **2:4b. O king, live forever.** This is a well-wishing address to the king.

5:11, 14. Wisdom. See **1:4, 17, 20. Wisdom.**

5:11. Nebuchadnezzar your father. The disputed phrases in Dan 5 which identify Belshazzar as Nebuchadnezzar's son read:

- "and the king, Nebuchadnezzar your father" (Dan 5:11);
- "to Nebuchadnezzar your father" (Dan 5:18); and
- "and you his son Belshazzar" (Dan 5:22).

The biblical tradition shows that many Judaean kings referred to the eponymous David as their father, as indicated in table 7. Nebuchadnezzar was the most prestigious and powerful of all the Neo-Babylonian kings. By being referred to as the son of Nebuchadnezzar, the model king, Belshazzar seeks to bolster the legitimacy of his claim upon the Chaldean throne. Jehu, king of Israel, is identified as the son of Omri on the Black Obelisk of Shalmaneser III. Jehu had no relationship with Omri. In fact, he became king by destroying the house of Omri (2 Kgs 9–10).

The author of Daniel was aware of the political customs of the Neo-Babylonian royal family. He was also aware of the Hebrew Bible's traditions (see table 7). Moreover, the Hebrew word *bēn* and its Aramaic cognate *bar* could mean "son," "grandson," "descendent," "cousin," or someone of remoter and metaphorical relationship. Also, *'bûk* (Dan 5:11, 18) could refer to "your father," "your grandfather," or "your ancestor."

---

68. Josephus, *Antiquities of the Jews*, 10.11.2.237.
69. Herodotus, *Histories*, 1.185–88, cited in Shea, "Nabonidus, Belshazzar," 133–49.

Table 7
BIBLICAL EPONYMOUS PRACTICE

Name of the King	Biological Father	Eponymous Father
Abijah (913–911/10 BC)	Rehoboam (1 Kgs 14:31)	David (1 Kgs 15:3)
Asa (911/10–870/69 BC)	Abijah (1 Kgs 15:8)	David (1 Kgs 15:11, 24)
Jehoshaphat (870/69–848 BC)	Asa (1 Kgs 22:41)	David (1 Kgs 22:50; 2 Chron 17:3)
Jotham (740/39–732/31 BC)	Azariah (2 Kgs 15:7)	David (2 Kgs 15:38)
Ahaz (732/31–716/15 BC	Jotham (2 Kgs 15:38)	David (2 Kgs 16:2; 2 Chron 28:1)
Hezekiah (716/15–687/86 BC)	Ahaz (2 Kgs 18:1)	David (2 Kgs 18:3; 2 Chron 29:2)
Josiah (641/40–609 BC)	Amon (2 Kgs 21:25)	David (2 Kgs 22:2; 2 Chron 34:2, 3)

5:13. Captives. See **2:25. Captives.** After residence in Babylon for nearly seventy years, Daniel, a high-ranking official, is still identified on racial grounds as one of the captives from Judah. See also 6:13.

5:17. Your gifts for yourself. Daniel objected to Belshazzar's gifts. Perhaps he knew that the fall of Neo-Babylonia was imminent. In light of this, Epicharmus (ca. 550–460 BC), a Greek dramatist and philosopher, rightly concluded that "the wise man must be wise before, not after."[70] Daniel clearly understood that Belshazzar's offer was not going to last. Belshazzar, however, prevailed upon Daniel to accept his gifts (Dan 5:29).

5:21. Dew of heaven. See **4:15, 23, 25. Dew of heaven.**

5:25–28. Deciphering the inscription. Scholarly debate regarding the inscription on the wall in Dan 5 concerns its reading and decipherment. The interpretation of the inscription is puzzling.[71] The reading, as indicated by the text, is as follows: $m^e n\bar{e}$' $m^e n\bar{e}$' $t^e q\bar{e}l$ $\hat{u}parsin$ (Dan 5:25). This differs from the interpretation of $m^e n\bar{e}$' (Dan 5:26), $t^e q\bar{e}l$ (Dan 5:27), and $p^e res$ (Dan 5:28). The second $m^e n\bar{e}$' in v. 25 has been considered as dittography[72] (inadvertent duplication by a careless scribe).

---

70. Wectar, "Three Wise Men Quote."
71. Zimmermann, "Writing on the Wall," 201–7.
72. Collins, *Daniel*, 250.

The Aramaic *mn'* is *mnh* in Hebrew and *mna* in Greek.⁷³ The Akkadian *manū*, "mina," contained sixty shekels.⁷⁴ In the Elephantine papyri *tql* (line 5) is a spelling variant of *šql* (line 3) and the equivalent of the Babylonian *šiklu* which can be understood as the Hebrew noun "shekel" or verb "weigh."⁷⁵ *Pᵉres* is an Akkadian *parsu*, "a half-mina," and is attested on an eighth-century BC Panammu inscription discovered near Zenjirli in 1888.⁷⁶

David Brewer attempted to read the inscription as numbers, that is, *Mina, Mina, Shekel, Peresh* (60, 60, 1, ½). This added up to 121½, but failed to depict what these numbers would imply in relation to the chronology of Daniel.⁷⁷ The interpretation or meaning of the words on the wall as given in Dan 5:26–28 makes more sense. It is also in keeping with the historical developments of the book.

5:27. Weighed in the balances. Daniel 5:27 states metaphorically that Belshazzar was weighed in the scales and found lacking. From the New Kingdom in Egypt (1550–1090 BC), the papyrus of Hu-nefer depicted the god Anubis leading the deceased toward the balance, where his heart would be weighed against Maat and the results recorded by Thoth.⁷⁸ According to this, the dead are pronounced righteous if their good works outweigh their weaknesses. The dead's weaknesses are cleared by rituals and magic.

WEIGHING TAMESIA'S HEART
In ancient Egypt they believed that a person's thoughts and emotions were finally weighed against Maat, a tiny goddess of truth. Maat judged the dead by weighing the truthfulness of their hearts against her ostrich feather. If the heart was heavier, then it would be destroyed and the individual would not have afterlife. (Courtesy of Toledo Museum of Art)

---

73. Collins, *Daniel*, 251.

74. Gibson, *Textbook*, 2:83.

75. Cowley, *Aramaic Papyri*, 30–31.

76. Gibson, *Textbook*, 2:80–81, 83.

77. Brewer, "Mene mene teqel uparsin," 310–16. Cf. also to Wiig, "Mene, mene, tekel-ufarsin," 26–35.

78. ANEP, 210, 326, fig. 639; and Wilkinson, *Complete Gods and Goddesses*, 216.

It has also been argued that October 12/13, 539 BC, "the date of the fall of Babylon[,] comes immediately after the annual morning rising of the constellation Libra, which in Akkadian was called *zibānītu* 'the scales.'"[79] Therefore, Daniel is thought by some scholars to have used traditional astrological lore to depict the fall of Neo-Babylonia. Daniel's interpretation, however, seems to lack Babylonian influence. Instead, it remains consistent with the message of the book.

5:28 Medes and Persians. See **6:8, 12, 15, 17. Medes and Persians.** The Medes and Persians appear in that order in the book of Daniel. They are portrayed as a single kingdom. They displaced the Neo-Babylonian Empire in 539 BC and became a world power until they were defeated by the Greeks in 331 BC.

5:30. Belshazzar murdered. James Wellard suggested that Dan 5 be read as a fable and argued that Belshazzar was "killed in battle on the western bank of the Tigris fighting against the army of Cyrus the Persian."[80] Contrary to Wellard, the biblical text recounts that Belshazzar was killed in Babylon on the night of the fall of the Neo-Babylonian Empire (Dan 5:30). Since there is no positive evidence to support Wellard's theory, there seems to be no reason to deny the traditional understanding in both the Bible and Xenophon that Belshazzar was present in Babylon when the city fell.

Isaiah (740–686 BC) foretold about Cyrus and the fall of Babylon (539 BC) with astounding precision (Isa 44:27—45:2). The Euphrates River flowed through the city of Babylon and divided the city into two halves. In chapter 5 of the book of Daniel, we find the author's account of the fall of this mighty city. Herodotus[81] and Xenophon[82] also give the account, explaining how the army of Cyrus got into the city. Babylon had high and impenetrable walls surrounded by moats.[83] Cyrus stationed part of his army where the Euphrates River entered into Babylon, and another part where the river flowed out of the city. He instructed both groups to watch for the water level to drop. They were then to enter through the riverbed and take the city. Cyrus withdrew with the rest of the army to an upstream location on the Euphrates River, out of sight from the city of Babylon. Here the army dug trenches to divert the river.

79. Wolters, "Riddle of the Scales," 177.
80. Wellard, *Babylon*, 183.
81. Herodotus, *Herodotus*, 1.190–92.
82. Xenophon, *Cyropaedia*, 7.5.13–36.
83. See the Building Inscription of Nebuchadnezzar in Rogers, *Cuneiform Parallels to the Old Testament*, 368.

Xenophon explains that Cyrus had good intelligence with regard to what went on in Babylon. He had learned that it was time for a certain festival during which all the inhabitants of the city were "accustomed to drink and revel all night long."[84] On the very night of the festival (cf. Dan 5), Cyrus opened his trenches, and the Euphrates was diverted (cf. Isa 44:27, 28; Jer 51:36, 37). His men marched in and took the city of Babylon without military conflict. Part of the Cyrus Cylinder records that Marduk got Cyrus "into his city Babylon without fighting or battle" to "put an end to the power of Nabonidus the king who did not show him reverence."[85] See Rev 16:12. Xenophon points out that Gobryas and Gadatas led the troops to the palace and found the king "already risen with his dagger in his hand."[86] They slew the king along with those who were around him (cf. Dan 5:30; Jer 50:35–38). That very night, October 12/13, 539 BC, Belshazzar was killed when the Medes and Persians invaded and took over Babylon (Dan 5:30). The Nabonidus Chronicle briefly indicates that "on the sixteenth day Ugbaru, governor of the Guti, and the army of Cyrus (II) entered Babylon without a battle."[87]

The sixth verse of Byron's poem, "Vision of Belshazzar" (1815),[88] was composed in light of Dan 5 and summarizes the story as follows:

> Belshazzar's grave is made,
> His kingdom pass'd away,
> He, in the balance weigh'd,
> Is light and worthless clay;
> The shroud his robe of state,
> His canopy the stone;
> The Mede is at the gate!
> The Persian on his throne!

5:31. Darius the Mede. See **6:1. Darius.** At the age of sixty-two Darius the Mede features in the book of Daniel as a recipient of the Neo-Babylonian kingdom on October 12/13, 539 BC.

---

84. Xenophon, *Cyropaedia*, 7.5.15.
85. Arnold and Beyer, *Readings from the Ancient Near East*, 148.
86. Xenophon, *Cyropaedia*, 7.5.29.
87. Grayson, *Assyrian and Babylonian Chronicles*, 109–10, lines 15–16.
88. Hilton, "Babel Reversed," 99; and Ashton, *Byron's Hebrew Melodies*, 179.

Chapter 6

PLOT AGAINST THE INNOCENT

THE MEDO-PERSIAN ADMINISTRATION UNDER Cyrus the Great took over from Neo-Babylonia in 539 BC. Darius the Mede featured as king in Babylon under the auspices of Cyrus the Great. It has been difficult to identify this Darius the Mede besides what the Bible says about him. However, the lack of external evidence on some individuals or events does not necessarily mean that they are not historical. Darius the Mede established an ingenious administration policy over all his provinces but his immutable laws failed to protect vulnerable citizens.

6:1. Darius. The identity of Darius the Mede (Dan 5:31; 6:1–28; 9:1–2; 11:1) is a puzzle to biblical scholarship. Daniel 11:1, which obviously refers to Darius the Mede, is attested at Qumran in 4QDan^c. The name is also familiar as *Da-ri-ia-muš* (Akkadian),[1] *daryhwš* (Aramaic on the Bisitun Inscription),[2] or *Dârayavauš* and its variant *Dâravayahauš* (Old Persian on the Bisitun Inscription).[3]

Darius the Mede has been dismissed by some scholars as a fictional character created by a "conflation of confused traditions."[4] Many scholars have not accepted this dismissal. These have attempted to identify Darius the Mede, who featured at the collapse of the Neo-Babylonian Empire

---

1. Voigtlander, Bisi*tun Inscription*, 11. From the Bisitun Inscription it can be noted that the trilingual text has paragraphs, each of which begins by saying "Darius the King says . . ."

2. Greenfield and Porten, *Bisitun Inscription of Darius the Great*, 64–68.

3. King et al., *Sculptures and Inscription*, 1–210.

4. Sparks, "On the Origin," 46.

(Dan 5:31; 6:1–2). Two suggestions have formed the basis for most of the discussion about Darius the Mede.

John Whitcomb first proposed the idea that Darius the Mede was to be identified with Gubaru/Gobryas, the provincial governor of Babylon.[5] Whitcomb discussed several cuneiform documents that attest to this Gubaru but evidence was not in favor of his proposal. Donald J. Wiseman presented the second proposal. He identified Darius the Mede with Cyrus by translating Dan 6:28 as follows: "Daniel prospered in the reign of Darius, even (namely, or i.e.) the reign of Cyrus the Persian."[6] Of the two major proposals for the identity of Darius the Mede, Whitcomb's has gained more popularity among biblical scholars. Still, there is no consensus on the identity of this Darius.

Several other historical names have been suggested as individuals to whom Daniel might have referred when he wrote of Darius the Mede. These include Cyrus II or Cyrus the Great (559–530 BC); Astyages (585–550 BC); Cyaxares II, son of Astyages; Gubaru/Gobryas and/or Ugubaru (539 BC); Cambyses II (530–522 BC); and Darius I or Darius/Hystaspes the Great (522–486 BC).[7]

Cambyses II and Darius I (who was a Persian and not a Mede) can quickly be disqualified as possible candidates for being Darius the Mede. Each of these came into kingship long after the fall of Babylon, which is the time when the real Darius the Mede is said to have reigned.

Gubaru/Gobryas and/or Ugbaru can safely be dismissed from the list because all the cuneiform evidence which mention him identified him as a governor of Cyrus/Babylon. He is never mentioned as a king.

Wiseman reads the Hebrew *waw* in Dan 6:28 as explicative, so as to identify Darius the Mede as the same person with Cyrus II.[8] This reading, however, is not supported by the text. Wiseman's view also takes Darius as Cyrus's Median name, or throne name.

Neither Astyages nor his son Cyaxares II has satisfactorily met the criteria for matching identity with the person of Darius the Mede.[9] Josephus stated that Darius the Mede was the son of Astyages. Josephus further

---

5. Whitcomb, *Darius the Mede*, 24.

6. Wiseman, "Some Historical Problems in the Book of Daniel," in *Notes on Some Problems*, 12.

7. McDowell, *Daniel in the Critics' Den*, 69–78; Shea, "Nabonidus Chronicle," 1–20; Grabbe, "Another Look," 198–213; Colless, "Cyrus the Persian," 113–26; and Albertz, "Darius in the Place of Cyrus," 371–83.

8. Wiseman, "Some Historical Problems in the Book of Daniel," 12–16.

9. "Additional Note on Chapter 6" (*SDABC*, 4:814–17).

believed that this Darius had another name among the Greeks.[10] William H. Shea concluded his search for the identity of Darius the Mede by affirming that Darius should be identified with Ugbaru, and that his reign lasted only for a week in 539 BC, when he met his untimely death.[11] There is too much significant information in the biblical text on Darius the Mede for anyone to suggest that he did not exist, or that he reigned only for a week. It is logical to postpone drawing conclusions on this personage until such a time as further archaeological or extrabiblical evidence on him is made available.

Darius is the only king in the book of Daniel whose age (Dan 5:31), father's name (Ahasuerus/Xerxes) (Dan 9:1), nationality (Dan 5:31; 9:1; 11:1), and administrative strategy (Dan 6:1–2, 25) are stated. He is referred to as king about thirty times (Dan 6; and Dan 9:1). This may indicate that he was a real, historical person known to the author. Therefore, questions regarding the identity of Darius the Mede are not resolved by suggesting various individuals with whom to identify him. It is reasonable to acknowledge his existence as a historical person known to the author of Daniel. This we do in anticipation that archaeological or extrabiblical evidence highlighting Darius the Mede will surface in the future.

Many impressive archaeological artifacts were accidentally lost through the years in the ancient Near East. For example, F. Fresnel, J. Oppert, and F. Thomas made important researches at Babylon, Birs Nimroud, Khorsabad, and other places. They loaded the treasures of art and inscriptions on rafts and floated them down the Euphrates to ship them to Europe. Unfortunately, due to "sheer carelessness and mismanagement," the rafts overturned and they lost all the collection in the river in the 1852 expedition.[12] These finds have never been recovered. It is possible that many artifacts which attest to some historical individuals in the book of Daniel could also have been lost one way or the other.

That Darius the Mede "was made king" (Dan 9:1; cf. 2 Kgs 24:17) over the realm of the Chaldeans implies that he was invested with kingship by someone superior to himself. Similarly, the verb "received" (Dan 5:31) indicates that Darius accepted the kingship from someone.

The Medes were under the Persians from 550 BC. Darius the Mede may, therefore, have been made a king over the Babylonian province under the auspices of Cyrus II. Such an arrangement was not uncommon in the

---

10. Josephus, *Antiquities of the Jews*, 10.11.4.248.

11. Shea, "Search for Darius the Mede (Concluded)," 97–105. It has also been suggested that Darius the Mede died "within two years of the fall of Babylon." See White, *Story of Prophets and Kings*, 556, 557.

12. Rogers, *History of Babylonia and Assyria*, 1:165.

ancient Near East. In the Behistun Inscription, for instance, Darius I, son of Hystaspes, was made king.[13]

According to the biblical text, Daniel continued his state administrative role through the reign of Darius, and also through that of Cyrus the Persian (Dan 6:28). The text also mentions only the first year of the reign of Darius the Mede (Dan 9:1–2).

Darius was trapped into a political ruse by two of his chief administrators and the satraps. These jealous officials wanted to get rid of Daniel, who was one of the three chief administrators (Dan 6). Taking advantage of the new administration, the officials planned that no one in the king's entire realm should petition anything from any god or person except from Darius for a period of thirty days.

Herodotus tells of another Median king, Deioces (ca. 715–647 BC), who also had imposed intrusive restrictions on his subjects. It is on record that

> Deioces built these walls for himself and around his own palace; the people were to dwell without the wall. And when all was built, it was Deioces first who established the rule that no one should come into the presence of the king, but all should be dealt with by the means of messengers; that the king should be seen by no man; and moreover that it should be in particular a disgrace for any to laugh or to spit in his presence.[14]

The Persian court continued to maintain certain restrictions (Esth 4:11).

Darius the Mede was a legislator who could not change what he decreed (Dan 6:8, 12, 15; cf. Esth 1:19; 8:8). He was also an administrator with a high sense of accountability (Dan 6:2). The fact that the text claims that Darius wrote a letter to all nations "in all the earth" (Dan 6:25) should not confuse anyone. The Aramaic *'r'ā*, like its Hebrew cognate *'ereṣ*, can also mean "world," "land," "country," "territory," or "ground."[15] Hammurabi designated himself *šar kiššati*, "king of the universe," implying his whole domain.[16]

The Nabonidus Chronicle states that, at the fall of Babylon, Gobryas (*Ugbaru*), the governor of Gutium, installed governors in Babylon.[17] It is

13. Kent, *Old Persian*, 11–157.

14. Herodotus, *Herodotus*, 1.99.

15. BDB, 75–76, 1083; and Holladay, *Concise Hebrew and Aramaic Lexicon*, 28, 398.

16. In the prologue to his laws Hammurabi also declared himself "the king who has made the four quarters of the world subservient." *ANET*, 165, col. v, line 10.

17. *ANET*, 306.

clear that Gobryas is referred to as governor and never as king. Governors reported to the king.

6:1–7. Satraps. In the Persian Empire (550–330 BC) the satrap or governor was in charge of a local province (satrapy). The entire realm was divided into satrapies in order to effectively administer taxation policies. Satraps had royal command in their respective territories. They were involved in both civil and military affairs in their region. They consistently communicated with the king, either to give the king the reports from their regions or to circulate the king's announcements. The provinces or satrapies were reorganized or adjusted from time to time.

Daniel 6:1 indicates that Darius the Mede appointed 120 "satraps" over the whole kingdom. *Herodotus* 3.89–96 says that Darius, the son of Hystaspes (522–486 BC), divided his dominions into twenty satrapies. Xerxes, during the time of his reign (486–465 BC), divided his kingdom into 127 provinces stretching from India to Cush (Ethiopia) (Esth 1:1). Josephus remarked that Darius the Mede had three presidents whom he set over 360 provinces.[18] The different records on the satraps or provinces may lack consistency in their numbers, but they do show that each ancient ruler adopted the administrative strategy of dividing the kingdom into smaller areas for accountability.

6:2–7. Presidents. The Aramaic masculine plural noun *sārᵉkîn*, "presidents," "overseers," "prefects," "chief ministers," or "administrators," appears in the Old Testament only in this passage in Daniel. The word is a loanword from Persian language which means head or chief. This is a title given to three officers appointed by Darius to monitor the work of the 120 satraps. The Persians were renowned for their taxation, and Daniel and the other two presidents may have been given the responsibility to safeguard the king from losing taxes. Daniel outshined all the officers in his service.

6:4. No error or fault. Daniel had served for decades as a top government official. The culture of his day was prone to corruption in every way, but they could not pick up even a simple mistake made by him, either personal or in the line of duty. Moral integrity is possible when a person has unwavering commitment to God.

6:5, 8, 15. Law of Daniel's God. See also **2:9. Law.** The first five books in the Old Testament are the Torah, the law of God. Daniel was well versed in the law of his God. He was also knowledgeable of other regulations and

---

18. Josephus, *Antiquities of the Jews*, 10.11.4.249.

rituals that had to do with health, social life, religion, and sacrifices. His life and conduct reflected this. Exodus 20:3–17 (Deut 5:7–21) has the Ten Laws inscribed by God on stone (Exod 34:1). Now the jealous court officials suggested crafting something with regard to the law of Daniel's God and use it against Daniel. This they could accomplish when the law of God is counteracted by a Medo-Persian law.

The idea by Daniel's colleagues was to let Daniel break the law of his God and get punished for that. The text also mentioned the laws of Medo-Persia, which could not be repealed once in effect (Dan 6:8, 12, 15, 17). However, the same text hints of an attempt by an ambitious king to change the law of Daniel's God (Dan 7:25). Daniel was well informed with the legislative matters of his day.

6:7. Lions. In the ancient Near East, the lion was used as a symbol for royalty and power. An Egyptian pharaoh had a pet lion that he took with him on war campaigns. King Solomon's throne was decorated with twelve lions, one standing at the end of each of its six steps and two lions standing beside each armrest (1 Kgs 10:19–20). In Assyria kings used to hunt lions. The Babylonians were known for keeping lions in a park outside the city. Nebuchadnezzar decorated his processional way with glazed brick reliefs of striding lions. From Assyrian, Neo-Babylonian, and Medo-Persian times, lions were loose and could be seen by local people in places.

6:7–24. Lions' den. The story of Daniel in the lions' "pit" or "den" (Dan 6:7, 12, 16, 17) has been considered by some scholars as a work of fiction.[19] It has been suggested that in the Babylonian tradition "lions are not really lions; they stand for human adversaries. The 'pit of lions,' in its sole Babylonian occurrence, is a metaphor for the hostility and competition among the scholars at court"[20] (cf. Ps 57:4–6).

In several Neo-Assyrian correspondence letters, and in the Neo-Babylonian wisdom literature, successful court scholars presented themselves as righteous sufferers.[21] Some biblical scholars have drawn parallels between these and Dan 6. Moreover, the words "lions' pit," used in Dan 6, are also attested in a Neo-Assyrian king's correspondence letter: "Day and night I pray to the king in front of the lions' pit."[22]

---

19. Hartman and Di Lella, *Book of Daniel*, 55–61, 196, 197.
20. Toorn, "In the Lions' Den," 627.
21. Toorn, "In the Lions' Den," 626–40.
22. Parpola, "Forlorn Scholar," in Rochberg-Halton, *Language, Literature, and History*, 262–63, line 39.

In consideration of the concepts presented above, some scholars conclude that Daniel's pit of lions is a metaphor for the hostility and competition among scholars at court. In light of this, we must ask what archaeology contributes to the understanding of a lions' pit in the book of Daniel. Was such a thing in existence during the time of the Neo-Babylonian Empire?

Fortunately, Donald J. Wiseman helps us here. He discovered the meaning of the word *šūšubātu*, "ambush," as it occurs in the chronicle concerning Neriglissar.[23] This contribution has made it easier to understand the appearance of *šūšubātu* in earlier Neo-Assyrian and Neo-Babylonian chronicles of the kings.[24] Even though there is no archaeological evidence for animal pits, the use of *šubtu* in connection with hunting animals has been suggested to mean an "animal pit" for trapping animals.[25]

Grayson argued that it is "probable that the meaning 'ambush' was derived from the meaning 'pit,' the word for the device to be used to ambush an animal."[26] Therefore, it is reasonable to assume that the Babylonians dug out pits for animals, and such pits could be closed with a stone. Ancient literary finds reveal that the Assyrians and the Babylonians would cage lions for release when the king or prince wanted to hunt them as a trial of royal prowess.[27]

Ezekiel 19:4, 8-9 mentions the trapping of lions in pits. Some features of this account are similar to Dan 6:7, 12, 16, 17. Karel van der Toorn points out that the story of Daniel's confinement in the lions' den, and his subsequent deliverance by divine intervention, is not an unusual idea.[28] Such stories circulated in ancient times. The motif of the pit of lions can be traced

---

23. Wiseman, *Chronicles of the Chaldean Kings*, 74-77, line 7; Grayson, "Ambush and Animal Pit in Akkadian," in University of Chicago, Oriental Institute, *Studies Presented to A. Leo Oppenheim*, 91; and Grayson, *Assyrian and Babylonian Chronicles*, 103-4, line 7.

24. For the Neo-Assyrian and Neo-Babylonian periods, see respectively King, *Chronicles Concerning Early Babylonian Kings*, 2:35-36, chronicle 3 rev., lines 5-9, and 2:43-44, chronicle 4 rev., lines 1-7.

25. Grayson, "Ambush and Animal Pit in Akkadian," in University of Chicago, Oriental Institute, *Studies Presented to A. Leo Oppenheim*, 93. See also *ANET*, 47, 75; the Gilgamesh Epic relates the use of pits in hunting animals. From the late Uruku Period (ca. 3500-3200 BC), a basalt stele was discovered which had a relief of two identical people (or it could be the same individual depicted) hunting lions; see Kuhrt, *ANE*, 1:23.

26. Grayson, "Ambush and Animal Pit in Akkadian," in University of Chicago, Oriental Institute, *Studies Presented to A. Leo Oppenheim*, 94.

27. Barnett, *Sculptures from the North Palace*, plates V, IX, XIII, XV; and Wiseman, *Nebuchadrezzar and Babylon*, 112.

28. Toorn, "Scholars at the Oriental Court," in Collins and Flint, *Book of Daniel*, 1:37-54.

back to Babylonia. First Maccabees 2:60 commented that Daniel was spared from the lions because of his innocence. The apocryphal story of Bel and the Dragon alludes to the biblical story in Dan 6. This story has Daniel with the lions in the pit for seven days.

The Arabic al-Qazwini, although a late source from the thirteenth century AD, carried an article on the site of Babil (Babylon):

> Bābil: the name of the village which formerly stood on one of the branches of the Euphrates in 'Irāḵ. Currently, people carry off the bricks of its ruins, and there exists a well known as "the Dungeon of Dānyāl" [Daniel] which is visited by Jews and Christians on certain yearly occasions and on holidays. Most of the population hold the opinion that this dungeon was the well of Hārūt and Mārūt.[29]

It is interesting to note that tradition has continued to perpetuate the story of Daniel in the lions' den. This may indicate that such an event could well be historical.

6:7, 10–13. Prayer. See **9:3. Praying Daniel.** Prayer is the primary way of communicating with God on anything. It can be verbal or nonverbal. Daniel continued his prayer life despite human threats or interference.

6:8, 12, 15, 17. Medes and Persians. Several scholars have presented the Medians and Persians separately in the chronology of the kingdoms in Daniel. However, in the book of Daniel the Medes and Persians, hence Medo-Persia, are always mentioned together and in that order (Dan 5:28; 6:8, 12, 15; 8:20). While the order in Daniel is the Medes and Persians, the book of Esther reverses it to the Persians and Medes (Esth 1:3, 14, 18, 19).

Paragraph 14 of the Behistun Inscription reads: "I reestablished the people on its foundation, both Persia and Media and the other provinces."[30] Under any circumstances, it is clear that the relationship between the Medes and Persians was long-standing in that they were both of the ancient Iranian culture.

Scholars could understand Medo-Persia in Daniel as a single kingdom by taking into consideration related ancient evidence. The Sippar Cylinder of Nabonidus,[31] the last Neo-Babylonian king, recounts the conflict between the Medes and Persians that resulted in Cyrus II's victory in 550 BC. Cyrus

---

29. Awad, "Bābil," in Gibb et al., *Encyclopaedia of Islam*, 1:846.

30. English translation of Paragraph 14 (1.61–71) of the Behistun Inscription of Darius I is quoted from Edelman, *Origin of the "Second" Temple*, 354.

31. *COS*, 2:310–13.

II eventually absorbed the Medes into the Achaemenid Empire (550–330 BC). Medo-Persia always appears as a single kingdom in the book of Daniel. Croesus, king of Lydia (560–546 BC), inquired from a Pythian priestess on the duration of his sovereignty. The priestess replied:

> Lydian, beware of the day when a mule is lord of the Medians
> Then with thy delicate feet by the stone-strewn channel of Hermus
> Flee for thy life, nor abide, nor blush for the name of a craven.[32]

The prediction in this text uses animal imagery similar to the book of Daniel. Cyrus may have been metaphorically referred to as "a mule" because he was of mixed extraction. His father was Persian while his mother was Median.[33]

Herodotus pointed out that the Medes, along with other nations, continued to pay the annual tax to the Persians.[34] The Medes also continued to play a subordinate role during the Achaemenid era.

In the reliefs at Persepolis, the Medes were portrayed with short curled beards, domed felt caps, knee-length leather tunics, and high-laced shoes. They were depicted as armed with rectangular shields and short swords cased in decorated scabbards.[35] One of the reliefs from the Apadana at Persepolis depicts the alternating Persians and Medes (521–486 BC).[36] This relief highlights the fact that Medo-Persia was a unified political force just as they were presented by Daniel. A foundation tablet inscribed by Xerxes (485–465 BC) states that Media was under Persia.[37]

---

32. Herodotus, *Herodotus*, 1.55.

33. See Yamauchi, *Persia and the Bible*, 79; and also, the discussion below on Cyrus II the Persian. The term "mule" is also attested in the fragment of Megasthenes cited below.

34. Herodotus, *Herodotus*, 3.90–96.

35. Yamauchi, *Persia and the Bible*, 57.

36. Yamauchi, "Persians," in Hoerth et al., *Peoples of the Old Testament*, 111.

37. *ANET*, 316.

PERSEPOLIS ROYAL GUARD
The palace relief of King Darius I (ca. sixth–fifth century BC) shows life-size royal guards. The wall carving depicts a Mede and a Persian alternating respectively in ceremonial army attire. (Credit: Zev Radovan)

In Daniel's first reference to Medo-Persia, it was represented by the chest and arms of silver (Dan 2:32). Medo-Persia was later represented by a bear which had three ribs in its mouth (Dan 7:5), and then by a ram with two horns (Dan 8:3, 4). Raymond Hammer stated that the two horns of Dan 8:3 indicate the author's "knowledge of the combined Medo-Persian Empire, although elsewhere we have seen a tendency to think of Median and Persian empires as separate entities."[38]

That the bear was raised on one side may possibly suggest the imbalance of power between the Medes and Persians. Goldingay was of the opinion that the three ribs may suggest the greedy, expansionist policy of these nations.[39] Some have suggested that the ribs represent the ravenous nature of this beast.[40] Others contend that the ribs stood for specific nations like the Assyrians, Medes, and Persians,[41] or Babylonians, Medes, and Persians.[42] It is most unlikely that two of the ribs would represent Medo-Persia. Lacocque thought the ribs could represent Nebuchadnezzar, Evil-Merodach, and Belshazzar.[43] Joseph Alobaidi took the ribs to be cities in Turkey like Harran, Nesibin, and Shahrezor.[44]

38. Hammer, *Book of Daniel*, 84.
39. Goldingay, *Daniel*, 186.
40. Charles, *Critical and Exegetical Commentary*, 178.
41. Hippolytus, "On Daniel" (*ANF*, 5:177–91).
42. Archer, *Jerome's Commentary on Daniel*, 74.
43. Lacocque, *Book of Daniel*, 140.
44. Alobaidi, *Book of Daniel*, 528.

There is another interpretation which is in keeping with the expansion of Medo-Persia in the first millennium BC. In this view, Babylonia, Lydia, and Egypt, three nations conquered by Medo-Persia, are seen as being represented by the three ribs.[45]

The fragment of Megasthenes (358–280 BC) seems to carry a prophecy by Nebuchadnezzar concerning the future of his kingdom:

> It is, moreover, related by the Chaldeans, that as he went up into his palace he was possessed by some god; and he cried out, and said: "Oh! Babylonians, I Nabucodrosorus (Nebuchadnezzar) foretell unto you a calamity which must shortly come to pass, which neither Belus my ancestor, nor his queen Beltis, have the power to persuade the Fates to turn away. A Persian mule shall come, and by the assistance of your gods shall impose upon you the yoke of slavery; the author of which shall be a Mede, the foolish pride of Assyria. Before he should thus betray my subjects, Oh! that some sea, or whirlpool, might receive him, and his memory be blotted out forever; or that he might be cast out to wander through some desert, where there are neither cities nor the trace of men; a solitary exile among rocks and caverns, where beasts and birds alone abide. But for me, before he shall have conceived these mischiefs in his mind, a happier end will be provided."[46]

It is to be noted that when the Greeks first came in contact with the Medes and Persians, they simply referred to both of them as the Medes.[47] Likewise, both the Medes and Persians could also be designated just as Persians. Daniel deciphered the inscription on the wall and told Belshazzar that the Neo-Babylonian kingdom would be given to Medo-Persia (Dan 5:28). It is well to note that the fall of Babylon in 539 BC took place long after the defeat of the Medes by Persians in 550 BC. Therefore, the Medes and Persians appeared as the next single unified kingdom which followed Neo-Babylonia.

Cyrus may have entrusted to his vassal king, Darius the Mede, rulership over the province of Babylon. It is therefore chronologically untenable to view Medo-Persia as separate or successive kingdoms after 539 BC, for

---

45. Pusey, *Daniel the Prophet*, 165; and Wright, *Daniel and His Prophecies*, 151. See "They Helped"; "Three Ribs," *SDABC*, 4:251, 821.

46. Cory, *Ancient Fragments of Phoenician*, 71–72, quoted in Sack, *Images of Nebuchadnezzar*, 32.

47. Widengren, "Persians," in Wiseman, *Peoples of Old Testament Times*, 316; cited in Yamauchi, *Persia and the Bible*, 57.

by this wrenching asunder of Media and Persia great violence is done to chap. viii., where the unity of the Medo-Persian kingdom is so distinctly affirmed, first in the vision, where it appears as a ram with two horns of which the higher is seen springing up last, and secondly in the words of the interpreting angel, "The ram which thou sawest that had the two horns, they are the kings of Media and Persia."[48]

According to the chronology of the book of Daniel, Medo-Persia became the next kingdom after the fall of Neo-Babylonia in 539 BC (Dan 5:30; 6:8, 12; 8:20). Medo-Persia continued to rule until it suffered defeat by the Greeks in 331 BC.

It seems scholars may understand the main concern of Daniel more clearly if they regard Medo-Persia as a single unified force that toppled Neo-Babylonia in 539 BC. The fact that the books of Daniel and Esther, along with impressive archaeological evidence, show the Medes and Persians together is a major clue for interpreters when constructing the chronology of the four kingdoms in Daniel.

6:8, 12, 15, 17. Laws of Medes and Persians. Medo-Persia had laws which, when put into effect, could not be revoked (Dan 6:8, 12, 15, 17; cf. Esth 1:19; 8:8). Daniel's consignment to the lions' den could not be nullified (Dan 6:17). The irreversibility of Persian law is illustrated by an event from the time of Darius III (336–330 BC). This king erroneously sentenced a certain Charidemus to death. Even though he regretted it afterward, there was no way to reverse what he had done by his royal authority.[49]

The Neo-Babylonian laws were less stringent. Nebuchadnezzar issued a decree for all wise men to be killed in Dan 2:12, 13. This order was not carried out because Daniel talked to the king himself (v. 16). Again, Nebuchadnezzar declared that no one should speak amiss against the God of the three young men who survived the fire (Dan 3:29), but nobody took him seriously.

Despite the consistency shown in upholding the immutability of the Medo-Persian law, it seems that those in authority had ways and means for evading the irreversibility of the law, if they wanted to. The Persian law did not allow a man to marry his sister under any circumstances. Cambyses II (525–522 BC), who was enamored by his sister, found a way out of this restriction while he was in Egypt.[50] He consulted his counselors who

---

48. Boutflower, *In and Around*, 4.
49. Siculus, *Diodorus of Sicily*, 17.30.
50. Herodotus, *Herodotus*, 3.31.

concurred that the law forbade such a practice. However, these counselors found a law that the Persian king might do whatsoever he wished to do. On this basis Cambyses married his sister.

Another evidence of this ability to circumvent the "immutability" of Persian decrees is the case of Darius the Mede, who issued a decree for all people to fear and reverence the God of Daniel (Dan 6:25–27). Despite this, the Medo-Persians continued to show their fidelity to Ahura Mazda.

6:10. Daniel's upper room. Excavations in ancient Babylon seem to offer more light on Daniel's place of prayer. In Dan 6:10, Daniel prayed in his own house. Specifically, he prayed $b^{e\,}illiṯeh$, "in his roof-chamber" or "roof room."[51] It is clear that $b^{e\,}illiṯeh$ (cf. Akkadian $elû$, "upper")[52] is an architectural term that might refer to an upper room or a room in the upper story. In the city of Babylon houses were usually closely crowded together in the narrow streets. It is most likely that the houses did not have windows toward the streets. Each house had a small courtyard or garden in the front. A house was flat-roofed and could have two or three stories. Herodotus indicated that some Babylonian houses consisted of three to four stories.[53] Daniel's upper room had windows which opened in the direction of his homeland.

When the Jerusalem temple was first dedicated, Solomon remarked that people would come to pray there (1 Kgs 8:31, 33). Believers in distant lands needed only to "pray towards this place" (1 Kgs 8:30, 35, 38, 42, 44). Specifically, Daniel and the others who were taken into captivity would pray toward their homeland, Jerusalem, and the temple (1 Kgs 8:46–48).

6:10, 11. Prayed. Daniel's consistent habit of praying was noticed by those associated with him. When prayer to his God became a capital offense, Daniel chose to continue praying just as he had always done. He opened the windows of his upper room toward Jerusalem and prayed three times a day (Dan 6:10). The opening of windows during prayer is reflected in the Babylonian Talmud, which asserts that "a man should not pray save in a room which has windows."[54] Daniel's prayer practice balances the two biblical extremes. He avoided both the hypocritical ostentatious public prayers (Matt 6:5) and the dilemma of being ashamed of God in times of persecution (Matt 10:33; Mark 8:38; Luke 9:26). Daniel chose to continue

---

51. Such a place offered favorable conditions for prayer; see also the Qumranic Temple Scroll, cols. 30–31; Acts 1:13; 9:37, 39; 20:8; and Collins, *Daniel*, 268.

52. Fuhs, "עלה," *TDOT*, 11:94.

53. Herodotus, *Herodotus*, 1.180.

54. *Babylonian Talmud*, 34b.

his normal religious life despite threats. His three friends (Dan 3) likewise refused to compromise their allegiance to their God.

Daniel prayed three times a day (Dan 6:10), a practice common in biblical times (Ps 55:17). Traditional Persian religion emphasized praying three times a day. While several religions promoted prayer three times a day, Zoroastrianism demanded praying five times a day. Muslims also pray five times a day, at dawn, midday, afternoon, sunset, and night. Archaeology points out that the Qumran community may have had a similar custom to the biblical praying (1Qs 10:1–7; 1QH 12:3–9; 1QM 14:12–14). Praying three times a day was an adopted tradition for $T^e fillāh$, "prayer," by the orthodox Jews as outlined in the Mishnah:

> the morning $T^e fillāh$ [may be said] until midday. R. Judah says: Until the fourth hour. The afternoon $T^e fillāh$ [may be said] until evening. R. Judah says: Until the middle of the afternoon. As for the $T^e fillāh$ of the evening, it has no fixed time. The additional $T^e fillāh$ [may be said] at any time of the day.[55]

6:13. Captives. See **2:25. Captives.** Those who accused Daniel for not complying with the king's requirements chose to address him as one of the captives rather than as one of the three governors.

6:17. Stone. Darius the Mede placed his seal upon the stone that covered the mouth of the lion pit into which Daniel was thrown. The high-ranking officials of the kingdom also sealed the stone with their personal signets.

How can an interpreter of this text understand the sealing of the stone? Fortunately, archaeologists have discovered many sealed tombs scattered throughout the ancient Near East.[56] From the sealing done on such tombs we may obtain clues to help us understand what Darius the Mede and his officials might have done (Dan 6:17; cf. Lam 3:53; Matt 27:64–66). Perhaps ropes, bricks, small stones, grooves, poles, or pins were used to fasten the stone over Daniel's den. Wet clay or wax could have been plastered over or around the stone which covered the mouth of this den, pit, or cave. Darius the Mede, along with his officials, may have stamped their signet or cylinder seals all over the wet wax or clay, which was then left to dry.

The sealing of the stone at the entrance of the den of lions could also indicate that Daniel's fate was irrevocable.

---

55. *Babylonian Talmud*, 4.1.
56. Roaf, *Cultural Atlas*, 84–86; Hawass, *Valley of the Golden Mummies* (2000); and Mattingly, "Tomb," *Eerdmans Dictionary of the Bible*, 1319–320.

6:17. Signet ring. For state business the early Persian kings used cylinder seals. On the other hand, they used either the signet rings or stamp seals for personal business. Recovered evidence show that seals usually had graphic pictures of the Persian king killing ferocious animals while he is being protected by the winged sun disc, which was a symbol for the god Ahura Mazda. See also Dan 12:4, 9.

6:18. Fasting. See 9:3. **Fasting and mourning rites.** The king abstained from food, entertainment, and sleep the night Daniel was thrown in the lions' den. In ancient times the main reason for fasting was to express penitential mourning to gain favor of the deity. The king might have been remorseful over being tricked into signing a law against an innocent person. See Esth 6:1.

6:20. Was your God able to deliver you from the lions? After a restless and sleepless night of wishing for Daniel's survival, King Darius hurried very early to the site and called in anguish to the sealed den of lions. From inside, Daniel responded to the king. He was alive. Daniel explained that his God had sent an angel to shut the lion's mouths (see Dan 6:22; Ps 34:7; 58:6). Stories of such divine deliverance circulated in the ancient Near East. A mid-first-millennium BC story tells of an innocent person who declared that "it was Marduk who put a muzzle on the mouth of the lion who was eating me"[57] (cf. Dan 6:19–23; Ps 58:6). Another man who was delivered is reported to have responded: "Marduk deprived my pursuer of his sling and turned aside his slingstones."[58] A colossal Babylonian statue of black basalt shows a lion standing upon a human being.[59] Excavations further show that lions were depicted on the walls of the Ishtar Gate and major buildings in Babylon. The lion was also Marduk's special symbol. Babylonians often called a lion "the dog of Ishtar."

---

57. Wiseman, *Nebuchadnezzar and Babylon*, 112.
58. Wiseman, *Nebuchadnezzar and Babylon*, 112.
59. Von Reber, *History of Ancient Art*, 81.

PLOT AGAINST THE INNOCENT

LION OF BABYLON
(Picture by Siegfried Horn, Courtesy of HAM)

6:21. O king, live forever. See 2:4b. O king, live forever.

6:24. Killing the families of the guilty. The story of Daniel in the lions' den ended on a sad note. The men who had accused him were thrown into the same den, along with their wives and children. These unfortunate people did not survive (Dan 6:24). The practice of killing the wives and children along with guilty men was common in Persia[60] (Esth 9:24–25). This practice was also illustrated in the Hebrew Bible (cf. Exod 20:5; Josh 7:24; Jer 23:34).

Intaphrenes was one of seven men accused of rebelling against the Persian King Darius I (522–486 BC). He wanted to personally talk it over with the king, as was required by the law, but the palace gate wardens would not allow him access because the king was with one of his wives. Intaphrenes cut off the gate wardens' noses and ears. Darius I then seized him with all his sons and household for plotting a rebellion.

Subsequently, Intaphrenes's wife came continuously to the palace gates, weeping and lamenting until her actions triggered the king's compassion. The king told her that he would grant pardon to only one of her imprisoned kinfolk, whomsoever she would choose. After counsel she chose her brother.

Darius I was amazed at the woman's decision, and asked her why she would choose her brother instead of her dear husband or one of her sons. She said to the king, "Another husband I may get, if heaven so will, and other children, if I lose these; but my father and mother are dead, and so I can by no means get another brother; but this is why I have so spoken."[61] Darius I was pleased with this answer. He granted the woman her request

---

60. Herodotus, *Herodotus*, 3.119; and Marcellinus, *Ammianus Marcellinus*, 23.6.81.
61. Herodotus, *Herodotus*, 3.119.

and also granted her the life of her eldest son. The rest of the imprisoned family members he killed.

In light of this story, the practice of the killing of the families of the guilty in Daniel reflected an ancient social reality.

6:25. Peoples, nations, and languages. See **3:4, 7, 29. Peoples, nations, and languages.** The message to be communicated was intended to reach all people everywhere. "Peoples, nations, and languages" is an all-inclusive language. Communication of a critical message was intended to reach all people in the whole realm. See Rev 14:6, 7.

6:25, 27. In all the earth. See **4:1, 10–23, 35. In all the earth.** The letter King Darius wrote to all people in all the earth could have been intended to get to all people in his empire.

6:25. Peace. See **4:1. Your peace be increased.** Ancient letters began by pointing out the addressees and then the greeting. "Peace be multiplied to you" was the common salutation.

6:27. Heaven. See **2:18, 19, 28, 37, 38. Heaven.** King Darius wrote that the God of Daniel was the God who does signs and wonders in heaven and on earth. God demonstrates His power and glory both in heaven and on earth to deliver and rescue people.

6:28. Prospered. The verb *tsalach* means to be successful, profitable, or prosperous in any area of life. In the Old Testament it is God who grants success or prosperity (Josh 1:8; Ps 1:3; Neh 2:20). It is also acknowledged that there are some people who may prosper without moral integrity (Ps 37:7; Jer 5:28; 12:1; Dan 11:27). The Dead Sea Scrolls (DSS) use *tsalach* as a warning that if anyone disregards God's statutes there would be no success guaranteed in anything that person does (Damascus Rule 13:21; cf. Prov 28:13). King Darius called Daniel "the servant of the living God" (Dan 6:20). It was because of Daniel's fidelity and commitment to God that God was with him in all he did and was granted success.

6:28. Cyrus the Persian. See **10:1. Cyrus, king of Persia.** This Cyrus, king of Persia, was mentioned earlier by the prophet Isaiah, the son of Amoz, to be God's shepherd who would fulfill God's plan for Jerusalem (Isa 44:28; 45:1). Daniel was an outstanding official in the Neo-Babylonian Empire. He continued to serve well even when Cyrus the Persian took over in 539 BC. Cyrus's peaceful victory over Babylon in 539 BC is described in the Cyrus Cylinder. He also set the captives free to go back to their respective homelands. Cyrus gave a decree in 538 BC that allowed Jewish captives to go back and rebuild Jerusalem.

Chapter 7

POLITICAL SUCCESSION

THERE IS A CLEAR transition in the biblical text from this point on that focuses on Daniel and his personal dreams. The tension here is that Daniel, who was renowned for interpreting dreams or solving enigmas, now struggles to understand his own dreams. The theme of the succession of nations presented by King Nebuchadnezzar in Dan 2 continues with Daniel being the main player in dreaming and seeking for meaning. The message is clear but veiled in the imagery that is rich in significance to the ancient Near East reader. Many finds attest to the fact that Daniel was accurate on delineating the political developments.

7:1. First year of Belshazzar. See **5:1. Belshazzar, identity.** Nabonidus (556–539 BC) was Belshazzar's biological father and king of Neo-Babylonia after he seized power from Labash-Marduk through a coup in 556 BC. He angered some priests and common people when he neglected worshiping Marduk, the local god in preference to the moon god, Sin. In his sixth year of reign (550/549 BC), Nabonidus left the city of Babylon for Tema in Saudi Arabia where he lived for ten years. He left his son Belshazzar in charge while he was away. So, 550/549 BC is Belshazzar's first year in Babylon.

7:1. Visions of his head. See **8:1. Vision.** The relationship between visions and dreams is very close both in the ancient Near East and the biblical text. Daniel's visions came at any time of the day. Visions were direct communication with the divine beings. Visions were more vivid and dramatic than dreams.

7:1. Daniel's dreams/visions. Daniel's visions and dreams occupy the last half of his book. There is a paradigm shift in the last half of the book of Daniel. The author, who was an expert in interpreting the king's dreams, now becomes the dreamer who pleads for interpretation (specifically, understanding) from someone else. He is extremely baffled and devastated by his own dreams (Dan 7:28; 8:27). In typical apocalyptic genre, the prophet himself does not understand his own apocalyptic dreams or visions.

Daniel had dreams and visions during the first year of Belshazzar, king of Babylon (550/549 BC), and he put them on record (Dan 7:1). A subsequent vision followed in 548/547 BC, the third year of Belshazzar (Dan 8:1). In 536 BC, the third year of Cyrus, Daniel had another vision while he was at the bank of the Tigris River (Dan 10:1–4). Like Gen 41, the text of Daniel shows that the dreams, or parts of them, could be repeated to communicate the same message through different symbols.

7:2. Four winds of heaven. See **2:35. Blowing winds of Daniel.** The Mesopotamians saw the world as having four principal points. To these they gave ethnic labels. They called north "Subar," south "Sumer," west "Amurru," and east "Elam," with Babylon at the center.[1] The concept of the four cardinal points is also used in Dan 7:2; 8:8; 11:4. The *mappa mundi* is the only surviving cosmographic map of Babylon made in Mesopotamia in the first millennium BC. This map places Babylon at the center of the universe.[2] Now housed in the British Museum, the *mappa mundi* shows the earth as round and enveloped by water, and there are other cities inscribed on the tablet as well. Such an exalted position was not only assumed for Babylon but for the other less important cities also. In a night vision, Daniel saw the four winds that stirred up the Great Sea (Dan 7:2). The motif of the blowing winds is common in the biblical tradition (Jer 49:36; Ezek 37:9; Dan 7:2; 8:8; 11:4; Jonah 1:4; Zech 2:6; 6:5; Matt 24:31; Mark 13:27; Rev 7:1; 20:8).

According to several extant sources, the four winds of heaven seem to denote the wind that blows from the four cardinal points of the world. The Rassam cylinder, written in 700 BC, is a record on Sennacherib's palace building. It states that he placed fifteen gates "toward the four winds," that is, three gates facing to the north, a total of seven to the south and to the east, and five to the west.[3] The imagery of the disturbed sea in Dan 7:2 may be related to Babylonian and Canaanite mythology.[4] The Enuma Elish

---

1. Champdor, *Babylon*, 15. See also Hallo and Simpson, *Ancient Near East*, 21–23.

2. Nemet-Nejat, *Daily Life in Ancient Mesopotamia*, 94–97; and Van de Mieroop, *Ancient Mesopotamian City*, 43.

3. Luckenbill, *Ancient Records of Assyria and Babylonia*, 2:170–71.

4. Longman III, *Daniel*, 181. See Enuma Elish, the Akkadian Creation Epic in

specifically mentions the South Wind, the North Wind, the East Wind, and the West Wind. The destructive fourfold wind is compared with the Whirlwind, the Hurricane, the Cyclone, or the matchless wind.[5] There is, however, nothing in this myth to warrant any source material for Daniel's imagery.

PAZUZU
In ancient Mesopotamia (ca. eighth century BC), Pazuzu was a home demon, a domestic spirit, a wild, wandering wind demon and also the king of evil spirits. (Credit: Zev Radovan)

The idea in Dan 7:2 is that of a turbulent whirlwind which agitates the sea. The sea was always perceived as dangerous, especially when it was agitated by winds (Job 38:8; Ps 89:9; 107:23-29; Jonah 1:4; Acts 27:14-20). Nabonidus related that "at the command of Marduk, the great lord, the four winds arose, [great] whirlwinds, (and) the sand which covered that city and temple was removed."[6] The gods are said to have stirred the winds that uncovered the foundations of the temple. The four winds in Nabonidus's inscription may be viewed as symbolic, depending on how one views Nabonidus's dream.

The four winds in Dan 7:2; 8:8; 11:4 could also be highly symbolic and might represent the religiopolitical unrest and instability (or the agents of

---

ANET, 60-72, 501-3; *COS*, 1:390-402; and Arnold and Beyer, *Readings from the Ancient Near East*, 31-50. The Baal Cycle contains the struggle between the storm god Baal, the sea god Yam, and the underworld god Mot. *ANET*, 129-42; *COS*, 1:241-74; and Arnold and Beyer, *Readings from the Ancient Near East*, 50-62.

5. *ANET*, 66, Tablet 4, lines 42-49.

6. Bezold, "Two Inscriptions of Nabonidus," 86-101, col. II, line 10. See also Beaulieu, *Reign of Nabonidus*, 48, 89, 95.

POLITICAL SUCCESSION

sociopolitical change) in the whole region surrounding the Mediterranean Sea.

7:2, 13, 27. Heaven. See **2:18, 19, 28, 37, 38. Heaven.** The four winds of heaven are the four cardinal points.

7:2. Great Sea. Daniel had a dream or vision (Dan 7:2, 3) in which four different animals emerged from "the Great Sea" (Aramaic *yammā' rabbā'*).

The ancient Near Eastern territory has five main bodies of water. The five seas which border the wider Mesopotamian region are the Black Sea to the northwest, the Caspian Sea slightly to the northeast, the Persian Gulf to the east, the Mediterranean Sea to the west, and the Red Sea to the south. While the animals Daniel saw in this vision represented four kingdoms in succession, Neo-Babylonia, Medo-Persia, Greece, and Rome, all of the animals came out from just one of the seas in the area, the Great Sea. The identity of this Great Sea in Daniel has been a puzzle to scholars. C. F. Keil and F. Delitzsch[7] and other more recent scholars rejected the biblical evidence for identifying the Great Sea with the Mediterranean Sea. Such scholarship preferred to take the Great Sea of Dan 7:2, 3 to be a "mythic" sea belonging only in legends.

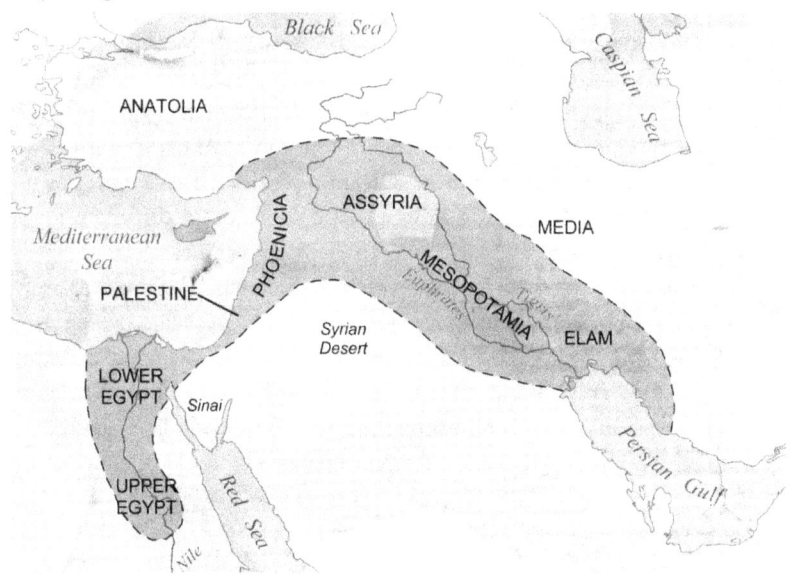

MAP OF THE FERTILE CRESCENT.
The Ancient Near East is marked by five seas in the area.
(Credit: Zev Radovan)

---

7. Keil and Delitzsch, *Ezekiel and Daniel*, 637.

James Montgomery was quite certain that the "Great Sea" was not the Mediterranean, although he acknowledged that the term was so used in Josh 1:4 and other texts.[8] He confused the term "the Great Sea" with "the great deep," "sea," or "abyss" of Amos 7:4; Isa 51:10; and Rev 17:8.[9] Montgomery's conclusion also failed to acknowledge contemporary evidences apart from the Bible which indicate that the Mediterranean Sea is the same as the Great Sea.

John E. Goldingay[10] has argued that more general terms like "the sea" (Isa 5:30; 27:1; Jer 51:42; Ps 74:13; 89:9; Job 26:12; Rev 21:1) and "the great deep" (Gen 7:11; Isa 51:10; Amos 7:4), were used in reference to some mythic or legendary sea.

It is important to remember that Daniel's dream was highly symbolic. In order to understand the symbols correctly, we must be careful to identify the components of the dream accurately. We must let the biblical and archaeological sources speak for themselves.

The Hebrew Bible refers to "the Great Sea" on different occasions. One of the outlined boundaries to the land of Israel in Josh 1:4 was "and until to the Great Sea, toward the setting of the sun." This is obviously the Mediterranean (Latin *medius terra* means "midland")[11] Sea. Similarly, Num 34:6-7; Josh 9:1; 15:47; 23:4; and Ezek 47:15, 20; 48:28 all geographically identify the Mediterranean Sea as the Great Sea. The same sea was also known as the Western Sea (Deut 11:24; 34:2; Joel 2:20), or the Sea of the Philistines (Exod 23:31). The identity of the Great Sea as the Mediterranean Sea is also supported by one of the Dead Sea Scrolls, Genesis Apocryphon (1QapGen 21:16). Any further attempt at sustaining an alternative view has not been meaningful. Taking all of this textual evidence into consideration, it seems clear that Dan 7:2, 3 is referring to the Mediterranean Sea.

Several archaeological finds also identify the Mediterranean Sea as the Great Sea. A foundation stone has been found which was laid by Shamshi-Adad I (ca. 1808-1776 BC), king of Asshur and Old Babylonia. This stone designated him as the builder of the temple of the god Asshur. The stone also states that Shamshi-Adad I brought peace to the land between the Tigris and the Euphrates. Lebanon is identified as a land of the shore of the

---

8. Montgomery, *Book of Daniel*, 285.

9. Montgomery, *Book of Daniel*, 285. See Gardner's summary in "Great Sea of Dan VII 2," 412-15. Gardner not only confused the Great Sea and the great deep, she also ignored the archaeological evidence for identifying the Great Sea. Further, Gardner attempted to revive Hermann Gunkel's 1895 thesis that there is correspondence between Enuma Elish and Dan 7. See her "Daniel 7, 2-14," 244-52.

10. Goldingay, *Daniel*, 160.

11. Lubetski, "Mediterranean Sea" (*ABD*, 4:664).

Great Sea.[12] A broken slab found at Calah was inscribed with Adad-Nirari III's (810–783 BC) expedition to Palestine. The territory of his conquest is said to stretch from the Great Sea of the rising sun (Persian Gulf) to the Great Sea of the setting sun (Mediterranean Sea).

Part of the inscription reads:

> Property of Adad-nirari, great king, legitimate king, king of the world, king of Assyria . . . conquering from the Siluna mountain of the Rising Sun, the countries Saban, Ellipi, Harhar, Araziash, Mesu, the (country of the) Medians, Gizilbunda in its (full) extent, the countries of Munna, Persia (*Parsua*), Allabria, Apdadana, Na'iri with all its regions, Andiu which lies away in the *pithu* of the mountains with all its regions, as far as the Great Sea of the Rising Sun (and) from the banks of the Euphrates, the country of the Hittites, Amurru-country in its full extent, Tyre, Sidon, Israel (^mat^*ḫu-um-ri*), Edom, Palestine (*Pa-la-as-tu*), as far as the shore of the Great Sea of the Setting Sun, I made them submit all to my feet, imposing upon them tribute.[13]

Egyptian literature uses the term *w3ḏ-wr*, or "Great Green," for any sea in general. This was applied to the Mediterranean Sea as well as *p3ywm '3 n Ḥ3rw*, "the Great Sea of Syria-Palestine" (*Ḫuru*).[14]

The British Museum houses a large stone block called the India House Inscription. This block, inscribed all over with ancient cuneiform writing, was discovered in the ruins of Babylon sometime before 1901 and given into the custody of the East India Company in Baghdad, from whence it obtained its name. In this inscription (col. ii, lines 15–16),[15] as well as in the Wadi Brisa Inscription (lines 3–4),[16] Nebuchadnezzar identified the Mediterranean Sea as the upper sea and the Persian Gulf as the lower sea.

We have seen that both the biblical text and several ancient Near Eastern inscriptions give evidence that the Mediterranean Sea is the body of water called the Great Sea. The Mediterranean Sea is bordered by Africa to the south, Asia to the east, and Europe to the north. This location gives it the international, maritime, and geopolitical prominence implied by the author of Daniel.

---

12. Grayson, *Assyrian Royal Inscriptions*, 1:19–21; and *COS*, 2:259.
13. *ANET*, 281.
14. Lubetski, "Great Sea" (*ABD*, 2:1091–92).
15. Rogers, *Cuneiform Parallels to the Old Testament*, 364–65.
16. *ANET*, 307.

7:3-8. Four great beasts. Scholarly debates center mainly on the identity of the kings represented by the beasts. There are also differing views on the background of the imagery of Dan 7. From the chaotic Great Sea (Mediterranean Sea) emerged successively the four grotesque and unique beasts (Dan 7:3). The author described the first three beasts by comparing them to familiar animals: a lion with eagles' wings, a bear with three ribs in its mouth, and a leopard with four wings on its back, respectively (Dan 7:4-6). Interestingly, Nebuchadnezzar had been likened to a lion (Jer 4:7; 49:19; 50:17) and also an eagle (Jer 49:22; Lam 4:19; Hab 1:6-8; Ezek 17:3, 12; Dan 4:33). The biblical text also uses the raging waters/seas metaphorically, comparing hostile nations to turbulent waters; cf. Isa 8:5-8; 17:12-14; Ps 46:1-6; Hab 3:8-10, 15.

In Assyrian, Babylonian, and Persian times, "winged bulls and winged lions, both with human heads flanked thrones and entryways."[17] Such unusual creatures are reported also to appear in dreams. Mesopotamian art and sculpture display a wide range of winged and hybrid creatures. The fourth beast was not only bizarre, unparalleled, and difficult to describe, but frightful, terrifying, and exceedingly strong (Dan 7:7). The author is more puzzled and fascinated with this one than any of its predecessors (Dan 7:19-28). Nevertheless, the text states that the four beasts are four kings who shall come from the earth (Dan 7:17).

The scholarly attempt to understand the imagery of Dan 7 in light of some archaeological finds is very much appreciated, although there is no consensus regarding the origin of the imagery. Hermann Gunkel was the first one to suggest that the beast imagery from the Hebrew Bible had its prototype in the Enuma Elish, the Babylonian Creation Story.[18] This idea was quickly dismissed. New views suggested that the background of Dan 7 was either Ugaritic[19] or Canaanite mythology.[20] Opinions on the historical background of the imagery continued to differ and different theories were suggested.

Helge S. Kvanvig argued for the Akkadian "Vision of the Netherworld" as the background of Dan 7.[21] His ideas were snubbed by Collins,

---

17. Walton et al., *IVP Bible Background Commentary*, 741.

18. Gunkel, *Creation and Chaos*, 205-14; and Collins, "Stirring Up the Great Sea," in Van der Woude, *Book of Daniel*, 121. See the text of the Enuma Elish in *ANET*, 60-72, 501-3. Cf. Lucas, "Source of Daniel's Animal Imagery," 161-85.

19. For the Ugaritic myths that are associated with Daniel see *ANET*, 129-42; Smith, *Ugaritic Baal Cycle* (1994); Matthews and Benjamin, *Old Testament Parallels*, 19-45; and *COS*, 1:241-71.

20. Emerton, "Origin," 225-42.

21. Kvanvig, *Roots of Apocalyptic*, 389-555. For the text of the Vision of the

who pointed out that the Akkadian text has "neither sea nor clouds; there is no opposition between the hybrid gods and the human figure, no destruction of a monster and no conferral of everlasting dominion."[22]

The beasts are believed to have been derived either from Hos 13:7–8, the ancient Near Eastern *Mischwesen* (hybrid creatures), astrology, the languages of the treaty curses,[23] or the Vision of the Underworld.[24] These ideas will be briefly discussed in relation to the book of Daniel which also uses animal symbolism.

In Hosea God metaphorically likens Himself to the lion, the leopard, the bear, the lion repeated, and a wild animal that would destroy Israel (Hos 13:4–8). The animals appear in a similar order to Dan 7. However, it is most unlikely that the context in Hosea would allow a background to the succession motif used in Daniel.

The idea that Dan 7 depended on the ancient Near Eastern *Mischwesen* was proposed by Martin Noth, who noted some examples in ancient Near Eastern iconography of animals with four wings and several heads.[25] However, only representations of the lion with eagle features and feet like those of man are attested in the iconography. No bear or leopard has been recovered with the characteristics specified in Daniel. Moreover, the ancient Near Eastern iconography has no association with a sea.

It has also been suggested that the animal visions of Dan 7 and 8 show close affinity to the *Shumma izbu*, "if an anomaly," text series.[26] This collection of ancient Mesopotamian divination texts speaks of unusual human and animal births which are interpreted to have a bearing on the future affairs of both individuals and the state. However, Daniel uses animal symbolism to outline successive historical world empires from his time to the time of the end. In contrast, the *Shumma izbu* texts give random prognostic omens without any bearing on world chronology. They present the fate which might befall an individual or nation following the birth of an unusual animal.

Netherworld, see *ANET*, 109–10.

22. Collins, "Stirring Up the Great Sea," 131.

23. Day, *God's Conflict*, 153–57.

24. For the text of the Vision see *ANET*, 109–10; and Kvanvig, *Roots of Apocalyptic*, 390–91. For the discussion of this view see Kvanvig, *Roots of Apocalyptic*, 389–441; and Collins, "Stirring Up the Great Sea," 122, 128–31.

25. Noth, *Laws in the Pentateuch*, 210–11.

26. For the texts see Leichty, *Omen Series Šumma izbu* (1970); and also Porter, *Metaphors and Monsters*, 16–42.

A. Caquot suggested that astrology might have influenced the writer of Daniel with regard to animal representations.[27] He sought to identify the astrological or zodiacal symbols associated with the ancient Near Eastern religions. His argument was weakened by lack of explicit corresponding parallels from the different astrological systems that might have served as the background to Dan 7. Also, astrology has no association with the sea.

Thorne Wittstruck pressed for the idea that the language of the Sefire I A treaty curses, which deal with devouring animals, be considered. He thought these might have elements which led to the beast imagery in Dan 7.[28] James A. Rimbach[29] and John Day[30] refuted Wittstruck's arguments. These scholars pointed out that only the leopard is common to the lists in Dan 7 and the Sefire I A treaty text. They argued further that the textual evidence of the treaty would not support the modifications necessary to fit his conclusions.

Collins indicated that the biblical tradition has sea dragons and monsters whose religio-historical background must be considered in understanding the beasts of Dan 7.[31] Despite this insight, some of the beasts and dragons in the Hebrew Bible (Job 9:13; 26:12-13; 41:1; Ps 74:13-14; 89:9-12; 104:25-26; Isa 27:1; 51:9-11; Ezek 29; 32) do not include the same representations as those in Daniel. On the other hand, the use of animals to represent kingdoms in the Hebrew Bible cannot be denied (Ps 87:4; Isa 30:7). The bizarre imagery of the beasts and their use to symbolize successive ancient Near Eastern kingdoms is unique to Daniel.

The hypothesis that Dan 7 had its background in the Ugaritic or Canaanite milieu fails to "account for the significant differences in description, function, and especially contextual relations"[32] between these texts. The animals in Dan 7 appear in a declining order of their potency and ferociousness. This serves to indicate the nature and political competency of the successive kings they represent. The metals of Dan 2 and the animals of Dan 7 and 8 share the same motif of the declining successive kingdoms.

---

27. Caquot, "Sur les quatre bêtes," 5-13; and also Day, *God's Conflict*, 154-55.

28. Wittstruck, "Influence of Treaty Curse Imagery on the Beast Imagery," 100-2. Wittstruck used the translation of the Sefire Treaties I A, lines 30-31, and Sefire Treaty II A, line 9 from Fitzmyer, *Aramaic Inscriptions of Sefire*, 2-3, 12-17, 53-58.

29. Rimbach, "Bears or Bees?," 565-66. Rimbach emphasizes the point that the text is badly damaged; where the word *dbhh*, "bear," is emended, only the final *h* is visible. Further, the proposed *nmrh*, "panther," in the text is even more uncertain.

30. Day, *God's Conflict*, 153-54.

31. Collins, *Daniel*, 295.

32. Ferch, "Daniel 7 and Ugarit," 81.

The identity of the four kingdoms in Dan 7 has long stimulated scholarly discussion. The poorly preserved 4Q552 mentions Babel and Persia but is not explicit on the rest.[33]

The enigma is solved by considering the kingdoms clearly identified in the book of Daniel and analyzing the biblical text in light of the history of antiquity. The four hybrid animals likely represent Neo-Babylonia, Medo-Persia, Greece, and the fourth kingdom, Rome (Dan 2:40; 7:23), respectively. The main thrust of the book of Daniel, therefore, is the chronological succession of kingdoms from the time of Nebuchadnezzar to the time of the end.

7:4. Lionlike beast. In Daniel's vision he saw a beast like a lion which had wings of an eagle (Dan 7:4). This lionlike beast and its characteristics correspond to the Babylonian Empire, the first of the four empires, each of which is represented by a different beast (Dan 7:17).[34]

It is interesting to note how archaeological finds can illuminate the interpreter's conception of the lion symbolism in Neo-Babylonia. The symbol of a lion was commonly used in Babylon.[35] The lion was the symbol for the Babylonian royalty and corresponds with the head of gold (Dan 2:32, 38), which represented Neo-Babylonia. It was also the symbol for both Marduk and Ishtar. Excavations in Babylon have revealed that during the time of Nebuchadnezzar the walls of the Processional Way, which ran from the Ishtar Gate to the Temple of Marduk, were decorated with glazed figures of striding lions. Each lion was about $3^{1}/_{2}$ feet (1.05 meter) high, about $6^{1}/_{2}$ feet (two meters) long, and they were about 120 in number.

Mesopotamian art from ancient times has many pictographs, statues, and figurines of lions that were made either for decorative or ceremonial purposes. It has been noted that the background of the animal imagery in Dan 7 could be the ancient Near Eastern treaty curse imagery. Various characteristics and habits of the lions are seen on cylinder seals, stone bowls, bricks, clay tablets, stamp seals, and sprouted vessels.

In the Wadi Brissa rock relief, the heroic Nebuchadnezzar is depicted contending with a lion.[36] This idea was adopted from the Assyrian motif which is displayed in the palatial reliefs and royal seals where the

---

33. Vermes, *Complete Dead Sea Scrolls*, 575.

34. See table 4.

35. Koldewey indicated that "among other signs more symbolic in character are the lion, the double axe, and the symbol of Marduk, a triangle on a shaft, either alone or combined with other stamps," in *Excavations at Babylon*, 80.

36. Börker-Klähn, *Altvorderasiatische Bildstelen und vergleichbare Felsreliefs*, plate 259.

THE BOOK OF DANIEL

king dispatches a lion. Austen Henry Layard discovered a winged lion at Nineveh.[37] Layard also reported that by the time of his visits, lions (commonly *leonina persicus*, "Persian lion," and *felis leo goojratensis*, "Indian lion") were often loose and could be seen on both banks of the Tigris and Euphrates Rivers. Two Neo-Babylonian period cylinder seals show Marduk in combat with a winged lion, and also with a winged eagle-headed lion.[38] The wings of an eagle on the lion in Dan 7:4 might have been intended to portray its swiftness. The hybrid lion and its symbolism depicted by Daniel is not a far-fetched idea, but a reflection of a motif which was utilized in the ancient times. He used animal symbolism to portray political reality.

7:4, 17, 23. Earth. See 4:1, 10–23, 35. **In all the earth.** To be lifted up from the earth can also imply to be lifted up from the ground or land. The lionlike beast was lifted up from the ground to be enabled to stand on the ground.

7:5. Bearlike beast. The bearlike beast that had three ribs in its mouth (Dan 7:5) represented the Medo-Persian kingdom which succeeded Neo-Babylonia in 539 BC. It corresponds to the chest and arms of silver in Nebuchadnezzar's image (Dan 2:32, 39). It also corresponds to the two-horned ram in Dan 8:3–4, 20.

Conflicting suggestions have been put forward as to what the three ribs stood for.[39] The difficulty is caused by the fact that the writer did not include them in the interpretation (Dan 7:15–17). There seems to be a consensus among interpreters that the three ribs stood for nations defeated by the Medo-Persian Empire, but opinions continue to differ on the identity of those nations. In light of this, then, the three ribs then represent the three main nations that were conquered by the Medo-Persian Empire. These nations were Lydia (546 BC),[40] the Neo-Babylonian Empire (539 BC),[41] and

---

37. Layard, *Nineveh and Its Remains*, 1:72; see also vol. 2 of the same book, pp. 349–50, for the discussion on the sculpture of a human-headed lion ministering to the king.

38. Langdon, *Semitic Mythology*, 5:281–82.

39. Hippolytus suggested the three ribs to represent the Assyrians, Babylonians, and the Medes. Hippolytus, *Kommentar zu Daniel*, 200. On the other hand, Jerome thought they stood for Babylonians, Medes, and Persians. Alobaidi identified the three ribs to represent three cities, viz., Harran, Nesibin and Shahrezor, in *Book of Daniel*, 528.

40. *ANET*, 306; Grayson, *Assyrian and Babylonian Chronicles*, 107, col. 2, lines 15–17; Herodotus, *Herodotus*, 1.53–56, 74–86; Xenophon, *Cyropaedia*, 7.1.2; and Yamauchi, *Persia and the Bible*, 81–84.

41. Yamauchi, *Persia and the Bible*, 85–87.

Egypt (525 BC).[42] The bear fits well with the Medo-Persian aggressively greedy character.

7:6. Leopard-like beast. The third hybrid beast looked like a leopard (Dan 7:6). It corresponds to the belly and thighs of bronze in Dan 2:32, 39, and the goat in Dan 8:5–8, 21. The goat is identified as Greece in Dan 8:21. The horn would represent Alexander the Great. The leopard had four heads and four wings on its back (cf. Ezek 1:5–9). The four heads correspond with the four horns which replaced the he-goat's prominent horn (Dan 8:5, 8).

The leopard is not attested in the extant ancient Near East art, although its appearance is suggested on a frieze contest of fighting animals and a bull-man.[43] The wings may depict the swiftness of the kingdom. The four heads/horns could be the four main protagonists who shared Alexander's kingdom after his untimely death. Alexander's army generals, Cassander, Lysimachus, Ptolemy, and Seleucus, divided up and ruled the kingdom after his death.

7:7–8. Strange beast. The fourth beast in Dan 7:7–8 corresponds to the legs of iron and the feet which were of mixed clay and iron (Dan 2:33, 40). This beast is described as "dreadful and terrible" (Dan 7:7). The Vision of Amram (4Q544 1:13) describes the frightening angel of darkness similarly as "dreadful and terrible." Such linguistic similarities serve to show that the scribes at Qumran were familiar with the writings of Daniel. The next world power after the collapse of Greece was unnamed by the author. This kingdom is identified only as the fourth kingdom (Dan 2:40; 7:7, 23) in the chronological succession after the fall of Neo-Babylonia. The Roman Empire displaced the Greeks from world dominance. As the fourth kingdom in the text of Daniel, the Roman Empire is therefore represented by the dreadful fourth beast. Among other characteristics, this bizarre beast had ten horns. The ten horns of the fourth beast represent these ten kingdoms. Three of the ten horns were displaced by a little horn which appeared later (Dan 7:8, 20, 24). Ancient history reveals that the Roman Empire was invaded by ten kingdoms, namely: Alamanni, Anglo-Saxons, Burgundians, Franks, Heruli, Lombards, Ostrogoths, Suevi, Vandals, and Visigoths. The author of Daniel observed a little horn rising up from the Roman Empire and displacing three of the ten kingdoms. History has it that when the papal Rome came into prominence, it displaced the Heruli (AD 493), Vandals

---

42. Herodotus, *Herodotus,* 3:10–15; Yamauchi, *Persia and the Bible,* 95–105; and Lloyd, "The Late Period (664–332 BC)," 383.

43. *ANEP,* 220, no. 678; cited in Collins, *Daniel,* 298.

(AD 534), and Ostrogoths (AD 553). These kingdoms were destroyed because they supported Arianism, a rival religion against papal Rome.

The author of Daniel was most fascinated by the little horn and its activities. This last horn received more of the author's attention than the others. Some works have attempted to draw literary parallels between the little horn of Daniel and several figures in ancient Near Eastern mythology.[44]

Opinions still differ on the identity of the fourth kingdom. The Grecian scheme sees the list as Babylon, Media, Persia, and Greece, while the Roman scheme has Babylon, Medo-Persia, Greece, and Rome. If Daniel's chronology is followed, Media and Persia are one kingdom represented by the two-horned ram (8:20). This kingdom is displaced by Greece, which was represented by the one-horned goat (8:21). From world history, scholars have pointed out that the Roman Empire was the next world power after it conquered Greece.

7:7, 8, 11, 20, 21, 24. Horns. See **8:3, 5, 8, 9, 21. Horns.** *Qerenain*, "horns," refer to animal horns. The animal uses its horns to fight and defend itself. The horns here are symbolic; they represent kings (Dan 7:24; Rev 17:12) of the fourth kingdom, the Roman Empire.

7:9, 10, 26. Court scene. The location of the court scene where mobile thrones[45] were set up and subsequently occupied is not clear (Dan 7:9-10). The judgment vision portrayed by Dan 7 seems to take place in heaven. The setting, or casting of the thrones, may imply the calling to order of the court session. First Kings 22:10 presents the idea of mobile thrones.

Court scenes are familiar in the biblical tradition (cf. 1 Kgs 22; Ps 122:5; Isa 6; Ezek 1-2; Rev 4-5). At the court scene the people, the holy ones of the Most High, would receive the kingdom (Dan 7:27). A great number of ancient literary texts,[46] iconography,[47] stelae,[48] and seal impres-

---

44. See Walton, "Anzu Myth," in Collins and Flint, *Book of Daniel*, 69-89; and Gane, "Hurrian Ullikummi," in Cohen et al., *Birkat Shalom*, 485-98.

45. Doukhan prefers translating the Aramaic plural *korsāwān* "superthrone" (Dan 7:9) rather than "thrones"; see his *Secrets of Daniel*, 113.

46. Examples of this literature include the Story of Nergal and Ereshkigal, *COS*, 1:384, 387, 389, 390; the Epic of Creation, 1:396, 397; *ANET*, 12-23, 120-28, 142-49, 288-90, 357, 389; 575, line 161; 584, line 66; 586, line 89. Adad-Nirari, king of Assyria, reported, "I solemnly took my seat upon the royal throne." Luckenbill, *Ancient Records of Assyria and Babylonia*, 1:117.

47. See Ur-Nanshe, king of Lagash, plate following in Kramer, *Sumerians*, 64.

48. The Stele of Hammurabi from Susa shows Shamash, the sun god, sitting while Hammurabi, king of Babylon, is standing before the god; see Frankfort, *Art and Architecture*, 120-21. See also the statue of Gudea, king of Lagash, and the stele of Hammurabi, following p. 266 in Roux, *Ancient Iraq* (1992).

sions[49] depict the concept of enthronement with either kings or gods sitting on the thrones.

Daegeuk Nam explored the Sumerian, Akkadian, Hittite, Ugaritic, and Egyptian sources which relate enthronement scenes in the ancient Near East.[50] An example of the setting up of thrones for special occasions can be viewed on the relief of the Babylonian king, Nabuapaliddina (870 BC). This relief was recovered from the temple of Shamash in Sippar.[51] Nabuapaliddina's relief furnishes insights on the setting up of a throne that can be correlated to the setting up of thrones in Dan 7.

Some interpreters have remarked that the court scene in Dan 7 must be understood through some parallels in the Ugaritic literature[52] or the Babylonian Marduk mythology.[53] Some important parallels may be drawn between the biblical text and the Ugaritic myth of struggles between Baal and Yamm (Sea).[54] Even so, Collins acknowledged that there is no exact prototype anywhere for Dan 7.[55]

The Ugaritic or Canaanite myth and Dan 7 share some remote resemblances and incidental correspondences which are obviously outweighed by the explicit significant differences. On the whole, the ancient literary texts on myths do not provide adequate evidence for inspiring Daniel's court setting.

7:9, 13, 22. Ancient of Days. The term "Ancient of Days" (Dan 7:9) is one of the epithets for Daniel's God. It can be equated to: "Eternal Father" (Isa 9:6); "Everlasting God" (Gen 21:33; Ps 90:2); "God afore time," or "God of Old" (Deut 33:27; Hab 1:12); and "Everlasting King" (Jer 10:10). At Ugarit, El is described as "king father of years," or "father of years."[56]

The Ancient of Days took His seat and the court session began. The text described His appearance in human characteristics. He sat down, He had a robe, and His hair was white as snow. Whenever the Hebrew Bible has

---

49. For cylinder-seal impressions which display either kings or gods sitting on thrones, see Frankfort, *Art and Architecture*, 45, 90.

50. Nam, *"Throne of God" Motif*, 59–118. Nam cites and discusses the extant literature about kings or deities ascending to the thrones in the ancient Near East.

51. Mettinger, "YHWH SABAOTH," in Ishda, *Studies*, 119–21.

52. Emerton, "Origin," 225–42; and Morgenstern, "Son of Man,'" 65–77.

53. Morgenstern, "'Son of Man,'" 65–77; Nickelsburg, "Son of Man" (*ABD*, 6:137–41); and Dalley, *Myths from Mesopotamia* (1989).

54. *ANET*, 129–142; Thomas, *Documents from Old Testament Times*, 128–33; Gibson, *Canaanite Myths and Legends*, 37–81; Arnold and Beyer, *Readings from the Ancient Near East*, 50–62; and *COS*, 1:241–74.

55. Collins, *Daniel*, 77.

56. Cross, "'ēl,'" *TDOT*, 1:245. Cf. "head of days" in 1 En. 46:1–2; 47:3; and 98:2.

portrayed God in a recognizable form, it has used human characteristics to describe Him (Exod 15:3; Ezek 1:26-28).

There are some parallels between Canaanite imagery and Dan 7. In ancient Canaanite myth, Baal, the cloud rider, is juxtaposed with the Son of Man in Dan 7, while the Ancient of Days is allegedly matched with the Canaanite god El. Both the Ancient of Days and El sit on their thrones and destroy their enemies. One of the striking differences is that Baal is not invested with kingship as is the biblical son of man (Dan 7:13, 14). Recovered images of Baal are many and different, but there has not been found an image of the Ancient of Days, the God of Daniel.

7:10. Books were opened. The Aramaic word translated "books" here, *siprin*, also means "writings," "scrolls," "documents," "letters," or "evidence." What are the books that were opened (Dan 7:10) on this judgment scene? It is worth noting that the other books mentioned by the author of Daniel include the Book of Truth (Dan 10:21) and the Book of Life (Dan 12:1). The record book (Ps 149:9; Isa 65:6), that is, "the Tables of fate," according to Mesopotamian religion,[57] is basically a register of human behavior and activities. In addition, there could also be the book of memorable works (Neh 13:14; Mal 3:16).

Daniel refers to the motif of divine books. This motif is also found in:

- The Hebrew Bible
    - Exod 32:32
    - Ps 56:8; 69:28; 87:6; 139:16; 149:9
    - Isa 65:6
    - Jer 17:1
    - Mal 3:16
- The New Testament
    - Luke 10:20
    - Rev 20:12
- The Apocryphal literature

Several other documents that share the idea of divine books include:

---

57. Nabu is the god of writing and is believed to write an individual's destiny on a tablet. Black and Green, *Gods, Demons and Symbols*, 133-34.

- Qumranic literature: Examples of divine documents that are mentioned at Qumran include 1QpHab 7:1; 1Q34 3:2, 7; 4QDibHam 3:12ff.; 4QDibHam 6:14; CD 3:3; 20:19; and possibly 1QM 12:2.
- Rabbinic literature: This includes also the Jewish pseudepigraphic writings and other collections of rabbinic interpretive traditions.[58]
- Egyptian religions: The Egyptian Book of the Dead is accorded divine authorship and is believed to be a product of Thoth, the god of writing. It is a collection of spells which serves as a guide to the deceased on the way to the judgment day and next world.[59]
- Babylonian religions: The epilogue to the laws of Hammurabi calls for anyone with a case to come to his statue and read what is inscribed on the stele as the norm for justice. The stele records that the words of the law were endorsed by the gods Marduk and Shamash.[60]

There is a selection of books at the judgment scene (Dan 7:10; Rev 20:12). What is written in the books stands as valid evidence for or against the individual concerned. The fate of the person is decided on what the record says. The concept of books at a judgment scene is most likely based on both the biblical and Mesopotamian traditions. The author of Daniel shows that he understood both the biblical and Mesopotamian judicial traditions. The vision of the judgment given in Dan 7, however, reinforces the recurrent motif of the chronological succession of the kingdoms. It affirms that the earthly kingdoms shall be destroyed and eventually replaced by a divine kingdom. Also, the judgment in Dan 7 brings the transition from the fourth beast kingdom, Rome, to the divine dominion (Dan 2:34, 35, 44, 45; 7:13, 14, 27; 12:1–4).

7:13. Son of man. The Ancient of Days took His throne, judged, and destroyed the last of the four beasts (Dan 7:9–11). Following this event, "the (one) like the son of man" was escorted with the clouds of heaven to the court scene for His kingship investiture (Dan 7:11–14). Who this individual was and the origin of the epithet "son of man" still preoccupies biblical scholars.

Richard N. Longenecker argued that Jesus was the son of man in Daniel.[61] W. Sibley Towner took the son of man and the saints of the Most High

---

58. Volz, *Jüdische Eschatologie von Daniel bis Akiba*, 266.

59. Brunner, *Altägyptische Religion*, 130–33, 150; and David, *Religion and Magic in Ancient Egypt*, 261–62.

60. *ANET*, 178, rev. xxv.

61. Longenecker, "Son of Man," 151–58; Schmidt, "'Son of Man,'" 22–28; and

to be representatives who would encourage others with the good news of God's victory over evil.⁶² The Old Greek text of Daniel does not render the expression "son of man" as being synonymous with "man." The expression is however taken as "an idiom of choice for conveying the specialized meaning of 'frail human' or 'vulnerable human.'"⁶³

A quick survey of the Hebrew Bible shows the two forms in use, *bēn ᵉnôš*, "son of man" (Ps 144:3), and *bēn ādām*, "son of man" (appears ninety-three times in Ezekiel and fourteen times elsewhere in the Hebrew Bible: Num 23:19; Job 16:21; 25:6; 35:8; Ps 8:4; 80:17; 146:3; Isa 51:12; 56:2; Jer 49:18, 33; 50:40; 51:43; Dan 8:17).

These Hebraic occurrences have been suggested as the antecedents to the Aramaic *kᵉ bar ᵉnāš*, "like son of man," in Daniel and also the messianic figure in the New Testament.⁶⁴ The expression "a likeness in appearance like a man" (Ezek 1:26) corresponds linguistically to "like a son of man" (Dan 7:13).

The son of man in Dan 7:13 was accompanied by clouds when He appeared. See Acts 1:9-11; 1 Thess 4:16, 17; and Rev 14:14. This may indicate that He was a divine figure. He was also associated with the apocalyptic messianic figure. Similar apocalyptic views are echoed in 1 En. 46:1-8 where the son of man is depicted as "the elect one," "the righteous one," and "the anointed one." The concept of the son of man can be comprehended better in light of some archaeological discoveries from the ancient Near East.

The earliest extrabiblical attestation of "son of man" is on the Aramaic Sefire Stele III, line 16, which is dated before 740 BC.⁶⁵ Other Aramaic leather and papyrus documents exist, including those from Elephantine and Sakkara, as well as the Nabataean, Palmyrenian, and Hatrian. In these documents the indefinite *'nš* is attested to mean both "man" collectively and also "a man," or "somebody" in the singular⁶⁶ (cf. Dan 5:5; 7:4; 6:7, 12). Also *'nš* can be used as a pronoun as in Dan 3:10; 5:7; 6:12.⁶⁷ Likewise, the determinative *ᵉnāšā* appears both in a general sense in Dan 2:43; 4:16; 7:8

Wenham, "Kingdom of God and Daniel," 132-34.

62. Towner, "Were the English Puritans," 46-63.

63. Lemcio, "'Son of Man,'" 44.

64. Gelston, "Sidelight on the 'Son of Man,'" 189-96; and Patterson, "Key Role of Daniel 7," 260.

65. Donner and Röllig, *Kanaanäische und aramäische Inschriften*, 1:44-45, Inscription 224.16.

66. Sjöberg, "בן אדם und בר אנש," 57-65, 91-107; Kraeling, *Brooklyn Museum Aramaic Papyri*, 226-227; see Papyrus 8, line 5, אנש אחרן "somebody else"; and line 8, לא אנש "nobody"; and Colpe, "ὁ υἱὸς τοῦ ἀνθρώπου" (*TDNT*, 8:402).

67. Colpe, "ὁ υἱὸς τοῦ ἀνθρώπου" (*TDNT*, 8:402).

and also in a collective sense in Dan 4:17, 25, 32, 33; 5:21; and Ezra 4:11. As a definite plural *bᵉnēy-ᵉnāšā*, "the sons of men," occurs twice in Dan 2:38 and Dan 5:21.

In light of this, the Aramaic expression *kᵉbarᵉnāš* or its equivalent is clearly descriptive and implies "one like a son of man," or better still, "like one in human form."[68] The description *kᵉbarᵉnāš* therefore can be linguistically equated to "a likeness in appearance like a man" (Ezek 1:26). It may also be associated with the fourth person in the furnace of fire whom Nebuchadnezzar recognized as "like the son of gods (Dan 3:25).

In the Qumranic literature the appellation *bar ᵉnôš* (1QapGen 21:13) was used in an indefinite sense to mean either "no man," "someone," or "no one."[69] The variant *br 'nš* (11 QtgJob 26:2–3), which was a translation of *bēn 'ādām* (Job 35:8), was used in a generic sense to mean "a human being."[70] The phrase *bn 'dm* or *bn h'dm* in the singular was collectively used for "human race" or "mankind" (1QH 4:30 or 1QS 11:20 [4Q184 4:4]). Its plural equivalent *bny 'dm* carried a similar meaning (1QS 11:6, 15; 1QH 2:24; 4:32; 4Q181 1:1; 11QPsᵃ 24:15; etc.), just as does *bny 'yš* (1QS 3:13; 4:15, 20, 26; 1QM 11:14; 4Q184 1:17).[71] Another occurrence of *br 'nš* is attested in 11QtgJob 9:9, where it also means "a human being."

The appearance of the phrase "son of man" in Qumranic writings serves to confirm that the expression was still in common use in the first century BC or AD in Palestine.[72] The figure of the son of man in Dan 7:13, as well as in the apocryphal writings 1 En. 37–41 and 4 Ezra 13, was assumed to be a hypostatization of *kᵉbôd Yahweh*, "the glory of Yahweh," appearing in "a likeness in appearance like a man" in Ezek 1:26–28; 8:2–4.[73] This idea affiliated the son of man with the divine or messianic being. While such an association cannot be completely denied, it is also important to consider that the expression *bēn 'ādām*, which occurs some ninety-three times in Ezekiel, always referred to Ezekiel himself in the same way it refers to Daniel in Dan 8:17. It is clear then that the one like the son of man who was escorted in the clouds to the Ancient of Days is unquestionably a divine being and not Daniel. Still, the one like the son of man who was invested with kingship

---

68. See "Like the Son of Man" (*SDABC*, 4:829).

69. 1QapGen 21:13 is a paraphrase of Gen 13:16 which used *' yš* in an if-clause, contrary to the fact to mean "no one" literally; see Fitzmyer, *Wandering Aramean,* 148.

70. Fitzmyer, *Wandering Aramean*, 148.

71. Haag, "ben 'ādhām" (*TDOT*, 2:161).

72. Fitzmyer, *Wandering Aramean*, 148.

73. Kim, "'Son of Man,'" 18. See also Ferch, *Son of Man in Daniel Seven*, 88–94.

is to be distinguished from the angelic being Gabriel (Dan 8:15; 9:21; 10:18; 12:6–7), who is also described in similar language.

Ziony Zevit associated the son of man in Dan 7:13 with the angel Gabriel.[74] His proposal, that Gabriel was the same as the son of man, failed to account for the identity of the individual who ordered Gabriel to explain the vision to Daniel (Dan 8:16).

Alternatively, the figure of the "son of man" was thought to have originated from the wisdom literature. This included but was not limited to Prov 1–9, the apocryphal Sirach, Wisdom of Solomon, and 1 Bar. 3:9–4:4.[75] Such an affiliation may have served to stimulate an interest in a human messianic figure. One such candidate was Judas Maccabees.[76] Several theories on the origin and identity of the "son of man" have attempted to place the background of Dan 7 in the ancient Near Eastern mythological setting.

The range of the sources and parallels considered is not only complex but covers a wide spectrum. It includes some similarities with certain Babylonian, Egyptian, Iranian, Hellenistic, gnostic, Canaanite, biblical, and apocryphal literature.[77] The comparative method used in the analysis of Dan 7 and related ancient literature has attempted to consider the genre, semantic patterns, styles, and relationships between words and phrases.[78] However, it can be noted that "Son of Man" was a common term which appeared in different contexts where it could have many special meanings.

The Babylonian story of Adapa[79] is associated with Dan 7 in that Adapa was entitled *zēr amelūti*, "the seed (shoot) of mankind" or "human offspring."[80] While Adapa's designation corresponds to "the Son of Man," in Dan 7, the context and functions of both texts have significant differences.[81] Moreover, Adapa was not invested with judicial powers. His identity did not

---

74. Zevit, "Structure and Individual Elements," 385–96.

75. Ferch, *Son of Man in Daniel Seven*, 89–90.

76. Colpe, "ὁ υἱὸς τοῦ ἀνθρώπου" (*TDNT*, 8:423).

77. The literature is sizeable on the discussion of the various proposals and the arguments for or against the association of the motif of the son of man with different ancient traditions. It is not necessary to repeat all the arguments here, but see Colpe, "ὁ υἱὸς τοῦ ἀνθρώπου" (*TDNT*, 8:400–77); Manson, "Son of Man in Daniel," 171–93; Ferch, *Son of Man in Daniel Seven*, 40–107; Day, *God's Conflict*, 151–77; and Caragounis, *Son of Man*, 35–60.

78. Kvanvig, *Roots of Apocalyptic*, 443.

79. The story of Adapa is extant in four fragments known as A, B, C and D. Of these B came from the el-Amarna archives and is dated fourteenth century BC while the rest were retrieved from Ashurbanipal's library. See Clay, *Neo-Babylonian Letters from Erech*, 3:40–41, plates iv and vi; and *ANET*, 101–3.

80. Langdon, *Sumerian Epic of Paradise*, 47; and *ANET*, 102, text D, line 12.

81. Ferch, *Son of Man in Daniel Seven*, 44.

involve the kind of end-time theological implications suggested in what the Son of Man did.[82]

Some scholars assume that the Babylonian chaos myths influenced the composition of Dan 7. Even if this were true, the "agreement of individual motifs does not prove the identity of the persons to whom they are attached."[83] Comparative analysis of the term "Son of Man" in Daniel and other archaeological literary works remains inconclusive in the scholarly discussions. The author of Daniel may well have been aware of the son-of-man imagery in the ancient literature, but he seems to have used the expression consistently with its biblical prototypes. The Son of Man in Daniel is therefore depicted as a divine being with apparent messianic characteristics.

7:14. Peoples, nations, and languages. See 3:4, 7, 29. **Peoples, nations, and languages.** The "one like Son of Man" is inaugurated to have sovereign power over all humans everywhere. See Rev 4 and 5.

7:15. Visions of my head troubled me. In the last six chapters of the book of Daniel the tables are turned. Daniel had been instrumental in interpreting Nebuchadnezzar's dreams and Belshazzar's enigmatic inscription. However, he was so stunned by his own dreams or visions that he looked for help with the interpretation (Dan 7:15, 16). It is interesting to note the tension presented between Daniel the statesman and Daniel the private man. The statesman is full of wisdom and knowledge. He understands other people's visions and dreams (Dan 1–6). The same Daniel struggles to understand his own personal dreams and visions (Dan 7–12).

7:22. Judgment. The judgment or court scene in Dan 7 follows the horrifying activities of the little horn (Dan 7:8, 11, 20–26). The Ancient of Days appears in the court scene for judicial intervention on behalf of the saints of the Most High (Dan 7:22). "The thrones" (or "superthrone"[84]) were cast, or set, and occupied (Dan 7:9). Then the court proceedings led to "the judgment," "verdict," or "justice" which "was (favorably) given to the saints of the Most High" (Dan 7:22).

In Israel, God presents himself as the giver and guardian of "justice" or "legal decision" (Ezek 45:9). He defends His people against threats from without. It is acknowledged that the victories of Israel are called "the righteous acts of God" and they are thus an outworking of His judicial decisions[85]

---

82. Colpe, "ὁ υἱὸς τοῦ ἀνθρώπου" (*TDNT*, 8:409).
83. Colpe, "ὁ υἱὸς τοῦ ἀνθρώπου" (*TDNT*, 8:409).
84. Doukhan, *Secrets of Daniel*, 113.
85. Herntrich, "OT Term משפט" (*TDNT*, 3:925).

in favor of His people. This can best be understood from the perspective of the old Semitic tribal belief which views God as the judge with dual responsibilities. He is seen as both legislator and legal representative (Isa 51:4; Jam. 4:12). He effects social justice in the tribe and also intervenes for it in times of war. See Isa 33:22; 35:4; and Acts 10:42.

The ancient Near East is quite familiar with judgment scenes. The root *dîn* appears in all Semitic languages denoting the verbal meaning "to judge."[86] It is interesting to note that the Qumran texts present *dîn* in parallelism with *mšpt*, "judgment," "justice" (1QH 9:9).[87] An overview of the Mesopotamian contest literature reveals that two disputants could come before a judge to have their issue settled.[88] At Ugarit, Dānī'ilu judged the widow's case and made decisions regarding the orphan.[89] In Mesopotamia there are times when a judgment scene occurs before a deity who renders a decision.[90] The judgment given in Dan 7 carries the motif of reward and punishment, which are awarded by the deity to the deserving parties.

7:25. Law. See **2:9. Law.** and **6:5, 8, 15. Law of Daniel's God.** To intend to change times set by God and the law of God is to attempt an impossibility. What God established with His own divine authority cannot be tempered with by any religious or political power.

7:25. For a time and times and half a time. This parallels Dan 12:7 and also Rev 11:2, 3; 12:14; 13:5. In Dan 4:16, 23, 25, 32, "seven times" stand for seven literal years. "Times" in Dan 7:25 is plural of "duality" in Aramaic, therefore it implies doubling, that is, two times. Therefore, the total time implied in Dan 7:25 as three and a half times points to three and a half years. The lunar calendar which was followed by both Jewish and Babylonian years has 360 days. The three and a half years total to 1260 days which should be considered in prophecy as literal years (Num 14:34; Ezek 4:6). The time frame of 1260 years extended from AD 538 to 1798 when the Roman church persecuted God's faithful people. Jesus had also announced that the gentiles would trample Jerusalem until the times of the gentiles are fulfilled (Luke 21:24).

7:26. Until the end. Daniel 7:26 seems to indicate that the little horn's power to cut off and destroy shall be taken away *'ăd-sôpā'*, "until the end." This

---

86. Hamp, "דין *dîn*" (*TDOT*, 3:187).
87. Hamp, "דין *dîn*" (*TDOT*, 3:189).
88. Denning-Bolle, "Wisdom and Dialogue," 229–230.
89. *COS*, 1:346.
90. Denning-Bolle, "Wisdom and Dialogue in the Ancient Near East," 230.

means that the little horn would continue to rule until the end, but without its former power and prestige. The word *sôp* is a late synonym for *'et qeṣ*, "time of the end." Both words mean "the end," usually of time.[91]

7:28. Alarmed. See 8:27; 10:8. It seems going through dreams and visions for Daniel was quite a traumatic experience. Daniel reported that he was left puzzled, faint, sick, and frail on several occasions when he had his dreams and visions. A similar situation is reported on an Aramaic ostracon from Elephantine dated 400–300 BC. A man was detained from his home and he wrote his wife to give her some interim instructions. In this letter the man begins by relating his frightening dream: "Now, indeed, I beheld a dream, and from that time on, I was exceedingly feverish. Then a vision appeared; its words: 'Peace!'"[92] Daniel evinces overwhelming characteristics of divine and human encounter in his dream/vision narratives.

---

91. BDB, 693, 893.
92. COS, 3:218.

Chapter 8

VISION IN TIME AND LOCATION

More on Daniel's complex visions and his apparent struggle for understanding what was going on is displayed here. Several ancient locations are mentioned showing that the writer was well acquainted with his geography. Extant evidence helps clarify the message that the central theme is the sequence of the historical kingdoms.

8:1. Third year of Belshazzar. 547 BC; see **5:1. Belshazzar, identity**, and **7:1. First year of Belshazzar.** While Nabonidus, his father, was away for ten years, Belshazzar was in charge of running the affairs of Babylon. Belshazzar was on the throne from 550 BC to 539 BC when Babylon fell to the Medes and Persians.

8:1. Vision. In 547 BC Daniel had a vision while he was probably in Susa by the Ulai river. *Chazon*, "vision," is an Aramaic loanword borrowed into Hebrew. It denotes a visual experience. The verb form of this word appears twice on a Kilamuwa inscription from Phoenicia. In fact, in the Semitic languages of the ancient Near East, there are many extant inscriptions that relate dreams and visions of individuals who claim to have had interaction with different deities. Vision is revelation by a divine being. It is that supernatural manifestation of God communicating His message to an individual (Dan 5:5). In the book of Daniel, it is mainly the author who had the visions. Daniel resembled the characteristics of other biblical individuals when he received visions.

VISION IN TIME AND LOCATION

A distinction must be made between a dream and a vision. A vision is more dramatic and its effects on the person involved may be quite traumatic. The person may be physically overwhelmed, puzzled, frightened, sick, or can faint so as to be without any strength left (Dan 8:17, 27; 10:16). A vision can be physical or metaphorical. The vision that is physical can be seen and experienced personally as opposed to something that is only perceived in the mind. A person can see objects, angels, or God (Dan 7:9) in a vision. Seeing the vision and hearing the word are both from God. It is God's prerogative to choose the person who is to receive the vision (Amos 3:7). God continues to dispense dreams and visions to the very end of time (Joel 2:28). Ezekiel 7:26 reports of people seeking for a vision from a prophet or seer through whom God communicates. Some self-proclaimed prophets could also claim to have visions from God but the Bible condemns them (Jer 14:14; 23:16). Usually visions are seen at night, but as we see in Daniel, they can happen anytime and anywhere (Dan 2:19; 10:4–7).

Qumran documents show a blurring distinction between a dream and a vision. In fact, 4QAmram fragment 1:10 calls Amram's vision a dream vision. 1QapGen 19:14 indicates that Abram had a dream revelation, but in 1QapGen 22:27, it says that Abram received a vision and not a dream. Also, the Teacher of Righteousness receives revelation from God but did not claim to be a prophet. The visions of Daniel predicted with astounding precision the political developments from his contemporary world to the end of time. The author himself struggled to understand his visions but received assistance from divine beings.

8:2. Shushan/Susa. Whether or not Daniel was physically in the king's palace at Shushan/Susa, is difficult for scholars to determine. It is most probable that a high-ranking official like Daniel had occasions to be in Susa in person. Susa (Akkadian $^{kur}Šū$-$šá$-$an/Šu$-$šu$-un, Hebrew Šušan) was a city in the ancient province of Elam (Dan 8:2). Susa (modern *Shush*) is located to the southwest of the city of Dizful at the edge of the Khuzistan flood plain in southwestern Iran. Susa was built on the 'Ulai or Eulæus River[1] (Dan 8:2). The Ulai River/Canal flowed past the northern part of ancient Susa, the capital of Elam, which later became the winter capital for the Persians.

According to a Babylonian Chronicle, Nabopolassar (626–605 BC) sent back to Susa the Elamite gods that were once looted by Ashurbanipal, king of Assyria, in 646 BC.[2] Some fragmented texts from Susa indicate that

---

1. Sayce, "Elam, Elamites," in Hastings, *Dictionary of the Bible*, 1:675.

2. Wiseman, *Chronicles of Chaldean Kings*, 51, Chronicle BM 25127, line 16; also see *ANET*, 303–5; and Grayson, *Assyrian and Babylonian Chronicles*, 17, 18, 87–90, Chronicle 2, lines 16–17.

Susa was under the Babylonian jurisdiction during the times of Nebuchadnezzar II (605–562 BC), Amel-Marduk (561–560 BC), and Nergal-shar-uṣur (560–556 BC).³ This, however, is difficult to validate considering that this information comes only from the imperial Babylonian administration. For the Persian administration, Susa served as the principal royal residence and had extraordinary palaces.

Daniel stated that his vision of the ram and the goat (Dan 8:2) was in Belshazzar's third year (547 BC). He indicated that he saw himself at the citadel of Susa in the province of Elam. Josephus, who was probably following the biblical text, related this incident in these words:

> [Daniel] wrote and left behind him what made manifest the accuracy and undeniable veracity of his predictions; for he saith, that when he was in Susa, the metropolis of Persia, and went out into the field with his companions, there was, on the sudden, a motion and concussion of the earth, and that he was left alone by himself, his friends flying away from him, and that he was disturbed, and fell on his face, and on his two hands, and that a certain person touched him, and, at the same time, bade him rise, and see what would befall his countrymen after many generations.⁴

By 550 BC the Elamites went under Persian rule. Darius I (522–486 BC) made Susa a vital ceremonial and cultural cosmopolitan city. Susa retained this status until the Persian Empire was destroyed by Alexander the Great.

Ran Zadok identified at least two Judaeans who appeared as witnesses in deed records from Susa, *Ia-hu-ú-šarra (LUGAL)-uṣur(URÚ)* s. of Šamaš-iddina (494/3 BC) and *Šá-ab-ba-ta-A+A* s. of *Nabû-šarra-bulliṭ*, Susa (493/2 BC).⁵ Montgomery questions whether Daniel was in Elam *in corpore*, "in the body," or *in spiritu*, "in the spirit."⁶ Unfortunately, archaeology cannot explicitly determine that. It is possible that Daniel might have visited Susa in person. It is equally possible that he was there only in vision. Daniel claims to have had the vision of the ram and the goat while he was in Elam (Dan 8:2).

---

3. Carter and Stolper, *Elam*, 54.
4. Josephus, *Antiquities of the Jews*, 10.11.7.269.
5. Zadok, *Earliest Diaspora Israelites and Judeans*, 46, 47.
6. Montgomery, *Book of Daniel*, 324–28, esp. 325. Montgomery argues that Daniel was in Elam in vision only; 325–26.

8:2. Citadel. The "castle," which could also be called "fortress" or "palace," appears in its varied forms in Dan 8:2. It is also mentioned in 1 Chr 29:1, 19; 2 Chr 17:12; 27:4; and Neh 2:8; 7:2. This can be compared with the phrase "the Fortress in Shushan" in Neh 1:1 and Esth 1:2, 5; 2:3, 5, 8; 3:15; 8:14, 15; 9:6, 11, 12, 14, 15, 18. The "fortress" is probably a loanword from the Assyrian *bîrtu*, "fortress."[7] The Persian word is *bâru* which is equivalent to Sanskrit *bura* or *bari*.[8] From ancient times, the citadel was a military stronghold, a heavily protected and impenetrable city of safety for the king and the people.

A Phoenician inscription dated the beginning of the seventh century BC found at Karatepe, the modern province of Adana, Turkey, indicates the accomplishments of Azatiwada, an agent of the king of the Danunians. This Azatiwada gives the reasons for building castles. He writes: "I built strong fortifications in all the far regions of the borders, in places where they had been evil men, gang leaders, of whom not one man had ever been a vassal to the house of Mopsos; but I, Azatiwada, placed them under my feet. And I built fortifications in those places so that they, the Danunians, might dwell in the ease of their hearts."[9]

As the capital city, Susa had the fortifications that could protect the people from the enemy. Usually, the enemy would lay a siege to the fortress until they could break through into the city. From the seventh century BC Susa continued its role as a cultural and ceremonial center but its strongholds served as refugee camps rather than political or military headquarters.

8:2. Elam. In the Bible "Elam" appears as a proper personal name (Gen 10:22; 1 Chr 1:17; 8:24; 26:3; Ezra 2:7, 31; 8:7; 10:2, 26; Neh 7:12, 34; 10:14; 12:42) as well as a geographical place (Isa 11:11; 21:2; 22:6; Jer 49:34–39; Ezek 32:24). Chedorlaomer, king of Elam, once dominated the valley of Sodom and Gomorrah for years until his vassal kings there rebelled against him (Gen 14).

Elam stretched east of Mesopotamia from the Caspian Sea to the Persian Gulf. An eighth-century BC Armenian text reads: "A land of Asia is that of the Elymaeans, that is Khuzastan, which the Greeks call Šošanik,

---

7. BDB, 108.

8. BDB, 108. Sanskrit is an Indo-European language which was developed around the end of the fourth century BC. Agnes and Guralnik, *Webster's New World College Dictionary*, s.v. "Sanskrit." There is also a suggestion that Sanskrit was used from 1200 BC onwards.

9. *COS*, 2:149.

after the city Šošan."¹⁰ Strabo reports that Susis (Susa) was part of Babylonia but the Elamites were in conflict with the Susians and the Uxii.¹¹

8:2–3, 6, 16. Ulai River. An excellent example of the value of archaeological discoveries in resolving scholarly debate is seen in the discussion generated by the different translations of Dan 8:2. Some scholars have objected to calling the Ulai a river or canal in Daniel. The ancient Greek versions of the Old Testament, such as Aquila, Symmachus, Theodotion (which omits Ulai), and the LXX, are not consistent in their translation of the Ulai river or stream of Dan 8:2. The text states that Daniel located himself "by the Ulai River." Different translations render Ulai as a "river," "stream," "conduit," "water course," or "canal."¹² This is the location where Daniel received the vision of the ram and the goat (Dan 8: 2, 3, 6, 16). The phrase "by the Ulai River" appears only in Dan 8:2.¹³

The debate centers on the legitimacy and linguistic history of the word ʾubal, "canal" or "river" (Dan 8:2, 3, 6). ʾUbal shares the same consonants with ʾabul, "city-gate," which may have come from the Akkadian loanword ʾabullu, "city-gate."¹⁴ The temptation is great to imply that Daniel had his vision by the gate of Ulai (Dan 8:2). Some scholars prefer to take ʾulai (Dan 8:2) as the adverb "perhaps,"¹⁵ which would serve to convey the idea of hope. This reading would allow the text to express only a wish or hope. The suggested reading for the complete phrase, ʿal ʾubal ʾulai, would then become "by the city-gate perhaps." Although it may be possible to translate the text in this way, it violates not only the context but the literary integrity of the text as well.

Archaeology has unearthed several ancient Assyrian and Babylonian texts which mention ʾulai as a river. Therefore, it is reasonable to conclude that Daniel stood in person by the river or canal Ulai.

For example, a stele reported that Shutruk-Nahhunte, king of Elam (ca. 1165 BC), crossed the Ulai River into Mesopotamia and captured seven hundred towns. He then forced the citizens to pay him tribute.¹⁶

---

10. Potts, *Archaeology of Elam*, 7, quoted in Marquart, *Ērānšahr nach der Geographie*, 137.

11. Strabo, *Geography of Strabo*, 7:15.3.12.

12. Holladay, *Concise Hebrew and Aramaic Lexicon*, 2.

13. אובל=יובל (Jer 17:8); BDB, 385; and Wilson, *Old Testament Word Studies*, 359. In Isa 30:25 and 44:4, *yibal* seems to share the same meaning with ʾubal.

14. Waterman, "Note on Daniel 8:2," 320; Ginsberg, *Studies in Daniel*, 57; and Arnold, "Ulai" (*ABD*, 6:721).

15. Lacocque, *Book of Daniel*, 157.

16. Roaf, *Cultural Atlas*, 148.

Another inscription on a *kudurru*, "a boundary stone," granted Nebuchadnezzar I (1124–1103 BC) some landrights. This inscription also recorded the battle Nebuchadnezzar I had with the Elamites at the bank of the Ulai River.[17]

The Bull Inscription from the Palace at Nineveh recorded the battle of Sennacherib, king of Assyria (704–681 BC), against some Chaldeans ʳÚ-la-a na-a-ru šá kib-ruša ṭabu, "by the Ulai, a river whose bank was good, the battle line was drawn up."[18]

In 653 BC the Assyrians killed Teuman (Tepti-Humban-Inshushinak, an Elamite) in a battle on the banks of the Ulai River. They brought back his head to their king, Ashurbanipal, who displayed it in Arbil and Nineveh.[19] Ashurbanipal claimed to have beheaded Teuman and numberless other warriors and "made their blood flow down the river Euläus (Ulai), and dyed its water like wool."[20] The discovery of the ancient Assyrian writings has contributed greatly to our understanding of the ancient Near East and the book of Daniel as well.

In the Akkadian sources which use the ancient cuneiform writing system, the Ulai is known as *u-la-a*.[21] In various Greek texts it is called Εὔλαιος, "Ulai," a river or canal of Elam.[22] The Ulai River ran through the northern part of ancient Susa, the capital of Elam, and is said to have been an irrigation canal branching off Choaspes River (modern Kerkha) towards the Coprates River (modern Abdizful).[23] Considering this, the ancient textual evidence supports the existence of a river or canal known as Ulai. Therefore, Daniel's reference to such a place should not be dismissed out of hand.

8:3. Ram. There was nothing unusual with this ram except that one horn was higher than the other. The writer continues with his theme of successive earthly kingdoms to correspond with Dan 2 and Dan 7. (See table 4.) To make things really easy, the author reveals that the ram symbolically represented the kingdom of Media and Persia (Dan 8:20). The two horns are the two kings. In 550 BC Cyrus, king of Persia, defeated Media and the two kingdoms became confederates. In the chronology of Daniel, the Medes

---

17. King, *Babylonian Boundary-Stones*, 32, col. 1, lines 18–23, 28, quoted in Saggs, *Babylonians*, 125–27, 178.

18. Luckenbill, *Annals of Sennacherib*, 75, lines 87–88.

19. Roaf, *Cultural Atlas*, 191.

20. Harper, *Assyrian and Babylonian Literature*, 106.

21. Luckenbill, *Annals of Sennacherib*, 75, line 87; Waterman, "Note on Daniel 8:2," 319–20; and Parpola, *Neo-Assyrian Toponyms*, 366.

22. BDB, 19; Pliny, *Natural History*, 6:27; and Layard, *Discoveries in the Ruins*, 146.

23. Waterman, "Note on Daniel 8:2," 319–20; and Arnold, "Ulai," 6:721.

and the Persians always appear as one power. The pushing by the ram depicts the Medo-Persian expansion to dominate a larger territory than any of the kingdoms preceding it. In later literature, when the signs of zodiac were associated with countries, the ram was also associated with Persia.[24]

8:3, 5, 8, 9, 21. Horns. The Old Testament uses *qeren*, "horn," to denote animal horn(s). Horns are the focus of the animal's power. Animals use their horns as effective weapons. Horns (*shofar*, sg.) were used as signaling or musical instruments (Josh 6:5; Dan 3:5, 7, 10, 15) and flasks (1 Sam 16:1; 1 Kgs 1:39). Our contemporary idea that some animal horns, like those of a rhino, have some magical and medicinal value is foreign to the Old Testament practice. In Semitic languages, the horn is also used metaphorically to denote strength, kingship, courage, pride, power, victory, fertility, abundance, and kingly majesty. While animal teeth and claws are understood as instruments for violence and force, the horn symbolizes physical might and power. The DSS also use the horn as a symbolical expression to imply power and strength. God will cut off the horn of His enemies (1QH 7:22). Archaeological evidence shows that horns were put on the four corners of altars to symbolize the presence and power of God. The blood that atoned for the sins was smeared on the horns. At Qumran, 11QT 16:2, 16; 23:12 also mentions the smearing of blood on the horns of the altar. Some Mesopotamian gods are horned, and good examples include the sun god Shamash and moon god Sin.

All the kingdoms that succeeded Neo-Babylonia are represented by animals that have horns which depict their lust for power. Daniel describes several animals with horns (Dan 7:7; 8:3, 5). In Dan 8:20, 21, the two horns of the ram represent the kings of Media and Persia. Usually, goats have two horns. The goat of Dan 8:5 had one conspicuous horn to depict a political reality. Alexander was a sole Greek king and when he died, his kingdom fragmented into four divisions, each administered by one of his generals. What must be seriously considered in Daniel's chronology is the sequence of the world empires as represented by the animals in Dan 7 and Dan 8. When the Greek Empire collapsed, it was followed by the Roman Empire. Daniel's vision details a bizarre animal with ten horns, and the eleventh horn that appears later to uproot three of the original horns (Dan 7:7). The ten horns represent the ten kings in the Roman Empire. The eleventh horn, or "a little one," belongs to the fourth animal which represents Rome, the fourth kingdom since the fall of Neo-Babylonia in 539 BC.

---

24. Walton et al., *IVP Bible Background Commentary*, 742.

When God gave Jehoiakim, king of Judah, to Nebuchadnezzar (Dan 1:2), God removed His protection from His people and "cut off in fierce anger every horn of Israel" (Lam 2:3) and threw down "in His wrath the strongholds of the daughter of Judah" (Lam 2:2). God cuts off the horn of the wicked. Psalm 75:5 discourages lifting up the horn against God. In the last half of the book of Daniel animals represented nations and horns the rulers of those nations (Dan 7:7—8:21).

8:4. Pushing west, north and south. Daniel saw a ram which had two horns, one higher than the other. The ram was charging toward the west, north, and south, implying that it was coming from the east. This, according to Papyrus 967 and 4QDan^a, could simply mean that the empire represented by the ram was "butting" in all directions.[25] This suggests waging war. Iconography from the ancient Near East provides a wide variety of caps, helmets, or crowns that have horns attached, and these were worn by deities.[26] The horns symbolized the strength of a goring ox which also implied victory (1 Kgs 22:11). The goring of an animal was common. In fact, the Old Testament has some laws concerning goring animals (Exod 21:28, 29, 31, 32, 36).

While Daniel was watching the ram, a he-goat with one horn between its eyes sprang suddenly from the west, furiously raging against the ram. Gabriel came and pointed out to Daniel that the ram represented the kingdom of Medo-Persia (Dan 8:20), and the he-goat represented Greece (v. 21). History's fulfillment of this prophetic clash between the ram and the goat was the battle at Gaugamela (331–330 BC) where Darius III (336–330 BC) was defeated by Alexander the Great (330–323 BC).

---

25. Collins, *Daniel*, 330.
26. *NIDOTTE*, 3:19.

GREEK AND PERSIAN BATTLE
The Nered Monument, ca. 390 BC, is a marble panel depicting a battle scene with Greeks and Persians. (Credit: Zev Radovan)

8:5. Male goat. In the ancient Near East goats were widespread and valuable. Goats appear in Mesopotamian art. Besides this, many figurines, plaques, clay models, and glyptic objects show goats being used for portraying different motifs.[27] In Persia the goat was a symbol for royalty, although in later literature the ram was the astral sign of Persia. The goat is also identified as symbolically representing the kingdom of Greece (Dan 8:21). See table 4.

A goat is less discriminatory in the vegetation it eats and is characteristically stronger and more destructive than sheep. In Dan 8:5, the male goat had a notable single horn that protruded from between its eyes. The conspicuous horn was its first king, Alexander the Great (Dan 8:21). The goat's horn that broke into four pieces echoes Dan 7:6 which points to the fall of the Greek Empire into the hands of four generals Lysimachus, Cassander, Seleucus, and Ptolemy who contested for the kingdom after Alexander's untimely death. The Greek kingdom was the third in Daniel's chronology.

8:5. Whole earth. "The whole earth" implies the distance covered by Alexander the Great as he advanced to the east where he encountered the Medes and the Persians.

8:8. Four winds of heaven. See **7:2. Four winds of heaven.** "The four winds of heaven" refer to the four cardinal directions where the kingdom of Alexander the Great spread.

8:9. Out of one of them. The implication here is that the little horn came out of one of the four winds of heaven, that is, out of one of the four cardinal directions. Daniel 8 presents the picture of the little horn differently from

27. Vancil, "Goat, Goatherd" (*ABD*, 2:1041).

the presentation in chapter 7. The writer talks about the Ram (Dan 8:2–4), which stands for Medo-Persia (Dan 8:20), and the Male Goat (Dan 8:5–10), which is Greece (Dan 8:21, 22). Several scholars make a compelling argument that the goat's one horn represents Alexander the Great. The breaking of the horn into four represents, of course, Alexander the Great's four successors. The four horns were "toward the four winds of heaven" (Dan 8:8). The little horn came "from one of them" (Dan 8:9), that is, from one of the four winds.

The syntactic difficulty in Dan 8:8–9 is caused by the attempt to determine whether the little horn came from one of the four horns of the Greek kingdom or from one of the four winds of heaven. To what does Dan 8:9 refer when it says "from them" (particle preposition suffix third-person masculine plural)? Does it refer to the four horns or the four winds?

Interestingly, the syntactic ambiguity is resolved by recognizing the link between the last part of Dan 8:8, "toward the four winds of the heavens," and the beginning of v. 9, "and from one of them." Doukhan suggests that "through the use of the four winds Daniel alludes to the four beasts. In the mentioning that the horn comes from one of the winds, he is implying that it originates in one of the beasts. The prophet purposely makes no mention of the beasts in order to keep the attention of his readers solely on the ram and on the goat."[28] Doukhan's insightful remark here seems to support the idea of a single little horn in the entire book of Daniel.

The little horn is seen first in Dan 7:8. This same little horn appears in Dan 8:9. In chapter 7 there are "the four winds" which vigorously stirred the sea. The little horn came forth from one of the four beasts which came out from the sea. The four winds in chapter 7 appear in chapter 8, and "from/out of them" came forth the little horn. Even though the destructive and ruthless beast with ten horns, from whence comes the little horn, is omitted in chapter 8, the winds are the same ones in both chapters.

Hasel concluded that "the syntax is gender-matched, and identifies the origin of the 'little horn' as moving forth from one of the directions of the compass—from one of the four winds of heaven."[29] Martin Pröbstle, who presents a grammatical-syntactic analysis of Dan 8:9–14, comes to a similar conclusion. Pröbstle demonstrates that the syntactic arguments, along with the contextual, literary, and structural syntheses, show that the "arguments

---

28. Doukhan, *Secrets of Daniel*, 125. See also Gzella, *Cosmic Battle and Political Conflict*, 112–14.

29. Hasel, "'Little Horn,'" in Holbrook, *Symposium on Daniel*, 390.

for 'the four winds of heaven' as referent outweigh the arguments for the 'four (horns)' as referent."[30]

All of the characteristics and activities of the little horn in Dan 7, 8, and 11 refer to just one power. This power, according to the chronological sequence of the events in Daniel, comes after the Greek kingdom. William H. Shea further demonstrated "why Antiochus IV is not the Little Horn of Daniel 8"[31] by tracing various interpretive views on the subject. Observations indicate that those who refer to Antiochus IV Epiphanes as the little horn do so "not very judiciously."[32]

8:9. Beautiful (land). The land that God gave to Israel was described as beautiful or glorious (Jer 3:19; Ezek 20:6, 15; Zech 7:14; Dan 11:16, 41). This refers to Palestine, the land promised to the decedents of Abraham (Gen 12:1-9). Other biblical texts that name the land beautiful include Ps 48:1-2; 50:2; 106:24; and Lam 2:15. The geographical boundaries of Palestine outlined in Num 34:1-12 and Ezek 47:15-20 continued to be fluid through the centuries. Mesopotamia dominated over Palestine from the Neo-Assyrian times (730s BC) through the Neo-Babylonian times (605-539 BC) to the Persian times (539-331 BC). Then the kingdom of Greece dominated the area from 331 BC until they were conquered in 168 BC by the Roman Empire, the fourth and last kingdom according to Daniel's geopolitical outline. The Roman Empire integrated Palestine into its realm in 63 BC. However, the little horn came from the fourth kingdom, the Roman Empire (Dan 7:8), and caused some problems in the beautiful land (Dan 7:23-25; 8:9-12). These included the desecrating and destroying of the temple, and persecuting people who were committed to the God of Heaven.

8:10. Stars. See also **12:3. Like the stars forever and ever.** The biblical text use "stars" both literally (Gen 1:16; Deut 4:19; Ps 147:4) and figuratively (Gen 15:5; 22:17; 26:4; Exod 32:13; Num 24:17; Job 38:7; Rev 1:20; 2:1). The context of the passage dictates the meaning. The dragon (Rev 12:9) drew a third of the stars of heaven to the earth (Rev 12:3, 4). In Dan 8:10 the little horn cast down some of the host of heaven and the stars to the ground and trampled them. The little horn originates from the fourth beast which is the fourth kingdom in Daniel's chronology (Dan 7:7, 8). The fourth kingdom is the Roman Empire. Horns represent kings (Dan 8:20, 21). The little horn

---

30. Pröbstle, "Truth and Error," 1:126; see esp. pp. 90-133.

31. Shea, *Selected Studies on Prophetic Interpretation*, 31-66. See also Boutflower, *In and Around*, 2-5.

32. Newton, *Observations on the Prophecies of Daniel*, 166.

represents a Roman king who will be notable for persecuting stars (saints) of God (Dan 7:19–21). Roman emperors like Nero (AD 54–68), Vespasian (69–79), Titus (79–81), and Diocletian (284–305) outrageously murdered the faithful followers of God. The pope rose to unprecedented political and religious power from AD 538 to 1798, and during this time the Roman church became notable for its horrendous persecution of the saints of God. The author of Daniel is pointing out to a historical fact (Dan 8:24).

8:11, 13, 14. Sanctuary. God ordered the building of a place where He would dwell among the people (Exod 25:8). The first such construction done by Moses was portable and moved from place to place. The sanctuary allowed people to gather for worshiping and sacrificing under the administration of the priests. This tripartite structure housed the ark (innermost section), the lampstand, the table for bread, and an incense altar (middle section), and the laver and altar for sacrifices were in the outer section. Other equipment, vessels, utensils, and treasure were housed in the adjacent storage rooms. Many people who looted or robbed temples went for such objects (1 Kgs 14:25, 26; 2 Chr 12:9; Dan 1:1, 2).

Archaeological excavations show many temples in ancient Mesopotamia, Egypt, and Syria-Palestine. Kings were responsible for building temples for housing the gods, offerings, and collected war booty from other foreign temples. In about 953 BC Solomon completed building the House of God (1 Kgs 6) or House of Holiness/Sanctuary (2 Chr 36:17), commonly known as the First Temple in Jerusalem. This temple, sitting on a mountain (2 Chr 3:1), was in use until destroyed by Nebuchadnezzar in 586 BC. Zerubbabel (516 BC) in the postexilic era reconstructed this temple, and it is known as the Second Temple. It remained in continuous use until King Herod, beginning in 20 BC, renovated it and expanded it. In AD 70, the Romans under Titus demolished and burned down this temple (Dan 9:27; 11:31). Its remains have never been recovered with the exception of what is famously known as the Western/Wailing Wall. Of all the writings from Qumran, the Temple Scroll sheds light on the sanctuary, especially its holiness and purity. If anyone profaned the sanctuary, he or she would have "the iniquity of mortal guilty" (Temple Scroll 35:8–9). The sanctuary was a holy place and the center for the nation. To destroy it was to disable the nation in running religious and socioeconomic life.

8:11–14. Desolate sanctuary. See 9:17, 18, 26; and **11:31. Abomination that desolates.** Jerusalem and the temple were completely razed down and burnt by Nebuchadnezzar in 586 BC. No evidence has been recovered on the temple in Jerusalem. The temple vessels were carried off to Babylon

(Dan 1:2; 5:2, 3, 23). In keeping with the prayer of Solomon (1 Kgs 8:22–53), Dan 9:17-19 pleads with God to intervene and reestablish the sanctuary services in Jerusalem and so revive worship again.

Some temple inscriptions from Assyria relate of the anointing of a temple that was to be repaired by one of the future kings. Daniel understood that the temple would be rebuilt and restored but a wicked person would desolate the sanctuary again in the future. The destructive work on the temple and its services would be done by the rulers from the fourth kingdom as depicted by Daniel's chronology of world empires. See Dan 11:31, 36-39; 12:11.

In the *Verse Account of Nabonidus*, the priests of Marduk accused Nabonidus of making an abomination by placing the statue of the god Nanna in the temple of Marduk. As a result, this text indicates that Marduk invited Cyrus, king of Persia, to come and displace Nabonidus from the Babylonian throne in the sixth century BC.

An expression that has puzzled many is the last part of Dan 9:27. It reads: "And on a wing of abominations shall come one who makes desolation even until the decreed end shall be poured out on the one that desolates" (cf. Dan 8:13; 9:17; 11:31; 12:11).

The phrase "the abominations of desolation," "the abomination that desolates," or "the desolating abominations" has been considered a word play on Ba'al Shomem, "Lord of Heaven." This is the Syrian equivalent of the Greek Zeus Olympus.[33] The implication is that foreign sacrifices to strange gods will be made in the Jerusalem temple. Unfortunately, the conclusion is therefore drawn that this text was fulfilled when Antiochus IV Epiphanes (175-164 BC) persecuted the Jews and sacrificed swine and other unclean animals on the Jerusalem altar (1 Macc 1:20-61; 2 Macc 6:2). Antiochus Epiphanes IV also desecrated the temple but he was from the third kingdom (Greece) according to Daniel's chronology. The desolation of the sanctuary in Daniel is done by one of the kings from the fourth kingdom (Rome). By the time of Jesus, the desolation of the sanctuary was still anticipated (Matt 24:15) and was fulfilled when Titus destroyed the temple in AD 70.

8:13. One speaking to another. Daniel 8:13-14 seems to show the concept of a dream within a dream. While the vision of the ram and the goat was in progress, it was interrupted by a divine being. This interpreter was asking another divine being about the time framework for the disruption of the sanctuary services (Dan 8:13). A dream that is interpreted in a dream was considered as certain. The fact that the vision of the 2,300 evenings

---

33. Collins, *Daniel*, 357.

VISION IN TIME AND LOCATION

and mornings intercepted the dream of the ram and the goat may seem to indicate that it is definite.

8:13. How long? The question "How long?" is also attested in the Neo-Babylonian Prayer of Lamentation to Ishtar.[34] Lines 56–59 of the prayer read:

> How long, O my Lady, shall my adversaries be looking upon me,
> In lying and untruth shall they plan evil against me,
> Shall my pursuers and those who exalt over me rage against me?
> How long, O my Lady, shall the crippled and weak seek me out?

Further, lines 93–94 read:

> How long, O my Lady, wilt thou be angered so that thy face would be turned away?
> How long, O my Lady, wilt thou be infuriated so that thy spirit is enraged?
> Turn thy neck which thou hast set against me; set thy face [toward] good favor.

The person offering this prayer expresses affliction and frustration against the goddess Ishtar for nonresponse. The prayer is asking for the restoration of some forfeited prosperity so that people may praise the goddess for that. The supplicant here sought out for personal favor from the goddess. However, in Dan 8:13 the question "How long?" demands to know the time the sufferers are to endure the atrocities of the persecuting little horn power.

8:14. 2,300 days. The 2,300 days here are to be understood as 2,300 literal years, a day for a year in biblical prophecy principle (see Num 14:34; Ezek 4:6). This time frame is given in answer to the question "How long?" in Dan 8:13. A detailed explanation about this time is given by the angel Gabriel in Dan 9:20–27. Crucial is the beginning point of this prophetic time. As ancient history indicates, the 2,300 years begin in 457 BC when Artaxerxes I gave a decree to build the city of Jerusalem (Dan 9:25).

8:16. Gabriel. See 9:21. Angels have names. The Hebrew name "Gabriel" means "the man of God," "God is Superior," "God is my Warrior," or "God is Mighty."[35] This is the first mention of the name of an angel in the Bible. Gabriel preeminently specializes in dealing with apocalyptic mysteries (Dan 8:15–26; 9:21–27). He was sent to enlighten Daniel on his puzzling

---

34. *ANET*, 384–85, lines 59, 93, 94; cf. Dan 12:6. See Collins, *Daniel*, 335.
35. *TLOT*, 1:299.

dreams and visions. He also faced resistance on his Persian mission and had to be assisted (Dan 10:13). Later, Gabriel went to announce the birth of John (Luke 1:11–20) and of Jesus (Luke 1:19, 26), after fourteen generations of Jewish people who came back from Babylonian captivity (Matt 1:17). The War Scroll discovered from Qumran depicts Gabriel as one of the archangels who stand before the throne of God. The other angels named are Michael, Sariel, and Raphael. Some apocryphal literature mention Gabriel and also name other angels who are believed to be God's messengers.

8:17, 19. Time of the end. The sequence of the four kingdoms in Daniel would terminate at the end of time (Dan 12:4, 9, 13). At that time God would set up His kingdom, which would remain forever (Dan 2:44; 7:13–14, 18, 22, 27). J. J. Collins asserted that the last part of the book of Daniel is "dominated by the expectation of an 'end' to a degree that has no parallel in the Psalms or earlier Prophets."[36] Hammurabi intended his laws to last *a-na wa-ar-ki-a-at u-mi*, "to the end of time," which implied that his laws should be observed forever.[37]

In the Hebrew of the book of Daniel, *'et*, "time," appears sixteen times (Dan 8:17; 9:21, 25; 11:6, 13, 14, 24, 35, 40; 12:1 [4x]). Its Aramaic counterparts are *'iddān* (Dan 2:8, 9, 21; 3:5, 15; 4:16, 23, 25, 32; 7:12, 25) and *zᵉmān* (2:16, 21; 3:7, 8; 4:36; 6:10; 13; 7:12, 25). The temporal usage of *'et qeṣ*, "the time of the end," in the entire book of Daniel (Dan 8:17, 19; 11:40; 12:4, 9, 13) can be distinguished from other time periods or events specified by the writer (Dan 1:5, 15, 18; 4:29, 34; 7:28; 9:24, 26; 11:6, 27, 29, 35, 45; 12:6, 8). Also, "appointed time/s" or "fixed day/s" (Dan 8:19; 11:27, 29, 35; 12:7; cf. Hab 2:3) could refer to a fixed time, definite time, or event.

The Aramaic equivalent of the Hebrew *qeṣ* is *qeṣāṯ*, "end" or "part."[38] Nebuchadnezzar was walking in his palace "at the end of twelve months" (Dan 4:29). In Dan 4:34, "and at the end of days" refers to the "seven times" or specifically "seven years" of Nebuchadnezzar's exile from the throne. The Aramaic phrase *bᵉʾaḥᵃrit yômayyā*, "in the latter days" (Dan 2:28), is the equivalent of the Hebrew *bᵉʾaḥᵃrit hayyāmim*, "in the latter days" (Dan 10:14). Both of these phrases can be understood in light of their context.

The time of the end in Daniel should be viewed in light of the political developments he describes. The feet and toes of iron and clay in Nebuchadnezzar's image represent the divided kingdoms of the time of the end, which would be displaced by God's eternal kingdom (Dan 2:41–44).

36. Collins, "Meaning of 'The End,'" in Attridge et al., *Of Scribes and Scrolls*, 91.
37. Pfandl, *Time of the End*, 118.
38. Holladay, *Concise Hebrew and Aramaic Lexicon*, 420.

VISION IN TIME AND LOCATION

In the Qumran texts, the time of the end appears in numerous texts but the context often indicates the specific time frame meant. The 4QHalakhic Letter (4Q397), fragments 14-17, col. 1, line 6, mention the things that would happen *bᵉahᵃri[t] hayyāmim*, "at the en[d] of days."[39] The *pesher* on Habakkuk (1QpHab 7:1-2) states that "God told Habakkuk to write down the things that are going to come upon the last generation, but the fulfillment of the end time he did not make known to him." Also, 1QpHab 7:7-12 tells of the men of truth who would appear at the end time. In the Dead Sea Scrolls, "the end" occurs over one hundred times. Here it conveys the meaning that is found in the late sections of the Hebrew Bible: "'span of time, historical period,' not 'time' generally or 'beginning/opening'"[40] (cf. Dan 11:6, 13; CD 7:21; 20:23; 1QS 4:18; 1 QH 3:38; 6:29). Some scrolls show that "the end" was used to denote a particular historical time period. Good examples are the scroll comments on Dan 9:26 which state: "And its end (shall be) with a flood and until the end (shall be) war." See 1 QM 11:8; 1QS 4:25; CD 1:5 cf. 5:20; 1QH 5:11-12; cf. Ezek 4:4-5).[41] "The end" can denote the specific time either in the future or in the past.

In short, Daniel's "time of the end" concept is best understood in contrast to the ancient literary works cited in this discussion. The "time of the end" in the ancient literary sources generally refers to either a specified time frame or future time. The term "time of the end" in the book of Daniel, however, specifically refers to that eschatological period of time leading to the ultimate end. It speaks of the time when God will completely destroy the earthly kingdoms and establish his own.

8:20. Kings of Media and Persia. See **11:1-2. Median and Persian kings.** Several kings of Media and Persia were involved with the captives from Judah. Some of these kings were instrumental in issuing decrees to let the Jewish captives go back to their home country and build the temple and all necessary infrastructure there.

8:21. Greece. See **10:20. Prince of Greece**; and **Dan 11:3-19. Greek kings.** The interaction of "Javan" (Greece, cf. Gen 10:4) and the ancient Near East in antiquity is still an ongoing discussion among several scholars. There is ongoing debate as to when Greece came in contact with the ancient Near East, and also how it fits into the geographical and political landscape of that region. As regards the book of Daniel, the debate is more focused on the presence of some Greek instruments in Nebuchadnezzar's orchestra

---

39. Martinez and Tigchelaar, *Dead Sea Scrolls Study Edition*, 2:802-3.
40. Talmon, "קץ" (*TDOT*, 13:83).
41. Talmon, "קץ" (*TDOT*, 13:85).

in Babylon (Dan 3). There are also questions regarding the placement of Greece in the chronological succession of the historical kingdoms in Daniel (Dan 8:21; 10:20; 11:2). However, the interaction of Greece with ancient Mesopotamia is highlighted through several ancient discoveries.

Intriguing evidence shows that trade between Greece and the ancient Near East increased from the tenth century BC through the Persian period.[42] Greek pottery, inscriptions, personal names, and other merchandise dating from the tenth century BC onwards have been found in several sites in Egypt, Mesopotamia, Palestine, and Syria[43] (cf. Ezek 27:13, 19).

Some Greek mercenaries who were drafted into the Egyptian army were used against the Neo-Babylonians in 616 and 605 BC.[44] Another Greek mercenary named Antimenidas served in Nebuchadnezzar's army and took part in the destruction of Ashkelon in 604 BC.[45] A Neo-Babylonian tablet text (Babylonian 28186) records some Greek carpenters receiving food rations in Babylon.[46] Moreover, the architectural designs in Nebuchadnezzar's throne room show some Greek influence.[47] These archaeological discoveries show that Greece was in contact with the ancient Near East at least as early as the first half of the first millennium BC.

The author of Daniel discusses social and political developments involving Greece using different symbols for that kingdom. Gabriel reported that the goat the author had seen in a vision (Dan 8:5–8) represented the kingdom of Greece. He said that its great horn, which later broke into four, was the first king (Dan 8:21). The kingdom of Greece is also symbolized by the belly and thighs of bronze in the image dreamed by Nebuchadnezzar (Dan 2:32, 39).

---

42. McRay, "Greece" (*ABD*, 2:1094). See also Grabbe, "Of Mice and Dead Men," 120–25.

43. Waldbaum, "Greeks in the East," 1–17; Bienkowski, "Greeks" (*DANE*, 134); *ANET*, 284, 285; and Lipiński, "Cypriot Vassals of Esarhaddon," in Cogan and Eph'al, *Ah, Assyria...*, 58–64.

44. Boardman, *Greeks Overseas*, 51, 115; and Bienkowski, "Greeks" (*DANE*, 134).

45. Quinn, "Alcaeus 48 (B 16)," 19–20.

46. *ANET*, 308.

47. Koldewey, *Excavations at Babylon*, 104, 105; and Lloyd, *Archaeology of Mesopotamia*, 228.

ALEXANDER THE GREAT IN BATTLE
Sculpture from the fourth century BC. Sarcophagus from the Royal Necropolis of Sidon, Lebanon (today in the Istanbul Archaeological Museum) shows Alexander the Great in battle. (Credit: Zev Radovan)

In Daniel's dreams and visions, Greece is represented by both the leopard with four wings (Dan 7:6) and the goat (Dan 8:5–8). Daniel 8:21 identifies a significant king of Greece who would topple the Medo-Persians. In fact, Cyrus the Great, king of Persia, conquered the Ionian Greeks at Lydia and Ionia in 547/546 BC, but in 331 BC, the Persian Empire fell to Alexander the Great at the battle of Gaugamela.[48]

In Daniel's prophetic review of the historical kingdoms, Neo-Babylonia is displaced by the Medo-Persians (Dan 5:28) in 539 BC. Greece is the power which in turn displaced the Medo-Persians (Dan 8:20, 21; 11:2–4) in 331 BC.

8:26. Shut/seal up the vision. See also **12:4, 9. Seal.** Daniel had multiple visions which he described in the first person in chapters 7–12. The Daniel portrayed in chapters 1–6 "had insight in all visions and dreams" (Dan 1:17). The Daniel seen in the last half of the book anxiously sought for help from celestial beings to interpret his puzzling visions and dreams (Dan 7:15, 16; 8:15, 16; 9:21, 22; 10:14; 12:8). A recurrent motif with the visions in this second section is Daniel's repeated confusion and inability to understand what he had been shown (Dan 7:28; 8:27; 12:8).

Despite expressing eagerness to understand what was told him by the angelic being, Daniel was commanded, "But you, shut up/keep closed the vision for (it is) for many days" (Dan 8:26). In Dan 9:24 there was a time element "to seal up vision and prophecy." Similar commands also appear in

---

48. Briant, *From Cyrus to Alexander*, 795–800.

Dan 12:4: "But you Daniel, shut up/keep closed the words and seal the book until the time of the end." Again, in Dan 12:9: "Go! Daniel, for the words (are) shut up/kept closed and sealed until the time of the end." The vision of Daniel had to be sealed at that time because it had to do with the time of the end. It was to be publicized when the time to do so had arrived. The book of Revelation has seals broken, thus allowing the message to be revealed because it was the appropriate time to do so (Rev 5:1–9; 6:1–12; 8:1). Also, Rev 22:10 forbids the sealing of the prophetic message of the book because it was the time of the end and the message was to be broadcast.

Shalom M. Paul pointed out that the keeping in secret and sealing of literary works expressed in Daniel could also be understood in light of Akkadian scribal technical practices in Mesopotamia.[49] Paul indicated that the term *kakkū sakkū*, derived from Akkadian verbs *kanāku*, "to seal," and *sakāku*, "to be clogged" or "stopped up" (said of the ears), appears in several Akkadian texts, for example: "[. . .]. *kakku sakku šû libittu šû* '[. . .],'" "It is hidden and obscure. It is a brick,'" and "*Ḫītāku miḫilti abni ša lām abūbi ša kakkū sakkū ballū*," "I [Ashurbanipal, king of Assyria] have examined the inscriptions on stone (dating) from before the Flood that were sealed, obscure, and confused."[50] Thus, the sealing of a document was a preventive measure to protect it from being altered or publicized before its intended time or audience.

8:27. Fainted and sick. See **7:28. Alarmed.** During the encounter with divine beings the prophet often had some traumatic physical manifestations that would last even after the vision.

---

49. Paul, "Daniel 12:9," 116.
50. Paul, "Daniel 12:9," 116–17.

Chapter 9

PROPHETIC PRACTICE

This chapter highlights the expectation that prevailed among the Jewish captives that the duration of their captivity would come to an end someday. Through prayer Daniel seeks to make this happen. However, by means of divine intervention he was able to discover more complex issues on their restoration than he ever anticipated. Architectural finds in the city of Jerusalem show a determined effort by captivity survivors to recover from religious and political impotence. Evidence of Daniel's personal religious practice is in keeping with the context of the theme of the book.

9:1, 2. In the first year of Darius. 539 BC is the year Babylon fell to the Medes and Persians. 538 BC is Darius' first year.

9:1. Darius the son of Ahasuerus. See **6:1. Darius.** Of all the kings in the book of Daniel, Darius is the only one whose personal information is mentioned. So far, no archeological evidence on his person has been recovered.

9:2. Books. In Hebrew *separim* means "missives," "letters of instruction," "requests," or "commission." Probably this ancient word was borrowed from Assyrian *shipru*, which meant "missive" or "message." These were the writings, documents, or written instructive letters that had scriptural authority. By the time of the Babylonian captivity, the books of the Torah were considered sacred part of Scripture along with some historical books, psalms, and writings from the prophets. The canon had not reached its final form at this time. Even though Jeremiah was Daniel's contemporary, his writings were considered the word of God. The study of the sacred writings helped in understanding the history of the nations and the prospects of the people's present and future. Different ancient religions had writings they considered as Scripture to guide the believers' lives and practice.

9:2. YWHW. The name "YHWH," the official and only God for the Israelites, appears only in the context of prayer in Dan 9:2, 4, 10, 13, 14, and 20. The appellations 'aḏōnāy, "Lord," 'ēl, "God," and 'elōhim, "God," are used in the book in the place of YHWH. Prior to the Persian period there was a deliberate effort not to vocalize YHWH but to replace it in the reading with various appellations. Aramaic letters from Elephantine in Egypt (ca. 400 BC) had the shortened forms *yhw* and *yhh* for the divine name.[1]

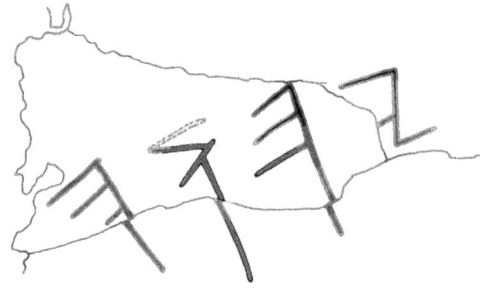

YHWH
The four letters of the divine name in Hebrew. (Credit: Zev Radovan)

The original YHWH in Hebrew is commonly known in Greek as the Tetragrammaton, i.e., the four Hebrew letters, *yod*, *he*, *waw*, and *he*. This was written without any vowels, a practice which led to a total loss of the pronunciation of the divine name. The attempt to vocalize or supply vowels to the name YHWH is derived from Exod 3:14 where YHWH revealed himself as "I am who I am." His existence is not bound by time limits. The transcription "Yahweh" is a scholarly convention that was crafted from Greek transcriptions such as *Iaoue/Iaouai* and *Iabe/Iabai*.[2] Humans use epithets or titles as names for God. No one knows the real name of God. Daniel declared: "Blessed be the name of God forever and ever" (Dan 2:20).

In most English translations "YHWH" is rendered as "Lord," "Lord God," "Lord," or "God." The Hebrews used a causative stem, *hyh*, in the sense of "to sustain, to bring into being, to establish."[3] After the Sinai covenant, a careful study of proper names gives evidence that the Hebrews reduced the

---

1. *ANET*, 491–92.
2. *DDD*, 910.
3. Obermann, "Divine Name YHWH," 320.

name "YHWH" to more familiar forms by formulating various derivatives of the names for deities. This tradition still prevailed in the time of Daniel.

From the 1982 archaeological excavations in Jerusalem, fifty-one bullae were found which contained many names ending in the suffix *-iahu*. This suffix, which designates a deity, occurs forty-one times. A good example is one inscribed "belonging to *Azariahu* so/n of *Hilkiahu*"[4] (1 Chr 9:11). The suffix *-iahu/yahu* is very common on ostraca and seals from the ninth and eighth centuries BC through the time of Nebuchadnezzar.

Assyrian royal annals have *ia-úḫa-zi*, "Ahaz,"[5] *az-ri-ia-a-ú*, "Azariah,"[6] and *Ḫa-za-qi-ia-ú/Ḫa-za-qi-a-ú*, "Hezekiah."[7] These names of Hebrew kings include the short forms of YHWH. There is literary evidence from the fifth century BC giving names in which references to the biblical deity are embedded. Such theophoric names include some Jewish principals and witnesses at Murashu in Nippur.

Linguists argue that the divine name "YHWH" was derived from the Hebrew root *hyh*, "to be." The vocalization of YHWH seems to have been based upon the theophoric names that contained part of the divine name either at the beginning or at the end. The names that have part of the divine name *yehô-* at the beginning include *yehôyāqim*, "Jehoiakim" (Dan 1:1), *yehôyākin*, "Jehoiachin" (2 Kgs 24:8), and *yehôyādā'*, "Jehoiada" (2 Sam 8:18). Good examples of names that have part of the divine name *-yāh* at the end are *ḥananyāh*, "Hananiah," and *'azaryāh*, "Azariah" (Dan 1:6, 7, 11; 2:17).

The modern reading "Jehovah" is associated with Petrus Galatinaus, a confessor to Pope Leo X (AD 1513–21), who transliterated "YHWH" into Latin "JHVH" in AD 1518 and is said to have used the vowels of Adonai to come up with the hybrid vocalization "*Iehouah*" or "Jehovah."[8] In the Hebrew Bible the name "YHWH" is never followed by a word in the genitive and neither is it prefixed by an article or suffixed by a possessive pronoun.

Ran Zadok affirms that the most reliable way of identifying Judeans in the Babylonian documents from 620–350 BC is the theophoric element *yhw* in the names of the people. "*Yhw*" is rendered in Babylonian cuneiform as "IA-A-HU-U" and "IA-A-MA."[9] Zadok points out that over four hundred

---

4. Shiloh, "Group of Hebrew Bullae," 27–34.

5. Schrader, *Cuneiform Inscriptions and the Old Testament*, 249.

6. Thomas, *Documents from Old Testament Times*, 53–54.

7. Schrader, *Cuneiform Inscriptions and the Old Testament*, 277–98.

8. See Thompson, "Yahweh" (*ABD*, 6:1011); Millard, "Yahweh" (*DANE*, 324–25); and *TDOT*, 5:501–2.

9. Zadok, "The Earliest Diaspora: The Judeans in Babylonia and Their Neighbors," (2004). Zadok points out that over four hundred such theophoric names have been identified.

such theophoric names have been identified. However, the theories that try to enunciate "YHWH" confirm that its vocalization was lost in antiquity.

Two Egyptian texts from the times of Amenophis III (fourteenth century BC) and Rameses II (1279–1213 BC) mention "Yahu in the land of the Shosu-beduins."[10] This land can be identified as Edom and Midian. The biblical texts in relation to this assertion include Deut 33:2; Judg 5:4; and Hab 3:3. These texts do not necessarily indicate that Edom and Midian or their vicinity is the place of YHWH's origin. The so-called Kenite hypothesis states that Moses got acquainted with YHWH during his stay with the Kenites in Midian and later introduced Him to Israel. This hypothesis, however, fails to account for the patriarchal traditions and the origin of the Israelites where YHWH featured.

Several other ancient discoveries are relevant to the discussion regarding Daniel's God. YHWH is attested as the official God of Israel on the Moabite Stone written by Mesha, king of Moab, in the ninth century BC.[11] Some ostraca from Lachish and Arad mention the name of YHWH. One such ostracon that seems to have come from the Jerusalem temple reads: "To my lord Eliashib: May Yahweh grant thy welfare! And (as) of now, give Shemariah half an aurora (of ground) and to Kerosi give a quarter aurora and to the sanctuary (give) what thou didst recommend to me. As for Shallum, he shall stay at the temple of Yahweh."[12]

A Hebrew inscription on a stone votive bowl dated eighth century BC is inscribed: "(Belonging) to Obadaiah, son of Adnah; may he be blessed by Yahweh."[13]

At Kuntillet 'Ajrud about fifty kilometers from Kadesh Barnea, Hebrew inscriptions have been found which date back to the ninth-to-eighth century BC. These inscriptions are on a wall plaster, on two large pithoi (storage jars), and on a stone vat. The subject seems to be YHWH of Samaria and his Asherah (a Semitic mother goddess). These finds have sparked a lively debate as far as their meaning and implications for the Israelite religion.[14]

Despite the mention or association of the name "YHWH" with a cultic goddess on an inscription, there is no attestation for this in the Hebrew Bible. The pictures of Bes, the Egyptian god, and a female deity may have

---

10. *DDD*, 911.

11. *ANET*, 320–21.

12. *ANET*, 569.

13. Dever, *What Did the Biblical Writers Know?*, 184.

14. Meshel, "Kuntillet 'Ajrud–An Israelite Religious Center in Northern Sinai," *Expedition* 20 (1978) 50–54.

no relationship with the inscriptions, and moreover, Asherah was never recognized or officially worshiped in Israel.

Another dedicatory formula mentioning YHWH was found on an inscription from a tomb at Khirbet el-Qôm (biblical Makkedah, 6.5 miles east-southeast of Lachish).[15] A seal, *lmqnyw 'bd.yhwh*, "belonging to *Miqneyaw*, the servant of *yhwh*," probably belonged to a priest who served in the sanctuary (cf. 1 Chr 15:18, 21).[16] Two seventh-century BC silver amulets recovered from Ketef Hinnom in Jerusalem contained the priestly benediction of Num 6:24–26.[17] This benediction mentions the name of YHWH just as it is found in Dan 9:4. YHWH is Daniel's God. Daniel calls Him the God of Heaven (Dan 2:28, 37, 44) or the great God (Dan 2:45). In the sixth century BC the Persians popularized the title "God of Heaven" for Ahura Mazda, the chief god for Zoroastrianism, a religion that has both monotheistic and dualistic beliefs.

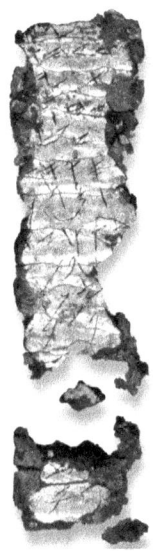

KETEF HINOM AMULET
Silver Amulet containing the divine name—YHWH, dating from the beginning of the sixth century BC, found in Jerusalem. The inscription written in ancient Hebrew contains the text of a prayer, the so-called "priestly benediction" (Num 6:24–26). The amulet is the earliest object with an inscription containing the divine name ever found. (Credit: Zev Radovan)

15. Zevit, "Khirbet el-Qôm Inscription," 39–47.
16. *TDOT,* 5:502.
17. De Souza, "Ketef Hinnom Silver Scrolls," 27–39.

THE BOOK OF DANIEL

Although YHWH's epithets and appellations are shared with the Canaanite and ancient Near Eastern pantheon, Daniel and his colleagues did not recognize other gods in Babylon except YHWH (Exod 20:3; Deut 6:4). Surprisingly, Nebuchadnezzar (Dan 2:47; 3:26, 28-29; 4:2-3, 34-37) and Darius (Dan 6:16, 25-27) seem to have finally acknowledged the God of Daniel and his fellow captives.

It is clear that when Nebuchadnezzar spoke of God, he used "some expression that is fitting in the mouth of a gentile,"[18] while Daniel used the expression that would convey more meaning to the king. YHWH has supremacy over other gods and nations. Evidence shows that YHWH was widely known in the ancient Near East as the only God for the Israelites.

9:2. Jeremiah the prophet. Daniel understood from the writings of Jeremiah that the time of the Babylonian captivity would last about seventy years (Dan 9:2; cf. Jer 25:11-12). The prophet Jeremiah (*yirmĕyāhû* "Yahweh loosens the womb?")[19] was born in Anathoth, possibly modern Anata or its vicinity (Jer 1:1). He is thought to have lived approximately from 640-580 BC. During his lifetime Neo-Assyria was displaced from its political dominance in the region by Neo-Babylonia.

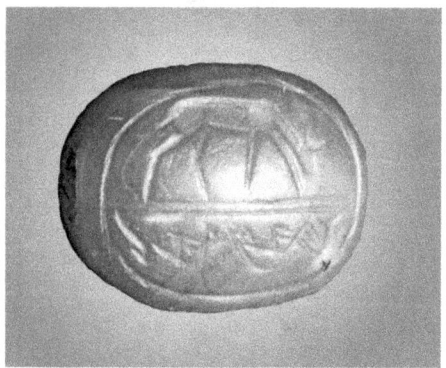

JEREMIAH SEAL
A Hebrew seal decorated with a deer and inscribed "*lyirmeyahu*," "belonging to Jeremiah," dating from the eighth century BC. (Credit: Zev Radovan)

Jeremiah was a survivor of the destruction of Judah in 587/6 BC. His prophetic career outlined in Jer 1:2-3; 25:1-3 (627-586 BC) made him an international geopolitical analyst who faced outrageous reaction and

---

18. Jones, "Prayer in Daniel 9," 489.

19. BDB, 438, 941. Other suggested alternative meanings of *yirmĕyāhû* include "may Yahu raise up" (Noth, *Die israelitischen Personennamen*, 201) and "Yahu founded" (*HALAT*, 420); "Yahweh shoots" or "Yahweh establishes."

persecution from his audience. His writings are the best source of information on the activities of Nebuchadnezzar in relation to Judah in late seventh century BC to the first half of the sixth century BC. It has been noted that the Lachish letters, ration tablets of Jehoiachin, and the letter of King Adon to Pharaoh could all point to Jeremiah's age.

Other prophets who referred to the Babylonian activities in Judah include the eighth-century BC Micah (Mic 4:10) and Isaiah (Isa 13—14; 21). Habakkuk was Jeremiah's contemporary who likewise affirmed that the Babylonian captivity was punishment from God (Hab 1—2). The role of Jeremiah was pivotal to interpretation of the current geopolitical changes. According to Jer 27, ambassadors from Ammon, Edom, Judah, Moab, Tyre, and Sidon convened a meeting in Jerusalem under King Zedekiah some time in 593 BC. Here they consolidated their forces with the Egyptian Pharaoh Psametichus II (595–589 BC). They were hoping to inhibit Nebuchadnezzar's imperialism over their territories.

Jeremiah spoke about Babylon in a metaphorical as well as a literal sense. In Jer 25:26; 51:41, "Sheshak" is a cryptogram for Babylon.[20] Jeremiah equated the tenth year of Zedekiah's reign to the eighteenth year of Nebuchadnezzar's reign, which was 588/7 BC (Jer 32:1–2).

Two bullae bearing seal impressions dated before the destruction of Jerusalem in 587/6 BC attest to two of the people mentioned in Jer 36. One was for Jeremiah's scribe Baruch and reads: "(Belonging) to Berekhyahu son of Neriyahu the scribe," and the other was for Jerahmeel, the king's son, "(Belonging) to Yeraḥme'el son of the king."[21] Likewise, Jeremiah gives a plausible list of some of Nebuchadnezzar's officials who played a major role in the military operations in Judah. Some of the names are preserved in Neo-Babylonian documents.[22]

---

20. Yamauchi, "Babylon," in Harrison, *Major Cities of the Biblical World*, 33. "Cryptogram" is the idea of coding Hebrew names through the literary technique called *atbaš*, i.e., substituting the first consonant of the Hebrew alphabet for the last one, the second for the next-to-last, etc.; for example: א־ת; ש־ב; ג־ר; etc.

21. Avigad, "Baruch the Scribe" (1978), 52–56; adapted in *BA* 42 (1979) 114–18; Avigad, *Hebrew Bullae*, 32; Shanks, "Jeremiah's Scribe and Confidant," 58–65; and King, *Jeremiah*, 95–97.

22. See commentary on **4:36. Royal officials.**

BARUCH SEAL
Hebrew bulla inscribed "(belonging) to berekhyahu son of neriyahu the scribe." Baruch, son of Neriah, is mentioned in the Bible as prophet Jeremiah's faithful friend and secretary (Jer 36:4, 8). (Credit: Zev Radovan)

From the onset of his career, Jeremiah warned the people that God would exile them because of their failing fidelity. In Jer 25:3 (cf. 1:2) he pointed out that twenty-three years had elapsed from the thirteenth year of Josiah, king of Judah (627 BC), "until this day" (605/4 BC), the fourth year of Jehoiakim, king of Judah (which is the equivalent of the third year of Jehoiakim in Daniel's reckoning).[23] He announced to the people assembled in Jerusalem that Nebuchadnezzar, king of Babylon, would invade and devastate the land (Jer 21:1–10).

Furthermore, the Judeans would go into captivity under the Babylonians for seventy years (Jer 25:11–12; cf. Dan 9:2). Jeremiah 29 contains the letter Jeremiah sent to the exiles in Babylon possibly in 597 BC, persuading them to settle down there. He assured them that after seventy years God would bring them back to Jerusalem. Jeremiah laments the final fall and destruction of Jerusalem in the biblical book of Lamentations.

The Babylonians finally destroyed Jerusalem in 586 BC. Nebuzaradan, the captain of the guard, treated Jeremiah with great respect. He offered to let Jeremiah go to Babylon, or stay with Gedaliah, the Babylonian appointee at Mizpah (Tell en-Naṣbeh). If neither of those choices pleased Jeremiah, Nebuzaradan told him he could go anywhere he wished. Jeremiah decided to stay with Gedaliah. He also received a present from the Babylonians for his prophetic ministry (Jer 40:5). In 582 BC Gedaliah was assassinated and Jeremiah was taken against his will to Egypt where he continued his prophetic role (Jer 43:5–13).

While in Egypt, Jeremiah foretold that Nebuchadnezzar would attack that land (Jer 46:13). In 566 BC the Babylonians are said to have

---

23. See commentary on **1:1, 2. Jehoiakim, King of Judah.**

unsuccessfully attacked Egypt during the reign of Ahmose/Amasis II (570–526 BC).[24] Jeremiah 50–51 bears oracles which were uttered against Babylon, telling of its coming destruction. The book of Jeremiah concludes by summarizing the fall of Jerusalem and King Jehoiachin's release from prison in 562 BC by Amel-Marduk, Nebuchadnezzar's son (Jer 52). While Daniel's focus was on Babylon, Jeremiah concentrated more on Judah.

9:2. Seventy years of captivity. In 539 BC Daniel understood from his study of the books that the Jewish captivity in Babylon would last for seventy years. He was led to believe that its end would probably coincide with the fall of Babylon. The passages he studied most probably included Jer 25:11–14 and 29:10 (see also Lev 26; Deut 4:15–40; 2 Chr 36:21, 22; Ezra 1:1; Isa 23:15–18; Zech 1:12; 7:5).

THE BOOK OF JEREMIAH
Page from the book of Jeremiah in Aleppo Codex, the earliest text of the Hebrew Bible written in the tenth century AD. Jeremiah was a contemporary to Daniel and his writings are in the Nevi'im (the Prophets).
(Credit: Zev Radovan)

In Dan 9:1–2 it is difficult to precisely determine the chronological framework of the seventy literal years. When do they begin or end? How do they fit into the historical timeline? Does the counting of the seventy years begin before Nebuchadnezzar's initial attack on Jerusalem in 605 BC, or in one of the subsequent years when the Babylonians attacked Judah? Do the seventy years begin at the final destruction of the temple in 586 BC?

---

24. See commentary on **11:42, 43. Egypt.**

A date or event which would mark the end of the seventy years may also be crucial in identifying this time frame. The number seventy remains perplexing in the sense that it could also be considered as a round number such as that used to indicate an individual's expected life span (cf. Ps 90:10; Isa 23:15; Jub. 23:15-16).

Determining whether the seventy years are to be considered literal or symbolic may underpin the understanding of that number. Those who strongly suggest that the seventy years of Babylonian captivity are symbolic have always struggled to fit these years into the historical framework. It must be acknowledged that Daniel is concerned with a historical reality. This leads to the consideration of the seventy years as a literal time frame.

Interestingly, a similar prediction to that of Jer 25:11-14 and 29:10 is found on the Black Stone of Esarhaddon, king of Assyria (680-668 BC). This inscription reads: "Until the days were elapsed that the heart of the great lord Marduk should be appeased and he would find peace with the country against which he had raged, 70 years were to elapse, but he wrote [11] years (instead) and took pity and said: Amen!"[25]

Recensions A and D of this inscription explain that while Marduk had initially decreed Babylon to be in desolation for seventy years from the time it was destroyed by Sennacherib in 689 BC, he relented after being appeased and in only eleven years Babylon was restored.[26] The seventy years appear on the Black Stone of Esarhaddon and also in the biblical text. However, there seems to be no literary interdependence or borrowing between these two texts. Nothing is mentioned in the biblical text about God cutting short the seventy years for the Jewish captivity. A passage in 2 Chr 36:21-23 seems to indicate that the seventy years of captivity were literal. These years were associated with the concept of Sabbath years in Lev 25; 26:31-35. In a desolated state, the land kept the Sabbaths. At the completion of the seventy years, Cyrus signed the declaration of Jewish independence (538 BC). This terminated the captivity, and the Jews were freed to go back to Jerusalem. Their mandate was to rebuild the city and reestablish themselves as a sovereign nation.

Ross E. Winkle suggested that the chronological framework of the seventy years stretched from 609-539 BC.[27] The difficulty with this assertion is that the biblical text does not give a clear-cut event to mark the beginning

---

25. *COS*, 2:306; and Luckenbill, *Ancient Records of Assyria and Babylonia*, 2:242-45, nos. 639-50.

26. Luckenbill, *Ancient Records of Assyria and Babylonia*, 2:242-45, nos. 639-50; Saggs, *Babylonians*, 159; and Lambert, *Background of Jewish Apocalyptic*, 7.

27. Winkle, "Jeremiah's Seventy Years for Babylon Part I," 201-14; and Winkle, "Jeremiah's Seventy Years for Babylon Part II," 289-99.

of the time period. Again, it is not clear whether the Jewish captivity ended with the fall of Babylon in 539 BC, with the Cyrus Declaration for Jews to go back to Jerusalem in 538 BC, or even later. Winkle's reconstruction of the seventy-years time frame seems plausible. However, he failed to explain first the futuristic thrust of Jeremiah's message in the temple which he dated to have taken place in 609 BC (Jer 25:8–11); and second, he did not discuss the important dates mentioned in Jer 25:3 in relation to his proposed date of 609 BC.

S. Douglas Waterhouse suggested that the seventy years ended in 536 BC, the third year of Cyrus according to Dan 10:1.[28] The seventy years may have begun when Nebuchadnezzar first attacked Jerusalem in 605 BC or at the final destruction of Jerusalem in 586 BC and ended when the returnees from the Babylonian exile resuscitated the land of Judah into productivity.

Josephus indicated that the first year of the reign of Cyrus was the seventieth year since his people were removed out of their own land into Babylon.[29] However, the author of Daniel seems to be more concerned with the chronological detail following the end of the Babylonian captivity. The main focus of the book of Daniel is the chronological succession of world imperial powers until the time of the end. This theme is recurrent in the entire text.

The datable events in the book of Daniel began in the third year of Jehoiakim, king of Judah (605 BC), and lasted until the third year of Cyrus, king of Persia (536 BC). These may reflect the time period Israel spent in captivity (Dan 1:1; 10:1). If the seventy years of exile are to be understood in light of the Sabbath years (2 Chr 36:21–22; Lev 25; 26:31–35), then they must have begun when the land of Judah ceased production. In this case, the seventy years would have ended when the exiled returnees resumed agricultural production on that land. Also, if the seventy years began in 586 BC, their end may be seen to have coincided with the completion and restoration of the temple by the returning exiles in 516 or 515 BC (Zech 1:12; 7:5).

9:2. Desolations of Jerusalem. Jerusalem was ignominiously destroyed by Nebuchadnezzar in 586 BC. Some historians and biblical scholars in the nineteenth century AD developed the idea (which is still perpetuated today) that Palestine then became completely "uninhabited and uninhabitable."[30]

---

28. Waterhouse, "Why Was Darius," in *To Understand the Scriptures*, 184, 185.

29. Josephus, *Antiquities of the Jews*, 11.1.1.

30. Barstad, *Myth of the Empty Land*, 15; Barstad, *Babylonian Captivity*, 80; and Stern, "Babylonian Gap: The Archaeological Reality," 273–77.

Perhaps Daniel's prayer in 539 BC had implications with regard to Judah, which was still devastated nearly seventy years after the captivity (Dan 9:2).

Robert P. Caroll popularized the concept of an uninhabited Palestine with his expression "The Myth of the Empty Land."[31] This idea may have been influenced by Hecataeus of Abdera. Hecataeus's Hellenistic-period *Aegyptiaca* (*History of Egypt*) indicated that a plague caused the Egyptians to expel the aliens to the land of Judah, which was completely uninhabited at that time.[32] It is possible that Hecataeus was aware of sweeping statements in the Jewish traditions (cf. 2 Kgs 25:21; 2 Chr 36:20-21; Jer 43:4-7; 52:27; Lev 26:34-35), which seem to show that the Jews returning from Babylonia in the Persian period found the land uninhabited.

The Neo-Babylonians brought into the city of Babylon many people and much *biltu*, "tribute," from distant subdued territories, but they seldom disbursed resources to the population centers in the outskirts of their empire. Thus, the city of Babylon became the center for economic, political, and religious affairs.

The Babylonians are thought to have either carried into exile or killed all the Judaeans. The land of Judah remained unpopulated and inactive from 586 BC until the Persian period. In fact, William Foxwell Albright suggests that the southern Judean hill country shows no signs of occupation from the exile until Roman or Byzantine times.[33]

When the Assyrians destroyed the Northern Kingdom of Israel, they embarked on extensive reconstruction and resettlement projects in the territory (2 Kgs 17:24). Many of the cities they once destroyed, they rebuilt, and also repopulated the vacant areas where the people had been deported. Ephraim Stern observed the fact that while the Babylonians came to destroy the Southern Kingdom of Judah and deported the population to Babylon, there is no indication of their occupation or reconstruction of the Judean territory. Scholars have commonly referred to this period as the Babylonian gap. Stern suggested that since there is no trace of any Babylonian activity in Judah after 586 BC, "in an archaeological parlance there is no clearly defined period called 'Babylonian.'"[34] Stern posited the idea that there was a strange archaeological gap after the final destruction of Jerusalem in 586 BC to the Persian period. Dever, however, argued that the biblical writers never supported an empty land concept.[35]

---

31. Carroll, "Myth of the Empty Land," 79-93.
32. Blenkinsopp, "Bible, Archaeology and Politics," 174.
33. Albright, *Archaeology of Palestine and the Bible*, 141, 142, 171.
34. Stern, "Babylonian Gap," 51.
35. Dever, *Did God Have a Wife?*, 293.

Before the untimely death of Gedaliah, the Babylonian protégé, he had encouraged the remainder of the people of Judah and some army personnel to settle in the land (Jer 40:9). In fact, some pilgrims from Shechem, Shiloh, and Samaria went to the destroyed temple in Jerusalem to offer sacrifices after the assassination of Gedaliah in 582 BC (Jer 41:4–7). Jeremiah reports of another trip to Egypt by some Judean survivors who were running away from Nebuchadnezzar's retribution (Jer 43:5–13). Nehemiah (445–433 BC) interviewed some Jewish visitors in Susa about the welfare of the Jews in Judah who had survived the Babylonian exile (Neh 1:1–3).

It is therefore possible that an insignificant population remained in the land of Judah, and that their settlement and economic activities are not traceable in the archaeological record. On the other hand, the prayer of Dan 9 seems to be a call for the reconstruction of Jerusalem and resettling of the people in the land of Judah after seventy years of captivity.

9:3. Praying Daniel. Prayer incorporates verbal and gestural communication with God. Prayer is a channel of communication in which the participants present their petitions to God in anticipation of His favorable intervention. The book of Daniel has several prayers. Daniel invited his friends to join him in prayer when they faced a death penalty (Dan 2:17, 18). In this prayer, they asked God to show them what Nebuchadnezzar had dreamed so that they and their peers might live.

Daniel prayed (Dan 9:4–19) after he discovered that there was no political inclination in Babylon to end the Jewish exile. He longed to see the fulfillment of the prediction by Jeremiah the prophet (Jer 25:11, 12; 29:10) that the exile would last for only seventy years. Daniel's prayer was intercessory and filled with historical and theological motifs from the Hebrew Bible. The Dan 9 prayer gives an "understanding of history as reward and punishment."[36] Before he finished praying, Gabriel came to answer his petitions (Dan 9:21). Although it has been suggested that Dan 9 was composed in Jerusalem as a liturgical piece between 587 and 538 BC, the prayer is typically exilic in its intent, framework, content, and terminology. The prayers in Dan 9, Ezra 9, and Neh 9 all deal with confession of national sins as well as pleading for God's favorable intervention on those who survived the exile.

9:3. Fasting and mourning rites. The ancient Near East had a wide range of practices and/or ceremonies with regard to expressing abject grief, self-abasement, and self-deprecation. Fasting was a customary sign of humbling oneself before the deity. In Dan 9:3 the author said: "So I set my face to

---

36. Jones, "Prayer in Daniel 9," 492.

the Lord God to seek (Him with) prayer, supplication, with fasting, and sackcloth, and dust." Fasting was often done in connection with making a special request to God. Daniel fasted as he requested wisdom in understanding Jeremiah's writings (Jer 25:11–14; 29:10).

Fasting as an expression of faith could be individual or communal, official (obligatory), or unofficial. It could be done as needed or on regular specified days and occasions. (See Dan 10:2–3 and Neh 1:4–11.) Duration of fasting and mourning depended on the gravity of the situation, one's piety or emotions, and the physical ability to endure. Fasting can be a penitentiary rite (Dan 9:3–16; Jonah 3:5–10). It is an attempt to elicit a positive response from God. It is also a way of improving one's spiritual condition. Science also shows that the human body can have substantial health benefits from fasting.

Some biblical texts that describe mourning rites include: the book of Lamentations; Isa 22:12; 51:9—52:2; Gen 37:34; 50:10; 2 Sam 3:31–35; 10:4–5; 13:31; 14:4; 2 Kgs 19:1; Ezra 9:3–5; 10:6; and Job 1:20; 2:8. The nonbiblical texts also include: the Curse of Agade; the Epic of Gilgamesh; the Poems about Baal and Anath; the Tale of Aqhat; a state letter of Hattušili III, King of the Hittites; a state letter of Tušratta, King of Mitanni; and the Mother of Nabonidus's Inscription.[37] It has been noted that mourning rites could incorporate "loud weeping (usually aided by professional wailing women), the tearing of clothes and donning of sackcloth, sitting or lying on the dirt, gashing the body, strewing dirt on the head, fasting, (and) abstaining from anointing with oil."[38]

The concept of tearing one's clothes was a way of laying aside one's former status and admitting to defeat. This usually prompted seeking for immediate divine intervention. Job tore his robe, shaved his head, and fell down to the ground to worship (Job 1:20). While in such desperation to seek divine help other people in the ancient Near East would keep their hair unkempt. Beaulieu (who cites Adad-guppi's inscription) argued that rituals of mourning were shared by all cultures in the ancient Near East.[39] Another mourning ritual is presented in Dan 10:2–3, following which a divine being came to illuminate Daniel regarding the problem he was presenting. The desperation of the participant hopes for divine intervention.

Ancient literature informs us that the Jews at Elephantine put on sackcloth, mourned, and fasted after their sanctuary was destroyed. Their fasting included abstaining from eating meat, drinking wine, anointing

---

37. See *COS*, 1:381–84.
38. Pham, *Mourning*, 23.
39. Beaulieu, *Reign of Nabonidus*, 120.

themselves, and having sexual relations. Some individuals smeared ashes or dust on themselves in contrition. Such a response to calamities and distress is reminiscent of Dan 9:3 and 10:2–3 and conforms to the prevailing practices of the time. When our contemporary Jewish people mourn, they incorporate the ancient mourning practices as well as putting on torn clothes, sitting on low chairs, and reciting prayers. The New Testament gives a different prescription on fasting and prayer (Matt 6:16–18).

Daniel 9:2–27 presents in a chiastic format (AB:C:B^{1}A^1) the cycle the practitioner goes through in the fasting or mourning ritual:

A Encountering a complex problem (v. 2);

  B Anticipating supernatural intervention (v. 3a);

    C Praying accompanied by contrition gestures (vv. 3b–19);

  B^1 Responding supernatural being (vv. 20, 21);

A^1 Resolving of complex problem (vv. 22–27).

9:3. Sackcloth. In the ancient Near East, sackcloth was made from either camel's or goat's hair. It was a coarse fabric, mostly brown or black, but worn as clothing during times of personal or national distress or mourning. It could be used also by the grieving person as a belt or loincloth. Sackcloth was uncomfortable but could be worn under or over one's clothes (2 Kgs 6:30). The suppliant in the Prayer of Lamentation to the goddess Ishtar complained: "One has made for me long sackcloth; thus, I have appeared before thee. The weak have become strong; but I am weak."[40] Daniel's personal penitence conformed to the cultural practice of his contemporary world.

9:4. Made confession. Daniel represented his nation and confessed the wrongs they had done which caused them to be sent into captivity (Lev 26:27–45). He was looking for restoration of the entire nation by asking God to reverse the unfortunate situation they had brought upon themselves. A speech by a certain Egyptian sage is dated 1580 BC to 1200 BC.[41] This writing is arranged in six poems that are divided into three parts. The first portion deals with an account of ordeals and calamities of the time. The second section consists of exhortations to the people urging them to repent by destroying their enemies and by fulfilling their religious obligations. The last section tells of an ideal monarch who would rehabilitate the country.

---

40. *ANET*, 384, lines 60, 61.
41. *COS*, 1:93–98.

It also lays a blame on an unnamed regnant who was responsible for the decline in social conditions in the nation. It then points to the fortunate conditions in store for Egypt once the nation is redeemed.

When an ancient nation became captive to another, the survivors usually sought for the reversal of their misfortune from their deity. The pain and discomfort of captive life would drive them to make amends with their deity. Confession, either personal or national, was sometimes accompanied by weeping, fasting, praying, and abstaining from luxury in many ways.

9:4, 27. Covenant. See also, 11:22, 28, 30, 32. The most common Hebrew expression used for establishing a covenant is *karath berith*, "cut a covenant" (Exod 23:32; Josh 9:6, 7, 11, 15, 16). "Cutting a covenant" was derived from the cutting of animals involved (Gen 15:9-10). The biblical text has often used *karath* without an object and the implication is clearly understood to express the idea of establishing a covenant (1 Sam 11:2; 22:8). In Daniel 9:26, *karath* is used without an object. It also implies without question that the Messiah himself would be cut or sacrificed to make a covenant with many people (Dan 9:27). The prayer and confession of sins are integral prerequisites for covenant renewal.

The biblical text is familiar with covenant making. It is the God of Israel who initiates and makes a covenant with His people (Exod 19-24). The biblical covenant is more than a mutual agreement between two parties. It is God who commands the covenant (Josh 23:16; Judg 2:20; Ps 111:9). The covenant with God is the commissioning of God's law to His people (Exod 24; Deut 4:13; 9:9). The commitment required by God to this covenant has no option for unfaithfulness. It is likened to the relationship of a wife and husband. Moreover, God's covenant with His people had signs, namely: Sabbath (Exod 31:12-18; Ezek 20:12-20); the rainbow (Gen 9:11-17); and circumcision (Gen 17:9-14).

The prophets were commissioned to remind the people to keep their covenant commitment with God. Catastrophic consequences would fall on the people should they lose their fidelity to the covenant stipulations (Deut 4:23-28; Hos 8:1; Dan 11:30). God's people were taken into captivity to Babylonia because they had failed maintaining faithfulness to the covenant (Deut 29:24-28; Dan 9:4-6). Going into exile was the most horrific consequence of the covenant curses (Lev 26:33; Deut 28:36; Jer 25:8-11).

The Rassam cylinder text, which is part of the annals of Ashurbanipal (668-ca. 627 BC), relates the breaching of a treaty. We read: "The people of Arabia asked one another, saying: 'Why is it such evil has befallen Arabia?', and they answered: 'Because we did not observe the valid covenant sworn to the god Ashur.'"[42] The three Sefire Inscriptions are eighth-century BC texts discovered at Al-Safirah (Sefire) near Aleppo in Syria. These inscriptions are good examples of extrabiblical evidence on the tradition of treaties and the entailed curses and blessings. Daniel's prayer acknowledged that God was still keeping His covenant even though Israel and Judah absconded.

9:6, 10. Your servants the prophets. The ancient Near East has some prophetic figures who featured as similar to the biblical prophets. Texts from Mari in Old Akkadian, Canaan (Taanach Letter), and Neo-Assyria show divine utterances which look like the Old Testament prophetic oracles.[43] A prophet communicates divine messages to the people, monitors the behavior of people, and preaches repentance. The frequent title for the prophet was "man of God." Israel had prophets as well as their neighbors (1 Kgs 18:4, 13, 40). Prophets of Israel were opposed to other prophets from elsewhere. Moreover, in Israel there was a class of self-styled prophets whom God had not commissioned (Jer 27:9). Such prophets were named "false prophets" but sometimes people liked their messages more than that of the prophet of God (Jer 23:9–40; 28:1–17). God spoke to His prophets through dreams and visions and He would not do anything without revealing His secrets to the prophets (Amos 3:7). The prophets spoke the word of God. Prophets often influenced political events, socioeconomic disparities, and religious reforms. Even though God sent prophets to Israel and Judah, persistent ignoring of their messages led the people into captivity.

Daniel is seen confessing the sin of disobeying God's messengers. Lamentations 2:20 laments the prophets who were murdered in the temple. The community at Qumran studied the "books of the prophets" (CD 7:17) and they were looking to the eschatological prophet mentioned in Deut 18:15 (1 QS 9:11).[44] All prophetic revelation came from the Holy Spirit. Lachish letters mention a prophet, probably Jeremiah, whose messages were being rejected by the political leaders. Babylonian captivity was a result of Israel and Judah's failure to heed the prophetic voice. In his prayer, Daniel acknowledges the mistake and prays for God to forgive the captives.

9:7, 14, 16, 18, 24. Righteous/ness. The LORD God is described as "righteous" (Dan 9:14). "Righteousness" is attributed to Him (Dan 9:7, 16). On the other hand, Daniel acknowledged that the exilic community's "righteousness" (Dan 9:18) was an inadequate basis for his prayer. Nebuchadnezzar was advised to break his sins with righteousness (Dan 4:27). Similarly,

---

42. Weinfeld, "*berith*" (*TDOT*, 2:269).
43. *TDOT*, 9:135–37.
44. *TLOT*, 2:710.

the Jewish exilic community was given time to end sin and bring in righteousness (Dan 9:24). It is possible to turn others to righteousness, as can be noted in Dan 12:3 (cf. Isa 53:11).

On his accession, or soon thereafter, the king in ancient times was obligated to show his public commitment to social justice by doing away with imbalances among the people, especially those who were in bad debt. Those whose debts were cleared were made right again in the society. Jesus seems to allude to this when he declared that he came to proclaim liberty to the captives and to those who were oppressed (Luke 4:18; cf. Isa 61).

The process for righting the imbalances created by debt in the society began with the invitation of royal officials to the capital for a briefing and distribution of the written enactments. Torches were lit to signal to the population that the royal proclamation was about to be made. The tablets that were inscribed with the debtors' obligations to their creditors were then collected and broken, thereby dissolving the debt. If any debtor and creditor would want their contract not to be nullified, they had to have the king formally affirm it. Thus, all whose debts were canceled were made right in the society; they were righteous.[45]

An Akkadian text, dated possibly to the seventh century BC, reflects how gods would deal with any king who failed in his responsibility of maintaining *kidinnu/kidinnūtu*, "civic rights."[46] A letter addressed to Esarhaddon, king of Assyria (680–669 BC), began with the words: "May the lord of kings look; that tablet (called) 'If the king does not heed justice . . .'"[47] Among such texts are examples from Nineveh and Neo-Babylonian Nippur. It is likely that the kings might have been exposed to these writings.

Nebuchadnezzar in 595 BC issued an official document condemning Baba-aḫa-iddina, son of Nabu-aḫḫe-bulliṭ. This prominent person had rebelled against the government. In the text, Nebuchadnezzar declares himself as one who "determines right and justice," and also as one responsible for destroying all criminals in his kingdom (cf. Dan 4:27; 5:19). Nebuchadnezzar is also characterized as *šar mēšarim*, "the just king," in the Wadi Brisa Inscription.[48]

Several West Semitic languages also attest *ṣdq* in various ways. Yehimilik, king of Byblos, was considered *ṣdq mlk*, "a righteous king," and

---

45. *TLOT*, 2:710.

46. Lambert, *Babylonian Wisdom Literature*, 110–15. Kidinnutu/kidinnutu literally means "divine protection"; Kuhrt, *ANE*, 2:612-21.

47. Kuhrt, *ANE*, 2:614.

48. *ANET*, 307.

yšr mlk, "an upright king."[49] Ṣedeq, a West Semitic god, is attested in the traditions around ancient Jerusalem.[50] Such personal names as *malkî-ṣedeq*, "Melchizedek" (Gen 14:18); *aḏōnî-ṣedeq*, "Adoni-Zedek" (Josh 10:1, 3); or possibly *ᵃḏōnî-bezeq*, "Adoni-Bezek" (Judg 1:5–7) show Ṣedeq as a theophoric element.[51] An eighth-century BC Phoenician bilingual inscription from Karatepe has Azitwadda of Adana boasting. He wrote, "Every king considered me his father because of my righteousness (*ṣdqy*) and my wisdom (*ḥkmty*) and the kindness of my heart (*nʿm lby*)."[52]

A seventh-century BC tomb inscription belonging to Agbar, the priest of the moon god in Nerab near Aleppo, recounted: "Because of my righteousness (*bṣdqty*) before him, he gave me a good name and prolonged my days."[53]

The Arabic *ṣadaqa* means "be true," "believe," or "hold to be true." *ṣidq*, on the other hand, is "truth." More importantly, in ancient poetry it was used to depict the male bedouin characteristics such as "courage," "dependability," and "competence."[54]

The Ethiopian language renders *ṣādĕq* as "good," or "just." *ṣĕdq* is rendered "justice," or "righteousness." In the Syriac, *ṣ* is replaced by *z* to have *zedqā*, meaning "what is right, responsible, instruction, prescription or duty."[55]

On the whole, it can be noted that the West Semitic languages, including the Hebrew, use *ṣdq* to cover a wide range of meanings. These include proper conduct, order, righteousness, legitimacy of succession, loyalty, favor, concession, and grant.

The root *ṣdq* occurs about 140 times in the Qumranic writings. The dominant motif is that the "salvific *ṣeḏāqâ* is a gift of God."[56] In the two copies of 4QWays of Righteousness[57] (4Q420 and 4Q421), *ṣdq* features prominently. It is associated with walking with God and with redemption. Righteousness could be studied in the same way as one might study the Torah.

---

49. *ANET*, 653.
50. Rosenberg, "God *Sedeq*," 162–65.
51. Rosenberg, "God *Sedeq*," 163.
52. *ANET*, 654; and Ringgren, "צדק," 12:242–43.
53. *ANET*, 661.
54. Ringgren, "Root SDQ in Poetry and the Koran," in Widegren, *Ex Orbe Religionum* 2:134–35; and Ringgren, "צדק" (*TDOT*, 12:243).
55. Ringgren, "צדק" (*TDOT*, 12:243).
56. Johnson, "צדק" (*TDOT*, 12:263).
57. *DJD*, 20:173–202.

The book of Daniel used the concept of righteousness in accordance to the range of meanings used in the ancient Near East. However, righteousness is also depicted as a quality of being which belongs to God. Being right with God first would lead to social justice and right actions towards fellow human beings. According to Daniel, one may be considered wise or understanding when one attains the righteousness of God and teaches others the same. The biblical text shows a distinction in righteousness. Human righteousness is good for nothing (Dan 9:18; Gen 38:26; 1 Sam 24:17; Jer 3:11; Ezek 16:51–52; Isa 64:6; Matt 5:20). On the other hand, God's righteousness is salvation to the believer (Gen 15:6; Dan 9:7; 12:3; Rom 1:17; 3:21–26).

9:7, 11, 20. Israel. See **1:3, 6. Israel and Judah.**

9:11. Curse. The ancient Near Eastern people believed that oaths and curses were sanctioned by gods. A curse was either conditional or unconditional. A conditional curse could be revoked and its effect nullified. The unconditional curse could be irreversible. The curse was always directed to the person who fails to act as anticipated by the person who utters the curse. A person could also curse oneself.

The most common curse uttered all over Mesopotamia on the offender was that the offender would die without leaving descendants or a name to be remembered. A similar curse brought the decimation of Eli's family in 1 Sam 2:31. A curse could also serve "as a legal vengeance against unknown thieves, perjurers, and accomplices (Judg 17:2f.; Lev 5:1; Zech 5:3; Prov 29:24)."[58] On the other hand, curses were perceived as helpful in securing an oath (Gen 24:41; Hos 4:2; Neh 10:30), contract (Gen 26:28; Ezek 17:19), or covenant (Deut 29:19–28). Curses were also a form of ancient insurance to protect certain objects or property. For example, someone could be cursed for stealing, vandalizing, breaking or abusing a monument, sculpture, stelae, or foundation deposits. People would refrain from committing atrocities in fear of being cursed. Micah believed the 1,100 pieces of silver he stole from his mother were cursed and so he returned them (Judg 17:2). The mother then reversed the curse by blessing him.

A Phoenician inscription dated 625–600 BC reads: "Mutas pronounced a mighty curse so that no one should illegitimately seize it—field or vineyard—from the possession of the family of Kulas among everything which Mutas had given him."[59] Among the Bedouins today is a customary practice that anybody missing something would say: "I hold the person

---

58. *TLOT*, 1:113.
59. *COS*, 3:138.

who finds this thing responsible for it. If he keeps it, may Allah cut him off from his property and his family."[60]

Curses were a major component in making suzerain/vassal treaties. As part of the agreement, curses were written down and effected on the party that defaults. Similarly, the God of the Hebrew people delineated curses and blessings for them (Lev 26; Deut 27–29). The people were aware of the consequences of breaking the covenant with God. However, provision was made that if they returned from their wickedness, God would rehabilitate them back. Daniel acknowledged that his people were under a curse because they broke their covenant with God. He was appealing for the reversal of the curses.

9:11. Oath. See 12:7. The Hebrew root *shbʿ* carries the meaning to "swear" or "cause to swear," while the noun is "oath."[61] The idea of oaths and curses is prominent in the covenantal relationships. An oath was a solemn and legal recourse that was to be taken seriously. It was taken as an obligation or at will. Once effected, the oath was binding and any defaulting was punishable. General oaths were used for trivial cases while solemn oaths were reserved for important events.

Mesopotamians appealed to their own gods when they were making oaths. When making a covenant, people swore. Making an oath assumes a future obligation and not the present situation. It is a promise one makes. For the Hebrews the oath was relevant in that God was the guarantor and guardian of the oath and would affect consequences on those absconding the obligations, and that God also obligates Himself in the oath to benefit His people.

Repeatedly Israel vowed that they would do what God required of them (Exod 19:8; Josh 1:16). They had been warned of the consequences for breaking the covenant with God (Deut 28:15–68). They would end up in captivity. However, God would give them His redemptive intervention if they encountered devastation and remembered to confess their sin. God promised to pardon them and restore them.

The community at Qumran did not depart much from the Old Testament concept of oath. The one who joins the community was bound with a solemn oath to keep the Torah (law) and not to sin (CD 8:15; 1QS 5:8; 1QH 14:17). Daniel acknowledged the fact that his people defaulted on the oath they had made to God. As a result, they were sent into exile for a specified time. His prayer is seeking the reversal of the exilic curse.

---

60. *TDOT*, 1:262.
61. *TLOT*, 3:1292.

9:11, 13. Law of Moses. See **2:9. Law.** The law of Moses comprised of the Pentateuch, the five books of the Old Testament. Moses authored these books. The Ten Commandments (Exod 20; Deut 5) are the moral code.

9:12. Judges. These were administrators of justice in the community. Mari texts show that in the ancient Near East judges were usually appointed by kings. The biblical text also points out the appointment of judges (1 Sam 8:1; 2 Chr 19:4-6). Their function included arbitrating in local disputes and also assisting in conducting military campaigns. Judges were either lawgivers, governors, or any such appointed officers that decided on social controversies and executed civil, religious, political, and social laws. Honesty and integrity were indispensable for judges. Paragraph 5 of Hammurabi's code stated that if a judge gave a judgment, rendered a decision, and/or deposited a sealed document, but later changed his mind or revoked that judgment, he was to be punished and would lose his credentials as judge.[62] In Israel judges were to make nondiscriminatory juridical decisions that aimed at maintaining peace, security, and justice in the community. Judges mainly settled disputes to establish the welfare of the widows, orphans, poor, strangers, or any unfortunate individual in their local territory. Daniel confessed that Israel went into captivity because the judges, along with all the other responsible authorities, had failed their duty. As a result, God disciplined the nation by sending them into captivity (Deut 4:27; 28:64; 2 Kgs 17:13-23). When the prescribed time for captivity was running out (Jer 50:33), Daniel prayed for the reversal of God's punishment on the people.

9:15. Egypt. See also Dan 11:8, 42, 43. The prayer in Dan 9:15 acknowledges Israel's historical deliverance from Egypt in the last half of the second millennium BC. The exodus of the Israelites from Egypt has long been debated and various formulations have been propounded by different scholarly persuasions. However, there is compelling evidence from the ancient Near East that show movements of large crowds from place to place.[63] Since God delivered Israel from Egypt, Daniel is praying for God to intervene and deliver the captives from Babylon.

9:17-18, 26. Desolate sanctuary. See **8:11-14. Desolate sanctuary.** Titus destroyed the temple in Jerusalem in AD 70. This fulfilled what Jesus was talking about in Matt 24:15. Ever since Titus destroyed the temple in Jerusalem, it was never rebuilt again.

---

62. *ANET*, 166.
63. Mazani, "Number of the Israelites," (1999).

9:21. Gabriel. See **8:16. Gabriel.**

9:21, 23, 24. Vision. See **8:1. Vision.** Visions are seen. Daniel labored to understand the visions he saw. The angel Gabriel often appeared to assist him to understand the visions.

9:24-27. Seventy weeks. The phrase *šābu'îm šib'îm* literally means "sevens seventy." This implies "seventy weeks" (Dan 9:24). The phrase is fraught with linguistic and syntactical issues which are the source of an ongoing debate among scholars. Mathematical computation on the seventy weeks should be done with caution.

The term *šābuî'm*, "weeks" (sing.), *šābûa*, "a period of seven (days or years)," "heptad," or "seven of years,"[64] is attested in some archaeological finds from Qumran, for example, in the Manual of Discipline (1QS) 10:7, 8.[65] The Pesher on the Periods (4Q180, 181) stated that Azazel would lead Israel astray for seventy weeks. The Greek Testament of Levi 16:1 quotes the Book of Enoch (1 En. 93:3-10; 91:11-17; cf. Jub. 50:4) as saying that "you will err for seventy weeks." The Testament of Levi, chapters 14-17,[66] relates some seventy weeks which are assigned for the priestly ministry, but it is difficult to associate the times of these seventy weeks with those of Dan 9:24-27.

The chronological key to locating the seventy-weeks' time period in history is this expression: "From the issuing of the order to restore and to rebuild Jerusalem to the Messiah the prince (shall be) seven weeks and sixty-two weeks," a total of sixty-nine weeks (Dan 9:25). The sixty-nine weeks give a total of 483 days/years. Likewise, the remaining one week (Dan 9:27) is equal to seven days/years. So, the seventy weeks amount to 490 days/years. The language in this passage permits this entire period to be 490 years (a day for year), a principle already at work in the biblical text (Num 14:34; Ezek 4:6).

9:24. Seal up vision and prophecy. See **8:26. Shut/seal up the vision**, and also, **12:4, 9. Seal.** Prophetic messages were to be unsealed or revealed only when the appropriate time had arrived. See Rev 22:10.

9:25. Command to build Jerusalem. History records four orders that were issued by the Persian kings with regard to Jews and Jerusalem. On the Cyrus

---

64. BDB, 988.

65. Hasel, "Hebrew Masculine Plural," 110. See Hasel, "New Light," 45-53; and Qimron, *Hebrew of the Dead Sea Scrolls*, 67.

66. Kee, "Testaments of the Twelve Patriarchs," in Charlesworth, *Old Testament Pseudepigrapha*, 1:793-94.

Cylinder, Cyrus the Great states that in "the holy cities beyond the Tigris whose sanctuaries had been in ruins over a long period, the gods whose abode is in the midst of them, I returned to their places and housed them in lasting abodes. I gathered together all their inhabitants and restored *to them* their dwellings."[67] In 538 BC Cyrus the Great granted Jews the permission to go back to their homeland and rebuild the temple (Ezra 1:2-4; 6:1-5; 2 Chr 36:22-23). The Jews did start a slow and gradual migration back to their homeland, but they did not work on rebuilding the temple (Hag 1:1-11).

In 520 BC, Darius I reaffirmed the decision made earlier by Cyrus the Great. He also commissioned the rebuilding of the temple (Ezra 6:1-12).

The third order was issued by Artaxerxes I in 457 BC. In response to this decree, Ezra, along with priests, Levites, singers, gatekeepers, temple servants, and a company of other people, went back to Jerusalem (Ezra 7:6-7, 11-17). Several archaeological discoveries may shed some light on this event. These include the Elephantine Aramaic Papyrus 6 that dated Artaxerxes I's first year as 465 BC.[68] This would make 458 BC his seventh year (cf. Ezra 7:7). According to the Egyptian system of reckoning, the Cairo Sandstone Stele seems also to have recorded the seventh year of Artaxerxes as 458 BC.[69] This, of course, was 457 BC according to the Jewish accession-year reckoning.[70]

The 70 weeks of Daniel 9:24-27

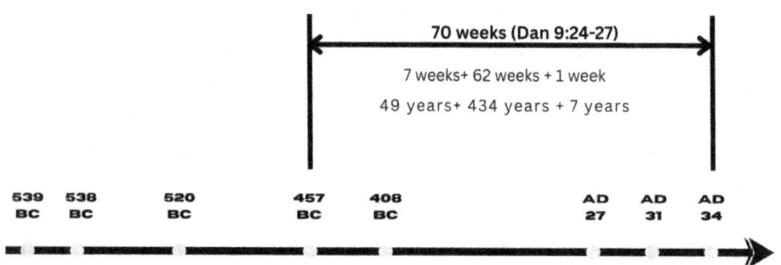

70 WEEKS OUTLINE

Three decrees to build the Jerusalem temple were offered by kings of Persia, Cyrus the Great, Darius I, and Artaxerxes I (Ezra 6:14). The decree issued by Artaxerxes I in 457 BC lines up well with the events outlined in Dan 9:24-27.

67. Arnold and Beyer, *Readings from the Ancient Near East*, 148.
68. Cowley, *Aramaic Papyri*, 15.
69. Horn and Wood, *Chronology of Ezra 7*, 142.
70. Horn and Wood, *Chronology of Ezra 7*, 124-27.

In 445/444 BC Nehemiah requested permission from Artaxerxes I to go to Jerusalem and rebuild the city and its walls (Neh 2:5).

Of these four decrees, one fits better all of the chronological events outlined: the decree issued in 457 BC by Artaxerxes I. It was issued in the seventh year of his reign (Ezra 7:7-9), and it harmonizes with Daniel's chronology (Dan 9:25). In Dan 9:24-27, the first epoch, forty-nine years (seven weeks), stretches from 457 BC to 408 BC.

9:25. Jerusalem built in troublesome times. During the Persian period, the population in Jerusalem was small. The inhabitants might have met with economic hardships, financial constraints, and religiopolitical intimidation. Archaeological discoveries relevant to this time period were found at Elephantine in Egypt. A well-preserved copy of the papyrus correspondence to Bagoas, the Persian governor in Judah, was sent by Yedoniah and the priests of the Jewish community at Elephantine in Egypt. Yedoniah petitioned for the rebuilding of the Jewish temple at Elephantine which had been intentionally destroyed in the fourteenth year of King Darius II (410 BC).[71] The letter was probably written in the seventeenth year of King Darius II, that is, 407 BC.[72] The priests at Elephantine informed Bagoas that they had also written another letter to Deliah and Shelemiah, the sons of Sanballat, the governor of Samaria.[73] Nehemiah started rebuilding the walls of Jerusalem in 445 BC and was met with strong opposition from Sanballat and Tobiah (Neh 2:10; 4:1-23; 6:1-14). Sanballat's sons are mentioned in the Elephantine letter. Daniel 9:25 alludes to the problems encountered in rebuilding Jerusalem, for "it shall be built (with) plaza and the moat even in the times of affliction."

The Elphantine correspondence shows that by 408 BC, Jerusalem was restored to its status and the call for the city's reconstruction was affirmed. The year 408 BC marks the end of the forty-nine years since Artaxerxes I's 457 BC decree to let the Jews go back to Judah.

The context of Dan 9:24-27 is the explanation of the vision in Dan 8:13-14. Daniel 9:24-27 is part of the answer to the other angelic being's question "Until when?" or "How long?" (Dan 8:13).

9:25. Messiah the Prince. From the time Artaxerxes I issued a command to rebuild and restore Jerusalem in 457 BC to the time when the Messiah the Prince shows up would be "seven weeks and sixty-two weeks," that is, 69 weeks, equivalent to 483 days/years. From 457 BC, 483 years lead to AD 26.

71. *ANET*, 491-92.
72. *ANET*, 492.
73. *ANET*, 492.

Transitioning from BC to AD has no zero ("0") year, so we add 1 to AD 26 and this bring us to AD 27 as the end of the 483 years. Jesus was baptized by John the Baptist in the Jordan River in AD 27. He began His three-and-a-half-year public ministry when Pontius Pilate (AD 26–36) was governor of Judea. See Luke 3:1.

2300 days/ years of Dan 8:14

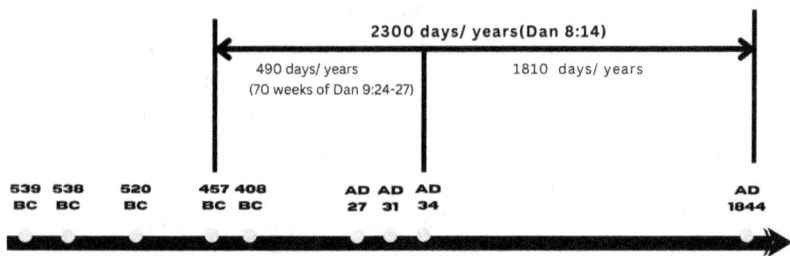

2300 DAYS/YEARS
The 2300 days/years begin in 457 BC with Artaxerxes I's decree to build and restore Jerusalem and end in 1844.

9:25. Square and moat. The expression in Dan 9:25 that Jerusalem shall be built with *reḥôb*, "a plaza," "square," or "broad open place," and *ḥārûṣ*, "a trench," "fosse," or "moat," has been the subject of an inconclusive scholarly discussion. The moat was a defense apparatus dug at the most vulnerable part outside the city wall to provide security from attackers. The plaza, on the other hand, was a social, business, and administrative center inside but near the gate of the city. The presence of these physical structures enabled a city to function autonomously.

The rebuilding of Jerusalem with a square and a moat has been taken to symbolize the restoration of the political and religious privileges which Jerusalem had lost, rather than the actual setting up of physical structures. Further, it has been suggested that the expression "square and moat" is a "euphemism for another Hebrew expression, *birah*, a word that apparently referred to both the physical temple and all of its associated institutions."[74] Archaeological finds, however, seem to show that the writer of Dan 9:25 may have been referring to the building of specific architectural structures in Jerusalem on a specified time schedule. The ancient architecture of Jerusalem may help in better understanding the expression.

---

74. Younker, "Daniel 9:25 Square and Moat," lecture (2001). See also Mazar, *Biblical Israel*, 111–12.

PROPHETIC PRACTICE

Ancient cities often had narrow streets. However, there was usually a public open space, especially near the main gate, for social activities, assemblies, business, and administrative purposes (Gen 19:2; 2 Chr 32:6; Ezra 10:9; Neh 8:1, 3, 16; Esth 4:6; Job 29:7; Dan 9:25).

There is no agreement on the meaning of *reḥôb weḥārûṣ*, "the square and the moat," in Dan 9:25.[75] Even so, the town plans of several cities in Palestine, including Beersheba, Dan, Lachish, Megiddo, and Samaria, had features that can be identified as a "square" and a "moat."

Excavations have often discovered benches near the city gates. In Jerusalem, *reḥôb*, "square," was connected with several places. The square was a public open space for commercial or legal transactions in the city. There was an open square before the Water Gate (Neh 8:1, 3, 16), and another next to the Gate of Ephraim (Neh 8:16). Also, there was an open square near the temple (Ezra 10:9). Daniel 9:25 may be referring to such installations. These may have been put in place in the mid-fifth century BC when Nehemiah built the walls under intensified opposition and harassment.

The word *ḥārûṣ*, "moat," is attested in the eighth-century BC Aramaic Zakir inscription[76] and also in the Copper Scroll from Qumran.[77] Archaeologists have found two moats that were dug into the bedrock in the northern part of the Temple Mount. These acted as part of the ancient defense structures. The northern moat runs under the present-day Sisters of Zion Convent. This moat has been dated to the Persian Period. The plaza has also been identified by Benjamin Mazar. Randall Younker's insightful conclusion is that "if the archaeological evidence has been interpreted correctly, it would appear that the construction of the Persian Period temple square, its walls and moat, were a fulfillment of Daniel 9:25 both physically and institutionally."[78]

Several moats have been found in the periphery of the ancient city of Jerusalem. From the times predating the Davidic conquest (2 Sam 5:6–10; 1 Chr 11:4–9) the Jebusite Jerusalem had a moat located to the north of the Ophel. This was an area that was later filled up when the city expanded northwards.

To the immediate north of the Temple Mount, a deep moat has been identified in which Herod installed the Struthion pool. This pool is still

---

. 75. Keil and Delitzsch prefer the expression to mean "wide space and also limited"; see *Ezekiel and Daniel*, 731. See Owusu-Antwi who has an elaborate discussion on these terms in *Chronology of Daniel 9:24–27*, 148–61.

76. Gibson, *Textbook*, 2:8, Inscription A, line 10; cited in Collins, *Daniel*, 356.

77. DJD, 3:289, Copper Scroll, col. 5, line 8.

78. Younker, "Daniel 9:25 Square and Moat," lecture, 2001. See also the Letter of Aristeas, vv. 83–120; Mazar, *Mountain of the Lord*, 65, 105.

visible today in the monastery of the Sisters of Zion. The moat (sixty feet deep and 250 feet wide) was cut in the rock bed as a defensive system for the northern part of the Temple Mount. This moat and the remains of a fortress adjacent to it may have existed during the First Temple period, but most probably it was built by the returnees from the Babylonian exile.

In 445 BC Nehemiah arrived in Jerusalem and mobilized the residents to embark on the reconstruction of the walls and defense systems of Jerusalem, but his efforts were constantly frustrated by the "hostility and interference of gentile neighbors."[79] Nehemiah oversaw the repair of the walls of the fortress complex and its two towers, Hananel and Mea (Neh 2:8; 3:1; 12:39). Contrary to the biblical text, Josephus proposed that the fortress was built by the kings of the Hasmoneans.[80] The Hasmoneans may have repaired the fortress later and named it the Baris.

If commentators are to make sense of the restoration and rebuilding of Jerusalem with a plaza and a moat (Dan 9:25), they must seriously consider the architectural finds in ancient Jerusalem. The name Jerusalem in Dan 9:25 refers to the physical city of Jerusalem and so should the architectural structures, the moat, and the plaza. Remains of the architectural structures attest to the physical reconstruction of Jerusalem by the returning exiles.

9:26. Messiah cut off. Jesus exercised his public ministry from his baptism in 27 AD for three and a half years. He was executed by Pontius Pilate, a Roman governor, in AD 31.

9:26. People of the prince who is to come. The Romans controlled Palestine from 63 BC onwards. Titus Flavius Vespasianus, the elder son of Vespasian, was born on December 30, AD 39. He served in the Roman army soon after his twentieth birthday. His father, Vespasian, was sent in AD 66 by Nero the emperor to quell the rebellion in Judea. Titus accompanied his father to Judea. Although very young, Titus distinguished himself and was accorded the honor to lead a third of the legions under his father. When Nero died on June 9, 68, he was replaced by Galba, who had an untimely death. Titus's father, Vespasian, was eventually appointed emperor of the Roman Empire on July 1, 69. Titus was eventually made a supreme commander of the Jewish war and in July 70, he attained victory over the Jewish militants. He destroyed the temple and carried some articles with him back to Rome in AD 71. His father elevated him to be a coruler. Later, on June

---

79. Geva, "Jerusalem" (*NEAEHL*, 2:717).

80. Josephus, *Antiquities of the Jews*, 15.403; and Ritmeyer and Ritmeyer, *Jerusalem in the Year 30 A.D.*, 17.

24, 79, Titus became emperor of the Roman Empire. However, Titus died suddenly of natural causes on September 13, 81. Titus is the prince of the Roman people who destroyed the temple in Jerusalem in AD 70 as implied in Dan 9:26.

9:26. Flood. See 11:10, 22, 26, 40. The semantic scope of *šeṭep*, "flood," in the Hebrew Bible includes both the literal and metaphorical meanings. The word occurs thirty-one times as a verb and six times as a noun. It is associated with the concepts of cleansing, rescuing, danger, and destruction. We have already noted that *šeṭep* has some similarities in sound and etymology with a number of other words:

- Akkadian *šaṭāpu(m)*, "preserve," "rescue life"[81]
- Arabic *šaṭafa*, "rinse (out)," "wash"[82]
- Egyptian *štf* which referred either to the watering of the land or the pouring out of a liquid in preparation for medication[83]
- Middle Kingdom (Egyptian) *ṯtf* which referred to the pouring out of liquids or the water that floods the land[84]
- Ugaritic (possibly) *štp* of which the meaning is uncertain[85]

In Dan 9:26 *šeṭep* is used as a common noun masculine singular absolute, but its meaning here is disputed. Koehler and Baumgartner acknowledged the syntactical ambiguity of the phrase *weqiṣṣô bašeṭep* here.[86]

Different textual emendations have been proposed. Some scholars would take *weqiṣṣô bašeṭep* as an independent phrase to mean "and his end will result in inundation," or "the end of it will be a cataclysm," while others prefer to extend the phrase to *habbā weqiṣṣô bašeṭep*, "and the end will come through inundation," or "its end shall come with a flood."[87]

In Dan 11:10, 22, 26, 40, *šeṭep* is used four times in a military context. All of the occurrences of *šeṭep* in Dan 11 seem to invoke a figurative usage. Archaeology informs us that at Qumran *šeṭep* is used in a military context.

---

81. von Soden, *Akkadisches Handwörterbuch*, 3:1203.

82. Wehr, *Dictionary of Modern Written Arabic*, 551; and Steingass, *English-Arabic Dictionary*, 455.

83. Erman, *Wörterbuch der aegyptischen Sprache*, 4:342.

84. Erman, *Wörterbuch der aegyptischen Sprache*, 5:411–12.

85. Dietrich, *Die keilalphabetischen Texte aus Ugarit*, 4.150, 1. Cf. Aistleitner, *Wörterbuch der Ugaritischen Sprache*, no. 2599; and Gordon, *Ugaritic Textbook*, 3:489, no. 2406.

86. *Hebrew and Aramaic Lexicon*, s.v. "שׁטף."

87. *Hebrew and Aramaic Lexicon*, s.v. "שׁטף."

Most translators understand that *šeṭep* is used in Dan 11 in a metaphorical sense. However, these translators differ when it comes to deciding with whom or what they will associate that word.

Daniel 9:24–27 is a symbolic passage so *šeṭep* cannot be isolated for a literal meaning. In the book of Daniel, therefore, *šeṭep* is used in a metaphoric sense in the context of war. This motif is already prevalent in the writings of Isaiah (cf. Isa 8:8; 28:2; 30:28). While the civil war continued in Jerusalem in AD 67 and AD 68, the Romans were ravaging the country such that "a flood of refugees and soldiers who had been driven out of Galilee, Peraea, and Idumaea rushed toward Jerusalem."[88] Similarities of imagery between Isa 8:7–8 and Dan 9:26 have been noted, and both passages can be understood metaphorically.

9:27. Sacrifice and offering. In all Semitic languages the root *zbḥ* is a general term which means "to slaughter for sacrifice." The verb and noun refer to an animal for sacrifice, a sacrificial ritual that comprises of slaughtering an animal, a libation, an offering, a meal, or a festival meal. On the other hand, *mnḥh* is "an offering," "a gift," "a present," a tribute," or "grain offering." In the ancient Near East sacrifice and offering were usually made to the deity or the dead. They were often presented at a specified sanctuary and time. Priests or other staff usually assisted people in the sacrificial process.

The Assyrian and Neo-Babylonian ritual texts refer to sacrifices as food for the gods. The practice of sacrifice and offering emanated from the idea that humans were created to be servants of gods. The value of the sacrifice and offering is in its symbolic role. What is sacrificed and offered on the altar is understood to be mediatory. The reasons for the sacrificial rituals include clearing personal or communal guilty, paying penalty for an offense, warding off evil or misfortune, appeasing gods, fellowship, thankfulness, asking for blessings, seeking divine favor, approval or intervention, and worship.

The Old Testament has extensive materials on sacrifice and offering. See, for example, Exod 25; Exod 35; Lev 1—27; and Num 7; 15; 28; 29. These writings are both descriptive and prescriptive.

The book of Daniel presents a unique motif about ending sacrifice and offering. Daniel 8:11–13; 11:31; and 12:11 indicate that the little horn power (from the fourth kingdom, Roman Empire, Dan 7:20–25) would do havoc against God's people and stop the sanctuary ritual of sacrifice. Daniel 9:27 points out that the Messiah would make a covenant with many people and bring the sacrifice and offering to an end. There are two contending parties

---

88. Sartre, *Middle East Under Rome*, 124.

to terminate the sacrifice and offering in Daniel. One uses force and persecution to stop sacrifice and offering, the other covenants with many people to end the sacrifice and offering. The little horn persecutes God's people to stop the sacrifice, while the Messiah is persecuted as He covenants with God's people to end the sacrifice and offering. In Dan 9:26 it is stated that the Messiah shall be cut off. This implies that the Messiah Himself will be killed as a substitutionary sacrifice for the people. The idea that the Messianic figure, on a specified timetable, would be sacrificed to end the sacrificial system for the people is unique to Daniel. See also Isa 53.

Chapter 10

CONTENDING POWERS

ACCORDING TO THE TEXT of Daniel on the chronology of political events, the Medo-Persian administration would dominate the ancient world for a while but would suffer defeat from the Greeks. This message is consistent with the political and historical developments in the ancient Near East. This Daniel strives to understand the proceedings that would happen in the future well after his day.

10:1. Third year of Cyrus. 536 BC. This is the third year since Cyrus took over the Babylonian kingdom.

10:1. Cyrus king of Persia. See 1:21; 6:28. Several archaeological discoveries highlight Cyrus II of Persia/Anshan or Cyrus the Great (559–530 BC). These include the Cyrus Cylinder,[1] Babylonian records,[2] and the Greek historians Herodotus[3] and Ctesias.[4]

---

1. The Cyrus Cylinder (BM 90920) was discovered at Babylon in 1879 and it highlights Cyrus II's imperial policy and administration over the nations he conquered; see *COS*, 2:314–16; and *ANET*, 315–16.

2. The Nabonidus Chronicle (BM 35382) relates the clash between the Median king, Astyages, and the Persian king, Cyrus. The chronicle continues to relate how Cyrus conquered Babylon. See Grayson, *Assyrian and Babylonian Chronicles*, 21–22, 104–11. The Cyrus Panegyric or the Verse Account of Nabonidus identifies Cyrus as king of all lands; see Smith, *Babylonian Historical Texts*, 83–97, plates v–x; and *ANET*, 312–15.

3. Herodotus (fifth century BC) wrote on the early life of Cyrus II; see *Histories*, 1.107–22.

4. Cited in Diodorus, *Diodorus of Sicily*, 9.23.

CYRUS CYLINDER
Cuneiform text mentions of Cyrus's policy of restoring deported people and rebuilding their temples in their home territories. Some Jewish people responded to Cyrus's policy to return to Judah to rebuild the temple (Ezra 1:2–5). (Credit: Zev Radovan)

A brick now housed in the British Museum has an inscription which reads: "Cyrus, king of the world, king of Anshan, son of Cambyses, king of Anshan. The great gods delivered all lands into my hands, and I made this land to dwell in peace."[5]

The name "Cyrus" comes from the Greek Κύρου. "Cyrus" is a corruption of the Old Persian *Kūrush*, the Elamite *Kurash*, or the Akkadian *Kurash(u)*.[6] The Hebrew transliteration of Cyrus is *Kôresh* whereas the Egyptian is *Kawarushu*.[7] Cyrus's father was Cambyses I, who was a Persian, and his mother was Mandane, who was the daughter of the Median king Astyages.[8]

Cyrus was credited as the founder of the Persian Empire. He was identified as the king of Persia in Dan 10:1, as well as in the Nabonidus Chronicle.[9] Cyrus inherited the kingdom from family predecessors. His father, grandfather, and great-grandfather were kings.

In 547 BC Cyrus conquered Asia Minor, the Greek cities, and Croesus, king of Lydia. Neo-Babylonia was the major power that resisted Cyrus, but in October of 539 BC (Dan 1:21) Cyrus conquered Babylon without

---

5. *NIV Archaeological Study Bible* (2005), 1283.
6. Yamauchi, *Persia and the Bible*, 72.
7. Yamauchi, *Persia and the Bible*, 72.
8. Yamauchi, *Persia and the Bible*, 79. Cyrus II is said to have been Darius the Mede's nephew "and commanding general of the combined armies of the Medes and the Persians." White, *Story of Prophets and Kings*, 523.
9. *ANET*, 306, col. 2, line 15.

military engagement. The Tomb of Cyrus is at Pasargadae,[10] in Iran. It once had the inscription: "O man, I am Cyrus the son of Cambyses, who founded the empire of Persia, and was king of Asia. Grudge me not therefore this monument."[11] Alexander the Great is said to have ordered the restoration of this tomb after he read the inscription.

TOMB OF CYRUS
Tomb of Cyrus the Great (559–529 BC), king of Persia, in Pasargadae, Iran. King Cyrus is amicably called "the anointed shepherd of Israel's God" (Isa 44:28; Isa 45:1). (Credit: Zev Radovan)

Cyrus's tomb has a room 3.5 meters long and 2.1 meters wide. It has the walls, floor, and the roof made of huge blocks of cut stone. The room stands on six tiers of massive white stones resembling marble. The whole structure rises eleven meters above the ground. The entrance to it has a narrow dark passageway which opens toward the west. The interior of the tomb has traces of a prayer niche, "*mehráb*," with an obliterated Arabic inscription of the Islamic period which reads: "In the Name of God, the Merciful, the Compassionate."

It is intriguing to note that the prophet Isaiah (740–681 BC) predicted events concerning Cyrus (Isa 44:28; 45:1, 13) about 150 years before he existed. The LORD God identified Cyrus as "His anointed" (Isa 45:1). This designation is similar to that of the Messianic figure. The LORD God also considered Cyrus as "My shepherd" (Isa 44:28) whose heart would be moved to fulfill a prophetic utterance that was made earlier by Jeremiah (Jer 25:12; 29:10; 2 Chr 36:22). A similar designation was also accorded Nebuchadnezzar (Jer 25:9; 27:6; 43:10).

In his first year of reign (538 BC), Cyrus made an edict for the rebuilding of the Jerusalem temple. At that time, he gave permission for any of the

---

10. Sami, *Pasargade*, 27–40; and Kuhrt, *ANE*, 2:661.
11. Bienkowski, "Cyrus" (*DANE*, 87).

Jewish captives who so wished to return to their native land (2 Chr 36:23; Ezra 1:1–2; 5:13–17).

During the time of Darius I (522–486 BC), Tattenai, the Persian governor for the Trans-Euphrates region, disrupted the temple building progress. Tattenai complained of what the Jews were doing in Jerusalem, and petitioned to have the royal records searched. The decree of Cyrus, written in 538 BC and legitimizing the reconstruction of the Jerusalem temple, was found. A memorandum giving the details of that decree was found at Ecbatana (Ezra 6:1–12). It is possible that anticipation of Cyrus's decree for the rebuilding of the Jerusalem temple motivated the prayer found in Dan 9.

10:1, 7, 8, 14, 16. Vision. See **8:1. Vision.**

10:2–3. Mourning. See **9:3. Fasting and mourning rites.** For twenty-one days Daniel prepared himself for an appropriate frame of mind to receive a special revelation from God. His contrition gestures were in keeping with religious practice of the day and continue to be widely utilized today by those who are in desperate need for divine intervention.

10:3. Anoint myself. In the ancient Near East it was a widespread practice for both men and women to smear themselves with aromatic substances. See Ruth 3:3 and 2 Sam 12:20. This was done for different purposes, including cosmetic, social, economic, medical, and religious needs. Scented oils and perfume manufacturing were good business. A promising market existed among the wealthy in different communities. Some of the aromatic products were very expensive.

The process of making the perfumes was very rudimentary. It began by the pleasantness of the smell of some substances. The mixture of some ingredients making perfumes was just by experimentation. Perfumes were mainly made from plants. Some animals, especially the Red Sea mollusk, were used for the manufacture of perfumes too. People made scented oils and perfumes from flower oils, gums, resins, roots of certain plants, and tapping trees to produce tears of resin that could be allowed to dry. Perfume boxes, clay jars, or elaborate alabaster jars were used for containers. Many of these vessels have been recovered by archaeologists.

The products for making the perfumes came from different parts of the ancient world. So, there were many trade routes that were used to distribute aromatic goods from place to place. Frankincense, bdellium, and myrrh came from Arabia (Isa 60:6; Jer 6:20); onycha from Red Sea mollusk; nard from Nepal; aloes, calamus, and saffron from India; cinnamon and cassia from Sri Lanka; galbanum from Iran; balm from Judah (Ezek 27:17) and Gilead (Jer 8:22; 46:11); and frankincense and myrrh from Somalia.

Scented oils and perfumes were used for cosmetics and for providing skin protection from the hot sun. They could also be used for embalming and funeral rituals. Daniel voluntarily abstained from the use of fragrant oils while he made his petition to his God. This practice of denying oneself luxuriant commodities in order to communicate pertinently with the divine has been known from antiquity.

10:4. Tigris River. The writer of the book of Daniel claims to have had a vision while he was standing "upon the side of the great river, which is Hiddekel" (Dan 10:4; 12:5-7). "Hiddekel" is the Hebrew name for the Tigris River. This name appears only twice in the biblical text (Gen 2:14; Dan 10:4). "Tigris" is the Greek name, adapted from the Old Persian *Tigra*. This is a word which originated from the Sumerian *Idigna/Idiglat*. The Assyrian/Babylonian (Akkadian) equivalent is *Idiglat/Idignat*, while Arabic/Aramaic is *Diglath*, and Turkish *Dicle*.[12]

In the creation story of Gen 2:14 the Tigris is the third tributary of the river in the garden of Eden which flows on the eastern side of Asshur (Assyria). The other rivers are the Euphrates, Pishon, and Gihon. While the names "Tigris" and "Euphrates" still exist today, the "Pishon" and "Gihon" are a mystery and this makes the effort to locate the garden of Eden ambiguous. There is a perennial spring called Gihon in the Kidron Valley to the east of Jerusalem (1 Kgs 1:33, 38, 45; 2 Chr 32:30; 33:14), but it is difficult to associate this spring with the Gihon River of Eden.

There are some suggestions that Eden might have been in the vicinity of the present waterheads of the Euphrates and the Tigris in eastern Turkey, or somewhere near the place where these two rivers are closest to each other, or in the alluvial plains leading to the Persian Gulf. However, the evidence to locate the biblical garden of Eden from the present geographical locations of the Tigris and the Euphrates must not be relied upon too heavily. In fact, Randall W. Younker observes that if the author's intention (Gen 7) was global (implied by the universal context of the narrative), then Noah's flood would have been understood to have wiped out all the preflood physical geography such that the "Euphrates" and "Tigris" Rivers we have today could just be names which survived from the oral tradition.[13] Many ancient Near Eastern tablets and inscriptions mention the Euphrates and Tigris

---

12. Jacobsen, "Tigris" (*IDB*, 4:642); Stefanovic, "Hiddekel" (*ABD*, 3:194); Edens, "Tigris" (*OEANE*, 5:206-9); and BDB, 293.

13. Younker, Horn Museum, Andrews University, Berrien Springs, MI, personal communication with author, April 24, 2006.

Rivers, their tributaries, the canals, and other rivers and seas in the area, but nothing has been found written yet on the names "Gihon" and "Pishon." To refer to the Tigris as "the great river" has been construed by some scholars as, at the least, misleading. Some feel that the author could be charged with "solecism or gross error."[14] The difficulty with Dan 10:4 is caused by the fact that on multiple occasions the Hebrew Bible refers to the Euphrates as the "Great River" (Gen 15:18; Deut 1:7; Josh 1:4). Further, the Syriac version of Dan 10:4 calls the river "the Euphrates" while the Masoretic Text has it as "the Tigris."

Although the Tigris is narrower and steeper than the Euphrates, surveys show that it drains a higher volume of water from the snowy mountain ranges in eastern Turkey and also the Zagros Mountains in Western Iran. The Tigris lies to the east of the Euphrates River. Its source is in the Taurus Mountains east of Turkey and it flows southeast for about 1,220 miles (1,950 kilometers). During earlier times it is possible that the Tigris emptied by itself into the Persian Gulf, but now it joins the Euphrates and together they flow for about forty miles (sixty-four kilometers) in what is known as the Shaṭṭ al-ʿArab. This river flows much faster than the Euphrates because of its steep gradient. It also carries a larger volume of water.

The Tigris can also be referred to as a great river in the sense that the name originates from the creation story (Gen 2:14), it carries more volume of water, and it flows faster than the Euphrates.

We do not know whether the author stood physically on the bank of the Tigris, or whether he was there only in vision. Either way, he indicates that other men were with him there on the banks of the river (Dan 10:4, 7).

10:5. Uphaz. Biblical interpreters, as well as archaeologists, have failed to identify Uphaz as a geographical place. In the biblical tradition "Uphaz" stands renowned for its quality gold (Jer 10:9; Dan 10:5). The identity of this ancient place, however, is ambiguous. The individual whom Daniel claims to have seen had his loins wrapped with fine gold from Uphaz (Dan 10:5). Collins argued that Uphaz in Dan 10:5 as well as in Jer 10:9 is a corruption of Ophir (Job 28:16; Ps 45:9; Isa 13:12).

It cannot be ascertained whether Uphaz was a nation, region, city, business center, or just a mine. In the biblical text, Uphaz appears as a proper noun without gender, number, or state. The context and syntax, however, show that it is definitely a geographical location. Deliberate effort has been made by different interpreters to identify Uphaz. Some have tried to associate it with another place, or to modify the word. The lack of evidence

---

14. Montgomery, *Critical and Exegetical Commentary*, 407.

supporting such modifications makes it difficult to reach a definite conclusion. Nevertheless, the word *'pz* appears on a Yemenite votive inscription where the context clearly indicates a quality of the metal gold.[15] Whether Daniel meant Uphaz or Ophir, it seems reasonable to conclude that the reference points to an actual geographical location which may have been renowned for its quality gold.

10:7. Great trembling. Daniel's companions by the River Tigris fled to hiding themselves because of their great trembling in the presence of a supernatural being. Great trembling can be experienced when panic and terror are at their height. Such extreme fear or panic/terror is always an unwelcome and unpleasant surprise. If the individual involved is not paralyzed with the fear, he or she can always escape away. Daniel could not run away because he was gripped with fear and could not do so (Dan 10:8-12). Surprisingly, his friends managed to disappear from the scene. In the ancient Near East panic terror was a common phenomenon and it often took place in war situations or in the context of a theophany. Recipients of bad news could also be traumatized by great trembling (Gen 27:33; 1 Sam 14:15; Ezek 26:16; 32:10).

10:8. Frailty. See 7:28. **Alarmed.**

10:13, 20. Prince of Persia. Daniel mentioned that he continued to serve in the royal court during the reign of Cyrus (539-530 BC; Dan 6:28). The vision by the Tigris River occurred in 536 BC, the third year of Cyrus (Dan 10:1). While Daniel fasted and prayed for three weeks (Dan 10:2, 3), a divine being was being opposed by the prince of Persia (Dan 10:12-13).

Opinions differ as to the identity of the prince of Persia. This person has been identified as the guardian or patron angel of Persia. Daniel 10:13, 20 raises for the first time the concept of "tutelary angels set over nations."[16] Such a suggestion is based on the fact that the word *śar*, "prince," "chief," "ruler," "official," "captain," "chieftain,"[17] is used for both human (Dan 1:7; 9:6, 8; 11:5) and angelic beings (Dan 8:11, 25; 10:13, 21; 12:1). On the other hand, some have identified Cyrus the king as the prince of Persia. Daniel 10:1 identifies Cyrus as the king of Persia. Related archaeological discoveries, which include the Behistun Inscription, the Nabonidus Chronicle, and the Cyrus Cylinder, also identify Cyrus as the king of Persia, and never as the prince of Persia.

---

15. Gregor, "Gold aus Ofir?," 19-22, quoted in Baker, "Uphaz" (*ABD*, 6:765).
16. Stevens, "Daniel 10," 410-31.
17. BDB, 978.

The Cyrus Cylinder records that Cyrus freed the exiled captives to return to their homelands.[18] The importance of the Cyrus Cylinder to the studies of Daniel is that it reflects the beginning of the fulfillment of what Daniel had prayed for (Dan 9:1–19). Cyrus also issued a decree for the reconstruction of the Jerusalem temple and the restoration of the vessels that were confiscated to Babylon (Ezra 1:1–4; 6:1–5; 2 Chr 36:22–23). The decree Cyrus gave for the reconstruction of the Jerusalem temple was recovered at Ecbatana during the time of Darius I (522–486 BC) when Tattenai was the Persian governor of the Trans-Euphrates province (Ezra 6:3–6).

It is therefore consistent with the text to take the prince of Persia (Dan 10:13) as a political figure who was obstructing the process of liberating the Jews from their captivity. Cambyses (530–522 BC) was Cyrus's crown prince, and might not have been in favor of Jewish autonomy. He seems to be the most probable candidate for the prince of Persia in Dan 10:13.

William H. Shea offered some insights on why Cambyses, son of Cyrus, could possibly be the prince of Persia mentioned by Daniel. Cambyses had political power and influence as a crown prince. He was very much opposed to foreign religious cults. He was zealous for Zoroastrianism and worshiped the god Ahura Mazda. He destroyed some temples of foreign gods in Egypt.

10:13, 21. Michael. See 12:1. Names of angels are rarely given. Michael here is depicted as one of the chief princes. This name appears only in apocalyptic passages (Dan 10:13, 21; 12:1; Jude 9; Rev 12:7). In Dan 10:13, an angelic being was resisted by the prince of Persia. Michael, "Who is like God?,"[19] is identified as "one of the first rulers" who responded to help the angelic being. Further, it is noted that Michael showed Himself courageous with Gabriel over the political developments in Persia. Michael is also identified as the great ruler who stands for Daniel's people in the time of distress at the end of the world (Dan 12:1).

The question to ask then is, who is this "Michael?" The Hebrew Bible has several individuals who bore the name "Michael." The onomastic list includes: Michael the father of Sethur, who was one of the twelve spies representing the tribe of Asher (Num 13:13); one of the members of the tribe of Gad was Michael who lived in Bashan (1 Chr 5:13, 14); a Levitical singer Michael, the son of Baaseiah (1 Chr 6:40); Michael, a chief and military leader of the tribe of Issachar (1 Chr 7:3); Michael, a Benjaminite from Jerusalem (1 Chr 8:16); Michael, the father of Omri of the tribe of Issachar

---

18. *COS*, 2:315, lines 28–36; and *ANET*, 316.

19. A similar name is *Mîkāyāhû*, "Who is like Yah?" The Assyrian proper names that fall into this category include *Mannu-kî-Rammân*, "Who is like Rammân?," and *Mannu-kî-ilu-rabu*, "Who is like the Great God?" See BDB, 567.

(1 Chr 27:18); Michael, one of the sons of Jehoshaphat (2 Chr 21:2); and Michael, a fifth-century BC Diaspora Judaean in Babylon whose son Zebediah led eighty of his kinsmen back to Jerusalem (Ezra 8:8).

The figure of the son of man in Dan 7:13 has been identified as Michael, one of the first rulers (Dan 10:13, 21; 12:1). Michael was named as one of the holy angels in the apocryphal 1 En 9:1; 10:11; 20:5. Further, Michael, who was the supposed son of man in Dan 7, was identified as Melchizedek in a text from Qumran, where He assumed military, judicial, and priestly roles (11QMelch 13-15).[20] Michael's name is popular at Qumran and throughout the intertestamental period literature where He is understood to be protector or guardian of God's people. In the Qumran War Scroll, Michael has purely a military office (1QM 9:15-16; and 1QM 17). He was also intimately associated with the Messiah in Rev 12:7. There He, along with His angels, defeated the dragon.[21] The Shepherd of Hermes identified Michael as Christ the Messiah.[22]

In the biblical text, therefore, Michael is identified with the anticipated Messianic figure. The Messiah was realized in the person of Jesus Christ (Dan 9:25-27). Michael is the heavenly prince mentioned by name in Daniel. Michael is "one of the chief princes (Dan 10:13); "prince of host" (Dan 8:11); and "the great prince who stands up" (Dan 12:1). In the New Testament Michael is the archangel who disputed with Satan over the dead body of Moses (Jude 9). He is also identified as the one who calls for the dead to rise (1 Thess 4:16). Michael appears when in direct confrontation with Satan; and Michael stands up to deliver God's children who are in trouble. In light of Scripture, Michael seems to point to the person of Jesus (Dan 12:1; John 5:28; 1 Thess 4:16).

10:19. Peace be to you. See **4:1. Your peace be increased.**

10:20. Prince of Greece. See **8:21. Greece.** Here is the announcement of the coming of the Greek rule to the ancient East. Alexander the Great (356-323 BC) was the son of Philip II, king of Macedonia, and the Epirote princess Olympias. At the age of fourteen Alexander served as his father's regent. He distinguished himself by commanding the left wing of the Macedonian army at the battle of Chaeronea in 340 BC. His father was assassinated in

---

20. For the text, see de Jonge and Van der Woude, "11 Q Melchizedek," 301-26; Milik, "Milkî-îedeq et Mikî-resa," 96-109; and Vermes, *Complete Dead Sea Scrolls in English*, 500-2.

21. Lacocque, *Book of Daniel*, 133.

22. Herm. Vis. 3; Herm. Sim. 8:3; 9:12, 7-8; Collins, "Son of Man and the Saints," 66.

336 BC and Alexander was crowned king at the age of twenty. He aligned himself with his father's generals Antipater and Parmenion. He successfully eliminated all opposition.

In 334 BC Alexander swiftly marched with his army across into Asia and engaged in battle at Granicus River with the Persian army. They had another battle again in 333 BC at Issus where Darius III actually fled and left his army. This was the initial defeat of the Persians but Alexander quickly moved his troops and passed through Syria and conquered Egypt in 331 BC. The Persian army attempted to obstruct Alexander's progress to the east. They engaged in battle with Alexander at Gaugamela in 331 BC. Here the Persian army suffered terrible defeat and Alexander marched and took over all of the Persian Empire. On June 10/11, 323 BC, Alexander unexpectedly died while in ancient Babylon, perhaps of malaria and excessive drinking. His kingdom was torn among four of his main generals.

In the chronological succession of the kingdoms in the book of Daniel, the Greeks are identified as the third kingdom that would follow the Medo-Persians. Alexander the Great is represented by the horn of the goat (Dan 8:5, 21) that broke up into four (Dan 8:8, 22). In Dan 10:20 Alexander is named as the prince of Greece, a title equal to the prince of Persia (Dan 10:13, 20).

10:21. Book of truth. This writing of truth could be a register or an enrollment. The Babylonians chronicled records for different purposes. Unfortunately, many of these documents were destroyed. The book of truth here could be the equivalent of the Babylonian Tablet of Destinies. Such a document contained the course of history or the cosmos and was usually entrusted to the custody of the gods. When the tablet was stolen then everything was said to be chaotic. The book of truth in Dan 10:21 had no human origin but was a divine record that no one could access or perceive what was written on it. The books mentioned in Daniel are divine and hold the destiny of humans (Dan 10:21; 12:1). See also Mal 3:16 and Rev 20:15.

Chapter 11

FIGHTS 'TIL END TIMES

A COMPLEX POLITICO-HISTORICAL AND socioreligious outline is presented in Dan 11. The narrative continues the discourse begun by Gabriel in Dan 10:21. The divine being had come to help Daniel understand (Dan 10:5–12) the developments which would take place in the ancient world leading to the time of the end. Caution should be exercised when applying current political developments or predicting of future sociopolitical events. Most of the key political figures in ancient history had similar behavior and actions. As history is sometimes said to repeat itself, some events in Dan 11 could possibly have multiple fulfillments. Interpreters should consider the chronological outline of the book of Daniel when dealing with Dan 11.

LITERARY PATTERN OF DANIEL 11

Vv. 1-2, Medo-Persian kings. Gabriel relates about the Medo-Persian kings. Notice that when Gabriel mentions the first encounter of the fourth Medo-Persia king with Greece in 480 BC to 479 BC where the Persians were initially defeated, Gabriel leaves discussing all the political events of the Medo-Persian Empire until its final fall. He moves on to talk about the Greeks, the next empire.

Vv. 3-19, Greek kings. Gabriel discussed political events of Greek kings. When Gabriel mentioned the Greeks provoking the Romans in 190 BC where the Greeks were initially defeated, Gabriel leaves discussing the rest of the history of the Greeks until their fall, but he moves on to talk about the Roman Empire, the next in sequence.

Vv. 20–45, Roman kings. Within the Roman Empire, verses 36–39 describe Christian Rome. Gabriel relates the political activities of the Roman Empire until "at the time of the end" (Dan 11:40). He talks about the king of the north and his final demise (v. 45). Again, Gabriel then stops discussing all the political activities of the Roman Empire during the time of the end until its final fall when the divine kingdom sets in. In light of this, the events of Dan 11 lead to the beginning of the time of the end. Gabriel finally moves on to talk about the closing of the time of the end (Dan 12:1–13). The book of Revelation discusses the religious and political developments during the time of the end.

CONTEXT OF DANIEL 11

The setting is in 536 BC, the third year of Cyrus (Dan 10:1). Daniel was by the River Tigris when he received the vision (Dan 10:4; 12:5–7). Gabriel (Dan 11:1, cf. Dan 9:1, 21) indicated that he had been involved in the local current affairs since the first year of Darius the Mede (539 BC). It is Gabriel who outlined the future events to Daniel. Consistent with the predictive message of the rest of the book, chapter 11 gives a synopsis of the Medo-Persian, Greek, and Roman kingdoms. The Neo-Babylonian kingdom is not discussed in Dan 11 because it had already fallen to the Medes and Persians in 539 BC (Dan 5).

11:1. Darius the Mede. See **6:1. Darius.**

11:1–2. Median and Persian kings. The vision of Dan 10 took place in 536 BC during the reign of Cyrus the Great. As shown in table 8, the history of antiquity confirms that the three kings (Dan 11:2) who succeeded Cyrus were Cambyses II (530–522 BC); the usurper Gaumata, who declared himself falsely as Bardiya or Smerdis (522 BC); and Darius I (522–486 BC).

KING DARIUS I
Limestone relief shows King Darius I (522–486 BC) sitting on the throne and holding a staff. Crown Prince Xerxes, guards, and attendants are behind him. Persepolis, Iran. (Credit: Zev Radovan)

The fourth Persian king after Cyrus was Xerxes I (486–465 BC) who invaded the Greek mainland in 480 BC. Xerxes I lost to the Greeks in a naval engagement in the Bay of Salamis. Herodotus commented on Xerxes I's military might.[1] He commanded troops collected from forty nations. Regardless of military prowess, the Persian army was defeated by the Greeks at Plataea and at Mycale in 479 BC.

Gabriel mentioned the encounter of the fourth Persian king with the kingdom of Greece (Dan 11:2) in 480 BC and 479 BC, and then moved on to discussing matters concerning the Greek kingdom. He did not discuss the political developments leading to the final fall of the Persian kingdom in 331 BC.

---

1. Herodotus, *Herodotus*, 8.75–100.

Table 8
KINGS OF PERSIA

KING	DATES OF REIGN
Teispes (of Anshan)	ca. 650–620 BC
Cyrus I (son)	ca. 620–590 BC
Cambyses I (son)	ca. 590–559 BC
Cyrus the Great (son)	559–530 BC
Cambyses II (son)	530–522 BC
Bardiya (Smerdis) (brother)	522 BC
Darius I (son of Hystaspes, grandson of Arsames, descendant of Achaemenes)	522–486 BC
Xerxes (son)	486–465 BC
Artaxerxes I (son)	465–424/423 BC
Darius II (son)	423–405 BC
Artaxerxes II (son)	405–359 BC
Artaxerxes III (son)	359–338 BC
Artaxerxes IV (Arses, son)	338–336 BC
Darius III (second cousin)	336–330 BC
Alexander of Macedon	330–323 BC

11:2. Kings will arise. Linguistic similarities have been noted between Dan 11 and the dynastic prophecy (dated Persian or Seleucid). The expression "The king of... shall rise..." has led some interpreters to conclude that both Dan 11 and the dynastic prophecy were *ex-eventu vaticinia* (foretold after the fact).[2] Nevertheless, the political struggles foretold in Dan 11 continued to be fulfilled long after the book was written. They also continue to fit into the course of history in a credible manner.

11:3–19. Greek kings. The Greek kingdom was represented by the bronze in Dan 2:32, a leopard in Dan 7:6, and a he-goat in Dan 8:5, 21. The first king, Alexander the Great (331–323 BC), is referred to as a mighty king in Dan 11:3. Alexander the Great was also represented by the single horn that was between the goat's eyes (Dan 8:5, 8, 21). The kingdom of Alexander the Great would be broken up and divided to the four winds of the heavens (cf. Dan 8:8; 11:4). See **7:2. Four winds of heaven.**

Josephus reported that Alexander was shown the book of Daniel. He was glad when he discovered from that book that the Greeks would conquer the Persians.[3] Alexander defeated the Persian army in 331 BC at Gaugamela, a city on the Tigris River in Assyria, two hundred miles north of Baghdad. When he died in Babylon on June 10/11, 323 BC, he left no legitimate heir

---

2. Grayson, *Babylonian Historical-Literary Texts*, 33, 35.
3. Josephus, *Antiquities of the Jews*, 11.8.5.337.

to his throne. For several years, there was a fierce struggle for succession in his kingdom. Several people claimed different parts of the kingdom and continued to fight for supremacy. Finally, Alexander's kingdom was divided between the main contenders (Dan 11:4). These four generals were known as the Diadochi: Cassander (Macedonia), Lysimachus (Thrace), Seleucus (Syria, Babylonia, and Asia Minor), and Ptolemy (Egypt). Each of these had declared himself king by 305 BC.

Gabriel focused on two of the four general divisions of the Greek kingdom (Dan 11:5-19). These two he characterized as the king of the north and the king of the south. The geography of the land of Canaan allowed easy invasions from the north and the south of that country. According to C. Mervyn Maxwell, the "king of the north" and the "king of the south" designate the persons controlling Syria and Egypt.[4] These two countries lie north and south of Jerusalem. Egypt, which is named in Dan 11:8, was under the Ptolemies from 305-30 BC.

Ptolemy I Soter (322-285 BC), the king of the south (Dan 11:5), claimed Egypt and its vicinity from 322 BC and ushered in a new dynasty there. He also took Jerusalem unopposed on a Sabbath day in 319 BC in his fight to establish hegemony over Palestine and Coele-Syria.

PTOLEMY I SOTER
Ptolemy I Soter—the founder of the Ptolemaic Dynasty of Egypt, after the death of Alexander the Great. (Credit: Zev Radovan)

---

4. Maxwell, *God Cares*, 1:284.

Seleucus I Nicator (321–280 BC) was a distinguished commander under Perdiccas, the protector of the kingdom after the death of Alexander in 323 BC. Perdiccas was murdered in 321 BC and Seleucus I Nicator became a governor in Babylon. He escaped to Egypt in 316 BC when he failed to withstand Antigonus who had been fighting to succeed Alexander. For some years, Ptolemy I was the host and protector of Seleucus I. Daniel 11:5 refers to Seleucus I as one of Ptolemy I's rulers who would be strong for him and rule independently. Seleucus I later claimed the northern part of Syria while Ptolemy I administered the southern part of that country. He then regained control over Babylonia in 312 BC and continued to have rule over all Syria.

Daniel 11:6 indicates that after a certain number of years the king of the north and the king of the south will make an agreement effected by a dynastic marriage. Berenice, the daughter of Ptolemy II Philadelphus (285–246 BC), the king of the south, married Antiochus II Theos (261–246 BC), the king of the north, who was already married to Laodice, his half-sister.[5] The struggle between the two rival queens is alluded to in Dan 11:6–9. Following the death of Antiochus II in 246 BC, Berenice and her infant son Antiochus were murdered (Dan 11:6) and war broke out (246–241 BC) between Berenice's avenging brother, Ptolemy III Euergetes (246–221 BC, one of the shoots of [Berenice's] roots; Dan 11:7), and Seleucus II Callinicus (246–225 BC), Laodice's son.

As indicated in Dan 11:7, Ptolemy III invaded Syria and its territories successfully (246–241 BC). He gained much of Mesopotamia but Seleucus II who had combined forces with his brother Antiochus Hierax blocked his progress. However, Ptolemy III received fifteen talents of silver from his new territories on the northern coast of Syria. He also managed to recover Egyptian divine statues and valuable works of art that were plundered from temples during the Persian rule and carried them back to Egypt (Dan 11:8). In his book, Daniel deals more with Egypt as it appears in some political dealings in the ancient Near East (Dan 11:8, 42, 43). Considerable archaeological data shows that Egypt was involved in the contemporary geopolitical affairs. See **11:42, 43. Egypt.**

Seleucus II unsuccessfully attempted to invade the Egyptian territory in 242 BC,[6] an incident referred to in Dan 11:9. His two sons (Dan 11:10) were Seleucus III Soter (225–223 BC), who was murdered by conspirators after a short reign, and Antiochus III the Great (223–187 BC), who succeeded his brother in 223 BC. Antiochus III marshaled a great army to wage war against Ptolemy IV (221–203 BC) at Raphia in Gaza on June 22, 217 BC

---

5. Whitehorne, "Antiochus" (*ABD*, 1:270).
6. Cary, *History of the Greek World*, 120.

but could not succeed (Dan 11:11–13). Polybius indicated that Ptolemy IV's army had 70,000 infantry, 5,000 horses, and 73 elephants, while that of Antiochus III had 62,000 infantry, 6,000 horses, and 102 elephants.[7] Ptolemy IV's soldiers were so elated by their success at Raphia that they would not take any more orders from him (Dan 11:12). It is possible that after his victory at Raphia, Ptolemy IV went to Jerusalem and entered the temple's holy of holies at the protest of the Jewish priests. An inscription found at Tell el-Firr, about seven kilometers from Beth Shean (ancient Scythopolis) in Israel, shows that Ptolemaios was holding certain lands in Coele-Syria and Phoenicia as a vassal of the Egyptian king. Ptolemaios attained this position after the seizure of these lands by Antiochus III (223–187 BC) in 200 BC.[8]

The Rosetta Stone (dated to March 196 BC) relates that Ptolemy V quenched a revolt by some residents of Lycopolis in Egypt. This rebellion at Lycopolis had done much damage to the temples and other citizens (Dan 11:14).[9] The Rosetta Stone serves to confirm that the Ptolemies controlled Egypt. The Ptolemies were Greek kings who ruled Egypt since the breaking of Alexander the Great's empire.

ROSETTA STONE
The Rosetta Stone inscribed in hieroglyphic (top), demotic (middle), and Greek (bottom). This inscription dating from 196 BC was a major tool in deciphering the Egyptian hieroglyphics. (Credit: Zev Radovan)

7. Polybius, *Histories*, 5.79.

8. Landau, "Greek Inscription Found Near Hefzibah," 54–70; and Walbank, *Hellenistic World*, 129.

9. See Rosetta Stone, English translation of the Greek text by Schoville, "Rosetta Stone in Historical Perspective," 17–18, lines 19–28; Andrews, *Rosetta Stone* (1984); and Quirke and Andrews, *Rosetta Stone* (1989).

In 202 BC Antiochus III invaded Coele-Syria and pushed the Ptolemaic forces back to the desert between Palestine and Egypt. He laid a famous siege on Gaza in the autumn of 201 BC (Dan 11:15). From 202-201 BC Scopas led the Ptolemaic forces to counteract the Seleucid occupation of Palestine and managed to recapture a number of places in southern Palestine. The king of the north, Antiochus III, would stay in the beautiful land [Palestine] (Dan 11:16). See **8:9 beautiful (land).** The struggle for occupying Palestine was finally settled at the battle of Panion, near the source of the Jordan River. There the Ptolemaic army under Scopas met the Seleucid army under Antiochus III. Scopas was defeated and Antiochus III repossessed Palestine for a long time that followed.

Antiochus III brought his daughter Cleopatra to the young Ptolemy V (aged sixteen) for marriage (Dan 11:17) at Raphia, the frontier of the Seleucid kingdom. This gesture brought about peace between these two warring kingdoms. Antiochus III then embarked on an expedition to the coastlands (Dan 11:18). He invaded Thrace in 194 BC and provoked the fury of the Romans. A long war was waged but in 190 BC Antiochus III was defeated at Magnesia by the Roman general Lucius Cornelius Scipio (vv. 18, 19). The Roman kingdom continued to be stronger and its decisive moment to become a world power came on June 22, 168 BC, when at the battle of Pydna the Roman army under General Aemilius Paulus completely defeated the Greeks under Persus, king of Macedonia.[10] The Greek kingdom is the third in Daniel's succession of kingdoms. It is symbolically represented by the belly and thighs of bronze (Dan 2:32, 39), a beast like a leopard (Dan 7:6), a he-goat (Dan 8:5-8, 21), and Greek kings (Dan 11:3-19).

We note again that when Gabriel (Dan 11:18, 19) refers to the defeat of the Greeks in 190 BC by the Roman power, he then leaves discussing all the political developments leading to the final fall of the Greek kingdom in 168 BC. He moves on to speak about this next kingdom which took the place of the Greeks in geopolitical dominance.

11:20-45. Kings of the fourth kingdom. The fourth kingdom is represented by the legs of iron and the feet and toes of iron and clay (Dan 2:33-35, 40-43). It is also represented by the fourth beast from which the little horn emanates (Dan 7:7-8, 23). The kings of Dan 11:20-45 belong to the fourth kingdom. According to Daniel's chronology, the fourth kingdom would last until the establishment of the divine kingdom at the end of time (Dan 2:35; 7:13, 14, 27; 11:20—12:1). The first three kingdoms are clearly identified in the book of Daniel. These are Neo-Babylonia, Medo-Persia, and Greece.

---

10. Plutarch: *Life of Aemillius Paulus,* 6:15-23; Livius, *History of Rome,* 44.41-46; Polybius, *Histories,* 29.14-21; and Holleaux, "Rome and Antiochus," 267-78.

The fourth kingdom remains unnamed. The author simply addresses it as the fourth kingdom. It was about this fourth kingdom that Daniel was most concerned. It will be noted for its horrendous activities. The fourth kingdom would displace the Greek kingdom, which was the third kingdom in the geopolitical successions outlined by Daniel (Dan 2:40; 7:23; 11:20-45; see table 4). History of antiquity shows that the Greeks were followed by the Romans as the next world power.[11] Daniel labored to understand the political significance and religious role of this Roman kingdom (Dan 2:33-35, 40-43; 7:7, 8, 11-12, 19-26; 8:9-12; 11:20-45).

The decisive moment for the Roman Empire to become a world power came on June 22, 168 BC, at the battle of Pydna. The Roman army under General Aemilius Paulus completely defeated the Greeks under Persus, king of Macedonia. Aemilius Paulus collected so much money into the public treasury that the people were no longer required to pay special taxes from his time until 43 BC. In fact, he was praised for his freedom of spirit and greatness of soul, and he was one who "would not consent even to look upon the quantities of silver and the quantities of gold that were gathered together from the royal treasuries, but handed them over to the quaestors for the public chest."[12]

Although he had conquered a large kingdom, Paulus did not add one drachma to his substance, but he was known to be very generous to others. Paulus "fell sick of a disease which at first was dangerous, but in time less threatening, though it was troublesome and hard to get rid of. Under the advice of his physicians, he sailed to Velia in Italy, and there spent much time in country places lying by the sea and affording great quiet."[13] He eventually returned to Rome to celebrate his recovery. After offering some sacrifices to his gods in the temple for his recovery, he went to his house to rest but all of a sudden "became delirious and deranged in mind, and on the third day after died."[14]

Paulus died in 160 BC, seven years after his victory over the Greeks. Daniel 11:20 alludes to him. His estate, which was divided between his two sons, hardly amounted to 370,000 drachmas. Regardless of the great riches of his kingdom which were at his disposal, he was known to have lived in so

---

11. Plutarch: *Life of Aemillius Paulus*, 6:15-23; Livius, *History of Rome*, 44.41-46; Polybius, *Histories*, 29.14-21; and Holleaux, "Rome and Antiochus," 267-278.
12. Plutarch: *Life of Aemilius Paulus*, 6:28.1-7.
13. Plutarch: *Life of Aemilius Paulus*, 6:39.
14. Plutarch: *Life of Aemilius Paulus*, 6:39.

great indigence that after his death the dowry was paid with difficulty back to his wife.¹⁵

The Roman kingdom was very strong although it was characterized by internal power struggles for a long time. Palestine was brought under the Roman control in 63 BC by the Roman general Pompey, who laid a siege on Jerusalem. Pompey and his men broke into the temple and "saw all that which it was unlawful for any other men to see, but only for the high priests."¹⁶ Pompey left Palestine under the Roman governor of Syria. When he returned to Italy, he lost his political career to his father-in-law Gaius Julius Caesar, although they had formed a political alliance.

Caesar was "a demagogue of genius and an astute politician, who strove to undermine the authority of the Senate and impose his will on the Republic."¹⁷ His two great political weapons were money and oratory. He bribed the influential people and purchased their support to attain the position of *Pontifex Maximus* ("High Priest"). Through intrigues he became a dictator from 59 BC to the Ides of March, 44 BC when he was murdered by his subjects. Daniel 11:21 seems to refer to Caesar's rule. He is identified as a contemptible person. Caesar was survived on the throne by his adopted son, Octavius, who was the grandson of his sister, Julia. Octavius eventually became known as Augustus Caesar (27 BC–AD 14). Augustus was succeeded by Tiberius Claudius Nero who became known as Tiberius Caesar (AD 14–37).

Augustus, along with Mark Antony, had named an Idumaean Jew, Herod the Great (37–4 BC), monarch over the kingdom of Judah. Herod the Great laid a long siege on Jerusalem and finally murdered Antigonus, the leader of the Hasmoneans, along with forty-five of his leading men. He executed the aristocratic members of the Synhedrion and massacred mercilessly many infants, members of the weaker sex, and the aged. He consolidated his power by an extensive building program in the country. He constructed the temple in Jerusalem to be one of the most splendid buildings in the ancient world. Herod the Great died in 4 BC. His sons took the kingship, Archaelaus (Judea, Samaria and Idumaea), Antipas (Galilee and Peraea), and Philip (Batanaea, Trachonitis, Auranitis, Gaulnatis, and Ituraea). Archaelaus's reign (4 BC–AD 6) was short-lived. After his death his territory was administered directly by the Romans.

Antipas, who was more cunning, ambitious, and a lover of luxury like his father, was known as Herod Antipas (4 BC–AD 39). During the reigns

---

15. Foster, *Dio's Rome*, 1:305.
16. Josephus, *Antiquities of the Jews*, 14.4.4.72
17. Fuller, *Julius Caesar*, 312.

of Philip (4 BC–AD 33/34) and Herod Antipas, while Tiberius Caesar was the Roman Emperor and Pontius Pilate procurator/governor of the Roman province of Judah (AD 26–36), Jesus, "the ruler of the covenant" (Dan 11:22; cf. 9:25, 26), appeared in Palestine. He was later executed at the hands of the Romans in Jerusalem in AD 31 (Matt 27:27–31, 35; Mark 15:1–15; Luke 23:1–23, 33; John 19:1–19).

11:20. Taxes. During the dominance over Palestine the Roman government was involved in the collection of *tributum soli*, "land tax," and *tributum capitis*, "poll tax."[18] The land tax was partly paid in kind and partly in money. The poll tax was levied on individual citizens as well on personal property. Men were required to pay taxes from the age of fourteen to sixty-five while women were required to pay from the age of twelve to sixty-five.[19] In the New Testament the denarius was associated with the paying of taxes (Matt 22:17–21; Mark 12:14–17; Luke 20:22–25). Emperor worship, census, and paying of exorbitant taxes were often the points of contention between the Jewish patriotic groups and the Roman authorities.

11:23-31. Continued religious and political struggles. Gabriel, the narrating angel, continued highlighting the historico-political and socioreligious developments in and around Palestine after the death of Jesus. These culminated in the destruction of the Jerusalem temple in AD 70 by the Romans. Josephus wrote on the war activities between the Jewish factions and the Romans with tantalizing detail.[20] The Roman domination over Judah continued mostly by appointed procurators, who were conferred with the right to administer justice or to impose the death penalty. These procurators were answerable to the emperor and were to serve the interests of the Roman Empire. See table 9.

Caligula (AD 37–41) took over from Tiberius as the emperor. He provoked the Jews by proposing to set up his statue in the temple of Jerusalem in AD 39/40. Following Caligula's assassination, Claudius (AD 41–54) assumed the office of the emperor. Claudius appointed King Agrippa (AD 37–44) to rule over Judea and the areas once administered by Herod the Great. Agrippa subscribed to some of the Jewish practices (Acts 26:2–3, 27, 28), but persecuted and put to death many Christians. He was successful in mollifying the Jewish patriots who were planning to wage war against the Romans. Claudius was poisoned at the instigation of his wife Agrippina,

---

18. Schäfer, *History of the Jews*, 106.
19. Schäfer, *History of the Jews*, 106.
20. Josephus, *Wars of the Jews*, bks. 2–7.

who then opened the way for her son Nero (AD 54-68) to be the next Roman emperor.

A fire broke out in Rome and Nero the emperor was highly suspect. In order to escape from the suspicion, Nero accused the Christians of setting the city on fire. A horrendous persecution arose against the Christians. They were killed in torments; "some were nailed on crosses; others sewn up in the skins of wild beasts, and exposed to the fury of dogs; others again, smeared over with combustible materials, were used as torches to illuminate the darkness of the night."[21]

The procurators continued to display the harshness of the Roman rule in Palestine. The procurator Gessius Florus (AD 64-66) plundered the temple treasury on April/May 16, AD 66 and imposed a temple tax of seventeen talents to punish the Jews he had been quarreling with over Caesarea. This provoked the fury of the Jewish patriots and it resulted in a deadly riot. Several Jewish patriotic groups, which included the Zealots along with some robbers, brigands, assassins, and malefactors who murdered for hire, fought against the Romans. They brutally murdered the Jews who seemed loyal to the Romans.

Table 9
ROMAN PROCURATORS IN PALESTINE

PROCURATOR	DATE
Coponius	AD 6-9
Marcus Ambibulus	AD 9-12
Annius Rufus	AD 12-15
Valerius Gratus	AD 15 26
Pontius Pilate	AD 26-36
Marcellus	AD 36-37
Marullus	AD 37-41
Agrippa I (King)	AD 37-44
Agrippa II (King)	AD 50?-92/93
Cuspius Fadus	AD 46-48
Tiberius Julius Alexander	AD 46-48
Ventidius Cumanus	AD 48-52
Felix	AD 52-60
Porcius Festus	AD 60-62
Albinus	AD 62-64
Gessius Florus (the last and worst of all)	AD 64-66

Florus responded to the demonstrators by indiscriminately killing about 3,600 people. He crucified many Jews, including the nobility and

21. Gibbon, *Triumph of Christendom*, 91.

Roman citizens. He then bade the remaining Jewish leaders to hold a reception in honor of the soldiers who had put down the revolt. This agitated the insurgents more and finally led to an open civil war. The Roman Empire was roused by the anti-Roman protests in Judah. Florus withdrew to replenish his forces. Cestius Gallus, the governor of Syria, came with about 30,000 men but failed to break through into Jerusalem. He finally withdrew. From Rome, Nero the emperor commissioned the commander Flavius Vespasian in February AD 67 to go and quell the insurrection in Jerusalem.

In the summer of AD 67 Vespasian started operating from the north of Palestine in Galilee and advanced to the east of Jordan in AD 68. When he was preparing to campaign against Jerusalem, he learned of the death of Emperor Nero on June 9, AD 68. Apparently, Galba was immediately chosen to succeed Nero, but he too died on January 15, AD 69. Ortho was appointed the next emperor, but he too died shortly after. The succession struggle in Rome affected the progress of the war in Palestine. Vespasian went south to Egypt to negotiate with the prefect Tiberius Julius Alexander to join forces against Jerusalem. However, Vespasian was eventually named the emperor of Rome, and this may have prompted Alexander to consent to send his forces to attack Jerusalem on July 1, AD 69.

11:24. Fortresses. The temple in Jerusalem was also used as a fortress during times of war. Under Titus the Romans destroyed it in AD 70. When Titus went back to Rome, he commanded Lucilius Bassus to take the other fortresses, the Herodium, Machaerus, and Masada, which were the stronghold of some Jewish militant groups (Dan 11:24). While the Herodium and Machaerus were easily overthrown, Masada resisted until April AD 74. The Jews suffered the difficult socioeconomic consequences of the war against the Romans for a long time that followed.

11:30. Kittim. The scholarly debate on Kittim focuses on whether its reference in Daniel is national, geographical, or figurative. The people of Kittim (cf. Gen 10:4) occupied the coastlands of the Aegean and the Mediterranean and also some parts of Macedonian Greece. Kittim/Chittim has been interchangeably used in the Hebrew text. As a place name, Kittim has been associated with Kition/Citium, a major Bronze-Age town near modern Larnaca which is located on the south-central coast of Cyprus. Kittim is mentioned on the stela of Sargon II (707 BC), now housed in the Vorderasiatische Museum in Berlin.

In Kittim they were known for their maritime skills during ancient times, and their influence was felt far and wide. The ships of Kittim roved the Mediterranean Sea and caused quite a stir in the region, as noted by

Dan 11:30 and other biblical writers (Num 24:24; Isa 23:1, 12; Jer 2:10; Ezek 27:6). Some Bible commentaries recovered at Qumran make reference to Kittim as a geographical location as well as a national term. The Qumran community believed that the priests of Jerusalem would compose the remnant whose riches and booty would be delivered to the hands of the army of Kittim. Probably the Romans were metaphorically implied here as the army of Kittim. For the Hebrews, the reference to Kittim may have included the islands and coastlands of the Aegean/Mediterranean Seas.

Several ostraca recovered from excavations at Arad demonstrate Judah's economic relations with Kittim just prior to Nebuchadnezzar's invasion in 598/7 or 588/7 BC. Specific instructions were given by the writer to Eliashib: "Give the *Kittiyîm* three baths of wine and write the exact date. And from what is left of the old wheat grind up one (*kor*) of wheat to make bread for them. Serve the wine in punch bowls."[22] The other ostracon directed to Nahum reads: "Go to the house of Eliashib, son of Oshiyahu, and get from him one (bath) of oil, and send it to m[e] in haste, sealing it with thy seal. On the 24th of the month Nahum delivered the oil into the hand of the *Kittî*."[23]

Porphyry, followed by Jewish writers and also Jerome, identified the ships of Kittim in Dan 11:30 as the Roman delegation under Marcus Popilius Laenas, who humiliated Antiochus IV Epiphanes and forced him to withdraw from Egypt. Such a reference to Kittim may be figurative but this theory lacks evidence.

A few other references to Kittim also appear in the apocryphal writings. In Jub. 24:28–29 we find Isaac's curse on the Philistines who were to suffer at the "hands of the Kittim." In 1 Macc 1:1 Kittim is identified as the location from whence Alexander the Great came when he defeated King Darius of the Medo-Persians.

11:31. Abomination that desolates. See 8:11–14. Desolate sanctuary. In the spring of AD 70, Titus was commissioned to deal with the Jews. He came to attack Jerusalem with around 60,000 soldiers. He laid a siege on the city and fierce fighting went on until Titus managed to break through all the fortifications and captured Jerusalem.

---

22. *ANET*, 569; Aharoni, "Hebrew Ostraca from Tel Arad," 1–7; and Aharoni, "Arad," 2–32.

23. *ANET*, 569; and Aharoni, "Use of Hieratic Numerals," 14–15.

TITUS
Marble bust of Titus who led the Roman soldiers in the destruction of the Jerusalem temple in AD 70. (Credit: Zev Radovan)

Titus suspended the temple daily sacrifice and burned the temple on August 29, AD 70. Daniel 11:31 (cf. 9:27b; 12:11) refers to the destruction of the temple by the Romans as "the abomination that desolates." During His time, Jesus had alerted His followers that the "abomination that desolates" mentioned by Daniel was still in the future (Matt 24:15; Mark 13:14).

ARCH OF TITUS
The panel from the Arch of Titus depicts Roman Soldiers in triumphant procession carrying the Golden Menorah and other artifacts looted from the Jerusalem Temple before it's destruction in AD 70. (Credit: Zev Radovan)

Titus captured the Antonia fortress, which was attached to the temple, on the day he took Jerusalem. Later, the Table of Showbread and the Seven-Branched Lampstand from the Jerusalem temple were displayed in Rome on the Arch of Titus. These later became the official emblems in the coat of arms for the state of Israel.

11:33, 35. Understand. See also **12:3, 10. Wise.** The Hebrew root *śkl* means to "be insightful," "be clever," "be wise," "understand." The word is common in wisdom literature and also in Qumran literature. The "emphasis often lies on the act of attentive observation, of perception and scrutiny, through which one becomes 'insightful'"[24] (Dan 9:13, 25; 11:33, 35). In the book of Daniel *śkl* is used interchangeably with *bîn*, "understand," "consider" (Dan 8:16, 17; 9:23; 10:11, 12, 14; 12:3, 10). Understanding here is related to God and is given by God. In Dan 9:22 Gabriel makes Daniel understand. At the time of the end those who understand will be given eschatological knowledge (Dan 12:10). The people at Qumran were very concerned with eschatological knowledge.

The term *maśkîl* (pl. *maśkîlîm*) refers to the one who understands or the office/rank of the teacher who helps others understand God. Influenced

---

24. *TLOT,* 3:1270.

by the Pharisaic sect, the title *Rabbi*, "teacher" or "master," became more prominent soon after AD 70. The *Rabbis* brought about religious reformation and influence to the Jewish nation. They could be identified as those who understand, discern, instruct, or spiritually guide the covenant community in the last days but would stumble and perish near the end of their career (Dan 11:32–35). Their contribution was in refocusing the nation to the Torah, the religious festivals, and establishing the canon of the Hebrew Bible which must have happened at Jabneh. Misunderstandings between the Romans and Jews and concomitant squabbles, revolts, and wars characterized the Roman occupancy of Palestine until the Arabs conquered Palestine in AD 634.

11:35. Refine. See **12:10. Refined.** The Hebrew verb *tsarap* means to "refine," "melt," "burn," or "dye fiery red."[25] It was mainly used for refining metals by removing dross. In the book of Daniel, the word appears in apocalyptic context (Dan 11:35; 12:10). It carries the concept that in eschatological times God's people will go through trying times that are meant to refine them from all contamination of sin. It refers to the fiery persecution of God's people by the fourth kingdom, the Roman Empire. See Jas 1:2, 3; and 1 Pet 4:12–19. Qumran writings follow the Old Testament use of the word but the purification there precedes being accepted into membership of the community.

11:35. Purify. See **12:10. Purified.** *Barar*, "purge," "purify," or "select," implies undergoing a physical or ritual process that makes a person clean or pure before God. This is portrayed as God's doing.

11:35. Made white. See **12:10. Made white.** The persecution of God's faithful people is a painful process to make them white, in the sense of being spotless, clean, and clear. The verbs "refine," "purify," and "made white" all appear in Dan 11:35; 12:10 and express the idea that enduring persecution will result in attaining the purity.

11:36–39. Christian/Papal Rome. While in Gaul in AD 312, Constantine is reported to have had a vision of the cross in the sky with words around it: *hoc signo victor eris*, "by this sign you will conquer."[26] This experience may have prompted him to think that the Christian God was the most powerful supernatural agent on earth. Further, Lactantius pointed out that Constantine was warned in a dream to inscribe the Christian monogram *Chi-Rho*

---

25. *TDOT*, 12:475.
26. Pamphilus, *Life of the Blessed Emperor Constantine*, 1.28–31.

on his soldiers' shields. He eventually ordered to stop the persecution of Christians. He made some legislative reforms which included religious tolerance and freedom. Constantine became the first Christian Roman emperor. He opened the door for the Roman Empire to have influence over the Christian church.

CONSTANTINE THE GREAT
Emperor Constantine (AD 306-37). During his reign, Christianity became the official religion of the Roman Empire and Constantinople became the new imperial capital. (Credit: Zev Radovan)

Although the Roman kingdom remained strong and powerful, its imperial unity was challenged by invasions of different groups of people. From the third century AD onwards, more and more tribes were engaged in power struggles and relocation, but the most prominent protagonists were the Franks (French), Alemanni (Germans), Burgundians (Swiss), Lombards (Italians), Anglo-Saxons (British), Visigoths (Spanish), Suevi (Portuguese), Vandals, Heruli, and Ostrogoths (the last three tribes were annihilated). This slowly weakened the Roman hegemony over some of the tribes. The upheaval and invasions in the Roman Empire continued such that even Emperor Justinian (527-65) was failing to consolidate his authority in the kingdom. Concurrently, the pope in Rome, who was solely involved in the affairs of the universal church, began to show interest in worldly affairs and politics.

The popes in Rome sponsored the Roman emperors to eradicate the tribal groups with which they had doctrinal differences. Such a move resulted in the extermination of the Arian Heruli in 493 initiated by the Roman emperor Zeno (474-91). Emperor Justinian (527-65) destroyed the Arian Vandals in 534 and drove away the Arian Ostrogoths in 538 (Dan 7:20, 24) and finally destroyed them in 553. The Justinian Code in 534 made the bishops of Rome prominent in administrative and judicial powers over heretics.[27] The bishops of Rome, backed up by the Justinian Code, rose to more ecclesiastical and political prominence effectively from 538 to 1798 (cf. Dan 7:25; Rev 12:6; 13:5). It was Pope Gregory the Great (540-604) who worked it out for the bishops of Rome to attain sovereignty in Rome and Italy. Unfortunately, on February 15, 1798, Napoleon Bonaparte's Army General Berthier arrested Pope Pius VI (John Angelo Braschi) while he was attending the anniversary of his exaltation in the Sistine Chapel in the Vatican, and exiled him to France.

Daniel 7:7-8 describes the fourth beast which had ten horns. According to the historical chronology, the fourth beast represents the fourth kingdom, Rome, and the ten horns, its ten kings (vv. 24-25). The ten horns represent the ten more prominent tribes listed above, and the uprooting of the three horns pulled from the beast by a little horn (Dan 7:8) represent the three tribes, the Heruli (AD 493), Vandals (AD 534), and Ostrogoths (AD 553), which were exterminated by the Roman popes through the Roman emperors. This clearly shows that the little horn represented the Roman papacy. Apparently, the Roman pope is the king who is discussed in Dan 11:36-39.

11:40-45. North and south contest. Daniel 11:40 onwards highlights the events leading to the time of the end. The difficulty with this passage is resolved when we realize that some events in this text may seem to have multiple fulfillments, since history is known sometimes to repeat itself. The events of Dan 11:40-45 led to the time of the end. This part of the book of Daniel corresponds with chapter 2:40-43. The Roman papacy will continue through the time of the end until the kingdom represented by the stone arrives (2:44-45).

Now the question one may ask is, what role do the ancient nations like Edom, Moab, Ammon, Egypt, Libya, and Ethiopia (11:41-43) play in the last days? These nations are mentioned in relation with the ancient kings of the north and of the south in Dan 11. As stated above, the kings of the north and south are identified by their geographical location from Palestine. Syria (north) and Egypt (south) have been on many occasions the main political protagonists in wrangles over the domination of Palestine. The events of Dan 11:40-45 led to the beginning of the time of the end as illustrated in the outline in Dan 8:14 and Dan 9:24-27.

---

27. Bemont and Monod, *Medieval Europe*, 108, 110. See also Miller, "Calculating the 1260-Year Prophecy," in de Souza et al., *Eschatology from an Adventist Perspective*, 559-72.

The Roman papacy continued to decline as the religiopolitical authority following the capture of Pope Pius VI in 1798 and his subsequent death in 1799. Following the French Revolution (mainly an attack against ecclesiastical authority), France maintained its position that it was an enemy of the pope and of the Catholic Church.[28]

The Mameluks ruled Egypt in the 1790s. They were not a stable political power and they sustained infightings that ruined Egypt. Under the leadership of Murad and Ibrahim, the Mameluks devastated their economy and destroyed French trade there. This attack on French merchants is implied in Dan 11:40. It provoked the fury of the French and made Napoleon plan to invade the land of Egypt.

On May 19, 1798 Napoleon undertook an expedition to Egypt with about 36,826 soldiers and 146 orientalists who were scientists, inventors, astrologers, technicians, interpreters, artists, painters, and skillful artisans, along with an armada of 13 ships (of-the-line), 14 frigates, 25 smaller military vessels, and 300 transports (Dan 11:40). He invaded and took Egypt, which was at that time ruled by the Mameluks under the auspices of the sultan of the Ottoman Empire.

On his march to Cairo, Napoleon had 30,000 men, with horses and camels (Dan 11:40). While he was operating in Egypt, he received news for him to return at once to France, because his wife Josephine was having a flagrant affair with Hippolyte Charles. Further, there was an impending invasion from the Syrian and Turkish opposition (Dan 11:44).[29] Eventually, he embarked on an expedition to Syria and wrote letters to Jaffa, Gaza, Ramleh, Jerusalem, and Damascus, warning them that he was passing through Palestine on his way to fight Syria (Dan 11:41).

On his way to Syria, Napoleon defeated and took the coastal cities, which included al-Arish, Gaza, Jaffa, Haifa, and Acre (Dan 11:45). Napoleon's Syrian expedition was fought in Palestine and not in Syria proper. However, the rest of Palestine, along with the lands east of the Jordan, that is, the territories of ancient Edom, Moab, and Ammon, did not suffer any attacks from Napoleon (Dan 11:41). Events led Napoleon to be exiled on St. Helena Island and he died there on May 5, 1821. Once again, when Gabriel mentioned the death of the king of the north (11:45), he leaves discussing all the developments of the fourth kingdom during the time of the end. He moves on to relate about the events at the end of the time of the end (Dan 12:1–13).

---

28. Thompson, *Napoleon Bonaparte*, 119.

29. Thompson, *Napoleon Bonaparte*, 115, 125–27; Britt III, *Wars of Napoleon*, 16; and Schom, *Napoleon Bonaparte*, 152.

11:41. Beautiful land. See 8:9. Beautiful (land).

11:41. Edom. The Hebrew Bible provides hints of Edom's political relations with Judah during the Babylonian period (Ezek 25:12-14; 35:1-15; Jer 27:1-8; 49:7-22; Obad 1-14; Ps 137:7; also cf. 1 Esd 4:45-50). The role of Edom in paving the way for the final conquest of Jerusalem by Nebuchadnezzar in 586 BC is not clear.

On the other hand, it seems that Edom became one of the refugee camps for some Jews who were fleeing from the fury of Nebuchadnezzar in 587/6 BC (Jer 40:11, 12). Later, the Edomites occupied southern Judah and became known as Idumaeans (Ezek 36:5). After the destruction of Edom, new population groups occupied the area. Some of these are the Nabateans of the fourth century BC to second century AD. The Nabateans moved in and made Petra their center. Even today Petra is a world-renowned tourist attraction.

Josephus mentions that Nebuchadnezzar subdued Ammon and Moab but is silent on Edom. Perhaps Edom cooperated with Nebuchadnezzar and did not suffer an attack. There are some destruction levels in Edom dating back to the sixth century BC. The Nabonidus Chronicle relates that Nabonidus destroyed [*uru A/U*]*du-um-mu*, which could be "the city of Edom."[30] A rock relief discovered in southern Jordan at Selaʿ shows a Mesopotamian king. This relief has been attributed to Nabonidus, and serves to confirm that he operated in the area. Evidence seems to show that Edom survived in the Persian period (539-332 BC). Evidence for Greek occupation in Edom is poorly represented by some potsherds from different sites. There are no Greek architectural remains in the area.

The Roman Empire annexed Edom around AD 106. During the Roman times there was much activity in the Edomite area. A number of Nabatean temples have been identified. The trade route flourished from the Gulf of Aqaba to the north via Petra. Edom continued to be occupied through the Byzantine times. Sometime between AD 630 and AD 640 Edom along with the whole territory east of Jordan was conquered by Islam, and later, the Umayyad dynasty was established in Damascus in AD 661. The region continued to be ravaged by concomitant wars and displacement of people for many centuries that followed. However, Dan 11:41 affirms the fact that Edom was not isolated from the contemporary geopolitical atmosphere of

---

30. See Grayson, *Assyrian and Babylonian Chronicles*, 105, 282; Beaulieu, *Reign of Nabonidus*, 166, 169; and John Lindsay argues that Edom may have cooperated with Nebuchadnezzar leading to the downfall of Jerusalem but Edom was obliterated from its economic and political career by Nabonidus; see his "Babylonian Kings and Edom," 23-39.

the region. Edom is mentioned in the book of Daniel as one of the nations, escaping from a ruthless foreign king (Dan 11:41). No more information is given regarding this incident. Edom may have been spared by different kings several times from the wars that ravaged that region. As ancient history indicates, Napoleon stormed Palestine and other areas when he was on his way from Egypt in 1799, but Edom and its neighbors were not part of his campaign.

11:41. Moab. G. A. Smith attempted to associate Moab with the Hebrew verb *yā'ab*, "to desire," making the participle of this verb *môāb*, "the desirable." In this case, *môāb* would simply be described as the desirable land or people.[31] Despite this, archaeological evidence shows the existence of the Transjordanian people of Moab as neighbors to Ammonites and Edomites. Even though the people of Moab were polytheistic, their national god was Chemosh (1 Kgs 11:33; Jer 48:7, 13, 46).

The Hebrew Bible relates the interaction between Moab and Israel/Judah as neighboring states which coexisted in the same geopolitical landscape. The ninth-century BC Mesha Stele highlights the longtime conflict sustained between Israel and Moab. The Moabites, like all of their neighbors, eventually fell into the hands of the Babylonians and Persians respectively. Not much is known about that successive imperialism.

---

31. Smith, "Moab" (*Encyclopedia Biblica*, 3:3166). Quoted also in Van Zyl, *Moabites*, 44–60; and Miller, "Moab and the Moabites," in Dearman, *Studies in the Mesha Inscription*, 1. For further etymologies on Moab see also Miller, "Moab" (*ABD*, 4:882).

MOABITE STONE
Moabite Stone or Mesha Stele, dated ca. 840 BC, is the longest extant royal inscription in the area of Palestine. King of Moab, Mesha, gives credit to his god Chemosh for deliverance from the control of Israel. (Courtesy of HAM)

Nebuchadnezzar might have invaded Moab on his way to Egypt in 582 BC and may have taken some captives from there into exile (Jer 48), while others may have taken refuge in Egypt. After the Persians, the Nabatean Arabs occupied the land of Moab from the fourth to the third centuries BC. Not much is known about Hellenistic Moab. The people of Moab disappear from history. Pompey's Syria-Palestine campaign in 64–63 BC subdued the territory of Moab and its neighbors to be under Roman rule for a long time that followed. For many centuries, minor and major wars were waged contesting the Holy Land region and its surroundings. Arabs invaded the area from about AD 630 onwards and dominated the region. In AD 1799 Napoleon concentrated on destroying the coast towns on his way from Egypt to fight the Turks and Syrians. He did not engage the territory of Moab and its immediate neighbors in war. By implying that Moab participated in contemporary social and political affairs, the author of Daniel reflects an awareness of the presence of these people in the region.

11:41. Sons of Ammon. The problem with the chief of the sons of Ammon (Dan 11:41) and the king of the north (Dan 11:40–45) is that both remain unidentified. This makes the dating of this event ambiguous. The text (Dan 11:41) is clear that the chief of the sons of Ammon would later escape the attack from an unidentified king of the north. There are no details regarding this political incident. However, impressive archaeological evidence shows that Dan 11:41 reflected the actual social and political situation of the Ammonites in their contemporary world. The Ammonites appear in both biblical and extrabiblical sources as a political force in the ancient Near East.[32]

AMAN ACROPOLIS
Remains of the Hercules Temple built by the Romans (AD 161–66) on the city acropolis in Aman (Philadelphia), Jordan. (Credit: Zev Radovan)

Ammon, Moab, Edom, and Judah all appear on a receipt of tribute from Palestine. The receipt dated to the time between Sargon II (721–705 BC) and Esarhaddon (680–669 BC) reads: "Two minas of gold from the inhabitants of Bit-Ammon ($^{mat}Bît$-Am-man-na-a-a); one mina of gold from the inhabitants of Moab (^{mat}Mu-'-ba-a-a); ten minas of silver from the inhabitants of Judah (^{mat}Ia-$ú$-da-a-a); [. . . mi]nas of silver from the inhabitants of [Edom] ($^{mat}[U$-du-$ma]$-a-a) . . ."[33]

An intriguing evidence for an Ammonite king (sixth century BC) is the royal seal inscribed b'lyš' mlk b[n 'm]n, which translates as follows: "[Belonging to] Ba'alis// King of// the B[nēi Ammo]n."[34] This king is also mentioned in Jer 40:14.

32. Fisher traces and analyzes the references to "Ammon," "Ammonites," and "Ammonitess," in "Ammon," 32–82, 235–53. Younker, "Rabbah" (*ABD*, 5:598–600); Younker, "Ammonites," in Hoerth, *Peoples of the Old Testament World*, 296–297; Younker, *Emergence of the Ammonites* (1997).

33. *ANET*, 301, c.

34. Becking, "Seal of Baalisha," 13–17; Becking, "Baalis," 15–24; Deutsch, "Seal of

The biblical text implicates Baalis, the Ammonite king, in the assassination of Gedaliah, the newly appointed Neo-Babylonian governor, at Mizpah (Jer 40:13, 14). A seal inscribed *lmlkm 'wr 'bd b'lyš*, "belonging to Milkom'ûr, servant of Baʿališʿa,"[35] was found by archaeologists in 1984 at Tell el-ʿUmeiri. At Ḥesbân in the summer of 1978 an ostracon (inscribed potsherd) was recovered with thirteen lines of script listing Ammonite personal names.[36]

On June 8, 2007, a seventh-sixth century BC Ammonite ostracon inscribed with a list of personal names with numbers was recovered at Tall Jalul excavation.[37] The archaeological data show that the Ammonites were a political force among their contemporary nations as implied by Dan 11:41. Some seals and inscriptions name about eleven Ammonite kings who reigned from 1000 BC until 581 BC when Nebuchadnezzar conquered Rabbah Amman.

Josephus[38] wrote that Ammon and Moab (and possibly Edom) were conquered by Nebuchadnezzar in 582/1 BC. It is not clear whether the people from those nations went into exile. Again, the Ammonites might have felt the Babylonian presence through Nabonidus. His military campaign to Syria in 553/2 BC could have included Ammon and the subsequent territories.[39]

The sixth-century BC rock relief at Selaʿ near aṭ-Ṭafilah in southern Jordan depicts a Mesopotamian king standing in front of three divine symbols. This figure has been identified with near certainty as Nabonidus (556–539 BC).[40] This relief may reflect the Neo-Babylonian political dominance in Jordan. In 2010 a 6.5-foot-tall basalt statue of an Ammonite king was discovered from the ancient capital of the Ammonites, Rabbah, the present city of Amman in Jordan.[41] This statue is larger-than-life and is believed to be from the early Iron Age.

Evidence show that the Ammonites continued to be a political power through the Persian and Greek times. Invasion of Arab groups in their

---

Baʿalis Surfaces," 46–49, 66; and Herr, "Is the Spelling," 187–91.

35. Herr, "Servant of Baalis," 169–72; and Younker, "Israel, Judah, Ammon and the Motifs," 173–80. Many more Ammonite inscriptions are in Aufrecht, *Corpus of Ammonite Inscriptions* (1989).

36. Cross, "Unpublished Ammonite Ostracon from Hesbân," in Geraty and Herr, *Archaeology of Jordan and Other Studies*, 475–89.

37. Younker, "Jalul 2007," 1–2; and Gane, "Jalul Ostracon I," 73–84.

38. Josephus, *Antiquities of the Jews*, 10.9.7.

39. Weippert, "Relations of the States," in Hadidi, *Studies in the History*, 102.

40. Dalley and Goguel, "Selaʿ Sculpture," 169–76. See also Hart, "Sela," 91–95.

41. Burnett, "Ammon, Moab and Edom," 31.

territory around AD 630 onwards may have displaced the Ammonites from history. Daniel's claim concerning a possible involvement of the Ammonites as a distinct, self-governing people group cannot simply be dismissed. Sons of Ammon are reported to have escaped the hand of the king of the north (Dan 11:41). This event may have multiple fulfillment since similar incidents occurred many times in the ancient nations. When returning from his expedition in Egypt in 1799, Napoleon did not attack Ammon because he focused more on the Syrian threat. What is important is that the event implied in Dan 11:41 points to the time of the end.

11:42, 43. Egypt. Many archaeological finds show that Egypt was involved in the ancient Near East's political, economic, social, and religious activities. Egypt's twenty-sixth dynasty (664–525 BC) founded by Psammeticus (664–610 BC) at Saïte is of interest as it relates to the imperial Neo-Babylonian Empire. A cuneiform text in the British Museum (BM 21901) recorded that the Egyptian and Assyrian armies pursued Nabopolassar's army in 616 BC but failed to attack him.[42] In a bid to control Palestine and Assyria, Pharaoh Necho II (610–595 BC) suffered defeat in battle with Nebuchadnezzar at Carchemish in 605 BC. From the time of this encounter, Egyptian influence in the area began to wane (2 Kgs 23:29; 2 Chr 35:20; Jer 46).

Some Egyptian names are listed for Babylonian rations on the tablets BM 57337 and BM 49785.[43] Several other people with Egyptian names are mentioned on these tablets. These individuals worked in Neo-Babylonia as *širkus* or "temple slaves" during the time of Nebuchadnezzar (BM 59410, BM 61993).[44] Babylonians then embarked on cleaning out the Egyptian presence from Assyria and Palestine. Finally, the Neo-Babylonian armies engaged the Egyptians in a critical battle at the Egyptian frontier, where both sides suffered terrible losses in 601 BC.

During the rule of Necho II's son, Psammetichus II (595–589 BC), Egypt kept a low political profile in support of Judah against Nebuchadnezzar's ravages over that land because Judah was already under the Neo-Babylonian domination (2 Kgs 24:7). Psammetichus II died and was replaced by his son Apries (589–570 BC), who revived the conflict between Egypt and Neo-Babylonia by interfering in Neo-Babylonian imperialism in Palestine. Apries supported Tyre and Sidon of Phoenicia and Jerusalem of Judah when they renounced their allegiance to Nebuchadnezzar. Even with the help of

---

42. Wiseman, *Chronicles of the Chaldean Kings*, 54–55. Other battles where the Egyptians were involved with the Babylonians took place in 610, 609, 606, 605, 601, and 568/7 BC; see Wiseman, *Chronicles of the Chaldean Kings*, 62–63, 66–71, and 94–95.

43. Wiseman, "Some Egyptians in Babylonia," 154–58.

44. Bongenaar and Haring, "Egyptians in Neo-Babylonian Sippar," 59–72.

some Greek mercenaries, Apries failed to ward off the Neo-Babylonian dominance in the west. With the fall of Jerusalem to Nebuchadnezzar in 587/6 BC, many Judaeans escaped to Egypt (2 Kgs 25:26; Jer 43:4-7).

Nebuchadnezzar continued having military conflicts with the Egyptians from 605 BC onwards. There is, however, no clear evidence to show how or when he invaded Egypt (cf. Jer 43:10-13; 46:13, 25-26; Ezek 32:11-16). Megasthenes and Berosus say that Nebuchadnezzar invaded Egypt, conquered Lybia and Iberia, and took many captives to Babylon.[45] The tablet (BM 33041) reports on Nebuchadnezzar staging a battle with Egypt in the thirty-seventh year of his reign (568/7 BC). No details about this military encounter can be intelligibly deciphered from this disappointingly fragmented document.[46] In light of this inscription, T. G. Pinches suggested that Nebuchadnezzar defeated Hophra/Apries in 572 BC and set Amasis/Ahmose on the Egyptian throne. He further indicates that Nebuchadnezzar might have taken the expedition to Egypt in 568/7 to suppress Amasis/Ahmose who was revolting from his vassalage. However, BM 952, a donation stela, helps establish 570 BC as Amasis/Ahmose's first year of reign.[47] Also, *Herodotus*, 2.162-69, 182, and *Diodorus Siculus*, 1.68.2-5 seem to relate that there was a civil war in Egypt in 570 BC when Amasis became king. This could have been implied on the Elephant Stelae of Amasis.

An inscription of Nebuchadnezzar (BM 45690) indicates that he defeated Egypt at some point in time. It reads: "What no one had done like this from time immemorial, they received from his pure hands for eternity, and constantly blessed his kingship . . . [In] conquering from Egypt to Ḫumê, Piriddu, Lydia . . . king of [distant] regions . . ."[48]

Nebuchadnezzar may have captured some Egyptians during military encounters and deported them to Babylonia. One of Nebuchadnezzar's Egyptian prisoners named Pusamiski was a keeper of the royal donkeys in Babylon. There are some place names in the region of Nippur in the fifth century BC which show Egyptian ethnic background for exiled groups of people. These names include *Nārušá^{lú} Mi-ṣir-a-a, Bīt^m Mi-ṣir-a-a, and Bīt^{uru} Mi-ṣir-a-a*.[49] Abundant evidence shows that Egypt was a significant political force in the ancient Near East. Evidence shows that Egypt continued

---

45. See Wilkinson, *Manners and Customs*, 1:119-20; and Josephus, *Against Apion*, 1.20.
46. See *ANET*, 308.
47. See Leahy, "Earliest Dated Monument," 184-85.
48. Lambert, "Nebuchadnezzar King of Justice," 9, 10 rev. col. V, lines 17-23.
49. Eph'al, "Western Minorities in Babylonia," 81.

political interaction with the ancient Near East down through the ages. Daniel 11:42, 43 relates Napoleon's expedition to Egypt and its neighbors.

11:43. Libyans/Lybians. In Dan 11:43 the Libyans are mentioned in conjunction with their neighbors, the Egyptians and the Nubians (Ethiopians). These are destined, according to the text, to be subdued by an unnamed king from the north. Megasthenes (358-280 BC) preserved information indicating that Nebuchadnezzar invaded Libya and Spain.[50] Libya is one of the countries listed on a tablet from Persepolis which Xerxes (485–465 BC) claims to have been given by his god, Ahuramazda.[51] This tablet may serve to illustrate the Persian political developments but may not have implications on Daniel 11:43.

The Libyans were known to be a part of contemporary international social, economic, religious, and political interactions (2 Chr 12:3; 16:8; Ezek 27:10; Nah 3:9; Matt 27:32; Mark 15:21; Luke 23:26; Acts 2:10). It is possible that Libya was subdued by various political powers in different time periods but the challenge for scholars is to identify the incident referred to in Dan 11:43. However, Napoleon's General Desaix was able by force to draft some Lybians into his French army and this could be implied by the text here.

11:43. Ethiopians. Again, the reference to Ethiopia in Daniel has challenged scholars who seek to ascertain the historicity of Dan 11:43. Following the invasion by an unidentified king from the north, Dan 11:43 figuratively states that the Ethiopians would be "by his steps." This implies that the Ethiopians would be "at his heels" or "in his train."[52] If the Ethiopians were subdued by a foreign king they could be plundered. In this case some of them would be dragged into captivity and slavery. From the fifth century BC to early Christian times, Ethiopia appears more often in the archaeological and epigraphic records. This shows that Ethiopia continued to participate in the geopolitical activities in the region. Some of these activities were implied by the author of Daniel.

---

50. Cory, *Ancient Fragments*, 71–72; and Sack, *Images of Nebuchadnezzar*, 32.
51. *ANET*, 316.
52. BDB, 857.

NUBIAN CAPTIVES
Relief depicting Nubian captives by Rameses II (1279–1212 BC), Abu Simbel, Egypt. It was the practice of ancient nations to take captives from those whom they had conquered. (Credit: Zev Radovan)

The Hebrew Bible uses the term "Kush/Cush" to refer to the southern land which is adjacent to Egypt. From ancient times the land of Cush was known to have been located between the second and fourth cataracts of the Nile Valley. The Greeks knew this land as *Aithiops*, "Ethiopia" (Jer 13:23; Acts 8:27). From the Roman times onward Cush was known as "Nubia/Abyssinia" and it comprised parts of the modern Sudan and Ethiopia in East Africa.

A certain Ethiopian, Ebed-melech, who lived in Jerusalem during the time of King Zedekiah (597–586 BC), was in charge of the eunuchs in the king's court. He parallels Ashpenaz of Dan 1:3. He pleaded with King Zedekiah to save Jeremiah from the pit (Jer 37—38). Ebed-melech might have been taken to Jerusalem as a slave. It was common that such people would be made eunuchs to serve in the king's court as in the case of Daniel and his friends (Dan 1).

11:43. In his steps. Figuratively, this expresses the idea of people being dragged into slavery or captivity against their will. While Napoleon was in Palestine fighting against the Turks and Syrians, he had left his General Desaix with some of the French forces to fight the Mameluks in Egypt (Dan 11:42). Desaix encountered Mameluk merchants who were bringing into Egypt black slaves from Abyssinia, Nubia (Ethiopia and Sudan), the borders of Lybia, and from as far as Timbuktu (Dan 11:43).[53] He managed to draft over 10,000 blacks into the French infantry. However, the French political power declined drastically. Despite this, their revolution prompted universal socioeconomic, religious, and geopolitical activities with repercussions continuing to the end of time.

11:45. Glorious holy mountain. This is where the Jerusalem temple was located (2 Chr 3:1). The temple was glorious and holy because it was the residence of the God of Israel. The presence of the temple made the land of Israel beautiful and glorious among all other lands (Dan 8:9; 11:16, 41).

11:45. Tents between seas. After his Egyptian expedition, Napoleon returned home to consolidate his forces. In the early 1800s he won several battles in Europe and became a great military icon. From 1812 Napoleon started having defeats from several fronts and was eventually exiled to the island of Ebla where he managed to escape back to France in early 1815. He organized another impressive army temporarily but suffered humiliating defeat against Wellington at the Battle of Waterloo on June 18, 1815. Napoleon was eventually exiled to St. Helena, an island off Africa where he died probably of stomach cancer on May 5, 1821. Daniel 11:45 seem to allude to the end of Napoleon's career.

11:45. Come to his end. Once the king of the north comes to his demise, the narrator in Dan 11 discontinued relating about the rest of the activities of the fourth kingdom, the Roman Empire, to the end of the world. He moved ahead to relate about the dramatic events at the closing of the time of the end in Dan 12.

---

53. Herold, *Bonaparte in Egypt*, 246–47.

Chapter 12

END OF THE TIME OF THE END

DANIEL 12 IS AN appendix to the vision in chapters 10 and 11. The author briefly focuses on how events will turn out at the close of the time of the end. This points to the fact that the political events outlined in Daniel outlive the author and stretch to the end of time. The text gives a synopsis of some of the dramatic events that occur at the end of this world's history.

12:1. At that time. This refers to the last part of the time of the end that leads to the dramatic closure of the history of the nations as outlined in the book of Daniel. This period is characterized by a brief but intense time of trouble such as never was on earth before. Immediately following that crisis, God's people will be dramatically delivered.

12:1. Time of trouble. This time of distress is unprecedented. The Bible gives hints about it (Jer 30:7; Matt 24:21). The last days of earth's history (Dan 2:42–45) are characterized by social upheaval, economic crisis, natural disasters, pandemics, political commotion, religious intolerance, manipulative fear, and moral depravity. The climax of these horrendous activities is the time of trouble. Revelation 16 is a synopsis of this terrible time of trouble. In this brief time of distress, just prior the end of the world, God unleashes the final judgments only on those who reject His offer of salvation. The Qumran community expected the time of distress to come, but believed that God would protect and deliver those whose names are inscribed in the book of life.[1]

---

1. 4QDibHam [504], VI-VII, in Vermes, *Complete Dead Sea Scrolls in English*, 366.

12:1. Michael. See 10:13, 21. Michael.

12:1. Delivered. See 3:15, 17, 28. Deliver. The Hebrew verb *malat* means to "escape," "deliver," or "flee to safety." The verb is used in the story of Lot who escaped the destruction of Sodom and Gomorrah (Gen 19:17, 19, 20, 22). Servants who came to Job and reported the bad news also used this verb (Job 1:15–19). This verb portrays the concept of moving from the place of danger to safety. At Qumran (4Q370 1.6) it is commented that the giants did not escape the flood (cf. Gen 6:1–7). CD 7:14 predicts that the members of the covenant community will escape in the future visitation.[2] The angel assured Daniel that God's people will escape at the time of the end (John 14:3; 1 Thess 4:16, 17).

12:1. Name is written in the book. This portrays the imagery of God keeping a register of all human activities (Isa 4:3; Luke 10:20; Phil 4:3; Heb 12:23). From time immemorial, the ancient Near East people believed that the deity recorded human behavior, either good or bad (cf. Eccl 12:13, 14). The writing of someone's name in the book depicts an assurance of salvation. The blotting out of someone's sin from the book of destinies also indicates divine forgiveness (Ps 51:1). What must be dreaded is to have one's name blotted out of the book of life (Exod 32:32, 33; Ps 9:5; 69:28; 109:13; Rev 3:5). Also, anyone turning away from the Lord will have, as it were, one's name written on the ground (Jer 17:13; John 8:6, 8). Of course, this leads the individual to eternal destruction.

The Instruction of Amenemope of Egypt (993–984 BC) is preserved in the British Museum Papyrus 10474 and also on an ostracon in the Cairo Museum. It warns that: "There is no ignoring of fate and destiny; do not let your heart go straying, every man comes to this hour."[3] The book of life (Dan 12:1; Luke 10:20; Phil 4:3; Rev 13:8; 17:8; 20:12, 15; 21:27) is an equivalent to the Akkadian *lē'ušu ša balāṭe*, "the tablet of life,"[4] which contains the list of those whom the judgment exonerates. The phrase *lē'ušu ša balāṭe* appears in several Akkadian texts. Those whose names are inscribed in the book of life are guaranteed salvation. This should be each person's goal in life.

12:2. The ones sleeping in the dust. Daniel 12:2 further develops the resurrection motif previously shared by some of the Hebrew Bible writers (1 Sam 2:6; Job 19:25–27; Isa 26:19; Ezek 37:1–14; Hos 13:14). There is a

---

2. *NIDOTTE*, 2:954.
3. *COS*, 1:118.
4. Waterman, *Royal Correspondence of the Assyrian Empire*, 386, letter 545, line 8.

linguistic affinity between Dan 12:2 and Isa 26:19. Isaiah speaks of "the dead," while Daniel euphemistically identifies them as "the ones sleeping." These texts share an eschatological hope. They speak of a future time when the dead are brought back to life again. Daniel uses the verbal adjective *yāšen*, "sleeping," as a euphemism for death. The Hebrew Bible repeatedly points to death as a sleep (Job 3:13; 14:12; Ps 13:3; Jer 51:39, 57). Inherent in this concept is the idea that the one who sleeps will rise up again.

First Kings 17:17-23; 2 Kgs 4:32-37; and 2 Kgs 13:21 are Hebrew Bible stories of dead people who were raised back to life (cf. Mark 5:21-43; Luke 7:11-17; John 11:1-44; Acts 9:36-43; 20:7-12). Ezekiel 37 is a vision of dry bones being resuscitated back to life. Revelation 20:4-6 relates about the first and second resurrection of the dead.

The idea of resurrection was already prevalent in the ancient Near Eastern religions. It is seen in the Canaanite fertility cult which celebrates the annual death and resurrection of the deity.[5] In particular, Mesopotamian records had the motif of divine kingship and a tree of life. These were associated with afterlife and resurrection. None of the ancient Near East ideas on resurrection are similar to what Daniel is portraying in his text. Some archaeological finds from Qumran broaden our understanding of "sleeping" in the context of Dan 12:2. At Qumran (1QS 7:10), *yāšen* is attested in the context of a punishment inflicted upon someone who is sleeping when the community meeting is in progress. The Messianic Apocalypse (4Q521) gives hope for the resurrection by stating that God "will heal the wounded, revive the dead and bring good news to the poor" (cf. Isa 61:1).[6] The ones *yāšen*, "sleeping," that is, dead, *yāqiṣû*, "shall be awakened," or *yāqûm*, "shall rise up."

Daniel 12:2 establishes the dual concepts of resurrection to eternal life for some, while others would experience a resurrection to everlasting shame and condemnation. See John 5:28, 29. In Dan 12:2, the elements of eternal reward and punishment appear for the first time. At Qumran it is clear that some people would be consigned to the angel of darkness (1QS 3:24) while others go to Melchizedek, the angel of light (11QMelch 1:8).

---

5. *ANET*, 129-42.
6. Vermes, *Complete Dead Sea Scrolls in English*, 391-92.

THE ONES SLEEPING IN THE DUST
The book of Daniel places more importance on the type of resurrection one would have at the end than on the way one died or was buried.
(Picture by Connie Gane, Courtesy of HAM)

Archaeology attests two main kinds of interment in ancient Babylonia. People could be buried in a designated cemetery. On the other hand, they might be interred under the floors of buildings or under roads. The dead were laid down three or six feet (one or two meters) under the ground. Neo-Babylonian burials included the double-pot burials, bathtub coffin burials, bathtub-bowls burials, jar burials, oval coffins, bowl burials, and earth graves. The book of Daniel places more importance on the type of resurrection one would have at the end than on the way one died or was buried. Daniel's belief in the resurrection of the body contradicted the Greek view of life after death or the immortality of the soul. It seems that Daniel received the assurance that though he would die, he would rise again to receive his inheritance at the end of time (Dan 12:13). Because of his anticipation of this personal experience, the resurrection of the dead in his book is literal. The hope for the resurrection of the dead holds a strong anticipation on Christians even today (John 5:25-29; 1 Cor 15:51-54; 1 Thess 4:16-17; Rev 20:5-6).

Two main traditions exist regarding Daniel's death. One says that Daniel died and was buried in Babylon. The other is proffered by Benjamin of Tudela, who visited the Holy Land in AD 1160. He claimed to have seen the Tomb of Daniel in the facade of one of the synagogues in Susa.[7] There were no remains in the traditional Tomb of Daniel.

12:3, 10. Wise. See also **11:33, 35. Understand.** In Dan 12:3, *maskilim*, "the wise," "the understanding ones," or "the instructors" (4Q298; 1QSb 1:1;

---

7. Benjamin, *Itinerary of Benjamin of Tudela,* i. 74-76; ii. 152-54.

4Q403; 4Q511; CD 13:7-8),[8] occupied an influential leadership position (1QS 9:12-26). Their duties included the fulfilling of the will of God and teaching the members of the *yaḥad* ("covenant community") the mysteries of wonder and truth. This would enable them to walk perfectly with one another. The understanding ones will shine "like the luminary" of the firmament.[9] See Isa 60:1-3 and Matt 5:16.

Those who understand will teach "the many" (Dan 12:3, 10). The learners were members of the covenant community (Dan 11:33, 39; 12:3, 10; Esth 4:3). In contrast, another group is identified as "the wicked," who do not want to comply with the teachings of those who understand (Dan 12:10). Steven Thompson clearly distinguishes these groups:

> The *maskilim* in Daniel seem to be discerners of the will of Yahweh, especially as it comes in apocalyptic format. They are also instructors to the covenant community, *harabbim*, during the time of the end. Partly by their response to the spiritual guidance from the *maskilim* the *rabbim* are polarized into two groups, the faithful and righteous ones, versus the *reshaʿim*, who having rejected wisdom are denied Yahweh's righteousness.[10]

12:3. Righteousness. See **9:7, 14, 16, 18, 24. Righteous/ness.** At Qumran, righteousness could be taught. This was the responsibility of the Teacher of Righteousness (CD 6:10-11; 1QpHab 8:1-3), who rigorously stressed election, sin, grace, judgment, and God's righteousness. Those who are righteous can assist others to be righteous as well.

12:3. Like the stars forever and ever. See also **8:10. Stars.** The ancient Near East is renowned for astrology, the study of stars and heavenly bodies and their movements to decipher messages from gods (Deut 4:19; Isa 47:13). Worshiping the sun, moon, and stars was widespread but forbidden in Israel. The biblical text, however, provides evidence that such a practice existed (2 Kgs 23:5). The focus of the biblical text is on the movement of stars (Isa 47:13; Matt 2:2, 9; 24:29; Jude 13; Rev 9:1), their countless number (Gen 22:17; Ps 147:4), and their brightness (Neh 4:21; Job 3:9; Ezek 32:7, 8; Ps 148:3; Jer 31:35), which points to the Creator's elegant power. The sole purpose of stars is to emit light. Figuratively, the righteous people who help

---

8. See DJD, 20:20-22; and 7:221.

9. Wolters prefers *zōhar* to mean "luminary," in "*Zōhar hārāqiaʿ* (Daniel 12.3)," 111-120.

10. Thompson, "Those Who Are Wise," 217.

others be righteous also will shine like stars. Notice that the stars are used here (Dan 12:3) for the purpose of comparison. See also Matt 13:43.

12:4, 9. Seal. See also **8:26. Shut/seal up the vision.** Sealing is a very important technical and symbolical process in the book of Daniel. Some ancient discoveries from the ancient Near East give a hint on the process and significance of sealing. The book of Daniel had to be sealed until the time of the end (Dan 12:4, 9; cf. Rev 5:1). The sins of the people of Jerusalem, along with Daniel's vision and prophecy, were to be sealed (Dan 9:24), as was the lions' den (Dan 6:17). The meaning of the verb *ḥāṯam* is "to seal shut" or "to affix a seal" while the noun has always carried the meaning "seal" and "seal ring."[11] Affixing a seal was a legal act. Seals were used to protect the contents of the legal documents such as contracts, wills, deeds of sale (cf. Jer 32:10-14), letters, and royal decrees (cf. Esth 3:12; 8:8-10). A sealed book could not be read (Isa 29:11). Sealing a book protected it from alteration or untimely disclosure of its contents. At Qumran they believed that David had not read the sealed book (Deut 17:17) which was hidden in the ark, and that is why he had many wives.[12]

Cylinder seal depicting a mythological deity fighting a lion and a bull, ca. 1000–539 BC, Mesopotamia, Neo-Babylonian. (Credit: Zev Radovan)

Archaeology informs us that signet seals were used for personal identification and authentication. Seals were usually used to make impressions on clay or wax. They were worn like a ring or attached to a cord so as to be hung around the neck. Seals were usually made of hard material which included bone, ivory, glazed pottery, glass, metal, wood, limestone, and clay. Such hard stones as onyx, jasper, and agate were more preferred

11. Otzen, "חתם" (*TDOT*, 5:263–64, 267).
12. Vermes, *Complete Dead Sea Scrolls in English*, 130.

for engraving seal symbols or letters for identifying the owner. Seals differed according to individual preference, authority, designs, and purpose. The main categories of seals were the scarabs, stamp (royal or individual names), and cylinder seals. Scarabs and stamp or signet seals were pressed on wet clay while the cylinder seals were rolled onto it. The stamp seals were used in Syria-Palestine, the scarabs in Egypt, and the cylinder seals in Mesopotamia.

It is reasonable to question how the sealing of Daniel's book can be understood. As already noted, seals served mainly as signature of ownership, and also to guarantee authenticity, identify contents of containers, safeguard property against theft, and ratify or legalize a commercial transaction. A seal usually had the name of the person with the individual's title and place of origin. A written scroll was rolled up and a string or thread was tied around it in one or several places. The scroll of Rev 5:1 had seven seals. In many cases ropes, strings, or threads tied an object, document, sack, box, basket, jar, envelope, or storeroom door. In this instance, a lump of clay or wax was applied to the tied knot of the ropes or strings, and the seal was pressed into the lump before it hardened and dried. See Job 38:14.

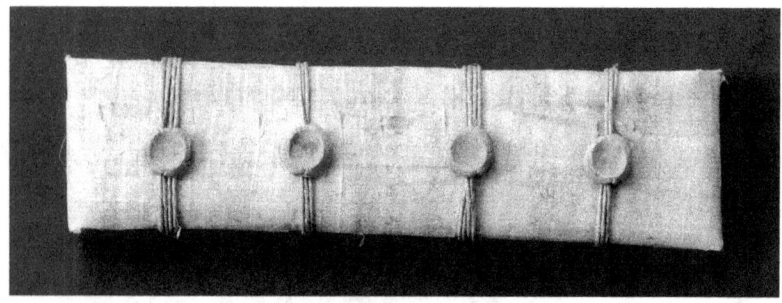

SEALED PAPYRUS SCROLL
(Credit: Zev Radovan)

The sealing of Daniel's book was meant to prevent the document from being read before its intended time. Such practice was common in the ancient Near East. Likewise, the sealing of a vision or prophecy (Dan 9:24) could imply that the vision or prophecy was not to be publicized until the appropriate time. The sealing of the people's sins in Dan 9:24 could symbolically imply putting an end to their transgressions. Seal imprints could be broken or destroyed when the appropriate time, occasion, or setting came (Dan 6:23; 12:4; Rev 6:3–12; 8:1; 10:2–8). Revelation 22:10 forbids that book to be sealed because it was the right time for the end-time message to be broadcast.

Archaeologists have recovered several seals in relation to Neo-Babylonia. Two Babylonian inscribed seals have been found in Palestine.[13] A cylinder seal belonging to Nabu Zabil, a scribe, was found out of context in Samaria. The other is a votive cylinder seal that was discovered at Tel Sheva in a crypt of the Persian period.

Many Babylonian seals were found which portrayed pictures or symbols rather than words. These were found in such places as Tel 'Ammal, Taanach, Tell Keisan, Samaria, Bethel, Ein-Gedi, Tell eṣ-Ṣafi, Transjordan in Edom (at Tawilan), in Moab, and in Ammon.

These epigraphic and non-epigraphic Babylonian seals are dated in the late seventh and sixth centuries BC. Among them are a number of well-known Neo-Babylonian motifs. There is "the palm-and-ibex motif; a hero struggling with ibexes with heads turned back; a wheel from which the winged *protomai* (busts) of a lion, ibex, and mountain goat project; a bird; a scorpion; and seals depicting simple geometric motifs."[14]

Many fake seals have been identified by archaeologists in the antiquities markets. The process of making a seal involved cutting the piece of material, "drilling the perforation, engraving the design, incising the inscription, and, finally, mounting the seal in a ring or threading it on a suspension cord."[15] Usually, the seal design was recessed or carved *intaglio* so that when it was impressed on either clay or wax, it would leave an elevated impression on the receptive surface.[16] The discovery of many Neo-Babylonian seals shows that Daniel recognized the sealing process as an important legal practice.

12:4. Time of the end. The expression "time of the end" is a technical term originating in, and specific to, the eschatological context of the book of Daniel. It refers to the final moments of earth's history just prior the establishment of God's new era. On the whole, the time of the end is to be understood in light of the chronological political kingdoms outlined in Dan 2:44, 45; 7:26, 27. Daniel's time of the end refers to the eschatological era which he saw as preceding the establishment of the divine kingdom.

12:5. Stood two others. Two people were considered the minimum number for witnesses in any case (Deut 17:6; 19:15; Matt 18:16). The two

---

13. Stern, *Archaeology*, 2:332–35. One seal impression was on a jar handle that was discovered at Tel Goren (biblical En-gedi) and it had a double-winged emblem with four Hebrew letters. The debate is on the dating and classification of this seal, which is similar to *lmlk* seal impressions; see Barkay, "King of Babylon," 41–47.

14. Stern, *Archaeology*, 2:334.

15. Hestrin and Dayagi-Mendels, *Inscribed Seals*, 8.

16. Collon, *Near Eastern Seals*, 11; and Magness-Gardner, "Seals, Mesopotamia" (*ABD*, 5:1062).

angelic companions here attend to authenticate the oath that was to be made. The one making the oath raised both hands toward heaven and swore (Dan 12:7), validating the announcement. An oath is a solemn declaration. Assyrian records have a divine oath taken by three men and three women before a council of judges, saying: "It is in truth that we speak. We shall not speak falsely. Should we speak falsely, let servants be taken from us."[17]

One of the two divine beings standing at the opposite banks of the river asked a question to the other one standing on the water to let Daniel know about the time frame for the events that were being discussed (Dan 12:6). The divine being swore by God and delivered the answer, signifying that what he said was verified and would take place as declared (v. 7). However, for humans, swearing is forbidden (Lev 19:12; Matt 5:33–37).

12:5–7. River. The author of Daniel uses the word *'ubal*, "river," "stream," "conduit," "water course," or "canal," for the Ulai in Dan 8:2, 3, 6. In Dan 10:4 he uses *nāhār*, "river" or "stream," for the Tigris. However, in Dan 12:5–7 the author uses *yᵉʾōr*, "river," "stream," or "watercourse of the Nile."[18] The noun *yᵉʾōr* appears about forty-five times in the Old Testament referring to the Nile. There are also such references in the apocryphal book of Sirach 39:22; 47:14; 24:27.

Since *yᵉʾōr* is an Egyptian loanword that was used singularly to refer to the Nile river or the stream of the Nile (Gen 41:1–3, 18; Exod 1:22; 2:3–5; 4:9; 7:15–28; 8:5–7; 17:5; Amos 9:5), it has been argued that in Dan 12:5–7, the author was referring to the Nile. The geography of the text would not allow such a reference. The author was still by the Tigris River where he received the vision (Dan 10:4). Moreover, the noun *nāhār* used for the Tigris has also been used for the Nile (Isa 19:5; Jer 46:7–10; Ezek 32:2). In light of this, biblical interpreters generally agree that the river in Dan 12:5–7 is the Tigris River mentioned earlier in Dan 10:4.

12:6. How long? See **8:13. How long?** Divine beings ask each other about when the events discussed would take place. The question is meant to help Daniel understand the time element of his vision.

12:6. Until the end. Here, "until the end" occurs in an eschatological context. This is also the case with the expressions "to the end" and "at the end of the days" in Dan 12:13. The expression in Dan 12:6 anticipates horrifying and inhuman activities of kingdoms opposed to God to continue until they are terminated at the end of time (cf. Dan 8:17, 19; 11:35, 40; 12:4, 9). In the

---

17. *COS*, 3:32.
18. BDB, 384.

Qumran scrolls the time of the end is considered also as "the time of judgment" (1QH 6:29–30) and it also occurs in an eschatological context. Here, it clearly points to the end of the time appointed by God, and the creation of a new time (1QS 4:25).

12:6. Wonders. The wonders in the biblical text refer to the extraordinary acts of God either cosmic or on behalf of God's people. Such wonders are the apocalyptic deeds that escape human logic but can only be understood as miracles. The wonders by God distinguishes Him from any other gods in the ancient Near East. In the Dead Sea Scrolls wonders are seen as God's work on creation and salvation. The Qumran group anticipated the eschatological intervention of God to bring about salvation to the community members and at the same time destruction of the wicked people. God's wonders in the biblical text bring deliverance to His people and at the same time judgment on His enemies.[19] On the other hand, in a negative sense, monstrosities by the Roman Empire, the fourth kingdom in Daniel's chronology that blow out human hope, are also viewed as wonders (Dan 7:19, 25; 11:36). In light of this, the wonders in Dan 12:6 refer to the incomprehensible evil activities done by the Roman kingdom that are opposed to God. This includes the persecution of God's faithful people.

12:7. Time, times, and half a time. See **7:25. For a time and times and half a time.**

12:7. Swore. See **9:11. Oath**; and also **12:5. Stood two others.** In the biblical text swearing of an oath is distinguished from making a vow (Ps 132:2). Swearing had to do with giving the assurance that one would keep his or her word or that something would take place.

12:10. Purified. See 11:35. Several verbs describe the concept of being purified. The root idea of the verb *barar* means to be clean, clear, free, pure, separate, to glitter, or to purge. In Ugaritic the verb form is used of metals, meaning to be pure, and also of slaves, implying to be free. The concept of being purified among ancient people covered social, hygienic, moral, and religious spheres of life. Lack of purity could result in isolation or even expulsion from the community. Many of the prayers, rituals, sacrifices, and offerings were presented to the deity in a bid to secure purity.

The method of being purified is not prescribed in Daniel's book. It could include sanctifying or consecrating oneself through careful spiritual preparation. The Bible already encourages the process that includes the

---

19. Mazani, *On the Plains of Moab*, 166–68.

washing of clothes (Exod 19:10, 14), taking care of physical bodies (Lev 15), making no contact with anything unclean (Num 19:11–22), and maintaining sexual morality (Lev 18:6–30). Daniel decided not to get defiled with food and drink (Dan 1:8). Those who are purified become holy just as God is (Lev 11:44; 19:2; 20:7, 26; Matt 5:48; 1 Pet 1:16).

A letter dated 418 BC sent by a certain Hananiah to the Jews in Elephantine, Egypt, gives instructions on the Passover. The third instruction in this letter cautions the Jews to "be pure, and take heed."[20] This instruction may have reference to the ritual preparation and readiness that was necessary for Jewish participants in the festival.

At Qumran the idea of purity appears in several documents.[21] In the Temple Scroll (11QTS 57:5, 8) army commanders should be truthful, God-fearing, and haters of unjust gain. The War Scroll (1QM 5:11, 14) refers to pure iron used for the blades of swords and pure horn for hilts. The Manual of Discipline (1QS 1:12) demands the community to purify their knowledge in the truth of God's precepts. The Thanksgiving Hymns (1QH 16:10) encourage everyone to keep their hands clean. Daniel 12:10 is quoted in 4Q174.

BOOK OF DANIEL
Dead Sea Scroll fragments containing some parts of the book of Daniel.
(Credit: Zev Radovan)

Being purified demands abstaining from all forms of moral pollution and defilement before God. The call to moral purity demands keeping away from all kinds of physical and spiritual contaminants (Isa 52:11;

---

20. *COS*, 3:117.
21. Vermes, *Complete Dead Sea Scrolls in English* (1997); and *NIDOTTE*, 1:773–74.

2 Cor 6:17). This must be taken seriously. God's people will make themselves ready (2 Cor 7:1; 1 John 3:3; Rev 7:14; 19:7, 8). Regardless of how, humans can never purify themselves (Isa 64:6; Eph 2:8–10). However, God's grace that brings salvation appears to everyone to teach each person to object to wickedness and to live righteously (Titus 2:11–14). Individual active participation is required in order to be purified.

12:10. Made white. In Semitic languages *laban*, "white," refers to a wide range of light colors including the white of snow, milk, teeth, and moon. It denotes that which is clear, bright, and light.[22] See Gen 30:35, 37; Exod 16:31; Lev 13; Dan 7:9; Zech 1:8; 6:3; and Rev 3:5. In Lebanese Arabic it refers either to the white of yogurt or the snow caps of the Lebanon mountains.[23] In theological usages whiteness relates to moral purity and symbolizes righteousness. Metaphorically, being made white points out to the forgiveness a penitent sinner receives from God (Ps 51:7; Isa 1:18). Daniel 11:35 and Dan 12:10 carry the idea that many people will endure persecution in order to be purified. The New Testament echoes this concept (Jam 1:2–4; 1 Pet 4:12–14). The godly will come out of the trying process refined, purified, and made spotless (Job 23:10), while the wicked will remain unrepentant (cf. Rev 9:20–21).

12:10. Refined. Daniel indicates that God's people shall encounter the refining process for their final readiness and completeness. The Hebrew verb *tsarap* means to smelt, purge, refine, test, burn, or dye fiery red.[24] From ancient times the verb was used of gold and silversmiths when refining metals. The process involved shoving metal material in the blazing furnace, liquefying it so as to separate pure metal from all dross (cf. Prov 25:4). Figuratively, *tsarap* is used in the biblical text to describe the process God uses to purify or refine His people (Isa 1:25; 48:10; Ezek 22:19–22; Dan 11:35; Zech 13:9; Mal 3:3). God uses His word to refine His people (Ps 12:6; Eph 6:17; Heb 4:12). To the very end of time, personal crisis, poverty, hunger, trials, temptation, disaster, disease, persecution, or war will be a fiery furnace for many people. Both the righteous and the wicked will go through the crucible of suffering (1 Pet 4:12–19) and come out showing their true substance (cf. Rom 5:3–5).

---

22. *NIDOTTE*, 2:754.
23. *TWOT*, 1:467.
24. *TDOT*, 12:475; and *TWOT*, 2:777, 778.

12:10. Wicked. The Hebrew substantive plural *rᵉšāʿîm* means "wicked people," "guilty," "evil," "unjust," "criminal," "impious," "unrighteous," "wrong."[25] It signifies their bad character and behavior that is targeted against God and the community they live in. A mythological tale from Egypt during the New Kingdom (1550–1069 BC), which was inscribed in the royal tombs of Tutankhamun, Seti I, Ramses II, Ramses III, and Ramses VI, carries the theme of human wickedness that arouses divine wrath and results in the destruction of humankind.[26] Such a theme is common in Mesopotamian and biblical literature. Indeed, God will deliver the righteous but the wicked will be annihilated.

The wicked are opposite to the wise, those who understand. At Qumran the wicked priest is opponent to the Righteous Teacher (1QpHab 5:9; 8:9; 9:1–11). According to Prov 10:27, wickedness is the antithesis of the fear of God.[27] Daniel 12:10 presents the wicked in the time of the end as a hopeless case; they will continue acting wickedly and will never come to understanding right doing (see Rev 9:20, 21; 22:11). Despite God's purifying and refining process, the wicked remain infested with moral impurities (Jer 6:29, 30). As long as the wicked people maintain that mindset and worldview, they will never be transformed to godlikeness. The wicked people fail in practical life to understand that "higher than the highest human thought can reach is God's ideal for His children. Godliness—godlikeness—is the goal to be reached."[28]

12:11. 1,290 days. These are 1,290 literal years, a day for a year in biblical prophecy (Num 14:34; Ezek 4:6). In AD 508 Clovis, king of the Franks, was converted to the Catholic faith. His conversion was significant in that it paved way for the union between church and state, leading to the dominance of the Catholic Church in the West. On the other hand, Clovis's move also encouraged the pope to keep rising to political and religious prominence, which was attained by AD 538. The 1,290 years began with this historical event in AD 508 and ended in 1798 when the French deported the pope and let him die in exile.

12:12. 1,335 days. Likewise, these are 1,335 literal years, a day for a year in biblical prophecy (Num 14:34; Ezek 4:6). The 1,335 years began on the same historical date with the 1,290 years, that is, in AD 508, and they ended in 1843. The end of the 1,335 years coincided with the ushering of the Millerite

---

25. *TDOT*, 14:1–2; *TLOT*, 3:1261–65; *TWOT*, 2:2222.
26. *COS*, 1:36–37.
27. *TDOT*, 14:6.
28. White, *Education*, 18.

Movement, a great religious awakening that focused on preaching prophecies on the soon return of Jesus.

12:13. Rest. The context here implies that Daniel was going to die before the end comes. The verb "rest" is used as a euphemism for dying. The dead are resting and waiting to be awakened to receive their reward (Dan 12:2). Rest continues as an apocalyptic theme that cherishes the hope that the dead faithful ones wait for the glorious blessedness of waking up back to everlasting life (Rev 14:13).

12:13. Your allotted portion, share, lot. The practice of casting lots (Hebrew *goral*) was used for both religious and secular functions as well as public and private affairs. Casting of lots guaranteed an impartial decision. It carried the concept of either chance and luck or recompense. A marked small stone or piece of wood was used. This was cast to the ground to indicate a desired outcome that had to be respected by the parties involved. More small stones or sticks were used as needed. These could be put into a receptacle, then shaken and drawn or cast to the ground to determine the decision. In some places, arrows could be used to cast lots.

The Old Testament endorses the practice of casting lots. It was a legitimate way of securing God's will on issues. In fact, when the lot was cast, its very decision was considered to have been from God (Prov 16:33). The priests used the Urim (curses) and Thummim (perfections), two cubic stones on their breastplate that were believed to have represented a "No" or "Yes" answer respectively, to indicate the will of God (Exod 28:30; Ezra 2:63; Neh 7:65; 11:1). Priests also cast lots to make important decisions (Lev 16:8). Joshua cast lots to distribute land to the tribes of Israel when they settled in Canaan (Josh 18, 19). The casting of lots or consulting the Urim and Thummim on the ephod were considered the final decision of God which could not be appealed against. It was believed that the individual's fate was in God's hands and this could be revealed through casting a lot. The practice of casting lots was still valid in the New Testament times (Matt 27:35; Luke 1:9; Acts 1:26).

Casting lots was widespread among the nations in the ancient Near East (Jonah 1:7; Esth 3:7), although there were several other ways that could be used to validate decisions. The Black Obelisk of Shalmaneser III of Neo-Assyria describes the practice of using lots. Nebuchadnezzar used divination as well as casting lots with marked arrows in his decision-making (Ezek 21:21). During the Late Egyptian era (664–332 BC), casting lots was considered a juridical exercise. Qumran literature presents casting lots in a figurative way to mean either punishment or reward. In fact, *goral qedhoshim,* "lot of the saints" (1QS 11:7), is *goral 'olam,* "everlasting destiny" (1QH 3:22), while *goral choshekh,* "lot of men of darkness" (1QM 1:11), is *goral 'aph,* "destiny of wrath" (1QH 3:27).[29] Several lot cubes made of either clay or bones have been recovered by archaeologists in Gaza and Tell Beit Mirsim.

DANIEL'S TOMB
Daniel's tomb monument in Susa, Iran.
(Credit: Zev Radovan)

Daniel 12:2 delineates the distinction between those who are going to be resurrected: each of the two groups will awake to their destiny (John 5:28, 29; Rev 20:4-6). Daniel himself is guaranteed to be raised at the end of time and his reward will be eternal life (Dan 12:13). Life is all about deciding for our destiny. In whatever way, at the end of time, God, the final arbiter of human behavior, will reward people according to the choices each one made in life, "whether good or evil" (Eccl 12:14; 2 Cor 5:10; Rev 22:12).

---

29. *TDOT,* 2:456.

Appendix A

THE COMPOSITION OF THE BOOK OF DANIEL

THE BOOK OF DANIEL has been the subject to ongoing debate among scholars. The identity of the author has been questioned. The relationship between the first half and the second half of the book has also been the subject of ongoing discussion.

Porphyry (ca. AD 232/4–304) questioned the historicity of Daniel, and the authenticity of the book that bears his name.[1] He suggested that the book of Daniel was written during the time of Antiochus IV Epiphanes (175–164 BC) by an individual who was in Judea. Porphyry argued that Daniel never predicted the future, but was simply narrating authentic history up to the time of Antiochus IV Epiphanes. In light of this, the writer of the book of Daniel has been "considered a 'palimpsestic author,' who used the texts transmitted to him in order to apply them to the situation of his own generation."[2]

The literary genre differences between the two sections of the book of Daniel have led some scholars to suggest multi-authorship. The debate over issues concerning the composition of Daniel continues to stifle progress towards understanding that book as a literary unit.

Fortunately, several archaeological discoveries provide extrabiblical data which can shed light on some of the problems encountered by those who seek to understand the composition of the book of Daniel. As already

---

1. Archer, *Jerome's Commentary on Daniel*, 15; and Collins, "Daniel, The Book of" (*ABD*, 2:30).

2. Polak, "Daniel Tales," in Van der Woude, *Book of Daniel*, 265.

shown in this work, the geographical places, historical persons, and enigmatic words and phrases in the text of Daniel can be understood better in light of related archaeological finds.

According to the internal evidence, the setting of the book of Daniel is mainly the Neo-Babylonian to Medo-Persian court (late seventh to sixth century BC). The events described stretch from the siege of Jerusalem in the third year of Jehoiakim, king of Judah (605 BC), to the third year of Cyrus, the Persian king ruling in Babylonia (536 BC).

Other contemporary historical figures are featured in the book. Those who interacted with the author include Nebuchadnezzar, king of Babylon (605–562 BC), the coregent king Belshazzar (550–539 BC), Darius the Mede (539 BC), Cyrus (559–530 BC), and Jeremiah (627–580 BC).

The book is attributed to Daniel, who appeared as a Jewish exile of noble birth (Dan 1:3, 6). No genealogical record exists for the author. Daniel 4:1–27, 34–37 appears as Nebuchadnezzar's first-person testimony, but vv. 28–33 could be the author's editorial comment. The first six chapters of the book are Neo-Babylonian and Persian court stories. The text reveals that the author must have been very well acquainted with the contemporaneous court system and its operations. The last six chapters describe in the first-person singular the personal dreams, experiences, and apocalyptic visions of the writer, which seem to build upon the first six chapters of the book.

Wayne Sibley Towner argued that the "radically divergent content of the two halves of the book"[3] of Daniel, which was written in two languages, is a reflection of a work by "several authors."[4] On the other hand, a comparative analysis by Zdravko Stefanovic attempts to show the thematic relationships between the two main sections of Daniel.[5] Stefanovic concluded that the historical section (chapters 1–6) and the prophetic portion (chapters 7–12) present the unified work of a single author rather than a fragmented collection of writings from different sources. Further, Stefanovic argued that the historical and prophetic segments of Daniel point to an early date of composition. The early type of Aramaic used in Daniel is also consistent with the earlier date for that book.

Opinions continue to differ with regard to the authorship of Daniel. Other individuals have been suggested as possible authors of Daniel's book. These include the Right Teacher of the Qumran community,[6] an anonymous

---

3. Towner, *Daniel*, 5.

4. Towner, *Daniel*, 5.

5. Stefanovic, "Thematic Links," 121–27. Among those who already see unity in the book of Daniel include Rowley, *Servant of the Lord*, 235–68; and Baldwin, *Daniel*, 35–46.

6. Trevor, "Book of Daniel," 89–102.

storywriter,[7] a second-century BC author,[8] multiple authorship,[9] and Daniel, a Jew in Babylonian exile.[10]

Despite the various ideas on authorship, the coherent nature of the text, its thematic consistency and ingenuity, and the supporting evidence from archaeological finds lead to the conclusion that the book of Daniel reflects a single author.

DATABLE EVENTS IN DANIEL

Some events in the book of Daniel can be chronologically ascertained and dated. Most of these historical incidents are attested in several contemporary ancient Near Eastern sources discovered by archaeologists. Such events can provide useful data for addressing the dating problem. The text of Daniel reveals that the author was cognizant of the prevailing situation in the Neo-Babylonian as well as in the Medo-Persian court. Daniel also provides information we cannot get from elsewhere.

The datable events shown in table 10 are contemporaneous with the author. These are useful in establishing the time during which the book of Daniel was written.

DATING PROBLEM

Scholars have inconclusively assigned the writing of the book of Daniel to different periods of time. The main views on the dating of Daniel are the traditional perspective which considers a sixth-century date for Daniel and the popular position which assigns the writing to about 165 BC. The irreconcilable opinions on the dating of Daniel have become more complex because the same evidences on the dating of the book have been used by some scholars in support of the earlier dates and by others in support of the suggested later dates for the composition of the text.

---

7. Lucas, *Daniel*, 313.

8. Talmon, "Daniel," in Alter and Kermode, *Literary Guide to the Bible*, 345–46; and Collins, *Daniel*, 24–26;

9. Di Lella, *Daniel*, 7–8; and Towner, *Daniel*, 6–8. In fact, Towner identifies the authors as Torah-true Jews, the *hasidim* (1 Macc 2:42; 7:13–17), in *Daniel*, 7.

10. Josephus, *Antiquities of the Jews*, 10.10–11; Longman III, *Daniel*, 21; Baldwin, *Daniel*, 18; Stefanovic, *Daniel*, 16–22; and Walvoord, *Daniel*, 11–12.

APPENDIX A

Table 10
DATED EVENTS IN DANIEL

DATE	EVENT
605 BC	Third year of the reign of Jehoiakim, king of Judah/Nebuchadnezzar besieged Jerusalem (Dan 1:1) Daniel and his friends, along with other Jewish captives and temple vessels, were taken to Babylon
604 BC	Appointment of students for the king's school (Dan 1:3–7)
603 BC	Nebuchadnezzar's dream in his second year of reign (Dan 2:1) Daniel recovered and interpreted the king's dream
602 BC	End of the three years of training set by the king (Dan 1:18) Daniel and friends entered the king's service (Dan 1:19)
602–536 BC	Daniel's service in the Neo-Babylonian and Medo-Persian courts (Dan 1:21)
593 BC	King Nebuchadnezzar assembles all people on the Plain of Dura to worship the golden image he had set up (Dan 3) Three instruments with Greek names are identified in the orchestra Shadrach, Meshach, and Abednego are rescued from the fiery furnace
550/49 BC	First year of Belshazzar (Dan 7:1) Daniel's dream of four marine beasts from the Mediterranean Sea
548/7 BC	Third year of king Belshazzar (Dan 8:1) Daniel's vision of the ram and the goat by the Ulai River/Canal
539 BC	Banquet and death of Belshazzar (Dan 5:1–30) Cyrus, king of Persia, takes Babylon (Dan 1:21) Darius the Mede receives the Babylonian kingdom (Dan 5:31)
539–530 BC	The reign of Cyrus, king of Persia (Dan 6:28)
539/8 BC	Darius the Mede's first year of reign under Cyrus, king of Persia (Dan 9:1; 11:1) Daniel's prayer in the first year of Darius the Mede (Dan 9:1) Angel visitor relating events of the first year of Darius the Mede (Dan 11:1)
536 BC	Third year of Cyrus, king of Persia (Dan 10:1) Daniel's vision while he was by the Tigris River

Some scholars advocate a pre-Maccabean era for the writing of the entire book of Daniel. Others prefer the Maccabean date (165 BC). Still, a few suggest that parts of Dan 1–6 are pre-Maccabean while the rest of the book may be Maccabean. The debate on Daniel's dating classified the arguments into the historical, literary or linguistic, theological, and exegetical categories. This analysis indicates that the use of archaeology as a means of understanding of the dating of Daniel has been underutilized.

Certain scholars have thought that the book of Daniel was written around 165 BC as a historical fiction. This theory assumes that the prophecy of Daniel was *vaticinium ex eventu* ("prophecy after the event"), designed to encourage the suffering Jews who were undergoing persecution by Antiochus IV Epiphanes.

A careful analysis of the themes and concerns of the book of Daniel show that the book was not written as a prophylactic document for people under the fire of persecution.

In the Hebrew Bible, Daniel is placed among *Ketûbîm*, "the Writings," and not among *Nebî'îm*, "the Prophets." This has been seen by some scholars to indicate that the book is not prophecy, but an apocalypse, and that it was written later than all the prophets.

In fact, the placement of Daniel in the Writings section of the Hebrew Bible or the *TaNaK* (*Tôrâh, Nebî'îm, Ketûbîm*) has nothing to do with the dating of the book. Daniel is placed in the same section as other earlier texts such as Job, Davidic psalms, and Solomonic writings. In the LXX Daniel is placed among the prophets. At Qumran, the Florilegium (4QFlor [4Q174]) indicates Daniel as a prophet, and the author of the book bearing his name. Josephus strongly indicated that in the first century AD Daniel belonged to the prophets in the second division of the Hebrew Bible canon. Other writers attest that by first century AD, Daniel was already considered a prophet (Matt 24:15; Luke 21:20; Mark 13:14).

The hymn in honor of the ancestors by Jesus Son of Sirach (Ecclesiasticus or Sirach 44–50) identifies some of the famous men in the Israelite history but does not mention Daniel in any way. This has been used by some as evidence for the late date for the book of Daniel. However, the names mentioned by Sirach do not appear in their chronological order, nor do they present a comprehensive list. Several key players in the writing of Israelite history are missing. Among these are Jehoshaphat, Ezra, and Mordecai, just to name a few. No renowned women are acknowledged in Sirach's entire text.

Several features of the book of Daniel have been cited as historical inaccuracies. These include:

- Internal dating data (Dan 1:1; 2:1; 7:1; 8:1; 9:1)
- Chaldeans as wise men (Dan 1:4; 2:2, 10–14)
- Nebuchadnezzar's building projects (Dan 4:30)
- Nebuchadnezzar's mental derangement (Dan 4:25, 28–33; 5:21)

APPENDIX A

- Identity of Darius the Mede (Dan 6:28; 9:1; 11:1)
- Identity of Belshazzar as king (Dan 5:1, 9; 7:1; 8:1)
- Identity of Belshazzar as the son of Nebuchadnezzar (Dan 5:2, 11, 18)

Discussing the above list in light of the archaeological evidence shows that these issues are not "in conflict with our other historical witnesses."[11] Rather, they indicate that the author of Daniel had unique information, and that he must have lived during the time he wrote about.

Linguists have studied the Hebrew and Aramaic of Daniel, along with some Greek and Persian loanwords used in the book. The purpose of this effort has been to determine whether the book belongs to an earlier time period or to the Maccabean date. Several experts in the Aramaic language have concluded that the Qumran Job Targum (11QtgJob) is dated to the second century BC.[12] Others place this document in the second half of the third century BC or the first half of the second century BC, and believe that its Aramaic is centuries later than that of Daniel and Ezra. In this case, the Aramaic of the book of Daniel would evidently point us to a much earlier date than the suggested 165 BC. Daniel's Aramaic and syntax have been attested by a number of scholars as belonging to the sixth century BC, and as being of Babylonian provenance.

Prior to the adoption of the Seleucid system in 311 BC, the ancient Mesopotamians had no fixed method for dating. They determined dates based on the reigning years of their rulers or proximity to important events. The book of Daniel used the Mesopotamian method of dating (Dan 1:1, 21; 2:1; 7:1; 8:1; 9:1; 10:1). The datable events in Daniel can be precisely ascertained when correlated with the contemporary Babylonian and Persian king lists and other relevant chronological conventions. See table 8 above. The Assyrian *limmu*-lists offer valuable astronomical data from 747–631 BC. They coincide with Ptolemy's Canon, which has the list of kings and their length of reign from Nabonassar, 747 BC, through Cleopatra VII's reign in 30 BC. These lists, along with the Neo-Babylonian and Persian dated economic texts and receipts, can be utilized to determine the datable material in the book of Daniel.

Some studies conclude that the stories in Dan 1–6 originated around seventh to sixth centuries BC during the time of the Babylonian exile, but that the apocalypses of Dan 7—12 were added around 165 BC. Nevertheless, more and more evidence show that the book of Daniel is a unified whole that must have been composed earlier than popular suggestions.

11. Collins, *Daniel*, 30.
12. Jongeling et al., *Aramaic Texts from Qumran*, 6; and Sokoloff, *Targum to Job*, 25.

Daniel was written in the sixth century BC since it contains more stories from that time than from the Hellenistic or Roman periods. If it had been written in the second century BC, as thought by some, then it should have had more of the Greek language, style, or literary motifs.

One of the main concerns of the author of Daniel was the looting and destruction of the Jerusalem temple (Dan 1:2; 5:2, 3, 23; 9:17). If the book had been written after the returning exiles had finished reconstructing the temple in 516/515 BC, it is most likely that the author would have highlighted this event. Careful examination of the archaeological evidence in relation to Daniel may show that the popular dating of the book (165 BC) has been misplaced by several centuries.

MULTILINGUALISM IN DANIEL

Daniel is usually classified as bilingual in the sense that the text is composed of two main languages, Hebrew and Aramaic, but there are several words in the text that were borrowed from other languages. Chapters 1–2:4a and 8–12 are predominantly Hebrew, whereas chapters 2:4b–7 are Aramaic. Mixed into the Hebrew and Aramaic passages are some Akkadian, Greek, and Old Persian words. These serve to show the author's linguistic skills. Further, this interlingual adaptability highlights Daniel's administrative experience with national and international affairs while he was in the Babylonian and Medo-Persian courts. The foreign words have been used to date the book of Daniel. The same evidence has been used in different ways by different scholars to advocate for either the sixth-century or second-century BC dates.

Some finds show that Daniel's multilingual document is not unique in the ancient Near East during the first millennium BC. A life-size statue was found of Hadad-yith'i, the ruler of Guzana, in the mid-ninth century BC in northern Syria. This statue has bilingual Akkadian-Aramaic inscriptions. In this case, the two versions were very similar in first half of the inscriptions, but the second half had wide-ranging differences.[13]

Bilingual texts from Asia Minor include writings in Lydian and Aramaic, and others in Greek and Aramaic. The excavations at Tel Dan (Arabic Tel el Qadi) uncovered a bilingual Greek and Aramaic dedicatory inscription which reads: "To the god who is in Dan, Zoilos made a vow."[14] The Tell

---

13. Mikaya, "Earliest Aramaic Inscription Uncovered in Syria," 52–53; and Millard and Bordreuil, "Statue from Syria," 135–41.

14. Donner and Röllig, *Kanaanäische und Aramäische Inschriften*, 2:309–10, no. 262; and Greenfield, "Aramaic Studies and the Bible," 128. See Biran, "Dan" (*ABD*,

Faḥariyeh inscription is also bilingual.[15] A trilingual inscription in Aramaic, Greek, and Lycian was found in the Sanctuary of Leto at Xanthos in 1973.[16]

The first extrabiblical reference to Elam appears in AD 1667. Samuel Flower discovered this reference in some cuneiform inscriptions at Persepolis.[17] These were deciphered in 1778 by Carsten Niebuhr, who indicated that the signs were trilingual. The languages included Old Persian, the Babylonian dialect of Akkadian and Elamite.[18]

The Rosetta Stone records a decree made by some Egyptian priests in 196 BC. These priests wrote of conferring honors on Ptolemy V Epiphanes. The inscription was written in classical Egyptian hieroglyphics, demotic, and classical Greek.[19]

Multilingualism in Daniel reflects a literary technique that was in common use in the ancient Near East in different time periods.

GREEK TRANSLATION OF DANIEL

The history of the translation of the Hebrew Scriptures into Greek remains unclear and debatable. The main source of information describing how the Greek translation came into existence is the apocryphal Letter of Aristeas or pseudo-Aristeas written in Alexandria a century or more after the translation was made.[20]

At issue is the credibility of the Letter of Aristeas as a reliable historical source of information regarding the Greek translation. The Letter of Aristeas has been charged with historical inaccuracies, questionable background, and unreliable dating. Other writers from Alexandria, Aristobulus, and Philo are not consistent with the Letter of Aristeas. They do, however, repeat its story, and this may in fact give Aristeas some credibility.

2:16–17); also Biran, "What Is Biblical Archaeology?," in Charlesworth, *Jesus and Archaeology*, 3.

15. Cross, "Paleography," in Zevit et al., *Solving Riddles and Untying Knots*, 393–409.

16. Greenfield, "Aramaic Studies and the Bible," 128; and Eichner, "Etymologische," 48–66. Bryce, "Recently Discovered Cult in Lycia," 115–27; Lemaire, "Xanthos Trilingual Revisited," in Zevit, *Solving Riddles and Untying Knots*, 423–32.

17. Potts, *Archaeology of Elam*, 5.

18. Potts, *Archaeology of Elam*, 5.

19. Budge, *Rosetta Stone*, 1–8; and Lloyd, "Late Period (664–332 BC)," 414–15.

20. Jobes and Silva, *Invitation to the Septuagint*, 34; and Shutt, "Aristeas, Letter of" (*ABD*, 1:380–82).

Interestingly, Josephus paraphrased the Letter of Aristeas and pointed out that it was circulating in Palestine in the first century AD.[21] Aristeas purports to write to a certain Philocrates. He describes to Philocrates the process of translating the Jewish Law into Greek in Alexandria during the reign of Ptolemy II Philadelphus (285–247 BC).

According to Aristeas, a certain Demetrius of Phaleron was the royal librarian. He came up with the idea and was later commissioned to translate into Greek the books of the Laws of the Jews. Ptolemy II Philadelphus sent a letter to the high priest in Jerusalem asking for translators. The Greek translation of the Hebrew Bible was the work of the seventy or seventy-two Jewish translators. Hence the designation "Septuagint" and its shorthand abbreviation "LXX."

Scholars are unsure of the date of the LXX, but based on the Letter of Aristeas and the six fragments from a work by Demetrius the Chronographer, it could be suggested to have been in the fourth to third century BC.[22]

The translations must have started with the Jewish Law or the Pentateuch and subsequently spread to cover the whole corpus of the Hebrew Scriptures. Ever since these manuscripts were first translated into Greek, other revisions or translations came from such as Aquila,[23] Theodotion,[24] Symmachus,[25] and others.[26] These continued to surface for use by either the Jews in the diaspora or the Jewish proselytes.

The text of the book of Daniel appears in two different Greek translations or versions. These are known as the Old Greek Daniel (OG-Dan or OG) and Theodotion Daniel (Th-Dan or θ). Both of these translations have the twelve chapters that are found in the Masoretic Text (MT). In addition, they include some apocryphal writings, namely, Bel and the Dragon, the Prayer of Azariah, the Song of the Three Hebrews, and Susanna. These works are discussed below. These writings are commonly called the Additions and

---

21. Josephus, *Antiquities of the Jews,* 12.2.1.11–118; and Josephus, *Against Apion,* 2.45–47.

22. Clancy, "Date of the LXX," 207; and Yarchin, *History of Biblical Interpretation,* 3–8.

23. Some fragments of Aquila's translation were discovered in the Geniza of the Cairo Museum. Kahle, *Cairo Geniza,* 3–33.

24. It is suggested that Theodotion lived in the second century and the use of the term "Theodotion" (Th) is purely a matter of literary convention. See McLay, "Double Translations," in Martinez and Vervenne, *Interpreting Translation,* 255.

25. Eusebius, *Ecclesiastical History,* 2:52–55.

26. The other Greek versions include the Quinta (έ), Sexta (ς) and the Septima (ζ) which were identified in Origen's research; see Eusebius, *Eusebius,* 1:262–64.

APPENDIX A

also appear in other ancient manuscripts including the Syriac Peshitta and the Latin Vulgate.

The OG-Dan and the Th-Dan approach the Masoretic Text differently. There are some areas where the OG-Dan and the Th-Dan are very similar to each other, but in some areas, they differ significantly. These two translations differ in the style of presentation, detail in the stories, points of emphasis, grammar, and vocabulary. Different renditions in the translations have been noticed between the OG-Dan and θ versions of Daniel. These have become known as the double translations. The double translation phenomenon is more noticeable in chapters 4–6. It is uncertain whether both versions were drawing from the same manuscript.²⁷

According to Irenaeus, Theodotion was a Jewish proselyte from Ephesus who translated the Hebrew Scriptures into Greek.²⁸ This version is commonly known today as Theodotion (θ). Theodotion revised the Old Greek version in light of the standard Hebrew text. He literally transliterated the Hebrew nouns into Greek. This translation of the book of Daniel was rated far better than the OG.

The second-century Papyrus 967 of the Chester Beaty 1931 collection and the eleventh-century MS 88 are good witnesses to the OG. All of the other extant manuscripts on the book of Daniel relied on Theodotion's translation. The Syriac text of Daniel also includes the apocryphal additions that were in the Greek translations. There are several extant versions of the Syriac Daniel. These include the Peshiṭta,²⁹ which seems to be in accordance with other ancient texts, the Syro-Hexapla,³⁰ and the Revised Peshiṭta of Jacob of Edessa.³¹ The Syriac text reflects the Old Greek text to a large extent.

---

27. McLay, "Double Translations," 255. McLay gives several examples of the double translations by comparing the MT, θ, and OG, e.g., Dan 4:29:
MT Dan 4:32/29 עשבא כתורין לך יטעמון
θ Dan 4:29 χόρτον ὡς βοῦν ψωμιοῦσί σε
OG-Dan 4:29 χόρτον ὡς βοῦν σε ψωμιοῦσι καὶ ἀπὸ τῆς χλόης τῆς γῆς ἔσται ἡ νομή σου
The underlined parts of θ and OG agree verbatim with the MT but the OG has the same underlined words repeated as a doublet in the following verse; McLay, "Double Translations," 257–58; see also Jeansonne, *Old Greek Translation*, 70–133.

28. Irenaeus, *Against Heresies*, 3.21.1, quoted in Dines, *Septuagint*, 84.

29. See Taylor, *Peshitta of Daniel* (1994). Taylor compares the Syriac text of Daniel to the Hebrew and the Aramaic and concludes that the Peshitta of Daniel is a direct translation from the Hebrew *Vorlage* in line with the Theodotion text, especially in the apocryphal additions. See also *Old Testament in Syriac, According to the Peshitta Version* (1991).

30. Vööbus, *Hexapla and the Syro-Hexapla* (1971).

31. Jenner, "Unit Delimitation," in Korpel and Oesch, *Delimitation Criticism*, 105.

Other witnesses to Daniel in addition to the MT include the Old Greek (OG), the extant copies of Daniel in the Dead Sea Scrolls corpus, and the New Testament (Matt 24:15; Mark 13:14; Luke 21:20). The Dead Sea Scrolls on Daniel do not show major disagreements with the MT.

In conclusion, there are some manuscripts which cannot be safely taken as witnesses to the book of Daniel. These include the apocrypha or the Greek Additions to Daniel and all the pseudepigrapha ascribed to Daniel. Some of this literature, however, presents unique material in relation to Daniel but should be used with caution.

SOURCES FOR THE STUDY OF DANIEL

The Hebrew Bible is one of several sources of information regarding the history of the Neo-Babylonian Empire. Scholars extract data for the reconstruction of this history from various ancient Near Eastern sources. These include mostly the Assyrian, Babylonian, and Medo-Persian archaeological and textual artifacts. These sources are essential for the study of Daniel. They can be further categorized as follows:

- *The Royal Correspondence*: The royal correspondence ranges from letters, seal inscriptions, building inscriptions, and votive inscriptions. The Assyrian Empire had more voluminous texts than the Babylonian. There are also letters to the Assyrian kings from individuals, temple administrators, and Assyrian authorities in Babylonia recovered in the archives at Kuyunjik and Nimrud, and these are dated from the eighth to seventh centuries BC.[32]

- *Monumental Inscriptions*: Examples of such monuments include wall reliefs and some inscribed *asuminētu ša galalu*, "stelas of polished stones," set up by Nabonidus (556–539 BC) in Sippar, Larsa, Agade, and Sippar-Anunìtum. These were to commemorate the restoration of their main temples or war victories.[33]

- *Architecture*: The architecture recovered from various parts of the ancient Near East remains impressive. Excavations have also unearthed some building inscriptions which offer relevant historical data.

---

32. Hallo, "Royal Inscriptions of Ur," 1–43; Clay, *Neo-Babylonian Letters from Erech* (1919); Parpola, *Letters from Assyrian and Babylonian Scholars* (1993); and Oates and Oates, *Nimrud*, 195–225.

33. Beaulieu, *Reign of Nabonidus*, 27–29. For the other texts see Clay, *Neo-Babylonian Letters from Erech*, 13–26, and the autographed texts, plates 1–200.

APPENDIX A

- *Chronographic Texts*: These can help in outlining historical events.[34]
- *King Lists*: These compilations include the Assyrian, Babylonian, Persian, and Egyptian king lists. More information can be gleaned from the chronicles as well as other documents and inscriptions.
- *Annals*: Such documents were normally commissioned by the king and can be useful for chronological purposes and also for deciphering information on the king's sociopolitical and socioreligious obligations. However, caution in using these annals must be exercised because of their propagandistic nature.
- *Pseudo-Autobiographies*: An example for the Neo-Babylonian period is the story of Nabonidus's mother, Adad-guppi, on two stelae found in Harran in 1906 and 1956 respectively. Adad-guppi narrates how she was devoted from her childhood to the gods Sin, Shamash, Ishtar, and Adad. She believed that these gods were in heaven. She further indicates that all her possessions were given by the gods.[35]
- *Prophecies*: These are considered as "prose composition consisting in the main of a number of 'predictions' of past events." Texts which belong to this category include: Marduk Prophecy, Šulgi Prophecy, Uruk Prophecy, and Dynasty Prophecy.[36] For the Neo-Babylonian period, see biblical prophecy books including Ezekiel, Jeremiah, Daniel, etc.
- *Historical Epics*: Such as *Atra-hasis*, *Enūma Elish*, *Eridu*, and *Gilgamesh*.[37]
- *Private Texts*: These may include letters by the king or his officials or other citizens. They can be useful historical documents which offer additional information on what was taking place during that time.[38]
- *Legal Documents*: These offer valuable dating information. Usually, the name of the reigning king, the date, and the place are included in a legally binding document. Marriage contracts are a good example.

---

34. See the Chronicles in Wiseman, *Chronicles of the Chaldaean Kings*, 1–96, also Plates I–XXI; and Grayson, *Assyrian and Babylonian Chronicles*, 8–192.

35. Gadd, "The Harran Inscription of Nabonidus," 35–92; and *ANET*, 560–562.

36. Grayson, *Babylonian Historical-Literary Texts*, 6. See also Longman III, *Fictional Akkadian Autobiography*, 131–146; *COS*, 1:480–481; Block, *Gods of the Nations*, 123–124; and Arnold and Beyer, *Readings from the Ancient Near East*, 215–217.

37. See *ANET*, 104–6, 44–54, 72–97; 104–6; 503–7, 512–13, 640–42; *COS*, 1:450–53, 458–60, 513–15, 550–52; and Arnold and Beyer, *Readings from the Ancient Near East*, 13–15, 21–50, 66–70.

38. Shiff has dealt more with private communication in "Nur-Sin Archive."

- *Economic Texts*: Some of these appear as deeds of sale, contracts, and receipts. These texts may be useful for asserting chronology, economic transactions, dating, and also for identifying the parties which were involved.[39]
- *Pseudo-Danielic Writings*: A large volume of pseudo-Danielic writings has been published but many such works continue to surface. These will be addressed later.

There are many myths from the ancient Near East that have shown some parallels and syntactical issues with the text of Daniel.[40] Even though it has been shown that the ancient myths and Daniel share some literary motifs and parallels, it has not been convincingly established that Daniel had any literary dependence upon them, or that he borrowed from any of them.

The Babylonian Chronicles are valuable for the reconstruction of the Neo-Babylonian history. They cover the years 626–623, 616–608, 608–605, and 605–594 BC. Unfortunately, the Babylonian Chronicles preserve nothing about Nebuchadnezzar's reign after 594 BC.[41] The chronicles leave out critical details in recording the events; for example, BM 21946 mentioned Nebuchadnezzar's invasion of Jerusalem on March 15/16, 598/597 BC, but does not give more information to highlight that historical event.[42]

Medo-Persia, especially under the Achaemenid administration (sixth to fifth centuries BC), offers some valuable archaeological and literary artifacts that have contributed to the understanding of the world of Daniel. In addition to these indigenous sources, there are some foreign ancient texts that offer information which is not found elsewhere in the study of Neo-Babylonia. Such secondary sources include the Arabic, Aramaic, Hebrew, Greek, and Latin sources. These highlight the history, culture, religion, economy, political administration, and military achievements of Neo-Babylonia, but they should also be used with caution.

In these sources there are some striking similarities with Daniel, but there are also irreconcilable differences in the descriptions of some of the

---

39. See Moore, *Neo-Babylonian Business and Administrative Documents*, 2–396; and Moore, *Neo-Babylonian Documents*, 3–71, and plates 1–75.

40. See *ANET*, "Egyptian Myths," 3–36; "Sumerian Myths," 37–59; "Akkadian Myths and Epics," 60–119; "Hittite Myths, Epics and Legends," 120–28; and "Ugaritic Myths, Epics and Legends," 129–55.

41. Kuhrt, *ANE*, 2:541, 592–93. For the texts of the chronicles see *ANET*, 265–317; Wiseman, *Chronicles of Chaldaean Kings* (1956); and Grayson, *Assyrian and Babylonian Chronicles* (2000).

42. Wiseman, *Chronicles of the Chaldean Kings*, 32–35, 73, reverse, lines 11–13; and Grayson, *Assyrian and Babylonian Chronicles*, 102, reverse, lines 11–13.

events. Berossus cited a complaint about the misinformation on the history of Babylon circulated by some Greek authors.[43]

Interestingly, W. G. Lambert remarked that there are no fully comparable extant Greek texts that were written before the book of Daniel.[44] It remains plausible to note that the material in the book of Daniel is more comparable to the Neo-Babylonian and Medo-Persian or earlier archaeological material than that of the later time periods. There is overwhelming evidence that some Babylonian materials in Aramaic were spread throughout the Hellenistic world.

The Greek classical historians fairly highlight the world of Daniel. However, some critical information from that time period remains unique to Daniel. It has already been pointed out that Herodotus, Ctesias, Strabo, Pliny, Diodorus, and others missed the concept that Nebuchadnezzar built Babylon to its grandeur in the sixth century BC.[45]

The Greek writers fail to explicitly present Medo-Persia as a unified kingdom after 539 BC as indicated in Daniel's text (Dan 5:28; 6:8, 12, 15; 8:20). The Greeks understood the succession of empires in the ancient Near East as Assyrian, Median, Persian, and then Greece.[46] In fact, for the Greeks, Babylon plays no significant geopolitical role. Babylon is even taken as an Assyrian colony by Ctesias.[47] However, some important items mentioned by the classical Greek writers which are not in Daniel include the hanging gardens of Babylon and lists of Neo-Babylonian kings and their years of reign.

Further, these classical writers also do not mention anything about a number of significant events:

- Nebuchadnezzar's dreams (Dan 2, 4)
- Nebuchadnezzar's lycanthropy (Dan 4)
- Belshazzar's inscription (Dan 5)
- Darius the Mede as king in Babylon (Dan 5:31; 6:1–28)

Daniel says that Belshazzar was killed on the night of the fall of Babylon (Dan 5:30). Xenophon does not provide the ruler's name but reports that the Persians killed the king the night they took Babylon.[48]

---

43. Burstein, *Babyloniaca of Berossus*, 28. See also Josephus, *Against Apion*, 1.20.142–44; and Grabbe, "Of Mice and Dead Men," 120–25.
44. Lambert, *Background of Jewish Apocalyptic*, 15.
45. Pfeiffer, *Biblical World*, 126; and Hasel, "Book of Daniel," 38.
46. Burstein, *Babyloniaca of Berossus*, 9.
47. Burstein, *Babyloniaca of Berossus*, 9. See also table 4.
48. Xenophon, *Cyropaedia*, 7.5.27–30.

In conclusion, Daniel can be understood as an earlier tradition that contains information which was lost to later writers. There are many informative extrabiblical sources available for highlighting the study of Daniel. A few of these sources have caused difficulties in understanding the content and the chronology of the book. Some of the data from such sources cannot be corroborated with the cuneiform sources. An additional problem is that some of the original classical texts have survived only in fragments, or in quotations by later writers. Megasthenes's work is lost except for a fragment of his writing. This appears as a quotation in Eusebius who got it from Abydenus. It reads:

> Abydenus, in his history of the Assyrians, has preserved the following fragment of Megasthenes, who says: That Nabucodrosorus (Nebuchadnezzar), having become more powerful than Hercules, invaded Lybia and Iberia, (Spain), and when he had rendered them tributary, he extended his conquests over the inhabitants of the shores upon the right of the sea . . . he expired, and was succeeded by his son Evilmarchus (Evil-Merodach), who was slain by his kinsman, Neriglisares (Neriglissor), and Neriglisares left a son, Labassoarascus (Labarosoarchod), and when he also had suffered death by violence, they made Nabannidochus king, being no relation to the royal race.[49]

Other documents in relation to Daniel have not been published. Many more such documents continue to surface as archaeologists continue their work. Sometimes these documents come from diverse and dubious backgrounds.[50] The interest in the study of Daniel intensifies as time goes on.

Some later ancient literary works relevant to Daniel were composed by various historians, scholars, geographers, and travelers from the classical Greek times to the early 1900s. The German Orient Society under the direction of Robert Koldewey (1895–917) organized archaeological work at Babylon.[51] Koldewey's extensive archaeological work can be taken as the benchmark for highlighting the book of Daniel.

More information on Nebuchadnezzar or the Chaldeans is also known from the collection of later antiquity literary sources. The Neo-Babylonian literature does not provide the historians with enough data on the political

---

49. See Sack, *Images of Nebuchadnezzar*, 31–32; Cory, *Ancient Fragments of the Phoenician*, 71–72; and Sack, *Neriglissar*, 4–5.

50. DiTommaso, *Bibliography of Pseudepigrapha Research* (2001); and DiTommaso, *Book of Daniel* (2005).

51. Koldewey, *Excavations at Babylon* (1917). See Klengel-Brandt, "Babylon" (*OEANE*, 1:251–56); and Tanner, "Ancient Babylon," 12–18.

APPENDIX A

developments of the ancient Near East region. The available sources have limitations in presenting the data because their authors seem to have had diverse personal interests other than the objective writing of history. Therefore, some of the sources should be used with caution (see table 11).

TABLE 11
SOURCES FOR THE STUDY OF DANIEL

AUTHOR	DATE	RELEVANCE TO DANIEL
Xenophanes of Colophon	ca. 550–500 BC	Illustrated the expansion of the Persian Empire.
Hecataeus of Miletus	ca. 500 BC	Had extensive travels in the Persian Empire including Mesopotamia. His two works, *Periegesis* and *Genealogiai*, are now lost. Herodotus refers to his genealogical record. Herodotus, *Herodotus*, 2.143.
Dionysius of Miletus & Charon of Lampascus	ca. 500 BC	Wrote Persian history and customs, but now lost.
Hellanicus of Lesbos	ca. 500 BC	Wrote *Persica* in two books covering the history of Assyria, Media, and the rise of Persia. Presents the Chaldeans as older people than the Persians.
Thucydides	Born ca. 460 BC	Mentioned Persian wars, King Cyrus, his son and successor Cambyses, and also that Darius I succeeded Cambyses. Finley, *Greek Historians*, 217–379; and Lesky, *History of Greek Literature*, 455–83.
Herodotus	Mid-5th century BC	Compiled accounts of his journeys and an extensive excursus on Babylonian history. Described layout of Babylon. His *Histories,* published between 430–425 BC, is the earliest surviving Greek account on the history of ANE.
Ctesias	ca. 5th century BC	Compiled history of Assyria and Persia, *Persica*, in twenty-three books through the help of Diodorus Siculus. He lived at the Persian court. He tried to discredit Herodotus.
Xenophon	ca. 427–355 BC	Compiled accounts of cities, history, legends, and stories. Traveled with Greek mercenaries through Asia Minor and upper Tigris and Euphrates Rivers. He wrote *Anabasis* and pro-Cyrus legends in *Cyropaedia*.

APPENDIX A

Hecataeus of Abdera	4th century BC	Questioned the origin of the Chaldeans and took them to be Egyptian colonists. Murray, "Hecateus of Abdera and Pharonic Kingship," 141–71; Wacholder, *Eupolemus*, 85–96.
Dinon of Colophon	4th century BC	Wrote a commentary on Ctesias's *Persica*.
Megasthenes from Ionia	Time of Seleucus I Nicator 312–280 BC	Wrote *History of India* but only a fragment is preserved. Discussed the sixth-century BC Neo-Babylonian list of kings but had more on Nebuchadnezzar. His work was cited by Abydenus and also Eusebius. Josephus, *Against Apion*, 1.20.
Pesudo-Democritus of Abdera	3rd century BC	Presented an account of Babylonian history, traditions, and culture.
Berossus, a Babylonian Priest	3rd century BC	Used ancient resources to compose the *Babylonica* which is now lost, but Josephus and Eusebius both preserved the fragmentary work. He wrote in Greek. Berossus's chronology corresponds with cuneiform documents. He dedicated his work to Antiochus Seleucus I (281–260 BC). His list of Neo-Babylonian kings agrees with cuneiform sources but is the only source informing us that Neriglissar was Amel-Marduk's brother-in law. See Burstein, *Babylonica of Berossus*.
Philo of Byzantium	250 BC	Described in detail the hanging gardens of Babylon.
Qumran Manuscripts	200 BC–AD 70	The Dead Sea Scrolls (DSS). The text of the canonical Daniel was among the discoveries.
Eupolemus	2nd century BC	Wrote on the kings of Judea by drawing data from 2 Kgs 24:12–13; 25:13–17 and possibly from apocryphal sources as well as Hellenistic writers like Hecataeus and Ctesias. Had informative but fragmentary account on Nebuchadnezzar's destruction of Jerusalem. Wacholder, *Eupolemus*.

Alexander Polyhistor from Miletus or Caria	Born 105 BC	Preserved fragments of Eupolemus's work, some of which were also preserved by Eusebius, e.g., the dynastic list of the Neo-Babylonian kings. Wacholder, *Eupolemus*, 44–52.
Diodorus Siculus, Pompeius Trogus, & Nicolaus of Damascus	1st century BC–AD	Compiled general international history from creation to their day.
Strabo	ca. 64 BC–AD 19	Wrote the *Geography*, which was more than just accounts of travel. His encyclopedic work covers the historical geography of the inhabited countries from the beginning of the Christian era. *Geography of Strabo*, 8 vols.
Flavius Josephus	Born AD 37	Wrote an autobiography, *Life of Flavius Josephus*, and in addition, *Antiquities of the Jews*, *War of the Jews*, and *Flavius Josephus Against Apion*. His writings covered Nebuchadnezzar and the fall of Jerusalem (cf. 2 Kgs 25:27–30; Jer 52: 31, 32) and give some information on Jewish and Neo-Babylonian history which is not attested elsewhere.
Pliny the Elder	1st century AD	Visited and described Babylon's walls, indicated that the Euphrates flowed through Babylon, and that it was rerouted by the Persians. He said that the temples were still standing and that the population was 600,000. Pliny, *Natural History*, 2:429–33.
Quintus C. Rufus	1st century AD	Visited Babylon and wrote that the hanging gardens were still visible. Rufus, *History of Alexander*, 5.1.35.
Lucian of Samosata	2nd century AD	Suggested in *The True Story* that Homer's birthplace was Babylon. Cyrus, son of Cambyses, is said to have transferred the kingdom of the Medes to the Persians and also to have subdued the Assyrians and Babylonians. *Lucian*, 2:415.

APPENDIX A

Claudius Ptolemy	2nd century AD	Authored Ptolemaic Canon which listed the Neo-Babylonian kings and the duration of their reign, but his work omits Labashi-Mardurk (556 BC). He seemed to have depended on Polyhistor who was, in turn, dependent on earlier historians. He gave some geographic descriptions of Mesopotamia. Sack, *Amel-Marduk 562–560 BC*, 11.
Justin	2nd century AD	Wrote *Dialogue with Trypho*, where he quoted Dan 7:9–27 and referred to Christ as the Son of Man.
Epistle of Barnabas	ca. AD 130	Wrote on Dan 7 and pointed out that the fourth beast was Rome.
Trypho	Mid-2nd century AD	Held views that Dan 7 pointed to the time after Antiochus IV Epiphanes.
Justin Martyr	Mid-2nd century AD	Was convinced that the little horn would appear well after Antiochus IV Epiphanes.
Irenaeus	AD 130–200	Wrote *Against Heresies* where he dealt with Daniel's major prophecies.
Abydenus	2nd/3rd century AD	He wrote about the Assyrians and incorporated information on Neo-Babylonian period by earlier writers but his book has not survived. In his writings he included fragments of Alexander Polyhistor and Megasthenes.
Hippolytus	AD 140–235	Wrote a commentary on Daniel in Greek ca. AD 202. He identified the little horn of Dan 8 with Antiochus IV Epiphanes.
Clement of Alexandria	ca. AD 150–220	Attempted to set up the chronology of ancient Israel from Dan 9:24–27.
Tertullian	AD 160–240	His *An Answer to the Jews* dealt with Dan 9 and he pointed to Jesus as the Messiah.
Julius Africanus	AD 160–240	Worked on the chronology of the figures mentioned in Daniel.
Origen	AD 185–254	Commented on Daniel in Greek and was translated into Latin, but the work is extant only in fragments.
Cyprian of Carthage	AD 200–258	Wrote much on Antiochus IV Epiphanes but without relating his work to Daniel.

Xenophon of Antioch	3rd century AD	Wrote the novel *Babylonian Matters*.
Soterichos	3rd century AD	Produced the novel *Experiences of Panthea, Babylonian Girl*.
Iamblichus	3rd century AD	Was author of the novel *Babylonian Story*, a story about lovers.
Porphyry	ca. AD 232/4-304	Wrote *Against the Christians* 15 vols. In vol. 12 he alleged that the book of Daniel was written by an unknown person during the time of Antiochus IV. He took the prophetic passages to be *vaticinia ex eventu* ("prophecies after the event").
Lactantius	AD 250-330	Wrote on the prophecies of Daniel and about the antichrist.
Eusebius of Pamphilius, Bishop of Caesaria	AD 260-339	Was a prolific writer. Among his works *Church History* and the *Chronicle* have been very influential. The *Chronicle* has thousands of ancient dates, also useful chronology and the history of the ancient Near East, the Assyrians, the Babylonians, the Egyptians, the Greeks, the Romans, and the biblical text. The *Onomasticon* gives a list of over 600 biblical geographical places. His *History of the Chaldeans, Assyrians,* and *Persians* offers useful information.
Ephraem Syrus	AD 308-73	Commentator on Daniel in Syriac.
Cyril, Bishop of Jerusalem	AD 315-86	Wrote about history as found in Daniel and that the Messiah was fulfilled in Christ.
Ephraat the Syriac Father	AD 337	Wrote a homily about Daniel praying in the lions' den. He added unsubstantiated extra details to the story of Dan 6. The Syriac text was published by Wright, *Homilies of Aphraates*, 1:66, 67. See also Gavin, *Aphraates and the Jews*.

APPENDIX A

Eusebius Sophonius Hieronymus (known as Jerome)	AD 340–420	Wrote on sixth-century BC Mesopotamian and Jewish history. Produced OT commentaries including *Isaiah* and *Daniel* with some unique insights, e.g., he mentioned in *Daniel* that Belshazzar was the son of Labashi-Marduk. In *Isaiah*, he pointed out that when Amel-Marduk wanted to get on to the throne after the death of Nebuchadnezzar, the state officials refused him to be crowned because they thought that Nebuchadnezzar might return. His works did not survive.
John Chrysostom	AD 347–407	Wrote a Greek commentary on Daniel.
Polychronius	AD 374–430	His commentary on Daniel in Greek survives in fragments.
Theodoret	AD 393–457	Wrote a commentary on Daniel in Greek.
The Venerable Bede	AD 672–735	Consulted available sources including the biblical text in his writings. Dealt with the Neo-Babylonian monarchy and commented on Jehoiachin, king of Judah. Quoted often from Jerome's commentary on Daniel and also from Josephus.
Anonymous clerical	7th century AD	The *Chronicon Paschale* named and discussed the Chaldean kings in the light of the biblical text. Narrated historical events from Adam to AD 629.
Georgius Syncellus	Late 8th/9th century AD	Wrote the *Chronographia* which traces events from Adam to Diocletian. He had king lists and discussed Nabopolassar through Nabonidus. Years for each king seem unreliable and he omitted Labashi-Marduk from his work.
Ibn Hawqal	10th century AD	Visited the site of Babylon and described it as a small village.
Benjamin of Tudela	AD 1160 & 1173	Was from Spain and traveled to Asia and China to see if Jews were adhering to the Bible. For him Babylon was only important in its relation to the Jews. Benjamin, *Itinerary of Tudela*.
Arabic source, al-Qazwini	13th century AD	Confirmed that Babil was the site of ancient Babylon.

Johann Schlitberger	AD 1396–1427	Was from Bavaria but became a Turkish prisoner of war. He visited Babylon, measured the walls, and recorded the city plans. His observations accord with those of Herodotus. He mistakenly took the ruins of Birs Nimrud (ancient Borsippa, south of Babylon) to be the Tower of Babel, an error found earlier in the Talmud, Sanhedrin 109a, Genesis Rabbah 38:11.
Annius?	15th century AD	In 1498 *Antiquitatum Variarum Volumina* was published in Venice. It had a list of Neo-Babylonian kings and unparalleled years of reigning. Thus: Nabugodonosor, annis 45; Amilinus Evilmerodach, annis 30; Filius hujus primus Ragassar, annis 3; Secundus Lab-Assardoch, annis 6; Tertius Baltassar, annis 5.
Leonard Rauwolff	AD 1574	The itinerary and notes of Rauwolff, a German doctor, indicated that he visited the site of Babylon and other Middle Eastern countries including Syria, Palestine, Armenia, Chaldea, and Mesopotamia. Ray, *Collection of Curious Travels*, 1.
John Eldred	AD 1583	An English merchant, took 'Aqar ruins (Dur-Kurigalzu) north of Babylon as the Tower of Babel. Hakluyt, *Principal Navigations*.
Anthony Shirley	AD 1599	Visited the site of Babylon and published his travel accounts in London in 1613. He attempted to describe what Babylon looked like in the time of Nebuchadnezzar.
Pietro Della Valle	AD 1614–46	Traveled in Mesopotamia, Persia, and India between 1614 and 1626. Visited Babylon in November 1616 and is said to have been the first person to give an accurate record of Babylon. He collected several cylinder seals. He discussed the multicolored glazed bricks. Valle, *Viaggi di Pietro Della Valle*.

APPENDIX A

Thomas Browne	AD 1658	Published the *Garden of Cyrus* where he discussed the hanging gardens of Nebochodonosor in Babylon and also the physical features of Babylon. His work is in line with some classical writers, Josephus, and the biblical text.
Athanasius Kircher	AD 1666, 1679	A historian from Europe who traveled to Egypt and Mesopotamia. He wrote *Obelisci aegyptiaci nuper inter Isaei Romani rudera effosi interpretio hieroglyphica* ("The hieroglyphic interpretation of recently excavated Egyptian Obelisks among the buried Isaei of Rome") (1666) and *Turis Babel* (1679).
Olfert Dapper	AD 1681	A Dutch scholar and printmaker whose book, *Umbständliche und eigentliche Beschreibung von Asia*, described Babylonia and made artistic copper engravings of Babylon the city, and the Tower of Babel.
Engelbert Kämpfer	AD 1686	Visited ruin sites in Iran. Kämpfer discovered that the Babylonian inscription was different from Old Persian and he gave the name *cuneatae*, "cuneiform."
Thomas Hyde	AD 1700	Wrote on Persian religion, *Historia religionis veterum Persarum* (1700).
Johann Bernhard	AD 1721, 1725	An Austrian baroque architect whose work, von Erlach's *Entwürf einer historischen Architectur*, had drawings of the city plan of ancient Babylon as recollected from classical writers. J. A. Delsenbach later produced copper engravings of Babylon and the ziggurat of Marduk from this work.
Fredrick Handel	AD March 27, 1745	*Belshazzar*, orchestral music performed in King's Theater, Haymarket, London. The text was written by Charles Jennens who drew words from Daniel, Jeremiah, Isaiah, Herodotus, and Xenophon. The theme was on God's punishment of the proud.

Voltaire	AD 1747	Authored *Zadig*, which deals with oriental tales with the setting in Babylon where the youth learn Chaldean science. This work shares much in common with the book of Daniel. Wrote *Semiramis*, 1748, and the novel *La Princesse de Babylone*, 1768.
Denis Diderot	AD 1751	Published *Encyclopedie: ou, Dictionnnaire raisonne des sciences, des arts et des metiers*, which has relevant entries on several topics on Babylon.
Carstein Neibuhr	AD 1761–68	Toured ancient Near East under Danish commission. Visited Babylon in December 1765. He took note of different building traditions in Babylon, Egypt, and Iran. Wrote *Reisebes-chreibung*, Copenhagen 1774–78, which was used by Georg Grotefend 1802–3, for deciphering cuneiform. Niebhur, *Travels Through Arabia and Other Countries* (1792).
Abbé de Beauchamp	AD 1780, 1790	He was a papal vicar who was commissioned to go to Babylon in 1780 and 1790 and reported on the surrounding people who were looting baked bricks and artifacts.
C. James Rich	AD 1808, 1811	Visited Baghdad in 1808 and Babylon, December 9–21, 1811. Gave accurate topography plans. Had excavations from 1811–17 and brought the finds back to England. Wrote *Narrative of a Journey to the Site of Babylon*, 1811; *Observation Connected with Astronomy and Ancient History, Sacred and Profane, on the Ruins of Babylon*, 1816; and *Memoirs on the Ruins of Babylon*, 1818.
Byron	AD 1815, 1821	His *Hebrew Melodies*, 1815, had several poems including "Vision of Belshazzar," and he also wrote the novel *Sardanapalus*, 1821.
Robert Ker Porter	AD 1818	Searched for the Tower of Babel in Babylon and adopted Herodotus's estimation of Babylon's size. Porter, *Travels in Georgia*.

APPENDIX A

John Martin	19th century AD	Paintings: *Belshazzar's Feast* (1820), *Fall of Nineveh* (1829) and mezzotints *Belshazzar's Feast* (1826) and *Fall of Babylon* (1831).
Eugène Delacroix	AD 1826-27	Painted *Death of Sardanapalus*.
Robert Mignan	AD 1827	Had minor excavations in Babylon and found an inscribed clay cylinder *in situ*. Mignan, *Travels in Chaldæa*, 122-37. Mignan made observations on the sites and remains of Babel, Seleucia, and Ctesiphon.
J. M. W. Turner	AD 1833-36	Watercolored landscape illustrations of the Bible, with an accurate depiction of the ruins of Babylon though he himself had never been in the Near East.
William K. Loftus	AD 1849-52	A geologist who excavated in Babylon in 1849 but abandoned his project prematurely. Loftus, *Travels and Researches*. Loftus has maps and an account of the excavations at Warka, the "Erech" of Nimrod, and Shush, "Shushan the Palace" of Esther, in 1849-52.
F. Fresnel & J. Oppert	AD 1852	Acquired many inscriptions, believed that the hanging gardens were in the hill of Amran ibn Ali, and tried to identify the Tower of Babel. Oppert drew a detailed map of Babylon in 1853 from trignometric calculations. This expedition lost all objects while being transported in the Euphrates.
H. C. Rawlinson & George Smith	AD 1854	Brief excavations in Babylon.
Gustave Courbet	AD 1854-55	Depicted Assyrians in his paintings, *Atelier the Painter* (1854-55), *The Meeting* (1855), and the lithograph *Portrait of Jean Journet* which had Sargon II as seen in the Khorsabad reliefs.
J. S. Buckingham	AD 1855	He thought he found in Babylon the hanging gardens described by Greek writers. Buckingham, *Autobiography of James Silk Buckingham*.
Paul Emile Botta	AD 1842-44	Carried out excavations in northern Mesopotamia. Albenda, *Palace of Sargon*.

A. H. Layard	AD 1817–94	Dug on the mound of Babel in 1850 and found late burials, and collected seals and inscriptions for the British Museum. Layard, *Discoveries in the Ruins*; Layard, *Discoveries Among the Ruins*; Layard, *Early Adventures in Persia*.
Hormuzd Rassam	AD 1876	Rassam promised to pay for significant finds. He got many clay tablets and the clay cylinder concerning Babylon being captured by Cyrus. Rassam's incentives increased the vandalism by the local people. Rassam, *Asshur and the Land of Nimrod* (1897).
Ernest Alfred Wallis Budge	AD 1887	Commissioned by the British Museum to curb the plundering of the ruins in Babylon but the effort was in vain. Budge, *Babylonian Life and History*.
Joséphin Péladan	AD 1895	Was a French artist who studied Mesopotamian artifacts and literature. Wrote the drama *Babylone* (1895).
Robert Koldewey	AD 1855–925	Carried out systematic excavations at Babylon. The excavations continued from March 26, 1899, to March 7, 1917. Koldewey, *Excavations at Babylon*.

DANIEL OUTSIDE THE BOOK OF DANIEL

In the Hebrew Bible: Noah, Daniel, and Job

Ezekiel's prophetic writings are dated 593–571/568 BC during the Babylonian captivity. Daniel is first mentioned in Ezek 14:14, 20. The date of this writing must have been in 592 BC. It appears, however, that Ezek 14:14, 20 offers chronological inconsistency by listing "Noah, Daniel, and Job," where Daniel is placed before Job. In view of this, the criteria used to assemble these three men together is questioned.

The other problem is that the biblical text seems to indicate that these three men would not be able to save their sons and daughters (Ezek 14:16). Noah had no daughters, and Daniel had no children at all. According to the biblical text, Job was a righteous man (Job 1:22; 2:10; 42:8), but he could not save his seven sons and three daughters from the destroying wind (Job 1:18, 19). After the loss of his property and children (Job 1:13—2:10), Job later had other children (Job 42:13–15). The context of Ezek 14 shows that the author cited the three men in order to make an illustrative hypothetical point (cf. Jer 15:1).

There are some archaeological finds that illustrate the righteousness implied by Ezekiel. On an inscription from Zinçirli dated about 730 BC, Barrakab, the son of Panamu, king of Sam'al and the servant of Tiglath-pileser III, boasted, "Because of the righteousness of my father and my own righteousness, I was seated by my Lord Rakabel and my Lord Tiglath-pileser upon the throne of my father."[52] While it may be true that Barrakab was appointed king on account of both his father's and his own merit, Ezekiel's point deals with the terms of salvation by God. Under God's terms, no individual's righteousness can save one's own children, or anyone other than oneself (cf. Ezek 18).

The Hebrew spelling *dāni'el* in Ezekiel has the consonant *nun* followed by the short vowel *hireq*, making the reading "Danel" possible. Some have attempted to avoid the rigor of exegesis by simply taking Ezek 14:14, 20 to refer to a Ugaritic Danel who might not have been the biblical Daniel. The different spellings of Daniel's name are not an issue here, for several names in the biblical text appear with spelling discrepancies, including that of the king of Babylon.[53]

In Ugaritic literature, there are no stories about Noah, Daniel, and Job like those found in the biblical text. The writer of Ezek 14:14, 20 is likely referring to biblical characters. Moreover, in Ezek 28:2-6, the writer seems to chide the prince of Tyre for regarding himself to be wiser than Daniel. This message must have been delivered in 587 BC. Nevertheless, to associate Daniel in Ezek 28:2-6 with Danel in the Ugaritic story of Aqhat is to stretch the evidence too far. There seems to be no connection between the fragments of Aqhat and the biblical text.[54]

New Testament Times

Reference is made to Daniel as a prophet in Matt 24:15 and Mark 13:14. This harmonizes with the way he was esteemed at Qumran (4Q174 Florilegium, col. 2, lines 1-3).[55]

Of interest is the citation of the recurrent expression "the abomination that causes desolation" from Dan 9:27; 11:31; 12:11. This was an incident that was still to be anticipated by the first century AD. Collins quoted

---

52. *ANET*, 655.
53. See commentary on Daniel **1:1. Nebuchadn/rezzar, the name.**
54. See Appendix B, "The Legend of Aqhat."
55. Allegro and Anderson, *Qumran Cave 4* (DJD, 5:54).

1 Macc 1:54 as the earliest passage interpreting the phrase in Daniel.[56] He concluded that "the abomination that causes desolation" referred to "the disruption of the Jewish cult by Antiochus Epiphanes"[57] which involved the placing of a structure on the great altar of sacrifice.

In fact, the futuristic thrust of Matt 24:15 and Mark 13:14 eliminates the association of "the abomination that causes desolation" with the second-century BC Antiochus IV Epiphanes. The historical event implied by Matt 24:15, 16; Luke 21:20; and Mark 13:14 is understood to have taken place in AD 70 when the Romans destroyed the Jerusalem temple.

The New Testament makes several allusions to the book of Daniel. G. K. Beale argued that Rev 1:19 is also a possible eschatological expression by allusion to Dan 2:28–29, 45.[58] The book of Daniel was taken as authoritative Scripture by New Testament times.

---

56. Collins, *Daniel*, 357.
57. Collins, *Daniel*, 357.
58. Beale, "Interpretive Problem of Revelation 1:19," 360–86.

Appendix B

DANIEL AND ANCIENT NEAR EASTERN LITERATURE

THE LEGEND OF AQHAT

IN 1929 ARCHAEOLOGISTS AT ancient Ugarit (Tell Ras Shamra on the Mediterranean coast in Syria) recovered some clay tablets with cuneiform script. These proved to be ancient Canaanite records, religious literature, and Hurrian administrative records. Also found were epics, letters, myths, and rituals. The religious texts from this archive have been of great interest to biblical scholars for a variety of reasons.

Of note is the appearance of the name "Dani'ilu" ("Daniel/Danel") in the text of Aqhat. Some parallels have been drawn between the biblical Daniel and King Dani'ilu in the legend of Aqhat (Aqhatu). Some have suggested that Dani'ilu was similar to the Daniel in Ezek 14:14, 20 and Ezek 28:3. It is apparent, however, that the spelling "Dani'ilu" differs from the biblical Daniel. The Aqhat text[1] relates the story of how Dani'ilu appealed from the gods to have a son. This son was Aqhat, who later became more prominent than his father. The central theme of the legend is what a son means to the father.[2] Dani'ilu clearly contrasts with Daniel with regard to the following:

- He is regarded as a *rapa'u*, "healer or savior" of the people.
- He sought for a son from gods (polytheistic).

1. Montgomery, "Ras Shamra Notes VI," 440–45.
2. Spiegel, "Noah, Daniel, and Job," 198.

- He gave gods food, drink, and sacrifices.
- He became sated with wine.
- He had a wife Danatay, a son Aqhat, and a daughter Pūġatu.
- He possessed a bow and arrow which he handed over to his son.
- He was a judge on social issues.
- He learned of his son's death.
- He cursed the environs of his son's murder.
- He cast spells.
- He could have been a king.

There is no biblical Daniel who can be associated with the person of the Aqhat myth. No correlations between the stories of Dani'ilu and Daniel can warrant any literary interdependence or borrowing. The two stories do belong to the ancient Near Eastern setting, and they share a few common motifs. Both speak of the putting on of sackcloth, of grieving, and of mourning. Ezekiel 14:14–20 states that the righteous father will not be able to save his child on account of his personal goodness. The Aqhat story is exactly the opposite: the father's intervention saves his son from death. Job did not save his own children; according to the biblical text, he ended up having another set of ten children (Job 42:12–15).

THE STORY OF AHIKAR/AHIQAR

The book of Ahikar/Ahiqar[3] contains the story[4] and proverbs of a sage who served as a scribe and counselor to two Assyrian kings. The kings he served were Sennacherib (704–681 BC) and his son Esarhaddon (680–669 BC). From the island of Elephantine on the Nile River in Egypt (near modern Aswan), some papyri fragments were found containing this story of Ahiqar. The fragments are dated about 500 BC.[5] Smaller fragments with demotic translations of the story of Ahiqar are dated to the first century AD. The

---

3. For the text, translation, and notes, see Cowley, *Aramaic Papyri of the Fifth Century BC* (1923); *ANET*, 427–30; and the newer translations which include Lindenberger, "Ahiqar," in Charlesworth, *Old Testament Pseudepigrapha*, 2:479–507; and Arnold and Beyer, *Readings from the Ancient Near East*, 189–91.

4. Variations/versions of the story of Ahikar are endless, and the literature that discusses them includes: Conybeare et al., *Story of Ahikar* (1923); Handel, "Ahikar" (*IDB*, 1:68); Kraeling, "Ahikar, Book of" (*IDB*, 1:68–69); and Vanderkam, "Ahikar/Ahiqar" (*ABD*, 1:113–15).

5. Cowley, *Aramaic Papyri* (1923).

story is probably of Assyrian origin, and was popular in the ancient Near East. It has a number of variations and is found in Arabic, Aramaic, Armenian, Ethiopic, Greek (associated with Aesop),[6] Old Turkish, Slavonic, and Syriac.

The polytheistic nature of the writings of Ahiqar makes the whole work stand in contrast to the monotheistic thrust in the book of Daniel. Ahiqar kills an innocent man to save the life of a reputable officer who had been condemned to die. Later that same officer saved Ahiqar's life by murdering an innocent eunuch. In contrast, Daniel pleads for and saves the lives of men condemned to death for failing to execute the king's orders (Dan 2:24).

On the whole, there is no clear intertextual dependence or borrowing between the story of Ahiqar and the story of the biblical Daniel. The two works do highly estimate the value a trained thinker had for the king in times of political emergencies. Although the two stories belong to the ancient Near Eastern milieu, they show no affinities close enough for anyone to assume the association of the two characters as one.

DANIEL AND RELATED UGARITIC LITERATURE

The formula "from generation to generation" is well attested in both Ugaritic and Hebrew.[7] It appears in the Aramaic text of Dan 3:33 and 4:31 (English: Dan 4:3 and 4:34, respectively). Other words and expressions shared between these two groups of literature include: "Dominion"—Line 10 of the Ba'al and 'Anat Cycle text reads: *tqḥ.mlk.'lmk.drkt. dt drdrk*,[8] "take *your* eternal kingdom, *your* everlasting dominion."[9] The noun *drkt*, "rule, authority,"[10] has been equivalently translated as *memšālāh* ["rule, dominion"] (Ps 145:13) and *šālṭān* ["rule, dominion"] (Dan 3:33/4:3 and 4:31/4:34);[11] and the word-pairs "reach/come" (Dan 7:13) are found in the

---

6. Aesop was either a Phrygian or Thracian but known as the inventor of Greek animal fables in the Eastern Mediterranean around the sixth to fifth centuries BC. See Aesop, *Three Hundred and Fifty Aesop's Fables* (1815); and the four fables of Aesop in Oates and Halpern, *Cat*, 309-11.

7. Rummel, *Ras Shamra Parallels*, 218.

8. Gordon, *Ugaritic Textbook*, 2:180; Text 68, line 10; and also Segert, *Basic Grammar of the Ugaritic Language*, 161 (Text 88.51).

9. See also *ANET*, 131, III AB A, line 10.

10. Segert, *Basic Grammar*, 184.

11. Rummel, *Ras Shamra Parallels*, 218.

Ba'al epic.[12] The similarity between Prince Ba'al as "a rider of clouds" and the son of man in Dan 7:13 has also been noted.[13]

The archaeological discovery of texts at Ras Shamra (Ugarit) revolutionized biblical studies. Scholars have identified the Ugaritic language as "a Canaanite dialect older than Hebrew, Phoenician, and the other known Canaanite dialects but sharing with them many common traits of morphology, vocabulary, and syntax."[14] It can be noted, therefore, that the similarities in the use of certain words or phrases was a common phenomenon in the ancient Near East Semitic languages. In view of this, it is acknowledgeable that the Aramaic and Hebrew of Daniel share certain words and phrases with other local ancient languages.

THE TEXT OF DANIEL AT QUMRAN

Archaeology has recovered about eight scrolls of the canonical book of Daniel at Qumran. Seven scrolls out of the eight originally contained the entire book. The two scrolls that were retrieved from Cave 1 are 1QDan^a and 1QDan^b. From Cave 4 came six scrolls, 4QDan^{a-e}, and 4Q174. Cave 6 had 6QDan (6Q7) only.[15] The scrolls were stored in clay jars.

The text on the scrolls follows mostly the Masoretic Text, but may differ in spellings of certain words. In the eight scrolls, each chapter of the book of Daniel is represented except for chapter 12.

The *Florilegium*, "anthology" (4Q174), contains fragments that cite Dan 12:10 and indicate that it was written in the book of Daniel. The texts of Daniel recovered at Qumran do not have the so-called Greek additions to the book of Daniel. About thirteen fragments retrieved from Cave 11 at Qumran contain the text commonly known as the Heavenly Prince Melchizedek (11Q13), which may have some references to the book of Daniel.[16] Such references may indicate that by Qumran times, the book of Daniel was viewed as authoritative Scripture. In addition, the references may also indicate that the book of Daniel was written much earlier than

---

12. Noted by Greenfield, "Hebrew Bible and Canaanite Literature," in Alter and Kermode, *Literary Guide to the Bible*, 551; see also *ANET*, 129–42.

13. *ANET*, 129–42.

14. Greenfield, "Hebrew Bible and Canaanite Literature," in Alter and Kermode, *Literary Guide to the Bible*, 545.

15. Sources for the texts include: Washburn, *Catalogue of Biblical Passages*, 136–39; DJD, 1:150–52; 3a:114–16 and plate xxiii; 3b: 23; 16:239–89; see also plates xxix–xxxviii.

16. Van der Woude, "11Q Melchizedek and the New Testament," 301–26; and Vermes, *Complete Dead Sea Scrolls in English*, 500–2.

APPENDIX B

what popular opinions suggest. Table 12 compiles the fragments of Daniel found at Qumran.

Table 12
QUMRAN SCROLLS ON DANIEL

Daniel	Scroll	Source	Notes
1:10–17	1QDan^a (1Q71)	DJD 1:150; Trever, *RQ* 19 (1965) 323–343.	Fragmentary, MT with a spelling variant in v. 16, זרעים for זרענים.
1:16–20	4QDan^a (4Q112)	Ulrich, *BASOR* 268 (1987) 17–37; DJD 16:239–43.	Surface of fragments flaked off. Variant reconstructions possible.
2:2–6	1QDan^a (1Q71)	DJD 1:150–51; Trever, *RQ* 19 (1965) 323–43; Mastin, *VT* 38 (1988) 341–46.	Fragmentary, MT with 4 variants, v. 2 ולכשדיים for כשדיים, v. 4 נחוה for נחוא, v. 5 ענה for ענא, and has די which is omitted in the MT.
2:9–11	4QDan^a (4Q112)	Ulrich, *BASOR* 268 (1987) 17–37; DJD 16:243.	Too fragmentary although column 1 top and right margins are preserved. No variants from other texts can be detected. Text too corrupt.
2:19–33	4QDan^a (4Q112)	Ulrich, *BASOR* 268 (1987) 17–37; DJD 16:244–46; *Of Scribes and Scrolls*, 29–42.	Probably column 4 of the original manuscript, with all four margins preserved. Parts of the surface have flaked. The text has numerous variants from the ancient MSS including the MT, Syriac OT, Arabic OT, LXX, and Theodotion translations.
2:33–46	4QDan^a (4Q112)	Ulrich, *BASOR* 268 (1987) 17–37; DJD 16:246–48.	Top and bottom margins of column 2 of the main fragment have been preserved. Many variants with mainly the MT can be noted and this could allow several reading options.

Daniel	Scroll	Source	Notes
2:47–3:2	4QDanᵃ (4Q112)	Ulrich, *BASOR* 268 (1987) 17–37; DJD 16:248–49.	Too fragmentary. Has variants from MT. ומכדנצר in 3:2 is a unique paleographical copying error. Regardless of the supralinear *dalet*, the spelling still differs from other ancient MSS, which read ונבכדנצר.
3:8–10?	4QDanᵈ (4Q115)	Pfann, *RQ* (1996) 37–71; DJD 16:279–80.	Fragment deteriorated and shrunk and this makes the paleographic diagnosis difficult.
3:23–25	4QDanᵇ (1Q72)	Pfann, *RQ* (1996) 63–64; DJD 16:281–82.	Text is fragmentary and has 5 spelling variations from the MT, v. 24 באתבהלה for בהתבהלה, v. 25 לנו for נבוכדנצר for נבכדנצר, v. 27 ושרבליהון for וסרבליהון, לנוא, and v. 28 ושזב for ושיזב.
3:23–25	4QDanᵈ (4Q115)	Pfann, *RQ* (1996) 37–71; DJD 16:281–82	Top and right margins of the fragment are extant on this MT.
3:27–30	1QDanᵇ (1Q72)	DJD 1:151–52.	Has 6 variations from mainly the MT, v. 27 עדה for אדת, v. 28 ומשן for מישן, v. 29 שימו for שים, כול for כל, אומה for אמה, and נגו for נגוא.
4:5–9	4QDanᵈ (4Q115)	Pfann, *RQ* (1996) 37–71; DJD 282–83.	Daniel's Babylonian name with an MT spelling is possible in v. 6. Fragmentary text.
4:12–16	4QDanᵈ (4Q115)	Pfann, *RQ* (1996) 37–71; DJD 16:283–84.	Too fragmentary but the text has MT characteristics.
4:29–30	4QDanᵃ (4Q112)	Ulrich, *BASOR* 268 (1987) 17–37; DJD 16:249.	Fragment has no notable variants.
5:5–7	4QDanᵃ (4Q112)	Ulrich, *BASOR* 268 (1987) 17–37; DJD 16:249–50.	Bottom margin of this fragmentary text is extant. Text extant. Has letter variations with most of the ancient manuscripts.

APPENDIX B

Daniel	Scroll	Source	Notes
5:10–16	4QDan^b (4Q113)	Ulrich, *BASOR* 274 (1989) 3–26; DJD 16:255–58.	Notable on this fragmentary text is one variant from MT in v. 16 תכול for תוכל.
5:12–14	4QDan^a (4Q112)	Ulrich, *BASOR* 268 (1987) 17–37; DJD 16:250–51.	Variants from MT in v. 12, ומדע for ומנדע, ושלתנו for שכלתנו, שתכחת for השתכח, and יקרא for יתקרי.
5:13–14	4QDan^a (4Q112)	Ulrich, *BASOR* 268 (1987) 17–37.	No variants from MT can be noticed on this very fragmented text.
5:16–19	4QDan^a (4Q112)	Ulrich, *BASOR* 268 (1987) 17–37; DJD 16:251.	Top and right margins and a stitched edge are extant. Two words in v. 18, עליא מלכותא, are written without word division. Two variants from the MT in v. 17 are ונבזבתך for ונבזביתך and ופשרה for ופשרא. Fragment looks contracted and split.
5:19–22	4QDan^b (4Q113)	Ulrich, *BASOR* 274 (1989) 3–26; DJD 16:259.	Fragment could have top margin of a column. For v. 22 only 2 tips of *lamed* are preserved. A single variant from MT and the Syriac OT is in v. 19? מהר [ים for מרים.
6:8–13	4QDan^b (4Q113)	Ulrich, *BASOR* 274 (1989) 3–26; DJD 16:259–60.	Bottom and left margins are extant. The hole between lines 16 and 17 might have been there before the writing. V. 10 כלקבל is without word division unlike in the MT, probably because of some morphological and etymological reasons. Variants from MT v. 11 קד[ם for בעלתה, עליתא[ב for קדמת; v. 13] אסרא for אסר and בעה[י for יבעהי.
6:13–22	4QDan^b (4Q113)	Ulrich, *BASOR* 274 (1989) 3–26; DJD 16:261–62.	Half of the column is preserved along with the left and right margins. See variants from other ancient MSS on Ulrich, *BASOR* 274 (1989) 12.

Daniel	Scroll	Source	Notes
6:27—7:4	4QDan[b] (4Q113)	Ulrich, BASOR 274 (1989) 3–26; DJD 16:263–64.	The 3 fragments here preserve the bottom margin of the column. There are clues for reconstruction of the text. Variants from the MT include 6:27 אלה חי for אלא חיא and v. 28 מן יד for מי[ד.
7:5–6?	4QDan[b] (4Q113)	Ulrich, BASOR 274 (1989) 3–26; DJD 16:264.	Too fragmentary, no variants from other ancient MSS.
7:5–7	4QDan[a] (4Q112)	Ulrich, BASOR 268 (1987) 17–37; DJD 16:251.	Variant from MT in v. 6 גביהא for גביה.
7:15–23	4QDan[d] (4Q115)	DJD 16:284–85.	Left and bottom margins extant. MT.
7:25—8:5	4QDan[a] (4Q112)	Ulrich, BASOR 268 (1987) 17–37; DJD 16:252–53.	Fragment retains the bottom and stitched left margin. Text shows two words in 8:1 crossed out by the scribe because they were an error. Several variants with other ancient MSS as noted in Ulrich, BASOR 268 (1987) 33–34; and DJD 16:253.
7:26–28	4QDan[b] (4Q113)	Ulrich, BASOR 274 (1989): 3–26; DJD 16:265–66.	Too fragmentary. No variants can be noted from other ancient MSS.
8:1–8	4QDan[b] (4Q113)	Ulrich, BASOR 274 (1989) 3–26; DJD 16:266–67.	V. 7 has a suprascript *waw* to act as a *mater lectionis* inserted by the scribe. Two variants from MT and BHS in v. 3 קרנים for קרנים והקרנים and v. 4 גדול for והגדיל.
8:13–16	4QDan[b] (4Q113)	Ulrich, BASOR 274 (1989) 3–26; DJD 16:267.	Top and right margin are extant. No textual variations can be noted.
8:16–17?	6QDan (6Q7)	DJD 3:116.	Too fragmented but there are a few noticeable letters. Written on papyrus, can also be identified with the siglum: pap6QDan.

APPENDIX B

Daniel	Scroll	Source	Notes
8:20–21?	6QDan (6Q7)	DJD 3:114.	Too fragmented but there are a few noticeable letters. Written on papyrus, can also be identified with the siglum: pap6QDan.
9:12–14	4QDan^e (4Q116)	DJD 16:288.	Fragmented, could be Daniel's prayer.
9:15–17	4QDan^e (4Q116)	DJD 16:289.	Right margin of the fragment text preserved.
10:5–13	4QDan^c (4Q114)	Ulrich, *BASOR* 274 (1989) 3–26; DJD 16:272–73.	Thin leather manuscript written on the hair side. Early semicursive was used. Top right and left margins preserved. Variants with MT and other ancient MSS are paleographical, morphological, and also orthographical.
10:8–16	6QDan (6Q7)	DJD 3:114–15.	Fragmentary but easy for reconstruction. Mainly MT. No variants from 4QDan^c. Written on papyrus; can be identified with the siglum: pap6QDan
10:13–16	4QDan^c (4Q114)	Ulrich, *BASOR* 274 (1989) 3–26; DJD 16:273–74.	The 4 margins are partially preserved. V. 15 has וכדב]רו for MT - וב.
10:16–20	4QDan^a (4Q112)	Ulrich, *BASOR* 268 (1987) 17–37; DJD 16:253.	Bottom and left margins extant. V. 19 has 3 variants from MT and other ancient MSS: החמדות for חמדות; ואמר (similar to Arabic OT, Syriac OT, Theodotion and LXX) for ואמרה; and דבר for ידבר.
10:21—11:2	4QDan^c (4Q114)	Ulrich, *BASOR* 274 (1989) 3–26.	Margins partially extant. Reconstruction misses most of the middle part of the MSS. A variant MT in 11:1, עמדתי for עמדי.
11:13–16	4QDan^a (4Q112)	Ulrich, *BASOR* 268 (1987) 17–37; DJD 16:253–54.	Bottom margin of the column is extant. Text similar to 4QDan^c but v. 15 ושפך differs from MT וישפך.
11:13–17	4QDan^c (4Q114)	Ulrich, *BASOR* 274 (1989) 3–26; DJD 16:274–76.	Right, left, and bottom margin of the column of the fragment preserved. Fragment wrinkled and makes reading doubtful.

Daniel	Scroll	Source	Notes
11:25–29	4QDan^c (4Q114)	Ulrich, *BASOR* 274 (1989) 3–26; DJD 16:276–277.	The right stitched and bottom margins of the column preserved. MT.
11:32	4QFlor (4Q174)	DJD 5:54–55.	ועם יודעי אלוה יחזיקו seems to be part of a parablepsis. MT reads: ועם ידעי אלהיו יחזקו.
11:33–38	6QDan (6Q7)	DJD 3:115–116.	Very fragmentary with only parts of words preserved. Written on papyrus, hence the siglum: pap6qDan.
12:10	4QFlor (4Q174)	DJD 5:54–55.	Daniel identified as a prophet and the author of the book which is partly quoted on this fragment of the *Florilegium*.

NONBIBLICAL QUMRAN TEXTS ASSOCIATED WITH DANIEL

The caves at Qumran in which the Danielic scrolls were found have been numbered for convenience in identifying the manuscripts found in each one, hence the designation 4Q placed before the number of each text found in Cave 4.

Qumran Cave 4 has yielded a number of documents written in Aramaic. About nine of these are nonbiblical documents[17] which have been associated with the canonical book of Daniel (Table 13). Closer examination shows that only four of these writings are somewhat related to the text of the biblical Daniel. The texts related to Daniel will be discussed below.

---

17. Brooke, "Parabiblical Prophetic Narratives," in Flint and Vanderkam, *Dead Sea Scrolls After Fifty Years* 1:290–301; and Collins, *Apocalypticism in the Dead Sea Scrolls*, 15–18.

APPENDIX B

Table 13
NONBIBLICAL QUMRAN TEXTS ASSOCIATED WITH DANIEL

MANU-SCRIPT	NUMBER	DATE COPIED	RELATION TO CANONICAL DANIEL
PrNab ar	4Q242	72–50 BC	No mention of the name "Daniel." The relationship is based on vague thematic associations between this document and parts of the canonical Daniel which are difficult to determine.
psDan[a] ar	4Q243	early 1st century AD	Classified as pseudo-Daniel. Has the Babylonian court setting and mentions the names of Daniel, Belshazzar, and the Chaldeans. Has the combination of past historical survey (unlike canonical Daniel) and future predictions.
psDan[b] ar	4Q244	early 1st century AD	Shares comments with 4Q243 above.
psDan[c] ar	4Q245	early 1st century AD	Has the name "Daniel." Has no relationship with 4Q243 and 4Q244 and no basis to associate it with canonical Daniel. Has a list of priests and kings not found in canonical Daniel.
Apocalypse ar	4Q246	last third of 1st century BC	No name of Daniel mentioned in this document. Certain themes that have New Testament language can somewhat be related to the canonical Daniel. DJD, 22:165–84. This text has allusions to the biblical Daniel. Collins, *Apocalypticism in the Dead Sea Scrolls*, 17–18. This document has also come to be known as the Apocryphon of Daniel. VanderKam, *BAR* 41 (2015) 51.

papApocalypse ar	4Q489	ca. AD 50	This text has 8 small fragments extant. On the basis of 2 words from 2 fragments, a possible relationship with the canonical Daniel: frag 1.1, וחזותה, "and its appearance" as in Dan 4:,8 and frag 1.2, וחזיתה, "and you saw," as in Dan 2:41; the two words also appear in other texts different from Daniel, e.g., the first, 1 En. 14:18, and the second, 1 En. 25:3; 46:4; 52:4. DJD, 7:10–11 and plate II.
DanSuz? ar	4Q551	late 1st century BC	Story of Suzanna taken as Dan 13 in the Apocrypha. Relationship with canonical Daniel is doubtful.
4 Kingdoms ar	4Q552	ca. early 1st century AD	Contains the 4-kingdom theme but not similar to canonical Daniel. The kingdoms are seen as trees and their chronology differs from that of Daniel.
4 Kingdoms ar	4Q553	ca. early 1st century AD	Shares the same comments with 4Q552 above.

THE PRAYER OF NABONIDUS

From Qumran Cave 4 archaeologists found several Aramaic fragments of another text. The reconstruction of these fragments and their translation, annotation, interpretation, and association with Dan 4 has attracted much attention from scholars. The extant text 4Q242 or 4QPrNab[18] is commonly known as the Prayer of Nabonidus. In fact, it does not contain any prayer at all, in spite of what those who reconstructed it would like anyone to believe.

Many other fragments were discovered in Cave 4 at Qumran. Among them were three manuscripts, 4Q243 (forty fragments),[19] 4Q244 (four-

---

18. "The Prayer of Nabonidus." Milik suggested this title when he published the manuscript in "Prière de Nabonide," 407–15. For the texts and translations of the Prayer of Nabonidus see Jongeling et al., "Prayer of Nabonidus from Cave 4," in *Aramaic Texts from Qumran*, 1:121–31.

19. Collins, "Pseudo-Daniel Revisited," 111–31; DJD, 22:97–121, 133–51; and Martinez, *Dead Sea Scrolls Translated*, 288.

teen fragments),[20] and 4 Q245 (four fragments),[21] which cite the name of Daniel.[22] Jozef T. Milik published only a few of these Aramaic fragments in 1956.[23] They were paleographically dated from 75–50 BC[24] to the Herodian period, that is, early first century AD.[25] These manuscripts also contain a list of the priests from one Qahath to one called Simon. There is a list of kings from David to Joash, and some eschatological remarks.[26] Despite the mention of Daniel and some of the kings, 4Q245, also known as 4Qps Dan^c ar,[27] has nothing to warrant its relationship with either 4Q243 and 4Q244 or the biblical book of Daniel.

4Q242 (4QPrNab), 4Q243, 4Q244, and 4Q245 do properly belong to the pseudepigraphal literary genre of the time. Due to the fragmentary nature of these manuscripts, their reconstruction has been debatable. The narrative depends largely on where one places the fragments.[28] As will be seen below, it is apparent that each redactor was influenced by the biblical story (Dan 4) in the reconstruction of the manuscripts.

4Q242 (4QPrNab) Text

1. מלי צ]ל[תא די נבני מלך]{} [ב]בל מלכ]א רבא כדי הוא כתיש הוה[
2. בשחנא באישא בפתגם א]לה[א בתימן [אנה נבני בשחנא באישא]
3. כתיש הוית שנין שבע ומן [די]שוי א]נה לחיוא וצלית קדם עליא[
4. וחטאי שבק לה גזר והוא יהודי מן [בני גלות על לי ואמר]
5. החוי וכתב למעבד יקר ור]ב[ו לשם א]להא עליא וכן כתבת אנה[

20. Collins, "Pseudo-Daniel Revisited," 111–35; Martinez, *Dead Sea Scrolls Translated*, 288–89; and DJD, 22:123–31, 133–51.

21. Flint, "4Qpseudo-Daniel ar^c (4Q245)," 137–50; and DJD, 22:153–64.

22. There is a claim that both 4Q243 and 4Q244 overlap and are possibly one document with 4Q245. For texts, translations, and commentaries, see Fitzmyer and Harrington, *Manual of Palestinian Aramaic Texts*, 4–9, 153; Eisenmann and Wise, "Pseudo-Daniel (4Q243–245)," in *Dead Sea Scrolls Uncovered*, 64–68.

23. Milik, "Prière de Nabonide," 411–15. However, Milik did not publish many other discovered fragments that were related to these.

24. The preferred dates for the copying of the script are 72–50 BC. See Cross, "Fragments," 260–64. Collins thinks the text is probably older than the second century BC in "Nabonidus, Prayer of" (*ABD*, 4:977).

25. Flint, "4Qpseudo-Daniel ar^c (4Q245)," 138, 140.

26. Flint, "4Qpseudo-Daniel ar^c (4Q245)," 140.

27. Flint, "4Qpseudo-Daniel ar^c (4Q245)," 140.

28. Cross mentioned "the proper placement of the fragments" in "Fragments," 260, but whatever placement one might come up with, it shows that there is a deliberate and conscious effort to relate this text to the biblical story in Dan 4.

6. כתיש הוית בשחנא באישא בתימן [בפתגם אלהא עליא ואנה]
7. שנין שבע מצלא הוית [קדם] אלהי כספא ודהבא [נחשא פרזלא]
8. אעא אבנא חספא מן די [הוית סב]ר די אלהין ה[מון]

Translation: (Note that amendments inserted by the redactor are in brackets.)

1. The words of the p[ra]yer which Nabonidus, king of [Ba]bylon, the great king, pray[ed when he was stricken]

2. with an evil disease by the decree of G[o]d in Teman. [I Nabonidus] was stricken with [an evil disease]

3. for seven years, and from [that] (time) I was like [unto a beast and I prayed to the Most High]

4. and, as for my sin, he forgave it (or: my sin he forgave). A diviner—who was a Jew o[f the Exiles—came to me and said:]

5. "Recount and record (these things) in order to give honour and great[ness] to the name of the G[od Most High." And thus I wrote: I]

6. was stricken with an evil disease in Teman [by the decree of the Most High God, and, as for me,]

7. seven years I was praying [to] gods of silver and gold, [bronze, iron,]

8. wood, stone (and) clay, because [I was of the opini]on that th[ey] were gods [].

The reconstructed Prayer of Nabonidus text above contains a few close similarities to the Dan 4 story. However, most of these similarities disappear when all of the amendments are removed.

The first-person common singular pronoun אנה, "I," does not appear anywhere in the fragments. The words in line 3, א[נה לחיוא וצלית קדם עליא "I was like unto a beast and I prayed to the Most High," are all supplied except for the first א on the first word. In fact, comparing Nabonidus to a beast is "not actually attested in the extant fragments,"[29] and has been observed as paleographically impossible. There is nothing in the surviving fragments that suggests the mention of a beast.[30]

On the same lacuna (damaged, missing, or unreadable portion) of the fragments Vanderkam suggested an altogether different reading אלהא עלי אנפוהי אנפוהי ואסא לי "God set his face on me, he healed

---

29. Collins, *Daniel*, 218.
30. DJD, 22:90.

APPENDIX B

me."³¹ Jongeling, Labuschagne, and van der Woude combined Cross and Vanderkam's reconstructions to have, לחיותא שוי אנה וצלית קדם אלהא עליא וכן "I came to be like the animals, but I prayed to God Most High."³² The unreadable space on the fragments does not allow this elongated reconstruction either.

There is no mention of the God of the Hebrews in the readable portion of the Prayer of Nabonidus. The redactor, who was obviously aware of the biblical story of Daniel, filled the unreadable space with the name אלהא. The reconstruction of אלהא in line 2 might have been calculated to meet the redactor's objective. In lines 3 and 5 the letters להא are added to a single surviving letter א to read "God." The plural אלהי in line 7 is questionable. אלהין in line 8 is the only clear evidence of the pantheon which has survived from the fragments.

In line 7 the fragments have "silver" and "gold," then some missing words, which are followed by the words "wood, stone and clay." Where there are some missing words, the redactor inserted נחשא פרזלא, "bronze, iron."

In his reconstruction above, Cross also supplied the word אלהי "gods" before this list so that it would match with Dan 5:4, 23, "gods of silver and gold, bronze, iron, wood and stone." This clearly establishes the fact that the redactors deliberately worked out the Prayer of Nabonidus in light of the biblical text in an effort to discredit the authenticity and early date for the composition of the book of Daniel.

Some other inconsistencies should be noted: In Dan 4 Nebuchadnezzar suffered from mental derangement, possibly "lycanthropy," which caused him to behave like an animal. Contrary to this, Nabonidus is said to have had a skin disease which irritated him. The *Verse Account of Nabonidus* (BM 38299) is a very fragmentary text from which a suggestion was made that *a-gu-ug šarru*, "the king is mad,"³³ referred to the madness of Nabonidus. However, it has been clearly shown that *a-gu-u* means "angry" or "wrath."³⁴

The stated time during which Nebuchadnezzar and Nabonidus were said to suffer afflictions should be noted. Nebuchadnezzar suffered for שבעה עדנין "seven times" (Dan 4:23, 32), while Nabonidus claims to have been afflicted for שנין שבען "seven years" (line 3). The time reckoning in

---

31. DJD, 22:88, 89.
32. Jongeling et al., *Aramaic Texts from Qumran*, 126–127.
33. Smith, *Babylonian Historical Texts*, 85, col. IV, line 5; and *ANET*, 314, col. iv.
34. Smith, *Babylonian Historical Texts*, 89, col. IV, line 5; and McNamara, "Nabonidus and the Book of Daniel," 141. *A-gu-ú* is used in reference to the violent current of water, that is, "a surging flow of raging water," "an angry surge of water," or "furious waves of water"; see *CAD*, A 1, 157–58.

Daniel is more difficult to interpret than that of the Prayer of Nabonidus, and this strongly suggests that Daniel's language could correlate with a much earlier tradition. שבעה עדנין of Daniel is part of an ancient prophetic language which calls for interpretation.

In light of the above discussion, some scholars believe that Dan 4 and the Prayer of Nabonidus could be the same event, but with differing details. This suggestion leaves us with questions regarding the dating and authorship of the two manuscripts.

- Which one of the two manuscripts is an earlier tradition?
- How is it that the Prayer of Nabonidus was not canonized, and yet it is featured at Qumran?

Either the story in Dan 4 or the Prayer of Nabonidus came directly from the event or a source relating the event. In light of this idea, the debate among scholars then centers on which of the manuscripts is more authentic, and which was written first.

In any case, the book of Daniel and the Prayer of Nabonidus present valuable data for biblical studies. In my opinion the most reasonable suggestion is that Dan 4 and 4QPrNab relate two different events, and that they contain complementary data.

The problem with 4QPrNab is in the reconstruction, which is done in light of the biblical text of Daniel. 4QPrNab draws its inspiration from several passages in the book of Daniel. Dissimilarities in content and literary structure between Daniel and the Prayer of Nabonidus indicate that these two accounts have less in common than what some scholars have suggested.

The Prayer of Nabonidus and the manuscript known as Bel and the Dragon do have some significant parallels with Dan 1—6. Collins has admitted, however, that, there is essentially no clear evidence of the supposed literary influence between any of these works.[35]

APOCRYPHAL ADDITIONS TO THE TEXT OF DANIEL

Several writings that the Roman Catholic Church considers to be holy and inspired by God are known as the "Additions" to the canonical book of Daniel. These writings are designated as deuterocanonical, from the Greek

---

35. Collins, *Apocalyptic Vision*, 6; and Hartman, "Great Tree and Nabuchodonosor's Madness," 81–82.

APPENDIX B

deuteros, "second," and *kanōn*, "a cane," "a measure," or "a rule."[36] No deuterocanonical literature was considered in the corpus of Scripture known as the biblical canon. Protestant Christians and Jews reject the deuterocanonical writings as uninspired, and reckon them as apocrypha, *apokryphos*, "hidden away" or "concealed."

Three documents found in the LXX are thought to be Greek additions to the canonical book of Daniel. These are The Prayer of Azariah and the Song of the Three Children, the History of Susanna, and Bel and the Dragon. Martin MacDonald has stated:

> It is likely that the additions to Daniel (Song of the Three Children, Susanna, and Bel and the Dragon), the extended portions of Esdras that were added to Ezra, and the epistle of Jeremiah (sometimes included as the last chapter of 1 Baruch) were added by the Jews in the first century B.C.E. or before and were a part of a popular Jewish collection of sacred writings before the church separated from Judaism.[37]

These Additions were rejected by the early Christian church. The Protestants termed them "apocrypha." The Roman Catholic Church accepted these documents at their council of Trent in 1546 and named them "deuterocanonical texts." These texts appear in the Douay Version, which is the official Roman Catholic Church's adaptation of the Holy Bible.

The Prayer of Azariah and the Song of the Three Children (sixty-seven verses) are composed mainly of the Prayer of Azariah and the Hymn of the Three Young Men. The sequence could be appropriate if these verses were inserted immediately after the canonical Dan 3:23. This manuscript was probably written during the Maccabean era and the original language remains unknown.

According to Dan 3, Shadrach, Meshach, and Abednego refused to bow down and worship the golden image Nebuchadnezzar set up on the Plain of Dura. In consequence, they were thrown into a furnace of fire. The sixty-seven verses of the Prayer of Azariah and the Song of the Three Children are supposed to have been the prayer and the hymn the three young men sang to their God after he miraculously delivered them from the fire. The canonical text states that Nebuchadnezzar finally declared that all the people should respect the God of Shadrach, Meshach, and Abednego or they would face destruction.

Carey A. Moore argued that the Prayer of Azariah was an independent document produced and circulated after 163 BC. He maintained that it had

---

36. Moulton, *New Analytical Greek Lexicon*, s.v. "δεύτερος," and "κανών."
37. MacDonald, *Biblical Canon*, 101.

nothing to do with the canonical Dan 3.[38] Further, Moore explained why the Prayer was inappropriate for the context of the canonical Dan 3:

> (1) the clumsy and repetitious character of the prayer's own introduction to itself in vv. 24–25 of the older LXX;
>
> (2) its use in v. 24 of the heroes' *Hebrew* names, whereas in the fiery furnace account of the MT their Aramaic names are always used (13 times);
>
> (3) the obvious inappropriateness of much of the prayer for its context; and
>
> (4) the logical and chronological misplacement of the prayer when compared to the narrative (3:46–51).[39]

Whether the story of Susanna is placed before the beginning or at the end of the canonical text (as in θ, Old Latin, Coptic, Ethiopic, or Arabic versions), it is still considered as strangely out of place. Susanna is a heroine who was condemned to be killed for having committed adultery. She is said to have been rescued by a young Daniel. The three stories in Bel and the Dragon have been characterized as lacking religious value. They do stress monotheism, but they ridicule paganism in view of Jewish religion. Whatever the status of the Prayer of Azariah, Susanna, and Bel and the Dragon with regard to the canon, these so-called Additions to Daniel have not been helpful in understanding or dating the book of Daniel.

DANIEL IN THE PSEUDEPIGRAPHA

Pseudepigraphal documents are falsely attributed to an ancient famous author. Such writings may have valuable information, but they are tainted with error and misconceptions. Charlesworth, who has done extensive editing of the literature dealing with the pseudepigraphal writings, defines the pseudepigrapha as

> those writings (1) that, with the exception of Ahiqar, are Jewish or Christian; (2) that are often attributed to ideal figures in Israel's past; (3) that customarily claim to contain God's word or message; (4) that frequently build upon ideas and narratives present in the Old Testament; (5) and that almost always were composed either during the period 200 BC to AD 200 or,

---

38. Moore, "Daniel, Additions to" (*ABD*, 2:19).
39. Moore, "Daniel, Additions to," 2:19.

though late, apparently preserve, albeit in an edited form, Jewish traditions that date from that period.[40]

The collection of the pseudepigraphal writings is voluminous. More such literature is continuously surfacing. There has been a deliberate effort by some scholars to show the relationship between these and the biblical text.[41] Charlesworth argued for the pseudepigrapha to be broadly understood as to include all Jewish, Israelite, or Christian writings claiming to be the word of God, and having been written from about 250 BC to AD 200 or later.[42]

Lorenzo DiTommaso further contended that "all post-biblical renditions of the Daniel story are in a sense retellings of the biblical version, regardless of their degree of drift from it."[43] It should be noted that this "drift" from the biblical text is the reason why responsible exegesis is always suspicious of the apocryphal and pseudepigraphal writings.

DiTommaso acknowledged that the bulk of the material in Daniel "is of a late enough date to assume the unambiguous precedence and thus the authority of its scriptural referent."[44] In view of this observation, it is reasonable to conclude that the pseudepigrapha and the apocrypha lack the authoritative aura of the biblical canon. It is, therefore, always safe to observe the distinction.

One well-distinguished literary genre in the pseudepigrapha is the apocalypses (*apokalypses*, "a disclosure," "a revelation," "a manifestation," or "an appearance"[45]). Pseudepigraphal literature such as 1 and 2 Enoch, 2 and 3 Baruch, 4 Ezra, Testament of Levi 2—5, Jubilees, Apocalypse of Zephania, and the Testament of Abraham is classified as the apocalyptic genre. The canonical book of Daniel is also considered to be apocalyptic.

Not much is known about the apocryphal fallen angel Dan'el/Danyul mentioned in 1 En. 6:7 and 69:2 respectively. Jubilees 4:20 does mention a Dan'el who was the maternal grandfather of one called Methuselah.

The apocalyptic pseudepigrapha are usually attributed to renowned ancient figures. Several reasons have been suggested as to why the writers

---

40. Charlesworth, *Old Testament Pseudepigrapha*, 1: xxv.

41. Charlesworth, *Old Testament Pseudepigrapha* (1983); and Kee, *Cambridge Annotated Study Apocrypha* (1994). For the apocryphal and pseudepigraphal writings found in the scrolls at Qumran see Vanderkam and Flint, *Meaning of the Dead Sea Scrolls*, 424–26.

42. Charlesworth, *Old Testament Pseudepigrapha*, 1:xxv; and Charlesworth, *Old Testament Pseudepigrapha and New Testament*, xi–xii.

43. DiTommaso, *Book of Daniel*, 50.

44. DiTommaso, *Book of Daniel*, 51.

45. *New Analytical Greek Lexicon* (1990), s.v. "ἀποκάλυψις."

chose to use a pseudonym. Collins pointed out that some writers chose to disguise their identity to avoid consequential retribution from authorities.[46] It is likely that as prophecy lost its popularity (Zech 13:2–6) after the Medo-Persian period (539–331 BC),[47] many writers may have been prompted to come up with some pseudonymous oracles.

Lastly, some writers may have employed pseudonyms in an attempt to attain prestige for their work. Some of these writers may have thought that their work would be included in the canon if it had the name of an ancient, well-regarded person. Some may have had a hidden agenda which they hoped to perpetuate through the assumed authority of a historical person. These works seem to be a deliberate effort to distort or discredit the biblical text. Whatever the reasons, the volume of such literature attributed to Daniel is overwhelming, and has caused significant trouble for those seeking to understand the biblical book.

DANIEL AS AN APOCALYPSE

The two Greek words *apo*, "from," and *kalyptō*, "to cover," "hide," or "veil," when joined become *apokalyptō*, which literally means to "uncover," "disclose," "unveil," "make bare," or "undo a package."[48] The macrogenre of the literature that is characterized by visions, dreams, symbolism, prophecy, historical outlines, human agents interacting with divine beings, eschatological cosmic events of destruction, and the transcendence of God has come to be known as the apocalypses. This has been loosely defined by J. J. Collins and others as the

> genre of revelatory literature with a narrative framework, in which a revelation is mediated by an otherworldly being to a human recipient, disclosing a transcendent reality which is both temporal, insofar as it envisages eschatological salvation, and spatial insofar as it involves another, supernatural world.[49]

Such a generic definition lacks some vital characteristics embedded in many of the apocalypses. Pseudonymity is one example, and it is used by several apocalyptic writers. Paraenetic discourses giving moral exhortation,

---

46. Collins, *Apocalyptic Vision of the Book of Daniel*, 67–71.

47. See Overholt, "Prophet, Prophecy," *Eerdmans Dictionary of the Bible*, 1087–88.

48. Oepke, "ἀποκαλύπτω" (*TDNT*, 3:560–92); and Thayer, *Thayer's Greek-English Lexicon*, 62. For other nuances and historical usage see Smith, "On the History," in Hellholm, *Apocalypticism in the Mediterranean World*, 9–20.

49. Collins, *Apocalypse*, 9; Collins, *Daniel: With an Introduction*, 4; and Collins, *Apocalyptic Imagination*, 5.

APPENDIX B

and mythical imagery, would be the other characteristics of the apocalyptic genre. Apocalypses are a macrogenre that can be broken down into subgenres with distinct themes, features, and content, which vary with each literary work.

The book of Daniel is considered to be one of the earliest works in the apocalyptic genre.[50] As noted above, chapters 1–6 exemplify a subgenre which works as preparatory background for chapters 7–12. The suggestion that the apocalyptic literature flourished from 250 BC to AD 250[51] fails to acknowledge such earlier biblical books as Isaiah, Ezekiel, and Zechariah. These books demonstrated some characteristics of the apocalyptic genre beginning from the eighth to the sixth century BC.[52] Earlier apocalyptic literature can be differentiated from the prophetic and wisdom traditions of ancient Israel. It is also distinct from the mythologies of the ancient Near East.[53]

That which was "shut up" and "sealed" in the book of Daniel (chapter 12:4, 9) until the time of the end has been "revealed" or "disclosed" in the book of Revelation (chapter 1:1). This verse in Revelation gives the first attested use of the word *apokalypsis* in reference to a specific type or style of writing.

The LXX used "was revealed" (Dan 2:19, 30; 10:1) regarding some mysterious historical developments that were to be known before they took place. The book of Daniel and the book of Revelation have much in common and can be studied one in light of the other. Some of the imagery in Revelation has its precedents in Daniel and other parts of the Hebrew Bible. Collins lists the Revelation, the Ethiopic Book of Enoch, 2 Apocalypse of Baruch, and 4 Ezra as a few examples of historical apocalyptic writings that are clearly dependent on Daniel.[54] Matthew 24, Mark 13, and Luke 24 are the New Testament apocalypses that give some reference to Daniel.

---

50. Collins, *Daniel*, 58. If the book of Daniel can be ascertained to have been written in the sixth century BC, then it assumes the title of being the earliest full-blown apocalyptic literature. Stuart Lasine considered Daniel's literary genre to have some social functions; see his "Solomon, Daniel and the Detective Story," 247–66.

51. Crawford, "Apocalyptic," *Eerdmans Dictionary of the Bible*, 72–73.

52. Hanson points out that some biblical prophetic books have prophetic eschatology "study of end-time events" and that apocalyptic eschatology was an outgrowth from this biblical prophetic eschatology. However, he emphasized the fact that "prophetic eschatology and apocalyptic eschatology are best viewed as two sides of a continuum" which thrives best in social and political conditions. See his "Apocalypses and Apocalypticism: Introductory Overview" (*ABD*, 1:280–82).

53. Crawford, "Apocalyptic," *Eerdmans Dictionary of the Bible*, 72.

54. Collins, *Daniel*, 58, 59.

Some themes in Daniel have parallels in other apocalypses, but it is difficult to detect direct dependence. Parallels to Daniel as seen in the book of Enoch include the eschatological era and the end-time judgment of the righteous and the wicked (chapters 1–5); the Messiah; the Son of Man; reckoning of time by the sun; the fate of the wicked (chapters 72–82); dream visions (chapters 83–90); and the blessedness of the righteous in contrast with the miserable end of wicked people (chapters 91–104).[55]

Generally, there are two types of apocalypses, namely, the historical and the otherworldly. The books of Daniel and 1 Enoch exemplify these respectively. The historical apocalypses have to do with the revelation of future developments that are fixed and may not change. Daniel's apocalyptic writing is not communicating a conditional future (Dan 4:27), although he wished that it might have been so. That which is revealed in his book is already certain and destined to take place (Dan 2:45). In Daniel there are no otherworldly journeys taken by the writer while in company of divine beings. In fact, the supernatural beings come to the furnace (Dan 3:25), to the lions' pit (Dan 6:22), and to explain visions to Daniel (Dan 8:15; 9:21, 23; 10:5; 12:5).

The apocalyptic messages in Daniel come through dreams and visions. Mysterious symbols are used. In the first half of his book, Daniel had skill in all visions and dreams and in any matter of wisdom and interpretation (Dan 1:17, 20). In the last half of his book, he is in desperate search for understanding. In this case, understanding could be obtained only through the help of the supernatural beings who came to explain the symbols.

The origin of the apocalypses has been a divisive matter among scholars. Some consider the apocalypses to be an outgrowth of either Old Testament wisdom or prophecy.[56] On the other hand, the history of religions views the apocalypses as a foreign element, possibly originating from Persian or Iranian and ancient Near Eastern myths.[57]

If the prophetic oracles that were in the biblical canon became the source material for some of the apocalypses, then it must be noted that the writers of the apocalypses may or may not have had different purposes and points of interest from those who inspired them. Some may have intended to supplement information unavailable from the ancient writers, but such

---

55. Isaac, "1 (Ethiopic Apocalypse of) Enoch," in Charlesworth, *Old Testament Pseudepigrapha*, 1:5–89.

56. Collins, *Apocalypticism in the Dead Sea Scrolls*, 4–7; Collins, "From Prophecy to Apocalypticism," in Collins, *Encyclopedia of Apocalypticism*, 130–34.

57. Clifford, "Roots of Apocalypticism," in McGinn, *Continuum History of Apocalypticism*, 3–29; Hultgård, "Persian Apocalypticism," in McGinn, *Continuum History of Apocalypticism*, 30–36; and Knavig, *Roots of Apocalyptic* (1988).

APPENDIX B

works are characterized mostly by the author's speculation and therefore raise suspicion.

A characteristic seen in many of the apocalypses is the tendency to "predict" events that may have already happened. This is commonly known as the *vaticinia ex eventu*. A second characteristic is prophecies. The third characteristic which we will consider is eschatological predictions—the foretelling of future signs of the end.

The prophecies found in Gen 15:13–16 and Dan 7, 8, 9, 10, 11 were mistakenly classified by Collins as *ex eventu*. His list of *ex eventu* prophecies also includes the following pseudepigraphal writings: Apocalypse of Abraham, Animal Apocalypse, Apocalypse of Weeks, Jub. 23:11–26, 2 Bar. 35—47, 53—77, 4 Ezra 11—12.[58]

The Persian writings, such as Bahman Yasht and the Bundahishn, provide examples of ways in which the *ex eventu* writings organized history into various time periods. This organization was intended to show that history was fixed and would happen as scheduled.[59] In such prophecies, Collins argued that the reader might be able to situate one's generation at the end of the chronological succession.[60] This is clearly not the case with the book of Daniel. Daniel 2 situated the Neo-Babylonian generation at the beginning of the chronological history, and all the subsequent time-line events point to an end time long after the Neo-Babylonian Empire had vanished into history (Dan 8:17; 10:14; 12:4, 9, 13).

Grayson describes some Akkadian prophecies as *vaticinia ex eventu*, presented by their authors as "a genuine attempt to forecast future events."[61] In light of this, scholars have noted a striking similarity in genre, style, and content between Dan 11 and some Akkadian prophecies. Several Akkadian texts that fall in this category include the Late Assyrian tablet from Assur, dated 614 BC, which reads:

> A prince will arise and rule for thirteen years. There will be an Elamite attack on Akkad and the *booty* of Akkad will be carried off. The shrines of the great gods will be destroyed. Akkad will *suffer* a defeat. There will be confusion, disturbance, and disorder in the land. The nobility will lose prestige. Another man

---

58. Collins, *Daniel: With an Introduction*, 11–14.

59. Hultgård, "Bahman Yasht," in Collins and Charlesworth, *Mysteries and Revelations*, 114–34; Collins, *Apocalyptic Vision of the Book of Daniel*, 39–43; Collins, "Sibylline Oracles, Book 4," in Charlesworth, *Old Testament Pseudepigrapha*, 1:381–89.

60. Collins, *Daniel: With an Introduction*, 11.

61. Grayson, *Babylonian Historical-Literary Texts*, 6. Lambert says that these texts appear "to give detailed predictions of future historical events" in "History and the Gods," 175.

who is unknown will arise, seize the throne as king, and put his grandees to the sword.[62]

Another text was found at Warka, Babylonian Uruk (biblical Erech), and it reads:

> After him a king will arise and will not judge the judgment of the land, will not give decisions for the land, but he will rule the four world regions and at his name the regions will tremble. After him a king will arise from Uruk and will judge the judgment of the land, will give decisions for the land. He will confirm the rites of Anu in Uruk.[63]

The Late Babylonian tablet now housed in the British Museum says:

> A re[bel] prince will arise ([...]) The dynasty of Harran [*he will establish*]. For seventeen years [he will exercise sovereignty]. He will oppress (lit. 'be stronger than') the land and the *festival* of *Esa*[*gil* he will *cancel*]. A fortress in Babylonia [he will build]. He will plot evil against Akkad. A king of Elam will arise, the scepter ... [...] He will remove him from his throne and ([...]) He will take the throne and the king who arose (from) the throne ([...]) The king of Elam will change his place ([...]) He will settle him in another land ([...)] That king will oppress (lit. 'be stronger than') the land an[d (...)] all lands [*will bring to him*] tribute. During his reign Akkad [will not enjoy] a peaceful abode.[64]

The Akkadian *vaticinia ex eventu* writings are meant either to justify the author's claims or simply to gain credibility from the readership.

Other examples of *vaticinia ex eventu* writings include the dynastic prophecy. This dynasty prophecy text is preserved on a fragment, tablet BM 40623 (BM 34903 could be its other piece). It relates the rise and fall of the nations. It refers to the fall of Assyria, the rise and fall of Babylon, the rise and the fall of Persia, and possibly the rise of the Greeks.[65] Text A relates of a chain of anonymous kings who are introduced by the formulaic statement: "A prince shall arise and rule for x years ... ."[66] Each incumbent king is either

---

62. Grayson and Lambert, "Akkadian Prophecies," 14, lines 9–15; and Lambert, *Background of Jewish Apocalyptic*, 10.

63. Lambert, *Background of Jewish Apocalyptic*, 10.

64. Grayson, *Babylonian Historical-Literary Texts*, 33, lines 11–24; and Lambert, *Background of Jewish Apocalyptic*, 12.

65. Grayson, *Babylonian Historical-Literary Texts*, 24–37.

66. *ANET*, 451–52, 606–7; Grayson and Lambert, "Akkadian Prophecies," 12–16;

APPENDIX B

good or bad but there is no regular pattern. The last part of the prophecy is lost. This makes it difficult to discover both its definite historical framework and the intention of the author. The other texts include the Uruk Text,[67] Marduk, and Shulgi Prophetic Speeches.[68] All of these texts have been thought to have some affinities or parallels to the Hebrew apocalypses.

A close analysis of the Akkadian prophecies in form, content, and function shows that they lack transcendental eschatology, which is the most dominant characteristic of the apocalypses.[69] These prophecies belong to a different genre than the apocalypses, although their historical outlines have some parallels with Dan 2, 7, 8, and 11.[70] Grayson concluded that this literature was valuable only for comparative purposes with the apocalypses.[71] Further, the Babylonian prophecies have no clear-cut purpose for their composition. They lack predictions that lead to a grand climax of history. They fail to present material of international significance. They have no affinity with the Hebrew apocalypses.

Scholars acknowledge the fact that Dan 1—6 claims to be from Neo-Babylonian and Medo-Persian periods.[72] There is no clear consensus on whether or not all of these stories came from the pen of a single author. Currently, more literary evidence and increasingly erudite scholarship show that the unity of the first six chapters of Daniel is to be viewed as a background to the last six chapters.

Whether the book of Daniel was written in the sixth or second century BC, it still carries its predictive force. The greater number of its predictions took place after the second century BC and the cosmic grand finale is still to come in the time of the end. Therefore, Daniel cannot be characterized as a *vaticinia ex eventu* ("prophecy after event") apocalypse. Its dream predictions are clearly *vaticinia ante eventu* ("prophecy before the event").

Biggs, "More Babylonian 'Prophecies,'" 117–32. See also Hallo, "Akkadian Apocalypses," 235–36; and Ringgren, "Akkadian Apocalypses," in Hellholm, *Apocalypticism in the Mediterranean World*, 379–80.

67. Hunger and Kaufman, "New Akkadian Prophecy Text," 371–75. Both Hunger and Kaufman concur that all these prophecies are dissimilar in both literary format and function (375).

68. Borger, "Gott Marduk," 3–24; and Ringgren, "Akkadian Apocalypses," in Hellholm, *Apocalypticism in the Mediterranean World*, 380–82.

69. Gane, "Genre Awareness and Interpretation," in Merling, *To Understand the Scriptures*, 144.

70. Gane, "Genre Awareness and Interpretation," in Merling, *To Understand the Scriptures*, 144–45.

71. Grayson, *Babylonian Historical-Literary Texts*, 21.

72. See the discussion in Appendix A, "The Composition of Daniel."

This study has shown the fulfillment of many of Daniel's predictions long after the book came into circulation. Some of the events portrayed in Daniel have not yet taken place as of this writing. Some of Nebuchadnezzar's (Dan 2) and Daniel's (Dan 7—12) dream predictions are not yet fulfilled. The eschatological stone of Dan 2:44-45 has not yet come to destroy the world and create a new order. The resurrection of the saints (Dan 12:2) has not yet taken place, and the saints have not yet received the kingdom (Dan 7:27).

PSEUDO-DANIELIC APOCRYPHAL APOCALYPSES

A large body of texts associated with Daniel has sporadically appeared from the Byzantine and mediaeval times. From this literature

> are Daniel texts where the action is related in the first person and there are third-person episodes about Daniel's life and times. There are Daniel apocalypses and apocalyptic oracles, Daniel astronomical and geomantic texts, Daniel mystery plays, and Daniel dream manuals. There are full-blown narratives involving that prophet, poems about him, and shorter traditions, embedded in a variety of formats, that touch on a particular aspect of life, deeds, or death. There are even tales that revolve around other figures from the Book of Daniel, such as Nebuchadnezzar, the three youths from the fiery furnace, and Susanna.[73]

These pseudepigraphal texts have little archaeological evidence to support them. Some manuscripts and the codices have been recovered from monasteries, libraries, museums, and private homes. It is possible that others will yet be discovered. The pseudepigrapha appear in various languages including Arabic, Aramaic, Armenian, Coptic, Ethiopic, French, Georgian, German, Greek, Hebrew, Italian, Latin, Middle English, Old English, Old Icelandic, Old Irish, Old Slavonic, Persian, and Turkish. The apocryphal literature associated with Daniel is classified into (a) the legenda, the third-person postbiblical narratives intended to retell or augment the biblical book of Dan 1—6; (b) the apocryphal apocalypses, the first-person writings pseudonymously ascribed to the biblical Daniel; and (c) the prognostica, which are basically the fortune-telling texts.[74]

---

73. DiTommaso, *Book of Daniel*, 12.
74. DiTommaso, *Book of Daniel*, 15-19.

APPENDIX B

Certain pseudepigraphal and apocryphal apocalypses[75] are assumed to be associated with the biblical book of Daniel. The connection to or association with the biblical Daniel remains "tangential at best."[76] These writings have some historical orientation, but this historical information is not always reliable. The apocryphal apocalypses generally present questionable extra information related to the book of Daniel which is mainly based on speculative traditions. The writers may have chosen Daniel as the supposed author so that their work would appear credible.

Below is a partial listing of the pseudepigraphal and apocryphal apocalypses:

Arabic

1. In *The Vision of Daniel as Related to Ezra, His Disciple* Daniel talks to his disciple Ezra about the vision which had historical implications. The document employs different animal symbols to relate the wars between Byzantium and Persia. There are also some Arabic conquests narratives. The Antichrist is hailed by Jews as the anticipated Messiah but he misleads many people through miracles. This Antichrist eventually destroys Enoch and Elijah. Finally, God intervenes by bringing the world to an end. The document has Christian overtones and is a ninth-century AD composition.[77] S. Amir Arjomand stated that the Quran is filled with both ecclesiastical and secular apocalypses, and the latter is tinted with political overtones.[78]

2. *The Apocalypse of Daniel on the Events After al-Mu'tamid*, dated approximately AD 934-47, reviews contemporary Muslim history in North Africa and the Arabian Peninsula. This apocalypse, written in eight sections, is part of the writings of Ibn al-Munādī who died in AD 947. It deals with Muslim history of the ninth to tenth centuries AD, conflicts between local and tribal messianic figures, war with the Byzantines, the messianic kingdom, and the history of the rule of

---

75. DiTommaso gives the latest list of twenty-four apocryphal apocalypses and valuable discussion on each in DiTomasso, *Book of Daniel*, 87-230. Another relevant work on this discussion is Martinez, *Qumran and Apocalyptic*, 137-61.

76. Henze, *Syriac Apocalypse of Daniel*, 23, n. 59.

77. For the text see Gottheil, "Arabic Version," 14-17; Macler, "L'Apocalypse arabe de Daniel," 265-305; and also Hall, "Vision of Ezra the Scribe," 537-41.

78. For some of the Quran apocalypses and bibliography, see Arjomand, "Islamic Apocalypticism in the Classic Period," in McGinn, *Encyclopedia of Apocalypticism*, 2:238-83.

the prophet Muhammad's grandsons. The end of the document has Daniel talking to an angel who declined to identify specific historical individuals.[79]

3. *The Vita Danielis* in the Lives of the Prophets is dated first century AD. This text is also available in Armenian, Ethiopic, Greek, Hebrew, Latin, and Syriac. Lives of the Prophets is probably from the late Second Temple period and presents biographies of the prophets. *The Vita Danielis* deals with Nebuchadnezzar's madness (Dan 4), and Daniel's death and burial. It concludes with an account of Daniel's predictions on the northern and southern mountains, and also the time of the end.[80]

4. *The Fourteenth Vision* of Daniel is possibly from 1200 AD. The extant manuscript is preserved in Coptic and Arabic in London, British Museum, Codex Or. 1314, folios 240r–251v [1374].[81]

5. *Malḥamat Dāniyāl*, "The Forecasts or Predictions of Daniel." There are copies preserved also in Hebrew, Persian, and Syriac.[82] The text MS 3808 is located in Cairo, Coptic Museum.

6. *The Book of Principles of Daniel the Sage* is also known as *The Principles of Interpretation of Dreams of Daniel*. Here is an anthology of predictions with regard to agriculture, astrology, astronomy, calendar, climate, and meteorology. These are tinted with eschatological and historical speculations which are associated with the dreams of both the biblical and apocryphal Daniel.[83]

7. Islamic *Kit āb al-Jafar*, "The Book of Numerology," is from the Islamic period. It tells of a Daniel who lived between the time of Noah and that of Abram. This person certainly cannot be the biblical Daniel. The main character of *Kit āb al-Jafar* is said to have authored some scientific writings, and some political predictions on kingdoms and

---

79. Cook, "Early Muslim Daniel Apocalypse," 55–96; and DiTommaso, *Book of Daniel*, 171–74, 471.

80. Extant text, MS Syr. 16, fols. 1–23 in the Union Theological Seminary, New York. Translations of *Vita Danielis* include: Hare, "Lives of the Prophets," in Charlesworth, *Old Testament Pseudepigrapha*, 2:389–91; and Satran, *Biblical Prophets in Byzantine Palestine*, 79–96, 121–28.

81. See the entry on **Coptic** below.

82. See the text and translation also by al-Masiḥ, "Fragmentary Farmer's Almanac," 5–9; and Tobi, "Judeo-Arabic Version," in Tobi, *Jews of Yemen*, 242–54.

83. For the discussion on the text see Bland, "On the Muhammedan Science," 123, 153; Seligson, "Daniel, in Arabic Literature" (*Jewish Encyclopedia*, 4:429). Further discussion and bibliography is provided by DiTommaso, *Book of Daniel*, 295–98, 482, 485.

end-time events. This Daniel is also said to have invented numerology, the ancient science of making predictions through numerical calculations.[84]

8. *Qur'at Dâniyâl* is a text on geomantics (a specialized divination) which is associated with Daniel. Geomantics is "divination by random figures formed when a handful of earth is thrown to the ground, or as by lines drawn at random."[85]

9. *Islamic Daniel Geomantic Texts* are a collection of divination texts which cover geomancy and the interpretation of dreams, all of which are associated with Daniel in one way or another. These texts appear also in Armenian, Persian, Syriac, and Turkish.[86]

Armenian

1. *The Seventh Vision of Daniel* is probably a seventh-century AD composition. The Armenian book of Daniel has six visions and this work adds a seventh. In this text, the angel Gabriel is said to have outlined history to Daniel from Constantius to Heraclius. The manuscript claims that these things happened in the third year of Cyrus the Persian, which is a date similar to that of Dan 10:1. The work is ambiguous, and the events it relates cannot be reliably dated.[87]

2. *Somniale Danielis* is a manual of dreams and their interpretations. These dreams are listed in alphabetical order. The manual was most probably composed in AD 300–500. This pseudonymous text is loosely associated with the biblical Daniel on the basis that he interpreted dreams.[88]

---

84. British Library in London, Code: Oriental 426 [Add.7473]; Seligson, "Daniel, in Arabic Literature" (*Jewish Encyclopedia*, 4:429); Arjomand, "Islamic Apocalypticism in the Classical Period" (*Encyclopedia of Apocalypticism*, 2:265, 278, n. 37); and DiTommaso, *Book of Daniel*, 296–97; 482–83.

85. *Webster's New World College Dictionary*, 4th ed. (2000), s.v. "Geomancy." DiTommaso indicates that the science of geomancy is "divination by means of figures and lines or geographic features"; *Book of Daniel*, 295, 468.

86. Several catalogue publications on geomantic texts are in DiTommaso, *Book of Daniel*, 468–70, 483–85, 503.

87. Two apocryphal MSS (No. 935 written in AD 1341 and No. 1635 written in the fifteenth century AD) of "The Seventh Vision of Daniel," are extant in St. Lazarus Library, the Armenian Monastery in Jerusalem. See also Issaverdens, *Uncanonical Writings of the Old Testament*, 306, 307, 324–48, or 1934 ed., pp. 249–65.

88. There are over 150 extant MSS of this text in several languages including English, French, German, Greek, Icelandic, Irish, Italian, Latin, and Welsh, but over one

3. *The Mors Danielis in the Names, Works, and Deaths of the Holy Prophets*[89]
4. *The Vita of the Three Children*[90]
5. *Daniel Geomantic Texts*[91]
6. *The Portion of Daniel the Prophet*, and many more.[92]

Coptic

The content of the Coptic *The Fourteenth Vision of Daniel* seems to follow the biblical book of Daniel as presented in the Alexandrian Codex. It adds the apocryphal stories of Bel and the Dragon as Visions 12 and 13 respectively. The fourth kingdom of Dan 7 becomes here the Arab kingdom, which is later split into nineteen divisions. The setting of the work is probably Egyptian during the Umayyad period, around eleventh century AD.[93]

Greek

Greek pseudo-Daniels are too many to enumerate here. Many more are yet to be identified.[94] They are also difficult to date. They seem to range from second century BC to medieval times. Significant examples include:

- Apocalypse of the Prophet Daniel on the end of the World or The Last Vision of the Prophet Daniel
- The Monk Daniel on the Seven Hills and on the Islands and Their Future
- Visions of Daniel on the Last Times and on the End of the World

---

hundred of these MSS are in Latin; see DiTommaso, *Book of Daniel*, 378–97; for text discussion, 236–59; and bibliography, 397–402. For the text see also Fischer, *Complete Medieval Dreambook* (1982).

89. Stone, *Armenian Apocrypha*, 164–66; and DiTommaso, *Book of Daniel*, 502.

90. Stone, *Armenian Apocrypha*, 154; Stone, *Selected Studies in Pseudepigrapha and Apocrypha*, 90–102.

91. DiTommaso, *Book of Daniel*, 468–70, 483–85, 503.

92. There are many Armenian apocryphal texts associated with Daniel and these may continue to surface; see Stone, *Il Caucaso* (1996), and DiTommaso, *Book of Daniel*, 503.

93. Meinardus, "Commentary on the XIVth Vision," 394–449; and Meinardus, "New Evidence on the XIVth Vision," 281–309.

94. Rydén, "Andreas Salos Apocalypse," 199–261.

APPENDIX B

- Discourses of John Chrysostom on the Vision of Daniel
- "The Narrative of Daniel," in Discourse of Methodius on the Last Days and on the Antichrist
- The Vita Danielis in the Life of the Prophets (Arabic, Armenain, Ethiopic, Greek, Hebrew, Latin, and Syriac)
- Diegesis Danielis
- Praedictiones Danielis
- Somniale Danielis
- Lunationes Danielis
- The Vision of Daniel on the Island of Cyprus
- The Vision of Daniel on the Blond Race
- The Visions of Daniel and Other Holy Men
- The Oracle of the Prophet Daniel on Byzantium
- The Proclamation of the Prophet Daniel
- The Vision and Revelation of the Prophet Daniel
- The Vision of Daniel on the Island of Crete

The Apocalypse of Daniel relates eighth-century AD Byzantine historical events. Three of these manuscripts are extant. Two of the manuscripts are complete, and one is only partial. The School of Medicine at Montpellier, France, houses one of the complete manuscripts. It is labeled "MS M" (fifteenth–sixteenth century). The second complete manuscript is in the Bodleian Library at Oxford, and is listed as "MS B" (Codex Canonicianus Nr. 19, folios 145–52 [sixteenth century]). The partial manuscript residing in the Bibliotheca Marciana in Venice, is MS V, Marc. Grec. VII 22, folios 14–16.

Many of the pseudo-Daniel texts share the title "The Apocalypse of Daniel."[95]

Hebrew

A medieval fragment retrieved from the Geniza in Cairo, Egypt, is entitled the "Vision of Daniel." It tells of a fourteenth vision of Daniel during the reign of Cyrus, king of Persia. Although the text has historical and

---

95. Zervos, "Apocalypse of Daniel," in Charlesworth, *Old Testament Pseudepigrapha*, 1:755–70.

apocalyptic parts, it does not mention the name "Daniel."[96] Other Hebrew pseudo-Daniels include:

- Daniel Poem,[97]
- Nevu'ot Daniel,[98]
- The Daniel-Tales in the Book of Yosippon.[99]

Persian

Qissayi Dâniyâl, "The History of Daniel," was written in Persian but transcribed in Hebrew. This work presents a Daniel who worked with Nebuchadnezzar, Cyrus and Darius. The document mentions the prophet Mohammed. It states that the Romans will destroy many people but the Messiah will come at the end and reign for 1300 years. The text was composed around AD 800–1090.[100]

The Book of Daniel (*Dāniyāl-nāma*)[101] attempts to reconstruct the history of the book of Daniel.

Slavonic

The Vision of Daniel must have been translated from the Greek. This is a historical narrative which shows some Byzantine characters and mentions the

---

96. A MS exists in the Jewish Theological Seminary, New York, Schechter Genizah fol. 5r-v entitled the Vision of Daniel. For the text and translations see also Starr, *Jews in the Byzantine Empire*, 134–35; and Buchanan, "Vision of Daniel," in *Revelation and Redemption*, 419–22.

97. Klein, *Targumic Manuscripts*, 37.

98. Text was discovered in the Cairo Genizah and is now housed in Sankt Petersburg, Russia. M. Ben-Sasson is editing it for publication. According to DiTommaso, the text is most probably Islamic; see his *Book of Daniel*, 184–85, 461; and Henze, *Syriac Apocalypse of Daniel*, 5n7.

99. Gaster, *Chronicles of Jerahmeel*, 200–24; Reiner, "Original Hebrew Yosippon," 128–46; and DiTommaso, *Book of Daniel*, 461–62.

100. Levy, "Danial-Nama," in Baron, *Jewish Studies*, 423–28; and Netzer, "Daniyal-nama and Its Linguistic Features," 305–14.

101. The MSS is in the British Library, London, Codex Or. 4743, fols. 2r–65r and also in the Hebrew University, Jerusalem, MS H2680 [1913]. For texts and translations see Baron and Marx, *Jewish Studies* (1935).

Arab conquest of Sicily in AD 827-28. The writings have an eschatological tone and could be dated to the ninth century AD.[102]

Syriac

1. One work, preserved only in Syriac, is titled *From the Young Daniel on our Lord and the End*. This text is from the second century AD,[103] and it contains the history of Bel and the Dragon. The text ascribes to Daniel a description of the events of the last days, drawing on events in Matthew 24, Mark 13 and Luke 21.

2. *The Syriac Apocalypse of Daniel* is one of several other apocalypses in Syriac. This manuscript is closely related to *From the Young Daniel on our Lord and the End*, and can safely be dated to around AD 629/630. The text claims to be the revelation of the prophet Daniel while he was in Persia and Elam. It portrays Daniel at the court of Nebuchadnezzar. Sennacherib defeats Babylon and Daniel escapes to Cyrus, who then comes to conquer Babylon. Darius becomes blind when he sees the temple treasure which had been looted from the Jerusalem temple. He goes to Jerusalem to the pool of Shiloah to regain his sight. There are also some eschatological visions attributed to Daniel.[104]

---

102. Srechkovic, "Zbornik Popa Dragolia," 10-11; and Istrin, *Otkrovenie Mefodiia Patarskago I*, 84-131, 156-58; and Alexander, "Appendix: English Translation of Slavonic Daniel," in Abrahamse, *Byzantine Apocalyptic Tradition*, 65-72.

103. The extant twelfth-century AD text is in the British Library, Codex Additional 18715, folios 239v-241r. For bibliography and discussion with regards to this text see Brock, "Jewish Traditions in Syriac Sources," 224, n. 48; and Martinez, *Qumran and Apocalyptic*, 158-61.

104. The Syriac Apocalypse of Daniel MSS is in the Harvard University Library, catalogued as Harvard MS Syr 42, folios 117r-122v (out of 125 folios) written in Serto; Henze, *Syriac Apocalypse of Daniel*, 1-2, 33-118; see also Goshen-Gottstein and Moshe, *Syriac Manuscripts* (1979); and DiTommaso, *Book of Daniel*, 113-23.

Appendix C

INTERPRETATION VIEWS ON DANIEL

THE MACCABEAN HYPOTHESIS APPROACH

THE MACCABEAN HYPOTHESIS STATES that the book of Daniel was compiled by unidentifiable second-century BC writer(s) who posed as a sixth-century BC prophet named Daniel. Further, it is postulated that the book was written after the events it purports to describe (*vaticinium ex eventu*) and that its message was spuriously crafted and presented as genuine predictive prophecy (*vaticinium ante eventu*). Those who subscribe to this idea also argue that the book was written around 165 BC to encourage Jewish patriotic resistance against the tyranny of Antiochus IV Epiphanes.[1] The Maccabean hypothesis claims have since developed into several strands of arguments. These theories seek to establish the later date for the writing of the book of Daniel, and also to discredit its historicity.[2]

---

1. Mastin, "Daniel 2:46 and the Hellenistic World," 80–93; Goldingay, "Book of Daniel," 45–49; Wenham, "Daniel," 49–52; and Archer, *Survey of Old Testament Introduction*, 423.

2. Jiří Moskala's study dealt extensively with the problems the Maccabean thesis encounters in the study of Daniel; "Book of Daniel" (1995).

APPENDIX C

HISTORICAL ARGUMENTS

A wide range of issues has been raised against the historicity of the text of Daniel. Among other things, skeptics have questioned the person of Daniel, Nebuchadnezzar's lycanthropy, Belshazzar's kingship, the Chaldeans, and Darius the Mede. Daniel 1:1 relates to the same date as Jer 25:1 and 46:2. These texts have been taken as contradictory of each other and therefore charged with historical errancy.[3] Other disputed dates include Dan 7:1; 8:1; and 9:1.

In the Jewish canon, Daniel is placed among the *Kethubim* or hagiographa rather than among the prophets. Daniel's placement in the *Kethubim* is interpreted to mean that it was written later than all the canonical prophets. In 170 BC Jesus ben Sirach (Ecclesiasticus) referred to all the prophets except Daniel, and this omission has been taken to mean that Daniel was not yet written at that time.

The major thrust of all these arguments has been to show that the book of Daniel was written in the second century BC. Literary and artifact discoveries have since refuted these arguments, showing that the book of Daniel is of earlier provenance than had been suggested.

LINGUISTIC ARGUMENTS

The book of Daniel is composed mainly in Hebrew and Aramaic, but the text also contains some Greek and Persian loanwords. The appearance of these foreign words in the text of Daniel has been viewed as evidence for a later date for the entire work.[4] Samuel R. Driver asserted that the appearance of some Greek words in Daniel demanded that the book should be dated after Alexander the Great had conquered Palestine.[5]

It was once believed that the word *kārôzā'*, "the herald" (Dan 3:4; 5:29) was a loanword from the Greek *kēryx*,[6] but it has been shown that the word comes from the Old Persian *khrausa*, "caller." The three Greek words that appear as names of musical instruments are: *qatrôs*, *pesanterin*, and *siphōnyāh/sûmphōnyāh* (Dan 3:5, 7, 10, 15). The last musical instrument is attested in Greek literature during the time of Plato (around 370 BC). This has been used to suggest that the book of Daniel was written after the fourth century BC.

3. See the discussion in Appendix A, "Dating Problem."
4. See the discussion in Appendix A, "Multilingualism in Daniel."
5. Driver, *Introduction to the Literature*, 508.
6. *BDB*, 1097.

The Assyrian king, Sargon II (722–705 BC), captured the Greeks who lived on the islands and sold them into slavery in the ancient Near East.[7] The Greek poet Alcaeus of Lesbos (ca. 600 BC) wrote about his brother, Antimenidas, who was drafted into the Babylonian army. Moreover, some Greek carpenters and shipbuilders, along with musicians from Ashkelon, were attested as recipients of Nebuchadnezzar's food rations. Apparently, Greek mercenaries, slaves, and Greek musical instruments existed in the ancient Near East long before the time of Daniel.[8]

The Greeks dominated the ancient Near East from 331–168 BC. There is the suggestion that the book of Daniel was composed after 170 BC. If this was the case, one would expect Daniel's book to be full of Greek expressions. Also, within the book would have been found Greek political as well as administrative terms, cultural customs, and other issues.[9] Instead, the book of Daniel has several words of Old Persian origin that relate mostly to government administration and politics.[10]

Examples of the Old Persian loanwords found in the book of Daniel include those attested in the Akkadian cuneiform:

- *'ăḥăšedārepăn*, "satraps" (Dan 3:2, 3, 27; 6:1, 2, 3, 4, 6, 7)
- *dāt*, "law," "decree" (Dan 2:9, 13, 15; 6:5, 8, 12, 15; 7:25)
- *detābăr*, "judges" (Dan 3:2, 3)

Examples of words found in sixth-to-fifth-century BC Elephantine papyri in Egypt:

- *pītegām*, "word" (Dan 3:16; 4:17)
- *'āzedā,*' "assured" or "certified" (Dan 2:5)
- *zăn*, "kind" or "type" (Dan 3:5, 7, 10, 15)
- *tīfetî*, "magistrate," "police officer" (Dan 3:2, 3)
- *rāzāh*, "the secret" (Dan 2:19, 27, 30)
- *gedāberăyā,*' "the treasure" (Dan 3:2, 3)

Other loanwords found in the book of Daniel include:

---

7. *ANET*, 284.

8. Archer, *Survey of Old Testament Introduction*, 431; Albright, *From Stone Age to Christianity*, 337; Yamauchi, *Greece and Babylon*, 92–94; and Yamauchi, "Daniel and Contacts," 37–47.

9. Archer, *Survey of Old Testament Introduction*, 432.

10. For the list of words see Kitchen, "Aramaic of Daniel," 35–44; and Archer, *Survey of Old Testament Introduction*, 432.

APPENDIX C

- *hăppăretemîm*, "the noblemen" (Dan 1:3)
- *păt-băg*, "food" (Dan 1:5)
- *ăpĕdĕn*, "palace" (Dan 11:45)
- *peṭăš*, "tunic," "garment," or "shirt" (Dan 3:21)
- *šerōš*, "root" (Dan 4:20, 23)
- *nĕberăšetā*,' "the lampstand" (Dan 5:5)
- *nebîzebāh*, "a present," "gift" (Dan 2:6; 5:17)
- *nĭdenĕh*, "sheath," "body" (Dan 7:15)
- *hădām*, "limb" (Dan 2:5; 3:29)
- *hămenîk*, "necklace," "chain" (Dan 5:7, 16, 29)

The presence of such Persian words in the text shows that the author was well acquainted with Persian affairs. He used the words in their proper context and meaning. The Old Persian words are dated 300 BC or earlier. They point to an earlier date for the book of Daniel.[11]

LITERARY ARGUMENTS

The apocalypses as a literary genre flourished from 250 BC to AD 250.[12] Many Jewish writings of this nature produced during this time include 1 Enoch, 4 Ezra, 2–4 Baruch, and the apocalypses of Abraham, Adam, Enosh, Paul, Sethel, Shem, and Zephaniah.[13]

The book of Daniel, which has been classified by some as apocalyptic literature, has also been considered a product of this time period by those who advocate for the Maccabean hypothesis. It has been strongly suggested that the book was written to console the Jews who were undergoing persecution by Antiochus IV Epiphanes. Such an argument is no longer tenable because there are stronger reasons for the writer to have come up with such a document during the most devastating time in that nation's history when Nebuchadnezzar murdered people, robbed and destroyed the temple, carried people into exile, and left the country devastated.

To assert that Daniel must have been written during the time in which most of the apocalypses were written also ignores the fact that the

---

11. Harrison, *Introduction to the Old Testament*, 1125; and Hasel, "Establishing the Date," in Holbrook, *Symposium on Daniel*, 127–28.
12. Crawford, "Apocalyptic," 72.
13. Charlesworth, *Old Testament Pseudepigrapha* (1983; 1985).

antecedents of apocalyptic literature can be found much earlier in the prophetic and wisdom traditions of ancient Israel and the mythologies of the ancient Near East. Daniel further develops apocalyptic motifs that were already raised by the other Hebrew writers.

Another distinct characteristic of the apocalyptic genre is pseudonymity—the idea of falsely ascribing one's writings to an ancient renowned individual. Many pseudepigraphal writings have claimed Danielic authorship, but evidence is lacking to consider, classify, or identify the canonical book of Daniel as pseudonymous. In the Hebrew Bible no pseudepigraphon could ever be accepted or considered as an authoritative work, for there was resistance to the interpolation of any new material in the text.

THEOLOGICAL ARGUMENTS

Proponents of the Maccabean hypothesis subscribe to a number of arguments. One such argument is that the book of Daniel shares some of the motifs and concerns occurring in the apocryphal and pseudepigraphal literature written during the intertestamental period. Such motifs include the concepts of angelology, resurrection, judgment, messianic figure, God's eschatological kingdom, deliberate avoidance of the name "YHWH," and penitential prayer and fasting.

Such works as Tobit (225–175 BC), the Testament of the Twelve Patriarchs (second century BC), the book of Enoch (first century BC), Susanna, the Vision of Isaiah (first century AD), and the Ascension of Isaiah (first century AD) have motifs similar to those of Daniel. It has been suggested that Daniel must have been written in the same time frame with the writings which share similar emphases.

Examination of the text of Daniel in light of the above-mentioned motifs shows that it has closer affinity to the other Hebrew Bible texts than the extrabiblical apocryphal and pseudepigraphal literature.

The role of angels in Daniel is consistent with what is found in the Pentateuch, historical books, and prophetic texts of the Hebrew Bible. Biblical angelology stands in "sharp contrast with extra-biblical intertestamental apocalyptic literature where angels of different kinds and ranks are bewilderingly teeming (see for example 1 En. 6:7–8; 9:1; 20:1–8; Tob 3:8, 16–17; 5:4; 8:3; 12:15)."[14]

The idea of the resurrection of both the good and bad in Dan 12:2 is biblically based, but the only extrabiblical text that mentions this is the Book of the Twelve Patriarchs (Judah 25:4–5).

14. Moskala, "Book of Daniel." (2007).

APPENDIX C

The Hebrew Bible contains many texts on prayer and fasting, the last judgment, the messianic figure, and God's eschatological kingdom, which are either reiterated or elaborated in Daniel. Archaeological and literary evidence shows that the book of Daniel seems to belong to the sixth-century BC provenance.

EXEGETICAL ARGUMENTS

The main exegetical concern for the proponents of the Maccabean hypothesis is with the startling predictions contained in the book. These they have dismissed as *vaticinium ex eventu*. The four-kingdom schema, the chronological succession of the earthly kingdoms, and their symbolism are a puzzle to them. All of the historical predictions are assumed to have been crafted by some author(s) who lived in the Maccabean times when Jews were militating against the Syrian hegemony. Chapter 11 of Daniel is taken as reminiscing on the Maccabean wars.

Antiochus IV Epiphanes looms large in the Maccabean hypothesis exegesis. He is assumed by these scholars to be the little horn of Dan 7:8 and 8:9. It is therefore necessary to discuss Antiochus IV Epiphanes in relation to the book of Daniel.

ANTIOCHUS IV EPIPHANES OMISSION

The person of Antiochus IV Epiphanes looms large in the minds of the scholars who subscribe to the Maccabean hypothesis. It is therefore necessary to address briefly the issues surrounding his role with regard to the interpretation of the book of Daniel.

The books of 1 and 2 Maccabees, Polybius,[15] and Livius[16] were some of the sources potentially available to Josephus as he was compiling the histories of the Jewish people.[17] First Maccabees 1:39 says, "Her sanctuary became desolate like a desert." Based upon this, Josephus suggested that Antiochus IV Epiphanes, and subsequently the Roman government, supplied the problems necessary to fulfill the "abomination that desolates" alluded to in Dan 8:13; 9:17, 27; 11:31; 12:11.[18]

---

15. Polybius, *Histories*, 6.29.27.
16. Livius, *History of Rome*, 44, 45.
17. See 1 Macc 1:10—6:17; 2 Macc 9; Josephus, *Antiquities of the Jews*, 12.5-9; 13.5.5; 13.7.2-4; 13.8.2; and Josephus, *Wars of the Jews*, 1.1.1-6.
18. Josephus, *Antiquities of the Jews*, 10.11.7.

Despite Josephus's point of view on Antiochus IV, some Jews still see the fulfillment of the "abomination that desolates" as referring specifically to the Romans.[19] Atrocities by pagan Rome included several incidents which would have been considered to be desolating abominations. These included:

- the proposal by Caius Caligula to erect an idol in the temple in Jerusalem
- the setting up of Roman standards in the temple
- the construction of the temple for Jupiter Capitolina by Adrian in AD 132
- the crushing of the Bar Kochba revolt
- the oppression of the Jews[20]

Scholars who study the book of Daniel have been more intrigued by Antiochus IV Epiphanes, the younger son of Antiochus III, than by any of the other Seleucid Greek kings. This fascination has popularized Antiochus IV Epiphanes as a major figure in the study of the book of Daniel.[21]

Hippolytus (AD 140–235) associated the activities of the little horn in Dan 8 and the king of the north in Dan 11 with Antiochus IV Epiphanes.[22] This idea was enlarged upon by Porphyry (AD 233–304), a Syrian sophist and neoplatonic philosopher who strongly suggested that Antiochus IV Epiphanes fulfilled the prophecies of Dan 9:27 and Dan 11:31.[23]

Jerome tried to object to Porphyry's views in *Jerome's Commentary on Daniel*. The debate begun by Porphyry over the identity and role of

---

19. Regardless of holding on to the opinion that Antiochus IV Epiphanes had a role to play in Daniel's writing, Josephus was also convinced that the Roman government would make Palestine desolate. Josephus, *History of Antiquity*, 10.11.7; see also Goldwurm, *Daniel*, 199; Ali, *Commentary on the Book of Daniel*, 34, 51, 64, 65; and Archer, *Jerome's Commentary on Daniel*, 32.

20. Josephus, *Antiquities of the Jews*, 134; and 1 and 2 Maccabees.

21. See arguments in favor of reading Antiochus IV Epiphanes in the text of Daniel in van Henten, "Antiochus IV," in van der Woude, *Book of Daniel*, 223–43. Cf. Broshi and Eshel, "Greek King Is Antiochus IV," 120–29; Vermes, *Complete Dead Sea Scrolls in English*, 388; and Vermeylen, *Ten Keys for Opening the Bible*, 161–66.

22. Hippolytus, "On Daniel," chaps. 4–7 (*Ante-Nicene Fathers*, 5:179).

23. Porphyry's twelfth book in his *Against Christians* series deals with Daniel, and it invoked an outrageous response from some of the early church fathers, including Eusebius and Jerome. See Shea, "Early Development," in Holbrook, *Symposium on Daniel*, 256–328. Shea analyzed the development of the association of Antiochus IV Epiphanes with the Danielic text before and after Porphyry.

Antiochus IV Epiphanes in the book of Daniel continues unabated.[24] The two issues most heatedly contested by scholars today are:

- the identification of Antiochus IV with the little horn of Dan 7 and 8, and
- whether or not Antiochus IV fits anywhere in Dan 11.

Unfortunately, the book of Daniel has been grossly misunderstood. This has, over time, resulted in erroneous interpretations of its theme and content, and the miscalculation of its mathematics and dating.

The outline of the four successive kingdoms in Dan 2, 7, and 8 began, according to the text, with Babylon. The text states clearly that Medo-Persia followed Babylon, and Greece followed Medo-Persia. Next, Daniel presents the fourth kingdom, which would subsequently fragment, and finally be destroyed and replaced by a divine kingdom.

The bizarre beast of Daniel 7 has ten horns. This beast represented the fourth kingdom (Dan 7:23). In this fourth kingdom the little horn came into prominence, displacing three of the ten existing horns. It is clear that the little horn comes from the bizarre beast which represents the fourth historical kingdom (Dan 7:23-25).

From the textual and historical evidence, it is very unlikely that Antiochus IV Epiphanes could be identified as the little horn. Antiochus IV Epiphanes was one of the Greek kings who ruled from 175-164 BC. The Greeks were conquered by the Roman Empire, the fourth kingdom (Dan 2:33-35, 40-43; 7:7, 19; 11:20-45).

According to the chronology of Daniel, Antiochus IV belonged to the third kingdom, which was represented by the belly and thighs of bronze (Dan 2:32, 39). It was also represented by a beast like a leopard (Dan 7:6), and the he-goat (Dan 8:5-8, 21). The anti-Jewish devastations instigated by Antiochus IV are insufficient to qualify him as the little horn of Daniel. As an illustration, Nebuchadnezzar seems to have had some of the characteristics of the little horn. He had worse atrocities done to Jerusalem and Judah than did Antiochus IV, but Nebuchadnezzar is never identified with the little horn according to Daniel's chronology, historical context, and logic. During the Second World War (1939-45) Adolf Hitler persecuted and orchestrated the genocide of about six million Jews in what is known today as the Holocaust, but in spite of this, Hitler cannot be identified with the little

---

24. See for example van Henten, "Antiochus IV as a Typhonic Figure in Daniel 7," 223-43; Gulley, "Why the Danielic Little Horn," 191-97; Collins and Flint, *Book of Daniel* (2002); and Harrington, "Antiochus," in *Eerdmans Dictionary of the Bible*, 68-69.

horn. The king to be identified as a little horn must fit all the description and characteristics defined by the text of Daniel.

Some identifying marks of the little horn in Dan 7 have been provided by several scholars[25] but a more elaborate list is as follows:

- It rose out of the **"fourth beast"** (Dan 7:8, 24).
- It appeared after **"ten"** other **"horns"** (Dan 7:24).
- It was **"little"** when it was first seen, but in time it became **"greater than its fellows"** (Dan 7:8, 20).
- It was to **"put down three kings"** so that, as it arose, **"three of the first horns were plucked up by the roots"** (Dan 7:8, 24).
- It had **"eyes like the eyes of a man, and a mouth speaking great things,"** and it spoke **"words against the Most High"** (Dan 7:8, 25).
- It was to **"wear out the saints of the Most High"** (Dan 7:25).
- It was to **"think to change times and the law"** (Dan 7:25).
- It was allotted special powers for **"a time, two times, and half a time"** (Dan 7:25).[26]

The little horn in Dan 11:36–39 does not fit Antiochus IV Epiphanes's end.[27] This part of Daniel can be viewed as "prophecy which fits in very badly if we restrict and apply it to the closing events of Antiochus's career."[28] The description of the king of the north in Dan 11:36–45 also contradicts Antiochus IV Epiphanes's religious practices. In conclusion, Antiochus should not be identified with that king.[29]

If Dan 11:40–45 is applied to Antiochus IV Epiphanes, then it was a "prophecy that was never fulfilled."[30] Prior to attempting to crush the Jewish opposition, Antiochus IV went to the east to raise funds for his military operations. There he failed to rob the temple of Artemis in Elymais because

---

25. Baldwin, *Daniel*, 140; Lucas, *Daniel*, 189–94; and Maxwell, *God Cares*, 1:122–43.

26. See Maxwell, *God Cares*, 1:127.

27. Smith, *Sanctuary and Its Cleansing*, 44. See also Pusey, *Daniel the Prophet*, 136–40.

28. Boutflower, *In and Around*, 3.

29. About Antiochus IV, Livy, 41.20.5, wrote, "Nevertheless in two great and important respects his soul was truly royal—in his benefactions to cities and in the honours paid to the gods," and also Polybius 26.1.10 concluded, "But in the sacrifices he furnished to the cities and in the honours he paid to gods he surpassed all his predecessors." Quoted also in Mercer, "Benefactions of Antiochus IV Epiphanes," 89–93.

30. Boutflower, *In and Around*, 3.

he was overpowered by the local residents. While returning from this failed venture, he went mad and died at Tabae in Persia in 164 BC.[31]

Second Maccabees 9:28 comments that Antiochus IV "came to the end of his life by a most pitiable fate, among the mountains in a strange land." When the activities in the text do not fit Antiochus IV, the defenders of a Maccabean date for Daniel take the passage (Dan 11:40–45) as merely the author's own "speculation."[32]

Antiochus IV Epiphanes has been misidentified as the little horn in the book of Daniel. To view Antiochus IV Epiphanes as the little horn is an *ad hominem* fallacy (a fallacy that appeals more to personal considerations than to logic), which has been subtly crafted into the interpretation of the book of Daniel. It has been used to deliberately disassociate the fourth kingdom (where the little horn actually originates) from the hermeneutics pertaining to the little horn. Scholars who posit this type of inaccurate inference, that Antiochus IV is the little horn, have distorted the basic theme and concerns in the book of Daniel.

In fact, the book of Daniel never mentions or alludes to Antiochus IV Epiphanes, and therefore the Maccabean hypotheses is not an accurate claim on the book of Daniel.

The chronology of the earthly kingdoms based on the image (Dan 2) and the animals (Dan 7; 8) has been distorted to accommodate Antiochus IV Epiphanes. For example, some scholars have argued that while Nebuchadnezzar was "the head of gold" (Dan 2:37, 38), Antiochus IV Epiphanes was "the toes" (Dan 2:41–43) as well as "the little horn" (Dan 7:8).[33]

Interpreting the text of Daniel in light of Antiochus IV Epiphanes has caused some scholars to argue that the theme of Daniel is to comfort beleaguered Jews during persecution by Antiochus IV. These scholars argue that compilers wrote the book in the second century BC.[34] Although these views are widely accepted today, the internal evidence from the text and the archaeological finds from the ancient Near East do not show Antiochus IV Epiphanies as playing a role in Daniel.

The appearance of Antiochus IV Epiphanes in the historical arena does not fit into the chronology of the book of Daniel. Antiochus IV came on the scene and then disappeared into history before the little horn arose. Antiochus IV belonged to the Greek (third) kingdom, whereas the

---

31. Polybius, *Histories of Polybius* 2:353, 433; Josephus, *Antiquities of the Jews*, 12.9.1; 1 Macc 6:1–17; v. 16 says he died in 163 BC; 2 Macc 1:13–17; 9:1–29.

32. Boutflower, *In and Around*, 4.

33. Redditt and Kruschwitz, "Nebuchadnezzar as the Head of Gold," 415.

34. For example, see, Di Lella, *Daniel*, 12–14; Hartman and Di Lella, *Book of Daniel*, 43–45; and Collins, *Daniel*, 62–65.

little horn king chronologically belonged to the fourth kingdom, Christian Rome (Dan 7:7-8). Antiochus IV persecuted the conservative Jews between 168 BC and 165 BC.[35] The little horn kingdom dominated for 1260 years (Dan 7:25),[36] that is, from AD 538 to 1798.

Daniel 7:26 indicates that the little horn's power would be taken away at the last judgment. The saints will then receive the eternal kingdom (Dan 7:27). The book of Daniel, therefore, does not mention, allude to, or implicate Antiochus IV Epiphanes in its historical outline.

The following observations demonstrate that Antiochus IV Epiphanes is not mentioned in the book of Daniel, nor is he to be associated with the little horn:

- The little horn rises from the last or fourth beast kingdom in Dan 7 (Roman Empire). Antiochus IV Epiphanes, a Greek king, belonged to the third beast kingdom, that of Greece. Chronologically he does not fit in Daniel's outline of history. Moreover, in Dan 7:14, 22, 26, 27, the little horn kingdom is followed by the last judgment, and the divine eschatological and eternal kingdom which will be received by the saints.[37]

- Antiochus IV Epiphanes was not a world power. He was just one of the Greek rulers. He did not completely eradicate or destroy three kingdoms when he rose into prominence (Dan 7:8, 24).[38]

- According to 1 Macc 1:54, Antiochus IV Epiphanes desolated and defiled the temple on 15 Chislev 167 BC. 1 Macc 4:52 stated that on 25 Chislev, 164 BC, the Jews reestablished the temple services. The time

---

35. Some prefer the dates 167–164 BC; see Whitehorne, "Antiochus" (*ABD*, 1:270–71).

36. Scholars point out that "time" in Dan 7:25 stands for a year (see for example Porteous, *Daniel*, 114; Collins, *Daniel*, 322; Walvoord, *Daniel*, 176; Lucas, *Daniel*, 194) which is a lunar calendar composed of 360 days (disputed by Lucas, *Daniel*, 193–94). The "times" would be double, amounting to 720 days, and one-half time would be 180 days. If all these days represent years (the day-year principle in biblical prophecy; see Num 14:31–35; Ezek 4:1–8) then 360+720+180=1,260 days, which, too, are a symbol of 1,260 years. The 1,260 years is the time the little horn power (Dan 7:25) was given for its devastating role. For the application of these years, see Montgomery, *Book of Daniel*, 313; and Stefanovic, *Daniel*, 281–82. Also, see Montor, *Lives and Times*, 2/1:489–90; and Maxwell, *God Cares*, 1:130–35.

37. Pusey, *Daniel the Prophet*, 118; Gulley, "Why the Danielic Little Horn," in Merling, *To Understand the Scriptures*, 192–93; and Shea, *Selected Studies on Prophetic Interpretation*, 31–66. See Stefanovic's *Daniel*, 322–23, 327–33.

38. See Braverman, *Jerome's Commentary on Daniel*, 90–94; Josephus, *Antiquities of the Jews*, 12.5–9; 13.5–8; Josephus, *Wars of the Jews*, 1.1.1–6; and Pusey, *Daniel the Prophet*, 118–20.

period during which the temple was nonfunctional is exactly three years and ten days. This does not fit any prophetic time outline in the book of Daniel. Efforts to associate the three years and ten days with the 2,300 days and evenings of Dan 8:14, or any other time frame in Daniel, have not been successful.[39]

- From the New Testament perspective in the first century AD (Matt 24:15–16; Mark 13:14; Luke 21:20), the abomination that desolates (Dan 8:11–13; 9:27; 11:31; 12:11) was still anticipated. It was fulfilled in AD 70 when Antiochus IV was long gone.[40]

The little horn must fit all of the biblical identifying marks—not just some of them. Antiochus IV fails to fit much of what Daniel says about the little horn. His inclusion in the interpretation of Daniel is a typical *ad hominem* fallacy which cannot be supported by history, the biblical text, or responsible hermeneutics.

THE MAJOR SCHOOLS OF INTERPRETATION ON THE BOOK OF DANIEL

Different schools of thought have developed through the years in an attempt to understand the book of Daniel. As a result, the major lines of interpretation of the book Daniel can be broadly categorized as preterism, futurism, historicism, and historical-criticism.[41] These approaches can differ widely in their approach to the text of Daniel, but they also overlap in many instances.[42] Each of these four lines has ignored archaeology as an interpretive resource for the book of Daniel. The nature of the text requires both symbolic and literal interpretation methods. The scholar seeking to understand and explain the book must move judiciously in determining the criteria used to distinguish that which is symbolic from that which is literal throughout the entire book.

---

39. Josephus, *Antiquities of the Jews*, 12.5.3–5; Gulley, "Why the Danielic Little Horn," 194–96; Ray, "*Abomination of Desolation* in Daniel 9:27," in Merling, *To Understand the Scriptures*, 209; Gane, *Altar Call*, 284–86; and Gane, *Who's Afraid of the Judgment?*, 83–85.

40. See Wright, *Daniel and His Prophecies*, 240–41.

41. Wright, *Daniel and his Prophecies*, xii–xxii; Ford, דניאל, 65; Maxwell, *God Cares*, 1:122; Shea, *Daniel 7—12*, 33; Shea, *Daniel 1—7*, 130; Hasel, "Interpretations of the Chronology of the Seventy Weeks," 3–63; and Núñez, *Vision of Daniel 8*, 429–432.

42. For broader interpretive differences see Davidson, "Biblical Principles for Interpreting Apocalyptic Prophecy," in du Preez, *Prophetic Principles*, 55.

INTERPRETATION VIEWS ON DANIEL

Preterism considers the predictive text of the book of Daniel *vaticinium ex eventu* and assumes that it has been fulfilled in the past.[43] Preterists mostly believe that all of the historical events in the book culminated in the person of Antiochus IV Epiphanes. This ruler is viewed as the anti-Christ. Some preterists believe that all of Daniel's prophecies were fulfilled in the second century BC. Other preterists regard the book of Daniel to have been a revelation from God, but take its historical fulfillment to have occurred from the sixth century BC up to the time of the first coming of Christ or the fall of the Roman Empire.[44] They outline the historical kingdoms mainly as Babylonian, Median, Persian, and Greek. Some preterists accept the supernatural element of Daniel, while others object to it.[45]

Futurists or dispensationalists believe that the predictive sections of the book of Daniel are *vaticinium ante eventu*, and that much of what has been written is yet to be fulfilled in the far future.[46] The point of departure for this approach is the outlining of the historical kingdoms of Daniel as Neo-Babylonian, Medo-Persian, Greek, and Roman.[47]

The proponents of futurism believe that the entire Christian era has no historical significance in relation to Daniel. They place a parenthesis or gap in the historical timeline from the first coming of Christ to about seven years before His second coming. They anticipate the fulfillment of most of Daniel's symbolical predictions in the last seven years of the earth's history.[48]

The Danielic authorship is accepted by futurists, and dated to the sixth century BC. There is no association of the little horn with either Antiochus IV Epiphanes or Christian Rome.[49] Instead, the person and activities of the little horn (Dan 7) are associated with the antichrist who is to be expected in the eschatological future.[50]

---

43. Interpreters who consider the book of Daniel to have been written in the second century BC are preterist. Examples of those who hold this view include Hartman and Di Lella, *Book of Daniel* (1977); Porteous, *Daniel* (1965); Goldingay, *Daniel* (1989); and Collins, *Daniel* (1993).

44. See Núñez, *Vision of Daniel*, 8, 11; and Pfandl, *Time of the End in the Book of Daniel*, 19.

45. See Ford, דניאל, 65.

46. Examples of such interpreters include: Leupold, *Exposition of Daniel*; Walvoord, *Daniel*; Archer, *Encyclopedia of Bible Difficulties*, 282–93; and Young, *Prophecy of Daniel* (1949). See also Hasel, "Interpretations of the Chronology of the Seventy Weeks," 13–25.

47. Archer, *Encyclopedia of Bible Difficulties*, 282.

48. Núñez, *Vision of Daniel* 8, 11; Shea, *Daniel 7—12*, 33; and Shea, *Daniel 1—7*, 130.

49. Bultema, *Commentary on Daniel*, 245–47.

50. Price, *Coming Anti-Christ*, 15–43.

APPENDIX C

Historicism views Daniel to have been a historic figure who lived in the seventh to sixth century BC. It accepts that Daniel was responsible for writing the book that bears his name. This approach takes the predictions of Daniel to cover the entire human history without any gap from the Neo-Babylonian times to the eschatological time of the end.[51] The predictions of Daniel are accepted as projecting a continuous historical timeline of the past, the present, and the future.[52]

Historical-Criticism rejects the idea that the book of Daniel is predictive, and that it is a revelation from God. It takes Daniel to be a *vaticinum ex eventu* apocalypse, or a reflection of the Jewish political and religious status quo during their persecution by Antiochus IV Epiphanes.[53] The role of Antiochus IV Epiphanes in the interpretation of Daniel is magnified, and he is identified as the little horn.[54] (See table 14.) The Maccabean hypothesis is the mark of this interpretive approach, although it cannot satisfactorily explain the dating of the book of Daniel. A second-century BC date is assigned for the final compilation to the book of Daniel, even though archaeological and textual evidence favor a much earlier time of writing.

The diversity of these four interpretation schools in the analysis of the book of Daniel has brought a wide range of ideas to the study (see table 14). These approaches have also brought many questions into the study of Daniel. To bring about a more coherent understanding of the book, an interpretive approach should use appropriate exegetical tools in a responsible manner when working with the text and the related archaeological and literary finds.

---

51. Archer, *Jerome's Commentary on Daniel*, 15–18; Charles, *Book of Daniel*, ix–xiii; Pfandl, *Time of the End*, 20; Ford, דניאל, 68–70; Shea, *Daniel 1—7* (1996); Shea, *Daniel 7—12* (1996); Doukhan, *Daniel* (1987); Doukhan, *Secrets of Daniel*, 41; and Stefanovic, *Daniel* (2005).

52. Shea, *Daniel 7—12*, 33; and Shea, *Daniel*, 130.

53. Montgomery, *Book of Daniel* (1927); Di Lella, *Daniel* (1997); Collins, *Daniel* (1993); see also Hasel, "Interpretations of the Chronology of the Seventy Weeks," 29–46; and Núñez, *Vision of Daniel 8*, 11.

54. Collins and Flint, *Book of Daniel*, 2 vols. (2002).

Table 14
THE FOUR INTERPRETATION STRAINS

	Historicist	Preterist	Futurist	Historical-Critical
Daniel 2:				
Gold	Babylon	Babylon	Babylon	Babylon
Silver	Medo-Persia	Media	Medo-Persia	Media
Bronze	Greece	Persia	Greece	Persia
Iron	Rome	Greece	Rome	Greece
Iron & Clay	Divided Rome	Seleucid Kings	Future Kings	Antiochus IV
Daniel 7:				
Lion	Babylon	Babylon	Babylon	Babylon
Bear	Medo-Persia	Media	Medo-Persia	Media
Leopard	Greece	Persia	Greece	Persia
4th Beast	Rome	Greece	Rome	Greece
10 Horns	Divided Rome	Seleucid Kings	10 Future Kings	Greek Kings
Little Horn	Papal Rome	Antiochus IV	Future Antichrist	Antiochus IV
Daniel 8:				
Ram	Medo-Persia	Medo-Persia	Medo-Persia	Persia
He-Goat	Greece	Greece	Greece	Greece
Little Horn	Papal Rome.	Antiochus IV	Future Antichrist	Antiochus IV
Daniel 11:				
vv. 1–2	Persia	Persia	Persia	Persia
vv. 3–19	Greece	Greece	Greece	Greece
vv. 20–39	Rome	Antiochus IV	Antiochus IV	Antiochus IV
vv. 40–45	Papal Rome	Antiochus IV	Future Antichrist	Antiochus IV

In the effort to understand the book of Daniel, the Maccabean hypothesis attempted to posit a second-century BC date for the document. Unfortunately, that has not brought forth a satisfactory reconstruction of ancient history. Daniel does not refer or allude to Antiochus IV Epiphanes at all. The book's socioreligious and historico-political emphases by far transcend the person and activities of Antiochus IV Epiphanes, who is erroneously identified as the little horn by some interpreters.

In conclusion, the major concern of the book of Daniel is the outline of the chronological succession of world empires leading to the time of the end when a divine kingdom will displace all of the earthly kingdoms.

BIBLIOGRAPHY

Ackerman, Susan. "'And the Women Knead Dough': The Worship of the Queen of Heaven in Sixth-Century Judah." In *Women in the Hebrew Bible*, edited by Alice Bach, 21–32. New York: Routledge, 1999.

———. "The Queen Mother and the Cult in Ancient Israel." In *Women in the Hebrew Bible*, edited by Alice Bach, 179–94. New York: Routledge, 1999.

Adams, Robert McCormick, Jr. *Heartland of Cities: Surveys of Ancient Settlement and Land Use on the Central Flood Plain of the Euphrates*. Chicago: University of Chicago Press, 1981.

Aejmelaeus, Anneli. "'Nebuchadnezzar, My Servant': Redaction History and Textual Development in Jer 27." In *Interpreting Translation: Studies on the LXX and Ezekiel in Honour of Johan Lust*, edited by F. García Martínez and M. Vervenne, 1–18. Bibliotheca Ephemeridum Theologicarum Lovaniensium 192. Leuven: University Press, 2005.

Aesop. *Three Hundred and Fifty Aesop's Fables*. Translated by G. T. Townsend. Chicago: M. A. Donohus, 1815.

Agnes, Michael, and David B. Guralnik, eds. *Webster's New World College Dictionary*. 4th ed. Foster City, CA: IDG, 2001.

Aharoni, Yohanan. "Arad: Its Inscriptions and Temple." *Biblical Archaeologist* 31 (1968) 2–32.

———. "Hebrew Ostraca from Tel Arad." *Israel Exploration Journal* 16 (1966) 1–7.

———. "The Use of Hieratic Numerals in Hebrew Ostraca and the Shekel Weights." *Bulletin of the American Schools of Oriental Research* 184 (1966) 13–19.

Aistleitner, Joseph. *Wörterbuch der Ugaritischen Sprache*. Berlin: Akademie, 1965.

Albani, Matthias. "The 'One Like a Son of Man' (Dan 7:13) and the Royal Ideology." In *Enoch and Qumran Origins*, edited by Gabriele Boccaccini, 47–53. Grand Rapids: Eerdmans, 2003.

Albenda, Pauline. *The Palace of Sargon, King of Assyria: Monumental Wall Reliefs at Dur-Sharrukin*. Paris: Editions Recherche sur les civilisations, 1986.

Albertz, Rainer. "Darius in the Place of Cyrus: The First Edition of Deutero-Isaiah (Isaiah 40.1—52.12) in 521 BCE." *Journal for the Study of the Old Testament* 27 (2003) 371–83.

Albrektson, Bertil. "On the Syntax of אהיה אשר אהיה in Exodus 3:14." In *Words and Meanings*, edited by Peter R. Ackroyd, 15–28. Cambridge: Cambridge University Press, 1968.

Albright, W. F. *The Archaeology of Palestine*. Harmondsworth: Penguin, 1949.

———. *The Archaeology of Palestine and the Bible*. New York: Fleming H. Revell, 1935.
———. *The Bible After Twenty Years of Archaeology, 1932-1952*. Pittsburgh, PA: Biblical Colloquium, 1954.
———. "Cilicia and Babylonia Under the Chaldean Kings." *Bulletin of the American Schools of Oriental Research* 120 (1950) 22-25.
———. *From the Stone Age to Christianity: Monotheism and the Historical Process*. 2nd ed. Garden City, NY: Doubleday, 1957.
———. "King Joiachin in Exile." *Biblical Archaeologist* 5 (1942) 49-55.
———. "The Seal of Eliakim and the Latest Preexilic History of Judah, with Some Observations on Ezekiel." *Journal of Biblical Literature* 51 (1932) 77-106.
Alexander, John Bruce. *Early Babylonian Letters and Economic Texts*. Babylonian Inscriptions in the Collection of James B. Nies 7. New Haven, CT: Yale University Press, 1943.
———. "New Light on the Fiery Furnace." *Journal of Biblical Literature* 69 (1950) 375-76.
Alexander, P. J. "Appendix: English Translation of Slavonic Daniel." In *The Byzantine Apocalyptic Tradition*, edited by Dorothy de F. Abrahamse, 65-72. Berkeley, CA: University of California Press, 1985.
Ali, Fadhil A. "Blowing the Horn for Official Announcement." *Sumer* 20 (1964) 66-68.
Ali, Japheth Ibn. *A Commentary on the Book of Daniel*. Edited and translated by D. S. Margoliouth. Oxford: Clarendon, 1889.
Allegro, John M., and Arnold M. Anderson. *Qumran Cave 4: I (4Q158-4Q186)*. Discoveries in the Judaean Desert of Jordan 5. Oxford: Clarendon, 1968.
al-Masiḥ, Y. 'Abd. "A Fragmentary Farmer's Almanac." *Les cahiers coptes* 10 (1956) 5-9.
Alobaidi, Joseph. *The Book of Daniel: The Commentary of R. Saadia Gaon: Edition and Translation*. New York: Peter Lang, 2006.
Andrews, Carol. *The Rosetta Stone*. London: British Museum, 1984.
Archer, Gleason L. Jr. *New International Encyclopedia of Bible Difficulties*. Grand Rapids: Zondervan, 1982.
———. *A Survey of Old Testament Introduction*. Chicago: Moody, 1994.
Archer, Gleason L. Jr., trans. *Jerome's Commentary on Daniel*. Grand Rapids: Baker, 1958.
Arjomand, S. A. "Islamic Apocalypticism in the Classical Period." In *The Encyclopedia of Apocalypticism: Apocalypticism in Western History and Culture*, edited by Bernard McGinn, 2:238-83. New York: Continuum, 1998.
———. "The Use of Aramaic in the Hebrew Bible: Another Look at Bilingualism in Ezra and Daniel." *Journal of Northwest Semitic Languages* 22 (1996) 1-16.
———. *Who Were the Babylonians?* Atlanta: Society of Biblical Literature, 2004.
Arnold, Bill T., and Bryan E. Beyer. *Readings from the Ancient Near East: Primary Sources for Old Testament Study*. Grand Rapids: Baker Academic, 2002.
Ashton, Thomas L. *Byron's Hebrew Melodies*. Austin, TX: University of Texas Press, 1972.
Aufrecht, Walter E. *A Corpus of Ammonite Inscriptions*. Lewiston: Edwin Mellen, 1989.
Avigad, Naaman. "Baruch the Scribe and Jerahmeel the King's Son." *Biblical Archaeologist* 42 (1979) 114-18.
———. "Baruch the Scribe and Jerahmeel the King's Son." *Israel Exploration Journal* 28 (1978) 52-56.

———. *Hebrew Bullae from the Time of Jeremiah*. Jerusalem: Israel Exploration Society, 1986.

———. "The Seal of Jezebel." *Israel Exploration Journal* 14 (1964) 274–76.

Awad, G. "Bābil." In *Encyclopaedia of Islam*, edited by H. A. R. Gibb et al., 1:846. 2nd ed. London: Luzac, 1960.

Baez-Camargo, Gonzalo. *Archaeological Commentary on the Bible*. Garden City, NY: Doubleday, 1984.

Bahat, D. *The Illustrated Atlas of Jerusalem*. Jerusalem: Israel Map and Publishing Company; New York: Simon & Schuster, 1990.

———. "Jerusalem." In *Oxford Encyclopedia of Archaeology in the Near East*, edited by Eric M. Meyers, 3:224–38. Oxford: Oxford University Press, 1997.

———. "The Western Wall Tunnels." In *Ancient Jerusalem Revealed: Expanded Edition 2000*, edited by Hillel Geva, 177–90. Jerusalem: Israel Exploration Society 2000.

Baker, Warren, and Eugene Carpenter. *The Complete Word Study Dictionary Old Testament*. Chattanooga, TN: AMG, 2003.

Baldwin, Joyce G. *Daniel: An Introduction and Commentary*. Tyndale Old Testament Commentaries. Leicester: InterVarsity, 1978.

Balz, Horst, and Gerhard Schneider, eds. *Exegetical Dictionary of the New Testament*. 3 vols. Grand Rapids: Eerdmans, 1990–93.

Bandstra, Barry L. *Reading the Old Testament: An Introduction to the Hebrew Bible*. Belmont, CA: Wadsworth, 2004.

Barkay, Gabriel. "The King of Babylon or a Judaean Official?" *Israel Exploration Journal* 45 (1995) 41–47.

Barkay, Gabriel, et al. "The Amulets from Ketef Hinnon: A New Edition and Evaluation." *Bulletin of the American Schools of Oriental Research* 334 (2004) 41–71.

Barkay, Gabriel, and Zach Dvira. "Relics in Rubble: The Temple Mount Sifting Project." *Biblical Archaeology Review* 42 (2016) 44–55, 64.

Barnett, Richard. *Sculptures from the North Palace of Ashurbanipal at Nineveh (668–627 B.C.)*. London: British Museum, 1976.

Baron, Salo W., and Alexander Marx, eds. *Jewish Studies in Memory of George A. Kohut*. New York: Alexander Kohut Memorial Foundation, 1935.

Barstad, Hans M. *The Babylonian Captivity of the Book of Isaiah*. Olso: Novus, 1997.

———. *The Myth of the Empty Land*. Olso: Scandanavian University Press, 1996.

Beale, G. K. "The Interpretive Problem of Revelation 1:19." *Novum Testamentum* 34 (1992) 360–86.

Beaulieu, Paul-Alain. "A New Inscription of Nebuchadnezzar II Commemorating the Restoration of Emah in Babylon." *Iraq* 59 (1997) 93–96.

———. *The Reign of Nabonidus, King of Babylon, 556–539 B.C.* Ann Arbor, MI: University Microfilms International, 1992.

Becking, Bob. "Baalis, the King of the Ammonites: An Epigraphical Note on Jeremiah 40:14." *Journal of Semitic Studies* 38 (1993) 15–24.

———. "The Seal of Baalisha, King of the Ammonites: Some Remarks." *Biblische Notizen* 97 (1999) 13–17.

Bemont, Charles, and G. Monod. *Medieval Europe: From 395 to 1270*. New York: Henry Holt, 1903.

Benjamin. *The Itinerary of Benjamin of Tudela: Critical Text, Translation and Commentary*. Translated by Marcus Nathan Adler. New York: Feldheim, 1964.

BIBLIOGRAPHY

Betlyon, John W. "Neo-Babylonian Military Operations Other than War in Judah and Jerusalem." In *Judah and the Judeans in the Neo-Babylonian Period*, edited by O. Lipschits and J. Blenkinsopp, 263–83. Winona Lake, IN: Eisenbrauns, 2003.

Bezold, C. "Two Inscriptions of Nabonidus." *Proceedings of the Society for Biblical Archaeology* 11 (1889) 86–101.

Biella, Joan Copeland. *Dictionary of Old South Arabic: Sabaean Dialect*. Harvard Semitic Studies 25. Chico, CA: Scholars, 1982.

Bienkowski, Peter, and Allan Millard, eds. *Dictionary of the Ancient Near East*. Philadelphia: University of Pennsylvania, 2000.

Biggs, Robert D. "More Babylonian 'Prophecies.'" *Iraq* 29 (1967) 117–32.

Biran, Avraham. "What Is Biblical Archaeology?" In *Jesus and Archaeology*, edited by James H. Charlesworth, 1–8. Grand Rapids: Eerdmans, 2006.

Black, Jeremy, and Anthony Green. *Gods, Demons and Symbols of Ancient Mesopotamia*. Austin, TX: University of Texas Press, 1997.

Blackie, John Stuart. *Homer and the Iliad*. Edinburgh: Edmonston and Douglas, 1866.

Bland, N. "On the Muhammedan Science of Tâbír or Interpretation of Dreams." *Journal of the Royal Asiatic Society of Great Britain and Ireland* 16 (1856) 118–71.

Blenkinsopp, Joseph. "The Bible, Archaeology and Politics or the Empty Land Revisited." *Journal for the Study of the Old Testament* 27 (2002) 169–87.

Bongenaar, A. C. V. M. *The Neo-Babylonian Ebabbar Temple at Sippar: Its Administration and Its Prosopography*. Istanbul: Nederlands Historisch-Archaeologisch Instituut te Istanbul, 1997.

Bongenaar, A. C. V. M., and B. J. J. Haring. "Egyptians in Neo-Babylonian Sippar." *Journal of Cuneiform Studies* 46 (1994) 59–72.

Borger, R. "Gott Marduk und Gott-König Šulgi als Propheten: Zwei prophetische Texte." *Bibliotheca Orientalis* 28 (1971) 3–24.

Börker-Klähn, J. *Altvorderasiatische Bildstelen und vergleichbare Felsreliefs*. Mainz: Philipp von Zabern, 1982.

Botterweck, G. Johannes, et al., eds. *Theological Dictionary of the Old Testament*. Translated by David E. Green et al. 17 vols. Grand Rapids: Eerdmans, 1974–2021.

Boutflower, Charles. *In and Around the Book of Daniel*. Grand Rapids: Zondervan, 1977.

Braun, Joachim. *Music in Ancient Israel/Palestine*. Grand Rapids: Eerdmans, 2002.

———. "Musical Instruments." In *Oxford Encyclopedia of Archaeology in the Near East*, edited by Eric M. Meyers, 4:70–79. Oxford: Oxford University Press, 1997.

Braverman, Jay. *Jerome's Commentary on Daniel: A Study of Comparative Jewish and Christian Interpretations of the Hebrew Bible*. Washington, DC: Catholic Biblical Association of America, 1978.

Brenner, Athalya. *The Israelite Woman: Social Role and Literary Type in Biblical Narrative*. Sheffield: JSOT Press, 1985.

Brewer, David. "*Mene mene teqel uparsin*: Daniel 5:25 in Cuneiform." *Tyndale Bulletin* 42 (1991) 310–16.

Briant, Pierre. *From Cyrus to Alexander: A History of the Persian Empire*. Winona Lake, IN: Eisenbrauns, 2002.

Brinkman, J. A. "Babylonia in the Shadow of Assyria." In *The Cambridge Ancient History*, edited by John Boardman et al., 2:1–70. 3rd ed. Cambridge: Cambridge University Press, 1991.

BIBLIOGRAPHY

———. *A Political History of Post-Kassite Babylonia, 1158–722 B.C.* Rome: Pontifical Biblical Institute, 1968.
———. *Prelude to Empire: Babylonian Society and Politics, 747–626 B.C.* Philadelphia: University Museum, 1984.
Britt, Albert Sydney III. *The Wars of Napoleon.* View Point Military History Series. Wayne, NJ: Avery, 1985.
Brock, S. P. "Jewish Traditions in Syriac Sources." *Journal of Jewish Studies* 30 (1979) 212–32.
Brooke, Alan England, et al., eds. *The Old Testament in Greek: According to the Text of Codex Vaticanus, Supplemented from Other Uncial Manuscripts, With a Critical Apparatus Containing the Variants of the Chief Ancient Authorities for the Text of the Septuagint.* 3 vols. Cambridge: Cambridge University Press, 1906–40.
Brooke, George J. "Parabiblical Prophetic Narratives." In *The Dead Sea Scrolls After Fifty Years: A Comprehensive Assessment*, edited by P. W. Flint and J. C. Vanderkam, 271–301. Leiden: Brill, 1998.
Broshi, Magen, and Esther Eshel. "The Greek King Is Antiochus IV (4QHistorical Text 4Q248)." *Journal of Jewish Studies* 48 (1997) 120–29.
Brosius, Maria. *Women in Ancient Persia 559–539 BC.* Oxford: Clarendon, 1996.
Brown, Francis, et al. *The Brown-Driver-Briggs Hebrew and English Lexicon with an Appendix Containing the Biblical Aramaic.* Peabody, MA: Hendrickson, 1999.
Brown, Raymond E. *Recent Discoveries and the Biblical World.* Wilmington, DE: Michael Glazier, 1982.
Brunner, Hellmut. *Altägyptische Religion: Grundzüge.* Darmstadt: Wissenschaftliche Buchgesellschaft, 1989.
Bryce, T. R. "A Recently Discovered Cult in Lycia." *Journal of Religious History* 10 (1978) 115–27.
Buchanan, George Wesley. *Revelation and Redemption: Jewish Documents of Deliverance from the Fall of Jerusalem to the Death of Nahmanides.* Dillsboro, NC: Western North Carolina, 1978.
Buckingham, James Silk. *Autobiography of James Silk Buckingham, Including His Voyages, Travels, Adventures, Etc.* London: Longman, 1855.
Budge, E. A. Wallis. *Babylonian Life and History.* 2nd ed. London: Religious Tract Society, 1925.
———. *The Rosetta Stone.* London: British Museum, 1955.
Bultema, Harry. *Commentary on Daniel.* Grand Rapids: Kregel, 1988.
Burnett, Joel S. "Ammon, Moab and Edom: Gods and Kingdoms East of the Jordan." *Biblcal Archaeology Review* 42 (2016) 26–40, 66–67.
Burstein, Stanley Mayer. *The Babylonica of Berossus.* Malibu, CA: Undena, 1978.
Butler, S. A. L. *Mesopotamian Conceptions of Dreams and Dream Rituals.* Münster: Ugarit-Verlag, 1998.
Buttrick, George A., ed. *The Interpreter's Dictionary of the Bible.* 4 vols. New York: Abingdon, 1962.
Caquot, A. "Sur les quatre bêtes de Daniel VII." *Semitica* 5 (1955) 5–13.
Caragounis, Chrys C. "History and Supra-History: Daniel and the Four Empires." In *The Book of Daniel in the Light of New Findings*, edited by A. S. van der Woude, 387–97. Leuven: Leuven University Press, 1993.
———. *The Son of Man: Vision and Interpretation.* Wissenschaftliche Untersuchungen zum Neuen Testament 38. Tübingen: Mohr, 1986.

BIBLIOGRAPHY

Carroll, Robert P. "The Myth of the Empty Land." *Semeia* 59 (1992) 79–93.
Carter, Elizabeth, and Matthew W. Stolper. *Elam: Surveys of Political History and Archaeology*. Berkeley, CA: University of California Press, 1984.
Cary, M. *A History of the Greek World from 323 to 146 B.C.* New York: MacMillan, 1939.
Champdor, Albert. *Babylon*. Translated by Elsa Coult. London: Eleks, 1958.
Charles, R. H. *Critical and Exegetical Commentary on the Book of Daniel*. Oxford: Clarendon, 1929.
Charlesworth, James H. *The Old Testament Pseudepigrapha and the New Testament*. Harrisburg, PA: Trinity, 1998.
———, ed. *The Old Testament Pseudepigrapha: Apocalyptic Literature and Testaments* 1. New York: Doubleday, 1983.
———, ed. *The Old Testament Pseudepigrapha: Expansions of the "Old Testament" and Legends, Wisdom and Philosophical Literature, Prayers, Psalms and Odes, Fragments of Lost Judeo-Hellenistic Works* 2. London: Darto, Longman and Todd, 1985.
Cheyne, T. K. "Dura." In *Encyclopaedia Biblica*, edited by T. K. Cheyne and J. Sutherland Black, 1:1142–43. London: Adam and Charles Black, 1899.
Clancy, Frank. "The Date of the LXX." *Scandinavian Journal of the Old Testament* 16 (2002) 207–25.
Clarke, E. G. *Targum Pseudo-Jonathan of the Pentateuch: Text and Concordance*. Hoboken, NJ: KTAV, 1984.
Clay, Albert T. *Miscellaneous Inscriptions in the Yale Babylonian Collection* 1. New Haven, CT: Yale University Press, 1915.
———. *Neo-Babylonian Letters from Erech*. Yale Oriental Series 3. New Haven, CT: Yale University Press, 1919.
Clifford, Richard J. "The Roots of Apocalypticism in the Near Eastern Myth." In *The Continuum History of Apocalypticism*, edited by Bernard McGinn et al., 3–29. New York: Continuum, 2003.
Clines, David J. A., ed. *The Dictionary of Classical Hebrew*. 5 vols. Sheffield: Sheffield Academic Press, 1996.
Cohen, A., trans. *The Babylonian Talmud: Tractate Berakot*. Cambridge: Cambridge University Press, 1921.
Colless, Brian E. "Cyrus the Persian as Darius the Mede in the Book of Daniel." *Journal for the Study of the Old Testament* 56 (1992) 113–26.
Collins, John J. *Apocalypse: The Morphology of a Genre*. Semeia 14. Missoula, MT: Scholars, 1979.
———. *The Apocalyptic Imagination: An Introduction to Jewish Apocalyptic Literature*. 2nd ed. Grand Rapids: Eerdmans, 1998.
———. *The Apocalyptic Visions of the Book of Daniel*. Missoula, MT: Scholars, 1977.
———. *Apocalypticism in the Dead Sea Scrolls*. London: Routledge, 1997.
———. "Current Issues in the Study of Daniel." In *The Book of Daniel: Composition and Reception*, edited by John J. Collins and Peter W. Flint, 1:1–15. Leiden: Brill, 2002.
———. *Daniel*. Hermeneia. Minneapolis: Fortress, 1993.
———. *Daniel: With an Introduction to Apocalyptic Literature*. The Forms of Old Testament Literature 20. Grand Rapids: Eerdmans, 1984.

———. "From Prophecy to Apocalypticism: The Expectation of the End." In *The Continuum History of Apocalypticism*, edited by Bernard McGinn et al., 64–88. New York: Continuum, 2003.

———. *Introduction to the Hebrew Bible*. Minneapolis: Fortress, 2004.

———. "The Meaning of 'The End' in the Book of Daniel." In *Of Scribes and Scrolls: Studies on the Hebrew Bible, Intertestamental Judaism, and Christian Origins*, edited by Harold W. Attridge et al., 91–98. New York: University Press of America, 1990.

———. "Pseudo-Daniel Revisited." *Revue de Qumrân* 17 (1996) 111–31.

———. "The Sibylline Oracles: A New Translation and Introduction." In *The Old Testament Pseudepigrapha: Apocalyptic Literature and Testaments*, edited by James H. Charlesworth, 1:317–472. New York: Doubleday, 1985.

———. "The Son of Man and the Saints of the Most High in the Book of Daniel." *Journal of Biblical Literature* 93 (1974) 50–66.

———. "Stirring Up the Great Sea: The Religio-Historical Background of Daniel 7." In *The Book of Daniel in the Light of New Findings*, edited by A. S. van der Woude, 121–36. Leuven: Leuven University Press, 1993.

Collon, Dominique. *Near Eastern Seals*. Los Angeles: University of California Press, 1990.

Conybeare, F. C., et al. *The Story of Ahikar from the Syriac, Arabic, Armenian, Ethiopic, Greek and Slavonic Versions*. London: C. T. Clay and Sons, 1898.

Coogan, Michael David. "Life in the Diaspora: Jews at Nippur in the Fifth Century B.C." *Biblical Archaeologist* 37 (1974) 6–12.

———. *West Semitic Personal Names in the Murasû Documents*. Cambridge, MA: Harvard Semitic Museum, 1976.

Cook, D. B. "An Early Muslim Daniel Apocalypse." *Arabica* 49 (2002) 55–96.

Cook, Edward M. "'In the Plain of the Wall' (Dan 3:1)." *Journal of Biblical Literature* 108 (1989) 115–16.

———. *Word Order in the Aramaic of Daniel*. Malibu, CA: Undena, 1986.

Cook, John Manuel. *The Persian Empire*. New York: Schocken, 1983.

Cooper, Jerrold S. *Pre-Sargonic Prescriptions*. Sumerian and Akkadian Royal Inscriptions 1. New Haven, CT: American Oriental Society, 1986.

Cornfield, Gaalyahu. *Archaeology of the Bible: Book by Book*. London: Adam and Charles Black, 1977.

Cory, Isaac. *Ancient Fragments of Phoenician, Chaldean, Egyptian, Tyraian, Carthaginian, Indian, Persian and Other Writers*. London: Pickering, 1876.

Cowley, Arthur Ernest. *Aramaic Papyri of the Fifth Century B.C.* Oxford: Clarendon, 1923.

Coxon, P. W. "The Great Tree of Daniel 4." In *A Word in Season: Essays in Honour of William McKane*, edited by J. D. Martin and P. R. Davies, 91–111. JSOT Supplement Series 42. Sheffield: Sheffield University Press, 1986.

Crawford, Sidnie White. "Apocalyptic." In *Eerdmans Dictionary of the Bible*, edited by David Noel Freedman, 72–73. Grand Rapids: Eerdmans, 2000.

Cross, F. M. Jr. *Canaanite Myth and Hebrew Epic: Essays in the History of the Religion of Israel*. Cambridge, MA: Harvard University Press, 1973.

———. "Fragments of the Prayer of Nabonidus." *Israel Exploration Journal* 34 (1984) 260–64.

———. "Paleography and the Date of the Tell Fahariyeh Bilingual Inscription." In *Solving Riddles and Untying Knots*, edited by Ziony Zevit et al., 393–409. Winona Lake, IN: Eisenbrauns, 1995.

———. "A Report on the Samaria Papyri." In *Congress Volume: Jerusalem*, edited by John A. Emerton, 17–26. VTSup 40. Leiden: Brill, 1986.

———. "An Unpublished Ammonite Ostracon from Ḥesbân." In *The Archaeology of Jordan and Other Studies*, edited by Lawrence T. Geraty and Larry Herr, 475–89. Berrien Springs, MI: Andrews University Press, 1986.

Curtis, John. "Gold Face-Masks in the Ancient Near East." In *The Archaeology of Death in the Ancient Near East*, edited by Stuart Campbell and Antony Green, 226–31. Oxford: Oxbow, 1995.

Dalley, Stephanie, ed. and trans. *Myths from Mesopotamia: Creation, the Flood, Gilgamish, and Others*. Oxford: Oxford University Press, 1989.

Dalley, Stephanie, and A. Goguel. "The Selaʿ Sculpture: A Neo-Babylonian Rock Relief in Southern Jordan." *Annual of the Department of Antiquities of Jordan* 41 (1997) 169–76.

Damerow, Peter, and Robert Englund. *The Proto-Elamite Texts from Tepe Yahya*. Cambridge, MA: Harvard University Press, 1989.

Dandamaev, M. A. *Slavery in Babylonia from the Time of Nabopolassar to Alexander the Great (626–331 BC)*. Dekalb: North Illinois University Press, 1984.

Daniels, Peter T. "The Decipherment of Ancient Near Eastern Scripts." In *Civilizations of the Ancient Near East*, edited by Jack M. Sasson, 1:81–93. New York: Charles Scribner's Sons, 1995.

Danrey, V. "Winged Human-Headed Bulls of Nineveh: Genesis of an Iconographic Motif." *Iraq* 66 (2004) 133–39.

David, Rosalie. *Religion and Magic in Ancient Egypt*. London: Penguin, 2002.

Davidson, Benjamin. *The Analytical Hebrew and Chaldee Lexicon*. Peabody, MA: Hendrickson, 2002.

Davidson, Richard M. "Biblical Principles for Interpreting Apocalyptic Prophecy." In *Prophetic Principles: Crucial Exegetical, Theological, Historical and Practical Insights*, edited by Ron du Preez, 43–73. Scripture Symposium Number 1. Lansing, MI: Michigan Conference of Seventh-day Adventists, 2007.

Day, John. *God's Conflict with the Dragon and the Sea: Echoes of a Canaanite Myth in the Old Testament*. Cambridge: Cambridge University Press, 1985.

de Jonge, M., and A. S. van der Woude. "11 Q Melchizedek and the New Testament." *New Testament Studies* 12 (1966) 301–26.

Denning-Bolle, Sara. "Wisdom and Dialogue in the Ancient Near East." *Numen* 34 (1987) 214–34.

———. *Wisdom in Akkadian Literature: Expression, Instruction, Dialogue*. Leiden: Ex Oriente Lux, 1992.

de Souza, Elias Brasil. "The Heavenly Sanctuary/Temple Motif in the Hebrew Bible: Function and Relationship to the Earthly Counterparts." PhD diss., Andrews University, 2005.

———. "The Ketef Hinnom Silver Scrolls: A Suggestive Reading of the Text and Artifact." *Near East Archaeological Society Bulletin* 49 (2004) 27–38.

de Souza, Elias Brasil, et al., eds. *Eschatology from an Adventist Perspective: Proceedings of the Fourth International Bible Conference, Rome, June 11-20, 2018*. Silver Spring, MD: Biblical Research Institute, 2021.

Desueza, Edmond F., and Judith Jones. *Conversations with Scripture: Daniel*. New York: Morehouse, 2011.

Deutsch, Robert. *Biblical Period Hebrew Bullae: The Joseph Chaim Kaufman Collection*. Tel Aviv: Archaeological Center, 2003.

———. "Seal of Ba'alis Surfaces: Ammonite King Plotted Murder of Judahite Governor." *Biblical Archaeology Review* 25 (1999) 46–49, 66.

Dever, William G. *Did God Have a Wife? Archaeology and Folk Religion in Ancient Israel*. Grand Rapids: Eerdmans, 2005.

———. "Iron Age Epigraphic Material from the Area of Khirbet El-Kôm." *Hebrew Union College Annual* 40/41 (1969–70) 139–204.

———. *Recent Archaeological Discoveries and Biblical Research*. Seattle: University of Washington Press, 1990.

———. *What Did the Biblical Writers Know and When Did They Know It?* Grand Rapids: Eerdmans, 2001.

———. *Who Were the Early Israelites and Where Did They Come From?* Grand Rapids: Eerdmans, 2003.

———. "Whom Do You Believe—The Bible or Archaeology?" *Biblical Archaeology Review* 43 (2017) 43–47, 58.

Dietrich, M. "Babylonian Literary Texts from Western Libraries." In *Verse in Ancient Near Eastern Prose*, edited by Johannes C. de Moor and Wilfred G. E. Watson, 41–67. Kevelaer: Butzon und Bercker, 1993.

———. *Die keilalphabetischen Texte aus Ugarit: einschliesslich der keilalphabetischen Texte ausserhalb Ugarits*. Translated by M. Dietrich et al. Teil 1. Kevelaer: Verlag Butzon & Bercke, 1976.

Di Lella, Alexander A. *Daniel: A Book for Troubling Times*. Hyde Park, NY: New City, 1997.

Dines, Jennifer M. *The Septuagint*. London: T. & T. Clark, 2004.

Discoveries in the Judaean Desert. 39 vols. Oxford: Clarendon, 1955–2002.

DiTommaso, Lorenzo. *A Bibliography of Pseudepigrapha Research 1850–1999*. Sheffield: Sheffield Academic, 2001.

———. *The Book of Daniel and the Apocryphal Daniel Literature*. Leiden: Brill, 2005.

Donner, H., and W. Röllig. *Kanaanäische und aramäische Inschriften*. 3 vols. Wiesbaden: Otto Harrassowitz, 1968.

Dougherty, Raymond Philip. *Nabonidus and Belshazzar: A Study of the Closing Events of the Neo-Babylonian Empire*. The Ancient Near East: Classic Studies. Eugene, OR: Wipf & Stock, 2008.

Doukhan, Jacques B. *Secrets of Daniel: Wisdom and Dreams of a Jewish Prince in Exile*. Hagerstown, MD: Review and Herald, 2000.

Driver, S. R. *The Book of Daniel*. Cambridge: Cambridge University Press, 1900.

———. *An Introduction to the Literature of the Old Testament*. Repr., New York: Charles Scribner and Sons, 1965.

Dyer, Charles H. "The Musical Instruments in Daniel 3." *Bibliotheca Sacra* 147 (1990) 426–36.

Edelman, Diana. *The Origin of the "Second" Temple: Persian Imperial Policy and the Rebuilding of Jerusalem*. London: Equinox, 2005.

Edens, Christopher. "Tigris." In *Oxford Encyclopedia of Archaeology in the Near East*, edited by Eric M. Meyers, 5:206–9. New York: Oxford University Press, 1997.

Edzard, Dietz Otto. *Gudea and His Dynasty: Royal Inscriptions of Mesopotamia, Early Periods*. Toronto: University of Toronto Press, 1997.

Eichner, Heiner. "Etymologische Beiträge zum Lykischen der Trilingue vom Letoon bei Xanthos." *Orientalia* 52 (1983) 48–66.

Eidem, J. "A Note on the Pulse Crops at Tell Shemshara." *Bulletin on Sumerian Agriculture* 2 (1985) 141–43.

Eisenmann, R., and M. Wise. *Dead Sea Scrolls Uncovered*. Rockport, MA: Element, 1992.

Ellis, Richard S. *Foundation Deposits in Ancient Mesopotamia*. New Haven, CT: Yale University Press, 1968.

Elwell, Walter A., ed. *Baker Encyclopedia of the Bible*. Grand Rapids: Baker, 1995.

Emerton, John A. "The Origin of the Son of Man Imagery." *Journal of Theological Studies* 9 (1958) 225–42.

Engel, Carl. *The Music of the Most Ancient Nations, Particularly of the Assyrians, Egyptians and the Hebrews: With Special Reference to Recent Discoveries in Western Asia and in Egypt*. London: W. Reeves, 1909.

Eph'al, I. "The Western Minorities in Babylonia in the 6th–5th Centuries B.C.: Maintenance and Cohesion." *Orientalia* 47 (1978) 74–90.

Erman, Adolf. *Wörterbuch der aegyptischen Sprache*. Leipzig: Hinrichs, 1926–31.

Eusebius. *Eusebius*. Translated by Philip Schaff and Henry Wace. Grand Rapids: Eerdmans, 1997.

Everhart, Janet. "Hidden Eunuchs of the Hebrew Bible." In *Society of Biblical Literature: 2002 Seminar Papers*, 137–55. Evanston, IL: American Theological Library Association, 2002.

Ferch, Authur J. "Authorship, Theology, and Purpose of Daniel." In *Symposium on Daniel*, edited by Frank B. Holbrook, 3–83. Daniel and Revelation Committee Series 2. Hagerstown, MD: Review and Herald, 1986.

———. "Daniel 7 and Ugarit: A Reconsideration." *Journal for Biblical Literature* 99 (1980) 75–86.

———. *The Son of Man in Daniel Seven*. Andrews University Seminary Doctoral Dissertation Series 6. Berrien Springs, MI: Andrews University Press, 1979.

Finkel, A. "The Pesher of Dreams and Scriptures." *Revue de Qumrân* 4 (1963–64) 357–70.

Finkelstein, Israel. Interview by Hershel Shanks. "A 'Centrist' at the Center of Controversy." *Biblical Archaeology Review* 28 (2002) 38–49, 64–68.

Finkelstein, Israel, and Neil Asher Silberman. *The Bible Unearthed: Archaeology's New Vision of Ancient Israel and the Origins of Its Sacred Texts*. New York: Free, 2001.

Finkelstein, Jacob J. "The Edict of Ammisaduqa: A New Text." *Revue D'Assyriologie et d'Archéologie Orientale* 63 (1969) 45–64.

Finley, M. I., ed. *The Greek Historians*. New York: Viking, 1959.

Fischer, Steven R. *The Complete Medieval Dreambook: A Multilingual, Alphabetical Somnia Danielis Collation*. Bern: P. Lang, 1982.

Fisher, James. "Ammon (עמון/עמוני) in the Hebrew Bible: A Textual Analysis and Archaeological Context of Selected References to the Ammonites of Trans Jordan." PhD diss., Andrews University, 1998.

Fitzmyer, Joseph A. *The Aramaic Inscriptions of Sefîre*. Rome: Pontifical Biblical Institute, 1995.

BIBLIOGRAPHY

———. *The Genesis Apocryphon of Qumran Cave I: A Commentary*. Rome: Pontifical Biblical Institute, 1966.

———. *A Wandering Aramean: Collected Essays*. Society of Biblical Literature Monograph Series 25. Missoula, MT: Scholars, 1979.

Fitzmyer, Joseph A., and D. J. Harrington. *A Manual of Palestinian Aramaic Texts: Second Century BC to Second Century AD*. Rome: Biblical Institute, 1978.

Flint, P. W. "4Qpseudo-Daniel ar^c (4Q245) and the Restoration of the Priesthood." *Revue de Qumrân* 17 (1996) 137–50.

Ford, Desmond. *Daniel*. Nashville: Southern, 1978.

Foster, Herbert Baldwin. *Dio's Rome: An Historical Narrative Originally Composed in Greek During the Reigns of Septimius Severus, Geta and Caracalla, Marcius, Elaga Balus and Alexander Severus*. New York: Pafraets, 1905.

Fowler, Jeaneane D. *Theophoric Personal Names in Ancient Hebrew: A Comparative Study*. Sheffield: JSOT Press, 1988.

Frame, Grant. "Chaldeans." In *Oxford Encyclopedia of Archaeology in the Near East*, edited by Eric M. Meyers, 1:482–84. Oxford: Oxford University Press, 1997.

Franken, H. J. *Excavations at Deir 'Alla*. Leiden: Brill, 1969.

Frankfort, H. *The Art and Architecture of the Ancient Orient*. New Haven, CT: Yale University Press, 1970.

Freedman, David Noel, ed. *Anchor Bible Dictionary*. 6 vols. New York: Doubleday, 1992.

Freedman, H., and M. Simon, eds. and trans. *Midrash Rabbah*. London: Soncino, 1939.

Fuller, J. F. C. *Julius Caesar: Man, Soldier, and Tyrant*. New York: Minerva, 1965.

Gadd, C. J. "The Harran Inscriptions of Nabonidus." *Anatolian Studies* 8 (1958) 35–92.

Gane, Roy E. *Altar Call*. Berrien Springs, MI: Diadem, 1999.

———. "Genre Awareness and Interpretation of the Book of Daniel." In *To Understand the Scriptures: Essays in Honor of William H. Shea*, edited by David Merling, 137–48. Berrien Springs, MI: Institute of Archaeology, 1997.

———. "Hurrian Ullikummi and Daniel's 'Little Horn.'" In *Birkat Shalom: Studies in the Bible, Ancient Near Eastern Literature and Postbiblical Judaism Presented to Shalom M. Paul on the Occasion of his Seventieth Birthday*, edited by Chaim Cohen et al., 485–98. Winona Lake, IN: Eisenbrauns, 2008.

———. "Jalul Ostracon I." *Bulletin of the American Schools of Oriental Research* 351 (2008) 73–84.

———. *Who's Afraid of the Judgment? The Good News About Christ's Work in Heavenly Sanctuary*. Nampa, ID: Pacific, 2006.

Gardner, Anne E. "Daniel 7, 2–14: Another Look at Its Mythic Pattern." *Biblica* 82 (2001) 244–52.

———. "The Great Sea of Dan. VII 2." *Vetus Testamentum* 49 (1999) 412–15.

Garsiel, Moshe. *Biblical Names: A Literary Study of Midrashic Derivations and Puns*. Ramat Gan: Bar-Ilan University, 1991.

Garstang, John. *The Hittite Empire*. London: Constable and Company, 1929.

Gaster, M., trans. *The Chronicles of Jerahmeel*. New York: KTAV, 1972.

Gavin, F. S. B. *Aphraates and the Jews: A Study of the Controversial Homilies of the Persian Sage in Relation to Jewish Thought*. New York: AMS, 1966.

Gelb, Ignace J., et al., eds. *The Assyrian Dictionary of the Oriental Institute of the University of Chicago*. 21 vols. Chicago: Oriental Institute of Chicago, 1956–99.

Gelston, Anthony. "A Sidelight on the 'Son of Man.'" *Scottish Journal of Theology* 22 (1969) 189–96.

BIBLIOGRAPHY

Geva, Hillel. "Jerusalem: Second Temple Period." In *The New Encyclopedia of Archaeological Excavations in the Holy Land*, edited by Ephraim Stern, 2:717-24. Jerusalem: Israel Exploration Society, 1993.

———. "Jerusalem: Tombs." In *The New Encyclopedia of Archaeological Excavations in the Holy Land*, edited by Ephraim Stern, 2:712-16. Jerusalem: Israel Exploration Society, 1993.

Gibbon, Edward. *The Triumph of Christendom in the Roman Empire*. New York: Harper & Row, 1958.

Gibson, John C. L. *Textbook of Syrian Semitic Inscriptions*. 3 vols. Oxford: Clarendon, 1971-82.

Ginsberg, H. L. *Studies in Daniel*. New York: Jewish Theological Seminary of America, 1948.

Giveon, R. *Les bédouins Shosou des documents égyptiens*. Leiden: Brill, 1971.

Goldingay, John E. "The Book of Daniel: Three Issues." *Themolios* 2 (1976-77) 45-49.

———. *Daniel*. Word Biblical Commentary. Dallas, TX: Word, 1989.

Goldwurm, Hersh. *Daniel: A New Translation with a Commentary Anthologized from Talmudic, Midrashic and Rabbinic Sources*. New York: Mesorah, 1980.

Gordon, Cyrus Herzl. *Ugaritic Textbook: Texts in Transliteration, Cuneiform Selections, Glossary, Indices*. 3 vols. Rome: Pontificio Instituto Biblico, 1998.

Goshen-Gottstein, and Henry Moshe. *Syriac Manuscripts in the Harvard College Library: A Catalogue*. Missoula, MT: Scholars, 1979.

Gottheil, R. J. H. "An Arabic Version of the 'Revelation of Ezra.'" *Hebraica* 4 (1887-88) 14-17.

Govier, Gordon. "Babylonian Official Mentioned in the Bible." *Artifax* 22 (2007) 15.

Grabbe, Lester L. "Another Look at the Gestalt of 'Darius the Mede.'" *Catholic Biblical Quarterly* 50 (1988) 198-213.

———. "A Dan(iel) for All Seasons: For Whom Was Daniel Important?" In *The Book of Daniel: Composition and Reception*, edited by J. J. Collins and Peter W. Flint, 1:229-46. Leiden: Brill, 2002.

———. "Of Mice and Dead Men: Herodotus 2.141 and Sennacherib's Campaign in 701 BCE." In *"Like a Bird in a Cage": The Invasion of Sennacherib in 701 BCE*, edited by Lester L. Grabbe, 119-40. Sheffield: Sheffield Academic, 2003.

Gray, John. "Social Aspects of Canaanite Religion." In *Volume du Congrès Genève 1965*, edited by G. W. Anderson et al., 170-92. Supplements to Vetus Testamentum 15. Leiden: Brill, 1966.

Grayson, A. K. "Ambush and Animal Pit in Akkadian." In *Studies Presented to A. Leo Oppenheim, June 7, 1964*. Edited by the University of Chicago, Oriental Institute, 90-94. Chicago: University of Chicago Press, 1964.

———. "Assyria: Ashur-Dan II to Ashur-Nirari V (934-745 B.C.)." In *The Prehistory of the Balkans, the Middle East and the Aegean World, Tenth to Eighth Centuries BC*, edited by John Boardman et al., 238-81. Vol. 3/1 of *The Cambridge Ancient History*. 2nd ed. Cambridge: Cambridge University Press, 1982.

———. *Assyrian and Babylonian Chronicles*. Texts from Cuneiform Series 5. Winona Lake, IN: Eisenbrauns, 2000.

———. *Assyrian Royal Inscriptions*. 2 vols. Wiesbaden: Otto Harrassowitz, 1976.

———. *Assyrian Rulers of the Early First Millennium BC II (858-745 BC)*. Assyrian Periods 3. Toronto: University of Toronto Press, 1996.

BIBLIOGRAPHY

———. *Babylonian Historical-Literary Texts*. Toronto: University of Toronto Press, 2017.

———. "Eunuchs in Power: Their Role in the Assyrian Bureaucracy." In *Vom Alten Orient zum Alten Testament*, edited by Manfried Dietrich and Oswald Loretz, 85–98. Kevelaer: Butzon & Bercker, 1995.

Grayson, A. K., and W. G. Lambert. "Akkadian Prophecies." *Journal of Cuneiform Studies* 18 (1964) 7–30.

Greenberg, Moshe. *Biblical Prose Prayer as a Window to the Popular Religion of Ancient Israel*. Taubman Lectures in Jewish Studies 6. Berkeley, CA: University of California Press, 1983.

Greenfield, Jonas C. "Aramaic Studies and the Bible." In *Congress Volume: Vienna 1980*, edited by J. A. Emerton, 110–30. Leiden: Brill, 1981.

———. "The Hebrew Bible and Canaanite Literature." In *The Literary Guide to the Bible*, edited by Robert Alter and Frank Kermode, 545–60. Cambridge, MA: Belknap, 1987.

Greenfield, Jonas C., and Bezalel Porten. *The Bisitun Inscription of Darius the Great, Aramaic Version*. Part I: Inscriptions of Ancient Iran. London: Lund Humphries, 1982.

Gregor, B. "Gold aus Ofir? Jer 10, 19 und einemianische Inscrift." *Biblische Notizen* 41 (1988) 19–22.

Grillot, François. "À propos d'un cas de 'Lévirat' élamite." *Journal Asiatique* 276 (1988) 61–70.

Gröndahl, Frauke. *Die Personennamen der Texte aus Ugarit*. Rome: Päpstliches Bibelinstitut, 1967.

Gulley, Norman R. "Why the Danielic Little Horn Is Not Antiochus IV Epiphanes." In *To Understand the Scriptures: Essays in Honor of William H. Shea*, edited by David Merling, 191–97. Berrien Springs, MI: Institute of Archaeology, 1997.

Gunkel, Hermann. *Creation and Chaos in the Primeval Era and the Eschaton: A Religio-Historical Study of Genesis 1 and Revelation 12*. Translated by K. William Whitney Jr. Grand Rapids: Eerdmans, 2006.

Gurney, Robert J. M. "The Four Kingdoms of Daniel 2 and 7." *Themelios* 2 (1977) 39–45.

Gzella, Holger. *Cosmic Battle and Political Conflict*. Rome: Pontificio Istituto Biblico, 2003.

Haklut, Richard. *The Principal Navigations, Voyages, Traffiques and Discoveries of the English Nation*. Edited by Irwin R. Blacker. New York: Viking, 1965.

Hall, I. H. "The Vision of Ezra the Scribe Concerning the Latter Times of the Ishmaelites." *Presbyterian Review* 7 (1886) 537–41.

Hallo, William W. "Akkadian Apocalypses." *Israel Exploration Journal* 16 (1966) 231–42.

———. "The Royal Inscriptions of Ur: A Typology." *Hebrew Union College Annual* 33 (1962) 1–43.

Hallo, William W., and K. Lawson Younger Jr., eds. *The Context of Scripture: Monumental Inscriptions from the Biblical World*. 3 vols. Leiden: Brill, 2000.

Hallo, William W., and William Kelly Simpson. *The Ancient Near East: A History*. 2nd ed. New York: Harcourt Brace, 1998.

Hammer, Raymond. *The Book of Daniel*. Cambridge: Cambridge University Press, 1976.

Hare, D. R. A. "The Lives of the Prophets." In *Expansions of the Old Testament and Legends, Wisdom and Philosophical Literature, Prayers, Psalms and Odes, Fragments of Lost Judeo-Hellenistic Works*, edited by James H. Charlesworth, 379–99. Vol. 2/2 of *The Old Testament Pseudepigrapha*. New York: Doubleday, 1985.

Harper, Robert Francis. *Assyrian and Babylonian Literature*. New York: D. Appleton, 1904.

Harris, R. Laird, et al., eds. *Theological Wordbook of the Old Testament*. 2 vols. Chicago: Moody, 1980.

Harris, Roberta L. *The World of the Bible*. London: Thames & Hudson, 1995.

Harrison, R. K. *Introduction to the Old Testament: With a Comprehensive Review of Old Testament Studies and a Special Supplement on the Apocrypha*. Grand Rapids: Eerdmans, 1969.

Hart, John. *Herodotus and Greek History*. London: Croom Helm, 1983.

Hart, Stephen. "Sela': The Rock of Edom." *Palestine Exploration Quarterly* 118 (1986) 91–95.

Hartman, Louis F. "The Great Tree and Nebuchodonosor's Madness." In *The Bible in Current Catholic Thought*, edited by John L. McKenzie, 75–82. New York: Herder & Herder, 1962.

Hartman, Louis F., and Alexander A. Di Lella. *The Book of Daniel: A New Translation with Introduction and Commentary*. Anchor Bible 23. Garden City, NY: Doubleday, 1978.

Hasel, Gerhard F. "The Book of Daniel and Matters of Language: Evidences Relating to Names, Words, and the Aramaic Language." *Andrews University Seminary Studies* 19 (1981b) 211–25.

———. "The Book of Daniel: Evidences Relating to Persons and Chronology." *Andrews University Seminary Studies* 19 (1981a) 37–49.

———. "Establishing the Date for the Book of Daniel." In *Symposium on Daniel*, edited by Frank B. Holbrook, 84–164. Daniel and Revelation Committee Series 2. Hagerstown, MD: Review and Herald, 1986.

———. "The Hebrew Masculine Plural for 'Weeks' in the Expression 'Seventy Weeks' in Daniel 9:24." *Andrews University Seminary Studies* 31 (1993) 105–18.

———. "Interpretations of the Chronology of the Seventy Weeks." In *The Seventy Weeks, Leviticus, and the Nature of Prophecy*, edited by Frank B. Holbrook, 3–63. Daniel and Revelation Committee Series 3. Washington, DC: Biblical Research Institute, 1986.

———. "The 'Little Horn,' the Heavenly Sanctuary, and the Time of the End: A Study of Daniel 8:9–14." In *Symposium on Daniel*, edited by Frank B. Holbrook, 378–461. Daniel and Revelation Committee Series 2. Hagerstown, MD: Review and Herald, 1986.

———. "New Light on the Book of Daniel from the Dead Sea Scrolls." *Archaeology and Biblical Research* 5 (1992) 45–53.

Hasel, Michael G. *Military Practice and Polemic: Israel's Laws of Warfare in Near Eastern Perspective*. Berrien Springs, MI: Andrews University Press, 2005.

Hawass, Zahi. *Valley of the Golden Mummies*. New York: Harry N. Abrams, 2000.

The Hebrew and Aramaic Lexicon of the Old Testament. CD-Rom ed. 1994–2001.

Heimpel, Wolfgang. "The River Ordeal in Hit." *Revue d'Assyriologie* 90 (1996) 7–18.

Henze, Matthias. *The Syriac Apocalypse of Daniel: Introduction, Text and Commentary*. Studien und Texte zu Antike und Christentum 11. Tübingen: Mohr Siebeck, 2001.

Herdner, A., ed. *Corpus des tablettes en cunéiforms alphabtiéques découvertes à Ras Shamra-Ugarit de 1929 à 1939*. Paris: Geuthner, 1963.
Herodotus. *Herodotus*. Translated by A. D. Goodley. 4 vols. LCL. Cambridge, MA: Harvard University Press, 1926.
Herold, J. Christopher. *Bonaparte in Egypt*. New York: Harper & Row, 1962.
Herr, Larry G. "Is the Spelling of 'Baalis' in Jeremiah 40:14 a Mutilation?" *Andrews University Seminary Studies* 23 (1985) 187–91.
———. "The Servant of Baalis." *Biblical Archaeologist* 48 (1985) 169–72.
Hesiod. *Works and Days*. Translated by David W. Tandy and Walter C. Neale. Berkeley, CA: University of California Press, 1996.
Hestrin, Ruth, and Michal Dayagi-Mendels. *Inscribed Seals: First Temple Period, Hebrew, Ammonite, Moabite, Phoenician and Aramaic, from the Collections of the Israel Museum and the Israel Department of Antiquities and Museums*. Jerusalem: Israel Museum, 1979.
———. "A Seal Impression of a Servant of King Hezekiah." *Israel Exploration Journal* 24 (1974) 27–29.
Hillers, Delbert R., and Eleonora Cussini. *Palmyrene Aramaic Texts*. Baltimore, MD: Johns Hopkins University Press, 1995.
Hilprecht, H. V., and A. T. Clay. *Business Documents of Murashû Sons of Nippur Dated in the Reign of Artaxerxes I. (464–424 B.C.)* 9. Philadelphia: Department of Archæology and Palæontology of the University of Pennsylvania, 1898.
Hilton, Michael. "Babel Reversed—Daniel Chapter 5." *Journal for the Study of the Old Testament* 66 (1995) 99–112.
Hippolytus. "On Daniel." In *The Ante-Nicene Fathers*, edited by Alexander Roberts and James Donaldson, 5:177–91. Peabody, MA: Hendrickson, 2004.
———. *Kommentar zu Daniel*. Translated by G. N. Bonwetsch. Berlin: Akademie Verlag, 2000.
Holden, Joseph M., and Norman Geisler. *The Popular Handbook of Archaeology and the Bible: Discoveries that Confirm the Reliability of Scripture*. Eugene, OR: Harvest, 2013.
Holladay, William L., ed. *A Concise Hebrew and Aramaic Lexicon of the Old Testament*. Grand Rapids: Eerdmans, 1988.
Holleaux, Maurice. "Rome and Antiochus." In *Rome and the Mediterranean 218–133 B.C.*, edited by S. A. Cook et al., 199–240. Vol. 7 of *The Cambridge Ancient History*. Cambridge: Cambridge University Press, 1970.
Hopkins, Keith. *Conquerors and Slaves: Sociological Studies in Roman History* 1. Cambridge: Cambridge University Press, 1978.
Horn, S. H. *Light from the Dust Heaps*. Washington, DC: Review and Herald, 1955.
———. "New Light on Nebuchadnezzar's Madness." *Ministry* (1978) 38–40.
Horn, S. H., and L. H. Wood. *The Chronology of Ezra 7*. Washington, DC: Review and Herald, 1970.
Horne, Charles F. *Babylonia and Assyria*. Vol. 1 of *The Sacred Books and Early Literature of the East*. London: Parke, Austin and Lipscomb, 1917.
Huffmon, Herbert Bardwell. *Amorite Personal Names in the Mari Texts: A Structural and Lexical Study*. Baltimore, MD: Johns Hopkins University Press, 1965.
Hultgård, Anders. "Bahman Yasht: A Persian Apocalypse." In *Mysteries and Revelations: Apocalyptic Studies Since the Uppsala Colloquium*, edited by J. J. Collins and James H. Charlesworth, 114–34. Sheffield: Sheffield Academic, 1991.

BIBLIOGRAPHY

———. "Persian Apocalypticism." In *The Continuum History of Apocalypticism*, edited by Bernard McGinn et al., 30–36. New York: Continuum, 2003.

Hunger, Hermann, and Stephen A. Kaufman. "A New Akkadian Prophecy Text." *Journal of the American Oriental Society* 95 (1975) 371–75.

Husser, Jean-Marie. *Dreams and Dream Narratives in the Biblical World.* Translated by Jill M. Munro. Sheffield: Sheffield Academic, 1999.

Isaac, Ephraim. "1 (Ethiopic Apocalypse of) Enoch." In *Apocalyptic Literature and Testaments*, edited by James H. Charlesworth, 5–89. Vol. 1/2 of *The Old Testament Pseudepigrapha*. New York: Doubleday, 1983.

Isbell, Charles D. *Corpus of the Aramaic Incantation Bowls.* Missoula, MT: Scholars, 1975.

Issaverdens, Jacques, trans. *The Uncanonical Writings of the Old Testament Found in the Armenian MSS of the Library.* Venice: Armenian Monastery of St. Lazarus, 1934.

Istrin, V. M. *Otkrovenie Mefodiia Patarskago I apokrificheskiia vidieniia Daniila v vizantiiskoi I salviano-russkoi literaturakh.* Moscow: Univ. Tip., 1897.

Jackson, Kent P., and J. Andrew Dearman. "The Text of the Mesha' Inscription." In *Studies in the Mesha Inscription and Moab*, edited by Andrew Dearman, 93–95. Atlanta: Scholars, 1989.

Jacobsen, T. "Tigris." In *Interpreter's Dictionary of the Bible*, edited by G. A. Buttrick et al., 4:642. Nashville: Abingdon, 1990.

James, Edwin Oliver. *The Tree of Life: An Archaeological Study.* Leiden: Brill, 1966.

Jastrow, Marcus. *A Dictionary of the Targumim, the Talmud Babli and Yerushalmi, and the Midrashic Literature.* Peabody, MA: Hendrickson, 2005.

Jeansonne, Sharon Pace. *The Old Greek Translation of Daniel 7–12.* Washington, DC: Catholic Biblical Association of America, 1988.

Jenner, K. D. "The Unit Delimitation in the Syriac Text of Daniel and Its Consequences for the Interpretation." In *Delimitation Criticism*, edited by Marjo Korpel and Josef Oesch, 105–29. Assen: Van Gorcum, 2000.

Jenni, Ernst, and Claus Westermann. *Theological Lexicon of the Old Testament.* 3 vols. Peabody, MA: Hendrickson, 1997.

Jobes, Karen H., and Moisés Silva. *Invitation to the Septuagint.* Grand Rapids: Baker Academic, 2000.

Johns, C. H. W. "Chaldea." In *Encyclopaedia Biblica*, edited by Thomas Kelly Cheyne and J. Sutherland Black, 1:720–21. London: Macmillan, 1899.

Johnson, Marshall D. *Making Sense of the Bible: Literary Type as an Approach to Understanding.* Grand Rapids: Eerdmans, 2002.

Jones, Bruce Williams. "The Prayer in Daniel 9." *Vetus Testamentum* 18 (1968) 488–93.

Jones, Ivor H. "Musical Instruments in the Bible, Part I." *Bible Translator* 37 (1986) 101–16.

Jongeling, B., et al. *Aramaic Texts from Qumran: With Translations and Annotations* 1. Leiden: Brill, 1976.

Joosten, Jan. "How Hebrew Became a Holy Language." *Biblical Archaeology Review* 43 (2017) 44–49, 62.

Josephus, Flavius. *Josephus: The Complete Works.* Translated by William Whiston. Nashville: Thomas Nelson, 1998.

———. *The Life Against Apion.* Translated by H. St. J. Thackeray. Cambridge, MA: Harvard University Press, 1926.

Kahle, Paul. *The Cairo Geniza.* Oxford: Basil Blackwell, 1959.

Kaiser, Walter C. Jr. *The Old Testament Documents: Are They Reliable and Relevant?* Downers Grove, IL: InterVarsity, 2001.
Kamphausen, Adolf. *The Book of Daniel.* Baltimore, MD: Johns Hopkins University Press, 1896.
Kang, Sa-Moon. *Divine War in the Old Testament and the Ancient Near East.* Berlin: Walter de Gruyter, 1989.
Kee, Howard Clark. *Cambridge Annotated Study Apocrypha.* Cambridge: Cambridge University Press, 1994.
———. "The Testaments of the Twelve Patriarchs (Second Century B.C.): A New Translation and Introduction." In *Apocalyptic Literature and Testaments,* edited by James H. Charlesworth, 775–828. Vol. 1/2 of *The Old Testament Pseudepigrapha.* New York: Doubleday, 1983.
Keil, C. F., and F. Delitzsch. *Ezekiel and Daniel.* Commentary on the Old Testament 9. Peabody, MA: Hendrickson, 1996.
Kent, Ronald G. *Old Persian: Grammar, Texts, Lexicon.* New Haven, CT: American Oriental Society, 1953.
Kenyon, Kathleen M. *Digging Up Jerusalem.* New York: Praeger, 1974.
Kilmer, Anne Draffkorn. "Music and Dances in Ancient Western Asia." In *Civilizations of the Ancient Near East,* edited by Jack M. Sasson, 4:2601–13. Peabody, MA: Hendrickson, 2000.
———. "The Strings of Musical Instruments: Their Names, Numbers, and Significance." In *Studies in Honor of Benno Landsberger on His Seventy-Fifth Birthday, April 21, 1965,* edited by Hans G. Güterbock and Thorkild Jacobsen, 261–72. Chicago: University of Chicago Press, 1965.
Kim, Seyoon. *"The Son of Man" as the Son of God.* Wissenschaftliche Untersuchungen zum Neuen Testament 30. Tübingen: Mohr, 1983.
King, L. W. *Babylonian Boundary-Stones.* London: British Museum, 1912.
———. *Chronicles Concerning Early Babylonian Kings* 2. London: Luzac, 1907.
King, L. W., et al., eds. *The Sculptures and Inscription of Darius the Great on the Rock of Behistûn in Persia: A New Collation of the Persian, Susian, and Babylonian Texts, with English Translations, Etc.* London: British Museum, 1907.
King, Philip J. *Amos, Hosea, Micah: An Archaeological Commentary.* Philadelphia: Westminster John Knox, 1988.
———. *Jeremiah: An Archaeological Companion.* Louisville: Westminster, 1993.
Kitchen, K. A. "The Aramaic of Daniel." In *Notes on Some Problems in the Book of Daniel,* edited by D. J. Wiseman et al., 31–79. London: Tyndale, 1965.
Kittel, Gerhard, and Gerhard Friedrich, eds. *Theological Dictionary of the New Testament.* Translated by Geoffrey W. Bromiley. 10 vols. Grand Rapids: Eerdmans, 1964–76.
Klein, Ernest. *A Comprehensive Etymological Dictionary of the Hebrew Language for Readers of English.* New York: Macmillan, 1987.
Klein, M. L., ed. *Targumic Manuscripts in the Cambridge Genizah Collections.* Cambridge: Cambridge University Press, 1992.
Klengel-Brandt, Evelyn. "Babylon." *Oxford Encyclopedia of Archaeology in the Near East,* edited by Eric M. Meyers, 1:251–56. Oxford: Oxford University Press, 1997.
Knavig, Helge S. *Roots of Apocalyptic: The Mesopotamian Background of the Enoch Figure and the Son of Man.* Neukirchen-Vluyn: Neukirchener Verlag, 1988.
Koldewey, R. *The Excavations at Babylon.* London: Macmillan, 1914.

Koehler, L., et al., eds. *Hebräisches und aramäisches Lexikon zum Alten Testament*. 5 vols. Leiden: Brill, 1965-95.
Komroff, Manuel, ed. *Contemporaries of Marco Polo*. London: J. Cape, 1989.
Korpel, Marjo C. A. "Fit for a Queen: Jezebel's Royal Seal." *Biblical Archaeology Review* 34 (2008) 32-37.
Kraeling, Emil G., ed. *Brooklyn Museum Aramaic Papyri: New Documents of the Fifth Century B.C. from the Jewish Colony at Elephantine*. New Haven, CT: Yale University Press, 1953.
Kramer, S. N. *The Sumerians: Their History, Culture, and Character*. Chicago: University of Chicago Press, 1963.
Kuhrt, A. "Ancient Mesopotamia in Classical Greek and Hellenistic Thought." In *Civilizations of the Ancient Near East*, edited by Jack M. Sasson, 1:55-65. New York: Charles Scribner's Sons, 1995.
———. *The Ancient Near East: c. 3000-330 BC*. 2 vols. London: Routledge, 1995.
Kvanvig, Helge S. *Roots of Apocalyptic: The Mesopotamian Background of the Enoch Figure and of the Son of Man*. Wissenschaftliche Monographien zum Alten und Neuen Testament 61. Neukirchen Vluyn: Neukirchener, 1988.
Lacocque, André. *The Book of Daniel*. Atlanta: John Knox, 1979.
Lambert, W. G. *The Background of Jewish Apocalyptic*. London: Athlone, 1978.
———. "Enmeduranki and Related Matters." *Journal of Cuneiform Studies* 21 (1967) 126-38.
———. "History and the Gods: A Review Article." *Orientalia* 39 (1970) 170-77.
———. "Nebuchadnezzar King of Justice." *Iraq* 27 (1965) 1-11.
Landau, Y. H. "A Greek Inscription Found Near Hefzibah." *Israel Exploration Journal* 16 (1966) 54-70.
Langdon, S. H. *Semitic Mythology*. The Mythology of All Races 5. Boston: Archaeological Institute of America, 1931.
———. *Sumerian Epic of Paradise, the Flood and the Fall of Man*. Philadelphia: University Museum, 1915.
Lasine, Stuart. "Solomon, Daniel and the Detective Story: The Social Functions of a Literary Genre." *Hebrew Annual Review* 11 (1987) 247-66.
Laughlin, John C. H. *Archaeology and the Bible*. London: Routledge, 2000.
Layard, Austen H. *Discoveries Among the Ruins of Nineveh and Babylon*. New York: Harper & Brothers, 1859.
———. *Discoveries in the Ruins of Nineveh and Babylon: With Travels in Armenia, Kurdistan and the Desert*. London: J. Murray, 1853.
———. *Early Adventures in Persia, Susiana, and Babylonia*. London: J. Murray, 1894.
———. *Nineveh and Its Remains*. 2 vols. New York: George P. Putnam, 1849.
Leahy, Anthony. "The Earliest Dated Monument of Amasis and the End of the Reign of Apries." *Journal of Egyptian Archaeology* 74 (1988) 183-99.
Leemans, W. F. *Foreign Trade in the Old Babylonian Period as Revealed by Texts from Southern Mesopotamia*. Leiden: Brill, 1960.
Leichty, Erle. *The Omen Series Šumma izbu*. New York: Locust Valley, 1970.
Lemaire, André. "Hebrew Inscriptions." In *The Renewed Archaeological Excavations at Lachish (1973-1994)*, edited by David Ussishkin, 4:2099-132. Tel Aviv: Emery and Claire Yass Publications in Archaeology, 2004.
———. "The Xanthos Trilingual Revisited." In *Solving Riddles and Untying Notes*, edited by Ziony Zevit et al., 423-32. Winona Lake, IN: Eisenbrauns, 1995.

Lemcio, Eugene E. "'Son of Man,' 'Pitiable Man,' 'Rejected Man': Equivalent Expressions in the Old Greek of Daniel." *Tyndale Bulletin* 56 (2005) 43-60.
Lemke, Werner E. "Nebuchadnezzar, My Servant." *Catholic Biblical Quarterly* 28 (1966) 45-50.
Lesky, Albin. *A History of Greek Literature*. New York: Thomas Y. Cromwell, 1966.
Leupold, H. C. *Exposition of Daniel*. Grand Rapids: Baker, 1969.
Levine, Baruch A. "Assyrian Ideology and Israelite Monotheism." *Iraq* 67 (2005) 411-27.
Levy, R. "Danial-Nama: A Judeo-Persian Apocalypse." In *Jewish Studies in Memorium of G. A. Kohut*, edited by S. W. Baron, 423-28. New York: Alexander Kohut Memorial Foundation, 1935.
Lindenberger, J. M. "Ahiqar." In *The Old Testament Pseudepigrapha: Expansions of the "Old Testament" and Legends, Wisdom and Philosophical Literature, Prayers, Psalms and Odes, Fragments of Lost Judeo-Hellenistic Works*, edited by James H. Charlesworth, 2:479-507. New York: Doubleday, 1985.
Lindsay, John. "The Babylonian Kings and Edom, 605-550 B.C." *Palestine Exploration Quarterly* 108 (1976) 23-39.
Lipiński, Edward. "The Cypriot Vassals of Esarhaddon." In *Ah, Assyria . . .: Studies in Assyrian History and Ancient Near Eastern Historiography Presented to Hayim Tadmor*, edited by Mordechai Cogan and Israel Eph'al, 58-64. Jerusalem: Magnes, 1991.
Lipschits, Oded, and Manfred Oeming, eds. *Judah and the Judeans in the Persian Period*. Winona Lake, IN: Eisenbrauns, 2006.
Livius, Titus. *The History of Rome*. 4 vols. London: Bell & Daldy, 1873.
Lloyd, Alan B. "The Late Period (664-332 BC)." In *The Oxford History of Ancient Egypt*, edited by Ian Shaw, 369-421. Oxford: Oxford University Press, 2000.
Lloyd, Seton. *The Archaeology of Mesopotamia from the Old Stone Age to the Persian Conquest*. London: Thames & Hudson, 1984.
Loftus, William K. *Travels and Researches in Chaldaea and Susiana*. New York: J. Nisbert, 1857.
Longenecker, Richard N. "Son of Man as a Self-Designation of Jesus." *Journal of the Evangelical Theological Society* 12 (1969) 151-58.
Longman, Tremper III. *Daniel*. Grand Rapids: Zondervan, 1999.
———. *Fictional Akkadian Autobiography: A Generic and Comparative Study*. Winona Lake, IN: Eisenbrauns, 1991.
Lucas, Ernest C. *Daniel*. Downers Grove, IL: InterVarsity, 2002.
———. "The Origin of Daniel's Four Empires Scheme Re-Examined." *Tyndale Bulletin* 40 (1989) 185-202.
———. "The Source of Daniel's Animal Imagery." *Tyndale Bulletin* 41 (1990) 161-85.
Lucian. *Lucian*. Translated by A. M. Harmon. 8 vols. Cambridge: Harvard University Press, 1959-67.
Luckenbill, Daniel David. *Ancient Records of Assyria and Babylonia*. 2 vols. Chicago: University of Chicago Press, 1926-27.
———. *The Annals of Sennacherib*. Chicago: University of Chicago Press, 1924.
Lundquist, John M. "Babylon in European Thought." In *Civilizations of the Ancient Near East*, edited by Jack M. Sasson, 1:67-80. New York: Charles Scribner's Sons, 1995.

MacDonald, Martin. *The Biblical Canon: Its Origin, Transmission, and Authority.* Peabody, MA: Hendrickson, 2007.
Macho, Alejandro Díez, ed. *Neophyti 1, Targum Palestinense ms. de la Biblioteca Vaticana 1.* Madrid: Consejo Superior de Investigaciones Científicas, 1968.
Macler, F. "L'Apocalypse arabe de Daniel: publiée, traduite et annotée." *Revue de l'histoire des religions* 37 (1904) 265–305.
Maekawa, K. "Cereal Cultivation in the Ur III Period." *Bulletin on Sumerian Agriculture* 1 (1984) 73–96.
Malamat, Abraham. "A New Record of Nebuchadnezzar's Palestinian Campaigns." *Israel Exploration Journal* 6 (1956) 246–56.
Manson, T. W. "The Son of Man in Daniel, Enoch and the Gospels." *Bulletin of the John Rylands Library* 32 (1950) 171–93.
Marcellinus, Ammianus. *Ammianus Marcellinus.* Translated by John C. Rolfe. 3 vols. LCL. Cambridge, MA: Harvard University Press, 1935–52.
Marcuse, Sibyl. *A Survey of Musical Instruments.* New York: Harper & Row, 1975.
Marquart, J. *Ērānšahr nach der Geographie des Ps. Moses Xorenac'i.* Berlin: Abhandlungen der königlichen Gesellschaft der Wissenschaften zu Göttingen, philosophische-historische Klasse, 1901.
Marsman, Hennie J. *Women in Ugarit and Israel: Their Social and Religious Position in the Context of the Ancient Near East.* Leiden: Brill, 2003.
Martin, W. J. "The Hebrew of Daniel." In *Notes on Some Problems in the Book of Daniel,* edited by W. D. Wiseman, 28–30. London: Tyndale, 1965.
Martinez, F. G., and E. J. C. Tigchelaar, eds. *The Dead Sea Scrolls Study Edition.* 2 vols. Leiden: Brill, 1997–98.
Martinez, Garcia F. *The Dead Sea Scrolls Translated: The Qumran Texts in English.* Grand Rapids: Eerdmans, 1994.
———. *Qumran and Apocalyptic.* Leiden: Brill, 1992.
Martinez, Garcia F., and E. J. C. Tigchelaar. *The Dead Sea Scroll Study Edition* 1. Leiden: Brill, 1998.
Mastin, Brian A. "Daniel 2:46 and the Hellenistic World." *Zeitschrift für die alttestamentliche Wissenschaft* 85 (1973) 80–93.
Matthews, Victor H., and Don C. Benjamin. *Old Testament Parallels: Laws and Stories from the Ancient Near East.* New York: Paulist, 1997.
Mattingly, Gerald L. "Tomb." In *Eerdmans Dictionary of the Bible,* edited by David Noel Freedman, 1319–20. Grand Rapids: Eerdmans, 2000.
Maxwell, C. Mervyn. *God Cares: The Message of Daniel for You and Your Family* 1. Nampa, ID: Pacific, 1981.
May, Herbert Gordon. "Three Hebrew Seals and the Status of Exiled Jehoiakin." *American Journal of Semitic Languages and Literature* 56 (1939) 146–48.
Mazani, Patrick. "The Book of Daniel in Light of the Ancient Near Eastern Literary and Material Finds: An Archaeological Perspective." PhD diss., Andrews University, 2008.
———. "Nebuchadnezzar's Deficits in Daniel 4:27 and His Response to Divine Promptings." *Journal of the Adventist Theological Society* 24 (2013) 59–74.
———. "The Number of Israelites at the Exodus Analyzed in the Light of Archaeological and Literary Evidence." Master's thesis, Seventh-day Adventist Theological Seminary, 1999.

BIBLIOGRAPHY

———. *On the Plains of Moab: Reflections for the End Times*. Bloomington, IN: Westbow, 2017.

Mazar, A. *Archaeology of the Land of the Bible, 1000–586 BCE*. Garden City, NY: Doubleday, 1990.

Mazar, Benjamin. *Biblical Israel*. Jerusalem: Magnes, 1992.

———. *The Mountain of the Lord*. Garden City, NY: Doubleday, 1975.

McComiskey, Thomas Edward. "The Seventy 'Weeks' of Daniel Against the Background of Ancient Near Eastern Literature." *The Westminster Theological Journal* 47 (1985) 18–45.

McDowell, Josh. *Daniel in the Critics' Den: Historical Evidence for the Authenticity of the Book of Daniel*. San Bernardino, CA: Campus Crusade for Christ, 1979.

McGovern, Patrick E. *Ancient Wine: The Search for the Origins of Viniculture*. Princeton: Princeton University Press, 2003.

McLay, R. Timothy. "Double Translations in the Greek Versions of Daniel." In *Interpreting Translation: Studies on the LXX and Ezekiel in Honour of Johan Lust*, edited by F. García Martínez, 255–67. Bibliotheca Ephemeridum Theologicarum Lovaniesium 192. Leuven: Leuven University Press, 2005.

McNamara, Martin. "Nabonidus and the Book of Daniel." *Irish Theological Quarterly* 37 (1970) 131–49.

Meinardus, O. "A Commentary on the XIVth Vision of Daniel from the History of the Patriarchs of the Egyptian Church." *Orientalia Christiana Periodica* 32 (1966) 394–449.

———. "New Evidence on the XIVth Vision of Daniel from the History of the Patriarchs of the Egyptian Church." *Orientalia Christiana Periodica* 34 (1968) 281–309.

Meissner, Bruno, and Wolfram von Soden. *Akkadisches Handwörterbuch*. 3 vols. Weisbaden: Otto Harrassowitz, 1965–81.

Mercer, Mark K. "The Benefactions of Antiochus IV Epiphanes and Dan 11:37–38: An Exegetical Note." *The Master's Seminary Journal* 12 (2001) 89–93.

Merrill, Eugene H. "Archaeology and Old Testament Biblical Theology: Their Interface and Mutual Informativeness." *Journal of the Adventist Theological Society* 26 (2015) 26–42.

Merry, W. W. *Homer: Odyssey*. Oxford: Clarendon, 1882.

Meshel, Ze'ev. "Kuntillet 'Ajrud—An Israelite Religious Center in Northern Sinai." *Expedition* 20 (1978) 50–54.

Mettinger, Tryggve N. D. "YHWH SABAOTH—The Heavenly King on the Cherubim Throne." In *Studies in the Period of David and Solomon and Other Essays*, edited by Tomoo Ishda, 109–38. Winona Lake, IN: Eisenbrauns, 1979.

Mignan, Robert. *Travels in Chaldæa, Including a Journey from Bussorah to Bagdad, Hillah, and Babylon, Performed on Foot in 1827*. London: H. Colburn and R. Bentley, 1829.

Mikaya, Adam. "Earliest Aramaic Inscription Uncovered in Syria." *Biblical Archaeology Review* 7 (1981) 52–53.

Milik, J. T. "Milkî-ṣedeq et Milkî-reša' dans les anciens écrits juifs et chrétiens." *Journal of Jewish Studies* 23 (1972) 95–144.

———. "Prière de Nabonide et autres écrits d'un cycle de Daniel: Fragments Araméens de Qumrân." *Revue Biblique* 63 (1956) 407–15.

Millard, A. R. "Daniel 1—6 and History." *Evangelical Quarterly* 49 (1977) 67–73.

———. "Large Numbers in the Assyrian Royal Inscriptions." In *Ah, Assyria . . .: Studies in Assyrian History and Ancient Near Eastern Historiography Presented to Hayim Tadmor*, edited by Mordechai Cogan and Israel Eph'al, 213-22. Jerusalem: Magnes, 1991.

Millard, A. R., and P. Bordreuil. "A Statue from Syria with Assyrian and Aramaic Inscriptions." *Biblical Archaeologist* 45 (1982) 135-41.

Miller, James E. "Dreams and Prophetic Visions." *Biblica* 71 (1990) 401-4.

Miller, J. Maxwell. "Moab and the Moabites." In *Studies in the Mesha Inscription and Moab*, edited by Andrew Dearman, 1-40. Atlanta: Scholars, 1989.

Miller, Nicholas P. "Calculating the 1260-Year Prophecy." In *Eschatology from an Adventist Perspective: Proceedings of the Fourth International Bible Conference: Rome, June 11-20, 2018*, edited by Elias Brasil de Souza et al., 559-72. Silver Spring, MD: Biblical Research Institute, 2021.

Mingana, A. "A New Jeremiah Apocryphon." *Bulletin of the John Rylands Library* 11 (1927) 352-95.

Mitchell, T. C. "The Music in the Old Testament Reconsidered." *Palestine Exploration Quarterly* 124 (1992) 124-43.

Mitchell, T. C., and R. Joyce. "The Musical Instruments in Nebuchadnezzar's Orchestra." In *Notes on Some Problems in the Book of Daniel*, edited by D. J. Wiseman et al., 19-27. London: Tyndale, 1965.

Montgomery, James A. *A Critical and Exegetical Commentary on the Book of Daniel*. International Critical Commentary. New York: Charles Scribner's Sons, 1927.

———. "Ras Shamra Notes VI: The Danel Text." *Journal of the American Oriental Society* 56 (1936) 440-45.

Montor, Artaud de. *The Lives and Times of the Roman Pontiffs: From St. Peter to Pius IX*. Translated and edited by William Hayes Neligan. 2 vols. New York: D. & J. Sadlier, 1866.

Moor, Johannes C. de. *The Rise of Yahwism: The Roots of Israelite Monotheism*. Leuven: Leuven University Press, 1990.

Moore, Ellen Whitley. *Neo-Babylonian Business and Administrative Documents*. Ann Arbor, MI: University of Michigan Press, 1935.

———. *Neo-Babylonian Documents in the University of Michigan Collection*. Ann Arbor, MI: University of Michigan Press, 1939.

Moran, William L., ed. *The Amarna Letters*. Baltimore, MD: Johns Hopkins University Press, 1992.

Morgenstern, Julian. "The 'Son of Man' of Daniel 7:13f.: A New Interpretation." *Journal of Biblical Literature* 80 (1960) 65-77.

Moskala, Jiří. "The Book of Daniel and the Maccabean Thesis." Paper presented at the Seventh-day Adventist Theological Seminary, Andrews University, Berrien Springs, MI, April 20, 2007.

Moulton, Harold K., ed. *The New Analytical Greek Lexicon*. Grand Rapids: Zondervan, 1990.

Mounce, William D., et al., eds. *Mounce's Complete Expository Dictionary of Old & New Testament Words*. Grand Rapids: Zondervan, 2006.

Mulzac, Kenneth D. "Gedaliah." In *Eerdmans Dictionary of the Bible*, edited by David Noel Freedman, 487-88. Grand Rapids: Eerdmans, 2000.

Muraoka, Takamitsu, and Bezalel Porten. *A Grammar of Egyptian Aramaic*. Leiden: Brill, 1998.

Murray, O. "Hecateus of Abdera and Pharonic Kingship." *Journal of Egyptian Archaeology* 56 (1970) 141–71.

Murtonen, A. *The Appearance of the Name YHWH Outside Israel.* Helsinki: Suomalaisen Kirjallisuuden Seuran Kirjapainon Oy, 1951.

Myers, Eric M., ed. *The Oxford Encyclopedia of Archaeology in the Near East.* 5 vols. New York: Oxford University Press, 1997.

Mykytiuk, Lawrence. "Archaeology Confirms 3 More Bible People." *Biblical Archaeology Review* 43 (2017) 48–52.

Nam, Daegeuk. *The "Throne of God" Motif in the Hebrew Bible.* Seoul: Institute for Theological Research, 1994.

Negev, Avraham, and Shimon Gibson, eds. *Archaeological Encyclopedia of the Holy Land.* New York: Continuum, 2001.

Nemet-Nejat, Karen Rhea. *Daily Life in Ancient Mesopotamia.* Peabody, MA: Hendrickson, 2002.

Netzer, A. "Daniyal-Mama and Its Linguistic Features." *Israel Oriental Studies* 2 (1972) 305–14.

———. "Dāniyāl-Nāme: An Exposition of Judeo-Persian." In *Islam and Its Cultural Divergences: Studies in Honor of Gustave E. Von Grunebaum*, edited by G. L. Tikko, 145–64. Chicago: University of Illinois Press, 1971.

Neusner, Jacob. *Esther Rabbah I: An Analytical Translation.* Atlanta: Scholars, 1989.

———. *The Talmud of Babylonia: An Academic Commentary* 1. Atlanta: Scholars, 1994.

Newton, Isaac. *Observations on the Prophecies of Daniel and the Apocalypse of St. John.* Edited by S. J. Barnett. Lewiston: E. Mellen, 1999.

Nichol, Francis D., ed. *The Seventh-day Adventist Bible Commentary.* 7 vols. Rev. ed. Hagerstown, MD: Review and Herald, 1976.

Niebhur, Carsten. *Travels Through Arabia and Other Countries.* Translated by Robert Heron. Edinburgh: R. Morisson and Son, 1792.

Nir, Rivka. *The Destruction of Jerusalem and the Idea of Redemption in the Syriac Apocalypse of Baruch.* Atlanta: Society of Biblical Literature, 2003.

Noth, Martin. *Die israelitischen Personennamen.* Hildesheim: Gg Olms, 1966.

———. *The Laws in the Pentateuch and Other Studies.* Translated by D. R. ap Thomas. Edinburgh: Oliver & Boyd, 1966.

Núñez, Samuel. *The Vision of Daniel 8: Interpretations from 1700 to 1800.* Berrien Springs, MI: Andrews University Press, 1987.

Oates, Joan. *Babylon.* London: Thames & Hudson, 1979.

———. "The Fall of Assyria (635–609 B.C.)." In *The Assyrian and Babylonian Empires and Other States of the Near East, From the Eighth to the Sixth Centuries B.C.*, edited by John Boardman et al., 162–93. Vol. 3/2 of *The Cambridge Ancient History.* Cambridge: Cambridge University Press, 1991.

Oates, Joan, and David Oates. *Nimrud: An Assyrian Imperial City Revealed.* London: British School of Archaeology in Iraq, 2001.

Oates, Joyce Carol, and Daniel Halpern. *Cat: A Gathering of Stories, Poems, and Miscellaneous Writings about Cats.* New York: Penguin, 1992.

Obermann, Julian. "The Divine Name YHWH in the Light of Recent Discoveries." *Journal of Biblical Literature* 68 (1949) 301–23.

Oded, Bustenay. *Mass Deportations and Deportees in the Neo-Assyrian Empire.* Wiesbaden: Dr. Ludwig Reichert Verlag, 1979.

Oelsner, Joachim, et al. "Neo-Babylonian Period." In *A History of Ancient Near Eastern Laws*, edited by Raymond Westbrook, 2:911–74. Leiden: Brill, 2003.
Oepke, Albrecht. "ἀποκαλύπτω." In *Theological Dictionary of the New Testament*, edited by Gerhard Kittel, 3:560–92. Grand Rapids: Eerdmans, 2006.
Oppenheim, A. Leo. *Ancient Mesopotamia: Portrait of a Dead Civilization*. Chicago: University of Chicago Press, 1979.
———. "Hammurabi." In *Interpreter's Dictionary of the Bible*, edited by G. A. Buttrick, 2:517–19. New York: Abingdon, 1962.
———. *The Interpretation of Dreams in the Ancient Near East, with a Translation of an Assyrian Dream Book*. Philadelphia: American Philosophical Society, 1956.
———. "Nebuchadnezzar." In *Interpreter's Dictionary of the Bible*, edited by G. A. Buttrick, 3:529–30. New York: Abingdon, 1962.
———. "A Note on Ša reši." *Journal of the Ancient Near East Society* 5 (1973) 325–34.
Ouaknin, Marc-Alain. *Mysteries of the Alphabet: The Origin of Writing*. New York: Abbeville, 1999.
Overholt, Thomas W. "King Nebuchadnezzar in the Jeremiah Tradition." *Catholic Biblical Quarterly* 30 (1968) 39–48.
Ovid. *Metamorphoses*. Translated by Frank Justus Miller. Cambridge, MA: Harvard University Press, 1984.
Owusu-Antwi, Brempong. *The Chronology of Daniel 9:24–27*. Adventist Theological Society Dissertation Series 2. Berrien Springs, MI: Adventist Theological Society, 1995.
Pamphilus, Eusebius. *The Life of the Blessed Emperor Constantine from 306 to 337 A.D. Ecclesiastical History*. London: Samuel Bagster, 1845.
Parpola, S. "The Forlorn Scholar." In *Language, Literature, and History: Philological and Historical Studies Presented to Erica Reiner*, edited by Francesca Rochberg-Halton, 257–78. AOS 67. New Haven, CT: American Oriental Society, 1987.
———. *Letters from Assyrian Scholars to Kings Esarhaddon and Assurbanipal*. 2 vols. Kevealer: Neukirchen-Vluyn, 1970–83.
———. *Neo-Assyrian Toponyms*. Kevealer: Butzon & Berker, 1970.
Parpola, S., ed. *Letters from Assyrian and Babylonian Scholars*. Helsinki: Helsinki University Press, 1993.
Parpola, S., et al., eds. *The Prosopography of the Neo-Assyrian Empire*. The Neo-Assyrian Text Corpus Project. 2 vols. Helinski: Neo-Assyrian Corpus Project, 1998.
Paton, W. R., trans. *Polybius: The Histories*. 6 vols. LCL. London: William Heinemann, 1923–27.
Patterson, Richard D. "The Key Role of Daniel 7." *Grace Theological Journal* 12 (1991) 245–61.
Paul, Shalom M. "Daniel 12:9: A Technical Mesopotamian Scribal Term." In *Sefer Moshe*, edited by Chaim Cohen et al., 115–18. Winona Lake, IN: Eisenbrauns, 2004.
Pearce, Laurie E. "How Bad Was the Babylonian Exile?" *Biblical Archaeology Review* 42 (2016) 49–54, 64.
Perrin, Bernadotte, trans. *Plutarch's Lives: Dion, Brutus, Timoleon and Aemilius Paulus* 6. Cambridge, MA: Harvard University Press, 1961.
Peshitta Institute, ed. *The Old Testament in Syriac, According to the Peshitta Version*. Edited on behalf of the International Organization for the Study of the Old Testament by the Peshitta Institute. Leiden: Brill, 1991.

Pfandl, Gerhard. *Daniel: The Seer of Babylon*. Hagerstown, MD: Review and Herald, 2004.

———. *The Time of the End in the Book of Daniel*. Berrien Springs, MI: ATS, 1992.

Pfeiffer, Charles F. *The Biblical World: A Dictionary of Biblical Archaeology*. Grand Rapids: Baker, 1966.

Pham, Xuan Huong Thi. *Mourning in the Ancient Near East and the Hebrew Bible*. JSOT Supplement Series 302. Sheffield: Sheffield Academic, 1999.

Philostratus. *The Life of Apollonius of Tyana*. Edited and translated by Christopher Jones. Cambridge, MA: Harvard University Press, 2006.

Pinches, Theophilus Goldridge. *The Old Testament in the Light of the Historical Records and Legends of Assyria and Babylonia*. London: Society for Promoting Christian Knowledge, 1903.

Pliny. *Natural History*. Translated by H. Rackam and W. H. S. Jones. 10 vols. LCL. Cambridge: Harvard University Press, 1961.

Polak, F. H. "The Daniel Tales in Their Aramaic Literary Milieu." In *The Book of Daniel in the Light of New Findings*, edited by A. S. Van der Woude, 249–65. Leuven: Leuven University Press, 1993.

Porten, Bezalel. "The Identity of King Adon." *Biblical Archaeologist* 44 (1981) 36–56.

Porten, Bezalel, and Ada Yarden. *Textbook of Aramaic Documents from Ancient Egypt*. Winona Lake, IN: Eisenbrauns, 1986.

Porteous, Norman W. *Daniel: A Commentary*. Old Testament Library. Philadelphia: Westminster, 1965.

Porter, Paul A. *Metaphors and Monsters: A Literary-Critical Study of Daniel 7 and 8*. Lund: CWK Gleerup, 1983.

Porter, Robert Ker. *Travels in Georgia, Persia, Armenia, Ancient Babylonia*. London: Longman, 1821–22.

Potts, Daniel T. *The Archaeology of Elam: Formation and Transformation of an Ancient Iranian State*. Cambridge World Archaeology. Cambridge: Cambridge University Press, 1999.

———. *Mesopotamian Civilization: The Material Foundations*. Ithaca, NY: Cornell University Press, 1997.

Powell, Marvin A. "Sumerian Cereal Crops." *Bulletin on Sumerian Agriculture* 1 (1984) 48–72.

———. "Wine and the Vine in Ancient Mesopotamia: The Cuneiform Evidence." In *The Origins and Ancient History of Wine*, edited by Patrick E. McGovern et al., 97–122. Amsterdam: Gordon and Breach, 1996.

Price, Randall. *The Stones Cry Out: What Archaeology Reveals About the Truth of the Bible*. Eugene, OR: Harvest House, 1997.

Price, Randall, and H. Wayne House. *Zondervan Handbook of Biblical Archaeology: A Book by Book Guide to Archaeological Discoveries Related to the Bible*. Grand Rapids: Zondervan, 2017.

Price, Walter K. *The Coming Anti-Christ*. Neptune, NJ: Loizeaux Brothers, 1985.

Prinsloo, G. T. M. "Two Poems in a Sea of Prose: The Content and Context of Daniel 2:20–23 and 6:26–27." *Journal for the Study of the Old Testament* 59 (1993) 93–108.

Pritchard, James B. *Recovering Sarepta, A Phoenician City*. Princeton, NJ: Princeton University Press, 1978.

Pritchard, James B., ed. *The Ancient Near East in Pictures Relating to the Old Testament*. Princeton, NJ: Princeton University Press, 1954.

———. *Ancient Near Eastern Texts Relating to the Old Testament*. 3rd ed. with supplement. Princeton, NJ: Princeton University Press, 1969.

———. *The Ancient Near East: Supplementary Texts and Pictures Relating to the Old Testament*. Princeton, NJ: Princeton University Press, 1969.

Pröbstle, Martin. "Truth and Terror: A Text-Oriented Analysis of Daniel 8:9-14." 2 vols. PhD diss., Andrews University, 2006.

Pusey, Edward B. *Daniel the Prophet: Nine Lectures Delivered in the Divinity School of the University of Oxford*. New York: Funk & Wagnalls, 1885.

Qimron, Elisha. *The Hebrew of the Dead Sea Scrolls*. Atlanta: Scholars, 1986.

Quinn, Jerome D. "Alcaeus 48 (B 16) and the Fall of Ascalon 604 B.C." *Bulletin of the American Schools of Oriental Research* 164 (1961) 19-20.

Quirke, Stephen, and Carol Andrews. *The Rosetta Stone: Facsimile Drawing*. New York: Abrams, 1989.

Rabinowitz, Isaac. "*Pēsher/Pittārōn*: Its Biblical Meaning and Its Significance in the Qumran Literature." *Revue de Qumran* 8 (1973) 219-32.

Rainey, Anson F. "Chaldea, Chaldeans." In *Encyclopaedia Judaica*, edited by Cecil Roth, 5:330-31. Jerusalem: Macmillan, 1971.

Rassam, Hormuzd. *Asshur and the Land of Nimrod*. New York: Eston & Mains, 1897.

Rawlinson, H. *The Cuneiform Inscriptions of Western Asia*. London: British Museum, 1861.

Ray, John. *A Collection of Curious Travels and Voyages in Two Tomes* 1. Microfilm. Ann Arbor, MI: University Microfilms, 1975.

Ray, Paul J. Jr. "The *Abomination of Desolation* in Daniel 9:27 and Related Texts: Theology of Retributive Judgement." In *To Understand the Scriptures: Essays in Honor of William H. Shea*, edited by David Merling, 205-13. Berrien Springs, MI: Institute of Archaeology, 1997.

Reade, J. "Neo-Assyrian Monuments in Their Historical Context." In *Assyrian Royal Inscriptions: New Horizons in Literary, Ideological, and Historical Analysis*, edited by F. M. Fales, 143-68. Rome: Istituto per l'Oriente, 1981.

Redditt, P. L., and Robert R. Kruschwitz. "Nebuchadnezzar as the Head of Gold: Politics and History in the Theology of the Book of Daniel." *Perspectives in Religious Studies* 24 (1997) 339-416.

Reiner, Erica. *Your Thwarts in Pieces, Your Mooring Rope Cut: Poetry from Babylonia and Assyria*. Ann Arbor, MI: Horace H. Rackham School of Graduate Studies at the University of Michigan, 1985.

Reiner, J. "The Original Hebrew Yosippon in the Chronicle of Jerahmeel." *Jewish Quarterly Review* 60 (1969-70) 128-46.

Rendsburg, Gary A. "'Someone Will Succeed in Deciphering Minoan': Cyrus H. Gordon and Minoan Linear A." *Biblical Archaeologist* 59 (1996) 36-43.

Rengstorf, K. H. "ἑπτά." In *Theological Dictionary of the New Testament*, edited by Gerhard Kittel, translated by Geoffrey W. Bromiley, 2:627-35. Grand Rapids: Eerdmans, 2006.

Resig, Dorothy D. "Cuneiform Tablet Confirms Biblical Name." *Biblical Archaeology Review* 33 (2007) 18.

Rimbach, J. A. "Bears or Bees? Sefire I A 31 and Daniel 7." *Journal of Biblical Literature* 97 (1978) 565-66.

Ringgren, H. "Akkadian Apocalypses." In *Apocalypticism in the Mediterranean World and the Near East*, edited by David Hellholm, 379-86. Tübingen: Mohr, 1979.

———. "The Root ṢDQ in Poetry and the Koran." In *Ex Orbe Religionum: Studia Geo Widengren, XXIV mense apr. MCMLXXII quo die lustra tredecim feliciter explevit oblata ab collegis, discipulis, amicis, collegae magistro amico congratulantibus*, edited by F. S. G. Widegren, 2:134–42. Leiden: Brill, 1972.

Ritmeyer, Leen, and Kathleen Ritmeyer. *Jerusalem in the Year 30 A.D.* Jerusalem: Carta, 2004.

Roaf, Michael. *Cultural Atlas of Mesopotamia and the Ancient Near East*. New York: Facts on File, 2000.

Rogers, Robert Williams. *Cuneiform Parallels to the Old Testament*. New York: Abingdon, 1926.

———. *A History of Babylonia and Assyria* 1. New York: Eaton and Mains, 1901.

Rosenberg, Roy A. "The God *Sedeq*." *Hebrew Union College Annual* 36 (1965) 161–77.

Roth, Martha T. *Babylonian Marriage Agreements 7th–3rd Centuries B.C.* Neukirchen Vluyn: Neukirchener, 1989.

Roux, Georges. *Ancient Iraq*. London: Penguin, 1992.

Rowley, H. H. *The Aramaic of the Old Testament: A Grammatical and Lexical Study of Its Relations with Other Early Aramaic Dialects*. London: Oxford University Press, 1929.

———. *Darius the Mede and the Four World Empire in the Book of Daniel*. Cardiff: University of Wales Press, 1959.

———. *The Servant of the Lord and Other Essays on the Old Testament*. London: Lutterworth, 1952.

Rummel, Stan, ed. *Ras Shamra Parallels*. Rome: Pontificum Institutum Biblicum, 1981.

Rydén, L. "The Andreas Salos Apocalypse: Greek Text, Translation and Commentary." *Dumbarton Oaks Papers* 28 (1974) 199–261.

Sack, Ronald H. *Amel-Marduk 562–560 B.C.: A Study Based on Cuneiform, Old Testament, Greek, Latin and Rabbinical Sources*. Neukirchen-Vluyn: Neukirchner, 1972.

———. *Images of Nebuchudnezzar: The Emergence of a Legend*. Toronto: Associated University Press, 1991.

———. *Neriglissar, King of Babylon*. Neukirchen-Vluyn: Neukirchener, 1994.

Saggs, H. W. F. *The Greatness That Was Babylon: A Sketch of the Ancient Civilization of the Tigris-Euphrates Valley*. New York: Hawthorn, 1962.

———. *Babylonians: Peoples of the Past*. Berkeley, CA: University of California Press, 2000.

Sami, Ali. *Pasargade: The Oldest Imperial Capital of Iran*. Translated by R. N. Sharp. Shiraz: Musavi, 1956.

Sartre, Maurice. *The Middle East Under Rome*. Cambridge, MA: Belknap, 2005.

Sasson, Jack M. "King Hammurabi of Babylon." In *Civilizations of the Ancient Near East*, edited by J. M. Sasson, 2:901–15. New York: Charles Scribner's Sons, 1995.

Satran, David. *Biblical Prophets in Byzantine Palestine: Reassessing the Lives of the Prophets*. Leiden: Brill, 1995.

Sayce, A. H. "Elam, Elamites." In *Dictionary of the Bible*, edited by James Hastings, 1:674–76. New York: Charles Scribner, 1908.

Schäfer, Peter. *The History of the Jews in the Greco-Roman World*. London: Routledge, 2003.

Schmidt, N. "The 'Son of Man' in the Book of Daniel." *Journal of Biblical Literature* 19 (1900) 22–28.

Schom, Alan. *Napoleon Bonaparte*. New York: HarperCollins, 1997.

Schoville, Keith N. "The Rosetta Stone in Historical Perspective." *Journal of the Adventist Theological Society* 12 (2001) 1–21.

Schrader, Eberhard. *The Cuneiform Inscriptions and the Old Testament*. London: Williams and Norgate, 1885.

Schrader, Eberhard, et al., eds. *Keilinschriftliche bibliothek: Sammlung von Assyrischen und Babylonischen Texten in umschrift und übersetzung* 3/2. Berlin: Reuther & Reichard, 1890.

Segert, Stanislav. *A Basic Grammar of the Ugaritic Language: With Selected Texts and Glossary*. Berkeley: University of California Press, 1997.

Seligson, M. "Daniel, in Arabic Literature." In *The Jewish Encyclopedia*, edited by Isidore Singer, 4:429. New York: Funk and Wagnalls, 1903.

Selms, A. van. "The Name Nebuchadnezzar." In *Travels in the World of the Old Testament*, edited by M. S. H. G. Heerma van Voss et al., 223–29. Assen: Van Gorcum, 1974.

Shanks, Hershel. "A 'Centrist' at the Center of Controversy." *Biblical Archaeology Review* 28 (2002) 38–49, 64–68.

———. "Ein Gedi's Archaeological Riches." *Biblical Archaeology Review* 34 (2008) 58–68.

———. "Jeremiah's Scribe and Confidant Speaks from a Hoard of Bullae." *Biblical Archaeology Review* 13 (1987) 58–65.

Shea, William H. "Daniel 3: Extra-Biblical Texts and the Convocation on the Plain of Dura." *Andrews University Seminary Studies* 20 (1982) 29–52.

———. *Daniel 1—7*. Abundant Life Bible Amplifier. Boise, ID: Pacific, 1996.

———. *Daniel 7—12*. Abundant Life Bible Amplifier. Boise, ID: Pacific, 1996.

———. *Daniel: A Reader's Guide*. Nampa, ID: Pacific, 2005.

———. "Early Development of the Antiochus Epiphanes Interpretation." In *Symposium on Daniel*, edited by Frank B. Holbrook, 256–328. Washington, DC: Biblical Research Institute, 1986.

———. "Nabonidus, Belshazzar, and the Book of Daniel: An Update." *Andrews University Seminary Studies* 20 (1982) 133–49.

———. "Nabonidus Chronicle: New Readings and the Identity of Darius the Mede." *Journal of Adventist Theological Society* 7 (1996) 1–20.

———. "The Search for Darius the Mede (Concluded), or, The Time of the Answer to Daniel's Prayer and the Date of the Death of Darius the Mede." *Journal of the Adventist Theological Society* 12 (2001) 97–105.

———. *Selected Studies on Prophetic Interpretation*. Daniel and Revelation Committee Series 1. Silver Spring, MD: Biblical Research Institute, 1992.

Shiff, L. B. "The Nur-Sin Archive: Private Entrepreneurship in Babylon." PhD diss., University of Pennsylvania, 1987.

Shiloh, Yigal. "A Group of Hebrew Bullae from the City of David." *Israel Exploration Journal* 36 (1986) 16–38.

———. "Jerusalem (Topography)." In *New Encyclopedia of Archaeological Excavations in the Holy Land*, edited by Ephraim Stern, 2:701–12. Jerusalem: Israel Exploration Society & Carta, 1993.

Siculus, Diodorus. *Diodorus of Sicily*. Translated by C. H. Oldfather. 12 vols. LCL. London: W. Heinemann, 1933–67.

Sjöberg, Erik. "בן אדם und בר אנש im Hebräischen und Aramäischen." *Acta Orientalia* 21 (1950-51) 57-65, 91-107.
Smith, G. A. "Moab." In *Encyclopedia Biblica*, edited by T. K. Cheyne and J. Sutherland Black, 3:3166-75. London: Adam and Charles Black, 1902.
Smith, Mark S. *The Ugaritic Baal Cycle: Introduction with Text, Translation and Commentary of KTU 1.1–1.2*. Vol. 1. Supplements to Vestus Testamentum 55. Leiden: Brill, 1994.
Smith, Morton. "On the History of ΑΠΟΚΑΛΥΠΤΩ and ΑΠΟΚΑΛΥΨΙΣ." In *Apocalypticism in the Mediterranean World and the Near East*, edited by David Hellholm, 9-20. Tübingen: Mohr, 1989.
Smith, Sydney. *Babylonian Historical Texts: Relating to the Capture and Downfall of Babylon*. London: Methuen, 1924.
———. "Notes on the Assyrian Tree." *Bulletin of the School of Oriental Studies* 4 (1926) 69-76.
———. "The Relation of Marduk, Ashur, and Osiris." *The Journal of Egyptian Archaeology* 8 (1922) 41-44.
Smith, Uriah. *The Sanctuary and Its Cleansing*. Battle Creek, MI: Steam, 1877.
Snyder, Franke, et al. "What the Temple Mount Floor Looked Like." *Biblical Archaeology Review* 42 (2016) 56-59.
Sokoloff, Michael. *The Targum to Job from Qumran Cave XI*. Ramat-Gan: Bar-Ilan University, 1974.
Sparks, H. F. D. "On the Origin of 'Darius the Mede' at Daniel v. 31." *Journal of Theological Studies* 47 (1946) 41-46.
Spiciarich, Abra. "The Jerusalem Diet." *Biblical Archaeology Review* 44 (2018) 43.
Spicq, Ceslas. *Theological Lexicon of the New Testament*. Edited by James D. Ernest. 3 vols. Peabody, MA: Hendrickson, 1996.
Spiegel, Shalom. "Noah, Daniel, and Job, Touching on Canaanite Relics in the Legends of the Jews." In *Essential Papers on Israel and the Ancient Near East*, edited by Frederick E. Greenspahn, 193-241. New York: New York University Press, 1991.
Srechkovic, P. S. "Zbornik Popa Dragolja." *Spomenik* 5 (1890) 10-11.
Starky, J. "Une tablette araméene de l'an 34 de Nabuchodonosor." *Syria* 37 (1960) 99-115.
Starr, Ivan, ed. *Queries to the Sungod: Divination and Politics in Sargonid Assyria*. Helsinki: Helsinki University Press, 1990.
Starr, J. *The Jews in the Byzantine Empire 641-1204*. New York: B. Franklin, 1970.
Stefanovic, Zdravko. *The Aramaic of Daniel in the Light of Old Aramaic*. Journal for the Study of the Old Testament 129. Sheffield: Sheffield Academic, 1992.
———. *Daniel: Wisdom to the Wise, Commentary on the Book of Daniel*. Nampa, ID: Pacific, 2007.
———. "Thematic Links Between the Historical and Prophetic Sections of Daniel." *Andrews University Seminary Studies* 27 (1989) 121-27.
Steingass, F. *English-Arabic Dictionary*. London: Crosby Lockwood and Son, 1882.
Stern, Ephraim. *Archaeology of the Land of the Bible: The Assyrian, Babylonian, and Persian Periods 732-332 BCE* 2. New York: Doubleday, 2001.
———. "The Babylonian Gap." *Biblical Archaeology Review* 26 (2000) 45-51, 76.
———. "The Babylonian Gap: The Archaeological Reality." *Journal for the Study of the Old Testament* 28 (2004) 273-77.

Stern, E., ed. *The New Encyclopedia of Archaeological Excavations in the Holy Land.* 4 vols. Jerusalem: Israel Exploration Society & Carta, 1993.
Stevens, David E. "Daniel 10 and the Notion of Territorial Spirits." *Bibliotheca Sacra* 157 (2000) 410–31.
Stevens, Marty E. *Temples, Tithes and Taxes: The Temple and the Economic Life of Ancient Israel.* Peabody, MA: Hendrickson, 2006.
Stolper, Matthew W. "A Note on Yahwistic Personal Names in the Marashu Texts." *Bulletin of the American Schools of Oriental Research* 222 (1976) 25–28.
Stone, Michael Edward. *Il Caucaso: cerneira fra culture dal Mediterraneo alla Persia.* Spoleto: Presso la sede del Centro, 1996.
———. *Selected Studies in Pseudepigrapha and Apocrypha with Special Reference to the Armenian Tradition.* Leiden: Brill, 1991.
Stone, Michael Edward, trans. *Armenian Apocrypha Relating to Patriarchs and Prophets.* Jerusalem: Israel Academy of Sciences and Humanities, 1982.
Strabo. *The Geography of Strabo.* Translated by Horace Leonard Jones. 8 vols. London: Willian Heinemann, 1917–33.
Stronach, David. "The Imagery of the Wine Bowl: Wine in Assyria in the Early First Millennium B.C." In *The Origins and Ancient History of Wine*, edited by Patrick E. McGovern et al., 175–95. Amsterdam: Gordon and Breach, 1996.
———. *Pasargadae: A Report on the Excavations Conducted by the British Institute of Persian Studies from 1961 to 1963.* Oxford: Clarendon, 1978.
Swain, J. C. "The Theory of the Four Monarchs: Opposition History Under the Roman Empire." *Classical Philology* 35 (1940) 1–21.
Tabouis, G. R. *Nebuchadnezzar.* London: Routledge, 1931.
Talmon, S. "Daniel." In *The Literary Guide to the Bible*, edited by Robert Alter and Frank Kermode, 343–56. Cambridge, MA: Belknap, 1987.
Tanner, J. Paul. "Ancient Babylon: From Gradual Demise to Archaeological Rediscovery." *Near East Archaeological Society Bulletin* 47 (2004) 12–18.
Taylor, Richard A. *The Peshiṭta of Daniel.* Leiden: Brill, 1994.
Thackeray, H. S. J., trans. *The Letter of Aristeas.* London: Society for Promoting Christian Knowledge, 1918.
Thayer, Joseph H. *Thayer's Greek-English Lexicon of the New Testament.* Peabody, MA: Hendrickson, 2003.
Thiele, Edwin R. *The Mysterious Numbers of the Hebrew Kings.* New rev. ed. Grand Rapids: Kregel, 1994.
Thomas, D. Winton., ed. *Documents from Old Testament Times: Ancient Texts and Translations.* New York: Thomas Nelson and Sons, 1961.
Thompson, J. M. *Napoleon Bonaparte: His Rise and Fall.* New York: Oxford University Press, 1969.
Thompson, Steven. "Those Who Are Wise: The *Maskilim* in Daniel and the New Testament." In *To Understand the Scriptures: Essays in Honor of William H. Shea*, edited by David Merling, 215–20. Berrien Springs, MI: Institute of Archaeology, 1997.
Tobi, Joseph. "A Judeo-Arabic Version of the Predictive Book Malhamat Daniyal." In *The Jews of Yemen: Studies in their History and Culture*, edited by Yosef Tobi, 242–54. Leiden: Brill, 1999.
Torczyner, Harry. *The Lachish Letters.* 4 vols. London: Oxford University Press, 1938.

Torrey, Charles C. "Medina and ΠΟΛΙΣ, and Luke i. 39." *The Harvard Theological Review* 17 (1924) 83-91.
Tov, Emanuel. *The Text-Critical Use of the Septuagint in Biblical Research*. Jerusalem: Simor, 1997.
Towner, Wayne Sibley. "Completion of the Publication of Some Fragments from Qumran Cave 1." *Revue de Qumran* 19 (1965) 323-44.
———. *Daniel*. Atlanta: John Knox, 1984.
———. "Poetic Passages of Daniel 1—6." *Catholic Biblical Quarterly* 31 (1969) 317-26.
———. "Were the English Puritans 'the Saints of the Most High'? Issues in the Precritical Interpretation of Daniel 7." *Interpretation* 37 (1983) 46-63.
Trevor, John C. "The Book of Daniel and the Origin of the Qumran Community." *Biblical Archaeologist* 48 (1985) 89-102.
Ulrich, Eugene C. "Daniel Manuscripts from Qumran Part 1: A Preliminary Edition of 4QDan^a." *Bulletin of the American Schools of Oriental Research* 268 (1987) 17-37.
———. "Daniel Manuscripts from Qumran Part 2: A Preliminary Edition of 4QDan^b and 4QDan^c." *Bulletin of the American Schools of Oriental Research* 274 (1989) 3-26.
———. "The Text of Daniel in the Qumran Scrolls." In *The Book of Daniel: Composition and Reception*, edited by J. J. Collins and Peter W. Flint, 2:573-85. Leiden: Brill, 2002.
Unger, E. *Babylon: die heilige Stadt nach der Beschreibung der Babylonier*. Berlin: Walter de Gruyter, 1931.
Valle, Pietro Della. *Viaggi di Pietro Della Valle*. Brighton: Gancia, 1843.
Van Beek, Gus W. "Jemmeh, Tell." In *New Encyclopedia of Archaeological Excavations in the Holy Land*, edited by Ephraim Stern, 2:667-74. Jerusalem: Israel Exploration Society & Carta, 1993.
Vanderhooft, David Stephen. *The Neo-Babylonian Empire and Babylon in the Latter Prophets*. Atlanta: Scholars, 1999.
Vanderkam, James C., and Peter W. Flint. *The Meaning of the Dead Sea Scrolls: Their Significance for Understanding the Bible, Judaism, Jesus, and Christianity*. New York: HarperCollins, 2002.
Van de Mieroop, Marc. *The Ancient Mesopotamian City*. Oxford: Clarendon, 1997.
———. *A History of the Ancient Near East ca. 3000-323 BC*. Malden, MA: Blackwell, 2004.
Van der Toorn, Karel. "In the Lions' Den: The Babylonian Background of a Biblical Motif." *Catholic Biblical Quarterly* 60 (1998) 626-40.
———. "Scholars at the Oriental Court: The Figure of Daniel Against Its Mesopotamian Background." In *The Book of Daniel: Composition and Reception*, edited by J. J. Collins and P. W. Flint, 1:37-54. Leiden: Brill, 2002.
Van der Toorn, Karel, et al., eds. *Dictionary of Deities and Demons in the Bible*. Grand Rapids: Eerdmans, 1999.
Van der Woude, A. S. "11Q Melchizedek and the New Testament." *New Testament Studies* 12 (1966) 301-26.
VanGemeren, Willem A., ed. *New International Dictionary of Old Testament and Exegesis*. 5 vols. Grand Rapids: Zondervan, 1997.
Van Henten, Jan Willem. "Antiochus IV as a Typhonic Figure in Daniel 7." In *The Book of Daniel in the Light of New Findings*, edited by A. S. van der Woude, 223-43. Leuven: Leuven University Press, 1993.

BIBLIOGRAPHY

Van Zyl, A. H. *The Moabites*. Leiden: Brill, 1960.
Velázquez, Efrain. "An Archaeological Reading of Malachi." PhD diss., Andrews University, 2008.
Vermes, Geza. *The Complete Dead Sea Scrolls in English*. New York: Penguin, 1997.
Vermeylen, Jacques. *Ten Keys for Opening the Bible: An Introduction to the First Testament*. New York: Continuum, 2000.
Voigtlander, Elizabeth von. *The Bisitun Inscription of Darius the Great: Babylonian Version 2/1*. London: Lund Humphries, 1978.
Volz, Paul. *Jüdische Eschatologie von Daniel bis Akiba*. Leipzig: Mohr, 1903.
Von Rad, G. *Wisdom in Israel*. Nashville: Abingdon, 1972.
Von Reber, Franz. *History of Ancient Art*. New York: Harper and Brothers, 1882.
Von Soden, W. *Akkadisches Handwörterbuch*. 3 vols. Weisbaden: Harrassowitz, 1965–81.
Vööbus, Arthur. *The Hexapla and the Syro-Hexapla: Very Important Discoveries for Septuagint Research*. Stockholm: Estonian Theological Society in Exile, 1971.
Wacholder, Ben Zion. *Eupolemus: A Study of Judaeo-Greek Literature*. Jerusalem: Hebrew Union College—Jewish Institute of Religion, 1974.
Walbank, F. W. *The Hellenistic World*. Cambridge, MA: Harvard University Press, 1982.
Waldbaum, Jane. "Greeks in the East or Greeks and the East? Problems in the Definition and Recognition of Presence." *Bulletin of the American Schools of Oriental Research* 305 (1997) 1–17.
Walker, C. B. F. *Cuneiform: Reading the Past*. Berkeley, CA: University of California Press, 1987.
Walton, J. H. "The Anzu Myth as Relevant Background of Daniel?" In *The Book of Daniel: Composition and Reception*, edited by John J. Collins and Peter W. Flint, 1:69–89. Leiden: Brill, 2002.
———. "The Four Kingdoms of Daniel." *Journal of the Evangelical Theological Society* 29 (1986) 25–36.
Walton, John H., et al., eds. *The IVP Bible Background Commentary: Old Testament*. Downers Grove, IL: InterVarsity, 2000.
Walvoord, John F. *Daniel: The Key to Prophetic Revelation*. Chicago: Moody, 1989.
Washburn, David L. *A Catalogue of Biblical Passages in the Dead Sea Scrolls*. Leiden: Brill, 2003.
Waszink, J. H., ed. *Quinti Septimi Florentis Tertullian: De Anima*. Amsterdam: J. F. Meulenhoff, 1947.
Waterhouse, S. Douglas. "Why Was Darius the Mede Expunged from History?" In *To Understand the Scriptures: Essays in Honor of William H. Shea*, edited by David Merling, 173–89. Berrien Springs, MI: Institute of Archaeology, 1997.
Waterman, Leroy. "A Note on Daniel 8:2." *Journal of Biblical Literature* 66 (1947) 319–20.
———. *Royal Correspondence of the Assyrian Empire*. Ann Arbor, MI: University of Michigan Press, 1931.
Watts, James W. "'This Song' Conspicuous Poetry in Hebrew Prose." In *Verse in Ancient Near Eastern Prose*, edited by Johannes C. de Moor and Wilfred G. E. Watson, 345–58. Kevelaer: Butzon und Bercker, 1993.
Wectar. "Three Wise Men Quote." Pinterest, pin. https://www.pinterest.com/pin/3448137195361844/.

Wehr, H. *A Dictionary of Modern Written Arabic*. Edited by J. M. Cowan. Weisbaden: Harrassowitz, 1979.

Weinfeld, Moshe. "'Justice and Righteousness' in Ancient Israel Against the Background of 'Social Reforms' in the Ancient Near East." In *Mesopotamien und seine Nachbarn*, edited by Hans-Jörg Nissen and Johannes Renger, 2:491–519. Berlin: Dietrich Reimer, 1982.

———. "Semiramis: Her Name and Her Origin." In *Ah, Assyria . . .: Studies in Assyrian History and Ancient Near Eastern Historiography Presented to Hayim Tadmor*, edited by M. Cogan and I. Eph'al, 99–103. Jerusalem: Magnes, 1991.

Weippert, Manfred. "Relations of the States East of the Jordan with the Mesopotamian Powers During the First Millennium BC." In *Studies in the History and Archaeology of Jordan III*, edited by Adnan Hadidi, 97–105. Amman: Department of Antiquities, 1989.

———. "Semitische Nomaden des zweiten Jahrtausends." *Biblica* 55 (1974) 265–80.

Wellard, James. *Babylon*. New York: Saturday Review, 1972.

Wellesz, Egon. *Ancient and Oriental Music*. London: Oxford University Press, 1960.

Wenham, David. "The Kingdom of God and Daniel." *Expository Times* 98 (1987) 132–34.

Wenham, Gordon J. "Daniel: The Basic Issues." *Themelios* 2 (1977) 49–52.

Westenholz, Joan Goodnick. "Babylon—Place of Creation of the Great Gods." In *Royal Cities of the Biblical World*, edited by J. G. Westenholz, 197–233. Jerusalem: Bible Lands Museum, 1996.

Whitcomb, John C. *Darius the Mede: A Study in Historical Identification*. Grand Rapids: Eerdmans, 1959.

White, Ellen G. *Education*. Nampa, ID: Pacific, 1952.

———. *The Story of Prophets and Kings*. Boise, ID: Pacific, 1943.

Widengren, Geo. *The King and the Tree of Life in Ancient Near Eastern Religion (King and Saviour IV)*. Uppsala: Lundequistska Bokhandeln, 1951.

———. "The Persians." In *Peoples of Old Testament Times*, edited by D. J. Wiseman, 312–57. Oxford: Clarendon, 1973.

Wiig, Arne. "Mene, mene, tekel-ufarsin." *Svensk Exegetisk Årsbok* 58 (1988) 26–35.

Wilkinson, J. Gardner. *The Manners and Customs of the Ancient Egyptians* 1. New York: Dodd, Mead and Company, 1878.

Wilkinson, Richard H. *The Complete Gods and Goddesses of Ancient Egypt*. London: Hudson & Thames, 2003.

Williams, George. *The Holy City: Historical, Topographical and Antiquarian Notices of Jerusalem* 1/1. London: John W. Parker, 1849.

Wilson, E. J. *The Cylinders of Gudea*. Kevelaer: Butzon and Bercker, 1996.

Wilson, Kinnier J. V. *The Nimrud Wine Lists: A Study of Men and Administration at the Assyrian Capital in the Eighth Century B.C.* London: British School of Archaeology in Iraq, 1972.

Wilson, R. D. "The Aramaic of Daniel." In *Biblical and Theological Studies*, edited by Princeton Theological Seminary, 261–306. Princeton: Princeton University Press, 1912.

———. *Studies in the Book of Daniel*. New York: Fleming H. Revell, 1938.

Wilson, William. *Old Testament Word Studies*. Grand Rapids: Kregel, 1980.

Winkle, Ross E. "Jeremiah's Seventy Years for Babylon: A Re-Assessment. Part I: The Scriptural Data." *Andrews University Seminary Studies* 25.2 (1987) 201–14.

———. "Jeremiah's Seventy Years for Babylon: A Re-Assessment. Part II: The Historical Data." *Andrews University Seminary Studies* 25.3 (1987) 289–99.

Wiseman, Donald. J. *Chronicles of Chaldaean Kings (626–556 B.C.) in the British Museum*. London: British Museum, 1956.

———. *Cylinder Seals of Western Asia*. Illustrations by W. Forman and B. Forman. London: Batchworth, 1959.

———. *Nebuchadrezzar and Babylon*. Oxford: Oxford University Press, 1995.

———. "Some Egyptians in Babylonia." *Iraq* 28 (1966) 154–58.

———. "Some Historical Problems in the Book of Daniel." In *Notes on Some Problems in the Book of Daniel*, edited by Donald J. Wiseman et al., 9–18. London: Tyndale, 1965.

Wittstruck, Thorne. "The Influence of Treaty Curse Imagery on the Beast Imagery of Daniel 7." *Journal of Biblical Literature* 97 (1978) 100–2.

Wolters, Al. "The Riddle of the Scales in Daniel 5." *Hebrew Union College Annual* 62 (1991) 155–77.

———. "Zōhar hārāqîaʿ (Daniel 12.3) and Halley's Comet." *Journal for the Study of the Old Testament* 61 (1994) 111–20.

Wright, Charles H. H. *Daniel and His Prophecies*. London: Williams and Norgate, 1906.

Wright, W. *The Homilies of Aphraates, the Persian Sage: The Syriac Text* 1. London: Williams and Norget, 1869.

Xenophon. *Anabasis*. Translated by Carleton L. Brownson. Cambridge, MA: Harvard University Press, 1998.

———. *Cyropaedia*. 2 vols. Translated by Walter Miller. Cambridge, MA: Harvard University Press, 1923.

Yadin, Yigael. *The Art of Warfare in Biblical Lands in the Light of Archaeological Study*. Vol. 2. New York: McGraw Hill, 1963.

Yamauchi, Edwin M. "Babylon." In *Major Cities of the Biblical World*, edited by R. K. Harrison, 32–48. New York: Thomas Nelson, 1985.

———. "Daniel and Contacts Between the Aegean and the Near East Before Alexander." *Evangelical Quarterly* 53 (1981) 37–47.

———. "The Eastern Jewish Diaspora Under the Babylonians." In *Mesopotamia and the Bible*, edited by Mark W. Chavalas and K. Lawson Younger, 356–77. Grand Rapids: Baker, 2002.

———. *Greece and Babylon: Early Contacts Between the Aegean and the Near East*. Baker Studies in Biblical Archaeology. Grand Rapids: Baker, 1967.

———. *Persia and the Bible*. Grand Rapids: Baker, 2000.

———. "Persians." In *Peoples of the Old Testament World*, edited by Alfred J. Hoerth et al., 107–24. Grand Rapids: Baker, 2003.

Yarchin, William. *History of Biblical Interpretation*. Peabody, MA: Hendrickson, 2004.

Yardeni, A. "Remarks on the Priestly Blessing on Two Ancient Amulets from Jerusalem." *Vetus Testamentum* 41 (1991) 176–85.

Young, Edward J. *The Prophecy of Daniel: A Commentary*. Grand Rapids: Eerdmans, 1949.

Younker, Randall W. "Ammonites." In *Peoples of the Old Testament World*, edited by Alfred J. Hoerth et al., 293–316. Grand Rapids: Baker, 1998.

———. "Daniel 9:25 Square and Moat." Lecture, Andrews University, Berrien Springs, MI, October 2001.

---. *The Emergence of the Ammonites*. Ann Arbor, MI: UMI Dissertation Services, 1997.

---. "Israel, Judah, Ammon and the Motifs on the Baalis Seal from Tell el 'Umeiri." *Biblical Archaeologist* 48 (1985) 173–80.

---. "Jalul 2007." *The Institute of Archaeology: Siegfried H. Horn Museum* 28 (2007) 1–2.

Zadok, Ran. *The Earliest Diaspora Israelites and Judeans in Pre-Hellenistic Mesopotamia*. Tel Aviv: Tel Aviv University Press, 2001.

---. "The Earliest Diaspora: The Judeans in Babylonia and Their Neighbors." Lecture, Horn Archaeological Museum, Andrews University, Berrien Springs, MI, October 5, 2004.

---. *The Jews in Babylonia During the Chaldean and Achaemenian Periods According to the Babylonian Periods*. Haifa: University of Haifa Press, 1978.

---. *On West Semites in Babylonia During the Chaldean and Achaemenian Periods: An Onomastic Study*. Jerusalem: H. J. & Z. Wanaarta, 1978.

---. "The Origin of the Name Shinar." *Zeitschrift für Assyriologie* 74 (1984) 240–44.

---. "The Representation of Foreigners in Neo- and Late-Babylonian Legal Documents (Eighth Through Second Centuries B.C.E.)." In *Judah and the Judeans in the Neo-Babylonian Period*, edited by Oded Lipschits and Joseph Blenkinsopp, 471–589. Winona Lake, IN: Eisenbrauns, 2003.

Zawadzki, Stefan. *The Fall of Assyria and Median-Babylonian Relations in the Light of the Nabopolassar Chronicle*. Delft: Adam Mickiewicz University Press, 1988.

Zeitlin, S. "Dreams and Their Interpretation from the Biblical Period to the Tannaitic Time: An Historical Study." *Jewish Quarterly Review* 66 (1975–76) 1–18.

Zervos, George T. "Apocalypse of Daniel." In *The Old Testament Pseudepigrapha: Apocalyptic Literature and Testaments*, edited by James H. Charlesworth, 1:755–70. New York: Doubleday, 1983.

Zevit, Ziony. "The Khirbet el-Qôm Inscription Mentioning a Goddess." *Bulletin of the American Schools of Oriental Research* 255 (1984) 39–47.

---. "The Structure and Individual Elements of Daniel 7." *Zeitschrift für die alttestamentliche Wissenschaft* 80 (1968) 385–96.

---. "The Use of עבד as a Diplomatic Term in Jeremiah." *Journal of Biblical Literature* 88 (1969) 74–77.

Zimansky, Paul. "Archaeology and Texts in the Ancient Near East." In *Archaeologies of the Middle East: Critical Perspectives*, edited by Susan Pollock and Reinhard Bernbeck, 308–26. Malden, MA: Blackwell, 2005.

Zimmermann, Frank. "The Writing on the Wall: Dan. 5.22f." *Jewish Quarterly Review* 55 (1964) 201–7.

INDEX

Note: Page numbers in *italics* indicate figures, and page numbers in **bold** indicate tables in the text

1260 days, 176
1,290 days/years, 280
1,335 days/years, 280–81
2,300 days/years, 191

accession system, 2–3, **3**, 42
accusation, 83
Adad-Nirari III, 161
afterlife, 270
Agrippina, 248–49
Akitu festival, 110, 115–17, 123
Alexander the Great, 236–37, 241–42, 244
Alobaidi, Joseph, 147
Amel-Marduk, 104
Ammonites, 260–63
Ancient of Days, 169–70
angels, 94–95
animal(s)
  bones, 19–20
  horns (*See* horns)
  as kingdoms, 60, 62
  See also beasts
anointing oneself, 231–32. *See also* perfumes
Antigonus, 243, 247
Antiochus III the Great, 243–45
Antiochus II Theos, 243
Antipas, Herod, 247–48
Antony, Mark, 247
Apries, 263–64
Aramaic language, 47–50

Arioch, 54
Artaxerxes, 89
Ashpenaz, 27
Ashurbanipal, 76
Assurbanipal, 127
astrologers/astrology, 40, 129, 272
Atrahasis, 72
at that time, 268
Azatiwada, 181

Baalis, 262
Babylon, 97–101
  ancient ruins, 98
  Benjamin of Tudela on, 101
  city gates, 100
  Herodotus on, 99
  interment or burials, 271
  Jewish captivity, 205–7
  topographical features, 99–100
  See also Neo-Babylonian Empire
Babylonian seals
  cylinder, *273*, 275
  epigraphic and non-epigraphic, 275
bag-pipe, 77–79
barley, 35, 36
battle
  of Carchemish, 1, 3–4, **5**, 76, 263
  of Chaeronea, 236
  of Panion, 245
  of Pydna, 245, 246
  of Waterloo, 267
bearlike beasts, 166–67

INDEX

beasts, 101–2, 162–68
  bearlike, 166–67
  dreadful and terrible, 167–68
  leopard-like, 167
  lionlike, 165–66
Behistun Inscription, 50–51, 141, 234
Belshazzar, 129
  banquet, 122–23
  biological father, 156
  first year, 156, 178
  gifts, 134
  great feast, 114–15
  identity, 106–8
  as king of Babylon, 108–14
  murder of, 136–37
  as Nebuchadnezzar's son, 133
  offering, 120–22
  wine, 117
  wives and concubines, 118–20
  See also Neo-Babylonian Empire
Benjamin of Tudela, 101, 271
Berenice, 243
Berossus, 5
besieging enemy cities, 17–18
biblical eponymous practice, **134**
boanthropy, 95
book of life, 269
  name is written, 269
book of truth, 237
books, 170–71, 197–98
Brewer, David, 135
British Museum, 119, 229, 263
  Assyrian bas-relief, 115
  Chronicle 5, Tablet BM 21946, 4
  gold face masks, 69
  India House Inscription, 161
  Instruction of Amenemope of
    Egypt, 269
  mappa mundi, 157
  Nebuchadnezzar inscription, 23
  wooden object ornamented with
    lapis lazuli, 114–15
burials, 271
burning by fire, 80–83

Caesar, Augustus, 247
Caesar, Julius, 247
Cairo Sandstone Stele, 220
Caligula, 248
Cambyses II, 139, 149–50, 239
Canaanite fertility cult, 270
captives, 29, 56–57, 134, 151
Caquot, A., 164
Caragounis, C. C., 61
casting lots, 281–82
Chaldeans, 33–34
  language, 32
  wisdom and knowledge, 32–33
Christians, 254–56
Chronicles of Jerahmeel, 102
citadel, 181
Claudius, 248–49
Cleopatra, 245
Clovis, 280
Code of Hammurabi, 51–52, 52, 81
Collins, John J., 2, 49, 69, 162–63,
    164, 169, 192, 233
Colossus of Rhodes, 67
concubinage, 119
concubines, 118–20. *See also* wives
confession, 211–12
conjurers, 40
Constantine, 254–55, 255
court scenes, 168–69
covenant, 212–13
Croesus, 146
curse, 216–17
cylinder seals, 274
  Babylonian, 273, 275
Cyprus Stela of Sargon II, 59
Cyrus Cylinder, 26, 27, 73, 118, 137,
    154, 219–20, 228, 229, 234–35
Cyrus II, 140, 145–46
Cyrus the Great, 40, 154–55, 207,
    220, 239

Daniel
  Aramaic of, 47–50
  blowing winds of, 64
  as chief prefect, 65
  death of, 271
  Nebuchadnezzar honoring, 65
  place of prayer, 150
  as a top government official, 134,
    142
  upper room of, 150

INDEX

Darius I, 139, 141, 153–54, 220, 239
  limestone relief, *240*
  Naqsh-i-Rustam inscription, 86
  palace relief, *147*
Darius II, 221
Darius the Mede, 137, 138–42
Day, John, 164
dead as righteous, 135
Dead Sea Scrolls (DSS), 154, 160, 193, 277
dedication, 71–72
defiling/defiled ones, 38–39
Deioces, 141
Delitzsch, Franz, 41, 159
deliver/delivered, 85, 269
Desaix, 265, 266–67
desolation of sanctuary, 189–90, 218
destroying people, 86
dew of heaven, 95
divine books, 170–71
  motif of, 170
dreams
  within a dream, 190–91
  interpretation of, 42–44
  Nebuchadnezzar, 44–46
  omens, 42–43
  prognostic, 42
  revealing of, 55
  symbolic message, 42
  types, 42
  See also vision
Driver, Samuel R., 48
dynastic marriage, 243

earth, 53–54, 88–89, 186
Ebed-melech, 266
Edom, 258–59
Egypt, 26, 60, 243, 263–65
  black slaves, 266–67
  dream interpreters, 44
  exodus of Israelites from, 218
  Great Sphinx at Giza, 67, *68*
  magicians, 39–40
  Mameluks, 257, 266–67
  Merneptah, 58
  Napoleon's expedition, 257, 259, 263, 265, 267

Nebuchadnezzar invading, 3–4, 9, 15
  Ptolemy III and, 243
  Shinar, 25
  Zedekiah and, 12–13
Elam, 181–82
Ellis, Richard, 50
Epicharmus, 134
Esarhaddon, 44, 261
escaping, 269
Etemenanki cylinder, 21–22, 72–73
Ethiopians, 265–66
eunuchs, 27–28
Euphrates River, 136, 232–33
Ezekiel, the prophet, 14–15

fasting, 152, 209–11. *See also* mourning rites
feast, 114–15
fiery furnace, 80–83, 86
Fitzmyer, Joseph, 48
flood, 225–26
Florus, Gessius, 249–50
flute. *See* pipe/flute
foods, 34–36
four-kingdom schema, 58–62
fourth kingdom and kings, 245–48
four winds of heaven, 157–59, 186
Fresnel, F., 140

Gabriel, 191–92
Gallus, Cestius, 250
Garsiel, Moshe, 91
gazers, 57–58
Gedaliah, 13–14
generations, 90
gigantic images, 58, 67–69
goats, 186
God
  of Babylonians, 84–85
  changing times and seasons, 56
  of Daniel, 24
  at final party, 122–26
  holy, 93
  hymns to, 55–56
  images, 67–70
  of Nebuchadnezzar, 24, 93
  revealing secrets, 55

399

INDEX

godliness/godlikeness, 280
gold
  chain, 129
  face masks, 69
  image of, 67–70
  vessels, 118
Goldingay, John E., 160
grain offering, 64
Grayson, 102, 144
great image, 58. *See also* gigantic images
Great Sea, 159–61
Great Sphinx at Giza, Egypt, 67, *68*
great trembling, 234
Grecian Scheme, 62
Greece/Greek kingdom, 60–61, 193–95
  battle of Pydna, 245, 246
  fall of, 186, 245
  he-goat representing, 185
  kings, 238, 241–45
  mercenaries, 194
greetings, 89–90
Gregory the Great, 256
Grotefend Cylinder, 97
Gunkel, Hermann, 162

hammelṣar, 39
Hammer, Raymond, 147
Hammurabi, 51–52
harp, 76, 77
Harran Inscriptions of Nabonidus, 109, 111, 132
Hasel, Gerhard F., 48
heart, 95
heaven, 54
  Bible on, 54
  dew of, 95
  four winds of, 157–59, 186
Hebrew, 47
  adjectives, 28
  of Daniel, 40–41
  as human language, 41
Hebrew Bible, 133
  beasts and dragons, 164
  burning by fire, 80
  death as a sleep, 270
  Edom and, 258

furnace, 86
Great Sea, 160
Kush/Cush, 266
Moab and Israel/Judah, 259
wives and concubines, 119
herald, 72
Herodotus, 34, 36
  on Astyages, 43
  on Babylon, 99
  on Darius I, 50
  on golden image/statue, 69–70
  on gold used in Babylon, 59
  on Medes, 146
  on wine, 36, 37
  on Xerxes I, 240
Herod the Great, 26, 247
Hezekiah, king of Judah, 7–9
holy gods, 93
horn(s), 74–75, 168, 184–85
  ten, 167, 184, 187, 256
How long?, 191, 221, 276
humiliation, 105
hymns to god, 55–56

iconography, 185
ideograms, 32
images, 58, 67–70
incense, 64–65
  bronze shovel, 65
  ingredients, 65
India House Inscription, 25, 59, 97, 99, 161
iniquities, 96
inscription
  deciphering, 134–35
  of Neferhotep, 65
  See also specific inscription
Instruction of Amenemope of Egypt, 269
interpretation of dreams, 42–44
Isaiah, 9, 136
Ishtar Gate, 66, *66*, 152, 165
Israel, 29. *See also* Judah
Istanbul Stele of Nabonidus, 57

Jehoiachin, 10–12, 14, 56, 130, 199, 203, 205
  ration tablets, 11, *11*, 203

400

INDEX

Jehoiakim, 9–10, 207
  binding of, 9
  third and fourth years of reign, 1–3
Jeremiah the prophet, 1, 56, 101, 202–5
Jerusalem, 17, 219–24
  archaeological finds, 19–20
  Babylonian attacks, 1, 17–19, 26
  desolations of, 207–9
  Nebuchadnezzar besieging, 17–19
  population, 221
  rebuilding with square and moat, 222–24
  See also Nebuchadnezzar
Jerusalem temple
  architectural descriptions, 25–26
  Babylonian plundering, 26–27
  utensils, 26
  vessels, 25, 26–27
Jesus, 221–22
  execution, 224
  public ministry, 224
Jews, 83–84
  prosecution, 249
  purity for, 278
  seventy years of captivity, 205–7
  See also Judah
Johanan, 13–14
Johnson, Marshall D., 61
Josephus, 1
Judah, 1, 29
  Babylonian attack, 15–17
  Babylonian names among Judean exiles, 31
  children of, 29
  Israel and, 29
  social distinctions, 29–31
  young men of, 31
  See also Jerusalem
Judahtown, 30
judges, 218
judgment, 175–76
Jursa, Michael, 103
Justinian, 255
Justinian Code, 255–56

Keil, C. F., 159
kingdoms
  animals as, 62
  chronological, 62, **63**
  four-kingdom schema, 58–62
  See also specific kingdom/empire
kings of Persia, **241**
Kitchen, K. A., 78
Kitharas, 76
Kition/Citium, 250
Kittim, 250–51
Klein, Jacob, 116
Koldewey, Robert, 98
kudurrus, 53
Kuhrt, A., 82
Kvanvig, Helge S., 162–63

Lachish letters, *16,* 16–17, 89
land tax, 248
language and literature, 31–32, 39
Laodice, 243
law(s), 50–53
  of Daniel's God, 142–43, 176
  of Hammurabi (*See* Code of Hammurabi)
  of Medes and Persians, 149–50
  of Moses, 218
  Neo-Babylonian, 149
Layard, Austen Henry, 166
Lebanon, 160–61
legumes, 35–36
leopard-like beasts, 167
Libya, 265
Libyans/Lybians, 265
lion(s)
  den/pit of, 143–45
  as dog of Ishtar, 152
  as a symbol for royalty and power, 143
lionlike beasts, 60, 165–66
literature. *See* language and literature
Longenecker, Richard N., 171
lots, casting of, 281–82
lycanthropy, 95
lyre, 76–77

Maat, *135, 135*
magicians, 39–40, 47
malat, 269
Mameluks, 257, 266–67

INDEX

Manual of Discipline
  idea of purity, 278
  seventy weeks, 219
mappa mundi, 93, 97, 98, 157
Marduk-apla-iddin, 8
marriages
  bigynous/bigamous, 120
  contracts and laws, 119
  monogamous, 119
  polygynous, 120
Martin, W. F., 41
maskilim, 271–72. *See also* wise (understanding ones or instructors)
Maxwell, Mervyn, 242
Mazar, Benjamin, 223
Mazar, Eilat, 7
Mediterranean Sea, 160–61
Medo-Persia (Medes and Persians), 60, 136, 145–50
  Behistun Inscription, 145
  kings, 193, 238, 239–41, *240*
  laws, 149–50
  nations conquered by, 148
  ram representing, 183–84, 185
  as a single kingdom, 146
Megasthenes, 104, 148, 264, 265
Merneptah, 58
Messiah the Prince, 221–22
Messianic Apocalypse, 270
metals, 58–59
Micah, 9
Michael, 235–36
Millerite Movement, 280–81
Mischwesen (hybrid creatures), 163
Moab, 259–60
Montgomery, James, 160
moral integrity, 142
mourning, 209–11, 231. *See also* fasting
musical instruments, 73–79, **75**
  bag-pipe, 77–79
  categorization, 73–74
  harp, 76, 77
  lyre, 76–77
  pipe/flute, 76

Nabonidus, 156, 262
  dream, 46
  extended expedition to Tema, 129
  Harran Inscriptions of, 109, 111, 132
Nabonidus Chronicle, 109–12, 115–17, *116*, 123–24, 126, 137, 141, 229, 234, 258
Nabopolassar, 4, 5, **5**, 91–92, 120, 179, 263
nāhār, 276. *See also* river
name is written in the book, 269
Napoleon I, 256
  Egyptian expedition, 257, 259, 263, 265, 267
  exile and death, 257, 267
  Syrian expedition, 257, 266
Nebuchadnezzar, 87–89
  administration, 104
  Babylonian Chronicle, 1, 2, *4*, 9
  battles/conflicts, 1, 5, 57, 264
  boanthropy, 95
  building projects, 5, 98
  daily offerings, 23
  death and succession, 104
  dreams, 44–46
  Edom and, 258
  Etemenanki cylinder, 21–22, 72–73
  gigantic/great image of, 58, 68–69
  god of, 24
  Grotefend Cylinder, 97
  Hattu campaign, 57
  honoring/awarding individuals, 65
  humiliating people at will, 105
  inscription praising, 23
  invasion of Palestine, 9–10
  law, 52–53
  lycanthropy, 95
  moral uprightness for, 97
  name, *20*, 20–21, **21**
  palace, 91–93
  as servant of deity, 21–24
  son of the gods, 86
  stele, 22
Nebuzaradan, 13, 103, 204
Necho, 1
Necho II, 3, 263
Neo-Babylonian Empire, 1–5
  accession system, 2–3, **3**, 42
  chronology, 5–7

402

INDEX

diet and foods, 34–36
education system, 31–32
kings, **105**
language and literature, 31–32, 39
vegetables, 36
See also Belshazzar; Nebuchadnezzar
Nero (AD 54–68), 249, 250
night vision, 55
Nile, 276
nobles, 28–31
non-accession time reckoning, 2–3, **3**

oath, 217, 276, 277
offering. *See* sacrifice and offering
omens, 42–43
ones sleeping in the dust. *See* resurrection
Oppert, J., 140
ostraca. *See* Lachish letters
oxhorns, 75

palace of Nebuchadnezzar, 91–93
  brickwork, 92
  buildings, 92
Palestine
  Adad-Nirari III's expedition to, 161
  battle of Panion, 245
  as beautiful land, 188
  Canaanite temples, 25
  geographical boundaries, 188
  Napoleon's Syrian expedition, 257, 266
  Nebuchadnezzar's invasion of, 9–10
  Seleucid occupation, 245
Patercilius, Velleius, 61
Paul, Shalom M., 196
Paulus, Aemilius, 245, 246
Perdiccas, 243
perfumes, 231–32. *See also* anointing oneself
Persus (king of Macedonia), 245, 246
Pesher on the Periods, 219
Philip II, 236–37. *See also* Alexander the Great
Pilate, Pontius, 224
Pinches, T. G., 264
pipe/flute, 76

Pius VI, 256
Plain of Dura, 70–71
poll tax, 248
Polybius, 244
Pontifex Maximus, 247
popes, 255–56
Potts, D. T., 35–36
Prayer of Nabonidus, 101
praying/prayers, 150–51, 209
presidents, 142
prince of Persia, 234–35
prophets, 213
  false, 213
  Israel, 213
  traumatic physical manifestations, 196
Psammetichus I, 60, 263
Psammetichus II, 263
Ptolemy II Philadelphus, 243
Ptolemy III Euergetes, 243
Ptolemy I Soter, 242, *242*, 243
Ptolemy IV, 243–44
Ptolemy V, 244, 245
purity/purification, 254, 277–79
  demands of being purified, 278–79
  documents reflecting, 278
purple clothing, 129
Pusamiski, 264

queen/queen mother, 129–33

ram, 183–85
refining/refined, 254, 279
rest
  as an apocalyptic theme, 281
  as dying, 281
resurrection, 269–71
righteousness, 97, 213–16, 272
Rimbach, James A., 164
Rim-Sin, 82
river, 276
Roman Empire
  battle of Pydna, 245, 246
  Christians and popes, 254–56
  decisive moment, 246
  Edom and, 258
  horns representing kings, 168, 184
  integrating Palestine, 188

INDEX

Roman Empire *(continued)*
   kings, 239, 246–48
   land tax, 248
   monstrosities as wonders, 277
   religious and political struggles, 148–50
   upheaval and invasions, 255
Roman Scheme, 62
Rosetta Stone, 244, *244*, 290
Rowley, H. H., 48
royal officials, 102–4

sackcloth, 211
sacrifice and offering, 226–27
sanctuary, 189–90
   desolation, 189–90, 218
   as a holy place, 189
Sargon II, 261
satraps, 71
scarabs, 274. *See also* seals
Scipio, Lucius Cornelius, 245
Scopas, 245
seals, 273–75
   Babylonian, *273*, 275
   categories, 274
   fake, 275
   imprints, 274
   Judean, 30
   material, 273–74
   purpose/usage, 273
seasons, 56
Sefire Inscriptions, 29, 213
Seleucus I Nicator, 243
Seleucus II Callinicus, 243
Seleucus III Soter, 243
Selms, A. van, 91
Sennacherib, 7, 34, 83–84, 132
Septuagint, 90
seven (the number), 95–96
seven times, 85–86, 96, 176
seventy weeks, 219
seventy years of captivity, 205–7
Shamash (sun god of the Babylonians), 46, 88, 121–22, 169
Shamshi-Adad I, 160
Shea, William H., 235
Shinar, 24–25
Shishak, 26

Shumma izbu, 163
Shushan/Susa, 179–80
Sibylline Oracles, 61
signet rings, 152
signet seals, 273, 274
Siloam Inscription, 7–8
silver vessels, 118
sixty-nine weeks, 219
Smith, G. A., 259
son(s)
   of Ammon, 260–63
   of the gods, 86
   of man, 171–75
sorcerers, 47
sorcery, 47
stamp seals, 274
Starkey, John L., 16
stars, 272–73
   astrology, 272
   biblical text, 188
   figurative meaning, 272–73
Stefanovic, Zdravko, 49
steward, 39
stone, 151
   sealing of, 151
stump and roots, 95
Sura, Aemilius, 61
Susa. *See* Shushan/Susa
swearing, 276, 277
syllograms, 32

Tattenai, 231
taxes, 248
Teacher of Righteousness, 272
Tell el-Firr, 244
temples
   kings building, 189
   treasure, 25
   vessels, 25, 118
   See also Jerusalem temple
Temple Scroll from Qumran, 38
   purity, 278
   sanctuary, 189
Ten Commandments, 218
ten days, 39
ten horns, 167, 184, 187, 256
Tertullian, 45
Thanksgiving Hymns, 278

INDEX

Thomas, F., 140
Thompson, Steven, 272
three and a half times, 176
Tigris River, 232–33, 276
Timbuktu, 267
time of the end, 192–93, 275
time of trouble, 268
Titus, 224–25, 251–53
Tomb of Daniel, 271, 282
Towner, W. Sibley, 171–72
tree, 93–94
    stump and roots, 95
trouble, time of, 268
tsarap, 279
turbans, 86

Ulai River, 182–83
understanding, 253–54. *See also* wise (understanding ones or instructors)
until the end, 176–77, 276–77
Uphaz, 233–34
upper room of Daniel, 150

vegetables, 36
Vespasian, 224, 250
vessels, 118
vision, 156, 175, 178–79, 219
    Daniel having, 156, 157
    dream *vs.*, 156, 179
    night, 55
    sealing up, 195–96
    See also dreams

War Scroll from Qumran
    Gabriel, 192
    idea of purity, 278
    Michael, 236
watcher, 94–95. *See also* angels
Waterhouse, S. Douglas, 207
Wellard, James, 136
well-wishing, 89–90. *See also* greetings
wheats, 35, 36
Whitcomb, John, 139
white/whiteness
    making people, 254, 279

metaphorical usage, 279
theological usages, 279
whole earth, 186
wickedness/wicked people, 272, 280
Wilson, R. D., 48
wind(s)
    as a cleaning agent, 64
    four, of heaven, 157–59, 186
wine, 36–38
    Belshazzar, 117
    Nabonidus Chronicle, 117
    social function, 117
    spiced, 38
Winkle, Ross E., 206–7
wisdom, 32–33, 54
wise (understanding ones or instructors), 253–54, 271–72
Wiseman, Donald J., 139, 144
witnesses, number of, 275–76
Wittstruck, Thorne, 164
wives, 118–20. *See also* concubines; marriages
women
    Neo-Babylonian society, 30–31
    queen/queen mother, 129–33
    wives and concubines, 118–20
wonders, 277
worship, 64, 79–80
writing name in the book, 269
writing on the wall, 127–29

Xenophon, 38, 115, 136–37
Xerxes, 50, 142, 146, 240, 265

yaḥad, 272
YHWH, 198–202
Yohanan, R., 46
Younker, Randall, 223

Zadok, Ran, 30, 180, 199–200
Zarathushtra (Zoroaster), 59
Zedekiah, 12–13, 266
Zerubbabel, 26
Zevit, Ziony, 174
ziggurat, 94, 100
zither, 76

www.ingramcontent.com/pod-product-compliance
Lightning Source LLC
Chambersburg PA
CBHW071227290426
44108CB00013B/1311